10.03 — Barnes + Noble 11-66 (Kniffin)

TRAVELS IN THE AMERICAN COLONIES

TRAVELS

IN THE

AMERICAN COLONIES

EDITED UNDER THE AUSPICES OF THE NATIONAL
SOCIETY OF THE COLONIAL DAMES
OF AMERICA
BY
NEWTON D. *Dennison* MERENESS

Antiquarian Press, Ltd.
NEW YORK
1961

First published 1916

Reprinted by Antiquarian Press, Ltd. 1961

Library of Congress Catalog Number 61-8045

Edition limited to 750 copies

19763

CONTENTS

CONTENTS

CUTHBERT POTTER'S JOURNAL OF A JOURNEY
FROM VIRGINIA TO NEW ENGLAND, 1690

INTRODUCTION

VIRGINIA was but slightly affected by the fall of the Stuart régime in 1688, but in consequence of the overthrow of the Andros government in Massachusetts, the uprising under Leisler in New York, and "great depredations committed by the Indians" in those parts, the Council of Virginia, on the 5th of June, 1690, resolved to send a messenger northward with instructions "to ascertain the truth of matters in New England and New York." Colonel Cuthbert Potter was forthwith named for the mission and on the 24th of the following month Governor Nicholson announced to the Council that the Colonel had agreed to perform the service for £60.

Colonel Potter was practicing law in Lancaster County, Virginia, as early as 1653, and three years later his name appears among the justices of the Lancaster County Court. In later years he was one of the large landholders of Middlesex County and was closely associated with Ralph Wormeley, a leading member of the Council. The narrative of his journey to New England shows that he was an advocate of strong government. Shortly after making that journey he removed in his own sloop, the *Hopewell*, to the Island of Barbados, where, as stated in his will, dated June 20, 1691, he was "suddenly seized and taken with bodily sickness." In return for his ill treatment in Boston the Governor and Council of Virginia warned the Government of Massachusetts that as "contrary to the Acts of Parliament divers goods are imported into New England not directly from England, and that no Collector is in New England, we have ordered that any ships bringing European goods hither from New England must produce their cocquets from England or be proceeded against at law."

An official copy of this journal has been preserved in the Public Record Office, London: Colonial Office, Class 5, No. 1305, pp. 176–179.

MR. POTTER'S JOURNALL FROM VIRGINIA TO N. ENGLAND

A Journall and Narrative of a Journey made by me Cuthbert Potter from Middx[1] County in Virginia to Boston in New England.

July 6. In the Evening I departed from the honble Ralph Wormley Esqre his house in a Shallop but having very rainy, Stormey weather, It was Sunday morning following before I could get to Casparas Harmans in Bohemia [2] and there tarried all day.

July 14. I took horses and guide and went to New Castle, that night, 'tis accounted 30 miles, I met with Mr. Williams the Collector deliver'd him his Letter, and discours'd him about the trade Betwixt the head of the Bey and that Town for tobacco, he told me there had been formerly much tobacco brought over to that Town, but now not so much, he had lately seised some tobacco that had been brought, but by others I perceived It is frequently carried over to that Town.[3]

July 15. I went from New Castle to Chester alias Uplands accounted 20 miles by water.

July 16. I went from Chester to Philadelphia by water accounted 20 miles more. I met President Loyd [4] and Mr. Plowman, and deliver'd their Letters also Mr. Markham,[5]

[1] Middlesex.

[2] Augustine Herrman, the founder of Bohemia Manor, at the head of Chesapeake Bay, died in 1686 and his second son, Casparus Herrman, took possession of the manor house in June, 1690.

[3] There was at this time a Maryland export duty on tobacco of two shillings per hogshead.

[4] Thomas Lloyd, president of the Provincial Council of Pennsylvania.

[5] William Markham, secretary of the Provincial Council of Pennsylvania.

Mr. Delaval [1] Mr. Barbery and Mr. Ducay with whom I discourst some time, the two last forced to fly from York.[2]

July 18.   I went from thence by water 30 miles up to the falls [3] and stopt about half an hour at Mr. Penns and lodged that night at Mr. Wheelers.

July 19.   I took horses and guid[e] for Eliza [4] Town being 72 miles, but reached no farther than Onions.[5]

July 20.   I went from Onions to Eliza Town, there having been very much rain, in sight of Collonel Townlies [6] my horse fell with me, and by Gods mercy I escaped drowning having been twice under water wet all my linnen and papers.

July 21.   I tarried all day with Mr. Townley, dried my linnen and papers, and left two or three letters with him for some New York gentlemen that were then escaped into East Jersey which he promised to deliver with his own hand.

July 22.   I went to New York by water, 16 miles, pre-understanding the severity they used in that Town towards strangers by securing and searching them, with the assistance of the watermen I put my portmanteaus on board a ship in the harbour and went privately ashore to Mr. Thompsons, and so soon as it was night that I could get my Portmanteaus on shore, I deliver'd all the letters I had for the Gentlemen in those parts.

July 23 *and* 24.   I was brought acquainted with most of the honest Gent : of that Town who very much deplored the present state of affairs there,[7] but generally exceeding Joy-

---

[1] John Delavall, a member of the Council of the City of New York. He subsequently removed to Philadelphia, became a member of the Philadelphia Council in 1691, and a member of the Provincial Council in 1692.

[2] New York.   [3] Trenton.
[4] Elizabeth.   [5] Mr. Onions.

[6] Col. Richard Townley, who came to Virginia with Lord Effingham in 1683, removed to Elizabeth Town in 1684, and married the widow of Philip Carteret in 1685.

[7] The Leisler uprising.

full for the welfare of this our honorable Governor,[1] every one speaking highly in his commendacion, and earnestly wishing for the arrival of Governor Slaughter there, which might put a period to their present distraccions. I was inform'd the Indians had cut of a small village,[2] near Fort Albany which caused the Inhabitants to keep a very strict watch and guard, the alarm of the French Pyrates being then upon the Coast, caused them to prepare a force for their defence, and all the masters of ships then in harbour and all the Gentlemen of the Town were by the Governor [3] sent for to consult the present safety, who most willingly assented for the common good to use their utmost endeavours to oppose and resist the common enemy, by which means Lashler [4] could find no time to send for me as was inform'd he intended and I expected.

July 25. I took horses and guide for New England, and that night went to Horsneck [5] being 40 miles.

July 26. I went to Fairfeilds [6] being 25 miles, and very bad way and tarried there the next day being Sunday.

July 28. Major Gold [7] provided me horses to Guilford being 42 miles.

July 29. I went to Sebrook [8] being 20 miles : It rained very fast all day.

July 30. I went from Sebrook to New London being 20 miles where I understood Major Winthrop was gone for Albany,[9] I deliver'd his letter to his brother Major Palmes,[10]

---

[1] Francis Nicholson, who, in 1689, was made Lieutenant Governor of the Dominion of New England with residence at New York, was appointed Lieutenant Governor of Virginia in 1690.

[2] Schenectady.   [3] Jacob Leisler.   [4] Leisler.

[5] West Greenwich.   [6] Fairfield.

[7] Major Nathan Gold, a member of the Connecticut Court of Assistants.   [8] Saybrook.

[9] Major-General Fitz-John Winthrop was commander of the New York-Connecticut expedition that set out in the spring of 1690 against Montreal but was soon abandoned because of desertion by the Indians and lack of supplies and means of transportation.

[10] Major Edward Palmes was a brother-in-law of Major Fitz-John Winthrop.

and took his receipt, was told that the French Pyrates had come to an anchor before the town, but finding too great an appearance to oppose them, they departed without doing any dammage, the Inhabitants there seeming no way in dread of the French Indians, In respect Major Winthrop with a convenient force was then gone for Albany.

July 31. I went from thence to Bulls in the Narragansit Government being 45 miles.

August 1. I hired a shallop, and went for Newport in Rode Island being 10 miles, where I met Mr. Brinley,[1] Mr. Newbery and Mr. Clark, and deliver'd them their Letters and left Mr. Smith's letter with Mr. Brinley.

August 2. I went for New Bristoll being 16 miles, the next day being Sunday I tarried at Mr. Lavins.

August 4. I took horses and guide and went for Boston being 50 miles, about midnight I got to the Townsend — there lay, in the morning I went into the Town to Md Usher and Mr. Jeffreys, and deliver'd them their letters.

August 6. I waited on the Governor Bradstreet,[2] and deliver'd him the Letter for that Government, who did not then open it, I told him it came from the Present Governor of Virginia, and requested an answer to which he replyed he was going to the Councill and then I should be sent for and have an answer. I rested there two or three dayes and in the mean time deliver'd what Letters I had for other Gentlemen in the Town, I went to Salem and waited on Major Brown, and deliver'd the Letters I had for that place then return'd to Boston, and waited on Bradstreet the Governor who told me he would write back to our Governor and shortly after I received his Letter, there I caused 700 copies of his Majesties Letter to the Bishop of London to be printed and disperst them all along according to order : In which time they were very busy in setting forth their Fleet for Canada, which consisted of 32 ships and vessels of all sorts, and 2200 men which set sail about the 9th.

[1] Francis Brinley was the leader of a Rhode Island faction favoring strong government.

[2] Simon Bradstreet was governor of Massachusetts in 1689–92.

August 9. The people [are] generally much dissatisfied with their present Government, and blame it very much for all their sufferings, which have happen'd onely through their ill management of affairs and sending away Sir Edmond Andrews,[1] that caused all those great losses to the Eastward. I went over to Cambridge and Charles Town, where I deliver'd all the Letters I had for those places, and having spent some time in discoursing severall Gentlemen and others, I generally observ'd that many who had been for, were now inveterate enemies to the present Government.

August 13. I prepared to return for Virginia, but hearing a rumour or whispering that the Governor had order'd officers to seize, and search me for Letters and papers I went and informed Collonel Shrimpton and Collonel Dongan what I had heard, who said they did not think that they would be so unworthy, yet they stopt Mr. Peacock and severall others. I went to Governor Broadstreet, and acquainted him what I had heard touching my self, he replyed he had heard nothing of it, he was going to the Councill and if any such thing was intended he would acquaint me with it, and in the time the Governor was at the Councill, Officers were sent out to seize, search me and my papers.

August 14. The officers found my Portmanteaus at Mr. Seawards where I intended to take horse, and brought them away, but as it happened by chance I met them in the street, and demanded by what power they seised my goods, they shewed an order of Councill, but would not let me read it. We went into Monks at the Anchor, I there demanded a copey of their order, but they refused and two of them took me into a private room, search'd my pockets and breeches, found severall letters and papers which they took, but gave me leave to lock them up in my portmanteau, they then sent to the Councill, who order'd me to be brought in the afternoon so I was dismist for the Present, and went home

[1] Sir Edmund Andros, governor of the Dominion of New England from April 1688 until his deposition by the people of Massachusetts in April 1689.

to dinner, then took out those letters and papers I had saved about my breast and back, in the afternoon I attended at the coffee house till near four of the clock then I was sent for by an Officer, when I came the Governor told me, there were a great many seditious people, about the Town, dispersing scandalous papers tending to the subversion of the present Government, and that they had reason to fear some of them kept correspondence with the enemy. They were at great charge in fitting out their fleet, which would cost them near 50 or 60,000 pounds so it behooved them to be carefull, they had made an order to stop and examine all Strangers, and see what papers and pamphlets they had against the Government. I desired to see the order, and have a copey of it that I might give an account to those that send me, they replyed I was before them which was sufficient, and bid me open my Portmanteau. I refused and began to argue the affront offered to our honorable Governor, whose pass I shewed, was chid and called sawcy, and a smith was sent for to break my locks, which done the Officers turn'd out all my papers, and linnen, the papers lying all before them on the table, they then bid me to with draw with the rest of my things. I replyed I could not carry them my self, they ordered an officer to carry them to the coffee house where I waited untill they broke open and perused what they pleased, then sent for me and told me they found cause to stop some letters, they sent for Mr. Jeffreys and ordered him to give security to answer next Court, turned the publick Notary out of Office, kept about five or six letters directed to the Right Honble Governor of this Colony, besides other papers, examined my being at Cambrige and Charles Town, shewed me Bradstreet's letter broke open, and told me they would write next day to the Governor, bid me take the remainder of my papers, and so dismist me.

August 15. I waited on the Governor Bradstreet, and importuned him for his pass, that I might be no more molested, which having received from him with a Letter to this honorable Governor, I took my leave and came to Mr. Billings at night.

August 16. I came to New Bristoll where I staid with Mr. Jno Smith, Captain Andrews and some others.

August 17. I came to Newport where I stayed wind bound till 23d.

August 23. I took a sloop for Long Island, and was seven dayes in getting within three miles of Flushing.

August 30. I took horses and guide for New York, I tarried there all day and received answers of those letters I had deliver'd, but was advised that Milburn [1] the present deputy Governor would seize all my papers as I was ready to depart, I forthwith got a boat and hands and came in haste away.

Sept. 1. In the morning I got to Collonel Townlies in Eliza Town, with whom I tarried two dayes expecting some Friend from York, with letters but they came not.

Sept. 3. I came from Collonel Townlys to Mr. Onions.

Sept. 4. I came to the falls and thence to Burlington.

Sept. 5. I came to Philadelphia was with Mr. Loyd, Mr. Markham, Mr. Delaval, and Mr. Test.

Sept. 6. I came to Chester thence to Newcastle, and there tarried the next day.

Sept. 8. I came to Casparas Harmans at Bohemia where I tarried three dayes before I could hire a boat.

Sept. 12. I hired a boat and came from Casparas Harmans, down the Bey [2] but by contrary wind and weather, I could not attain into Rappa [3] River till the 24th day of the moneth,

Sept. 24. On which I by the blessing of God safely arrived, at the house of the honorable Ralph Wormley Esqre. Memorandum :

When I was in Boston I understood there was great plenty of Canary wine, and discoursing with several Gentlemen there they told me they had four ships with Canary wine, two of which belonged to Bristoll. I was asked twenty four

---

[1] Jacob Milborne.
[2] Chesapeake Bay.
[3] Rappahannock.

pounds a pipe but told by others I might have my choice of good wine for Eighteen, and in the time I was at Salem, waiting on Major Brown I met with a master of a small vessell, that was lately arrived from Spain, belonging to Salem, who treated me with a Glass of good wine, and anchovies, and told me he had made twenty pounds a hogshead of that little tobacco he had with him and that he came directly from Cales.

[*Endorsed*]
> *1690*
> Mr. Potter's Journall from
> Virginia to New England.
> Received 29 January 1690/1.

JOURNAL OF DIRON D'ARTAGUIETTE, 1722–1723

INTRODUCTION

LOUISIANA, comprising the French possessions in the Mississippi Valley, was granted in 1717 by the Regent, the Duke of Orleans, to the Western Company, the grant being a part of John Law's project for replenishing the exchequer of France when the wars of Louis XIV's reign had brought that country to the verge of bankruptcy. The charter made the Company proprietors of the territory for twenty-five years, promised it full ownership of all mines that should be opened during that period, and full title to all lands that should be peopled. The Company was to enjoy the exclusive right of trade within its territory and to have a monopoly of the beaver trade with Canada. The Crown was to pay a bounty on vessels constructed in Louisiana for carrying goods to France, and for ten years the import duty on goods from Louisiana was to be but one half of that levied on goods from other French colonies. The Company was authorized to provide armed vessels for the protection of its trade, to construct forts within its territory, to make treaties with the Indians, to appoint officers, and to enact necessary statutes. The colonists were promised the same liberties and immunities as they enjoyed in France and exemption from taxation by the Crown.

The charter required that the stock of the company be divided into shares of 500 livres each, payable in exchequer bills, and that every holder of fifty shares be entitled to a vote in the board of directors and to one additional vote for each additional fifty shares. Law was made director-general and 200,000 shares were issued. Subsequently the Western Company was merged with another of Law's institutions, the Royal Bank, and with the East India Company. For a brief period shares were fifty per cent or more

15

above par, but security for the stock was almost wholly lacking, the Royal Bank failed in 1720, and fear for his life drove Law from France.

The Company, however, did much for the growth of the colony. Bienville, who for years had been its leading spirit, was appointed governor; the white population increased from a few hundred in 1717 to more than five thousand in 1721; and settlements were established on concessions of the Company at Baton Rouge, Natchez, Natchitoches, Pointe Coupée, Cannes Brulées, Tunicas, Bayagoulas, on the Yazoo River, on Pascagoulas Bay, and at other places. In 1721 the Duke of Orleans intrusted the direction of the affairs of the Company to three commissioners, and they appointed Diron d'Artaguiette inspector-general. Artaguiette, as royal commissary in the colony, defended Bienville against malicious attacks in 1707. He was one of the board of directors of the Western Company, and was the founder of Baton Rouge. His journal was a report to the Commissioners on conditions in the colony in 1722–1723 as observed by Artaguiette at New Orleans and while on a tour of inspection up the Mississippi to the Illinois Country.

There is a transcript of the journal in the Library of Congress which was made from a copy in the Archives Nationales, Paris: C 13 C 2, ff. 18–269. The translation is by Miss Georgia Sanderlin.

JOURNAL OF DIRON D'ARTAGUIETTE

Journal from the 1st of September to the 11th of the same month

SEPT. 1. New Orleans. There died here Monsieur Macée, chaplain of the ship L'Avanturier.

Sept. 2. We have been informed that six men — habitants or traders — had deserted from this post and that a detachment, commanded by Sr. De St. Esteve, had gone out in search of them.

Sept. 3. We have learned that Sr. de St. Esteve arrived at Fort Louis [1] three days after his departure and that he had brought back the six deserters, who made no resistance. They were only put in chains for a short time.

Sept. 4. An officer, accompanied by four fuzileers, set out to carry a large packet of letters, which he delivered in the bayou [2] to the master of a canoe. The latter immediately departed for Fort Louis du Biloxcy. [3]

Sept. 5. A man named Traverse, living in New Orleans, was today let out of prison. The cause for which he was imprisoned was this. This man had built a house in New Orleans. This house was not set in accord with the alignment of the streets, as he had built it before the plan had been proposed. M. Peauger [4] had it torn down. Traverse being not well pleased about this, presented a petition to the council, asking them to recompense him for his house in order that he might have the means to build another. M.

[1] Fort Louis was on the site of the present Biloxi, Mississippi.
[2] Bayou Saint John, on the south side of Lake Pontchartrain.
[3] The capital of Louisiana was at this time removing from Biloxi to New Orleans.
[4] M. de Pauger, engineer, assistant to M. de Latour, the chief engineer.

Peauger had him sent for, and, after having regaled him with a volley of blows with his stick, had him thrown into prison, with irons about his feet, and today this man has come out of prison almost blind.

Sept. 6. We have been informed that twelve soldiers and three sailors — the soldiers from the Company of St. George — had deserted. These people had made an agreement with the skipper, who was steering a canoe in which were Messieurs Dharcourt and Nolan, the former the treasurer, and the latter an officer, who were going from Mobile to Fort Louis. The skipper running very close in shore, these gentlemen asked him where he was going and why he was not carrying them on their journey, upon which the skipper replied that the currents were carrying them ashore. Having arrived at the Pointe des Chutaux, twelve soldiers came to them with bayonets at the end of their guns, and asked them civilly to lend them their canoe, they having a long journey to make, and to give them a present of some flasks of brandy. These gentlemen, seeing themselves the weaker party, responded, also civilly, that they (the soldiers) were the masters. The soldiers took the canoe and some flasks of brandy and set sail, leaving these gentlemen and their effects behind.

Sept. 7. Today the ship L'Avanturier was preparing to sail for France, but M. Bienville[1] detained her to see what news there was from France, three ships having recently cast anchor in the roads of Fort Louis.

Sept. 8. Nothing of interest took place.

Sept. 9. M. Delatour,[2] having some small jobs to be done, sent for four soldiers, but all refused to come.

Sept. 10. Today at two o'clock in the afternoon, the ship L'Avanturier was to have set sail, but a heavy wind, contrary and violent, having sprung up, her departure was put off until tomorrow.

[1] Jean Baptiste le Moyne, Sieur de Bienville, Governor of Louisiana in 1701–1713, 1718–1724, and 1733–1743, and founder of New Orleans.

[2] M. de Latour was lieutenant-general of Louisiana and chief engineer.

The same day Sr. Feaucon Dumanoir, director of the Concession of the Malouins,[1] presented us with the memoirs set forth below. You will see there the grievances which they have to allege against the company,[2] what it has made them suffer in spite of the conventions and agreements made between them. You will also see enumerated the things which are absolutely necessary for the establishment of the colony.

Grievances

1. The lack of lodgings and store-houses, which the company ought to furnish to the concessionnaires immediately upon their arrival.

2. The lack of a hospital for the sick.

3. The lack of goods to trade with, and necessary to have, so as to secure fresh provisions to restore those who have been enfeebled by their journeys and to feed others.

4. The lack of such supplies as flour, wine, meat and brandy.

5. The lack of boats and vessels for transportation to the said concessionnaires. From this deficiency have arisen many inconveniences, to wit:

That the concessionnaires have remained upon arid sand for eight months. This stay has been the cause of their consuming the whole food supply intended for their establishments, the company being in want almost continually. That all the greater part of the workmen have died in extreme wretchedness for lack of fresh provisions and lodgings, being exposed to injury from the weather and from the cold through lack of clothing and storehouses, not having the materials for making the latter. The greater part of the goods of the said concessionnaires have rotted or have been plundered, damaged or stolen.

[1] Merchants of Saint Malo who had a grant or concession of land near the site of the present Natchez, Mississippi.

[2] The Western or Mississippi Company by whom the concessions were made; at the head of it was John Law.

As to the seizure of the food supplies of the concessionnaires, which the Company has made:

6. As soon as the concessionnaires had found themselves lodged and had storehouses in which to put their goods under cover, which they had made while consuming their food supplies, the company had immediately seized them, forcing open the doors of the storehouses and lodgings, although the goods of the said concessionnaires were still within.

7. Although the company had sent here many food supplies and much merchandise, both for trading purposes and otherwise, the council of this place replied nothing worth while to the demands of the concessionnaires, and yet the convicts had more of them than was for their good.

8. Note, I beseech you, that there are among the concessionnaires those who, for a year, have had from the company only 25 quarters of flour, 3 casks of white wine and perhaps about 30 pistoles worth of merchandise, in spite of the fact that the company has received more than 8000 quarters of flour, 600 casks of wine, 300 quarters of meat, and an infinite quantity of merchandise. They prefer to support a great number of people in idleness rather than to feed and maintain the concessionnaires, who are the pillars and the base of the establishment of this colony. One notes today two concessions in particular — that of the Sr. Dumanoir, which is in a condition to receive four or five hundred negroes, having supplies sufficient for two years, and that of Sr. Ceard, both of which form the ground-work upon which this establishment rests and which deserve to be sustained more than they have been up to the present time. As to the protest of the letters of exchange drawn by Sr. Du Manoir and Sr. Ceard upon M. Colly, in favor of Messrs. Hubert Trefontaine and Massy for the purchase of their dwellings, situated at the Natchez and at the Chapitoulas, the council ordered the seizure of the effects of the said concessionnaires, parties neither heard nor called, to which the said Sr. du Manoir made much opposition, representing that if these effects were seized he would be without the power to continue his enterprise, and that he would be obliged to abandon it alto-

gether. To this the council made no reply, permitting the seizure to proceed, with no desire to put a stop to these evil prosecutions and chicanery. It is proper to remark here that for an establishment as large as this one, such seizures interrupt the course of work, discourage the inhabitants and make them abandon everything. This would bring about total and irremediable ruin to the whole country. In regard to Sr. Ceard: In order to avert the seizure of his effects, he was forced to enter into a very onerous agreement with Monsieurs Trefontaine and Massy. This does not encourage the inhabitants to carry out the plans which they have made.

9. That the concessionnaires have been obliged to go up to their lands at their own expense, even to paying the sailors for working the boats which the company furnished them.

10. That they also had to provide themselves with vessels to bring their effects up the river.

11. As to the fact that they paid no attention to the number of people which each concession has, giving as large food supplies to the concessions which have only 60 or 80 men as they give to those which have 200. The same is also the case with merchandise of all kinds.

12. As to the enormous expenses which the concessions have made because of the failure to execute the contracts made with them, I can assure you, Gentlemen, without any partiality, that if the concessions are sustaining themselves, the credit for it is due alone to the steadfastness of those who direct them here, and to the manner in which the colonists have conducted themselves throughout the whole enterprise. The concessions of St. Catherine produced this year 2000 quarters of grain and 1000 hogsheads of tobacco, and so on.

Memorandum of the things which are necessary for the establishment of this colony and which are absolutely indispensable, to wit:

1. That the company should send here great numbers of negroes (there being no French) to clear the land.
2. That the colony should never be allowed to suffer for

lack of flour, as the country does not yet produce any wheat, nor will it produce it for three or four years, and then only after much clearing and cultivation.

3. By sending a great force of negroes, to the number of about 4000 to 5000, they could hope soon to make returns for them to France in rice, indigo, tobacco, silk and other things which they might produce.

4. That the colony should not be permitted to lack for wine or brandy, until the time when every one is permitted to plant vines and they should be producing — a thing the company has forbidden.

5. Salted meat; the country in some seasons not being sufficiently supplied with buffalos to support the colony.

6. Shot, powder, bullets and salt, which the colony has lacked every year, in order to profit in winter from the abundance of game and to preserve the meat after one has obtained it by hunting.

7. Butter; because the country has not enough bears to supply it with oil.

8. Trading goods; not being able to dispense with these because they are needed to purchase meat from the Indians.

9. Assortments of cloth and everything that is necessary to maintain the French of both sexes and the negroes and slaves, and that each thing should be given in proportion to the supply.

10. That the merchandise and food supplies coming from France, also the negroes, should be divided equally among all the concessionnaires and inhabitants in proportion to the number of each.

11. That the company should send into this colony Frenchmen who have a thorough knowledge of indigo, tobacco and silk, and also vine-dressers, wheelwrights, shoemakers, tool-makers, carpenters, cabinet-makers, coopers, and other workmen, so that the concessionnaires and other inhabitants should have them at hand when they need them.

12. That the company should procure a great number of all sorts of cattle in order that each person should have some for his own establishment.

13. That the company ought to think first of enriching the inhabitants before it can even think of drawing any profit for itself. The inhabitants once enriched, the company will find itself to be suddenly reimbursed for its advances, and it would make a large production upon which it would have a large profit, for if one counts upon stifling the inhabitant at the first moment he begins to breathe — I mean to say, if one forces the inhabitant to give to the company his first crops for nothing — this will not be the means of making him discharge his debt, but on the contrary, it will only thrust him deeper into the abyss, by which method the company will lose its advances and throw the country into the same condition in which it was formerly.

14. That the articles of merchandise should be sold to the inhabitants at the same rate and in the same proportion as the inhabitants will sell their commodities; for if the company sells its merchandise at a profit of 200 or 300 per cent., it is necessary also that the company receive at the same profit the commodities of the inhabitants in proportion to what its merchandise brings, the company deducting both the expenses of its houses and the incidental expenses of the merchandise.

15. That justice should be rendered equally to all without prejudice, revenge or distinction. The company being sure of the success of this colony, as we show by the proofs we send to it, it ought not to hesitate one moment to procure the necessities above specified, if it wishes to see the colony in a little while rise to a flourishing condition.

Sept. 11. I learned today at the home of M. Peauger, the engineer, where I had gone to find out why it was that M. Delorme wrote to Sr. Bhonneau, formerly my secretary, to make an agreement for him with a man called Drapeau, to build him a pigeon-house within the enclosure about the house which Sr. Bhonneau lent him. M. Peauger informed me that it was because M. Delatour had employed for over two months more than sixty workmen (men paid by the company) to clear up his land, to build a pigeon-house and to make over a frame which M. Delatour had taken to make him a house and which was intended for a 60-foot storehouse, the said frame belonging to the company, and that apparently M. Delorme did not wish to imitate in that respect M. Delatour, who had no fear as to causing expense. The same day, at half-past five in the morning, the ship L'Avanturier set sail from New Orleans.

Sept. 12. New Orleans. The ship L'Avanturier set out about 6 o'clock this morning, but was obliged to moor to the shore a half league below N. O.,[1] not being able to proceed on account of violent and contrary winds. The same day at four o'clock in the afternoon, there also set out two passenger-boats, one commanded by Klaziou and the other by Carron, which went no farther than the L'Avanturier.

Towards ten o'clock in the evening there sprang up the most terrible hurricane which has been seen in these quarters. At New Orleans thirty-four houses were destroyed as well as the sheds, including the church, the parsonage and the hospital. In the hospital were some people sick with wounds. All the other houses were damaged about the roofs or the walls.

It is to be remarked that seven years ago there was a similar calamity which caused a terrible destruction at Massacre or Dauphine Island, where I was at the time.[2]

There were ten flat-boats broken up and sunk together with launches, canoes and pirogues, and in fact everything in port was lost. The wind came chiefly from the southeast. The ships, the Santo Christe and the Neptune, and two passenger-boats, one of which was being used as a powder-magazine, were damaged and grounded far ashore.

It is to be remarked that if the Mississipy had been high this hurricane would have put both banks of the river more than 15 feet under water, the Mississipy, although low, having risen 8 feet.

Sept. 13. The hurricane, continuing until mid-day, has

---

[1] New Orleans.
[2] This paragraph is in the margin of the manuscript.

not ceased to rage, but at noon, it having become much calmer, we learned from some people who had just come from the settlements of Srs. Trudeau and Coustillas, that the houses there were blown down and their crops lost. The same day, in the evening, we learned that three pirogues had been lost up toward the Tensas,[1] five leagues above New Orleans. These pirogues were loaded with fowl, Indian corn and other goods which a man called Poussin, living at the Thonniquas,[2] was coming down here to sell.

Sept. 14. We are working hard here to repair the damage which the hurricane has caused. The same day we learned from some pirogues which were coming down from above that at the Cannes Bruslées [3] the houses, barns and sheds, had blown over and the crops badly damaged.

Sept. 15. All the past night patrol was sounded, a workman of the company having informed M. Bienville that a party was being formed to desert. They say that he even named the leaders. They were intending to seize the pirogues and boats and go to the lower end of the river and take the passenger-boat of Kerlaziou. The same day at noon there arrived a passenger-boat, commanded by du Clos. It was loaded with goods for the company.

Sept. 16. We have been informed that a boat was lost the night of the hurricane toward Bay St. Louis.[4] The people on board escaped to shore.

Sept. 17. We have been informed by the Chaouachas [5] that a boat called the Postillion, belonging to Sr. Dumanoir, had been sunk for lack of a launch which he had asked from Sr. Fouquet, Captain of the L'Avanturier, but which he refused

[1] Taensa Indians, who were closely related to the Natchez.
[2] The Tonica Indians inhabited the region of the lower Red River and there was a post named for them on the Mississippi, about six miles above the mouth of the Red.
[3] Cannes Brulées, on the Mississippi River, about fifteen miles above New Orleans. The Company had made a concession here to the Marquis d'Artagnac.
[4] Now Galveston Bay.
[5] A small tribe of Indians on the east bank of the Mississippi about thirty miles above New Orleans.

to give him. This boat has a deck and will be used to take transports to Natchez where the Sr. Dumanoir has a settlement.

Sept. 18. This morning Sr. Peauger had a quarrel with M. Delatour on the subject of the work which the latter has had done, the former having reproached the latter for having employed the workmen of the company to do his building, when they did not have there a church in which to put God under cover (these are the words which he used) nor a hospital in which to put the sick.

Sept. 19. Today the two men accused of having plundered the storehouse were questioned and they confessed everything. The bayou, which is situated a league from here and by which one goes and comes from Biloxcy to this place, has overflowed by about two or three feet, by reason of the hurricane. The waters having subsided, they found upon the surface of the water many dead fish, which caused a great stench.

Sept. 20. A decree was issued this morning by which the commandants and directors *order that all the inhabitants of this place must have their houses or land enclosed by palisades within two months or else they will be deprived of their property and it will revert to the company.*

The same day we were informed that there had been seized at Mobile a launch *loaded with merchandise which belonged to a man called Durant, storekeeper at the above-mentioned place. He was sending it to St. Joseph's Bay to trade with the Spaniards.*

Sept. 21. We have been informed that the ship Le Dromadaire is in the Mississipy and that the ship L'Avanturier departed the 18th of last month.

Sept. 22. We have heard nothing of interest.

Sept. 23. Counsel was held concerning the two men accused of having plundered the stores *and who had been questioned on the 19th of the present month. They were condemned to be hanged and to be strangled until life was extinct. This sentence was executed the same day, at four o'clock in the afternoon.*

Sept. 24. We have learned by means of a canoe which arrived from the lower part of the river that the two ships, the Loire and the Deux Freres, which had set out from the roads of the Isle aux Vaisseaux a few days before the hurricane to come to N. O.,[1] had returned there without having suffered any damage. They say also that all of the houses and storehouses which are in Fort Louis were either blown down or damaged and that the sea rose 7 or 8 [feet] more than is ordinary, and that it had partially inundated the place.

Departure from N. O. for the Cannes Bruslées

Sept. 25. I set out from New Orleans to go to Cannes Bruslées. The same day I spent the night at the house of Sr. Massy where I noticed that the greatest injury which the hurricane had done there was to their houses which it had completely destroyed. The crops are not in such a hopeless condition; the rice, which was only in flower, having straightened up again. The loss to the colony, however, will be very considerable, because there was a great deal of rice ready to cut but which is entirely lost.

Cannes Bruslées

Sept. 26. I arrived at Cannes Bruslées where I found all of the houses and barns blown down and not fit to be used. We set to work to repair the loss and to build sheds for the workmen and the grain.

Sept. 27. The continual rains which fall here prevent us from getting in our crops and cause a considerable loss.

Sept. 28. The report that the ships had returned to the road of Fort Louis without having been damaged and that four passenger-boats belonging to the company had been stranded on the beach, has been confirmed.

Sept. 29. I have learned that at New Orleans the troops complain greatly because they are not given any meat and

---

[1] New Orleans.

yet they see it given to the workmen of the company and to the convicts.

Sept. 30. *and the last day.* There are two pirogues full of traders who carried some young poultry to New Orleans.

Continuation of the 30th and last of September

Two pirogues full of voyageurs, who were carrying some young poultry and other produce to New Orleans, were lost in the hurricane between Natchez and Thonniqua.

Continuation of the Journal for the Month of October, 1722.

Oct. 1. We learned from a pirogue which arrived today from the Natchez that the hurricane had committed the same ravages there as down here.

Oct. 2. The report has been confirmed by a pirogue which arrived here from Fort Louis that the two vessels, the Loire and the Deux Freres, had put back there after the hurricane; that all the houses had been damaged; that the passenger-boat commanded by a certain Beau had been sunk on the shoals off the Isle aux Chats; that the six sailors who were on board had been drowned; the Captain with an attendant [1] saved themselves on the main yard, where they passed a day and night exposed to the violence of the waves which nearly maimed them; the passenger-boat commanded by du Clos went ashore on Isle au Chevreuil; the Spidouelle, commanded by Bhonneau, was stranded on the flats of the Bay of St. Louis; the passenger-boat commanded by Fontaine went ashore among the pines, large trees, near Fort Louis; these brigantines belonged to the company and were anchored in the roads of Fort Louis; all the other boats, canoes and pirogues which were at Fort Louis are wrecked, sunken or useless; they are working with all possible diligence to repair these brigantines or passenger-boats, and they did this under the direction of M. Delorme,[2] the director, whom they do expect here soon.

[1] *Mousse.*
[2] M. De l'Orme, a principal agent of the Company.

Oct. 3. The ship, Le Dromadaire, is about two leagues from New Orleans.

Oct. 4. We have learned that the two ships, the Loire, and the Deux Freres, are in the Mississipy, one of them having remained at Fort Louis to partially unload so as to be able to supply the needs of Massacre Island and Mobile, as well as other ports.

Oct. 5. The ship Le Dromadaire, commanded by Fillart, arrived about noon at N. O. It is loaded with one hundred barrels of salt, which had remained at Fort Louis, and with lumber which had been worked up at the said place; not that there is a dearth of it here, but this is wood which was all squared and it was thought worth while to ship it to N. O.

Oct. 6. M. Bienville has forbidden all the inhabitants to go to cut wood within the cypress groves, especially those which are near N. O., without his written permission; those upon whose land there are groves are excepted.

Oct. 7. I have learned that Sr. Feaucon Dumanoir, director of the company, and Monsieurs Colly and associates, had raised the ship Postillon, which we said in the Journal of the past month, was lost in the hurricane at his settlement among the Chaouackas on the Mississipy.

Oct. 8. They are working at New Orleans on the organization of two companies, one for M. Pradel and the other for M. Bourmont, who is going as commandant to the Mysourys, but who is very ill at N. O.

Oct. 9. The commandant and engineers have discharged within the last few days forty laborers who were certainly poor workmen. Some of them are joining the companies which are being formed and about which I have just spoken in the entry of the preceding day. Others are hiring themselves to work for the inhabitants.

Oct. 10. The Chonnicas [1] Indians, to the number of twenty, both men and women, led by their head chief,

[1] Tonica.

today sang the Calumet [1] to M. Bienville, who presented them with the usual presents.

Oct. 11. We have learned that the two ships which were coming to unload at New Orleans, are only six leagues from there, which gives excellent hopes, as there was beginning to be a lack of everything.

We have learned from a certain Marie le Cadet, an officer in the concession of the Marquis Demezieres, that the hurricane which wrought such destruction here was not felt at all at their settlement, which is on the Wachita River.

Oct. 13. The troops garrisoned at New Orleans grumble greatly because they have been reduced for so long a time past to eating dry bread, and because they cannot get any meat for the money which is paid them; nor can they get any merchandise, which they procure only with difficulty in the company's stores.

Oct. 14. By the three last ships which have arrived, it is said that M. Bienville had received orders not to give passage to France to anyone whomsoever, whereupon several people, having gone to find Monsieurs Bienville and Delatour, to ask for it, they were told that it was very much better to give passage to reputable people, who had business in France and who doubtless would take it by force if they refused to give it to them.

Oct. 15. The two ships, the Loire and the Deux Freres, are two leagues from N. O.

Oct. 16. The continual rains which we are having here prevent the completion of the rice harvest.

Oct. 17. The wife of a certain German laborer in the concession of Monsieur the Count D'Artagnan, is dead at this place.

Oct. 18. The two ships, the Loire and the Deux Freres, arrived at New Orleans today about 3 o'clock in the afternoon, after having saluted the city (if it can be called by

[1] I do not explain what Calumet means because they are well acquainted with the term in France. (A note in the margin of the manuscript.)

that name) the one with nine guns, the other with seven, and they were returned from N. O. by one gun only.

Oct. 19. Two men, named Marlot and Boutteux, the former storekeeper of the company and the latter formerly storekeeper of the concession of M. Law, are, it is said, tormented every night by spirits which appear to them, maltreat them and create disorder. The people believe that they are the spirits of those two men who were hanged, as I explained in the Journal of last month, because Marlot performed the duties of being procureur (public prosecutor) and Boutteaux made the accusations against them. It is easier to believe that it is some of their enemies, for those gentlemen, the clerks, make more enemies than they should.

Oct. 20. *The store-house which M. Delatour, lieutenant-general of Louisiana, was having made over into a house for himself, will not serve him for this purpose. M. Bienville, Commandant general, having set himself against it with some haughtiness, has completely fallen out with M. Delatour on account of this matter and because of some other subjects for jealousy. This lumber has been reserved to build the director's house.*

Oct. 21. We have learned that two men, Langevin by name, father and son, Canadians, living among the Illinnois, with two French servants and an Indian slave, had been captured on the Mississipy (it is not said where) by the Chicachats [1] with whom we are at war, and that they had carried them off to their village, from which place these Frenchmen had written to M. Bienville that they were being well treated by the Indians, that the latter only asked for peace, and that they had told them that they would not give them up unless peace was made, and that they could so inform the great French chiefs.

Oct. 22. Monsieurs Bienville and Delatour have today issued a warning to every one [not] to go on board the two ships, the Loire and the Deux Freres, without having a written permission from them.

[1] Chickasaw Indians.

Oct. 23. We have learned from a pirogue full of Frenchmen, which arrived from the Illinois, that the Rock Indians [1] and those of the Pimitéouy [2] had been attacked by the Fox [les Renards], an Indian nation, who killed a score of them and several women and children. The Renards had come "en village," that is to say, with their wives and children. The Ilinnois defended themselves very well since they killed, so they say, more than 120. M. de Boisbriant [3] having learned all these things resolved to go to the rescue of these Ilinnois, whom their enemies held besieged, and he departed with a hundred Frenchmen [in boats and pirogues]. MM. D'Artaguiette [4] and Tisne, captains of infantry, with De L'Isle, an ensign, and some other subalterns, accompanied him. He then ordered Bourdon, a Canadian living at the Ilinnois, to take the forty Frenchmen who remained and proceed by land until he came close to the Pymiteouy, where they would meet. Bourdon added to the 40 Frenchmen 400 Ilinnois Indians. M. Boisbriant left as a guard for Fort de Chartres [5] a man named Mellicq, lieutenant of a company, and some soldiers. But their journey was not long. M. Boisbriant learned when forty leagues up the Rivière des Illinois that the enemies had withdrawn. This made him turn back. The detachment which Bourdon commanded returned a few days afterward, but in a pitiable condition, having suffered severely from hunger on account of the bad leadership of *Bourdon who is not fit for this sort of employment and is more skilful at goading oxen in the ploughing than in leading a troop of warriors.*

[1] Savages du Rocher, a tribe of Illinois Indians closely associated with the Peorias; they were also known as Prairie des Roches Indians.

[2] Illinois Indians inhabiting the village of Pimitoui on the Illinois River, near the mouth of the Fox.

[3] Pierre Duqué de Boisbriant, a cousin of Bienville, and the first commandant of the Illinois Country.

[4] Pierre d'Artaguiette, either a son or younger brother of Diron d'Artaguiette.

[5] Fort Chartres on the east bank of the Mississippi in what is now Monroe County, Illinois. It was built by Boisbriant in 1720.

Oct. 24. The report has been confirmed that the men called Langevin, father and son, of whom we spoke in the entry of the 21st of the present month, had been taken by the Chicachats, and that it was at the Ecorres à Prudhomme [1] when they were ascending to go to the Ilinnois, and that they had been very well treated by the Indians, who did them no harm, and who even carried Langevin, the father, for four days because he was ill and could not walk. He died of sickness four days after his arrival at the village of the Chicachats. This is surely a sign that the Indians want peace, for when a prisoner cannot work, it is their custom to kill him.

Oct. 25. A pirogue arrived from the Yazous which told us that the Sieur de Grave, who is in command at that post,[2] had received the Calumet from the Chicachats and had made peace with them.

We beg the commissioners of the King to correct these errors and any others which will be found in these journals, because we have no time to revise them.[3]

Oct. 26. We have learned that at the Natchez a few days ago an Indian of that nation, owing something to a certain Fontaine, a sergeant in the troops, went to see him. This Frenchman, having demanded a settlement of his debt, the Indian replied that he did not yet have a payment for him, upon which the Frenchman flew into a passion. The Indian leaped upon his gun and aimed it at the Frenchman. Seeing this, the wife of the Frenchman ran out and called the guard, who arrived, and seeing this Indian, who kept his gun aimed all the time, they shot him dead and wounded another with a thrust of the bayonet. Some other Indians who came up carried off the dead man and led the wounded man away, grumbling. The same day at five o'clock in the evening a man named Guenot, an officer in the concession

---

[1] On the east bank of the Mississippi at the Chickasaw Bluffs.

[2] Fort de St. Pierre des Yazous, which was erected in 1718 on the Yazoo River about twelve miles from its mouth.

[3] This paragraph is in the margin of the manuscript.

of MM. Collys and associates, returning from there on horse-back to his dwelling, a league distant from the fort, was shot by a Natchez Indian. The ball entered his shoulder and lodged in his arm above the elbow. Although severely wounded, he would not let them probe for the ball, but returned to his home to get the wound dressed.

Oct. 27. We have learned that the Natches Indians have killed one negro and wounded another. The two negroes belong to the concession of the Srs. Collys and associates.

Oct. 28. We have been informed that the Natchez Indians every day offer insults to the French who are in this port, and that they have even attacked twenty soldiers, who had been detailed to go to meet a cart which was coming from the settlement of the Sieur Guenot to get things and the people who drove it had been attacked by the Natchez.

Oct. 29. Sr. du Tisne, a captain of the infantry in the Ilinnois, passed through here. He was accompanied by his wife, who comes from Canada, and they are going to New Orleans to take passage for France. He has confirmed everything which we have said since the 23rd of the present month.

Oct. 30. A Jesuit, the Father Boulanger, who comes from the Ilinnois on business for the mission which they have at the Ilinnois, passed through here. He has also confirmed all of the above from the 23rd of the present month until today.

Oct. 31. We have learned from a pirogue which has just come from the Houmas,[1] an Indian village, 23 leagues above New Orleans, that the head chief of the Natches, called the Great Sun,[2] with a band of his people who were coming from New Orleans, had sung the Calumet for M. Bienville, but having learned what had taken place at Natchez, he

[1] A Choctaw tribe of Indians.
[2] They claim that the family of their chiefs are descended from the sun. That is why they bear the name. (A note in the margin of the manuscript.)

had resolved to return with all of his people to his village without having been willing to open up their minds to the French, nor to offer any opinion on this affair.

Continuation of the Journal for the Month of November, 1722.

Cannes Bruslées

Nov. 1. Sieur Pailhoux,[1] who performed the functions of Major General in this place, passed here yesterday, about ten o'clock in the evening, in a boat, manned with twelve men. He is going in haste to Natches by orders of M. Bienville, to quell the disturbances which are taking place there. He is travelling day and night and does not stop at any place.

Nov. 2. We have been informed by a war chief from the Colapissas,[2] an Indian village situated 12 leagues from New Orleans, that the chief of the Natches Indians had been held, together with several of his people, by the order of this war chief, because, he tells us, it was said that the Natches had killed and were continuing to kill the French, and that it was right, since they had the chief ones of the nation among them, to hold them until the French chiefs should reach a decision respecting them. This is a mark of attachment to the service of the French which deserves praise.

Nov. 3. I have learned that this same war chief of the Colapissas was going down to New Orleans to make a present to M. Bienville of some fowl and Indian corn, to the end that he [M. Bienville] should permit his nation to seize the medicine man of the village of the Ouachas,[3] living among the Tensas, ten leagues distant from N. O., who had undertaken to cure the great chief of the Colapissas,

---

[1] Paillou, Major-General of Louisiana.

[2] Choctaw Indians. The name is also spelled Acolapissas.

[3] Washa Indians. Their village at this time was on the east bank of the Mississippi a few leagues above New Orleans.

but who, on the contrary, had put into his body the teeth of serpents and other evil things. This is the belief of these Indians. It is to be remarked that when a medicine man among them takes a patient and does not cure him, they kill him [the medicine man].

Nov. 4. Today M. Delorme, the director, arrived at New Orleans. The ship L'Alexandre, one of the last three arriving, which had remained at Biloxcy to discharge part of its freight in order to supply the needs of the posts of Fort Louis and Mobile, has entered the Mississipy.

Nov. 5. We have learned from a pirogue arriving from the Natchez that the Indians of that section had killed three Frenchmen. We learned from the people who were in this boat that they had neither seen nor had any knowledge of Sr. Pailhoux. The war chief of the Colapissas has come back by here and had informed us that M. Bienville is very ill and that he speaks to no one, and as a consequence that he [the war chief] had not been able to have any audience with him concerning those things of which we have spoken.

Nov. 6. A boat which came down from the Arkansas (and which is one of those which the Sr. De Tonty brought up to the Ilinnois and of which I spoke in the entry of July 18) has informed us that they had put in at the Arkansas. There are twelve men, all sick. The Sr. De Tonty had put the load from this boat into three others. They also say that this convoy was growing weaker every day for lack of salt and other fresh provisions, and that they did not believe it could reach the Ilinnois.

Nov. 7. The great chief of the Natchez, accompanied by ten or twelve men from his nation, has arrived here. This chief is called the Great Sun (we have explained why in the Journal of October). He escaped from the Colapissas and returned home, where having learned of these disturbances, he had set out with all speed and is going to New Orleans so as to prove himself innocent of all these disorders.

Nov. 8. We have learned that the Sr. Pailhoux, of whom

we speak in the first entry of the 1st of this month, had put in at the village of the Hommas. We do not know why or what reason he can have for this manœuvre.

Nov. 9. We have learned by a pirogue which comes down from the Natches that the people of that nation had killed, the 6th of this month, three Frenchmen and that nearly 200 Indians from the same nation had come to the settlement *of the Sr. Dumanoir (the one which he bought from Sr. Hubert) and had killed thirty head of cattle belonging to the said concession, and a man called La Rochelle, formerly a workman* in the same concession.

Nov. 10. The Sieur Pailhoux passed back by here in a canoe manned with fifteen men, and four pirogues, each manned with six men. It is loaded with arms and other munitions of war and is going to the Natchez to quell the disturbances or to make war upon that nation.

Nov. 11. There passed here a boat, manned with eighteen men who are going as a reinforcement against the Natches, in case it is necessary to make war upon those Indians. They told us that M. Bienville was drawing near his end.

Nov. 12. We have learned from Fort Louis that Kerlazious, captain of a passenger-boat, who had come down to pilot the vessel L'Avanturier out of the Mississipy, and of whom we speak in the Journal of September, had gone to Fort Louis where he had loaded with flour and other things to carry to Mobille for the company; that Sr. Boispinel, engineer, had embarked upon it, with all his effects, that this brigantine, having arrived in the Mobile Bay was invested by thirty armed men, among whom were twelve habitants and the rest soldiers, sailors or convicts, who took possession of the brigantine, and as Kerlazious threatened them, they put him on shore after having maltreated him severely, and themselves set sail.

Nov. 13. There passed here a pirogue which was coming down from the Natchez, which confirmed all that we have said concerning that post, and that the Indians of that nation were continuing to create disturbances. The Sr.

Guenot, of whom we spoke at the end of last month as having received a shot in the shoulder, was in this boat. He is going to New Orleans to be treated.

Nov. 14. We have learned from New Orleans that M. Bienville continues very ill and that *MM. Delatour and Delorme* were not to be seen and that they *did not attend to any business.* We do not know *why.*

Nov. 15. We have learned that Sieur de Pontual as he was returning from Biloxcy to New Orleans had been assassinated near the Isle aux Chats, by a man named La Borde, a trader.

Nov. 16. *The clerk of the ship Le Dremadaire died today from a sword wound which he received in a fight with the clerk of the ship the Deux Frères.*

Nov. 17. We have learned that M. Bienville is much better.

Nov. 18. We have been informed that the Colapissas had taken as slaves a great part of the village of the Ouachas. The rest had escaped to the French. I explain this matter in the entry of the 3rd of the present month.

Nov. 19. Sr. Delatour, an officer of the troops at New Orleans, passed here about six o'clock in the evening on his way to the Colapissas in haste to order those Indians to restore the Ouachas, whom they had made slaves, and to live in peace with them.

Nov. 20. The man named La Borde, who assassinated Sr. Pontual, has just been arrested at New Orleans. There are many other affairs to his account.

Nov. 21. *Sieur Damerval, a detailed officer commanding at Pensacola, went to the Bay of St. Joseph to reclaim the French deserters who were there. He brought back fifteen in consideration of three hundred piasters, which he paid for the expenditure which those deserters had made.*

Nov. 22. We have learned that at New Orleans it is a plague to get anything from the stores. Many respectable people can get nothing, not even brandy nor wine. It is only the friends who have any, although there is plenty of it for private individuals, like, and for example, Rossard, the notary, who some days past gave an entertainment at which was drunk a cask of wine and of the best.

Nov. 23. We have learned that Sr. Coustilas, an officer of the troops at N. O., who has a very fine place a league below, had presented a request to the council to have on his pay certain articles of merchandise, such as toiles de platille, etc.

The council replied that if he had any piasters they would give him what he asked for. To which Sr. de Coustilas replied that they paid him only in copper money and that it ought to have currency.

Nov. 24. We have learned that there are ninety people sick at N. O., with fevers and with other diseases, and that M. Bienville is much better.

Nov. 25. They are engaged in the trial of that La Borde who killed Sr. de Pontual, of which I spoke in the entry of the 15th of this month. He has undergone an examination in which he confessed that he had killed him.

Nov. 26. A boat, which is going to the Tensas to take on Indian corn for the company passed here. It informed us that yesterday there was a workman of the concession and a sailor who had had a keel-hauling at N. O. for having insulted a man named Drilland, disbursing clerk.

Nov. 27. M. Chateaugué,[1] king's lieutenant of the province, commandant at Mobile, brother of M. de Bienville, has arrived at New Orleans.

Nov. 28. Two Spanish ships, loaded with troops, have arrived at Isle Dauphine otherwise [known as] Massacre Island. They are going to Pensacola to take possession.

Nov. 29. M. Delatour, the officer who went to the Colapissas to reconcile them with the Ouachas, has passed here on his way back after having restored peace between these two nations, in accordance with his orders.

Nov. 30. *All of the prisoners whom Sr. Damerval, the officer, had brought back, have been set at liberty, having had for sole punishment a few days in prison.*

---

[1] Sieur Jean Baptiste Lemoyne de Chateaugue.

Continuation of the Journal for the Month of December, 1722

From New Orleans.

Dec. 5. The ship L'Alexandre has arrived at New Orleans.

Dec. 10. M. Guilhet, director of the company, died here of an attack of apoplexy, which lasted only 18 hours, at the end of which he gave up the ghost and was buried the same day.

Dec. 11. Several bundles of merchandise, belonging to Sr. Pasquier, an officer, have been seized. Sr. Marlot, a clerk at New Orleans, was involved, and they [Pasquier and Marlot] were sending that merchandise to St. Joseph Bay, a Spanish colony, to be sold.

Dec. 16. A brigantine, with twelve soldiers, commanded by Sr. de Moüy, an officer, has set out. It is loaded with the best merchandise from the magazines, which they are going to [use in] trade with the Spaniards; we do not know for whose account. From the 16th to the 21st of the same month we have been occupied with taking from the magazines of the company the things necessary for our trip to the Ilinnois.

Departed from New Orleans for the Ilinnois.

Here in the margin will be given the number of leagues.[1]

Dec. 22 — 3 leagues. We departed from New Orleans in a boat manned with fourteen men, nine soldiers and the rest sailors, accompanied by a pirogue manned with six men belonging to a certain Dulongpré, a Canadian living at the Ilinnois, who is returning there under our escort. The same day we reached the Chapitoulas and put in for the night.

Dec. 23 — 2 leagues. Early in the morning, our men having taken to the oars, we continued our journey, and came to the Cannes Bruslées, where we arrived about 11 o'clock in the morning, and spent the night.

[1] The date and the distance traveled each day are in the margin of the manuscript. It is to be noted, however, that the number of leagues in the margin differs in some instances from that in the text.

Dec. 24 — 1 league.   We set out about four o'clock in the evening and camped for the night a league above.

Dec. 25 — 6 leagues.   We departed early in the morning and had gone only a league when we perceived two boats coming down on the current, in one of which was Sr. Pailhoux, major-general, who is descending from the Natchez with his detachment [which he had taken] to make peace (as I have already explained in the Journal of last October). He told us nothing except that peace was made by the time of his arrival at the Natchez.

The same day we came for dinner with the Tensas, which are on the left in ascending, where Sr. Delaire has a little shack.   This Delaire was director of a concession which has not succeeded.

A quarter of a league back from this concession are the Chaouachas,[1] an Indian nation, which is abandoning this land on account of their disputes with the Colapissas respecting their medicine man.   A half league higher up on the same side and on the bank of the Mississipy, there are three little villages of Germans, commanded by Sr. Darensbourg. They may be about 300 in number, including the women and children.   They are the remnant of that multitude of Germans whom the company had sent here and who have, for the most part, died of destitution.

The same day at half past four in the evening we arrived at the village of the Colapissas, which is on the right as you ascend and there we spent the night.   This village is composed of 150 warriors.   Their chief occupation is that of planting great quantities of Indian corn which they sell to the French in exchange for merchandise.

Dec. 26 — 4 leagues.   We left the Colapissas about 10 o'clock in the morning, and passed on to the Petits Colas, three leagues distant from the last village.   There was in this place a house belonging to the Marquis d'Ancenys, which had been abandoned, and where at present lives the

---

[1] The Chaouachas were closely associated with the Ouachas or Washas.

Sr. De Chavagne, who has some negroes whom he employs in raising food crops.[1]

The same day an hour before sunset we put in for the night a league above.

Dec. 27 — 6 leagues. About 6 o'clock in the morning our men, having taken up their oars, we continued our journey and came for the night to the little village of the Hommas Indians, which is situated on the right as you ascend. A half league above is the great village of the Hoummas, of the same nation, and between these two Indian villages, there are eight French settlements which are engaged in raising food crops. This nation has in all 300 warriors, and works in the same way as the Colapissas.

Dec. 28 — 5½ leagues. We left about seven o'clock in the morning and arrived for breakfast at the fork of the Chetimacha,[2] which is on the left as you ascend, distant a league and a half from the Houmas. This is a branch of the Mississipy, which empties into the sea. We put in for the night four leagues above that.

Dec. 29 — 4 leagues. We continued our route, the weather being cold and gloomy, and came for dinner to the Bayagoulas,[3] a settlement which the Sr. Du Buisson exploits. It is on the left; a league and a half back is the village of the Chetimachas,[4] with whom we made peace in 1719. This nation has about 100 warriors, great eaters of the crocodile, or alligator, which they catch with considerable skill. When they see one of these animals in the water (they call them amphibious) they plunge after them and put one hand on the lower jaw and the other on the upper jaw, and they bring them in this way to the shore, where they kill them. I have seen some which were 17 feet long, including the head and the tail. This animal has no vertebra. Two leagues above the Bayagoulas, we camped for the night.

[1] *Vivres.*　　　　[2] Grand River in Louisiana.
[3] Here a village of the Bayagoulas, a Choctaw tribe of Indians, had been nearly exterminated by the Taensas in 1706, and the site was subsequently chosen for a concession to Paris Duvernay.
[4] A Choctaw village.

Dec. 30 — 6 leagues. We left about 6 o'clock in the morning and passed Menchaeg, which is on the right as you ascend, distant five leagues from the Bayagoulas. It is a branch of the Mississipy, which empties into Lake Ponchartrain, but so obstructed with wood that it is almost impossible to cross. However, there have been some traders who have crossed it by cutting away much of the wood. We spent the night three leagues above this place.

Dec. 31 — 2 leagues. We set out at day-break and came to Dirombourg, or Baton Rouges, which is on the right as you ascend. These are the first bluffs or steep banks which we have found on the Mississipy.

January, 1723

Jan. 1. We have remained here, being forced to do so by the rain which has not stopped all day.

Jan. 2 — 4 leagues. We left about 11 o'clock in the morning in a strong north wind and put in for the night at the Isle d'Ibervile. This is the first island there is in the main branch of the Mississipy.

Jan. 3 — 2 leagues. At 7 o'clock in the morning our men took their oars and we arrived for breakfast at the beginning of the Pointe Coupée bluffs, which are on the right as you ascend, where there is a settlement belonging to the Marquis Demezieres, which is almost abandoned. From there we forced our oars in order to stem a very strong current which runs from the bluffs to Pointe Coupée, and from there to the settlement of M. Collys, which is on the right as you ascend, a half league above, where we spent the night. There are at this settlement about twenty French and twenty-five negroes who cultivate rice, beans, potatoes, and other things necessary to life.

Jan. 4 — 5 leagues. We left this place and came for breakfast to the Rivière de la Chaudepisse, two leagues distant from the last settlement. Three leagues above that place we put in for the night.

Jan. 5 — 6 leagues. About 7 o'clock in the morning we

embarked and at dinner time reached the portage de la Croix. From there it is only two leagues by land to the Indian village of the Thonniquas, although it is ten by water. We camped two leagues above.

Jan. 6 — 4 leagues. Our men having resumed their oars, we reached by dinner time the Trois Chenaux [1] (these are formed by two islands) and continuing from there we put in for the night at the entrance of Red River, which is on the left as you ascend, where we found Father Boulanger, a Jesuit missionary from the Ilinnois, who was returning there in a pirogue manned with seven men and loaded with supplies for the convent. Those good fathers, who are at the Ilinnois, always attentive to increase their patrimony and never satisfied with it, had detailed him (Boulanger) in order that he, while attending to their affairs, might ask for them the ownership of a salt mine which is two leagues from the Kas Kas Kias. This they have not obtained. I do not know whether they had conscientiously any reason to ask for this, but I can affirm that for this purpose they availed themselves of the least skilful of all the Jesuits. This Reverend Father Boulanger had left New Orleans eight days before our boat (that is to say, before we left).

Jan. 7 — 2 leagues. We continued our route, accompanied by the pirogue of the reverend Jesuit father, and by that of Dulongpré, who have the firm intention not to leave us until [we reach] the Ilinnois, and arrived at the village of the Thonniqua Indians, which is situated on the right as you ascend. There may be in this village 200 warriors who live on hunting and Indian corn, which they raise. There are some of them who have a smattering of Christianity, but just as they were commencing to appreciate the Word of God, Father Davion [2] left them, to such a degree did his own interests outweigh those of charity. We spent the night in this place. There are also in this village fifteen French places which raise rice, beans, maize and other vegetables necessary to life. Their greatest trade is in poultry, which they go to New Orleans to sell.

[1] Three Channels.   [2] Antoine Davion.

Jan. 8 — 2 leagues. About 10 o'clock in the morning we left the Thonniquas, which is two leagues above, on the same side, where we spent the night and purchased some Indian provisions. In this place we hired an Indian hunter to go with us as far as the Arkansas.

Jan. 9 — 3 leagues. In the morning the pirogue of the Reverend Father and of Dulongpré joined us. They had remained at the first village of the Thonniquas to secure provisions. We then continued our journey and arrived at dinner time at the Chesnal du Diable, where the rain compelled us to spend the night. The salt meat which we brought for ourselves and our crew has given out. Our hunter does not kill anything and we have no hope [of getting food] until [we reach] the Yazous. It is above this post that the good hunting begins.

Jan. 10 — 5 leagues. We set out about 7 o'clock in the morning and put in for the night at La Bature au Chevreuil.

Jan. 11 — 5 leagues. Weather clear and cold. Our men resuming the oars, we continued our route and put in for the night at the Trois Chenaux, which is five leagues distant from the Natchez.

Jan. 12 — 5 leagues. We continued our journey. About noon we passed the white bluffs which are on the right as you ascend. It is to be remarked that from Bâton Rouges to Natchez there runs the same chain of mountains, which meet in two or three places on the banks of the Mississipy. The same day we came to spend the night at the Natchez.

Jan. 13. The fort of Natchez is a rather sorry fort of piles the size of a leg, where there are two small, mounted pieces of iron cannon, with only a brass swivel gun. Its form is square, having four bastions. It is situated at the top of the hill, which is nearly 400 feet high. There are [in the country] around this fort, which is all hills and valleys, several good habitants, who cultivate maize, beans, and other vegetables in quantity. They labor principally at tobacco raising, which grows there very fine and [is] good and abundant, but the scarcity of negroes among them prevents them from pushing forward this industry, which would be very profitable to them and advantageous to the colony.

Jan. 14. We summoned the Natchez chiefs to supply us with provisions, which they agreed to do; also the chief of the Tyous. This is a small nation which has its village a league to the south of the fort. This nation is not very large, consisting of only 50 men bearing arms. It has the same language as the Thonniquas and does not differ from them in any way as to customs.

Jan. 15. We went to the settlement of St. Catherine, belonging to MM. Colys and Company, which is a league back from the fort of the Natchez. We did not notice anything in particular there except a water mill which is on a little river which passes through the middle of this settlement. The houses are very ordinary and very badly built. The Sr. Dumanoir Feaucon, who is director of this concession, has two officers and a surgeon, together with some Frenchmen and negroes. I will not put them down here because I have made a special enumeration of them which will be found joined hereto. The officers employ the Frenchmen and negroes in cultivating the land so as to grow Indian corn, beans, potatoes, and other necessities of life. The land there is very fine and good, and is the same kind from New Orleans to here. They employ their Frenchmen and their negroes in the cultivation of tobacco of which they gather every year a fairly good quantity.

Jan. 16. We were invited to go to the Terre Blanche, a settlement formerly the Company's, belonging to M. Le Blanc, to be present at the appraising of the houses and other effects which the company left to M. Le Blanc. This appraising was very badly done because a house which was worth 800 livres was valued at only 200 livres, and an entirely new bridge which certainly cost more than 2000 livres to build [was valued at] 20 ecus and so on with the rest.

We did not notice anything in particular except the land, which is very fine and good, and where one can make a very fine settlement, for the culture of tobacco and Indian foods.

The Natchez Indians are situated a league back from the fort, and are scattered along in little villages to a distance of two leagues from the aforesaid fort. These Indians number perhaps 500 warriors. They live on Indian corn which they raise and from their hunting, which consists of deer, wild turkeys, ducks, geese and other game. They also kill buffaloes, but they have to go a very long distance to find them. These are the only Indians among whom I have noticed any kind of religion. They adore the sun from which they claim that their chief is descended, and they have a temple where they keep a sacred fire, which is never extinguished, several savages being assigned to the care of the temple and to keeping up this fire. They have several festivals. One among others which they call "La Thonne," is a little like our village festivals in France. The great chief, who is called the Great Sun, is absolute, having the power of death over his subjects. It is a wonderful thing how this great chief has only to say to one of his subjects that he must die for that subject to kill himself. When this great chief dies, about a hundred [people], both men and women, kill themselves. They die of their own accord in order that (so they say) they may go to serve their great chief in the other world. It is only the great chiefs who are buried in the temple of which I have just spoken. There is among this nation a squaw chief who has as much authority as the great chief. This squaw ordinarily marries a puant, that is as we would call a man who does not go to war, and at the very most he can only, after he has arrived at this distinction, take the rank of noble. Furthermore, upon the death of his wife, he must strangle himself, and with him as many people as if he died a great chief. It is from this squaw chief that the Great Suns are born and that they are perpetuated. Nevertheless their subjects render them infinite respect and blind obedience.

It is also to be remarked that the children of the Great Sun can only take the title of "spirits," and are not allowed to attain to the degree of great suns. It seems that, as I said, the Natchez Indians were scattered about in little villages, each of these villages has a chief or little sun, with a squaw chief, who are subordinate and obedient to the Great Sun and to the Great Squaw Chief, whom they do not fail to greet with yells. These yells are more than a secular adoration. There are in this nation three orders. The first consists of the great sun, the great squaw chief, with the spirits; the second, the nobles, who include the warriors, and certain families, who have cut the throats of five or six of their children at the death of the great chief or the great squaw chief, for in this way they acquire their nobility. The French are little by little weaning them away from these barbarous customs. The third order comprises the puants, who are men considered as not being warriors, as I have already said.

Polygamy is in practice here and among all the Indian nations which I have seen, but especially among these. The chiefs and the nobles can take as many wives as they please, but for the puants, when they have one, it is a good deal. Here the men do not leave their wives, but the wives leave the men to marry others, without the least complaint being made by those whom they leave. It is necessary, however, to make an exception in the case of the great sun: his wives may not leave him without his consent.

The women are fairly passable [as to looks] for Americans, and are all precocious in matters of love. One sees among them very few girls, twelve years old, who have not several lovers, all of whom they make happy. They blacken their teeth with a certain root, a practice which is greatly esteemed among them. This, together with their tawney color, renders them rather disagreeable to those who are not prejudiced in their favor. Nevertheless, they have rather regular features, and generally like all the Frenchmen, to whom they refuse none of their favors, in return for a few glass beads or other trifles; but the malign influences of Venus are so common that those who are wisest restrain themselves and go bridle in hand. They know how to cure all sorts of venereal diseases and have healed numerous Europeans.

In the house of the great chief (generally all of their houses are made in the shape of a dome, with neither chimney nor window, and only one door) in the evening, by the light of a cane torch, when the chief so orders, a sort of comedy is performed. There are some which one can look at and which are very bizarre, but there are some also which are full of all sorts of license and in which they make no difficulty in representing the most indecent actions. So much for what I more especially observed at the Natchez, both among the French and among the Indians.

I do not recount here the war which our French have had with these Indians. I have made a separate Journal concerning this which will be found joined hereto.

Jan. 17. I have made my review as inspector at Fort Rosalie of the Natchez.

Jan. 18. The Indians have commenced to bring us provisions, and we have endeavored to take a census of all the inhabitants.

Jan. 19. There arrived here in a pirogue a man by the name of Lehoux, clerk of the company at the Arkansas. He is going down to New Orleans to secure some things for the subsistence of the troops, not having any at all in his stores. The same day about four o'clock in the afternoon, this Lehoux left here.

Jan. 20. Two hours before day there arrived from the Yazous a boat manned with ten soldiers in charge of a sergeant, which is carrying a half score of workmen for Terre Blanche. These people are from the concession of M. Le Blanc. They are abandoning the post of the Yazous because of the sickness there, and the company of Bernaval will go to the fort of the Yazous.

Jan. 21. We have finished the transportation of our Indian provisions, which consist of Indian corn, some crushed and other ground into meal, and we are getting ready to depart.

Jan. 22 — 3 leagues. We left the Natchez about 2 o'clock in the afternoon in company of the boat of which I have just spoken, and which is returning to the Yazous, of the pirogue of the Reverend Jesuit Father, and that of Dulongpré, and we put in for the night three leagues above the Natchez.

Jan. 23 — 6 leagues. Fine weather. Our men took up the oars about noon. A good wind from the south assisted us until evening, when we put to shore to camp for the night.

Jan. 24 — 6 leagues. The stiff breeze holding, we came by dinner time without rowing to the Petit Gouffre, which is a bluff where a great eddy is formed, which is very dangerous when the waters are high. Two leagues above this spot we put in for the night.

Jan. 25 — 5 leagues. Fine weather. The wind being in the north, our men took up their oars and we came in time for dinner to the Grand Gouffre, so called because of the great currents which form whirlpools when the waters are high. We camped for the night on an island two leagues above this spot.

Jan. 26. We set out about 7 o'clock in the morning. Heavy currents, which is why we have made only four leagues.

Jan. 27 — 3 leagues. Early in the morning, our people having resumed their oars, we continued our journey. At noon the rain having caught us, we were obliged to seek shelter.

Jan. 28 — 4 leagues. The rain continued this morning until about 11 o'clock, when, it having suddenly ceased, we continued our journey and made four leagues.

Jan. 29 — 3 leagues. Cold weather. Our people having taken their oars, we continued our journey. Strong currents, together with a violent north wind; nevertheless we reached for the night a little island about two leagues from the mouth of the Rivière des Yazous.

Jan. 30 — 2 leagues. Weather dark and cold. We departed about 10 o'clock in the morning and camped at the entrance to the Petite Rivière des Yazous.

Jan. 31. Weather clear and fine. About 9 o'clock in the morning we set out and arrived about noon at Fort de

St. Pierre des Yazous, which is three leagues up this river, on the right. The concession of M. Le Blanc is in this same place.

February, 1723

Feb. 1. We stayed at Fort St. Pierre des Yazous, which is on a bluff. The plan of the Fort is square, having four bastions surrounded by a little moat about six feet wide and three feet deep. The commandant, who is M. Degrave, has his house in the fort, as do also the officers and the soldiers, who form two companies. It is at this fort where I have seen the best disciplined troops and where the duty is performed with exactitude, thanks to the attention of the commandant. These two companies are to go to the Natchez, as I have already said. A league above Fort St. Pierre, on the bank of the river, and on the same side, there are three Indian villages, which hardly make one. They are the Yazous, the Aufaugoulas and the Couroyes. The last are going to establish themselves on the Rivière des Ouatchitas. These nations number in all perhaps 200 warriors, who form a sort of little republic, living without recognizing any chiefs. I will say nothing of their manners and customs. I stayed there too short a time to enlighten myself concerning them. Their manner of living is sufficiently like that of the Natchez.

Feb. 2. About 9 o'clock in the morning I made my review as inspector. The same day we learned from the Yazous Indians that the Chectas,[1] an Indian nation, our allies, had entirely destroyed the largest village of the Chicachats, our enemies.

Feb. 3. About 10 o'clock in the morning we set out from Fort St. Pierre des Yazous and put in for the night at the entrance of that river, where we joined the Jesuit father and Dulongpré, who were awaiting us there with their pirogues.

Feb. 4 — 5 leagues. We departed about 8 o'clock in the morning and spent the night five leagues above.

---

[1] Choctaws.

Feb. 5 — 3 leagues. Our men took up their oars about 7 o'clock in the morning and we went about a league when we put to shore, and found several huts of the nation of Couroye Indians, whom I have already said were on the Rivière des Yazous. They were hunting. As we had no meat, we bought some buffalo, bear oil, and other meat in exchange for powder, shot, knives and other things. We put in for the night at the usual hour, which is an hour before sunset. We figured we had made three leagues.

Feb. 6. · Our men having taken their oars, we continued our journey against rather strong currents, and camped four leagues above.

Feb. 7 — 5 leagues. It being Sunday before Lent, the Reverend Father Boulanger, the Jesuit, said mass for us after which we embarked and continued our journey. At 11 o'clock in the morning we perceived a little fire on the other side of the river at the end of the cove, which we were not able to reconnoitre because of the strong currents and [on account of] which, after we lost two leagues of our way, we continued our route and camped opposite a little island, having made five leagues, during the day.

Feb. 8. All the past night it did not stop raining, and, the rain continuing, we have been obliged to stay here, where we noticed numerous tracks, all fresh, of buffalo, which induced us to go hunting, and to dispatch our Indian [to hunt], who has killed nothing.

Feb. 9. The rain fell all the past night and continued this morning, which obliged us to remain here.

Feb. 10. The rain having ceased, we continued our journey, and, three leagues above, we found seven pirogues loaded with meat which Canadian traders, established at the Ilinnois, are taking down to New Orleans to sell. They told us that diseases had been very prevalent among the Ilinnois, and that many Canadians had died. Rain having overtaken us in this place, we passed the night here. The Reverend Father Boulanger, the Jesuit, has sold many things, such as clothes and linen, at a profit of 400 per cent.

Feb. 11. Weather fair and cold. We remained here

with the canoes of the Canadians to dry our clothes which were wet through and through.

Feb. 12. Fine weather. Our men having resumed their oars, we departed about 7 o'clock in the morning. A good current and we put in for the night three leagues above.

Feb. 13 — 2 leagues. We departed about 8 o'clock in the morning and about noon we perceived on the other side of the river a herd of wild cattle, [buffaloes], which were coming there to drink, a thing which induced us to cross over and to go ashore so as to kill some of them; but these animals, having scented us, we could not approach them. From this place we came to pass the night at a little island, which is a little above the Petite Pointe Coupeé, where our Indian killed us a young roe.

Feb. 14. We set out about 7 o'clock in the morning, after having heard the mass of Father Boulanger, and arrived at a little island, which is a league above, where we waited for a certain Legras, a Canadian from the pirogue of Dulongpré, and a Yazous Indian, who had departed this morning. As these two men did not return, we were obliged to camp and to fire off a gun at intervals.

Feb. 15. It rained all last night and this morning, and although we have fired the gun many times, it has not been responded to, which makes us think that some misfortune must have happened to those men or that they had lost their way. The rain continued all day and did not cease until evening, when we began again to fire off our guns, which were responded to, shot for shot, but night having come, we did not send out to investigate these shots, not knowing whether they came from our enemies or from the two men. The same day we noticed that the water had risen 3 feet.

Feb. 16. Fine weather. The man called Dulongpré, a Canadian, sent his pirogue manned with four men to investigate the shots which had been heard yesterday evening. Our men, having dried all their clothing, we set out about 11 o'clock in the morning and spent the night on a large island which is two leagues above, in the hope of finding some buffaloes. The water rose last night 8 feet.

Feb. 17. We are in great need of meat. Our men begin to grumble,[1] and our Indian has hunted without having killed anything, which has determined us to leave for Grande Pointe Coupée to endeavor to kill some buffaloes, for we are reduced to Indian corn, without either meat or flour, and with no hope of killing any buffaloes from here to the Arkansas. That nation having come to hunt in these quarters, has caused these animals to withdraw into the back country.

The same day at noon we arrived at Pointe Coupée, hunting all the time, and we camped there as much to hunt as to wait for the Jesuit priest and Dulongpré, who joined us at three o'clock in the afternoon without having found the two men. This determined M. Diron [3] to propose to them to set out with some Frenchmen and two Indians to go to see what had become of these two men. The past night the water rose 5 feet.

Feb. 18. At day-break, Father Boulanger said mass, during which time we unloaded his pirogue and I ordered out nine Frenchmen and four Indians, and we embarked in the pirogue of the Reverend Jesuit Father, having left my secretary with fifteen men as a guard for my boat.

The same day at ten o'clock in the morning, after we had drifted three leagues, we perceived in the middle of the river two men on a raft (*cajeu*) made of three pieces of wood tied together. They were the two men for whom we were looking. They told us that they had gotten lost in a marshy country, full of canes, through which they had difficulty in seeing the sun so as to guide themselves; that they had been three days without eating; that the 4th day they had each killed a deer; that they had not been able to find the Mississipy; that this morning they had at last come upon the banks of it without being able to recognize the place in which they were, and that they had resolved

---

[1] *Tomber sur les dents.*

[2] Artaguiette, the author of the journal.

to make this raft (cajeu) so as to drift to the first post. They had still the half of a deer and a charge of powder, which they were saving to kindle a fire with. We put about, therefore, after having taken on these two men, and by dint of rowing rejoined our boat at three o'clock in the afternoon, and spent the night there. Last night the water rose 7 feet.

Feb. 19 — 5 leagues. We set out at day-break and passed the night five leagues above. Last night we noticed that the water had risen 3 feet. Today we killed three ducks.

Feb. 20 — 5 leagues. Early in the morning our men having taken to their oars, the weather being fine, we put in for the night at the usual hour five leagues above our last camp, where our Indians went to hunt and returned without having seen any animals. The past night the water rose 4 feet.

Feb. 21 — 6 leagues. At day-break the Reverend Jesuit Father said mass, after which we embarked and continued our journey, killed two ducks, and camped six leagues above. Today the water rose 4 feet.

Feb. 22. About 5 o'clock in the morning our men having taken the oars, we continued our journey and at noon we entered the Petite Rivière de Sotéhouy [1] or Arkansas, which is on the left as you ascend, and camped a league up it, looking as though it might rain. We killed two ducks. Last night the water rose 7 feet.

Feb. 23 — 6 leagues. All last night it thundered and lightened, and a little rain fell. That did not hinder us from setting out this morning at day-break. About 3 o'clock in the afternoon we passed a branch of this river, which empties into the Mississipy six leagues above that [branch] which we entered. We camped a league above.

Feb. 24. We left at sunrise and arrived at the village de Sotéhouy [2] about 9 o'clock in the morning. It is on the left as you ascend. The same day, at noon, Sr. La Boulaye,

[1] Named for a portion of the Quapaw or Arkansas Indians.
[2] Quapaw or Arkansas Indians.

commandant of the post, which is a league from here by land, and two by water, on the right as you ascend, came to see us.

Feb. 25. We have made a talk to the Indians and made them promise to furnish us some provisions.

The same day about 8 o'clock in the morning, the weather being gloomy, we departed, my secretary and I, and we had not gone a league when we came to the new village of the Arkansas, who lived not so very long ago twelve leagues higher up on the Mississipy, on the left, as you ascend. We embarked from there in a little pirogue to go to the settlement of M. Law, which is a quarter of a league distant by water from this village. We arrived there at 11 o'clock in the morning. We did not notice anything in particular. There are only three miserable huts, fourteen Frenchmen and six negroes, whom Sr. Dufresne, who is the director there for the company, employs in clearing the land. Since they have been on this land they have not even been able to raise Indian corn for their own nourishment, and they have been compelled to trade for it and to send even to the Ilinnois for it.[1]

The same day at 2 o'clock in the afternoon we embarked in a little Indian pirogue and arrived at about 4 o'clock in the evening at the post, where are the troops commanded by Sr. La Boulaye. There is no fort at all. The commandant there has only a little hut. There is also a sort of barn which serves as a lodging for the soldiers, who are very badly equipped in every respect. There are also in the vicinity of this post, on the banks of the river, many French habitants, who are all men dismissed from the concession belonging heretofore to M. Law. The Jesuit father baptised there two French children and performed two marriage ceremonies.

Feb. 26. In the morning I made my review at the completion of which I departed to join my boat, which had

[1] The Company granted John Law a concession twelve miles square on the Arkansas, he agreeing to settle upon it a colony of fifteen hundred Germans.

remained at the village of Sotéhouy two leagues below by water and one league by land. I found my detachment very much incensed at the Indians, who were playing a thousand tricks upon them. This forced me to make them promise to discontinue these practices, which promises they observed very religiously all the time that I remained there.

Feb. 27. I have had collected all the purchased provisions which have cost us rather dear. The nation of Arkansas was formerly separated into two villages, one on the banks of the Mississipy, 12 leagues from here as you ascend, called the great village of the Arkansas, and this one, which is on the Riviere de Sotéhouy, as I have already said. The first has come to establish itself near the second, on the same river. This nation has perhaps 300 warriors. They clothe themselves, as well as their women and children, in buffalo skins, and plant Indian corn, which is their principal food, together with their hunting, which consists of wild cattle, stags, deer and bear. These Indians worship the moon, to which they are accustomed to pray every evening. These are surely the coarsest and the most superstitious savages that I know in Louisiana. They have a method of healing their sick which is very peculiar. About a year ago almost all of them were afflicted with smallpox (a disease unknown among the Indians before the French came among them). Their medicine men, who are jugglers, begin by approaching the sick person, uttering at the same time horrible yells and making frightful contortions, which they continue for an hour, so as to conjure the evil spirit to depart. At the end of this time they pour over the sick person five or six pails of water, which was almost ice (for it was in the winter) after which they chase away the spirit with imprecations, and, acting as if they held it, they put it out of the tent, whereupon is concluded the treatment, which is twice a day, until the patient is either dead or cured. If he recovers, the juggler or medicine man is highly esteemed and well paid, but if on the other hand he dies, the medicine man receives nothing, but, on the contrary, he loses much of the respect which they formerly had for him.⌉

They believe in metempsychosis, with this reservation : that they believe that the soul of their relatives does not take up its abode in the wild animals which they kill or in their enemies. I have seen an Indian of this nation kill a buffalo and make a sign to several French people who were present not to come near until he had given numerous yells and had spoken some words which we did not understand, after which he told us that it was an enemy, who was in the body of this animal.

The women are passable for Americans, and are all very well-behaved, for I do not believe that there is a man in the colony who can boast of having had any gallant relations with any Arkansas girl or woman. The reason which is offered for this is rather curious, if one cares to believe the interpreters, who say that their men make them believe that they would die if they had the least intercourse with us. The women do all the work except the hunting which is the ordinary occupation of the men, as is also the dressing of the buffalo skins, upon which they paint designs with vermilion and other colors. These skins are very highly prized among the other nations.

Feb. 28. It rained all of last night and the rain continues, which has made us put off our departure until tomorrow.

March, 1723

Mar. 1 — 3 leagues. Early in the morning we set out from the village of Sotéhouy so as to continue our journey, having left there the Jesuit father and Dulongpré who are making a search for a young man who deserted from the pirogue of the Jesuit father.

Between nine and ten o'clock in the morning we entered the Mississipy by the upper branch and continued our journey with a favorable wind until about noon, when the wind having become contrary, we put to shore to await the two pirogues. We figured that we have made 7 leagues today, 4 in the Petite Riviere de Sotéhouy and 3 in the Mississipy.

Mar. 2. Fine weather. We were obliged to remain here to await the two pirogues of the Reverend Father and of Dulongpré, who did not join us until very late in the evening, without having found their man. The water rose 5 feet the past night.

Mar. 3 — 5 leagues. We departed early in the morning in company with the Reverend Jesuit Father and Dulongpré, to each of whom we had to give a man as otherwise they would not have been able to follow us. The same day we reached and camped at the old village of the Arkansas. The water rose 6 feet last night.

Mar. 4 — 2 leagues. We made two leagues today against a heavy current. The rain, which overtook us, was the cause of our having gone into camp alone, the Jesuit father and Dulongpré having gone on ahead because they make very poor progress.

Mar. 5 — 2 leagues. Our men having taken to their oars about 6 o'clock in the morning, we continued our journey and joined the Reverend Father and Dulongpré by breakfast. The weather was bad which was the reason we made only two leagues. The water rose 6 feet last night.

Mar. 6 — 3 leagues. We departed about 7 o'clock in the morning with heavy currents and a contrary wind. At noon the Reverend Jesuit Father and Dulongpré fell behind, not being able to follow us, which caused us to camp two hours before sunset so as to wait for them. We figured that we had made 3 leagues today.

Mar. 7. Fine weather. We were obliged to wait for the pirogues of the Reverend Father and Dulongpré, who joined us with great difficulty about 9 o'clock in the morning. We then continued our journey against heavy currents and camped 3 leagues above. Killed a bustard which gave us great pleasure, as we and our men were reduced to eating Indian corn with water and salt. We noticed that the past night the water had receded half a foot.

Mar. 8 — 2 leagues. We departed about 6 o'clock in the

morning and arrived about noon at Cap a l'Anguille, so called because of some travellers having caught eels there. This is a bluff which juts out into the Mississipy, on the left as you ascend. There we went ashore to make some oars, as we no longer had any spare [oars]. We spent the night there.

Mar. 9. We departed about 6 o'clock in the morning and arrived about 10 o'clock at the mouth of the St. Francois River, which is on the left as you ascend, where, having noticed some buffalo tracks, quite newly made, we resolved to camp and go hunting. Many of our Frenchmen having set off for the chase (we no longer had any Indians as they left us at the Arkansas) saw some buffaloes but were not able to kill them. We are, however, in great need of them as our men are beginning to get tired of boiled lean meat.[1]

Mar. 10 — 3 leagues. In the morning we had a little rain, which lasted until about 9 o'clock. This having ceased, we set out and travelled till an hour before sunset, when we camped for the night. We figured that we had gone 3 leagues. The water fell a foot last night.

Mar. 11 — 5 leagues. Weather gloomy and foggy. We departed about 7 o'clock in the morning. At noon with fine weather and a good south wind, we made a league by sail, without rowing. The Reverend Father and Dulongpré went ashore to hunt, and we continued our journey. About an hour before sunset we went ashore to camp for the night. We estimated that today we had gone five leagues. The water fell last night a foot and a half.

Mar. 12 — 2 leagues. We departed about 7 o'clock in the morning and arrived about 10 o'clock at the Chenal du Diable, where, having gone ashore to hunt, we killed a cow. At noon we were joined by the Reverend Father and Dulongpré, who have not killed anything. We gave them a part of our meat, and spent the night in the same place. The water fell last night a foot.

Mar. 13 — 3 leagues. The weather was gloomy, but it

---

[1] *Gras à l'eau sans graisse.*

did not hinder us from setting out about 8 o'clock in the morning, against heavy currents. We put in for the night three leagues above. As we were about to camp we perceived on the other side of the river a herd of buffaloes. The pirogue of Dulongpré crossed over, but they killed nothing. The water fell last night two feet.

Mar. 14. The Reverend Jesuit Father said mass this morning. A violent north by northwest wind with lightning and thunder, accompanied by rain, which continued all day. This forced us to remain here in spite of ourselves.

Mar. 15 — 4 leagues. We departed about 6 o'clock in the morning. Gloomy weather, which cleared. About noon fine weather and good currents. About an hour before sunset as we were about to camp, one of the Frenchmen went ashore and killed a buffalo. We camped for the night at the same place. We estimated that we had gone four leagues. The past night the water fell three feet.

Mar. 16 — 3 leagues. Fine weather and a good northwest wind brought us without rowing to the Rivière a Margot, where we had dinner. In this place we had a violent and contrary wind, which was the reason we made only one league. The hour for camping having come, we put to shore and killed a cow, which we were not able to take, the night having overtaken us. The past night the water fell two feet.

Mar. 17 — 2 leagues. Two of our Frenchmen went ashore (while we continued our journey) to look for the cow which they had killed yesterday, but they found that it had been entirely devoured by the wolves. They killed another and came to join us a league above our last camp, where they had gone ashore to search for it [the cow]. After we had divided it between the two pirogues and ourselves, we continued our journey and had not gone a league when a violent northwest wind forced us to go ashore to take shelter for the night.

Mar. 18. — A violent north wind blew the past night which increased this morning, and still continues. This has decided us to remain here.

Mar. 19 — 2 leagues. Weather gloomy and cold. We departed about 7 o'clock in the morning, and we proceeded until about noon when it began to snow. This obliged us to go ashore to camp. The snow continued until evening. About 2 o'clock that afternoon a hundred paces from us three buffaloes threw themselves into the water and crossed over to the other side.

Mar. 20 — 3 leagues. We set out about 7 o'clock in the morning. Gloomy weather and heavy currents. We journeyed till an hour before sunset when we put to shore to camp for the night. One of our men having gone about two arpents inland, killed a buffalo. We estimated that we had gone three leagues today.

Mar. 21 — 5 leagues. Palm Sunday. The Jesuit father said mass, after which we embarked and rowed until breakfast, when a southeast wind sprung up. We hoisted our sail and came without the use of oars to the Seconds Ecores a Prud'homme, where the wind having failed us we put to shore to camp. We estimated that we had made five leagues.

Mar. 22. The thunder, lightning and rain continued all of the past night. At 10 o'clock in the morning the rain ceased. The weather was still cloudy and cold. We were obliged to remain, the winds having gone around to the north and becoming violent.

Mar. 23 — 3 leagues. Weather cloudy and cold. However, we embarked and came in spite of the currents to eat dinner two leagues above, where we killed a fat she bear of enormous size. A league above we killed a buffalo. We camped there.

Mar. 24. All the past night it has not ceased to rain, and this morning the rain continuing, we have been obliged to remain.

Mar. 25. Fine weather. We departed about 7 o'clock in the morning, after having heard the mass of the Reverend Jesuit Father. We breakfasted on top of the Ecores a Prud'homme, and passed the night in spite of a heavy current three leagues above where we killed [incomplete]. This is the place where Langevin, father and son, were captured by the Chicachats. Some of the other Frenchmen who were in the same pirogue killed a buffalo. The past night the water rose a foot.

Mar. 26 — 4 leagues. Weather clear and cold. We set out about 6 o'clock in the morning against a heavy current, and ate dinner at the beginning of the Isle au Canadiens, where we saw a pirogue and some broken chests. From this place we went to spend the night a league above. We estimated that we had gone four leagues.

Mar. 27. About six o'clock in the morning, we departed, the weather was cloudy. We had not gone a league when we were forced to go ashore to seek shelter, the rain having overtaken us.

Our men went hunting and killed two buffaloes, about a league above. This induced us, the weather becoming fine, to embark so as to get the two buffaloes, and we determined to spend the night there in spite of the fact that the fine weather continued.

Mar. 28. We remained here to celebrate the holy Easter festival, and to give time to our men to make their devotions. The Reverend Father said high mass for us this morning, and, after noon, vespers. There were only two men in our boat who did not take communion.

Mar. 29. The Reverend Jesuit Father said mass for us this morning, after which we had hopes of continuing our journey but there came on a heavy rain which continued all day and which forced us to remain. The past night the water rose 4 feet.

Mar. 30. The lightning, thunder and rain continued without ceasing all last night. This morning the rain continues, which has made it impossible for us to depart. We noticed that the water had risen 3 feet since yesterday.

Mar. 31. Fine weather. We set out at day-break and had not gone a league when we met seven pirogues full of traders living among the Ilinnois, who had been hunting in the Riviere de Ouabache.[1] They are loaded with salt meat

---

[1] Ohio River.

and bear oil, which they are going to sell at New Orleans. They were not able to tell us any news from the Ilinnois as it had been four months since they left there. We camped in this place, both to write by this way to the sea [*i.e.* to avail ourselves of this opportunity of sending letters], and to dry our clothes. The past night the water rose 4 feet.

April, 1723

Apr. 1 — 4 leagues. At day-break the Reverend Jesuit Father said mass for us, at which the traders attended. After this was over we embarked and continued our journey. Heavy currents and contrary winds. However, we went four leagues today. After we had camped, one of our men went hunting and killed a buffalo. In this place Dulong-pré sent his pirogue back to the seat and put part of his people in our boat and part in the pirogue of the father; and the Reverend Jesuit Father got into our boat. The water rose last night 2 feet.

Apr. 2 — 4 leagues. We departed about 6 o'clock in the morning and proceeded until breakfast time, when, having seen a herd of buffaloes, our Frenchmen went after them and killed one which was found to be very fat.

Apr. 3 — 6 leagues. Fine weather. We set out about 5 o'clock in the morning and came to breakfast at La Petite Prairie, and from this place, in spite of heavy currents, we came to camp five leagues above.

Apr. 4. The fine weather continues. The Jesuit father said mass, after which our men taking up their oars we continued our journey and came to eat dinner at the place where Chesne, a Canadian, had been killed, together with an Arkansas. They were going up the Ilinnois from this place. We went on and camped a league above. The past night the water rose four feet.

Apr. 5 — 4 leagues. The Reverend Father said mass for us this morning, after which we embarked and continued our journey. At noon two of our men having wished to go hunting, lost their way. We waited for them, firing guns at intervals, which they heard. They joined us after having kept us waiting two hours and a half. We then continued our journey and camped at the usual hour, having made four leagues today. With much difficulty we found a place to camp.

Apr. 6 — 5 leagues. The water rose last night four feet. Fine weather and very warm. We departed at day-break and proceeded all day against heavy currents. We were until night before we could find any land to camp on, the two banks of the river being inundated. At length we found a little place about two arpents in size where we spent the night.

Apr. 7 — 3 leagues. We departed at day-break, the weather being fine, and journeyed until about 11 o'clock in the morning, when a south by southeast wind began to blow with violence, and we went a good league without rowing .when, the wind changing suddenly to the southwest, we undertook to cross, and when we were half way over we had a gust of wind west by southwest, which made us take water over the side. We were obliged to take down our sail and to finish the crossing with the oar. On the other side we found very fortunately a little bayou which we entered for shelter. The pirogue of the Reverend Jesuit Father was in very great peril and had much difficulty in joining us in the place in which we were. At length [the squall] having ceased we resolved to continue our journey so as to find a place to camp.

Apr. 8. All last night there was lightning in the west and this morning rain, which did not hinder us from setting out, and from going to the iron mine to hunt, as our men had no meat. We arrived there about 10 o'clock in the morning, and there we camped. As soon as we were on land our Frenchmen went hunting and killed two buffalo, two deer and a wild turkey.

Apr. 9. Weather clear and cold. We have been obliged to remain here so as to make oars and to give our men some rest.

Apr. 10 — 1 league. Gloomy weather. However we

departed about 7 o'clock in the morning, and, the rain having overtaken us, we were obliged to put ashore a league above. Our men went hunting and killed a buffalo, three wild turkeys and a young deer.

Apr. 11 — 4 leagues. All last night there was thunder and rain, which continued until about 11 o'clock in the morning, which having ceased, we embarked, after having heard the mass of the Reverend Jesuit Father, and put in for the night at the usual hour four leagues above our last camp.

Apr. 12 — 2 leagues. It rained all last night and continued this morning until noon, when we embarked to continue our journey. High winds and strong currents, in spite of which we reached the Riviere de Ouabache,[1] which is on the right as you ascend, where we camped. We noticed that this river had all overflowed, and that it pushes back the Mississipy, which is very low.

Apr. 13 — 8 leagues. Fine weather. We departed about 5 o'clock in the morning and came to eat dinner 4 leagues above the Ouabache at the place where the Sioux, an Indian Nation (who live towards the head of the Mississipy, a hundred leagues above the Ilinnois), had killed a man called Desnepveus, his wife, and two of his children. They were coming from Canada to establish themselves at the Ilinnois. From here we came to pass the night at the place where M. de Longuiel had been killed, [and] where we have been confirmed (in our opinion) that the Mississipy was very low. In this place we killed three bears. We estimated that we had gone eight leagues.

Apr. 14 — 6 leagues. Weather fine and cold. At daybreak we embarked and came in time for dinner to Cap a la Cruche, so called because a Canadian, in ascending to the Ilinnois from Isle D'Auphine had broken there a jug or an earthen pot. Here the north winds began to blow, which is the reason we made only two leagues, and camped. It is to be noted that from the Ouabache up to this point we

---

[1] Ohio River, to the lower part of which the name Wabash was then often given.

found no currents. The reason is, as I have said, that the Ouabache is high, the Mississipy very low, the former pushing back the latter.

Apr. 15 — 8 leagues. Fine weather. We set out at day-break, no current, the wind from the southeast. We went two leagues of the way without rowing, and came to pass the night a league below Cap St. Anthoine.

Apr. 16 — 8 leagues. Fine weather and a good south wind, which enabled us to round with shipped oars Cap. St. Anthoine where we had breakfast. This is a rock, round in shape, high and steep, so called because a company of traders have sojourned there during the feast of St. Anthony. The wind continuing we came without the use of oars to eat dinner at the Cap a l'Ail, so called because there grows there a great deal of garlic which is very good and which does not differ in any way from that of France. Here the wind left us. Our men took up the oars and we continued our journey to above Cap St. Cosme, where we spent the night. This is a high and steep rock, forming a point which juts out into the Mississipy, so named by M. de St. Cosme,[1] priest of the seminary of Canada, when he was descending from the Ilinnois to Mobile.

Apr. 17. At midday we arrived at the entrance of the Petite Riviere des Cascakias,[2] which is on the right as you ascend. It is two leagues up this river on the left (on the right is a border of high mountains) in a vast prairie that is situated the French village called the Cascakias, which is composed entirely of farmers who live there very comfortably. French wheat grows very well there and of a fine quality, of which they gather a fairly large quantity, which they sell for the subsistence of the troops. All the other vegetables necessary to life grow very well there. Their houses are all built of frame timbers on the ground. The chimneys are of stone, of which they could very easily build their entire houses, as the stone there is of very

[1] Jean Francois de St. Cosme, an early missionary to the Indians at Cahokia and Natchez.

[2] Kaskaskia River.

good quality and ready at hand, but the scarcity of men has prevented them from undertaking this work. Several inhabitants also have horse tread mills of their own with which they grind their French wheat. There is also a church there, which is certainly the finest in the colony. This church is ministered to by a Jesuit who performs the functions of curate and takes the tithes which are fairly large.

There is in this village a windmill made of wood, belonging to the Reverend Jesuit Fathers. It was formerly placed on the bank of the Petite Riviere, but as it got little wind in this place, they considered it wise to place it in the middle of the prairie, upon their own land, where it is certainly better off. The Jesuit priests have a little farm in this place, which they manage themselves. I do not give here the number of their cattle nor their other property, because I have put it in a general enumeration which will be found affixed hereto. It is six leagues by land and twelve by water from this village to Fort de Chartres. A league higher up on the same side on the road which leads to Fort de Chartres and upon the same river is found the settlement of Sr. Melicq, lieutenant of the company of Artaguiette, which he manages himself. They gather here French wheat, maize, beans, peas, pumpkins and other vegetables. From this place, continuing along the road to Fort de Chartres, at the upper end of the same prairie as that upon which Sr. Melicq is, a half league higher up on the bank of the same river, is the Indian village of the Ilinnois, who number about 200 warriors. From this village one goes on through beautiful wide prairies which are cut only by a few fringes of timber, to the above-mentioned Fort de Chartres.

Apr. 18 — 5 leagues. We set out from the mouth of the Petite Riviere and came to pass the night at the salt spring, which is on the left side of the Mississipy. (This is a fountain of salt water which has its ebb and flow like the ocean.) The habitants use it to make salt, which they make by boiling the water in caldrons till a certain amount has been boiled away, and when this is done, the water crystallizes of itself and forms a fairly good salt. They go there every year to get a supply of it.

It is only two leagues from here to the village of the Cascakias, although it is seven leagues in making the detour by the Petite Rivière. Upon leaving the Cascakias they make the west [1] and come upon the Mississipy, which they cross by means of pirogues, which they take care to have in readiness here.

From this salt spring going west fourteen leagues back is the region of the mines which M. de la Motte Cadillac,[2] formerly commandant of the country, had opened up about the year 1715. Before arriving at these mines, which are a chain of mountains in the middle of which flows a brook, one crosses over for about a half league a mountain which is all stone, as clear as crystal and very sharp.

Two leagues to the west of this mine is a river, called the St. Francois River. It is very beautiful. They claim that is the same St. Francois River which has its mouth twenty leagues above the Arkansas. This was a discovery which we had intended to make, but did not.

Apr. 19 — 5 leagues. We departed from this place and arrived at 5 o'clock in the afternoon at Fort de Chartres, which is on the bank of the Mississipy, on the right as you ascend. From the salt spring to Fort de Chartres is five leagues. Fort de Chartres is a fort of piles the size of one's leg, square in shape, having two bastions, which command all of the curtains. There are two companies of infantry in garrison commanded by M. de Boisbriant, Knight of the military order of St. Louis, first royal lieutenant of the province. There is a church outside of the fort and some dwellings a half league lower down on the same side as well as half a league above as far as little village of the Ilinnois where there are two Jesuit fathers, missionaries, who have a dwelling and a church. This little village which is called

---

[1] I mean to say they go to the west. (This note is in the margin of the manuscript.)

[2] Cadillac was governor of Louisiana in 1712–1716, while Antoine Crozat, the predecessor of the Western Company, was proprietor.

Mechiquamias[1] numbers perhaps about 200 warriors. From there one goes through a large and vast prairie a league and a half to the northwest where M. Renaut,[2] director of the mines, is established with two score Frenchmen, all laborers. This place is a quarter of a league distant from the Missisipy. There is a fort, with stakes the size of a leg. The shape is that of two horse shoes, one turning in and the other turning out, with two square bastions. There are in this fort a church, four houses, frame, and one of stone, which was begun last year but which the work of the mines prevented from being finished. About a half league to the east of this fort are two large marshes which in the winter time are covered with wild geese, bustards, ducks, teal, and other game. When we arrived Sr. Renaut had left, about the month of March of the present year, to go to a mine in the Riviere Maramecq,[3] with a detachment of ten men, commanded by a sergeant. He is still there and is working hard. We hope upon his return, which cannot long be delayed, that we shall learn the truth as to whether these mines are valuable. The trade of the inhabitants of the Ilinnois, who are Canadians, French or discharged soldiers, consists in selling their wheat and other products to the company for the subsistence of the troops, in exchange for merchandize (which they are obliged to fetch from New Orleans) which they trade to the Indians for quarters of buffalo, bear oil and other meats, which serve them for food or which they sell in exchange for merchandize. They also trade in skins, such as beaver, buck and deer, buffalo and bear skins, and other peltries, which they get very cheap from the Indians, and which they sell at a very high price to the traders who come down from Canada every spring and autumn, and who give them merchandize in exchange. For it is not necessary for them to rely upon having their needs supplied from New Orleans, whence very few convoys

[1] Michigamea.

[2] Philippe François Renault arrived at Fort Chartres in 1720 with 200 miners and artisans, and 500 negro slaves.

[3] Meramec River, which joins the Mississippi at Saint Louis.

come, and even when they do come they bring so few merchandizes that they are not nearly sufficient to pay a part of the debts which the company is obliged to incur every year. The Ilinnoise Nation was formerly numerous, but the continual wars, and principally the one against the Iroquois, a well-known and war-like nation, have so enfeebled them that they number at present not more than 700 warriors. They are scattered about in three villages — the Cascakias, the Mekchiquamias and the Cahokias. The last village is 18 leagues by land and 15 by water from Fort de Chartres. Here are four soldiers in garrison, commanded by Sr. de St. Anges.[1] One hundred and ten leagues from Fort de Chartres, up the Rivière des Ilinnois, there used to be two villages of the same nation, the Peorias and the Roches, but they were forced to abandon these villages and to withdraw to the above-mentioned villages, because of the Outagamis [2] nation or the Renards, who last year came clear to their villages to attack them. The Ilinnois are in general the handsomest and the best built savages that I have seen. Proud and arrogant at home, they are the most cowardly of men when they are out of sight of their own village. They live on maize and their hunt, which consists of buffalo, deer, roe, wild turkeys and other game, which is in abundance. They clothe themselves and also their women with buffalo skins, which they dress on the flesh side and leave the hair which is long and fine, but after a while when the French came among them, they began to learn the French way of dressing. They recognize a good and an evil spirit, to whom they give a few attributes. They believe also in metemsychosis. The Jesuit fathers who have for more than thirty years been among them, have up to the present failed in their attempts to make them understand that God made himself man and died for us. Their huts are oval in shape, surrounded and covered with mats which they make out of rushes which they get from the marshes. These huts have only one opening

[1] St. Ange, the father of Louis St. Ange de Bellerive.
[2] Fox.

through which they come in and go out and get the light. They carry them with them when they go to hunt, at which they are engaged for at least seven months of the year. They prepare their food in the filthiest manner and make no objections to eating after their dogs, which they have in great number, and which they eat when they have their war feasts.

The men concern themselves only with hunting and with making war, employing the remainder of the time in eating and in staining themselves (or in painting their faces) which they do with red, yellow, black, blue or other colors. Among them the most bizarre are considered the best painted. Their manner of making war is as barbarous as their persons. If they go to war and have the good fortune to capture any children, women or men, they kill them and remove their scalps, which they carry home in triumph. If they bring back any slaves, upon their arrival they are given over to the old men, who have the power to give them life or death. When they have condemned their prisoner to be burned they tie him to a boat and burn him — today one part of the body and tomorrow another, and sometimes for three days and three nights. I have seen some of these unfortunates, who kept singing up to their last breath.

It is to be remarked that if the chief of the party loses one of his warriors, be it by voluntary death or otherwise, or when they win the battle without losing a man, he must recompense the relatives of the dead warrior, and the relatives of the warriors who were in the war with this chief enter his hut and take whatever they find. They are at quits with him when they say, "My relative has aided thee to make a prisoner." This is why they are very often constrained to flee in order to avoid these persecutions. This is also why all of these people go to war and return without striking a blow. They recognize no chief. There are chiefs, however, but they have so little authority that they do not deserve to bear this title, for the last in the tribe considers himself as great a master as the first.

They marry very young. Here are all the ceremonies

which I have seen observed in their marriages. A good hunter (to be a good hunter is esteemed the greatest merit among them) who wishes to marry a girl to whom he perhaps has never spoken (the boys conversing very little with the girls) sends by his parents to the father of the girl a present of skins and other merchandize. If the present is accepted the parents of the girl take her in the evening to the hut of the groom. They can have several wives, except the converts who are not numerous, and even they prefer (so they say) to refrain from going to the good fathers rather than deprive themselves of the pleasure of having two or three wives.

The women occupy themselves with housework, in sewing and gathering the Indian corn, in dressing deer and buffalo skins and the rest of the time they do porcupine work, which is very well known in France (where a good deal of it has been sent). In return their husbands leave to them the say as to the buying and selling. The husband has full power and authority over his wives, whom he looks upon as his slaves, and with whom he does not eat. However, they separate one from the other, upon the consent of both parties. The married women indulge very little in gallantry (although they are all naturally inclined towards love) because of their fear of punishment, for their husbands, who are more jealous than the Spaniards, scalp them upon the least proof of their infidelity. As for the young girls, they are the mistresses of their own bodies (to use their own expression). The good Jesuit fathers are endeavoring as much as possible to instil virtue in them, but they have not as yet succeeded. I forgot to say that I have not seen any Indians who are more agile or who run more swiftly than the Ilinnois. They begin to exercise themselves from their earliest youth, which is of great advantage to them, escaping when they are hard pressed by the enemy. There are some (if one is to believe the Canadians) who have made forty leagues in a day. I have seen them go and return from the Cascakias to Fort de Chartres, which is ten full leagues, in four hours. This is an absolute fact.

I do not speak here of their dances. They are as barbarous as their manner of living is unrefined.⌈ Necessity
has forced these Indians to find many good simples for
healing their wounds or other accidents.⌉ As for the other
diseases which come from the corruption of the blood, they
did not have them at all before seeing the French.

They know also many roots from which they make very
good dyes, red, black and yellow. The climate of the
Illinois is very temperate and healthy, being 38° in latitude. The soil is very rich and fertile. It has never yet
failed to produce anything which has been planted in it.
It is to be remarked that the winter is very severe, since
the Mississipy freezes over and one has to cross it on the
ice to go to hunt on the other side. The stone there is
very good for building, and very common. It only needs
some men to work it. The fruits which I have seen are
some red plums which are very good. There are also some
apples the size of an egg, but very acid to the taste, and
some currants, which do not differ in the least from those
of France. There are some walnut trees which bear nuts,
but of a very bad taste. There is another kind of nut tree
which bears fruit just like a walnut but much smaller.
The shell is very thin and the inside is exactly like our
French walnut. They call this fruit the paquannes.[1] There
is another tree which does not grow any larger than a leg,
which bears a fruit called the asmine, which is almost like
the banana. The inside is entirely filled with little seeds
or nuts, which are the shape of a marsh bean, and very hard.
They taste very good.

The wood which I have seen is very fine, and suitable
for building, especially the walnut and the paquanier. The
mulberry trees here bear fruit similar to those of Europe.
The wood of the mulberry tree lasts for thirty years in the
ground, without rotting. There are two kinds of elms,
which are very beautiful, and two kinds of oak. The white
oak can be worked up very easily, but the other, which is

---

[1] This is the pecan.

red, is as hard as iron. There are also some grapes, which are very good and plentiful. Their vines climb to the top of the highest trees, and when one wishes to get the grapes it is necessary to cut down the tree, which is why one says commonly that they make the vintage with a hatchet.

Apr. 25. About 2 o'clock in the afternoon a man called Perilaud, clerk of the Ilinnois stores, ran a man named Morin, drummer for the company of Artaguiette, through the body with his sword, for having spoken impertinently to him. This Morin died a quarter of an hour after he received the blow, and Perilaud has been arrested.

Apr. 26. M. d'Artaguiette presented a request to M. Boisbriant in which he asked that he be permitted to testify against the said Perilaud. This request was responded to the same day with permission to testify.

Apr. 27 and 28. They have been occupied with the examination of several witnesses.

Apr. 29. In the morning, M. De Lisle, performing the functions of major of the above-mentioned post, in the capacity of King's procureur, conducted the examination of the accused.

Apr. 30. Three Miami Indians arrived here yesterday evening. We learned that the Wiatanons [1] Indians, living up toward the head of the Rivière de Wabache, were leaving that place to go to establish themselves at their old village of La Babiche, which is on a little river which empties into Lake Erie. The same day there arrived a party of 200 Illinois warriors, who were on their way to make war upon the Renards.

May, 1723

May 1. Two boats of the convoy of M. De Tonty, which they had detained here, set out last night, without orders, to return to New Orleans.

May 2. An Indian from the Cahoskias [2] arrived here, who told us that four Mysouri Indians had come to them

---

[1] Wea. [2] Cahokias.

and had said that as soon as their planting was finished they were going to come to pay their respects to M. Boisbriant.

May 3. The chiefs of the villages of the Cascakias, namely Kiraoueria, Michel and Mamentouensa, having heard the report that they were going to put to death the man called Perilaud, held in chains for having killed the man called Morin, came today to Fort de Chartres with a band of thirty men from their nation to ask for his pardon. We beg the Commissioners to refer to two sheets of paper joined hereto, where the harangues of these Indians and the responses are given at length.

May 5. We departed from Fort de Chartres for the Cascakias, where we arrived about 2 o'clock in the afternoon.

May 6, 7 and 8. I received visits from the reverend Jesuit fathers, and from all of the inhabitants.

May 9. I called together all the inhabitants of this village to whom I said that I had an order from the King to form a company of militia for the purpose of putting them in a position to defend themselves with greater facility against the incursions which the Indians, our enemies, might attempt, so I formed a company, after having selected four of the most worthy among them to put at the head. This company being under arms, I passed it in review the same day.

May 10. An Ilinnois Indian has informed us that the Renards were going toward the Rocher with the purpose of establishing themselves there.

May 11. We left the Cascakias about noon and arrived about 5 o'clock in the afternoon at Fort de Chartres, where we found a band of Indians from the village of the Choaskias,[1] who had come to ask for the pardon of Sr. Perilaud. There will be found on a sheet of paper affixed hereto their harangues and the replies which M. Boisbriant made to them.

May 12. The chief of the Indians from the Cahoskias presented me with a porcelain necklace, at the same time wishing me all sorts of happiness, and a fine journey and one free from enemies.

---

[1] Cahokias, near the site of the present city of Saint Louis.

May 13 *and* 14. The confrontation of the witnesses in the affair of Perilaud was continued. From this day until the 19th of the present month nothing of importance has taken place.

May 19. About midnight there arrived a party of Ilinnois Indians, who are carrying back with them the head and the scalp of a Chicachat.

May 24. The Mysouri Indians, a nation situated 100 leagues up this river, on the left as you ascend, have arrived here to see M. Boisbriant.

May 27. Day of the Feast of Our Lord.[1] The procession of the Blessed Sacrament was made, the troops under arms lining the streets. The same day about one o'clock in the afternoon M. Renaut, director of mines, arrived here from the Maramek mines where he went a month and a half ago to join the thirty or so Frenchmen who were working at getting out the ore. Sr. Renaut keeps at these mines, not without great expense, all Frenchmen, who have been there for more than six months. There is perhaps about six thousand pounds weight of lead melted down. These mines are situated to the northwest from Fort de Chartres, or ten leagues above. One enters the Petite Riviere de Maramek, which is dry for three fourths of the year. After having navigated for about sixty leagues through very strong rapids, one lands and goes five leagues inland. At this place is the mine where Sr. Renaut works. He has brought along some of this ore for the purpose of making some assays of it in our presence to send by us to his Royal Highness, my lord the Duke of Orleans.

May 28. Two Ilinnois Indians arrived here very late yesterday evening. They had set out about fifteen days ago to the number of thirty men to go to war against the Renards. They had not gone forty leagues from here when they were attacked by a part of the latter, who killed eleven of their men. The rest escaped.

May 31. The man called Perilaud, who killed the drummer, has been set at liberty.

[1] Corpus Christi.

June, 1723

June 1. At noon we perceived in the middle of the river a French canoe, with a man in it who seemed to us not to be rowing. We sent out a pirogue which brought back this canoe in which was a man called Ponpon, a soldier detailed to the Cahoskias. He had received two gun shots, one in the head and the other in the arm, and several other arrow shots and had his scalp torn off to the skull. In the stern of the canoe there was a bundle of skins, upon which there were two pairs of Indian mittens, and the vest of M. St. Ange, the son, in the pocket of which we found some letters from MM. St. Ange, father, and Mercier,[1] the priest, which informed us that the Renard Indians were coming with 300 men by land and as many by water to attack the village of the Cahoskias. They besought M. Boisbriant to send to their aid both men and provisions. At four o'clock in the afternoon the troops were put under arms for the distribution of powder and balls, and to see if the guns were in good condition. They began to cut down the large bushes and other things which would favor an approach to Fort de Chartres. About 11 o'clock at night there arrived from the Cahoskias two Indians and a Frenchman, who came by land. They told us that two Indians from their village, who were descending with M. St. Ange, the younger,[2] in the canoe which had been attacked, had returned to their village about an hour before sunset the day of the fight, one of them wounded in the calf of the leg by a gun shot and that these men had said that M. St. Ange and Ponpon were dead.

June 2. About 9 o'clock in the morning Sr. de St. Ange, the younger, whom the Indians believed to be dead, along with Ponpon, arrived here. He had two slight wounds. This is the account of the affair as he gave it to us : The last of May he had set out from the Cahoskias accompanied by the soldier, Ponpon and two Indians from this village. After he had drifted about a league above the Petite Riviere de Miaramek, they had found themselves attacked by two

---

[1] François le Mercier. [2] Louis St. Ange de Bellerive.

canoes, one manned with twelve men and the other with three, whom they recognized as Renards. These two canoes, giving them the chase and firing all the time, had forced them to attempt the crossing. The man Ponpon had been killed as soon as he had fired his first shot. Fortunately for them they noticed that the large canoe was completely disabled, there appearing in it no more than five men. Having crossed back to the other side of the Riviere de Maramek, a little above, the two Ilinnois Indians becoming angry, or growing tired of fighting, told him to put to shore so that they could fight to greater advantage. This St. Ange having done, the Indians no sooner saw themselves approaching the land than, without waiting for the pirogue to reach the shore, they leaped into the water and fled. M. St. Ange saw that the two Ilinnois Indians were fleeing. Seeing that the two hostile canoes were about to land, he adopted a plan of action and likewise disembarked and concealed himself fifteen paces from the Pirogue behind a large tree, when seven or eight hostile Indians throwing themselves upon the pirogue scalped Ponpon, and returned precipitately to their canoes, giving vent to frightful yells.

The Sr. de St. Ange about midnight crawled to the edge of the water to see if the pirogue was still there, but he could not find it. The first of June he had got down to the entrance of the Miaramek where he had made a raft (cajeu) for the purpose of drifting down, and arrived here, as I have already said.

June 3. There arrived here from the Cahokias two Indians, who brought us some letters from M. St. Ange, the elder, who is in command there, in which he tells us of the scarcity of provisions among them, and they beseech M. de Boisbriant to send them some, together with some reinforcements. I resolved to go there and in fact my departure was set for the next day.

June 4 — 5 leagues. We departed about 7 o'clock in the morning, after having heard mass. Our boat was manned with a sergeant and sixteen soldiers. I was accompanied by M. St. Thereze Ensign de Dutisnet my secretary, and Sr. de St. Ange, the younger, who had just been attacked.

The weather was fine. In spite of the strong currents we came to the upper end of the Isles de Perdues, where we spent the night. We estimated that we had gone five leagues.

June 4[1] — 7 leagues. About 4 o'clock in the morning we embarked and encountered strong currents. Having arrived at the island which is the nearest to the entrance of the Miaramek, we landed and found a man dead from a gun shot. His Manitou[2] was near him (this is a kind of bird of prey) and a piece of the skin of a little dog, which was also near him. A little further we found the tracks of another Indian, who appeared to be wounded above the left breast. We did not consider it wise to go to look for him. Our purpose was to go to the aid of the Cahokias, whom we believed to be at that very time in close battle with the enemy. This is why we continued our journey. We came to the mouth of the Petite Riviere de Miaramek which in the Ilinnois language means brill, a kind of fish, which is very good. We had dinner there, and, having embarked, we continued our journey. A league higher up, on the same side, that is to say on the left as you ascend, Sr. de St. Ange showed us the place where he had landed and where the Indians had scalped Ponpon. From this place we continued our journey and put in for night three leagues from the Cahokias. We estimated that we had gone seven leagues.

June 6. At day-break we embarked and came to get breakfast at the old village of the Cahokias, which is on the left as you ascend, a league and a half distant from the Cahokias. In this place we perceived a large pirogue, of French make, which was crossing over from the village of the Cahokias. We decided that they were some traders who were going with the Mysouri Indians to their home both to trade in horses and to buy skins. We then continued our journey and arrived about 10 o'clock in the morning at the post where Sr. de St. Ange is in command, with six soldiers. This is a wretched fort of piles where Sr. Mercier, priest of the

---

[1] June 5.
[2] This was his spirit. (A note in the margin of the manuscript.)

Foreign Missions has a house and a church. An eighth of a league higher up is the village of the Cahokias.

We had no sooner arrived than they told us that the Mysouri Indians in coming up the river from Fort de Chartres to this place had found, on the right side opposite the Riviere de Miaramek, a Renard Indian, recently killed, whose head they had carried off and given to the Cahokias. The same day I assembled the Indian chiefs of the Cahokias. They came accompanied by forty of their warriors, who, after they had told me that they were very glad to see me among them, sat down on the ground in a semi-circle and I addressed them as follows, M. Thaumeur, a missionary priest, being the interpreter.

"That I had come with my warriors both to aid them and to bring them provisions. That I thought that all the reports which they had sent to Fort de Chartres were false; that they should send out parties to discover with certainty whether the enemy were coming, and, in case they should have sure news of it, that they, together with their wives and children, should retire to the fort of the French, who would not fail to defend themselves vigorously; that I exhorted them to imitate the French and to defend themselves strongly against the common enemy; that for this purpose I was going to give them a French flag; that they ought, as soon as they were attacked, to send their best runners to Fort de Chartres and that their father, De Boisbriant, would not fail to come with all the French warriors to aid them." They answered me with a shout of joy and after they had given me their thanks, I dismissed them. The Cahokias are in $38\frac{1}{2}°$ of latitude, in a plain which is perhaps a league in width and two in length. This plain is bounded on the west by an island, which is a league in length and a half league in width; on the south and north by low woods; inland on the east there is a large marsh abounding in game and in fish.

The Rivière des Ilinnois which empties into the Mississipy eleven leagues from the fort of the Cahokias, on the right side as you ascend, flows from the northeast to the southwest.

The Rivière des Mysourys, which empties also into the Mississipy six leagues above the Cahokias, on the left side as you ascend, comes from the northwest.

In front of the Indian village of the Cahokias flows a little river, which separates the prairie from the island. It flows from the northeast.

June 7. About 7 o'clock in the morning we set out from the Cahokias with two score Indians, both men and women, who were going to see their relatives at the Cascakias. About three leagues from Fort de Chartres we met four Indian pirogues which were ascending the river. We identified them. They were Cascaskias who were reconnoitering (so they told us) to see if they could find any hostile trails. We arrived the same day about three o'clock in the afternoon at Fort de Chartres.

June 8. Sr. Renaut came to the Fort de Chartres to tell us that he had made several assays, which he showed us, and in which he had not found any traces of silver. He still has some to make, doubtless during the next few days.

June 9. Our boat set out from here to go to the Cascakias to load with maize for the subsistence of the troops.

June 12. One of the sailors from our boat arrived here, who informed us that in returning to this place the boat had sunk and that they were working to repair it.

June 15. Our boat arrived here with a very light load and leaking above the second streak.

June 17. We set out from Fort de Chartres for the Cascakias and arrived there the same day.

June 18. We careened our boat to give it a coat of tallow. We were informed the same day that the Cahokias had been besieged and that M. Boisbriant had sent three Frenchmen, the best runners, with ten Mekchiquamias Indians.

June 20. Towards evening the French and the Indians, of whom I have just spoken, arrived at Fort de Chartres, with a party of Cahokias, who brought with them two prisoners. They gave one to the Mekchiquamias and the other to M. Boisbriant to replace Ponpon, and a third, which they had burned, to the Cahokias. These three Indians were the same ones who had attacked M. St. Ange. They admitted that in this attack they had had four men killed and three wounded.

June 22. The prisoner who was given to the Mekchiquamias was burned for four hours at the end of which a Frenchman killed him with a gun shot. The one who had been given to the soldiers has had his head broken.

June 22. Our boat was loaded today, and we are getting ready to leave tomorrow.

June 27. (Sunday) We set out from the village of the Cascakias in company with another boat laden with maize for the concession of M. Law, which is at the Arkansas. We had ten men in our boat. The same day we came to spend the night at Cap a l'Ail [or Cape Garlic] where we killed a young roe.

June 28. At day-break we embarked and a little below Cape St. Anthoine we found swimming across a young roe. We took it on board and in spite of a violent head-wind, we reached the Isles a la Course, where we passed the night. At 9 o'clock in the evening our dogs, having scented either men or animals, barked all night long, and we kept ourselves under arms.

June 29. An hour before day-break, worn out from not having slept the previous night, we embarked and continued our journey. There was a strong wind and much rain, which lasted till noon, when, having perceived a buffalo we put to shore and killed it. The same day we came to pass the night at Wabache.

June 30. We departed about 5 o'clock in the morning. The weather was fair and very hot. About breakfast time we saw a buffalo crossing. We overtook it in the middle of the river and hitched our boat to it for more than a quarter of a league, after which we killed it. We took only the tongue. About noon we landed to go after a herd of more than a hundred buffaloes, both bulls and cows, of which we killed five and wounded more than twenty. We cut out only the tongues. Continued our journey and camped at the usual hour.

July, 1723

July 1. About 4 o'clock in the morning we embarked and had the pleasure of seeing both sides of the river lined with bulls and cows. About noon we landed on a sand bar to amuse ourselves with hunting. We brought down eight animals. We contented ourselves with cutting out their tongues. Continued our journey and camped at the usual hour.

July 2. At day-break our men took up the oars and we continued our journey. The weather was very hot. About noon we landed opposite a little prairie and went after a herd of nine [buffaloes], all of which we killed. Camped for the night in this place so as to dry the best of these animals.

July 3. About 6 o'clock in the morning we embarked and let ourselves drift so as to rest our men who had spent the night smoking their meat. In the evening, a little before camping, we killed four buffaloes, of which we took only the tongues.

July 4. At day-break we embarked and continued our journey. The weather was fine. The heat continued. About noon, wind being contrary, we perceived four boats and two pirogues full of Canadians. We fired some shots and went on shore to wait for them. It was M. Bourmont, who, with a company of fifty men, of whom M. Pradel was captain, was going up the river to the Mysouris. The same day at 4 o'clock in the afternoon I reviewed this company. We camped five leagues from the Ecores a Prud'homme. We learned from the convoy of the arrival of the Commissioners appointed by the King for the administration of the affairs of the colony at New Orleans.

July 5. We took leave of MM. Bourmont and Pradel and [the] others, and left them, we to descend the river and they to ascend. This convoy seems to me very badly conducted and has many sick. The great heat contributes largely to this. Furthermore, they hardly are given time to eat maize cooked in water, although they are surrounded by Buffalo. They tell me by way of excuse that they have not found any, but I am much more inclined to think that it is a case of laziness, for the most worthless Frenchman can kill a buffalo in this region. They told us that they had degraded one of their sergeants two leagues below for mutiny. We found him two leagues below resolved to die in the woods rather than to rejoin them [the convoy].

July 6. Early in the morning our men having taken up their oars, we continued our journey and came to spend the night at the Riviere a Margot, where we killed four buffaloes, of which we took only the tongues.

July 7. At day-break we embarked and continued our journey. About 10 o'clock in the morning, upon our left as we were drifting very close to shore, we perceived on the bank of the river a man who called to us in the language of the Mobile to come to him. We asked him, at the same time taking up our guns, if he was a Chicachat.[1] Our arms frightened him. He got behind a large tree and replied that he was a Chicachat. The same instant, seeing others appearing, he saluted them with eight gun shots which they returned with twelve shots, two of which hit the stern of our boat. Our boat kept on its way and we did not think it wise to shoot at them, as they were out of range, nor were we in a position to go to attack them on shore. The other boat was on the other side of the river and joined us immediately.

July 8. Early in the morning we embarked and continued our journey. The great heat continued to inconvenience us. Killed this morning a buffalo. About 5 o'clock in the evening we came upon a pirogue manned with six men, in which was the man Langevin who has been captured the year before by the Chicachats. Although we told him about the attack which we had had yesterday, he still resolved to continue his journey and go up the Wabache to salt some meat. He informed us that a party of Arkansas had fallen upon some French in the Riviere des Watchitas; that there had arrived at the Yazous two score Chicachats and two chiefs, called the Courceracs, to ask for peace; that

---

[1] Chickasaw.

the Natchez Indians were still continuing to kill the cattle belonging to the French, and that he even believed that these Indians intended to besiege the fort.

July 9. We embarked early in the morning, after having given to these Frenchmen a part of the meat which we had. About 9 o'clock in the morning we came upon three pirogues full of Arkansas Indians, who were going up the Petite Rivière St. Francois to hunt. About three o'clock in the afternoon we arrived at the village of the Arkansas. We found there three huts, and we were told that the others were coming back to form a village after the harvests were over.

July 10. At day-break we embarked and arrived about breakfast time at the first fork of the Rivière de Sotéhouy, where we had a squall, but it did not last long. We sent a Frenchman to the post so that men might be despatched to help in taking the boat back.

July 11. Six soldiers from the garrison of Sotéhouy arrived, and we embarked in the boat loaded with wheat and left the other one behind with four of our men. We proceeded to Sotéhouy where the captain delivered the wheat to Sr. Dufresne. We returned by land to the post of Sotéhouy where we spent the night.

July 12. I reviewed the troops of this post and took a census, as many inhabitants had established themselves there since my last review.

July 13. In the morning we departed and came to join our boat in which we embarked and rejoined the boat which we had left at the first fork. We entered the Mississipy and camped at the usual hour.

July 14. Early in the morning we embarked and continued our journey. The heat was very great. We had no longer any hope of killing any buffaloes. Camped at the usual hour near Pointe Coupée.

July 15. We departed about sunrise. The weather was fair and the sun's rays terrible. Two of our sailors were sick — one with the fever and the other with the scurvy.

July 16. At day-break we embarked. No meat to give

them [the men], a deer which was crossing most opportunely was killed. Camped at the usual hour.

July 17. The heat was intense the whole of last night, and the maraingouins, a kind of fly, which we call in France gnats, annoyed us so much that it was impossible to rest. This caused us to embark an hour before day. We arrived at noon at the entrance of the Yazous, where we left one boat, and manned another with ten oarsmen, and we arrived at the Yazous about 4 o'clock in the afternoon.

July 18. Early in the morning I made my review, as inspector, of the Fort Saint Pierre des Yazous, and we sent for the other boat so as to deliver to M. Livilliers the corn belonging to the company.

July 19. This morning the boat arrived here and the corn was delivered to Sr. Livilliers, who is without means of subsisting his garrison. It was from M. Petit Livilliers that [we learned] that M. Degrave had gone to New Orleans without orders. That since the departure of M. Degrave he had engaged the Aufaugoulas, Couroye and Yazous to remain there. They had intended to go and settle on the Rivière des Wachitas. That he had engaged the Tapoucha Indians to come and settle near the fort. This is a small Indian nation, which lived forty leagues up this river. They were going to come in the autumn. That he had sent to New Orleans two Chicachat chiefs and two other Indians. They had come to ask for peace, which he could not grant. He sent them to M. Bienville. They brought back with them a man called Parisien whom they captured at the same time they did Langevin.

July 20. About 6 o'clock in the evening we departed from Fort Saint Pierre des Yazous and reached the entrance of the river, where the other boat awaited us. We passed the night there.

July 21. At day-break we embarked and continued our journey. About an hour before sunset we landed in order to put on the kettle, having resolved to drift all that night.

July 22. We drifted all last night, not without striking against some trees where the current carried us and from which we had great difficulty in extricating ourselves. We passed, however, the Grand Gouffre. We continued our journey and arrived at the Natchez about two hours before sunset, where we found two boats. One had brought Srs. Desliette and Chepar, the former commandant of the fort of the Natchez, and the latter the captain of a company, and a detachment to reinforce this post. The other boat was going to the Yazous to bring some relief to this post.

July 23. In the morning I made my review, as inspector, of the post at Natchez. The same day I went to the settlement of the Sr. dumanoir Feaucon, where I reviewed a detachment of fifteen men, commanded by Sr. de Noyant, an ensign. This detachment comes from New Orleans for the purpose of preventing the Natchez Indians from troubling it [the settlement]. They [the Indians] continue to be hostile. In the evening we came back to the fort of the Natchez.

July 24. I went to the settlement of M. le Blanc where I did not tarry, as I had no business to attend to. About noon we embarked, having increased our company by the addition of the boat which had brought MM. Desliet and Chepar. The weather was fine. All night we drifted our three boats tied together.

July 25. About 8 o'clock in the morning we arrived at the first village of the Thonniquas, where we landed to put on the kettle. They told us that they had killed two Natchez Indians and burned one. These three Indians were drifting in a pirogue. They did not know where they were going. These Indians are building a fort so as to provide themselves with a defense in case the Natchez should come to attack them.

We remained there only long enough to cook our breakfast, after which we embarked and continued our journey. About sunset we came upon two pirogues. One was going to the Natchitoches and the other to the Thonniquas. They told us that sickness was very prevalent at New Orleans.

July 26. We drifted all the past night and came about noon to the Petite Pointe Coupée where there is a concession belonging to MM. Collys. We got dinner there, after which

88

we embarked and continued our journey. We arrived at Dirombourg about 8 o'clock in the evening, and slept there.

July 27. It rained all last night, and, the rain continuing, we were not able to set out until about 11 o'clock. We arrived about sunset at the Bayagoulas.

July 28. In the morning, in spite of the heavy rain, we started out, and continued our journey. We drifted all night.

July 29. We arrived about 5 o'clock in the evening at Cannes Bruslées, where we slept.

July 30. Early in the morning we reached New Orleans, where we arrived about noon. One cannot enter any house here without finding sick people. The ship **Galatée** has gone down a little below New Orleans in order to take on ballast. There is sickness on board. They say it is the purple fever.

July 31. We learned that during our voyage from the Illinois a band of more than fifty men had carried off two passenger-boats.

Aug. 1. I went to pay my respects to the Commissioners, who were all sick.

Aug. 2. We were informed that the Natchitoches Indians had intended to fall upon the garrison of the Natchitoches because M. St. Denys,[1] who is the commandant there, had broken the head of an Indian of this nation because he had killed about a year ago a man called Perrier. I have spoken fully of the death of this man in my journals, and in the memoirs which I drew up at the time of my trip to the Natchitoches.

Aug. 3. Sickness continues to carry off many people. They bury eight or nine persons every day.

Aug. 4. Everybody complains here of famine. Everyone seems to be discontented with the new administration.

Aug. 7. M. de Sauboye, one of the commissioners appointed by the King to administrate the affairs of the colony, died this morning and was buried about 5 o'clock in the afternoon with all of the ceremony due his worth and integrity.

---

[1] Juchereau de St. Denis.

Aug. 13.   M. Peauger, the engineer who had been for many months superintending the work at the establishment of the post of Balise, which is at the mouth of the Mississipy, arrived here about noon with a Spaniard who brought with him six thousand piasters to spend in merchandize.   He left at Balise a bilander manned with fourteen men in which he had come, and he comes from Vera Cruz.

Aug. 18.   The two Chicachat chiefs have left here to return to their homes by way of the Yazous.   M. Terrisse, an officer, with a detachment, accompanied them as far as that post.

Aug. 24.   There arrived here a band of Chectas, who were deputized by all of that nation to come and ask arms, powder and shot, from M. De Bienville so as to go to war against the Chicachats.

Sept. 2.   M. De Bienville went today to dine on board the Galathée, where he was received with a salute of nine guns.

Sept. 3.   We have been informed by the Thonniquas that M. St. Denys, commandant at the Natchitoches, had descended the river with all the Indians of this nation, and that he was persuading the Thonniquas to join him, to make an attack upon the Natchez.

Sept. 4.   We learned from a boat which arrived from Natchez that they were always on the alert and were constantly molested by the Indians of that nation, who had killed a horse, a cow and a pig belonging to the concession of St. Catherine, (and that within five or six days) and that all these things were most prejudicial to the inhabitants, who could neither gather their crops nor work, and that they were waiting for M. De Bienville or his orders to attack that nation. M. Bienville is making no preparations to go there.   We do not know why.

Sept. 5.   About 4 o'clock in the afternoon Sr. Allaire, an Englishman or an Irishman, was arrested and put on board the ship Galathée, to be taken to France.   They say that it was because he had written in favor of the colonists and against the government.   Others say that he was arrested as a spy. He had carried on a correspondence with the English and the Spanish so as to keep them informed of everything which was taking place in the colony. These papers have been immediately seized by the council here. This Allaire was formerly storekeeper in the concession of Mgr. Le Blanc, which he had left, and he was working at the time of his arrest for Sr. Duval, auditor of accounts. The people say that it was because Duval was not correct in his accounts and that the authorities wished to make Allaire tell what he knew about them.

Sept. 6. A man called Berard, living at New Orleans, was today condemned by M. De la Chaise, commissioner on the part of His Majesty for the execution of his orders in Louisiana, to pay a fine of 500 livres, to be applied to building a hospital for curing venereal diseases. It is for having bought in speculation, a note of 100 ecus for 13 piasters, and in addition the said Berard has been condemned to give to the bearer of the note of 100 ecus 27 piasters as full payment for the note. The judgment was very just as this Berard had been carrying on this sort of business for more than three years.

Sept. 7. A boat which was descending the river from the Natchez arrived here, from which we learned that the Indians of this nation were continuing to kill the cattle at the concession of MM. Colys; that they did not molest in any way the French who are there; that two hundred of their men had attacked the Thonniquas, whom they had beaten, and wounded the great chief in the arm, and that the second chief of this nation had died of disease.

Sept. 8. M. De la Chaise went today to the home of Sr. Marlot, former storekeeper, I mean chief clerk at New Orleans, where he found much merchandize from the stores. They examined him the same day to find out where these goods came from. They went also to the house of the maid servant of this Marlot, where they found much fine merchandize, which they seized. She will be made to tell where she got these goods and whence came this fortune.

Sept. 9. A pirogue full of Frenchmen who were coming down from the Ilinnois, has arrived here. They informed us that the Renard Indians had killed, opposite Fort de Chartres, two men named Sueur and Lafond, Canadians, who were hunting deer. These same Frenchmen were attacked on their way down, just as they were approaching the Ecore a Prud'homme, by a party of Chicachats. They have confirmed the entry of the 7th of the present month, in which I spoke of the Natchez. They spent one night with two hundred Natchez men, who were going to attack the Thonniquas, who have not done them any harm.

Sept. 10. We are preparing to embark on the ship Galathée and to leave tomorrow, the 4th [1] of the present month.

[1] 11th (?).

COLONEL CHICKEN'S JOURNAL TO THE
CHEROKEES, 1725

INTRODUCTION

THE Cherokee Indians occupied a prominent place in the early history of South Carolina. At the time of Colonel Chicken's visit they numbered upwards of 10,000, of whom not less than 3800 were among the best of Indian warriors. They were distributed among three settlements: the Lower Settlement, in what is now western South Carolina and northeastern Georgia; the Middle Settlement, in western North Carolina and northern Georgia; and the Upper Settlement, in western Tennessee and northern Alabama. Intercourse between the Cherokees and the government of South Carolina was begun in 1693 when twenty Cherokee chiefs visited Charleston to ask assistance against the Catawbas and the Congarees. A profitable trade with the Cherokees was begun about the same time. At first this was only in a private way, but in 1707 all Indian trade of the colony passed under government regulation, and in 1716, when for a short time it was made a public monopoly, Fort Moore, on the east bank of the Savannah about six miles below the present site of Augusta, Georgia, was erected for its protection. By a treaty with the Cherokees which was made that year it was agreed that both parties should carry their goods for trade to Fort Moore, the immediate consequence of which was that the Government established a pack-horse route from Charleston to that place and that the Cherokees cut a trail from their country thither along the east bank of the Savannah, a trail which was subsequently widened for the pack-horse train. Fort Congarees, on the Congaree River, a little below the present site of Columbia, was erected in 1718, and a shorter pack-horse route from Charleston to the Cherokee country was established. It passed through Dorchester, approached the Congaree opposite the mouth of the Wateree, crossed the Little Saluda about five miles from its mouth, passed the site of Fort Ninety-Six, and from thence led direct to Keowee, the principal town of the Lower Cherokees. It will be seen that Colonel Chicken went by the shorter route and returned by the longer one.

Colonel Chicken became prominent in Indian affairs in 1715, when, at the crisis of the war with the Yamasees, he, at the head of the Goose Creek militia, inflicted on those Indians a decisive defeat at "The Ponds." He was a member of the Board of Indian Commissioners in 1721–1723 and was sole Indian Commissioner in 1724–1731. The primary object of the mission of which he gives an account in his Journal, and on which he was sent by President Middleton, was to counteract the influence of French emissaries from Louisiana who had been among them, inciting them to war against the Creeks and seeking to win them from the English interest.

A manuscript copy of this Journal is in the Public Record Office, London; C. O. 5, 12, ff. 14–34, and the Library of Congress has a transcript which was made from this.

COLONEL CHICKEN'S JOURNAL TO THE CHEROKEES, 1725

Journal of the Comissr [1] for Indian Affairs on his Journey to the Cherokees and his proceedings there

Thursday the 17th day of June 1725.

I took my departure from my house at Goose Creek [2] about 7 of the Clock this Morning, and dined at the Honble Thomas Broughtons [3] and abt five of the Clock in the Evening I came to Mr. Jones's being about Twenty Six Miles from my house, where I staid til Monday the 21 Instant in Expectation of Mr. Eleazer Wigan's attending me at Mr. Peter St. Julien's [4] which was the place I Ordered the Cherokee Indians (then down) to go to from my house. And the said Wigan not coming according to my Expectation, I set away from Mr. Jones's the 18th Instant and abt five of the Clock in the Evening I came to John Hearn's Plantation where I Encamped for that Night.

Tuesday the 22d day of June 1725.

I sett away from my Camp abt Eight of the Clock in the Morning and abt half past four in the afternoon I came to

---

[1] Commissioner.
[2] Goose Creek was the name of a settlement which was established by the Huguenots in 1686 on Goose Creek, a branch of the Cooper River.
[3] Thomas Broughton was Speaker of the Assembly in 1725.
[4] Peter St. Julien's residence was near Dorchester. It was the first general stopping place on the trail northwest from Charleston and was at the point of divergence of the Creek trail from that leading through the valley of the Congaree and Saluda to the Cherokee country.

Capt. Charles Russells [1] who in a Short time after my stay at his house made Information to me as ffollows,

That David Doway Indian Trader when he was Last at his house, said that he would take his Oath that John Sharp some time before he came from the Cherokees went to one of the Towns in that Nation and took away what Skines he could get from the People of the Town and afterwards Obliged them to take what goods he thought fitt for the same and that One James Hitchins (the said Sharps hireling) was with him at the time of his so doing And on Considering the above Information I thought proper to send the following Letter to Majr Wm. Blakewey (who by Virtue of a Resolution of the General Assembly I Empowred to grant Lycences to the Traders dureing my Absence.

Sir —

Sometime after my Arrival here Capt. Russell made Information to me that he heard David Doway Indian Trader (now in Town) say that he would take his Oath that John Sharp Indian Trader (now in Town also) some time before the said Sharp came from the Cherokees went to one of the Towns in the said Nation, the Name of which he could not then call to mind, and took away what Skins he could get from the people of the Town and afterwards Obliged them to take what goods he thought fitt to give them for the same, and that one Ja. Hitchins, his hireling (who is now in Town) was with him at the time of his doing the same. This Information I thought would be proper to Acquaint you off therefore would not have you grant Sharp a Lycence til such time you hear further from me in the Cherokees where I shall take particular care to informe myself of the truth of this Affair and then Shall as soon as possible give you my Opinion thereon that you may Govern your self thereby; in the mean time I remain
Sir   Your Most humble Servant.

[1] Captain Charles Russell was the first commander of Fort Congaree, which was built in 1718 a little below the present site of Columbia for the protection of the Cherokee trade.

Wednesday the 23d and Thursday the 24th day of June 1725.

Stayed at Capt. Russells in Expectation of Mr. Eleazer Wigan's coming, And he coming according to Expectation We set away from Capt. Russells on Friday morning being the Twenty ffifth Instant in Compa [1] with the sd Wigan and John M ly Indian Trader and abt half past twelve of Clock at Noon We Crossed Beever Creek where We Stayed til three of the Clock in the afternoon and then set away and came as far as Sandy run being Six Miles further and making up our day's Journey in all Twenty ffour Miles here We Encamped for this Night having great Showers of Rain til next Morning.

Saturday the 26th day of June 1725.

We set away from Sandy run and about Twelve a Clock at Noon We Crossed the Congree Creek and were Obliged to Encamp for this Night (the Pack horsses being very much gauled) abt four Miles from the sd Creek which made Our day's Journey Sixteen Miles.

Sunday the 27th June 1725.

Set away from Our last Encampmt abt Seven of the Clock in the Morning and abt two of the Clock in the Afternoon We came to Beaver Dam and the Packhorses not coming up with us for some Considerable time and being late in the day We Encamped for this Night having Travilled this day 24 M.

Munday the 28th day of June 1725.

We set away from Beever Dam about Six of the Clock in the Morning and about twelve Clock at Noon We Crossed Saludee river [2] where We Stayed for Our Packhorses, which

---

[1] Company.
[2] What is now the Saluda River was formerly known as the Congaree and what is now the Little Saluda was in Colonel Chicken's time known as the Saluda.

were behind us, and they coming about two hours after us We found that Sevl of them were tired and it being late in the day We Encamped here for this Night and the day following in Order to rest our horses having travilled abt 15 M.

Wednesday the 30th day of June 1725.

Set away from Saludy river abt 10 of the Clock in the Morning and about Twelve Clock at Noon We came by Saludee old Town,[1] and Travilled as far as a place called half way Swamp being Eight Miles further from the said Town and making up Our days Journey Twenty ffour Miles.

Thursday the 1st day of July 1725.

Set away from half way Swamp abt Nine of the Clock in the Morning leaving John Neely and the Packhorses behind us and abt Six of Clock at Night We came to a Fort built at a place called Coronaclo Sanelo [2] where We lay all Night having Travilled this day about Twenty Seven Miles.

Friday the 2d day of July 1725.

The Weather proving very Rainy and having lost one of Our horses we were forced to Stay at Our Camp for this day, About 2 of the Clock in the afternoon two Indians came to the Fort from their hunting and Stayed wth us all Night designing to Accompany us to Keewohee and after a Short Stay wth us at the Fort, they went out to look for one of Our horses wch was lost and on their return they brought in a Deer which they Shott in looking for the horse.

[1] Saluda Old Town was a few miles west of the mouth of Little Saluda River.

[2] The trail passed the site of the present town of Ninety-Six (96 miles on the trail from the Lower Cherokee town of Keowee) at which there was at a very early day a private fort and trading house known as Gowdy's Fort.

Saturday the 3d day of July 1725.

Set away from Coronaclo Sanelo about Eight of the Clock in the Morning and about five of the Clock in the Evening We came to a Spring Eight Miles from the dividing Paths where we Encamped for this Night having Travilled in the rain all day 33 Mill's.[1]

Sunday the 4th day of July 1725.

Set away from Our Camp about Six of the Clock in the Morning and about four of the Clock in the afternoon We came to a Creek about Twenty Miles on this side Keewohee where I was Obliged to leave my Secry. and Son in Order to send them ffresh horses from Keewohee and Encamped myself with Mr. Wigan within Six Miles of Keewohee having Travilled this day 38 M.

Munday the 5th day of July 1725.

Set away from my Camp about five of the Clock this Morning and about Seven Clock I Arrived at Keewohee [2] and soon after I sent away Two ffresh Horses for my Secry. and Son.

At my Arrival here King Crow and the head men were out of Town at their Plantations and a Messinger being sent to inform them of my Arrival, they Imediatly repaired to Town and soon after, they after their Ceremonial way placed me in a Great Chair in the most Publick Place in the Town and set down by me themselv's faning me with Eagles Feathers and the Ceremony being over, the King made the following Speech to me:

That they long Expected a beloved Man of the English among them and that now they had sent me and that they were as glad to see me as if I had come from above.

[1] Miles.

[2] Keowee, the principal town of the Lower Cherokees; it was situated on the Keowee River in what is now Oconee County, South Carolina, about fifteen miles northeast of Walhalla. Fort Prince George was erected here in 1753.

I Answered them, that I was as glad to see them, and that I was come with a great talk from all the beloved men of the English and that I intended to give it to them as soon as they had gott together the head Men of as many of their Towns as they could and as soon as my Pack hors's Arrived.

They returned me thanks with a great deal of Joy and fired a Volley over my head and then King Crow taking me under the Arm lead me into Joseph Coopers house with a great deal of Ceremony, the head men at the same time following us and in a little time after my being in the house they presented me with their pipes to Smoak out of (it being their Custom).

Tuesday the 6th day of July 1725.

The King having given Orders to his Towns people to provide Provvissions for us, they accordingly this day presented me with some Fowles and Venison.

Wednesday the 7th day of July 1725.

This day Arrived here from the Settlemt Alexr. McCormick Indian Trader who informed me that he had left his Pack horses at the Congree [1] Creek and that he left mine at Wilsons Creek.

Thursday the 8th day of July 1725.

Sent the following Order to Saml. Brown Indian Trader.

To Mr. Samuel Brown Indian Trader —

You are hereby Ordered on receipt hereof to send down to Keewohee, Jno. Hewet, who I have Information is in your Employ and hath been in the Indian Country for a Considerable time without my leave or Lycence and Contrary to a Law in that Case made and provided. Hereof fail not as you will Answer the Contrary.

Given under my hand at Keewohee this
8th day of July Anno Dom. 1725.

[1] Congaree.

COLONEL CHICKEN'S JOURNAL

The following Accot was brought this day into Town by a Chickesaw fellow who made his Escape from his Enemies : That the ffrench Indians [1] had killed on the other side the Hills Six Chickesaw [2] Men four Women, Seven boys and Girls and two Cherookee Women.

Friday the 9th and Saturday the 10th of July 1725.

Nothing happened this two days worth my Observation.

Sunday the 11th day of July 1725.

I gave Orders to all the Traders in the Town to Attend me this Morning in Order to have the Service of the day read to them, and as a Duty Incumbent on me, I desired them to follow so good an Example beleiving they might be Negligent therein.

Monday the 12th day of July 1725.

Arrived here from the Catabaws William Ballow and one John Ellis Indian Traders and having Demanded their Invoice of goods, found that it Amounted to 1341 wt of leather at Indian Price and that they Traded for Majr Bowling in Virginia.

Tuesday the 13th day of July 1725.

Wednesday the 14 day of July 1725.

Nothing Occurred these two days for my Observation.

Thursday the 15 day of July 1725.

Arrived here from Tuccaseegee [3] Samuel Brown and John Hewet who I sent for by an Order of the 8th Instant.   And

[1] The Choctaws, in what is now Mississippi and western Alabama, were the principal tribe of Southern Indians that were at this time in the French interest.

[2] The Chickasaw Indians were the chief occupants of the country between the Cherokees and the Mississippi River. They maintained friendly relations with the English but were habitually at war with some of their neighboring Indian tribes.

[3] There was a Cherokee town of Tuckaseegee at the forks of the Tuckaseegee River in North Carolina.

having Examined the said Hewet in relation to his being among the Indians without my leave, I found that he was Employed by Mr. Marr and that after he had left the said Marrs Employ that James Millikin Indian Trader Employed him and gave him Orders to Trade by two Letters from the said Millikin which the said Hewet produced to me and having Considered the aforesd Information,

I gave Orders to the said Hewet to Stay at Keewohee til the said Milikin Arrived here from the Catawbaws at which time I informed him I should give him further Orders.

Friday the 16th day of July 1725.

This day came in here twelve head men of Tugelo Town.[1]

Came in from the Settlement David Doway and Andrew White Indian Traders.

Richard Hasford gave to me the following Information of which he took his Oath.

That in or about the Month of November Annoq Dom. 1724 When the said Hatton went to Noyouwee [2] that he the said Hatton told an Indian Woman in the same Town Named Peggy to tell the Indians that he had gott a paper from the English Governor that promised them men, and that if they asked for any that they must demand three hundred and that the said Hatton told them when they had pitched upon two men to go down to the English that they must give them in Charge to talk Strong to them and not to be affraid.

Signed   RICHD. HASFORD.

Arrived here from the Settlement Laufflin McBain Indian Trader.

The head men of Twenty one Towns being mett here together I had the Talk Interpretted to them.

---

[1] Tugaloo, a. Cherokee town at the confluence of Tugaloo River and Toccoa Creek in Habersham County, Georgia.

[2] Noyouwee, or Noyoee, was a Cherokee town at the head of Tugaloo River on the west border of Oconee County, South Carolina.

At a Meeting of the head men of Twenty one Towns whereof Crow is King Jo : Cooper and Eleazer Wigan Interpreters

I informed them that I was come a great way with a great talk from the English, that I beleived they have had Stories told them and I desired to know if they did not all know me.

A. They all knew me very well.

I informed them that I should have been glad to have had the headmen of all their Towns here, but as they were not come, I informed them that I was glad to see so many of them together as there was.

I likewise informed them that I should deliver the talk to them from all the beloved Men of the English and that as there was the head Men of Twenty one Towns present I hoped and Expected they would mind what I said to them.

A. It's very well and that they'll always harken good to the English talk.

The whole talk being Interpreted to them

They informed me that they did send down a talk to the English abt White Men and that they Expected them.

Q. What reason had you to Expect them or who was it that told You anything abt White Men coming among You ?

A. That they never heard it from any White Man but that when the King first recd his Comission and talk from the English it was therein say'd that the English would Consider of Assisting them agt their Enemies in Case they killed their Burtheners or other people belonging to them.

They informed me that now I had given the talk to them and that they would give me a General Answer at the Meeting of the head Men of the whole Nation.

I informed them it was very well and that I desired they would Consider well of the talk before the General Meeting and that they would make it known to all their people.

Which they Promissed to do And then they Severally took me by the hand and took their leavs of me.

Saturday the 17th day of July 1725.

Sent the following Letter to his Honour the President[1]:
May it please your Honour —

This Opportunity happening by two Burtheners who are
going to Mr. Hasford's Cowpen I thought it would be proper
to Acquaint your Honour of my Arrival here on Monday the
ffifth Instant where I have been Obliged to stay for this
Twelve day's for the head men's meeting together, the reason
of their not meeting sooner was because Provission is Scarce
here, and on Friday the 16th July I had the talk with the
head men of Twenty One Towns which has mett with the
Genl Satisfaction of them all and I hope will prove to the
Intire Satisfaction of the Government it being my whole
Study to bring it about. I intend (God willing) to set
away from hence the 18th Instant on my Journey over the
Hills where I intend to have the talk with the people of those
parts and there is to be a General Meeting of the head Men
of the whole Nation in the Middle Settlements to Consult
about a General Answer to our talk which I shall take care to
send down to your Honr as soon as possible and I hope your
Honour will be Speedy to me in your Expresses, Especially
in your Answer to me when you have heard from the Creeks,
that I may Compleat all Matters Comitted to my Charge.
As to what we have heretofore heard from the Traders in
Genl in Relation to our sending Men here, I do Assure your
Honr is groundless and that having talked to the Indians
about it I find by them that they never thought of any such
thing, but that it has been Infused into their heads by the
Traders here and particularly [by] a Man whom We have had
too much relyance on.

I hope your Honour will lay before the Assembly a Clause
to be Altered in the Indian Trading Law (wch is) that the
Traders be confined to Trade in any one or two Towns of their
own Choice there being Towns Sufficient for more Traders
than hath ever been here yet and not to run from Town to

[1] Arthur Middleton was president of the Council and acting
governor in 1725–1730.

Town which in my Opinion is a great Detriment to the Trade and will in a little time (if care be not taken) Create great disputes and Quarrells among the Traders which will be Ill Examples to the Indians and may prove of ill Concequence to the Country and it is my Opinion that the Principal is Sufficient to Trade on one Lycence Choosing two Towns to Trade, the Men they bring up with them being in General a loose Vagabond Sort of people and will not Stick out to say or do any thing among the Indians for the Lucre of a few Skines, so that I think the fewer of them their is the better and I am well Assured that it will be better for the Trade in General. If your Honour and Assembly Approves of this and can gett it past before I can depart hence and will send it to me I shall then Imediatly put it in force and I dont doubt but in a little time after that you will see the good Effect of it as well as the Traders Employers, I have nothing further to Advise your Honrs of at present but that there hath not been any hostillities Comitted here since the Departure of the Traders and that a few days agoe We had an Accot of the ffrench Indians doing some damage to the Upper People wch I intend to make use of in my discourse to them in hopes that it will keep them at Warr with all Indians in Amity with the French which these Lower people very very much approve off.

I desire your Honour will Render my best Services Acceptable to the Honble Council and Assembly in doing of which you'l Oblige

Your Honrs Most Obedt
Humble Servant.

Sunday the 18th day of July 1725.

We set away from Keewohee in Company with the Lower King, Eleazer Wigan, and Jos. Cooper about Ten of the Clock in the Morning and about Twelve a Clock at Noon We came to Tamautley [1] a Town Distant from Keewohee about 12 Miles where we lay all Night.

[1] Tomautley, Tomantly, or Tomassee was in a northwesterly direction from Keowee and not far from the North Carolina border.

About Eight of Clock at Night I went to the Town House and carryed along with me King Crow and the Two Linguisters And having Stayed there for some time King Crow made a Speech to the people of the Town and Rehearsed to them the Substance of the Talk I had with them and desired that they would not forgett it, that they might have it in mind at the General Meeting and withall telling them to Consider what a good thing it was to be ffriends with the English who they would always Stand by and bid them to remember what good times it was now to what it hath been before the English came among them. The King having done Speaking, the people in the Town house Returned thanks which are Words they use when they like any thing that [is] said to them.

Monday the 19th day of July 1725.

The Weather being very Cloudy and looking very likely to rain We did not set away from thence til Eleven Clock in the Morning and about half past five We came to Tuccareecho [1] distant from Tamantly about Eighteen Miles where we lay all Night.

Tuesday the 20th day of July 1725.

We set away from Tuccareecho abt nine of the Clock in the Morning and abt three in the afternoon We came to Old Estotoe [2] in the Middle Settlements being about Sixteen Miles from Tuccareecho where we lay all Night.

Wednesday the 21 day of July 1725.

Set away from old Estotoe about Eight of the Clock in the Morning and abt four of the Clock in the afternoon we came to Nocochee [3] w[h]ere was mett together the head Men of the

[1] Tuccareecho was also in a northwesterly direction from Keowee, but its exact location has not been determined.
[2] Old Estatoe on the Tugaloo River at the western extremity of South Carolina.
[3] The identity and location of this town has not been determined.

said Town and also of Six other Towns belonging to the Lower Kings Precincts who were not at Keewohee at the time of my giving the Talk to the head men of Several other Towns, And having given the Talk to them they seemed all very well Satisfyed therewth And then I informed them that I did not Expect an Answer to the talk at that time but hoped they would keep it well in mind that they migt Remember what I said to them at the General meeting of the head men of the whole Nation (of which I would give them Notice). I also informed them that as Crow was their King and made by them and Approved off by the English, that I Expected they would look upon him as such, otherwise they would be no people, and that the head men in all their Towns would take care to keep their Young Men under them and make them obey them in every thing.

To the foregoing talk they Answered in One Voice That they would take Notice of what I had say'd to them and that it was good.

Thursday the 22d day of July 1725.

This day King Crow left us and the rest of the head Men who Accompany'd Us in our path to the last of his Precincts that lies in Our path over the Hills and at their departure I called them together and informed them in the presence of the King that I Expected they with four or five Towns Adjacent to Keewohee would build a large house with a Corn house thereto in the said Town in such a place as their King should think fitt, in Order for the head men of his precincts meeting at any time when they had any thing to talk abt and to Entertain them at their coming thither as also to receive the White mens goods when they came there, and that Each Family should bring to the King Yearly for a publick Store a bagg or baskett of Corn to Entertain their head men at their Publick Meetings as well as Strangers.

They Answered to the above discourse that they would take care and get it done out of hand.

We were Obliged to Stay here this day the Weather proving very Rainy.

Friday the 23d day of July 1725.

Set away from Nocoochee abt 6 of the Clock in the Morning and abt Six at Night we passed by Tamautley in the Upper Settlements and came to Elejoy[1] being abt two Miles further where we lay all Night having Traviled this day thirty ffive Miles a road which is almost Impossible to Travile in and were Obliged to walk Several Miles of the way.

At my Arrival here was mett together the head men of five Towns in the Upper Settlements who after their Ceremonial way came and Sing'd before me and faned me with their Eagles tailes and seemed very much Joyed at my coming among them.

About Eight of the Clock at Night I went to the Town House there being all the head men and Others, And informed them by Linguisrs[2] that I Expected that the head men of every Town in the Upper Settlements would go over the Hills to their King where I should give them the talk and also that there would be a Meeting of the head men of the whole Nation at which I Expected they would be at and that they would remember what I said to them, when I had talked with them over the hills.

They in Answer to the above discourse said that they would take Notice of it.

Saturday the 24th day of July 1725.

This Morning came to me the head men of Elejoy who informed me that they were desirous to hear the talk in their own Town and that they had no Mind to go over the Hills.

I then Informed them after a Sharp Manner that I would not talk wth them in their own Town, and that as the head Men of the Lower Settlements had waited upon their King,

[1] Ellijay. There were several Cherokee towns of this name, but the one here referred to was most likely that in Macon County, North Carolina, near the site of the present town of Franklin.

[2] Linguisters or interpreters.

so I Expected they would wait upon their King he being of their own Choosing and Approved of by the English that they might be altogether and then there could be no Excuses from any of them in saying that they had not heard the Talk which was Usual among them, And having done saying any further, I desired that they would give me an Answer to what I had now said to them.

And the head Men having Considered among themselv's of what I had said to them made Answer — That they would send two head men and a Councelour out of Each Town and that they would be two Nights after me in my Journey Over the Hills.

I inform'd them that it was very well and that I was Glad they had given me so good an Answer.

Set away from Elejoy abt nine of the Clock this Morning and abt Ten of the Clock we came by little Teriquo [1] in the Middle Settlements being about Two Miles from Elejoy. We also passed by Conustee. About Twelve at Noon I took our Departure from thence and came about five Miles Short of a place called the Beaver Dam where we lay in the Woods for this Night having Travilled that day 25 Miles.

Sunday the 25th day of July 1725.

We set away from our Camp about five of the Clock in the Morning and abt three in the afternoon we Arrived at Great Terriquo [2] over the hills where we was mett by two head men of the said Town (the rest being all out a hunting). We Travilled this day about 25 Miles in a very bad road so that we were Obliged to walk for Several Miles over the hills.

This Town is very Compact and thick Settled which they are Obliged to, otherwise they would be Cut of by the Enemy who are Continually within a Mile of the Town lurking about the Skirts thereof and very often Cut of their People

[1] Little Tellico.
[2] Great Tellico, on Tellico River near its junction with the Little Tennessee.

and make their Escape. Here are two town Housses in this Town by reason they are the people of Two towns settled together wch are both Enforted and their houses which they live in all Muskett proof.

Munday the 26th day of July 1725.

We stayed at Terriquo all day, it proving rainy, and sent away Messingers to the King of these parts at Tunissee [1] about 16 Miles from hence to inform the King that I should be with him the next day following in Order to give out the Governours Talk to his people.

Tuesday the 27th day of July 1725.

The day proving very rainy we could not goe from hence according to the Message sent Yesterday to the King at Tunisee I informed the headmen at Terriquo that were at home that I Expected they would Accompany me to Tunissee where there King lived and where I intended to give them the English talk.

Wednesday the 28th day of July 1725.

We set away from Terriquo about Nine of the Clock this Morning and about ten of the Clock we had a Violent Shower of rain wch Caused the head men of Terriquo wch were along with me to return home and the Shower being over we set away and about one Clock in the Afternoon we Arrived at Tunisee where the King of the Upper people lives, and some time after my Arrival there I had their whole Ceremony used before me at which time the head Warriour of Tunissee got up and made the following Speech to me and the People of the Town.

That they must now mind and Consider that all their Old men were gone, and that they have been brougt up after another Manner then their forefathers and that they must

_____
[1] Tennessee, on Little Tennessee River, near its junction with the Tennessee.

Consider that they could not live without the English. As for his part and the Kings they allways are and will be loving and kind to the English for taking so much Notice of them in sending up one of their beloved men among them which they as Young Men had never seen before. Mind that if ever I dye you Pitch upon a Man among you that will talk to you for your own good as I do, and that he be a Man that will always Stick Close to the English who you have, and will always bee good to you and be sure You mind what I have now said to you.

The head Warriour having done Speaking they all returned thanks.

He then Ordered both Men Women and Children to take us by the hand as Brothers and ffathers to them.

Their whole Ceremony being over, I then informed the King and head Warriours that I had heard his good talk to his people and that I was come a great way with a great talk from the Governour and all the belov'd men of the English (their brothers) which I was ready to give out to them as soon as I had Notice that all the head men of the Towns had mett together. And then the head Warriour got up and told the People what I had said to the King which they in one Voice gave thanks to him for.

The King informed me that as soon as they had mett together he would let me know.

At Night the head Warriour being along with us at Supper and afterwards Smoaking two or three pipes of Tobacco gave us the following Accot of what had happened since Mr. Wigan had left them.

That about Six Nights agoe a Man and a Woman going over the river to geather some herbs to make Salt, the Man left the Woman for some small time in Order to go and Shoot a Turkey, and at his return back he Espyed some Enemies who he found had taken away the Woman he left behind him and the Man making his Escape Allarmed the Town who Imediatly got a party of Men and went out about 35 Miles agt the Enemy but could not come in Sight of them, they dividing in Small Numbers and the doggs which the people had a long with them runing before gott Sight of the Enemy and made a Sad Noise, the Enemy finding by the dogs that these people were Nigh them, they then took to their heels and gott away the Night coming on. They beleive there was five of the Enemy (one of which) they Suppose to have Struck out by himself with the Woman that was Carried away. That the begining of last Moon some of his people being a hunting down the river about 16 Miles discovered a great body of their Enemies, On which they immediatly sent in some of their people to Allarm the Town, who Immediatly dispatched away a party of Men in Canoes and when they came up with their own people that had first discovered the Enemy they sent out four ffresh look outs, who they told they would goe easily down the River and Land at some Convenient place, the lookouts in the mean time coming upon the Enemy, who were on the top of a Hill took them for their own people, thinking that they might be landed long before they gott there, and the lookouts calling to the Enemy (who they took for their own people) the Enemy made no Answer, and then they discovered they were the Enemy and said to one another, "lets run for it," and as they run the Enemy followed them and wounded one of them but he getting into a Thickett they were afraid to Venture after him, so that he made his Escape, the other three look outs keeping along came up with their own body of people and told them what had happened (on which) they took Measures to way lay the path for the Enemy wth thought to give them battle the next Morning, but the Enemy as they Supposed discovered them and Steared their Course from them in the Night and got away on which the people returned home without any Success.

After the relation of the foregoing Story he further said that they were hemed in all round with their Enemies and that if they were in Unity with the Southward Indians they should have no Enemy then to look after but the ffrench Indians who they could send out agt And then Venture to leave their Women and Children at home and also that they could then have room to Hunt.

Thursday the 29th day of July 1725.

Came in from Terriquo two of the head men of the said Town to hear the talk given to the King at Tunisee.

Friday the 30th day of July 1725.

Saturday the 31 day of July 1725.

Nothing Occured this two daies for my Observation.

Sunday the 1st day of August 1725.

Munday the 2d day of August 1725.

The head men of the following Towns being mett together at Tunisee I had the talk Interpreted to them.

Tunissee .	Terriquo .	Tallassee	Towns on this side the hills.
Suittico .	Coosaw		
Elejoy .	Tamantley . . .		Towns on the other side the hills.
Cheeowee	Conustee		

Towns wanting in the Upper Settlements:

Iwasee and Little Terriquo

I inform'd them by the Two Linguisters that I was sent a great way by the English with their talk for the good of the Cherookees and hoped that they would take Notice of it.

A. That they were glad to see me among them and that they would take Notice of no other talk but the English's.

The talk being Interpreted to them they returned thanks And then I Examined them as follows in relation to the Coosaw Man [1] being Recd by one of their Towns.

Q. What did the Coosaw Man which was recd by Terriquo Town say to the people of the said Town?

The Head Warriour of Great Terriquo made Answer as follows: That the Coosaw Man came to this Town with a Slave Woman that was taken from them by the Creeks and

---

[1] Kusa man, an inhabitant of the Upper Creek Town of Kusa, which was situated on the Coosa River in Talladega County, Alabama.

that Tusseegi omeco of the Coosaw Town in the Abeecoes [1]
Ordered her to come along with his Nephew which was the
sd Coosaw Man and to Sue for a peace for Six of their
towns, and one more wch had not heard of it with the
Cherokees.

The head Warriour of Terriquo also informed me, that
the reason the Woman was sent along [with] the Coosaw
Man was because there was a party of the Cherokees and
some Chicksaws gone out against the Creeks who coming up
with some of the Abeecoe Towns, a Cheeckesaw ffellow that
was among them, run away from the rest of the party, and
got with the Abecoe Towns, and gave the Abecoes an Accot
that the English had sent up an Army of White men and
Negroes to the Cherokees to goe agt the Creeks, and Advised
them to Enfort themselv's forthwith which was the reason
they sent the Coosaw Man and the Slave Woman to the
Cherokees.

Q. Why did you beleive an Idle ffellow who came to tell
you lies for if he had come for a peace he would have brought
some token with him?

A. That the Slave Woman which the Coosaw Man
brougt along with him was his Child, and that the Coosaw
Man informed him that if [they] approved of His Message
they would send all the Cherokees home which they had
Amongst them as Slaves at times, which made him believe
what the Coosaw man said to him.

I inform'd him that he might as well beleive any Idle
Fellow who perhaps might be sent from a body of their
Enemies (who might be near any of their Towns) to discover
what Number of people might be in them and if they found
they could have an Advantage over them then they would
Cutt you off before you could Defend yourselv's agt them.

A. That it was very true what I had said and that such
a thing might happen at one time or another.

Q. Why did you not Immediatly send to your King living
in the next Town to Yours and the rest of the people of your

[1] Abihkas, Upper Creek Indians inhabiting the valley of the
Upper Coosa.

Nation to lett them know that a Coosaw man was come into your Town?

A. That he did send a Messinger and was going to send another but the News of Quannissee being Cutt of by the people of the Coosaw Man's Nation made him run away in the Night after four days Stay wth him.

Q. What did you say to the Coosaw Man before he went away?

A. That he told him that there were Several of his people out at Warr and that if they killed any of the Coosaws or if the Coosaws killed any of his People that it must not be thought of.

Q. What discourse had you with him the time he was with you wch you say was four day's?

A. That he Advised him to be gone because he did not design he should go any further into the Towns, and that he Expected the King (who he knew would not Approve of his being there) having sent a Second Messinger to him.

I inform'd him that I found by his discourse that he was Conveyed away by him.

A. That if he had been Conveyed away by him that he would not have left his Gun and Coat behind. At which Answer all the rest of the head men at the Meeting Laughed at him wch is their way when any of their head men do any thing without the Consent of their King and the head men of the other Towns.

Q. How came you to Suffer your Young Men to go to Warr agt the Coosaws in so little a time after the Coosaw Man run away?

A. That they were Young Men and would do what they pleased.

The foregoing Answer gives me Strong reason to beleive that none of the People at Terriquo were willing to receive the Coosaw Man Except the head Warriour and some of the old men.

Q. Why did not you send the English word that a Coosaw Man was come to Your Town for a peace according to the Promise when you was last down and According to the promise of all the head men of your Nation that have been down to the English ?

A. That the Coosaw Man run away before the King and head men could meet together to Consult abt him so that they could not send down to the English.

This was all I could gett from the head Warriour he being so Confused at what he had done and at what I had say'd to him in the presence of the rest of the head men at the Meeting.

At my giving out the Talk when I came to that part of it wch relates to their making any Treaty with the French or their Indians, I thougt fitt to Add the following Article to it: That if any french Man comes among them that they Secure them because they do all they can to destroy them And that altho they do not come into Towns, Yet they come a great way wth their Indians (y[ou]r Enemies) in the path and down the river with a design to destroy your People.

To the foregoing discourse they gave the following Answer.

That they never will Suffer any ffrench Man Whatsoever to come amongst them, because they never had any love to them, and the King and the head Warriour of Tunnisee Spoke as follows :

That they remembred very well what the English Govr said to them when they were last down relating to the French, Which was to Secure them and to take their goods for themselv's Which they also made Answer and said they would be Sure to mind what the Govr said because they never had any Value for the ffrench nor never will.

I inform'd them that the 14th day of this Month I had Appointed to be the General Meeting at Elejoy and that I Expectèd they would all be there and that I should send as soon as they could get me a Messinger to go to the Lower King and headmen who had promised to mett as soon as they heard from me to give me a General Answer to the talk I had given them.

And then they all made Answer that they would be sure to be there and that they would before that time Consider well of what talk I had given them.

And then they Departed.

Came in this day from Kewohee Henry Guston and Ja: Millikin, Indian Traders.

Wednesday the 3d day of August 1725.

This Morning appeared before me Ja: Millikin and Henry Guston to Answer a Complt agt[1] them pursuant to my Orders of the 18th of July last in Relation to their Employing one John Hewet for one whole Year in the Indian Trade without my leave or Lycence which I proved before them by Two Letters from them to the said Hewet, wherein they Charge him not to Trade in the presence of any White Man for fear of his being discovered.

And the said Gustin and Millikin pleading that they Employed the said Hewet out of Charity and without any design of defrauding the Country or in Contempt of the Government and hoping that I would take their Case under Consideration and to Shew them as much favour as the Circumstance of the Case would Admitt of, and as would seem mett with me, Promiseing for the future to take care of any further Complt against them, And on Considering the above Complt I Ordered them to give me a Note for the Sum of Thirty pounds payable to the Country it being there due from the said Hewet who Traded for them a whole Year without any Lycence and they having given me their Note accordingly on Mr. Saml. Eveleigh Mercht I then dismist them of the Complt agt them giving them in Charge to take care for the future how they behaved themselv's, which they Promised to do.

Wednesday the 4th day of August 1725.
Thursday the 5th day of August 1725.
Friday the 6th day of August 1725.
Saturday the 7 day of August 1725.
Sunday the 8th day of August 1725.

[1] Complaint against.

Munday the 9th day of August 1725.

Nothing Occured these Six days for my Observation.

Tuesday the 10th day of August 1725.

We set away from Tunnisee about 9 of the Clock in the Morning in Company with the King of the Upper People and the head Warriours of the sd Town in Order to goe to the General Meeting and about four of the Clock in the Afternoon We came to Terriquo where we Stayed all Night and the next day.

Thursday the 12th day of August 1725.

Having Intelligence that the Cherekee Woman who came along with the Coosaw Man from the Abecoes was in this Town, I thought fitt to Examine her as Follows :

Who gave you leave to return to your own Nation again ?

A. That she had leave from Youho-lo-mecco a head Man of the Occacoochee Town in the Abecoes and that Six Nights before She came away the head Men of the said Town had a meeting with Several others but She could not tell what they mett about or that She was to be sent home And that She was Ordered first to come along by herself, by the Coosaw Mans Nephew.

Q. Did you hear that the Upper Creeks had any meeting about a peace with the Cherokees ?

A. No, but that she was Ordered by Youho-lo-mecco to talk with the Cherookees about a peace with them for the Summer gone, the Winter coming and the Spring following.

Q. Do You understand the Creek Language ?

A. Yes.

Q. Did You hear the head Men of the Towns where you was talk of a Peace ?

A. That She did, and that Six Nights before she came away they had a Meeting abt it but that she did not hear what they had Concluded on and that She was sent away by

You-ho-lo mecco when She was gathering of Wood, and that he Ordered his Nephew to come along with her.

Q. How many Towns did you Understand were for a Peace?

A. That all the Towns of the Upper People were for a Peace.

Q. Did You understand what made them desirous of a peace?

A. That they Supposed there was a great Number of their people killed by the Cherokees but that She finds Since she has been at home they were killed by the ffrench Indians which was their reasons for a peace.

Q. Do you know what Answer the Coosaw Man that came along with you had to Carry home with him in relation to his Message which was for a Peace?

A. That She beleived he run away before he had any Answer given him.

I inform'd her that I understood she was in the Town House when the people of Terriquo Town talked to him.

A. That she heard them say Nothing to him abt his Message and that they talked with him only about the path and his Journey to Terriquo Town.

I Observe that when any of these people (who are taken) return back to their own Nation that they are keept four day's and Nights in the Town house and that the people of the Town dance all the time, so that if there had been any thing said to the Coosaw Man (who was keept in the Town house also) that she must have heard it she being in the Town House along wth the Coosaw Man all the time of his Stay with these people.

Some small time before my Departure from Terriquo Arrived there three Chickesaws from their own Nation with a Message (as I was Informed) wch Occassioned my Enquiry about it and found it to be as follows:

That they were Sent to the Cherokees by their head men to give them an Accot that they heard by the way of the Toomes (a Settlement of the French Indians) that the Creeks had Concluded on a talk to cutt off Terriquo Town last Year.

That the Chickesaws have made a peace with the Chactaws but for no Longer time then they can have an Opportunity of Cutting a Number of The Chactaws off as they Served the Chickesaws some time agoe. That the Weeo-tee-noes, (the ffrench Indians) have lately killed the Chickesaw King which they little Expected they being at peace wth them and that they have also killed Several of their Men on the Broad river so that now they have declared open Warr with them. They also give an Accot that the broad river is full of Canoes with ffrench Indians in them and that they are all about in these parts.

That there was four White Men in the Chickesaw Nation and that they had sold all their goods, but three of them was gone down with 20 horse load of Skins and the other Stays to take care of what Skins is left behind and that they all Promised to be up again about this time.

We set away from Terriquo about 10 of the Clock this Morning and about 6 at Night We came a Mile Short of a place called Beaver Dam being about 24 M. where we lay in the Woods all Night.

Friday the 13th day of August 1725.

Set away from our Camp about 6 of the Clock in the Morning and abt one of the Clock in the Afternoon we came to Conustee having travilled this day 26 Miles.

Saturday the 14th of August 1725.

Stayed at Conuste all day having an Accot that the head men of the whole Nation were not mett at Elejoy according to their promise being about Eight Miles from hence.

Sunday the 15th day of August 1725.

Stayed at Conustee all this day having great Raines.

Munday the 16 day of August 1725.

The Weather breaking up and being very fair We set away from Conustee about 10 of the Clock in the Morning and about Twelve at Noon we came to Elejoy where was mett together the King and head men of all the Upper People in Order to be at the General Meeting at the said Town and in Expectation of meeting the King and head men of the Lower people who Appointed to be here two days after the time appointed for the General meeting.

Tuesday the 17th day of August 1725.

This Morning a Messinger was sent away to Jhoree [1] and Noocochee to inform the head men of the Lower people (who we had an Accot were mett at those places) that the King and head men of all the Upper People were mett at Elejoy and to know why they did not meet them According to the Appointed time for the General Meeting.

Wednesday the 18th day of August 1725.

Finding that the Upper people had not sent away Messingers to the Lower people according to their Promise Yesterday, I went my Self to them about it and desired to know their reasons for not sending to the Lower people.

They Answered that the King and all the head men of the Upper people were mett at the place and time appointed and that they have waited four Nights for the Lower people who had Notice of the time and place for the General meeting as well as they.

Q. I then asked them if they thougt it would take up too much time in sending Messingers to the lower people for the English to know their reasons for not meeting according to their promise, And then the head Warriour got up and Ordered two Messingers to go to Nocoo-chee where the head men of the Lower people were mett.

The Head Warriour of Tunnisee told me that he would Stay til the Messingers Returned and that if the Lower people did not come with them they would hear the talk and return home.

[1] Jore, on Iola Creek, an upper branch of the Little Tennessee.

I inform'd him that at the return of the Messingers I would give them the talk.

The two Messingers who were sent Yesterday to the Lower people returning Informed us that they mett a Messinger from the Lower people abt 15 Miles from hence who Informed them that the head Man of the Lower people were mett together at Nocochee and that they Expected to have the talk there (in Answer to which) the Messinger that went from hence Informed the other Messinger by my Order that the King and head men of all the Upper People were mett together at Elejoy being the place appointed by them all after the General Meeting and that I was very Uneasy at their not coming having Stayed Six days for them and that I designed the talk to be given them at no other place then Elejoy.

Arrived here one James Beemer with two other Men (by Name) Daniel Jenkins and Peter Wood Indian Traders who informed us that they set away from the Settlemts 13 days after us and that they were 29 daies on the Path to this Nation.

Thursday the 19th day of August 1725.

Waited at Elejoy all day in Expectation of the Lower people's coming and they not coming according to Expectation, The Head Men of the Upper People sent their King to me in the Evening to informe me that they had Waited here a long time for the Lower people and that they would wait one day longer and that if they didn't come in that time that they would have the Talk given them again, at which time they Should be ready with their Answer.

I inform'd the King that I hoped they would rest Satisfyed for one day longer and that if they did not then come I would give him and his head men the talk and that after I had had their Answer I intended to goe to the lower people from hence.

Friday the 20th day of August 1725.

This Morning I hired a Special Messinger to go in the path to Nocoochee til such time he mett the lower people and that if he mett them in the path to hasten them here, because the talk was to be given toMorrow Morning to the Upper people who had waited so long a time for them, And in Case he did not mett them to go to Nocoochee and if he found them there to inform them that I Expected they would keep all together til such time I came to them which (God willing) I designed on Sunday next before which time I intended to give the talk again to the Upper People and to have their Answer thereto.

The Messinger returning abt 6 of the Clock in the Evening Inform'd Us that he had mett the lower people who he said would be here this Night. And they having come Accordingly

I desired to know their reasons for their not coming sooner. They informed me that their King had set the time 6 Nights longer then I had set it before, and that the reason their King did not come along with them was because, he was out of Order in his Grind and that it was his Custome to Serve the head Men after this Manner at any of their meetings.

I plainly perceive by all the lower people that [they] have not any regard for their King, he being a Man (As I have been informed) that they never could rely on for truth which makes them so doubious of their being sent for at any time to hear the English talk.

MEMORANDUM :

That Daniel Jenkins is allowed as a Substitute to Thomas Booth Indian Trader provided the said Booth forthwith sends down to Charles Town John Hunt who is incerted in his Lycence, the said Booth having given his Note to the Country on Demand for the Sum of Ten pounds for the Endorsmt of the said Jenkins on the back of his Lycence it being the Country's due.

Additional Instructions to Thomas Booth and to all persons Interested or Indorsed in his Lycence and to every of them :

You are not on any Accot or pretence whatsoever to receive of any Indian or Indians any Sort or Quantity of

Raw Skines or Skines Undreast Either in the Vending of any Sort or Quantity of the goods to them or any other way's Whatsoever.

Saturday the 21 day of August 1725.

The King and head men of all the Upper Settlemts and of 24 Towns of the Lower Settlemts being mett together I had the talk given to them — recd their Answer thereto as follows :

At a Meeting of the King and head men of all the Upper Settlements and of 24 Towns of the Lower Settlemts at Elejoy.

Eleazer Wigan and Jo : Cooper Interpreters.

The King of the Upper people made the following Speech to me :

That they are all very glad the English have taken so much Notice of them in sending one of their beloved Men among them, That they have gathered a few Skines which they desired I would Accept of to do with them as I pleased.

That the head men of all the Towns in the Nation (Except a few of the Lower Towns) are now mett together to hear the English talk again and to give their General Answer thereto having already agreed upon it and that they are Unanimous in their Opinion.

After the King had done Speaking I inform'd them that as the head men were here altogether that I should give them the talk again and that I hoped they had Considered it well since I gave it them before because I Expected they would be very General in their Answer.

And the Talk being Interpreted to them, they called themselv's together and having Consulted for some time among themselves they made Choice of the head Warriour of Tunnisee to be their Speaker and to return the following Answer for them all :

That they heard some thing of White men being sent amongst them and that the White Men in the Nation Expected them as well as they.

That the Coosaw Man wch was recd by the head Warriour

of Terriquo made his Escape before the King or head Men of any other of the Towns had Notice of his being there, or Else they Should have known what to have done with him.

That they understood when the English Govr came in and their head men were down that the English had Traders amongst the Creeks as well as Among them, and that all was Streight and that the talk was given to both Nations.

I inform'd them that it was so with us Stil and that it will be so Stil if they make us Satisfaction as they find by the talk we have Demanded.

That after this time they shall hear from the Creeks and that if they dont Comply with Our talk (sent them) that they Expect to hear from the English and to know what they design to do.

That the Creeks do not only Abuse them, but also the English (their brothers) that they take away our goods and kill us and Shoot us and that now if the Creeks do not mind the Govrs talk that they are ready.

That the English go the path and that some times their people go along wth them, that the Creeks kill both their people and Ours (And what) must No Notice be taken of these abuses? Now We for Our parts never Robb the White Men or kill them but always hearken good to the English talk and that we are a people as well as the Creeks.

That if the White Men and the Creeks do Continue in ffriendshipp (it may be) that the Creeks may knock them on the head notwithstanding they are at peace with the English and then they'll use their pleasure in Continueing the War.

As for the ffrench they never had any love for them nor never shall and that if any of them comes amongst them that they'll Secure them because it was the English Govrs Orders to them when their King and head men were down.

That they have all their goods of the English and Arms to Defend themselves (without wch) they could not go to Warr and that they'll alway be ruled by them.

That what goods they have among them is made by the English and that they are Supplied with Impliments of Warr from them who they take for their Eldest brothers, and that when the Answer comes from the Creeks they Expect to hear from the English then they shall know whether they make Satisfaction to the English or not, and if they find the Contrary they are then ready to go against them as they did against the Tuskerorees.[1] They having done Speaking I thougt proper to put the following Questions to them :

Whether they would leave it to the English their Eldest Brothers (as they called them) that in Case the Creeks make us Satisfaction according to our talk whether they would Continue the Warr with them as it now is, or leave it to the English their brothers to make a peace for them if they think fitt for their good ?

A. That when the English have had an Answer to their talk from the Creeks and that when they have heard it they'll then Consider on it.

They having done Speaking I desired that if they all agreed to what the head Warriour of Tunnisee had said that they would all Speak in one Voice.

Which they did Accordingly. And then I gave them the following Additional talk :

I must inform You that I am Sorry to hear that its so hard for our Traders to get Burtheners among you when they want them and that when the difficulty of getting them is over that they'll not carry any burthens wth out being first payed and as I am informed very often leave their burthens half way of the place they are designed to be Carried to, So that the Traders are Obliged to pay double burthenage for every Pack.

If You would but Consider that the goods which are Carryed from Town to Town are for the good of the whole Nation and that you Assist one another in the Carriage of them, Your head men would not Suffer such ill Practices among your Burtheners. And further I would have you Consider among yourselv's how you can Expect our Traders will be able to bring goods Amongst you, if your Burtheners

[1] Tuscarora Indians.

impose on them as they have of late done and from this time they must not Expect to be paid til their Work is done and then you'l follow our English Custome. I must informe You that I have an Accot that Mr. Sharp one of Our Indian Traders amongst you came to one of the Towns of yr Nation in the Night time and took away what Skines was in the Town (and as I am informed) gave the Indians what he pleased for them. Now as your head men are altogether I Expect you [to] lett me know the truth of this Matter, that I may right the Persons that are injured being sent among you, to see that you have all Justice done you in Order that there may be a good Understanding betwixt you and us, who have always Esteemed you as our Brothers. Sometime agoe there was one Sawney Longe a Trader among You who went from Your Nation to the ffrench. I should be glad to know if you have anything to say against him because when your King and head men were Last down they did not care he should be Interpreter for them to the English.

I have of late found out an ill Custome among yr people which is their runing themselv's in debt to our Traders.

I must inform You that the English are always very ready to do anything for Your good, But as for trusting you any more, you must not Expect because when the Traders trust you, they Expect you'll pay them, and ask you for their Skines, which at that time you may not have by you, and then they Quarrell one with another and Create ill blood among you and them, which the English never love to hear of you being their Brothers, as you may plainly see by their letting you have goods farr Cheaper then any other Indians on the Main and by their treating you so handsomely when any of you go down to them, And I must inform you that Our Traders are Orderd not to take any more raw Skines nor trust for their goods so that you must dress and bring them to the Traders before they can give you goods for them. And You very well know that Our goods are always dressed to your hands.

Since now the King and all the head men of the Upper Settlemts and of 24 Towns of the Lower Settlemts are meet together I must give you in Charge to mind what the English have alway's said to you and particularly at this time and I hope there will always be so good an Understanding between yr King and head men, that they will mind what he says to them and that the head Men will mind and take care to keep the Young men under them. And then You will be a people and your King and head men will be looked on as such by your people and by us.

To the foregoing talk they returned the following Answer:

I[n] Answer to the Parragraph in relation to Sharp, the head Warriour of Tuegelo Spoak as follows: That he knew the whole Matter and that Sharp did not take away any Skines from any Indians but was gathering in his Debts from them.

As to the Parragraph relating to Sawney Long, They were Silent not carring to Complain of him.

As to Trust and raw Skines they made Answer that it was intirely the White Mens faults and that some of them followed the Indians in the Woods for their Skines and that they love them so well that they do not care if they take them raw or any other ways.

To the last Parragraph they made Answer That its what ought to be and that they intend to come into that Method otherwise they never will be a People.

After they gave me the foregoing Answer I returned them thanks for their present of Skines and Informed them that I did not come among them to receive any presents but to give them the English talk for their good, and to keep the Traders among them in good Order.

They answered
That it was their thougts that I should take the Skines because that when any of their head men go down to the English they always have presents made them and that now they have a beloved Man of the English among them, its good to make presents to him and to treat him as well as they can.

I informed them that as now I had done talking to them

I intended to take my leave of them, and then I wished them well, and safe home and desired them to keep a good look out agt their Enemies, And informed them that I should write down to the English Governour as soon as possible and then they would hear the Sooner from him, and that I would Acquaint them how ready and willing they were to meet to hear the English talk and how Civilly they had treated me.

I gave Orders to the head Warriour of Toxsoak[1] and Chagey[2] to Acquaint the head men of all the Towns, that have not been at the Meeting that I should meet them at Keewohee nine Nights hence to give them the talk in Order to have their Answer, Which they Promised to do.

I desired that when ever they sent any of their people abt business to the English that they might be head Warriours, that We might know how to Use them, and those were the people among them that We must take the most Notice of.

Sent Additional Instructions to Ja. Millikin, Andrew White and Eleazer Wigan Indian Traders debarring them from taking Raw Skines.

Sunday the 22d day of August 1725.

Having finished all Matters here I sett away abt ten of the Clock in the Morning and about Seven at Night We came to Nocoochee being about 34 Miles where we lay all Night.

Munday The 23d day of August 1725.

We set away from Nocoochee abt Seven of the Clock in the Morning and abt Seven at Night We came to Tuccarecho being about 27 Miles where We lay all Night.

[1] Toxsaah, a Cherokee village on Chatooga Creek, near its head in Oconee County, South Carolina.

[2] Chagee, a Cherokee village on Chatooga Creek, near its junction with the Tugaloo River.

Tuesday the 24th day of August 1725.

We set away from Tuccarecho about Eight of the Clock in the Morning and about ffive in the Evening we came to Tamusey being about 25 Miles where we lay all Night.

Issued Out Orders to Mr. Cornelius Dougherty, Wm. Cooper, Edward Kirk, John Neely and David Doway debarring them of taking Raw Skines.

Wednesday the 25th day of August 1725.

Gave the following Permission to John Savy and John Hewet:

You and Each of You are hereby permitted to Stay in the Indian Country til the return of Mr. David Doway from Charles Town who is to take out a New Lycence (in which) one of you are to be Indorsed or Inserted and The other to be Principal til which time you are not on any Accot whatsoever to Trade with any Indian or Indians and You and Each of you are to be of good behaviour during your Stay in the Indian Country on pain of Suffering the Utmost Severity of the Law in that Case made and provided.

Given under my hand this 25th day of Augt Anno Domo. 1725.

Set away from Tamausey abt 10 of the Clock in the Morning and about one in the Afternoon We came to Keewohee being about Twelve Mile.

Thursday the 26th day of August 1725.

Sent Additional Instructions to Mr. John Sharp and Alexr. McCormick debarring them from taking any raw Skines.

Gave the following Authority to Mr. Saml. Brown Indian Trader:

You are hereby Authorized and required as soon as you Arrive in the Catabaw Nation to Inspect into the Lycences of all persons trading there and an Accot thereof to take and return to me on Oath as soon as possible as also an Accot of all persons Trading or residing in those parts without my leave or Lycence and all persons in the said Nation are hereby required to pay due Obedience to these my Orders as they will Answer the Contrary at their Peril.

Given under my hand and the Seal of Office for Regulating Indian Affairs this 26th day of August Anno Domo. 1725.

Arrived here two Chickesaws from the Savannah Town [1] who came with a Message to the Cherokees to give them an Accot that the Cowetas [2] were gone in a body against the Yamassees and that the Upper Creeks designed to come up against the Upper Settlements of this Nation. And that they had this Accot from a Creek Indian who came down with a White Man to Savanah Town.

And having Examined the Chickesaws Concerning this Matter they gave me the foregoing Accot. I then informed them that I could not beleive what they had sayed because if it had been true I should have heard of it before now from the Comander of the Savanah Garrison or some of Our White Men.

Thursday the 26th day of August 1725.
Friday the 27th day of August 1725.

Issued to Capt. Wm. Hatton and to all persons in his Lycence Additional Instructions debarring them from taking raw Skines and also forbiding his two Packhorse men to Trade, it being Contrary to Law.

Issued out also to Mr. Richard Hasford, Mr. Sharp and

---

[1] Savannah Town, on the east bank of the Savannah River, six miles below the present site of Augusta, Georgia, was protected by Fort Moore.

[2] Kawitas, Lower Creeks in what is now Russell County, Alabama.

Mr. McComick Additional Instructions debarring them from taking raw Skines.

Saturday the 28th day of August 1725.
Sunday the 29th day of August 1725.
Munday the 30th day of August 1725.

Sent the following Letter together with a Copy of the General Answer to the talk to his Honour the President:

May it please your Honour —

Since my last to your Honour I have been Over the Hills and have given the Talk to the people of those parts and throughout the Towns in the Road there which I with a great deal of Satisfaction must inform your Honour has mett with its desired Effects as your Honour will see by the General Answer of the head men of the whole Nation herewith Inclosed Excepting of ten Small Towns the head men being all Out a hunting, so that I have given Orders to them to meet me at the Great dance here (called the Green Corn dance [1]) and then I shall have the talk Interpreted to them, and I cannot think they'll desent from the Answer of all the rest of the Towns they being so few in Number and their Towns so Inconsiderable. I have been very particular in my discourse to the Upper people Concerning the reception of the Coosaw Indian and find that he was recd by the head man of Terriquo (a Town over the hills) and that the King who lives but Sixteen Miles of them, had not the least Intelligence of it til such time the fellow run away altho he was with them four daies and its my Opinion that the Chief reason of his being recd there was because he brougt along with him a Woman (one of the head men of Terriquo's relations) wch they had taken from the Cherokees and I am very possitive that if it had come to the Ears of the King or head men of any other of the Towns before the

[1] The busk or green-corn dance was a solemn annual festival of eight days' duration. It was observed by both Creeks and Cherokees, was made the occasion of forgiveness and absolution of crime, and thought to be a time for a change of mind.

Fellow made his Escape that they would have Certainly destroyed him as they declared they would at the General meeting and Endeavoured as much as they could to Shame the head man of Terriquo when I particularly Examined him about it. I have also Examined the Cherokee Woman that came along with the Coosaw Man concerning the Creeks making a peace with these People and she informs me that Six Nights before She came away Several of the head men of the Upper Creeks had a Meeting abt it but that she could not learn what they had Concluded on, but informs me that all the Upper Creeks are very desirous of a peace with these people, having as they Suppose lost a great many of their people by them (which she finds since she has been at home) they are Mistaken in and says that they have lost most of their people by the ffrench Indians. I could not understand by her that the Coosaw fellow had any Private Message from the head Warriour of Terriquo to Carry home with him or from any of the Towns. She informed me that she was sent home by You-ho-lo-mecco a head man of Occacochee Town in the Abecoes and that the Coosaw man that came along with her was his Nephew and that he particularly gave her in Charge to talk with the Cherokees abt a peace for the Sumer gone, the Winter to come and the Spring following. This Sir, is the Chief of the Examination wch I thougt would be proper to Acquaint your Honr of and I must remark to you that Sevl of the men of Terriquo Town Went out to Warr and brougt in two Scalps just after the Coosaw man made his Escape which in my Opinion shows how little these people are for a peace. I had an Accot at Terriquo by three Chicksaw fellows that came in there just at my departure from thence that they and the Chactaws have made a Peace tho for no longer time then they can have a fair Opportunity in killing a Number of them as they Served the Chicksaws some time agoe. They likewise gave me an Accot that the Weeo-tee-nees (the ffrench Indians) have latly killed their King which they say they little Expected they being at peace with them and have now declared War agt them, they allso give me an Accot that the broad River is full of Canoes with ffrench Indians in them and that they are all about in these parts. How true this Information may be I cannot Assure your Honours because they are always known to be a people that run from one Nation to another Inventing what Stories they can to Amuse the people with, and I should be heartily glad if there could be some Means found out to prevent their being so much Carest by these people and their droping in amongst them as they do and I am very Jealous of the[ir] Over powering them at one time or another.

I must inform your Honour that the people in these lower parts have so little regard for their King that they do not in the least hearken to him and the reason of it is because he is a Man they can't rely on for truth and in my Opinion is more under the Comands of his Subjects then they are under him, which makes him very Undeserving of the Station he is in, and I am of Opinion that an old Indian called (breakerface) is the properest person for a King for these parts, he being a Man of resolution and was always known to be a good man to the English and I beleive will keep the Young men under a better Governmt then now they are.

I hope Your Honour will not forget laying before the Assembly what I mentioned to you in my last in relation to the Traders having the Liberty to send their Substitute from Town to Town to Trade in their behalfs which in my Opinion will be the Sole Means of Spoiling the Indians as well as the Trade, they having so little regard as to what they do amongst them or how they dispose of their Employers goods so they get but a few Skines, and having discoursed Several of the Traders themselves I find them to be of my Opinion and are very willing to have a Stop put to it, and to have the Towns divided amongst the Principal Traders. I must Assure your Honr that I should not press this Affair so much did I not see the ill Conveniences of it and I must take Notice to your Honour that last Year his Excellcy and some of his Majties Honble Council did not Approve of my granting so many Lycences and altho' there are not so many Lycences this year, Yet there is three times the

Traders, the persons Inserted therein being on the same
ffooting as the Principal and it was my Opinion on the
Comittee for drawing the last Indian Trading Act that they
would soon see the Ill Conveniency of Granting that Indul-
gence to the Traders wch was in Opposition to the Virginia
Traders who I am Certain cannot do any prejudice to Ours
in the way of Trade, there not being above two or three of
them and their goods no ways Sortable or Comparable to
ours. If the General Assembly do not Approve of Alter-
ing the Law after this Manner or after the Manner it was
last Year, I shall be very Apprehensive of some Unforseen
Misfortune. I am Sorry to inform Your Honour that the
Traders are not in the least Ashamed to make Publick their
trusting the Indians last Year for such Considerable Quantitys of goods as they did and tho' they have Instructions
to the Contrary and know the ill Consequences of it so well
as they do I have informed them that I intend to prosecute
all their Bonds which God willing I intend to do, and have
wrote to Majr Blakewey to deliver out their bonds to the
Kings Attorney to do with them as he shall think proper
and Wee all too well know the ill Consequences of Trusting
the Indians and have fattaly Experienced them. Two
daies agoe Arrived here from Savanah Town two Chickesaws (who as they Informed me) came with a Message to
the Cherokees from their people to give them an Accot
that the Cowetaws were gone in a body against the Yamasees
and that the Upper Creeks designed for the Upper Cherokees and that they had this Accot from a Creek Indian who
came down with a White Man to Savannah Town, If this
is truth, I Suppose Your Honr hath heard of it before now
from the Comander of the Savannah Garrison or some otherways. I beleive it would be very proper if your Honr
thinks fitt that there be four Coats and Shirts and four
pair of Stockins to be made Presents of One Coat, one Shirt,
and one pair of Stockings to the Upper King

To the Head Warriour of Tunnisee . . . . . . Ditto.
To the Head Warriour of Tugelo . . . . Ditto.
To Old Breakerface . . . . Ditto.

These are the Most Noted Men in the Nation and as the present is so Small I hope it will be sent them.

I have taken care to Speak to the Indians at their General meeting that they do not send anybody down to the English about business but such as are head Warriours and I must take Notice that the King of the lower people when he has a Mind to send anybody down to the English that its unknown to the Upper King and that he getts the Traders to write what they please to the Governmt abt the people which he sends down which I have told the Traders of and to take care how they impose on the Governmt as they have heretofore done. It is my humble Opinion that these people are so well Affected to us that they may be brought into any Measures the Governmt pleases and I must Assure yr Honour that I have been Recd every way by them with a great deal of Joy and I am Certain they have Ussed me with their Utmost Civillity. Your Honour will Receive this Letter by four Indians who I have given Orders to Wait at my house to know your Honours pleasure and I am in hopes Your Honour has heard from the Creeks and that you'l dispatch what is thought proper to me til which time, I shall be travilling from Town to Town and lear[n]ing all I can from the Indians. I Should not have sent four Indians had not two been afraid to come by themselvs and I have drawn on Collo. Parris [1] for a White Blankett Each which is much Cheaper then I could pretend to gett a White Man. Wee have an Accot that the Senecas have latly fallen on the Waccamaws [2] and Carryed away with them Several Slaves and that they are very thick in these parts, so that Mr. Brown (who is here) cannot get Burtheners to goe that way along with him. I must take Notice to your Honour that Sharp and Hatton have brougt up their Slaves altho' by Law they are to fforfiet one hundred pounds for so doing and I should think myself Negligent in my Duty if I did not Acquaint your Honour therewth and altho' Sharp hath your Honours leave Yet Hatton hath not, and it's my

[1] Alexander Parris was treasurer of South Carolina in 1712–1735.
[2] Indians dwelling in the region of the Lower Pedee.

Opinion that the Law ought to be punctually Complyed with in that Case because the Slav's that are now come up talk good English as well as the Cherokee Language and I am Affraid too often tell falcities to the Indians which they are very apt to beleive, they being so much among the English. As for the Skines which the Indians were pleased to make me a present of (and which I could not refuse without Affronting them) I know not how to gett them down without I have horses sent for them, Your Honour being well Acquainted with the bulk of an Indians Present of Skines. I intend (God willing) after I have recd the Governmts Comands and finished all Matters here to set away for Savana Town. Your Honour hath inserted in this Letter the Chiefs of my Journal and when any thing further Occurs Shall not fail of Acquainting the Governmt therewth. I have nothing further to Advise Your Honour of but desire you'l be pleased to render my best Services Acceptable to his Majties Honble Council and the Honble Gentlemen of the Assembly and You'l Oblige

Your Honours

Most Obliged humble Servant.

Sent the following Order bythe bearer of the foregoing Letter to Collo. Alexr. Parris Treasurer.

Sir —

Please to pay to the bearers each a Blankett, they having come down as runners on the Country Service and place it to the publicks Accot of Moneys recd on Accot of Indian Trading Lycences as the Law directs. I am

Sr Your most humble Servant.

Tuesday the 31 day of August 1725.

Wednesday the 1st day of September 1725.

Thursday the 2d day of September 1725.

Arrived here from Savanna Town Six Chickesaw man [1] three Women and two Children, who gave us an Accot

[1] Men.

that Collo Hastings was at Savana Town and that he went down to the English in Company wth Mr. Haines Indian Trader, and also that the Cowetaws were gone in a body against the Yamasees and that the Upper Creeks designed for the Upper Cherokees.

Friday the 3d day of September 1725.

Saturday the 4th day of September 1725.

This day being Appointed for the Green Corn dance the head men of Seven Towns that were not at the General Meeting mett here, and abt Eleven Clock in the Morning they came to me and brougt a few Skines with them and having appointed their King their Speaker He informed me that the Skines he brougt here were a present for me from the Towns that had not their head men at the General Meeting.

I informed them that I thanked them for their present, but that I did not come among them to receive any presents but to Settle a good understanding between them and the English (their Brothers) and that they were the people the English had most Value for.

I also told them that I did not doubt but that they had heard the talk and the Answer of the head men of all the other Towns and that if they Approvd of the Answer I desired they would all Speak in one Voice.

They Answered that they Approved of the Talk and the Answer I had had to it very well and that they had appointed their King to Speake for them, who Spoak as follows : That they were all well Satisfyed with the Talk and the Answer thereto, and that they all intended to be at the next meeting after I had heard from the English. I Answered that it was very well and that I was glad they Approved of what had been done and that as soon as I had heard from the English they should hear from me and then they took me by the hand and departed.

Sunday the 5th day of September 1725.

Munday the 6th day of September 1725.

This Morning came to me King Crow and some of his head men to Enquire w[ha]t was done with the boy they promised to redeem last Year. I told them that he was among the English learning to make Shoes and that according to their desire he would not be sent over the Great Water and that as soon as they had made a gathering among themselv's of Skines to pay for him that they might then have him again as soon as they pleased, at which they went away well Satisfyed, the King and head men having heard that I designed to goe to Togelo parts informed me that he with some of his head Men would Accompany me there.

MEMORAND :

That John Facey and Wm. Collins are Allowed as Packhorse Men to James Millikin Indian Trader, he having given an Order on Samuel Eveleigh Mercht in Charles Town payable to the Publick for the Sum of £20, it being required by Law for the Endorsement of the said Pack horse men.

Given under my hand and Seal the date above written.

Tuesday the 7th day of September 1725.

Wednesday the 8th day of September 1725.

About Seven of the Clock in the Evening came in here a Young ffrench ffellow with a Chickesaw Woman who Stayed til the Dusk of the Evening about a Mile from the Town being very much afraid of these people knocking him on the head before he could come to the Sight of some White Person.

Thursday the 9th day of September 1725.

Having Examined the French man in relation to his coming to these parts I thought proper to send the following Letter to his Honr the Presidt

May it please your Honr —

Yesterday about the hour of Seven of the Clock in the Evening came in here a Young ffrench Fellow with a Chickesaw Woman who I have Examined this day and find that last fall he deserted from the Garrison at Moville [1] and went to the Chactaws and hearing that the ffrench were in Pursuit of him, he came from thence to the Chickesaws where he mett with Mr. Chambers, one of Our Traders there, who he came down with to Savanna Town, where he was Secured by the Comander there who I suppose had wrote to your Honour to know Your pleasure Concerning him, but in the mean time the ffellow run away with the Chickesaw Woman he brought here along with him, who I found was taken Slave by the Chacktaws from the Chickesaws and that She was sold to the French from whom he brougt her away with a design to Sell her, or to keep her as his Wife. This Sir his Examination which I thougt would be very proper to send down to your Honour for fear he should vary therein.

This Morning mett together Several head men of this as well as other towns (who came here to the Great dance) to Consult about the ffrench ffellow who they had Concluded to knock on the head, saying that it was the English Govrs talk, and having asked my Advise therein, I told them it was not our talk to kill the ffrench [but] only to Secure them when they came among them wth goods and to send us word of their being amongst them, and having this Opportunity by Mr. Foulton, Indian Trader, I thought proper to send him down to your Honour to do with him as shall be thought proper, it being my Opinion that his Stay here would be very pernicious to the Country. As for the Chickesaw Woman that came along with him I have Informed the Chickesaws that they may have her again she having been taken a Slave from them. This day I am setting Out for Togelo [2] parts in Order to learn what I can of the people

[1] Mobile.

[2] Tugaloo; there was a Cherokee town of this name in Habersham County, Georgia, at the confluence of Tugaloo River and Toccoa Creek

there and when anything of Moment Occurs I shall not fail in sending to your Honour to give you Notice thereof.

I am

Your honrs Most Obedt humbe Servt.

Wee set away from Keewohee abt 10 of the Clock in the Morning and went to Tamausey where we Stayed for three daies.

Friday the 10th day of September 1725.

Came in here from Great Terriquo Andw White Indian Trader who gave us an Accot that the Enemy were all about the Middle Settlements and that a great body of them was discovered.

Saturday the 11th day of September 1725.

This day I had an Accot from Keewohee by a Letter from Edward Kirk Indian Trader that the ffrench ffellow and Chickesaw Woman came to Keewohee the 8th Instant [and] were run away, altho' I gave possitive Orders to King Crow to secure him well, and that there was some of these people That were gone out after him. About Seven of the Clock in the Evening came in here the Warr hoop with the peice of a Scalp of an Ittewager Indian from Tuccaseegee[1] parts.

Sunday the 12th day of September 1725.

This day came to me King Crow and gave me an Accot that he heard the French man and Chickesaw Woman were seen at Chagey abt Six Miles from hence.

I then gave Orders to him to Speak to the Warriours of this Town to send out to the other Towns and if possible to have him Secured til I should come down from Tolego parts.

Munday the 13th day of September 1725.

About two of the Clock this Morning I recd the following Letter from his Honour the President together with a

[1] There was a Cherokee town of this name in Jackson County, North Carolina, at the confluence of the forks of the Tuckasegee River.

Copy of Capt. Fitches [1] Journal from the Creeks and also a Copy of the Honble Councils Resolutions thereon with further Instructions to the said Capt. Fitch which were all Added to the Copy of the said Journal.

SIR —

Some few daies agoe I recd the Inclosed Journal of Capt. Fitch, his Proceedings with the Upper and Lower Creeks and the Several Letters Inclosed by which you will be fully Acquainted with every thing that has past in those parts. I have also dispatched away the resolutions of the Council to Mr. Fitch on his proceedings and further Additional Instructions as you will see them Added to the Lower part of the said Journal now sent you. I Expect to hear every day from you which Occasions this to be very Short, but as soon as I have recd further Advices from You I will take care to send You back our Opinion and Advice with further Instructions if Occasion. The Chief reason of my now sending Chester before that I had heard further from you is to give You Notice that the Creeks and Chactaws do design to fall on the Indians you are with, and thinking it to be an Advantage to them to know it I desire that you will take care that they Shall. If the Cherokees upon knowing this would raise a Strong party and keep out good Scouts they might give the Creeks such a blow as they would never be able to gett over, but if they dont, lett them take what falls. We have no News from England not having had any Vessell from thence or from any other part.

The Assembly dont sit til the twelfth of August and if you dont come down before that I will lay your Letter before the Genl Assembly and get the Alterations you Mention in the Indian Act.

I have Ordered Chester to call on Mrs. Chicken for Letters, they are all well.

I am with all due respects
Your Very humble Servant

AR. MIDDLETON.

August the 29th 1725.

[1] Tobias Fitch, who was on a mission to the Creeks similar to that of Chicken's to the Cherokees. See pp. 175–212, *post*.

Mr. Wigan —

Last Night I had an Accot from the Settlemt that there's an Army of the Chactaws and Creeks coming agt these people about Six Weeks hence, so desire you'l give the people of your Town and Terriquo an Accot of this and tell them to be in a readiness and to raise as great a party of men out of their Inland Towns as they can in Order to Defend their Frontiers Towns and also to keep out good Scouts that they may not be Surprised. I am

Your ffriend —

We set away from Tamusey abt nine of the Clock this Morning and About three of the Clock in the afternoon We came to Toxsoah and sent [1] away from thence (having Stayed there for some Small time) in Compa[ny] with King Crow and the head Warriour of the said Town and about four of the Clock in the afternoon we got to Nogouwee where we Stayed for some time.

Tuesday the 14th day of September 1725.

The head men of Six of the Adjacent Towns being Assembled together they desired that I would meet with them at Togelo being the most Antient Town in these parts and having mett the head men of Six Towns accordingly at the said Town they fired a Volly at my Entrance of their Council House and Ussed their Ceremony before me, which being done the King Spoak as follows:

That there was all the head Warriours of Six Towns mett together and then I proceeded to tell them as follows:

First. That they might remember that I told them in the Talk that the English had sent up a beloved Man to the Creeks to Demand Satisfaction of them for Robing Sharp as well as for all injuries they have done us and Especially to Our Traders.

Second. That I had now heard from the English about that Affair and that the Creeks had delivered up Mr. Sharps

[1] Set.

Slaves and had promised to make him Satisfacon for his goods and other things which they Robbed him of and that we were Satisfyed therewith at present.

A. Its very well.

Thirdly. That they may see how much care the English has taken of them in sending up to me a White Man on purpose to give them an Accot that there is no [1] body of the Chactaws who are to Joyn the Creeks and come against them and that they might Expect them in a Month or Six Weeks time if not Sooner.

A. That they are their Enemies.

Fourthly. That if you will take my Advise from the English You need not to fear any of Your Enemies and may preserve Your Women and Children at home and likewise your Corn in the ground.

A. That if the Enemy comes that they will defend their Towns til they are all dead.

Fifthly. That if you would but Consider among Yourselv's how Numerous you are and how little you would Miss the drawing out of Each Town in the Nation A Small Number of men, You would not talk of defending your Towns but would raise an Army of Men and Defend [yourselves from] your Enemies before they come Nigh your Towns and you cannot have a better Opportunity then now you have because the English have taken care to give You timely Notice of their design.

A. That they'l Consider when I have done talking to them abt this Matter in particular.

Sixthly. That the English had now and would always take care to lett them know the design of their Enemies and that if they did any Mischief they could not blame us.

A. That they are very thankfull to the English.

Seventhly. I must Advise you to keep out good Scouts to discover your Enemies path and to Watch their ways, and if you could but in the mean time draw out but Ten Men out of Each Town you would be able to give the Creeks

[1] Now a.

such a Blow that they would for ever after dread you, and then you would Show yourselv's like men and let your Enemies see that You are not Afraid of them.

After I had had the foregoing discourse with them They then informed me that they would all go and Consult together abt what I had said to them and that they would give me their Answer.

The King with three of the head men from their Consultation Informed Me that they had Consulted about what I had said to them and that they intended to sett[1] out Scouts forthwith in Order to discover the Enemy and that they had Concluded to send to the other towns in Order to mett them to Concurr abt what I had said to them.

I inform'd that it was very well done of them and that I was glad I had taken such Methods.

They informed me that when the head men of the Towns they had sent to had all mett together they should send out Several parties of Men severl waies in Order to discover the Enemy. I informed that unless they had a body of Men ready to go out against the Enemy when they were discovered that their Scouts would be but of little Service to them.

A. That they'll take care when the head men of the other Towns meet to Consult about raising a body of men.

I must inform You that if the Creeks were not Afraid of you that they would not have the Chactaws to joyn them against you and I cannot help giving you the best Advice I can in Order that you may be in a readiness to goe out against your Enemies, because its for your good that I do it, and the best way for You to discover Your Enemy is to have good Scouts before your Army.

A. That they'll Consider about it as soon as the head men they had sent for had mett them.

I informed them they must be as Speedy as posible and that in the mean time their Women ought to be prepairing fflower for their Journey.

[1] Send.

They then told me that they Understood the English and Creeks were Streight Stil because they had done as the English Ordered them, and that they need not to be Affraid, and that if the Enemy comes on them before they can gett a body it would not be the Englishes fault because they have given them Notice of it.

I inform'd them that we had given them Notice of their Enemies design and that as they are Our best ffriends We would have them raise an Army to go out agt them that they might lett them see that they are not Afraid of them and that they are Men.

The head Warriour of Toxsoah then Offered his Service in going out and said that he would gett what Men he could to goe along with him. I inform'd him that I was glad to see him so forward against his Enemies and that I hoped on a Consultation of them all that they would all follow his Example.

Wednesday the 15th day of September 1725.

Sent the following Letter to Mr. Eleazer Wigan at Tunisee.

MR. WIGAN —

Since my last to you I have had a Meeting with the head men of Six Towns in Togelo parts Concerning the Advice I have had from the Settlemt and having given them an Accot of the design of their Enemies I then proceeded to perswade them as much as possible to raise a body of men and to send out Scouts before them, and they having had some Consultation abt it Informed me that they would send to the other Towns in Order for them to meet and to Consult together and I am in hopes they'll Conclude to raise an Army and goe out, otherwise if any Accident happens to them they cannot blame us. The reason of my sending this is to desire you to Encourage the people in your parts to goe out in a body, and in Order thereto I Suppose they'll have a Meeting, at which I desire you'll be at and Lett me know what Steps they intend to take to prevent their Enemies doing them damage and I would have you Consult the long Warriour in particular abt this Affair hoping that he'll be for going out, and You must take care that they send a Message to these lower people to lett them know their resolution on this Affair, as these people have taken care to do to the people of your parts. You may inform them that I had an Accot from the English that the Creeks have made us Satisfaction according to our talk sent them and that Sharp will have full Satisfaction made him by them.

I must inform You that these people have been very thankfull to the English for giving them an Accot of the design of their Enemies and for sending up to them a White Man for that purpose. I Expect the same from the Upper people and must once more desire of you if possible to per-swade them to raise an Army of Men to Joyn these Lower people who I dont doubt but will be very ready to Joyn them. Pray lett me hear from you as soon as possible and what your people design to do.

I am   Your ffriend.

We set away from hence and went to Chagey in Order to View the Fortifications of that Town and upon Viewing them I found that round their town house is built a very Substantial Fort and that round the most part of the Town is built a Slight ffortification.

We returned in the Evening to Noyouwee.

About ten of the Clock at Night came in the Warr hoop from Estotoe and gave us an Accot that there was a body of the Enemy discovered and that they had made Sevl paths towards these Towns downwards. Some time after the Warr hoop came in I went to the Town house and gave the people of the Town all the Encouragemt I could agt their Enemy in case they Should Attack them and informed them that they would find the Accot the English have taken so much care to give them Concerning their Enemies would be true and that unless they would draw out a body of Men to keep them from their Towns that they would be a plague to them for this long time and might in all prob-abillity do them a great deal of Mischief.

A. That they had sent for all the head Warriours of the other Towns and that when they mett together they would Consult about it.

Tuesday [1] *the 16th day of September 1725.*

We set away from hence and went to Old Estotoe a large Town and very well ffortifyed all round with Punchins and also ditched on the Outside of the sd Punchins (wch Ditch) is Stuck full of light wood Spikes so that if the Enemy should ever happen to fall therein, they must without doubt receive a great deal of Damage by those Spikes. I also Observe that there are Sevl New fflankers made to the ffortificacõns of the Town and that the Town house is also Enforted.

We returned in the Evening to Noyouwee.

Friday the 17th day of September 1725.

We set away from Noyouwee and about three of the Clock in the Afternoon we came to Tamausey were [2] we Stayed for some time.

We had an Accot that the Scouts being in Number (one hundred) that went out after the Enemy were returned without any discovery.

Saturday the 18th day of September 1725.

This day was brougt to me by one of Capt. Hattons Slaves the Young ffrench Fellow that was to have gone down to Charles Town with James Fulton Indian Trader but made his Escape from Keewhohee the Night before.

We set away from Tamusey and came to Keewohee.

Sunday the 19th day of September 1725.

Munday the 20th day of September 1725.

Set away from hence William Hatton and Henry Guston Indian Traders in Order for Savanna Town.

[1] Thursday.   [2] Where.

Tuesday the 21 day of September 1725.

Went away from hence David Doway Wm. Cooper and one Daniel Kearle a Virginia Trader in Order for Savana Town.

Came in here from Togelo parts King Crow who informed us that all was quiet there and that they had not been troubled with the Enemy since we came from thence.

Sent the following Letter by John Chester to his Honour the Presidt.

May it please your Honour —

On Monday the 12th Instant I recd your Letter with a Copy of Capt. Fitches Journal and also his two Letters with one from Collo. Hastings and also a Copy of the Resolutions of his Majesties Honble Council on Capt. Fitches proceedings among the Creeks and I Assure your Honour that Nothing could have happened more to my Satisfaction then to hear that the Creeks have so fairly promised to make Satisfaction for the Injuries they have done us. I was at Tamusey when your Honrs Letter came to me and having perused it and the other papers that came therewith I immediatly sent away to Noyouwee and Suṁoned all the head men of Togelo parts to meet me where they should Appoint, which was at Togelo. The reason of my going to these parts was because I take the people thereabouts to be the most Turbulent in the Nation and also the most taken Notice of by the other Towns. After the head men had mett together I informed them I had recd Letters from the Governmt wherein I had an Accot that the Creeks had restored Sharps Slaves with some other things and had made the English such Satisfaction that they were Satisfyed therwth at present and withall telling them that the English had so much regard for them that they had sent a White Man on purpose to give them an Accot that there was an Army of the Creeks and that the Chactaws had Joined them in Order to come against them, and that it was my Advice to them that they should forthwith raise an

Army of Men in Order to meet their Enemy in the Woods and by that means they would be able to Defeat them.

After I had had the foregoing discourse with them they returned the English thanks and Imediatly sent away Messingers from Town to Town in Order to have a Consultation about what I had said to them but have not yet heard whither they have mett or what they have Concluded on. All the Towns in these parts are so well Satisfyed that I am well Satisfyed no Indian Enemy will ever Attack them if any of the people are at home, the people in these parts have taken care to send out Scouts and have promised me to keep them out and when the head men have all mett together they intend to see if they can Conclude on raising an Army in Order to goe out to meet their Enemy and say that they are not at all Afraid of them, and that they are Resolved to Defend their Towns to their Utmost, and I am Apprehensive it will be a hard Matter to gett them out of them, to go against their Enemy, but shall Endeavour as much as possible to Encourage them against them and to get them to goe out. Since I have given these people an Accot of their Enemy they have had Several Allarms and are now repairing their Forts in Expectation of them.

Soon after the Arrival of your Honours Letter I sent away to Mr. Wigan to give the people on the other side the Hills an Accot of the designed Expedition of the Creeks and Chacktaws and if possible to gett the head Warriour of Tunisee (the Most Noted Man in the Nation) to go out with a body of men and to Acquaint them that the Lower people were very thankfull to the English for giving them an Accot of their Enemies coming against them. I have not yet had an Answer from Wigan nither do I Expect one these Eight days. I have gott the ffrench Man again that I wrote to your Honr about. He was taken up by these people agoing to Terriquo on the other side the hills with some Chickesaws in Order for that Nation. I have taken care to send him to Savanna Town by some of the Traders who are going there. I intend (God willing) after I have recd your Honours Comands by the Indians and have

Executed them to sett away from hence to Savanna Town in Order to Supervize the Garrison there, an Accot of which as well as all other my proceedings shall be returned to Your Honour by   Your Honrs
                              Most Obliged humle Servt.

P.S. I dont perceive that the ⎫
people are in the least Surprised │
at the designs of their Enemy but │
Seem as Chearfull as can be Expectd. ⎭

Wednesday the 22d day of September 1725.

Thursday the 23d day of September 1725.

Friday the 24th day of September 1725.

Nothing happened this three daies but frequent Allarms of the Enemy tho nothing happened on Either Side.

Saturday the 25th day of September 1725.

Some time this Morning I went to the Fort in this Town which the people by my Orders were repairing and seeing the Work go on but Slowley, I desired to know of the King the reason of it, the Enemy being daily Expected; He informed me that the people would work as they pleased and go to Warr when they pleased, notwithstanding his saying all he could to them, and that they were not like White Men. I then asked him what his head men Signifyed if they would not mind what was said to them.

He told me that if they were going to the English they would mind then what was said to them, because they would be then in hopes of having some Cloath given them, but at their return home would soon forgett what the English said to them or what they were to do, He likewise told me it would be good if the English did not give them anything when they go down, because it would not Spoil them, and that they are always wanting to goe down to the English to see what they can get of them. You see (says the King) that they'll promise you to go to Warr (but its when they please) and that they will have their own way of Warring and that it would be good if the English would let them alone and see what they will do of themselv's and by that means they may grow better. About four of the Clock in the Afternoon came in the Warr hoop from Ouconey [1] with a peice of a Scalp of one of the Enemies Scouts, giving an Accot that Scouts being in Number Twenty four that went out from old Estotoe, and Toxsoah having come upon the tracts of three of the Enemy found they were made downwards towards the other Towns (on wch) they Concluded to waylay the Path thinking by that means to Catch the Enemy being three in Number returning back to their old tracts near Estotoe from Town to Town. William The head Warriour of Estotoe fired upon them and killed one of them and another of them Recd two Shotts in his body which they Suppose to be dead, the other made his Escape.

Sunday the 26th day of September 1725.

Munday the 27th day of September 1725.

Tuesday the 28th day of September 1725.

Wednesday the 29th day of September 1725.

Thursday the 30th day of September 1725.

This five daies the Enemy hath been tracked and Scouts sent out from hence after them tho no Discovery of the Enemy's persons.

This Morning came to me Sevl of the head men of the Town Complaining that the Sevl Traders horses are here Continually amongst their Corn and that they have already destroyed a great deal and desiring a Stop might be put to it they not being willing to Shoot any White Mans horse.

I told them that the English did not Suffer any such

---

[1] Oconee, a Cherokee village near the site of the present town of Walhalla in Oconee County, South Carolina.

thing and that if they would Shoot some of their horses they would take more care of them for the future, and that I should Speak to the white Men about it.

Friday the 1st day of October 1725.

Saturday the 2d day of October 1725.

Sunday the 3d day of October 1725.

Munday the 4th day of October 1725.

Came in here from the Middle Settlemts of the Upper people Richd. Hasford who informed me that Mr. White according to my Orders had given the Indians in those parts an Accot of the design of their Enemies and that he was a Linguister to the said White and that at Little Terriquo where was mett together at the Corn dance Several of the head men over the hills and also the Major part of the head men of the other Towns in the Upper Settlements who after hearing what Mr. White said to them returned the English thanks and sayed that they always found the English their Brothers and Especially at that time and that they would forthwith send out Scouts to make what discovery of the Enemy they could. The said Hasford likewise gave me an Accot that since my being over the Hills [t]here went out of Great Terriquo four Young Lads two of which went into the Corn ffields of the Cowsaw people and that the other two Stayed in the Woods, that one of the two that went into the Corn ffields Shot two Cowsaw Women and brougt their Scalps into the said Terriquo and that they had been out fifteen daies.

Recd by the hands of the said Hasford the following Letter from Mr. Eleazer Wigan, Linguister over the Hills.

September the 25th 1725.

Honrd Sr:
Your Letters one dated the 13th and the other the 15th [were delivered] by Mr. White on the 23d Instant, and Immediatly [I] had all the Warriours of the Towns on this

side the hills together at Terriquo where I delivered your Honrs Message to them in Publick and likewise [to] the long Warriour in Private, in the first place they return the Govern[or] thanks, and as he has thougt by his sending them word of it that they should fight them, that they are resolved so to do, and the Method they design to take is for to lett them come to their Towns, but not undiscovered, for they design to keep out lookouts every way and be ready to give them a Smash in their Towns First and then to gather all their Strength and follow them when they are upon their retreat with their Wounded men, and the Long Warriour would have the people in those parts do the same and dont lett them goe away and not follow them as they have always done. I shall write to your Honrs in three or four daies time again and til then I am

Your Honrs Most Obedt humble Servt.
ELEAZER WIGAN.

Tuesday the 5th day of October 1725.

Wednesday the 6th day of October 1725.

I went this Morning to the Town house and gave the King and head men an Accot of the Message I had recd from the Upper people in relation to their Enemies coming against them and their Method to prevent their being Surprized. The King in Answer said that they were thankfull to the English for taking so much care of them and that they would take care to keep out Scouts and that the Upper people might take their own Method as they would theirs.

Thursday the 7th day of October 1725.

Friday the 8th day of October 1725.

The King came to me at Night with a Linguister and by him informed me that there was four Chickesaws come in this Evening with a Message from their people as follows — That this is the first Message from them and that they may

Expect another and that soon after they may Expect a body of the Chickesaws in at Terriquo to Joyn the people in those Parts some time in the Spring in Order to goe against Okefuskee [1] and Cusetaw [2] Towns in the Creek Nation and that they would send down to their people in this Town to joyn a body of these lower people and to go in a body against the aforesd Towns and that they would not have any White Men to know it fearing it might come to the Knowledge of the Southward people. The King likewise told me that he thought it was good for me to know this Message because I could tell him then my Opinion of it. After the King had done Speaking I inform'd him that he very well know'd the Chickesaws never came Amongst them without they brougt some Story or another and that I should be glad if they would make their words good in Joyning these people and going against the aforesd Towns but that I very much feared, and that We had not so much Value for the Southward people as to give any Accot of their design as We had done them.

Saturday the 9th day of October 1725.

Sent by Richd. Hasford a Letter to John Sharp desiring him to give the people in Togelo parts a Charge abt repairing their Forts and keeping out Scouts and also to inform them of the Message I had received from the Upper people in relation to their Enemies, as is Expressed in a Letter which I Recd from Mr. Wigan the 4th Instant.

Sunday the 10th day of October 1725.

Munday the 11 day of October 1725.

Tuesday the 12 day of October 1725.

Sent the following Order to the Sevel White Men in the Nation.

[1] Oakfuskee, an Upper Creek town on the upper Tallapoosa River.

[2] Kashita, a Lower Creek town, on the Chattahoochee River.

To all White men Traders and Men in the Cherokee
    Nation :

Having had Several Complts to me and Especially by the
head Man of Tamusey that the Several White Men there
without any Manner of regard to the ffriendship betwixt us
and the Cherokees do Suffer their Several horses to destroy
and eat up their Corn which is Contrary to our good Will
towards them.

These are therefore to Charge and Comãnd all White
men as aforesd not to Suffer or Comitt such ill practices
for the future, having given the Indians a particular Charge
to Shoot any Such Horsses as may at any time hereafter
be seen in their Cornfields destroying their Corn or doing
them any such damages as they have heretofore done.

Given under my hand at Keewohee this 12th
day of October 1725.

Came in here from Great Terriquo Ja : Millikin Indian
Trader who Informed me that the person (who lately brougt
into the said Town two Womens Scalps) with Eight more were
gone out to Warr agt the Upper Creeks and that they had
been out Six daies and that they were to return in Twenty
daies from their sitting out.   He likewise gave us an Accot
that their Conjurer had given them Assurance of Success.   I
must remark that this is the Town that the Cowsaw fellow
was recd in by the head Warriour there and by no other of
the Town and I am very well Satisfyed that, that Town
would never come into a peace (Assurance of wch) We have
had since we have been here by their going out to Warr
daily against the Creeks.

Wednesday the 13th of October 1725.

This Morning I recd the following Letter from his Honr
the Presidt together with Sevl other Letters by one of the
Indians runners who I sent down to the Governmt and
who had left the rest abt 30 Miles off, there being one of
them Sick and travilled all Night in Order to gett in this
Morning.

September the 18th 1725.

Sir —

I have recd Your Packett dated the 30th of August 1725 by the four Indians you sent wth it and I Assure You I am very well pleased wth the Accot you give of Our Affairs amongst the Cherokees I doubt not but you have recd long before this the Packett I sent You by Chester, in which you are fully Informed of all that has past Amongst the Creeks and Afterwards here by his Majties Council, the Chief thing that now wants to be regulated amongst the Cherokees is the Indian Traders and we Approve very much of the Method you propose and we shall press it Close to the Assembly when they meet and in the Mean time things must lye as they are only on your leaving that Nation, that you give Express Orders to the Traders to Comply with the Trading Act. The Assembly Stands prorogued til the 12th of October and as I dont see that You can be of any further Service amongst those Indians for the present so I think it Advisable that you come down in Order to be in the house to press forward the regulations you propose. I believe I shall prorogue the Assembly for five or Six days longer and by that time you may be down but if you return by way of Savanna Town I shan't Expect you so soon, I would have sent the Coats etc. you wrote for but have not time but they shall be sent up to the head men you Mention. Since you left us We have had here thirty Spaniards from St. Augustine there Errand was about the ffort on Allata-maha[1] river and to settle the two bounds of the Governmt. But as we have never recd any Orders from home abt it So they are returned as they came.

I did give Hatton and Sharp leave to Carry up their Indians fellows, not Apprehending nor yet indeed that, that part of the Law was intended against any but those that went up to the Savanno[2] and Allatamahaw Rivers, or Negros by Land and not agt Indian Slaves with their Masters. If it is otherwise it is my fault and not theirs and I must take the blame from them but I am well Assured

[1] Altamaha. [2] Savannah.

I am in the right. Wee are very barren of News not having a Vessell from England since You left us but are in hourly Expectations of two or three from London. We have had a fine Summer and now as fine harvest weather as ever was known and the Crops a getting in a pace. You will receive Letters from Mrs. Chicken so I need not say anything of your Family. Mrs. Middleton Joins with me in Our best respects, and I am

Sir, Your very humble Servt

AR. MIDDLETON.

P.S. At the same time that I sent Chester up to you I dispatched Another up to the Creeks to Mr. Fitch but have not heard from thence Since.

Came in this day from Savanna Town Capt. Wm. Hatton, Mr. Wm. Cooper, David Doway, Henry Guston and one Daniel Kearl, a Virginia Trader.

Thursday the 11th day of October 1725.

About Twelve of the Clock at Night came in the Warr hoop giving an Accot that Six of the Southward people had fallen on Camp of the Chickesaws abt five Miles off who went out in the Catawba pathe the 13th Instant in Order to hunt and that they had killed a Chicksaw Man and wounded two Women of these people who were agoing with the said Chickesaws. Immediately the Town sent out a party of men After the Enemy and went to the Camp where the Chickesaws had taken up, and found one of them dead and two Women of their own people Wounded.

The party that went out of the Town followed the Enemy all the remaining part of the Night and some part of the day following but finding the Enemy were gone too farr to be Overtaken they returned home.

Came in here from Toogelo parts Richd Hasford who gave us an Accot that there had been four of the Enemy who went in the dead of Night to the Out Fortification of Estotoe old Town (three of wch) fired against the sd Fortification and made of[f] from the said Town. Immediatly the people of the Town went after the Enemy but could not come up with them, so returned home. I must take Notice that these people have been very brisk agt their Enemy and have never failed of making all the discoveries they could by sending out Scouts.

Friday the 15th day of October 1725.

Saturday the 16th day of October 1725.

Sunday the 17th day of October 1725.

Munday the 18th day of October 1725.

The King and head men of the Town hearing of my Departure from their Nation this day mett together and after a Consultation among themselv's they sent for me to meet them at a New House they had built and then they Appointed their head Warriour to Speak for them as ffollows :

1*st.* That they was very glad I was amongst them to do good for the whole Nation and that they'll always be good to the English, and that they should never find them rogues.

I Answered that I had found them good to the English since I had been amongst them and before and that they had Ussed me wth a great deal of Civillity and that whatever they had sayed to me, I had sent down to the English and had heard from them again and that I hoped they would mind what I had sayed to them, because it was for their good and to keep a good Understanding between them and the English who they might always depend would show themselv's as Brothers.

2*d.* That they are very thankfull to the English Governour for sending up a Streigt talk to them, and that they are well pleased with it and that they hoped there would be no Stories told the English for the future about them.

I Answer'd it was very well and that I should tell the English their Brothers how they had behaved themselv's since my Stay amongst them and that now I had given them the Streight talk from the English and that I did not doubt but that [they] would be a good people for the future if they would but take Notice of what I had sayed to them for their good. I likewise gave them in Charge that when any thing happened amongst them that the English should know of, that they would be first sure it was truth and then to send us word by two or three of their head men and by no other because they are the persons we take most Notice of.

I inform'd them that they might depend the English would always take care to give them Intelligence of the design of their Enemies when ever they had any Notice of it, and that we should never take so much Care of any other Indians because We have not so much Vallue for them.

3d. That I was not come amongst them to Trade but to give them the Streight talk in Order to make them a good people and to have a good ffriendship between them and us, and that if ever they were Misused by any of the White Men amongst them that they must Complain to the Linguisr that the English might hear of it and do them Justice.

I likewise told them that We Expected that whenever they had any thoughts of making a peace with their Enemies that the English should hear of it before they did any Such thing, because they would undertake to bring it about the best way for them and most for their good, and that it was the Promise of all the head men that were down when the English Gover[no]r first came in.

A. That if any Indians should come to them for a peace that they'll take care to let the English know it according to their Promise.

Tuesday the 19th day of October 1725.

[I] gave the following Order to Joseph Cooper Linguister on Alexr. Parris Esq. Treasurer:

SIR —

Please to pay to Joseph Cooper or Order on demand The Sum of Twenty ffive pounds being for his trouble as one of the Linguisrs to me in the Cherokee Nation and place it to the Publicks Accot of moneys recd by Virtue of the Indian Trading Act, as the said Act directs.

I am Sr Your Most humble Servt.

To the Honble Alexr. Parris }
Esq. Publick Treasurer.   }

Gave the following permission to Mr. John Savey.

To Mr. John Savey,

You are hereby permitted to trade on behalf of Mr. David Doway and Mr. Andrew White according to the Lycence and Instructions of the sd Doway and White and the Law now in being for the better regulation of the Indian Trade, the said White having Entred into bond to take out a Lycence for you in June next Ensueing from the date hereof and also for your good behaviour.

Given under my hand and the Seal of the Office for the better regulation of the Indian Trade this 19th day of October 1725.

Sent the following Letter to Mr. Eleazer Wigan, Linguister on the other Side the hills.

Mr. Wigan —

Since my last to you I have had Advices from the Settlemt and having finished all Matters in this Nation I intend to take my Departure on Sunday next. The reason of my sending this to you is to desire you'll Slip no Opportunity in Acquainting me with the Motions of the Indians in your parts and that you take great care that you do not Acquaint me with anything but what you are first Assured is truth, You very well knowing how we have heretofore been Amussed with fallcities and what Charge the Country hath been at to set those Stories in a true light.

I would have you Consult the long Warriour in all Affairs wch may relate to the Indians beleiving him to be a true ffriend to us for which reason we cannot too much Esteem him. You may tell him of my hearing from the Governent and that I have nothing further to Offer to these people having Already said what was delivered to me from the Governmt to them and what I have thougt for their good to make them a People and I hope they'll mind and follow what Methods I have laid before them for that purpose. In my last to you I have given you an Accot of some Affairs among the Creeks which I hope you have Interpreted to them, and told them that it is now with the Creeks and us as it was before, they having given us such Satisfaction as We are Satisfyed with at Present, as I told them it would be at the General Meeting. You may Inform the Long Warriour that the English would have sent him a present but that they could not gett what they designed for him ready before the Indians came away and that altho he hath it not yet, I shall take care that it Shall be sent him when ever I get down and have an Opportunity.

I have had an Accot from Savanna Town that the Woman that came here along with the French Man was run away with by him. She's a Chachama Woman and is a Slave to the Comander of the Garrison there, and I beleive She's some where in your parts so that you must Speak to the Warriours to have her Secured and I desire if they gett her that you'll send her down to Mr. Doway who has promised me to Convey her to the Owner by the first Opportunity. I cannot too much Caution you of letting me know the truth of all Affairs among these people (You being on Oath) the Nature of which I hope you are not unacquainted with. I shall take care to represent to the Country your Trouble as Linguister to me and as I cannot but beleive you have been and may be of Service so you need not doubt but on a true representation of yr Care and Fidellity to them that they'll readily requite you.

I have nothing further to Offer only to desire that you'l take care that the people in Your parts do Nothing of Moment relating to sending to the Governmt without first Consulting these lower people and I have already given them the like Charge and I cannot but take Notice that We have been too much Imposed upon by their sending down those that are not leading men and who the people take very little Notice of, when We send up any business to the rest of the Nation, and when its delivered by them.

I wish you health and Success in all Affairs.

And am   Your Assured ffriend.

Wednesday the 20th day of October 1725.

I set away from Keewohee having finished all Matters in the Upper and Lower Towns of the Cherokees and having Crossed the River the King drew up the Men in his Town and then made them fire a Volley as did the Several White men in the Town.

Tuesday the 26th day of October 1725.

We arrived at Savanna Town after Seven daies travilling from the Cherokees.

Thursday the 28th day of October 1725.

I proceeded to Supervise the Garrison and Accordingly gave Orders to the Comandr to Render an Accot of the Stores together with a Muster roll of the Men under his Comand.[1]

About Ten of the Clock this Morning We had an Accot by the Chickesaws that one of their people was killed by four of the Creeks at the Dividing paths being about thirty Miles from Savanna Town.

Friday the 29th day of October 1725.

The Petition of John Hows, to me directed, praying to have Access to the Garrison, he being of late debarred the same, and that he may be Allowed Some Provissions from the

[1] Fort Moore was built primarily for the protection of Indian trade and placed under the jurisdiction of the Indian Commissioner.

said Garrison, he having Nothing to Subsist himself withall and being ready to Starve. And having Considered the said Petition and the Circumstance of the said Hows and that he hath been a Man, who hath Appeared well in the World, tho' now rendered Uncapable of getting his bread, by reason of his Advanced Age and Sickness I thougt fitt to give the Comͫander of the sd Garrison the following Order on behalf of the Petitioner.

By etca.

To Major David Durham Comͫander of Fort Moore.

You are hereby Ordered to Supply Mr. John Hows with the same Allowance of Provissions as the Several Men under your Comͫand have at this Present time and likewise to lett him have Access to your Garrison til such time you have Orders from the Governmt to the Contrary.

Given under my hand and Seal this 29th
day of October Annoq. Dom. 1725.

The Comͫander renders an Accot of the Sevl Stores in the Garrison together with a Muster roll of the Men under his Comͫand ᵥ/ch were both Signed by the said Comͫander.

Report on the Garrison.

On Viewing the Garrison both within and without I find it to be in very good repair and that there is nothing wanting to be done thereto only Two Sheds to be repaired which are over two of the fflankers for wch they have provided Materialls in Order to repair them.

On Viewing the Several Stores in the Garrison I find that there's the Particulars as per a List delivered to me by the Comͫander and that they are in the Condition and Order as is therein Mentioned.

The Comͫander Informs me that they have Corn Sufficient to Supply the Garrison for the Ensueing Year which is not yet gath'red.

I must take Notice that by Articles of Agreemt between

Alexr. Parris Esq. and Capt. Charlesworth Glover that the said Glover is Obliged to furnish the Garrison for one Year from the date of the said Articles and that the Comander can't refuse the whole Years provissions in Case its Tendered by the said Glover to the Comander tho' at the same time the said Glover is not Obliged to Cure the sd Provissions, neither have they Salt at the Garrison to Cure it themselv's which is very much Wanted at this time being the Properest Season to kill meat for the Garrison.

The Several men being under Arms I had them called Over by the Muster Roll and found there was the full Complimt and that they were all Able men and fitt for Service, and that there Armes were in good Order.

By etca.

Additional Instructions to be Observed by the Comander of the time being of Fort Moore.

First. You are on Application made to you by any Principal Trader to Endorse on the back of their Lycences any one or more Packhorse Men Provided they make Oath that any person or persons who were Inserted or Indorsed in any of their Lycences at the time of their taking it out, have run away from them and that they cannot be without them or may be Sufferers by the Want of such men and provided also they give Security for the behaviour of such Packhorsemen dureing their Stay in the Indian Country and the Names of such Packhorse Men You are as Soon as possible to return to me or the Comissrs of the Indian Trade for the time being. And in Case any Trader should Apply to you for an Additional Packhorseman You are to insert one for such Trader Provided he hath not more then is Allowed by the Indian Trading Law and that he pay to you the Sum of ten pounds for the Use of the Country as the Law requires for the Endorsemt of such Packhorsemen and Enter into Bond to his Majesty for his good behaviour.

Second. You are from time to time, as you shall see Occasion, to repair your Garrison both within and without and as the Sevl Punchins on the Outside decay's You are to take care that there be New Ones to Supply those that are Decayed.

Third. In Case any Trader should have the Misfortune of bad Weather Whereby their goods or Skines may be damaged in Crossing the River You are to give them all the Assistance you can for the better preservation of their goods or Skines as aforesd.

Given under my hand and Seal this
30th day of October 1725.

The foregoing Instructions were then Signed and Delivered to the Comander together with a Copy of the Order in relation to Mr. Hows.

I thougt fitt to send the following Letter to Capt. Fitch by the hands of Florence Mahoney Indian Trader.

S[I]R —

On Thursday the 28th Instant We heard by the Chickesaws here that the Cowetaws have killed one of their people between the Dividing paths and Rosemary Branches and by what little discourse I have had with them Concerning it I find that their Inclinations are to retalliate the Creeks for it, So that I hope you'l take care that none of the Southward people come this way without they are resolved to Stand to the design of the Chickesaws and I hope you'll take care if there's any comes along with you to give them Notice of what I have writt You and to be very Cautious yourself, beleiving that if they have any Opportunity they'll treat You after the same Manner as the Southward people.

I am heartily glad to hear of your Success in Your Negotiations and in a short time I dont doubt but to have the pleasure of seeing You, in the Interim

I remain
Your very humble Servant.

The Squiril King with three head Warriours of the Chickesaws desiring to talk with me they accordingly came this Afternoon and then I proceeded to tell them as follows.

Elias Thomas, Linquisr.

That they knew I came here once a Year in Order to regulate the Affairs of the Indians and that if they had any thing to say to me I was then ready to hear them. And then the King Spoak as follows:

That they have heard the Talk of the White people for this many Years and that they have been down to the English Sevl times and heard the talk there and that they desire always to be at peace wth the White people and desire to have their own way and to take revenge of the red people and that it was their Young people that first broak out Warr with the White people.

I desired to know of them what Young people it was that broak out the Warr wth the White people.

They desired to know the reason of my Asking them a thing that past so long agoe.

I Answered them Angerly that it was a thing Still always a passing among them.

They Answered that there was Young men among them that were always playing the Rogue and that they could not help it.

And as to the Creeks they always thougt that they were their Youngest Brothers, and that now they are daily killing of them and that they intend to take their revenge and hope the White people will not take it at heart.

I Answered that We beleive them to be Our ffriends but that I did not know how the Creeks or Cherekees could take them for theirs when some of them were fitting[1] for the One and some for the other and have no Settlemt of themselv's nor will not Settle any where in a body Notwithstanding they had so often promised the English that they would (which if they did) they then might Expect protection from us, and that While they are as they are we could take them to be no more then Wild Wolves in the Woods Seeking their prey and that We could not mind them any longer then we were talking to them nor could not tell where to find them.

[1] Fighting.

They Answered that for the future they'd mind what the White people says to them and that they'll look out for a good place to Settle all together and that there is three or four old men among them that would make the Young men mind them for the future.

I then desired to know of them whether they could not think of a place themselv's to Settle on, on the other side the river and not to disturb our Stock as they daily did on this side the river and that we Expected when any Complts[1] is made to any of their headmen by any white man of any Damage done to the English by any of their Young men that they should Cause them that did the Mischief to make Satisfaction and to punish them in the presence of those that were damaged which would give us Assurances of their desire to be in ffriendship with the English, and that the Complt to be made to the Chief man of the White men that's in being and that if they are Nigh the Garrison that they bring the Offender to the Comander and that in Case any of the White men do them any damage that they Immediatly make Complt to the next White man they see, but if they are near the Garrison they are to Complain to the Comander and that they might Expect Justice done them in Order to keep a good Understanding between them and us and that we Expected the same from them.

That in Case they go on this side the river to hunt that they first come to the Comander to ask liberty and that they Acquaint him how many they are in Number, how long they intend to hunt, and at what place and to come to him at their return and to let him know if they are all returned or not, and that We Expected it from the head men of the Gang that were going to hunt and that the King be Answerable for them all if there's an[y] Damage done by any of them.

A. That they have heard what I had say'd to them and that when there people meets together they'll tell it to them and that they are very willing to keep Settled where they are, but that when they make any Corn the Packhorses get

<hr/>

[1] Complaints.

among it and eat it and that if all their people that are abroad would Settle Among them, that they would leave one half of their people at home to take care of their Women and Children and the other half might be out a hunting.

I Answered. That if any of the Traders Packhorses gott among their Corn and Destroy[ed] it that they should Immediatly Complain to the Comander of the Garrison who on hearing the Complt and finding it to be true would Order Satisfaction to be made them by the White Man that owned the horses, and that if any of their people should meet with any White Mans Horse in the Woods that they should not Meddle with them wthout Orders from the White man, and that in Case we found it Otherwise, that We should Expect Satisfaction from their King and that he'll take care to have the Offender punished and that in Case any of them Should take up Slaves that they are to bring them to the Comander of the Garrison and deliver them to him. And that they would be paid for so doing.

That the reason of my giving them such Cautions was because I was last Year an Eye Witness to some of the faults of their people, having found out One of them who Stole a horse and Saddle which I took from them at the Pallacholas on wch a White man went out upon, but was never since heard of and having had an Accot of some of them breaking open a White Mans Store at the Oconeys as also Sevl other Crimes done at other places which we were sure was done by their people.

A. That if their Young Men were drunk and Mad that they could not help it but that they'll take care for the future and keep them in Awe.

Q. What do you design to do with the Creeks if you meet them?

A. That they have lost Seven Men since the last Corn was planted between the Savanna Town and the Oconeys, and that if they meet with any of the Creeks in the path and find them too strong for them, that they'll be ffriends wth them, but that if they meet any in the Woods and think they can Manage them that they will Serve them as they Served their People.

I Answered. That as they pretend to be ffriends to the English, and say that whereever they found an Advantage they would kill the Creeks That we daily have and Should have White men coming down from the Creeks where there might be two or three or more of them along with the White Men that we Expected they would take care that none of their people Should Mollest any of the Indians that might at any time come down or go up with any of the White people.

A. That they know the White people Carry hunters along with them to keep them from hunger and that they had as good kill the White people as their Hunters.

I then told them that if they did we Should know it and that we should deem it as bad a Crime as that if they should kill any White People.

A. That if they found there was any hunters along with the White People that they would not hurt them, but if they mett any of the Creeks in the Woods by themselves they knowed what to do with them.

Sunday the 31st day of October 1725.

Wee set away from Savanna Town and on Wednesday the 3d day of Novr We Arrived at Goose Creek.

GEO: CHICKEN.

CAPTAIN FITCH'S JOURNAL TO THE CREEKS,
1725

INTRODUCTION

THE Creek Indians, at the time of Captain Fitch's mission, were settled chiefly in the region extending west by north from the middle and upper Chattahoochee River to the west border of Alabama. To the north and northeast of them were the Cherokees; to the northwest, the Chickasaws; and to the west and southwest, the Choctaws. Those in the region of the Coosa and Tallapoosa rivers were known as the Upper Creeks and those on the Chattahoochee as the Lower Creeks. The English at Charleston established a trade with the Creeks even earlier than with the Cherokees. But in 1714 the French built Fort Toulouse at the confluence of the Coosa and Tallapoosa. The Creeks thereupon began to trade with the French and although they continued to deal with English traders they assumed toward them an independent and often insolent attitude. President Middleton sent Captain Fitch to counteract French influence and to exact proper treatment of English traders. The Creek-Chickasaw trail ran northerly from Charleston to Dorchester, thence west by north to Fort Moore, westerly across the Ogeechee, Oconee, Ocmulgee, Flint, and Chattahoochee rivers, and again west by north from the Chattahoochee to Oakfuskee on the Tallapoosa.

Little is known of Captain Fitch prior to his discharge of this mission. He succeeded Colonel Chicken as Indian Commissioner and held that post in 1733–1734. In the latter year he was appointed a justice of the peace in Berkeley County.

There is a manuscript copy of his Journal in the Public Record Office, London: C. O. 5, 12, ff. 35–55, and a transcript made from this is in the Library of Congress.

TOBIAS FITCH'S JOURNAL TO THE CREEKS

AFTER a hard and Tiresome Journey I Arrived at the Oakefusky Town [1] in the upper Tallapoop's [2] being 17 days in my Journey there. I Arived *Jully the 9th* and was Received with a great many Serimoneys; The King of the said Town Takeing me by the hand Lead me To a house Where were Sitting all the head men of the Several Towns there about; And after passing Some Complements there was Some fowls Brought in and Set Before me; And Befor I was Suffered to Eat the King Made The Following Speach : "I am Glad to see you here In my Town But I am Sory that I Cannot Entertain you With Such as I am Entertained When I go Down to your Great Town; But I hope you will Except of Such as I have and you are very Welcom to it." My answer That ordinary Fair from On[e] Who is a Freind and has a Strieght heart is more Welcome To me then Greater Dainteys from On[e] Who profest Freindship To my Face But in his heart was my Enemys. *On Sunday. The* 11 *Jully* the sd King Summonds all his head men To Meet and made the Following Speach :

"Here is a Beloved man Come from the great King of the English and [we] must all provide for him that he may not Want any thing that our Town Can Supplye him with For When I was in his Town they did not think anything Too good for me; I do not Know the Reason of Our Treating White men as we do : For Mally [3] When any Beloved Man

[1] Oakfuskee, the principal town of the Upper Creeks, was situated on the west bank of Tallapoosa River, four miles below the mouth of Elkhatchee Creek, in Tallapoosa County, Alabama.

[2] The Upper Tallapoops were the Creeks inhabiting the region of Upper Tallapoosa River.

[3] Formerly.

[came] To us we used to go with [him] Wherever he went But now We act like Women more than Head Men; Therefore I hope you wil Take Notice of What I have Said To you and Check This Slight that Two many of you Sho the White men; before It becomes a Coustom to you."

On Munday the 12th I Tould the King To send for all the Kings and Principale Men belonging To the Abecas [1] and Tallopoops To met me in Eight days at your house and then [I] shall Deliver to them a great Talk that I have Brought up from my great King and Beloved Men Which was Imediatly don.

On Friday the Sixteenth I went To a Town Called the Oakechoys [2] Where I was very well Received and after being Intertained With the Best that his Town afoard; He Told the Lingister he had Somthing To Say unto me I answered him I was Ready To here anything That he had To say; he then Brought a boundale of Dear Skins and throwed them befor me and gave The following Talk:

"I am a True Freind to the English and always have Behaved my Self as such and I Find that When any of our People goes To your Great King That they Receive presents; I have not such Presents to give as we Receive from you But hope you wil except of Such as I have and through [3] I never was Down to see your great King Yet I am as Streight hearted as the Best of them that has been Down; for I do not find that the Talk your great King gives them Lastes any Longer than the present he maks them. As soon as the Present is wore out the Talk is forgotten."

Answer. "I am Sent here from my great King To know how [4] among you is his Freind and how [4] is not; You Say that you are a Freind, I hope I will find you So; But as To your present I must Tell you That my Great King did not Send me here to get presents neithere do I vont [5] them. I

[1] The Abecas, or Abihkas, were Upper Creeks inhabiting a town on or near the Upper Coosa River.

[2] Okchayi was an Upper Creek town on Oktchayi (now Kialaga) Creek, in the southeastern part of Coosa County, Alabama.

[3] Though.   [4] Who.   [5] Want.

ame Come To see my Kings Freinds and To know Who they be for as you say that your People minds my Kings Talk no longer then the presents last I Belive its very True and its for that Reason that I am Sent among You; For When your People are with my King they Tell Him that they are his Good Freinds as you Tell me now You are. But when they Come here the[y] Never Mind What They promise To my King When they are with him."

On Tusday the 20th According to appointment there Met at the Oakefusk'y Town 60 head men Representing Twenty Towns of the Abecas and upper Tallapoop's.

Answer. "We are all met According to your orders and are now Ready to here What you have to say to us; we have Bin a long Time Threatned with a Talk to be sent among us But its not Comeing after so many promises we had Now given over Expecting any; But we [are] heartely Glad to see you on our Land and very Thankfull to your Great King for Takeing Such Care of us, as to Send on[e] of his Beloved men To see us, You being the first White man That We have Seen Sent among us Since the peace was Made Through [1] we have Been often Threatned."

Answer. "I am very Glad to See you met According to appointment In order to here the great Talk That my Great King has sent To you by me." I then proceeded with the part Of my Instructions Where I was Directed To Demand Satisfaction for the Roberry Don Mr. Sharp at the Cherokey's and with the Following addition:

Pointing To Gogell Ey's Told him: "you pretend To Excuse that Rogus Action of yours that you was guilty off at the Cherokeys By Saying it was Don Rashly by the young people, But that Excuse will not do With our King for you are a man in years and ought To know better and Since you was the head of them People you Should have prevented thir Rogush proceedings. But you are So farr from Doeing that; That you Imbrace every oppertunity you have of doing us all the prejudice you Can and I Look upon you to be

[1] Though.

Such a Freind To the English That you had ane Opportunity you would now Serve me as you did the White man at the Cherokeys; But had that White man adyed [1] with the Wound that you gave him I do assure you That my King Would Requir no less Satisfaction Then Your Life and the Lives of all the head Men that was With [you]; and if your people should have Denied to Deliver you up Then my King Would have took Satisfaction with the Mussells of their Guns. But Since the man That you wounded is like to do well my King is so good as to be Content With your makeing Satisfaction for the Goods Taken away and your Sincear promisses Never to be guilty of the Like again. If we Should met any of your People from thir Towns, Plunder Them of there Skins, Kill or Wound your People, Could you then Think us To be your Freinds? I Belive not, yet this your People have don to us and at the Same Time Call themselves Freinds. But my King do not understand Such Freindship as that."

Gogell Eys Answer.

"I was at the first makeing a Peace with the English and have always Behaved my Self Like a freind, I Went Down To Warr against the Yeamases [2] in Behalf of the English and I have Now Been at warr against the Cherokeys and What you have s[ai]d against the White man is very True. I was not with my people when they Begun to Plunder the White man through I was thire head and When I found What they had Don I Thought that as there was a Breach made it Could not be Recalled and I did take Some of the Remains of The Goods For Which I am heartily Sory and will willingly Pay you for the Same and I do promise before you and The head Men that are here Present That I never Will be guilty of the Like Action While I Live. There is now in Our

[1] Died.
[2] Yamasees, who in 1715 effected a general massacre of English traders and settlers on the Carolina frontier, and subsequently, as allies of the Spaniards, continued in active hostility against the English.

Possession The Woman and her Children That We took from the White man which you may have and his Best Case of Pistoolls. But as for the Rest Off the Goods they are Cut and Distributed that we Cannot Return them any othere ways than by paying For them in Skins."

Then Spoke the Oakechoye [1] Capt. by order of the Whole Body :

"Since he that was at the head of that Mischieff that Happen'd at the Cherokeys has made so frank a Confession and has promised a Better Behaviour for the Time to Come We will all Contribute To paying of the White man for his Goods. But that this is not a Time of year To pay Debts in For there is not Skins in the Whole Nation To pay Half the Debt But by the Next Spring every on of them Shall be paid Into any hands You will order us."

"Since it is so with you I will Stay Till the Time you propose, you Delivering me now the Slaves and Pistools. But then you must rember [2] that if you are not Punctual To the Promise you make me How that then all this Talk is To No Purpose and I am of oppinnion That our King will look On you as Enemies and Treat you as such wherever He Metts You."

Hopeya-ha-chey Being appointed To Receive the Skins Declairs that, "When the Time Drawes near if you do not make Preparation, To pay in the Skins you now promise That I wil then goe Down to the English and let him know it And he may do with you as he thinks fit."

I then Proceeded To that part [of] my Instructions Relateing To a Peace With the Cherokeys etc.

Hobyhawchey [said] : "The Reason that I did not Send Down To your great King According to my Promise to him When I was Down To sue For a Peace with the Cherokeys Was that at my Return home I Summon'd my People Together And thought To have Consulted them According to your Kings Orders, but Before I Could get them To me[e]t The News Came in of what was Don to the White man

---

[1] Okchayi.   [2] Remember.

at the Cherokeys. I then Thought [it] Needless To Send Down to your King for I Expected Nothing Less then a Warr.

But as for a Peace With the Chericeys [1] at this Time we have no thought They haveing Latly Killed Several of the Leading Men of Our Nation; and till we have had Satisfaction We will heare of No peace; But as soon as our Corn is hard We Designe to be with them and after our Return if your King Will undertake To make a peace for us We will Readylie Except of it."

I then proceeded to that part of [my] Instruction Relateing to the amunition That Lies at Savana Town [2] and Designed For the Tallapoops That went against them Yamasses.

Tickhoneby Answers: "We never heared of any amunition For us only once Actcedentaly and then we answered Coll Heastins [3] and he Told us there was Non for us; Since That we never thought no more of it, had we knowen of any amunition Being there We should [have] Brought it Long agoe."

Ane Addition To Instructions.

"I must tell your Young Men that if it had not Been for us, you would not have knowen how to Warr Nor yet Have anything To Warr with. You have had nothing But Boes and Arrow's To kill Dear; You had no hoes or Axes then What you made of Stone. You wore nothing But Skins; But now you have Learn'd the use of Firearm's As well to Kill Dear and other Provissions as To War agst Your Enemies And yet you Set no greater Value on us who have Been Such good Friends unto you, Then on yr greatest Enemies this all you that are old men knowes to be True. And I would have you make your young men Sensable of it."

[1] Cherokees.

[2] Fort Moore, or Savannah Town, South Carolina, on the Savannah River six miles below Augusta, Georgia.

[3] Colonel Theophilus Hastings commanded in 1715 a company of North Carolina militia sent to aid South Carolina against the Indians. In 1716 he was the principal factor of the North Carolina Indian trade.

I then proceeded to the Lower people and Summons'd them To meet me On Munday the Second of August and accordingly the[y] Met, There being present old Brunnis and 45 head Men Who were all the principale head men of the Lower Creekes; I then Delivered the Talk in Relation to ther head Men Not paying their Respect To this Government, of their Being Desireous of other Trade Then what they had from this Government and all Maters Else Contained in my Instructions etca., Only Omiting that part Where the Tallapoopes did not agree to a Peace With the Cherekeys but I Tould them how far The upper people had Concur'd with it.

Oald Brimins answers: "The Tallapoop's and Abecas may do As they please But we have Nothing of Makeing a peace with The Cherokeys. For them men that was killed by the Cherokeys of Mine When the White people were there is not over w[it]h Me as yet, nor never shall be While there is a Cowwataid [1] Liveing."

Ane Addition to my Instructions.

"I am Informed that Some of You have Threatned Tickhonebys Life for goeing to warr against the Yamasses and there Killing On of your Freinds. I must tell you that Tickhonebey was Sent There by our King To Warr against his Enemies and if your Freinds will keep Company with our Enemies I know not how our king Can do to have Yamasses Killed, for as Shure as we Kill A Yamassee, he has a Relation or freind amonge The Creek's; Therefore Tickhonebe has Dun very will in Following Our kings orders and if you want Satisfaction It's of Our king that [you] must Seek it, and Since I am here I am Ready To answer every thing That my King has ordered Tickoneby to do or any person alse [2] and I desire The man that Vants Satisfaction for the Death of a Yamasse Would now Speak and then I am Shure to know my Freind That Loves the Yamasses so wel. Dont you know very well that our King has offered them Yamasses To make

---

[1] Lower Creek.   [2] Else.

a peace with them and they would not? But why was it? Because the[y] knew they had you to uphold them. But I do assure you that our King is a weary of this unserton peace. I therefore must know how [1] amongst you is our Freind's and Who is not. These Belowed [2] Freinds of Yours, the Yamasess, you will find befor I goe from hence it Will appear they are the people that have Latly Killed your very Good Freinds as well as ours and so have Lead it on the Floradays. I shal not say much To you about them lest You Should Think that I do it to sett you against them. Through I have heered a great Deal of that affair Since I have Been here, but I leave that To your own Selves To find out, Being Well asshured you will soon do it."

Oald Brimins answer.

"There is a great many Storys Come into this Nation but from Whence they come I Can not Tell. Somtimes I here that Your King is Joyning the Te   and Coming To Cut us of[f]. We that are head men give no Credit to these Storys But The Young Men may belive them for What I know and Likewise add to them. But I do now assure you in behalf of these head men that I have [heard] nothing of Leaving your Trade for We Desire there may be a Containuance of the Peace that is made. I must Confess we have not obayed orders as we Ought To have Don, But for the Time To Come When your King will order us We shal be Ready, and as For the Yamasees they shal soon know [who] our hearts is With. As my Son hollala is Dead There is not [one] Left of my Family But Sepey Coffee Who is fit To take upon him The Charge that I have, which is Two great a Charge for a man of my age. Tho I must Confess that Sepey Coffee has not been your Freind a great while but Rather a Freind To the French and Spaniards. But he has had so much said To him that he Will now prove as True to you as ever he did To them, and I hope your king will let him Succeed his Brother Since its the General oppinion of my People That he Should."

---

[1] Who.   [2] Beloved.

Sepe Coffees Speach.

"Tis True I have Been in the French and Spanish Interest A Great While and the first begining of it was When the warr was Brock out with you. The heads of the Whole Nation Sent me to the French and Spanards To make a peace wt them, and I did [so] and after That it[1] Created a farther Acquaintance and I assired[2] them of my Freindship in Particullar and have Containu'd to be their Frend according To my Promise. But Since I find that I disoblidge my Father and all other Freinds by it I have now Left thir Intrest and have not Been [with] any of them for some Time. I am Now Designed To Warr. My Father has oblidged me To go out with him against some of his enemies. Where it is [I] cant Tell But if, [I] Live to Return will, If I Can be admit'd, goe Down and See your great King." The Old King Confirm'd his Sons Speach.

August the 7th. Arived at the Pallachocola Town[3] Two Spaniards, on Negro, and four Commantle Indians where I met them in order to know ther Bussiness. The Spanyard was Shye of Comeing unto the Square for Some Time but The Negro Sat in the Square in a Bould Maner. At Length The Spanyard Came also into the Square. I Received them as Friend[s] knowing that they were Designed To the Cowweetaws[4] where I thought my Best Freinds to be. Sepe Coffee Seemed To Show The Spanyard great Favour Which he did to prevent There haveing a mistrust of his Freindship and Discover [what] it is [he] Designes against the Yamasees, as he Informed me afterward. *August the 8th.* The said Spanyard arived at the Cowweetaws and Brought with them Two Caggs of Spainish Brandy Which Soon put

---

[1] I.   [2] Assured.

[3] Apalachicola, a town of the Hitchiti, who were closely associated with the Creeks. It was situated on the west bank of the Chattahoochee nearly opposite the present site of Columbus, Georgia.

[4] Kawitas, who had two towns, Kawita (old town) and Upper Kawita, both on the west bank of the Chattahoochee, a few miles below Apalachicola.

the Town in a Confusion.   I went over To Cusseetaw Town [1]
and the nixt day Summonsed the heads of sd Town To meet;
according they did.   I then gave them the Following Talk:
"There is Arived at the Cowweetawes Two Spanyards,
On Negro and four Tommantle Indians.   I do not know
what their Bussines is But the Negro that they have Brought
with them I know to be a Slave Belonging To our Country
and therefore Designe This day To goe over and Take him.
I do not know whither The Cowweetaw's will like my
Takeing the Negro; I therefore Expect That you that are
head men will goe over with me and Carry Som of your
Warriours with you that if in Case the Cowweetaws should
opose me you may be ready to Stand by me.   I hope none of
you will Refuse this Since you say you are Freinds To my
great King, and by this you will in a great Meassure prove
your Freindship."

Answer from the head men.

"What you have Said is Good and [we] are Ready to goe
with you Not only To the Cowweetaws But where Else
where you will order us."
I then went over the River with 100 Cusseetaws and 10
White men heading them with my Flag flying, which put the
Cowweetawes in Such a Freight that there was not on head
Man to be seen when I Came to the Square.   I imediatly
Put Two Sentinalls at the Door where the Spanyards and
Negro [were] quartered.   When the Cowweetawes saw that
they found my Designes was against the Spanyards, and then
on of the head Men Came to the Square Who I Sent To
[tell] Old Brimins, Sepe Coffee, Chiglley, and as many more
of head men as was in the Town To Come to the Square;
accordingly they Imediatly Came and I gave them the
Talk as Followes:
"Here is Two Spaniard Come To your Town and has
Brought With them a Negro Beloning To my King who I
am now Designed To Take into my Possession and Send

[1] Kashita, which was on the east bank of the Chattahoochee
and two or three miles below Kawita.

Down into my Said King. The Reason that I Call you Together is That as the Negro is now under your Jurisdictione I am not Willing to Take him Till [I] Inform you of the Same, And if there is any among you That has any thing To say against it I Desire to know What it is and Who they be That makes any objections against it. The Negro is a Slave and tho he has Been Taken by the Yamasees and Lived among The Spanyards Yet that dis[1] not make him free. The Reason That I Brought These Cusseecaws is because our King has allways had a Better Charrecter of them then You, But I hope that You Will Convince me of that and Show me by your Behaviour That you are as good Freinds To my King as the Cusseetaws are."

Old Brinimis answers : "We have Nothing To say or doe In this affair. As you Say the Negro is a Slave you must Take him an Do with him what you please for although the is in my Town I have Nothing to Do with him nor no Body Else that is here and as To the Cusseetws being your Best Freinds I know the Reason of it. But I should be Glad if you would Show me on Instance Where the Cusseetaws has Expressed their Freindships in Better Termes Then we have Don."

I Then Sent and had the Negro [seized] and brought Into the Square, and the Spanyards there apeared in Behalfe of the Negro Assuring me that he was a Good Christian.

A Talk to the Spaniards.

"I am Sent here by the Government of Carolina To See our Freinds, The Creek Indeans, and To Transact affairs here for Our Said Government, and I am not To Suffer any white Man To Reside in this place without giveing me an account of his Bussines. I therefore Demand of you who Impower'd You To Come into This nation and for what purpose are You Come ? "

The Spanyards Answer.

"I have a Commission, which I here Lay befor you, To Impower me to Come here. Though I should not have Come

---

[1] Does.

here had not old Brinimes Sent for me. He did Send on[e] of his men Down to my Master the Governr of [St.] Augustine Desireing him To Send a man To him That he wanted To here[1] a Talk, and Likewise to Send a Talk To [St.] Augustin[e]; and that is my Arand here but I find that I have no Bussiness here and if I had Thought that I should have Been Received a[s] I am I should not have Come. They sent for a Talk and the Mouth that I Brought to Talk with them they have Suffered you To take from me. But since you say that he is a Slave its Right That every on ougat[2] To have their own. But if you will Take Two Indian Slaves for him I have them Ready for you; if not, let me know his purchase [price] and I will Redeem him to the Spanyard."

"Its need[less] for you To Contest about the Negro for he is not To be purchased. As To old Brmimis Sending for you its not So, For the old man himself Denies it. But this is only ane Excuse of your Own makeing. I do not Doubt But you have Some Lying Stories To tell the Indians as is Customary for you To do, and I should do you but Justice To Lie[3] you and Send where the Negro is agoeing. But Since I find you have a writeing Which I Belive is from your Governr I shal Excuse you at this Time."

He then asked live To go him[4] in a very Submisive manner. I Told him he might goe Where he pleas'd and So we parted.

On of the head men of Cawweetawes, Takeing Notice of the Discourse Between us, Came to me and asked What the Spanyard had Said.

I Tould him that the Spanyard Declaired that Old Brmimis had Sent for him and that he was Come to here a Talk from Brinimis, But had Brought no Talk with him.

The head mans answer.

"The Spanard Lyes. If you had not Been here we should have had Talk for Two or three days. But Being hear he is afear'd you will Tie him as you have don the Negro. They are often Comeing here with Talk and we never find any of

---

[1] Hear. [2] Ought. [3] Seize. [4] Home.

there Talks to be True, and I no of no on here that wonts any of their Talk; And if you Think it good they Shal never find the way home To Fetch an other Talk."

Answer. "What you Say is True. I Belive The Spanyards brings a great many Lies among You. But they and us is now Freinds, and its not our way to profess Friend[ship] with our Mouths and in our hearts To be Enemies. Altho I do not Doubt But if them Spanyards had Such ane offer against me they would Readylie except of it; But whenever We profess Friendship to any people we are allwise True to Our Words."

I then proceeded to give them the Following Talk, there being The King of the Tommantles in the Square:

"I am very Glad That I happen'd to be here at this Time To see your Kind Behaviour to the Yamasees who you Know to be our utter Enemies and all Dayly doing us all the Injury they Can. After all your promises to The Contrary, you Can not but think that I Take Notice of this since them very Yamasees That are now Sitting with you would Take my Scalp and all the rest of the White people that are here if they had ane oppertunity; and its you that Protects them In such action, for if you was not their Freinds they Would not Dare be our Enemies; and you can no longer Denie your Freindship to them Since I have now seen it with my own Eyes and must Tell you that I am oblidged To Take notice of this and Informe my King of your Behaviour, and how he will Like it You may Judge after your Repeated Promises to the Contrary."

I had no answer made to this which I Found afterwards was for Fear of Discovering their Designe against the Yamassee.

I was then Designed to set foreward To the Abecas but Soon, *the* 11 *August*, arived five Indeans from the Sinecaws,[1] Three of Which had Been Sent to the Sinecaws with a Talk and Been gone nine months which was three months longer Then there Time Limeted. They Brought Two Sineecaws who Brought the Following Talk To the Cowweetawes and other of the Lower Towns.

---

[1] Senecas.

"In answer to your proposalls of a peace with the Cherokeys we Can by no means Consent To. Neither do you upon any pretence Whatever Conclude a peace with the Cherokeys; Lest we Deem You our Enemies as we do them; for we have no peoble To warr Against nor Yet no Meal To Eat But the Cherokeys. But as You are part of Our Nation we Charge You To keep a peace With the English, you once had a warr with them and you gott Litle by it and had you Contained [1] it Longer it would have Been the worse for you. But as you are now at peace with them we aduise you to Continue so For the English are a people that we have had a long Experience of and have allwise found them to be True and Trusty Freinds and Faithfull To thir promise, which you will Likewise find if you Behave your Selves as Freinds to them and Continue your Freindship as we have Don.

"As to the Indians that Lives to the Southward of you, make a peace With a[s] many of them as you please, But Take Care That you oblidge all Such as you make a peace with That they Imediatly Remove and Setle naer you. By that you will have all your Freinds Ready To oppose your Enemies. That is the Method that We Take and we would have you do the Same. But be sure to use the White people well That Comes among you and never Forget your freindship to the English. While you do that your Faer [2] and ours is on. We here Send you a Token of Freindship." Which was Some painted garters.

On August the 12*th* I Sett away from the Cowweetawes and arived at the Lun-ham-ga Town in the Abecas 22d Instant, which is 186 mil's. I was there Received with a great many Serimony's and after Being hansomly Treated Hopeahachey made the Following Speach:

"We are the Uppermost People of this Nation and tho we ar at this Distance Yet our hearts is as naer to you as them that Leve naer then [3] we do; for tho we Latly had a Difference yet it was never our seeking nor yet our Desire; But we were Brought into it By the Tallopoops Coweetawes and

[1] Continued.   [2] Father.   [3] Live nearer than.

other of the Lower people. But as To the Robing of the White man at the Cherokeys we know nothing of it. Non[e] of our People was there and though the Lower Creeks has once Brought us Into a snare I do assure you we shal take better Care then to be Droven into the Like By the Lower Creeks or any others. We are very glad to see you here and tho we have not Such Intertainment To give you as you give us when we Come to you, yet such as we have we give you Freely; and we are very glad to see that you Can eat such as we Live on. When you are at home your Dyet is kept more under Command. Your Chatle are kept in large pens and Likewise your Sheep; your Turkeys and Ducks are at your Doores. Now with us its not so. We are forced to hunt and Take a Great deale of pains To get our provissiones befor we eat it, but we shall not think any Trouble Too much To get Intertainment for you while you Stay with us be it as long as it will, you Being the first Beloved Man that ever we Saw in our Town."

Just at this Time it happen'd that 300 of the Tallepoopes was marched To the Lower part of the Abecas on thire Jurney to the Cherekeys and Expected 200 of the Abecas To Joyne in warr against the Cherokeyes. I found that the Abecas was not designd To send any but Young men. I therefore gave them the Following Talk:

"I think that Since none of your head men Designes to Lead your young Men to Warr your Best way will be to put a Stop to thire goeing out, Least they Should be Lead on by the Tallopoopes To be guilty of Such Actiones as themselves has been in plundering our White man at the Cherokeys."

This Talk put a Stop to the Abecas goeing out and the Tallapoops armey was then Imediatly Reduced to 40 men Who proceeded to the Cherokeys.

Dureing my Stay at the Abecas they were Dayly Terrified by the Cherokeys and Chick'saws who are in Conjnction with them; the Abecas lost five of thire people while I was in thire Towns.

On Septr the 14*th* I Received aditionale Instructions from the Honable Arthour Middleton Esq., president, pursuant to which I Sumons'd all the head men of the Tallapoopes and Abecas. Accordingly They Mett [and] I gave them [the] Following Talk:

"My great King has Sent me a great Talk to give you which is the Reason that I Sent for you; and I am glad to See that you are So Mindfull of Our King as to Come and here his Talk. The talk I sent to my Great King in which you have promissed To make Satisfaction for the goods your people Took from our White man and [1] the Cherokeys is well Liked only that my King and Beloved men Expects that you will pay me Some part of them now before I goe from hence, Which Will Convince them that you Really Intend to pay the debt.

Answer. "You know that we have not Skin's among us, But if that will Convince your King we will gett what Skines is to be found among us and pay you before you leave us."

Ques. "My Great King Expects likewise that Since he has offered you to make a peace with the Cherokeys and that [they] Refuse it, that you wil not Concern your Self any Further therein Till you apply to him for the Same."

Answer. "We Cannot say anything about that for our people is not all at home. Some are gone to Warr; but at the Nixt Meeting You Shal have a Talk Relating to the peace w[i]t[h] the Cherokeys."

"My Great King Desires to know what Assureance You Can Give him that your young men do not Comitt the like Action againe."

Answer. "We belive that our Young people has and will Suffer So Sevearly for this that they will take Care how the[y] Bring themselves and Freinds in Trouble again. Beside we will Take Care that non of Our people Shal goe out to warr Without Sending Such Leading Men With them as we Can Trust, and if any of Our Young Men Will be So head Strong as not to follow orders and will Committ any Hostilletys on your people at the Cherokeys or Else Where We will then Deliver Such offenders to your King and he may do with them as he thinks fitt."

[1] At.

Ques. "My King likwise Demands Satisfaction for three of the Avecas that was Taken by the Cherokeys. Our King Saved thir Lives and gave his Cloath for them for which you have promised To pay him and never have don it. This and Some other things has made our King So Cross that he now Say's that he will not Suffer any more amunition to Come among you unless you will pay him what you owe him."

Answer. "We must have Some time to Consider of What you have Said to us and if you will appoint a Time to mett we will then give ane answer about the Slave Redeemed from the Cherokeys; for our King Hoby-o-haw-Chey not Being here, we Can say nothing Concerning it; but we hope that your King will not Stop the White mens bringing Goods among us, for unless You Supply us with goods and Anumition we are no people Neither shal we be able to pay Debts unless we Can be Supply'd with Amunition from You."

Ques. "I do not see how you can Expect any Favour from my king Since your peoples behaviour is Such to him; That Action Don at the Cherokeys, you pretend to say it was Don by Rash Young men. I would not have you think that I am To be Imposed upon by Lying Stories for you yourself know the Sleyamasees cheys warr Talk every Night to His Wariours were that the White people gave the Cherokeys Notice of your designes against them and that if they mett with white men there goods should be Taken from them. Now is this the Behaviour of a Freind? I Leave you To Judge, and what I say is True, and that you know for what I say I have from on of the people that was there.

So I hope That as there is Gogell eys and Several of his people is gone to warr against the Yamasees that you will be of Oppinion with me at there Return to take from them what Slaves they gett Towards makeing Satisfaction [and] in Case they are not Willing, To take them by Force, for I did not Come here to ask them men for anything that Realy Took the White mans Goods, they Being a percell of Inferriour Fellowes. I am Come to Talk with you that are the head men and its of you that my King Expects to be paid, Which will, and Nothing Else Can prevent my Kings makeing a Warr with you; So I now give you fourty Days To make answer to What I have Said To You, at which Time I hope you will Bring what Skins you Can gett and Comply wt my Kings Demands in Every Respect, That As we have Lived like Freinds So we may part. In doeing of which you will Serve none more then yourselves."

On Septr the 28th I Returned to the Cowweetawes, Expecting to mett[1] Cherokeys Leech-che, who I had Sent for to mett me with the White English Woman that he keeps as a Slave and Deliver her to me or I should find ways to oblidge him. She was not Come but in Two dayes Time arived on of the Lower town's people who gave the Following Account:

"Cherokeyes Laceeh-che was fully Designed to Come up and Bring with him all his Town and live amonge us, But when the Spanish Capt. heard of it he Came to Cherokey Leech Town and assured[2] Where he was goeing.

Cherokey-leech-che Answered: 'There is a Beloved man Come from the English to the Creeks and Sent for me to Come to him and I am agoeing to See what he wants wt me.'

The Capt.: 'But what are you prepareing those Counues[3] and othere Nessesaries for as you had a mind to leave your Setlemt?'

Cherokeys leech: 'I designe to goe and here the Beloved English man Talk and if it's good I Shal Remove and live amonge the Creek's where I have a great many Relations.'

Capt.: 'That is what we heard and therefore I am Sent to tell you from my King that the English man Who is at the Creeks was Sent on purpose to Justice You There and then by the assistance of the Tallapoops he is Lie[4] you and Your Women and Childreen Carry you down and Send You over the great Water.'"

This prevented Cherokey's Leech-ches Comeing to the Çreeks as the Lower people affirm. I found that the army agst The Yamasees had Been march'd Eighteen days and

---

[1] Meet. [2] Inquired. [3] Canoes. [4] Seize.

that a Message was sent by a Negro from the Governour of moveal [1] Chargeing the Creeks not to goe Out To Warr against The Yamasees. The Said Negro pursued the Army Two days and Turned Back 70 of the Warriour's that was Designed against the Yamases.

The old King Brmins Told me He had a Talk left by his Son Sepe Coffee for me Which was as followes:

"I am now goeing against the Yamasees and hope at my return To Show you that I am Realy your Freind and not the Spanyards nor French, and if your King S'ould [2] Send a Comission for me and if you Cannot Stay till my Return leave it with my Father. But I should be very glad to See you at my Return."

Brmins Speach before his head men and Derected To me

"I have now Sent my people against the Yamasees and my order to them is to take, Kill and Destroy all the Yamasees they meet with and in Case the Sparnyards S'ould assist the Yamases then to the Spanyards as Yamases; but wethar they will [have] any Success I cannot tell for there is a Massage Sent Down to the Yamases from the Lower Towns to give them an account of my peoples goeing out. This Should have Been Long agoe but your King never Sent a Talk to me before you Brought it. There has Been Several talkes here, But I would not have you Belive that I am to take a Talk from any man in this Nation for through [3] I am Old yet I am the head of this Nation and my mouth is good. I do not know the meaning that your King has Left of his former Customs for thire was never a head man made here but such as I would Recomend to your King. But now any young Fellow that gees Down and Tell[s] a Find [4] Story they [get] a Commission and then they Come here and they are head Men and at the Same Time No more [fit] for it then Doges. Where is all these men that has been Such Good Freinds to you? How many of them is gone Farr against Your Enemies? I sent to the Capts. and ordered them To gett ready and they would not on man goe out, nay they would not give the Variours [1] any thing to eat as they past The Town, and these are the people that wants the white peoples goods Cheeper then us because they are your Best Freinds.

Answer. "I am glad to hire [2] that your People is gone out with so good a Designe and hope they may have as Good Success. But as fore [3] my King appointing unproper men to be head men I know not how you Can bleam [4] him for these very Cussitawes when they are Down with Our King, They tell him they will goe to Warr With Our Enemies and if they will Talk Streight there and throw the Talk away When they Come here I know not how my King Can help that. Neither do I know Who among you he Can Depend on for by What I Can see the mot [5] of you are in one mind this day and another the nixt."

Octr the 26th. I left the Cowweetaws and on November the 1st I Came to the Oakefuskey town in the upper Talla-poopes which was the Time and place appointed to make payment for the Three Slaves Redeemed and likewise for Mr. Sharpes Goods. I Came here at 9 a Clock at Night and 150 head men and Warriours mett Expecting me, and after passing Some Complemts one Wm. Wood, who is a Tradeour in Said Town, Desird to Speake with me and Said: "This Company that you see hear has been met two days' and have not Slept any. We that are White men have Been very much Slighted by them and its my opinion that if you Reherse the same talk that you gave them last that we Shal be all murdered, for I heard a head man say Sitting In the Square that the Beloved man Talked much of Warr In his last Talk, that the White people once had a Warr and Why did they not keep it if they liked it; But that if the Beloved man would have warr They would give him warr. Ane other Replyed, ' Be easey, let him Come; We will here his Talk again, it may be Better.' If You have a mind to be easey you must Tye the Wariours; for they would not be

---

[1] Warriors. [2] Hear. [3] For. [4] Blame. [5] Most.

queit else." An other Reply'd, 'Take Care What you Say
that White man understands you. I do not Care what he
understands for if the Beloved man was here himself I
would Say As much.'"

I then turned to the Square and asked for letter[s] from the
Oakechey Capt. whom I had seen[1] to the Chocktaws on purpose to bring me ane account from them how the Tradeours
was Rec'd.

Capt. answer[ed] : "The White men are Well but they gave
me no Letters. Here is two head men of the Chocktaws that
has Brought you a token of peace and hope that your king
will look on them as Freinds and when the Whitemen Comes
Down Some of the Chocktaws kings Designes [coming]
Down to your king to pay thir Respects to him."

Novembr the 2d. The head men of Abecas and Tallapoopes mett, Being in Number 150 men; I went to the
Square and sd[2] as followes :

I am very Glad to see so many of you meet according to
apointmt. But before We proceed to any talk I must
Inquire who among you is Disturb'd at the last talk that I
gave You. I am Informed by the White man that Trades in
this Town that Some of you have Said I told you much of
Warr in my Last talk to you and that if I wanted warr you
would give it me. I should have took it well of you if you
had told me then what part of my Talk you disliked, for I
would then have Satisfied you, and you have had no need to
have bore it in mind so long. When my king sent me here
he thought he had Sent me to talk with head men and Warriours and therefore he did not send Talks to please Women
and Childreen. I dont Doubt but [that if] I had told you
that you were the Best freinds to my King and that he Loved
you very well but what this would a have pleased you.
But then this would not be the way To make all Streight
Between my king and you. For you yourselves know that
[you] have Been guilty of what you dare not Justifie, and if
my king should pass this by and take no notice of it, I am
Sure you Could not think that his heart was Streight with

[1] Sent. [2] Spoke.

you, but must think that [he] would bear it in his mind. I do suppose your discourse before the white man has been to Deterr me from Insisting uppon your promises. Tis true you may Choo's whither you will pay me what you promised me or no; but unless you do, I Can Assure you as I Told you before that my King will make a warr with you which I have in words from his own mouth, and like it how you will I Cannot help it, for I came here to tell you the Truth and that I shal doe. Tis true you [may] kill a few white men that is among you if you will, But I would not have [you] think that I am affeard to Dye. Since I am Sure my king will Revenge it on you; for if you was to do me any hurt I do assure you my king would never forgive you while on of you was Liveing."

The King of the Oakfuskys Answer.

"'Tis true we [were] Speaking pretty angre in the Square but it was about the Chickesaws and not about you, and the White man dis not understand our Talk. I do asure you We desire to have no Difference with you."

I then Called for the White man and made him give in the Indean Tongue the same words that he heard spoke in the Square by the head men, which by my Lingister agreed with what he Told me in English. When the Indeans found that he had Rehears'd it they Seem'd to [be] under Some Concern, but Still Denyed the words.

I then proceed[ed] to Receive What Skins they had Brought in, part for Mr. Sharp; then they Delivered 120 Skins telling me, "We are no[t] the people that was Concerned in the Plundering the White Man, nor yet had we any of his Cloths; but to let your king see that we doe Designe to see him paid we brought you these. The people that tooke the Coths are all out, either at warr, or a hunting; and as soon as they Come In, if we find they are not Willing to pay as they have promised then we will take from them Either Slaves or Skins and send them to Savana Town. This you may Tell your king he may depend on.

And as to the three Slaves Redeemed from the Cherokeys the skins has been paid long since, but we find the man in Whose hands the Skins Wes [1] lodged has Detained them; but you may depend they shal be paid this Spring.

To [2] a Peace with the Cherokeys we now apply to your king. For we now find its the Chickesaws that Injur's us and not the Cherokeys; so that if the Cherokeys will Send all the Chickesaws home out of there nation and bring a white man from your King with them down the Coossaw [3] River we will Trust them and Receive them in the Cossaw town, but not without a White man being with them.

Answer. "You see that I write everything down that you say, therefore I shal not forget your promisess, and hope that you will Remember as well to Comply with them. I Shal likewise take Care To Informe my king of What you Say in Relation to the Cherokeys."

Just at this Time arived 40 Warriours from the Cherokeys and Came Directly to me, and Said as followes:

"I have Been to Warr agst the Cherokeys and Lay 15 days about there Towns, waiteing ane opertunity to gett a Scalp, but to no Purpose for they ware in Forts as though they Expected our Comeing, and you must Certainly have given your king [an] Account of [our] Designes and he has Sent it to your Beloved man that is at the Cherokeys. Now I think its Strenge Freindship that you pretend to us When every opertunity that you have of apraizeing the Cherokeys of our Designes against them you make use of it to acquent the Cherokeys of the Same. But Since You Call yourselves our friends, why do not you give us ane account of the Cherokeys Designe against us? But that you never do."

Answer. "You know that at the first talk I gave you, I promised a peace with the Cherokeys In answer to what you Told me to send to my King and tell him that you Designed once more against the Cherokeys, and then you would Except of a peace if any king Would make it for you."

<hr>

[1] Were. 　　　 [2] For. 　　　 [3] Coosa.

"'Tis true we did tell you to send to your king, but then we thought we were Sending to our ffreind and not to the Cherokeys."

"According to your request I sent to my king What you desired me, but I would not have you think that my king ever Sent that newes to the Cherokeys or that he is so much more the Cherokeys freind then yours, for the Custome with us is the Same as with you; when there is any talk Sent down our King Calles the Beloved men Together and when they have Seen the Talk and Considered it amonge themselves then they give it out to Every Body and there might have happen'd Some Cherokeys Tradours down and [they] may [have] Carr[ied] the Talk home to the Cherokeys; for you find the Traders here When they Come from our great Town if they here any thing of the Cherokeys they tell it you, and its as like the others may tell the Cherokeys. But I would not have you think its my Kings doeings, for he is a greater freind to you then You think on."

Novembr the 3d. I came down to the lower Tallopoopes and there pursuant to my late Instructions did take a Negro Who as I Resited Turned Back 70 Warriours, the sd Negro Being near the French Fort and amonge those Indians who have the French Commission, Which are the very lower Tallopoopes and Mixt with the Stinging-lingo Indians. I then Sumons'd the head men To meet. Accordingly [they] did. It was a litle Surprizeing to them That I should Desire a meeting being ane English man. They Readily meet, and I gave them the following Talk:

"I am very Glad to see that you are Come to hear my Talk Which Indeed I did not Expect, Since you are Such Slaves to the French that you dare not Suffer our Traders to Come among you for fear of Offending our master the French Capt. Altho at the same time you Cannot get Cloth any other way then Comeing Where Our Traders are and Buy of them, for the French are not able to gett Cloath; And that is the Reasone they order you not to Suffer our White people to Come among you. Now its not soe with us. These people that we Call our Freind, as here is two with me, ask them if I ever Told them not to let the French Come Among them. I do not Endeavour to keep my Freinds like Slaves as the French do you. But I am willing they should be like free men as they be and if the French Can sell as Good Coths as we do and as Cheep let them buy of the French. But my Bussines with you is to tell you that I [have] here Taken a Negro Who is a Slave blonging to my great King and has Been Run from us a great while and lived with the French. Now I Expect that the ffrench will Endeavour to perswad you to take this negro from me if they Can. But I do now Tell you that this [is an] afair that Lives between the French Capt. and my Self, and [as] it dis not Concerne you I shall Expect that you will not medle Eithere on way nor other. If the French Capt. thinks he has a better right to the negro let him Come and Take him Since he has Twenty men in the Fort and I have but Ten here. But I doe Belive that if I should goe away now with the negro, the Capt. would Come and tell you that I Stole him and was Run away with him and that had I Stayed Longer he would Come and take hime from me. Now to Show that my Right to the Negro is good you goe and tell the Capt. That I Shal Stay in this Town four days to see if he has any[thing] to say to me."

Answer from the head man.

"Your Talk is very Good, and as to the Negro Since you say its your Slave you ought to have him and we have nothin to Say to him; but we will Send the Capt. word of what you Say and if he thinks its good he may Come and Talk wt you about him. For our part we are Indeans and will Differ with no White people."

Accordingly they Sent to the Capt. of the albaw-man fort.[1]

November the 4th. Capt. Sent the ffollowing Massage by on of his Subjects:

[1] Alabama Fort, or Fort Toulouse, which was erected by Bienville in 1714 near the confluence of the Coosa and Tallapoosa rivers.

"I am Come from the King of the Al-bawma fort to you To know by what Authority you have taken a Subject Belonging to the Crown of France and ane Inhabiter of the Governmt of Moveall,[1] and on whome the Governour of Moveall has ane Intire Value for and in case your Right to him is good to know what is the purchase [price] of him."

"You may goe back and tell your king, as you Call him, that I think his assistance is great to question my authority by which I proceed here. [It] is very Good and that he shall know if he Dispute it, and that I hope to give an account of my proceedings to the Governmt of South Carolina that Sent me here and not To your king, and as to the purchase [price] of the Negro its Two great to[2] the Governmt of Moveall To obtain."

November the 8th. I Went Back to the Tallapoopes where I Mett the Death hoop. I Imediatly Enquired the Meaning of it and found that the Abecas and Tallapoopes had Declared Warr against the Chickesaws, and had then Killed on Chickesaw Who lived among the Abecas; and [that it] was designed to Kill all that was Liveing among the Creeks.

Tickhomebey and Sixteen more Chickesaws aplyed themselves To me in this Manner : "Here is the Oakechoye Capt. Come from the Chocktawes and there has heard that the Chickesawes has latly Killed Some of the Creek people and Carried there Scalps to the Chickesaw Towns for which the Creeks has Killed on of our people and Designes to Kill all of us that is here. The Chocksaws[3] are not Reconcilled to our nation neither Can they gett Satisfaction of us without the assistance of the Creeks. So I hope as our Natne[4] is at peace with you that you will save our lives for I ame a True ffreind to the English and So will Continue."

I then Imediatly Sent Runers to the Abecas to forbide their proceedings, and likewise for the heads of the uper Tallopoopes To Come to me, Accordingly they did and

---

[1] Mobile.   [2] For.   [3] Choctaws.   [4] Nation.

on *No[vembe]r the* 10*th* I gave them The following Talk in the Tallasee Towne[1] in lower Tallapoopes:

"I understand that You have Declared a warr against the Chickesaws from only a Story that the Oakechoye Capt. have brought me from the Chicktaws.[2] We are but Just Getting ane acquantance with the Chocktawes, as yet we do not know them. Its very like that this may be don to set you against the Chickesawes that they may gett Revenge, Since they Cannot do it of themselves. What do you think the head men at the Chickesaws will think of me if I suffer you to kill there people that lives among you as Freinds? Doubtles they will think that I am not their Freind, neither Can I Expect them to use Our White people there as Freinds unless I Show my ffreindship now to these people that you are agoeing to kill Which I Charge you not to doe, and I am not against your killing those that Live with the Cherokeys. For I see they are Dayly killing of you and if you will goe to war against the Chickesawes I Cannot help it. I have nothing to say to That. But as the Dogg king is now at the Chocktaws I think you would do well to Stay till he Comes and here what he Says. Its like the Captain might mistake.

Answer. "We hear and your Talk is good. We will take it and wait as you say till the dog king Comes and then we shal know the Truth."

November the 12*th.* I Left the Tallopoopes and *the* 15 *Instant* Came to the Cowweetaws. The day after my arival here there Came a Tommantle man from Cherokeys Leech's town and gave the Following Account:

"Your people that is gone to War against the Yamases was disapointed finding the Yamases all in Forted. They Turned off and is gone to the Floradays. There is likewise four ships from Carolina loaded with all Sorts of provissions and Tradeing goods on purpose To Suply the Yamases, and there is Two English men Sent to the Yamases from the King of the English to make a Peace with the Yamasees,

---

[1] The Upper Creek town of Tallassee was on or near the site of the present town of Tallassee, Alabama.
[2] Choctaws.

Which is don; and there is now ten of the Yamases with them Two english men waiting to Meet your people When they Return and make a Peace With them. The Method proposed is that the Yamases Shal Deliver to you as many men as You lost with holatta to be put to Death and then to make a peace. Then the English proposses to erect a Fort at the fork of Hallatomahaw [1] River and there to Supply the Yamases with all Sorts of Goods and in order thereto they have already Brought Great Guns, Some of Which are Brass."

It happen'd a little time before this I was telling Old Brinins of Mr. Spotswoods [2] Runing to [St.] Agustine With a parcell of Trading Goods Which proved of Service.

Old Brunin's answer to the Commantle man.

"I am Surprized at your newes. I Cannot tell how to live [3] you. Since here is a Beloved man Who has latly Recd Letters from his king and if this had Been so I Should had heard it from him but you are On of our own Collour and the best of you will Lie. I shal here soon from my people and then shal know more of the Matter."

My Own answer to the Commantles Speach Derected [to] Brunin's and his Beloved men.

"I am very Glad that it happen'd so as we talk of the man that I told you was Run to [St.] Augustine before this Newes Came in, or you might have thought I told you a Lye For if there is any White English man with the Yamases it's the Same man that I told you of, and the Spanyards has Contrived this Storye to Save the Yamasees by puting this Englishman with them. But I Could wish your people knew my Mind; them Englishmen Should be used as Yamasees that [are] found with them. And as to a peace with the Yamases if my kind [4] had a mind to make any he Would not

---

[1] Altamaha.
[2] Alexander Spotswood, who was lieutenant governor of Virginia in 1710–1722.
[3] Believe.   [4] King.

Send to [St.] Augustine for it, but he would Send orders to me, being a more ready way.

The Gun's being Sent to the fork of halla to mahaw [1] River is Like the rest of the Story and I find its Contrived by the Spanyards only to make ane Exchange for Our Freind Hollatta and the rest of our Beloved men that was murdered with him by the Huspaw [2] King and his Warriour's.

Now I like the proposal they make of Exchanging and give-ing you as many Yamases as they have Killed of your people. But we must know what men they will Deliver up, whither they will Deliver the Huspaw King in Lew [3] of Hollataw and as many Yamases Warriours as we[re] killed with him; but instead of that they will give you Slaves or Some other Inferriour Sort of Fellows that they may Spare without being mist. But I hope you have more Value for your king though he is dead and Respect to his ffather then to Sweep him away as we doe horses for the Spanyards themselves would Laugh at you as well as at the Yamases for Such an act[io]n.

Old Brm'ns Your Talk is good, But I do not know what to think of these Two English men that is with the Yamases. For I know that will Surprize my people and they will not know what to doe, but you have Told us how it is. Lett them agree To what they will it shal be Spoilt at their Return."

I then proposed Runners to be Sent and apprise the army of this affaire. But the Old King was of Oppinion it would be very Uncertaine where to Meet the Warrioures and the Runners very much Endangered; but while we were Con-sidering of this affair there Came in two Runners from the Warriour's and gave the Following Account:

"The Pilot that we had, Carried us to a Fort in a Town Where we thought the Yamases were, and we fired at the Said Fort, Which alarmed ten Men that was Placed To Discover us which we past when they were asleep. Our

[1] Altamaha.
[2] Huspah was the chief of a band of Yamasee Indians of the same name.
[3] Lieu.

fireing awaked them and they Ran round us and gave Notice
to the Yamasees Who was Removed from this town Nigher
the Sea and had there Build a new fort which we found and
Attacked but with litle Success through[1] it happen'd the
Huspaw Kings Family was not all got in the fort and we took
three of them and fired Several Shott at the Huspaw king
and are in hopes have killed him. There Came out a party
of the Yamases who fought us and we took the Capt. We
waited three days about there Fort, Expecting to get ane
oppertunity to take Some More but to no purpose. We
then Came away and the Yamases pursued us. We fought
them and gained the Batle. We drove the Yamases unto a
pond and was Just Runing in after them where we Should a
had a great advantage of them but we discover'd about fourty
Spanyards armed on horse Back Who made Toward us wt
a White Cloth before them and as they advanced toward us
They made Signes that we Should fforbear fireing. Some
of our head men gave Out orders not to fire, But Steyamasiechie or Gogel Eys Told them it was spoilt and to fire away.
According we did, and the Spanyards fled. After that the
Yamases pursued us [and] gave us ane other Batle in which
they did us the most Damnadge. We have killed Eight of
the Yamases, on of which is the huspaw kings head Warriour
and have Brought off all thir Scalps. We have likewise
Taken nine of them a Live, Together with Several Guns,
Some Cloth, and Some plunder Out of there Churches,
Which you will See When the Warriours Come in."
We have Lost on our Side five men killed dead and six
wounded. When I found the Army so nigh there return I
was willing to prepare for my Comeing away [and] there being
a Negro then in the Pallachochole town Belonging to Andrew
Partoson of Port Royal that I thought to have Brought
down, I sent five White men to take him and bring him to
me. They Accordingly Took the Negro and had him, but
the King of the Town Cutt the Rope and threw it into the
fire and the King of sd Town Told the White men that they

[1] Though.

had as good Guns as they, and Could make as good use of them; upon which the white man Returned unto me.

I then thought, as the Warriours was not farr off, to wait till they Came in, before I Said any more about Said Negro.

November the 30th. Thomas Jones arived from the Chock-tawes and gave Following Account:

That after Being at the Chocktaws and purchast some Skines the hunters where he was, all went out a hunting, in Number 700, Who was to bring in Skins Sufficient to purchase all his goods. The sd Jones Left Thomas Wiggin and a Considerall qaintity goods in order to Trade with sd Indeans at there Return, and Jones Left the Nation. On John Gallespy being Ready at the Same time to leave the Nation with Jones would not but waited for the Coossaw [1] king of the Chocktawes, who had promised Gillespey to Come down to this governmt, and sd Gillespey waited on purpose for him or might have Brought off his Leather and horses as Jones did, but the sd Gillespey the 16th November Left the Chocktawes nation; And the 17 Instant the Chock-taws, as they belive, did fall on said Wiggin who was left in the Nation and did plund[er] and Take from him all the Said goods but with much to do did Escape. The Indeans did pursue the said Gillespey and Took from him Several horses loaded with Skins, wounded Several of the White men, and Killed One. The said Gillespey Came foreward With what horses was left him and mett with the Coosaw king who had apointed to Come Down with him. The Coossaw king Seeing of him Bloody Inquired the meaning of it. Gillespey Related to him what had hapen'd, Only omitting the death of the white man.

The Coossaw king Replyed: "If you will goe Back with me Your goods and horses shal be Restored Back to you againe and you shal not loose on Skin by what has hapen'd."

Then Gillespey told him that the worst of all, they had killed a White man. This seem'd to Surprize the King and he Said, "Now its all Spoilt; The horses and goods I Could

[1] Coosha was an important Choctaw town on Lost Horse Creek in what is now Lauderdale County, Mississippi.

have gott, but the man Cannot be Brought to Life. I have Been Several years Endeavouring to open the path to the English and thought it was now don, but find it as farr of as ever. There is three men of Ours gon to the Creeks to see your Beloved man and then [1] I Give over to be dead."

Gillespey told him that they should not be hurted, for though there was a white man killed He did not belive it was done by the Consent of the Chiefest of the Nation. Accordingly Gillespey mett the Three Indians and Sent Them home w[i]t[h]out hurt.

The Dogg king of the Oakefuskey Came to me at the same time and Said, "What the Chocktaws has Done is not good and I have heard that the Chocktawes makes as good slaves as Negros; if you think it will be good I will soon have some of them here. I have 100 men at my Command who are good Warriours and only wait for your orders."

"What you Say is Good, but I dare not send you to Warr Till my great King has heard what has hapen'd."

December the 28th. Hearing that the Warriours was naer the Lower towns I thought to goe down and meet them. I order'd my Lingister to make ready Which he Refused to do. It hap'nd That On William Hoge Just then was Come from the hovanys [2] who was a Better Lingister then the former John Molton. I took the Said hodge as Lingester and vent down to the Lower Towns. Sd hodge Being a Pack horse Driver to on John Cannaday, Who Molton was no ways Concerned with. Notwithstanding the Said Molton followed me to the Lower Town's and Just as I mett the head man that was Come from Warr, and had Begun to Talk with them, the sd Molton Came litle Better then Drunk and Interupted my Lingester, telling me that William Hodge was his servant and that I had Stole him, which he would make me know, and then told the Indeans that I was A Thieff, had Stole his servant and not to mind what I had Said To them for my Talk was not good. He then Turned to me and Told me that what Talks I had given while he was

[1] Them.   [2] Havana.

Lingester he would undoe for that the publick Intrust [1] was not So advantageous to him as his Own. I then Charged him to behave himself with more Respect and not to think he was Speaking to a privat man for by the Trust Reposed in me I Represent the Governmt of Carolina. His Reply was, "Dame you and the Governmt Both. The Worst that Can be don is to prevent my Comeing here Which is more than they Can doe for I Will Come." Which he Bound by his Maker. I was oblidged to Conceal my Lingester from him and Could Not have any Discourse with the Indeans. The day after I Returned to the Cowweetawes where the Said Molton Endeavoured to perswad my Kings not to speak any thing for Me. This he did When he was Sober, and When he found he Could Not prevail with him, he then prevailed with Some of the head men, as I Suppose, not to Talk with me by the said Hodges Interpretation. Accordingly Some of the Indeans Told me they did not hear the Said hodge and Desired they might have Molton to talk with them. I answered them, "I look upon Molton to be a Rogue and Not fitt to be Intrusted with any of my Talk, and if [you] Cannot here this Man You must goe to my king and Talk wt him. For I will Talk with You by noe othere then this." Sepe Coffee Hott and Chuggilley, who Told me the said hodge Could speak there Tongue neir as well as themselves, asked those that objected against him what part of the Talk they misunderstood and So made them asshamed of there Objections, and then They Could all here the Sd Hodge.

December the 15th. I Sent for all the Lower Towns head men to meet at the Cowweetaw; the Same day the Warriours arived at the Cowweetaws.

Old Brmins Speech to his Warriours.

"You are Returned from Warr and Some of Your men You have Left. Such things as them must hapen or you

---

[1] Interest.

would Be noe Warriours for if Men Should always goe out
To Warr against Enemies and never loose any men then old
Women would be good Warriours. But this is What makes
you warrioures. That you will goe into such Dangers
where you [are] sure some of you will Drop. But I hope this
is but a beginning as you have now made a war with the
Yamasees I hope you will Continue it while there is a
Yamasees Left on the land, Since In that you gett revenge
for your Selves and English Both [of] who[m] they have
Caused to Shead many tears as well as my self."

Sepe Coffee answers, "We have had but poor Success
but we hope The nixt Time to have Better. But a Warr I
do Designe To Continue against the Yamasses While I Can
gett Bullets and Powder for Skins. I Cannot say, I will
kill them all. Some may goe over the Great Water. But
there Shal not One Stay on this Land."

"I am very Glad to see you Return with no greater Loss
than you have which Indeed I did not Expect Since the
Yamases had Such Timely Notice of your Designes against
them. Its a wounder to me they did not do you a greater
deal more Damage But hope that you will Take some Course
with those That Sends Such newes to the Yamases. Amonge
us Such a man would be Tied to four mad horses and Draven[1]
to pices — as Should give Our Enemies ane Account of Our
Designes against them and at the Same Time pretend to be
Our ffreind. My king has Sent a Commission to King Sepe
Coffee to be Comander in Cheif of this Nation under his
Father Emprour Brmin's Derections, the meaning of which
Comission is to Take all orders that shall Come from my
king, to hear no talk But What Comes from him, and to be
Sure to put all his orders In Execution, and that all men in
this Nation is to pay the said Sepe Coffee due obedience as
there King dureing the Time that Sepe Coffee Containues to
be True and Trusty to my King and no Longer." And So
[I] Delivered his Comission and Likewise [one] to one Capt.
Hott, which was Intirely to the Satisfa'ne of all the heads
in Generall.

[1] Drawn.

Sepe Coffees Speech at Takeing his Comission.

"I do now take this with a Streight heart and you may Tell your King that I Shal not let it lie much in my house. But that it Shal be put in Execution, that is goe to War against his Enemies and mine and you may tell him that my heart is now Streight with him and So Shal Containue."

On December the 2d I gave them the following talk being the day I Left the Natione, there being 120 head men of the Lower Townes present:

"My king Sent me into this Nation to see every Town and To know Who among You are his Freinds and who are not. Accordingly I have Been throughout your Whole Natione and I am now agoeing to my king and Shal let him know What I am now agoeing to tell You.

The Negro Which I Took from the Spanyard in this Town did make his Escape from the White man that were Carring him Down and Returned to Squire Mickeo who Imediatly assisted him with Cunnue and provissions sufficient to Carry him to Saint Mallagoes. Now there Sitts the Squire, Let him Denie it if he dares, and then I will prove it to his Face. There is likewise a White girl that Belonges to us Whis [1] detaind by the Dogg King of the Pallachochola Town and is kept over the River in a Remute [2] pleace that no white man shal see her. Then [3] I Sent down to the Pallachocola Town and had a Negro Tied in order to Carry him to his master, the King of sd Town did Cut the Rope, threw it in the fire, and Told the whiteman That they had as good Guns as they had and Could make as Good use of them.

Now do you think that these lookes like Freindly Actions? Or do you think when I goe home and my king askes me if all the Creeks are his Freinds that I Can tell him they are? Noe I do assure you I Cannot. But I Shall tell him I look upon all people Below Capt. Hotts house to be Reather freinds To the Yamases then to us, for is [it] not plane that Squire Mickeo Sent to the Yamases to let them know of

---

[1] Who is. [2] Remote. [3] When.

Your Comeing? As I Tould you beffore Such a man with us would be Tore to pi[e]ces with mad horses. Thereffore if these people has a mind to Show thir freindship to my king Let Squire Mickeo's Town pay for that Negro he assisted away, Let the dog king Deliver the White girl, and let the pallachochola town pay for the Negro their King untied; without which I do not see how you Can Call Your selves frcinds to my king. Tis True you may Call yourselves freinds as You [say], but my king wants no Such freindship as is only Exprest with the Tongue and not by the Actions. I Would not have you think that I am Beging your Freindship for my king has Freinds Sufficient w[i]t[h]out you. I only want to know how [1] among you will be his Enemies and who [h]is Freinds, so I shal Expect when Seepe Coffee Comes down that he will Bring Satisfaction for the two Negroes and the White girl."

Sepe Coffee['s] Speech to the head men and Wariours.

"You here What the Beloved man say's. I do not find that any of you Denies what he says thereffore [as] I belive what he says to be all True and [that] his Demands is all Reasonable, So I hope you that are my Warriours will Stand be [2] me and See that all his Demands are Comply'd with."

I then left the Natione Leaving 120 Dear Skins in Sepe Coffees possession and four Slaves Belonging to Mr. Sharp which I Should have Brought with me but Receiving a Letter from the honable Coll. George Chicken Esquire where he adwised me of a Chickesaw being killed naer the Savana Town by the Creeks and that the Chickesaws was Resolved to Retal[i]ate it on the Creeks, I inform[ed] The Creeks of the Same, which was the Reason that they did [not] think it safe for the Burdeners To proceed with me But the said goods Should be Left and that Sepe Coffee Would bring them Down in the month of March when he Designes to be Down himself with five other head Men and fourty Warriours with him for

---

[1] Who. [2] By.

a guard. But he Desires that the guard may be Suffered to pass The Savana Garrisson and Came [1] as Low as Edisto River for he Lookes upon it as [being as] Dangerous between the Savana town and Edisto [as] any other part of the way.

I Left the Cowweetaws December the 2d and Brought with me a Negro as I have herein Resited and being Within 20 miles of the Savana Town left the sd Negro In Charge of two white men well arm'd and the negro Prisoned. Notwithstanding he got the white mens armes and Shot on John Sergant through the Brest and made his Escape.

As soon [as] the News Came to me at Savana Town I Dispactht ane Express to [the] Creek's and gave ane account of the Negros Escape and promised a peace of Strouds to any Indean that Should Bring the sd Negros head To on Florance Makhone, a Tradour at the Creeks, or a hundered pounds to any White man that Should Take him. Sepe Coffee promised he would do his Endeavour To have him taken and sent Runer To aprize The uper Creeks of the Same. The foregoing proceedings as·[2] a Just and True account

by TOBIAS FITCH.

This is a true Copy from the Originall.

Exãied [3] this 21st May 1726.

by Hen Hargrave, Depty Secty.

[1] Come.   [2] Are.   [3] Examined.

A RANGER'S REPORT OF TRAVELS WITH
GENERAL OGLETHORPE, 1739-1742

INTRODUCTION

GEORGIA was chartered in 1732 to save South Carolina from the French and Spanish, yet South Carolina begrudged the people of Georgia a share in the Indian trade. Georgia, on the other hand, being a prohibition province at that early day, objected to the sale of rum to the Indians, and expressly charged that the difficulties between the English and the Creeks arose from the failure of South Carolina to render "satisfaction for injuries done by their pedling traders." General Oglethorpe, who was the early guide of affairs in Georgia and who in 1738 was appointed commander in chief of His Majesty's forces in both Georgia and South Carolina, made it his first care to win the friendship of the Indians. On the 15th of June, 1739, he wrote the Georgia Trustees: "I have received frequent and confirmed advices that the Spaniards are striving to bribe the Indians, and particularly the Creek nation, to differ with us; and the disorder of the traders is such as gives but too much room to render the Indians discontented; great numbers of vagrants being gone up without licenses either from Carolina or us. Chigilly, and Malachee, the son of the great Brim, who was called Emperor of the Creeks by the Spaniards, insist upon my coming up to put all things in order, and have acquainted me that all the chiefs of the nation will come down to the Coweta town to meet me, and hold the general assembly of the Indian nations; where they will take such measures as will be necessary to hinder the Spaniards from corrupting and raising sedition amongst their people.

"This journey, though a very fatiguing and dangerous one, is quite necessary to be taken; for if not, the Spaniards, who have sent up great presents to them, will bribe the corrupt part of the nation; and, if the honester part is not supported, will probably overcome them, and force the whole nation into a war with England. The Coweta town, where the meeting is to be, is near 500 miles from hence [1]; it is in a straight line 300 miles from the sea. All the towns of the Creeks [2] and of the Cousees and Talapousees,[3] though 300 miles from the Cowetas, will come down to the meeting. The Choctaws, also, and the Chickasaws, will send thither their deputies; so that 7,000 men depend upon the event of this assembly. The Creeks can furnish 1,500 warriors, the Chickasaws 500, and the Choctaws 5,000. I am obliged to buy horses and presents to carry up to this meeting." [4]

The 16th of the following month he wrote the Trustees from Savannah: "The French and Spaniards have used their utmost endeavours to raise disturbances amongst our Indians and the not deciding clearly in the Act relating to them has given such Insolence to the Carolina Traders that the Indians have declared, if I do not come up to them they will take Arms and do themselves Justice and have ordered a General Assembly of all the Nations to meet me. I set out this night." [5]

Regarding the success of his trip Oglethorpe wrote from Augusta, September 5, 1739: "I am just arrived at this Place from the Assembled Estates of the Creek Nation. They have very fully declared their rights to and possession of all the Land as far as the River Saint Johns and their Concession of the Sea Coast, Islands and other Lands to the Trustees, of which they have made a regular Act. If I had not gone up the misunderstandings between them and the Carolina Traders fomented by our two neighboring Nations would probably have occasioned their beginning a war, which I believe might have been the result of this general meeting; but as their complaints were reasonable, I gave them satisfaction in all of them, and every thing is entirely settled in peace. It is impossible to describe the joy they expressed at my arrival they met me forty miles in the woods and la̎yd

---

[1] From Frederica. [2] Lower Creeks.
[3] The Cousees and Talapousees were Upper Creeks.
[4] Henry Bruce, *Life of General Oglethorpe*, pp. 207–208.
[5] *Collections* of the Georgia Historical Society, Vol. III, p. 80.

Provisions on the roads in the woods. The Express being just going to Charles Town, I can say no more but that I have had a burning fever of which I am perfectly recovered."[1]

While at Augusta Oglethorpe received a communication from England informing him of the declaration of war against Spain and instructing him to "annoy" the Spaniards. The Ranger's *Report* is an account of his travels with Oglethorpe to the Indian Assembly at Kawita (Coweta) on the Chattahoochee River and in attendance upon Oglethorpe during his operations against Saint Augustine and in defense of the Georgia coast from Spanish invasion.

The *Report* is among the Stowe Manuscripts in the British Museum, and a transcript which was made from this is in the Library of Congress.

[1] *Collections* of the Georgia Historical Society, Vol. III, p. 81.

A RANGER'S REPORT OF TRAVELS WITH GENERAL OGLETHORPE, 1739–1742

*A Report having been raised by W. C. Esqr. that General Ogle-
thorpe had no Rangers in Georgia but two or three that he
kept to defray the Expence of Servants, The Author of the
following Account (having been a Ranger in Georgia and
Constantly paid as such) Submits it to any Candid Person
whether such Report is not without Foundation and
absolutely false.*

His Excellency Genl. Oglethorpe making a Tour into the
Indian Nations to Establish Peace between them and the
English ordered me to attend him it being about four Hun-
dred Miles through the Woods, *July the 8th* we began our
Journey and went by Water as far as Ebenezer. The General
took Horse and Rode to the Uchee Town [1] he having sent the
Boat round there where we arrived *July the 19th. July the
24th.* The General set out with about twenty Five Persons
in Company and some Indians all well Armed, it being very
Necessary so to be, for not long before a Party of the Choctau
Indians came down to the General who gave them Presents
and they staid amongst the English as Friends, but did not
prove so, for in their Return home, they met two English
Men who traded among the Indians, one of these they killed
and shot three of the others Fingers off, however he made his
Escape to a Town of the lower Creeks, Who upon hearing
his Relation of what the Choctau's had done, imediately
armed themselves and went in pursuit of the Choctau's
whom they find encamped round a Fire ; The Creeks imediately charged them, killed a great many and took the rest

[1] A town inhabited by Uchee Indians and situated on the
Savannah River, thirty-five miles above Ebenezer and seventy
miles above Savannah.

Prisoners. The General had also at this time two of the Choctau Indians with him who had put themselves under his Protection for fear of the People of the Creek Nation who would have killed them for the Barbarity of their Countrymen to the two English Traders. But now I return to our Journey, which we Continued being Supplied with Venison by the Indian Hunters, and also Wild Honey of which they took Plenty. *July 27th.* We arrived at Great Ogeechee River which we Swam our Horses over and The Packhorse Man got his Things over in a Leather Canoe which they carry for that Purpose and at every River where they are to use it, they stretch it with Stakes made on Purpose. *July the 28th.* The Things being all got over the River we set forward, The Indians killing plenty of Deer and Turkeys for our Refreshment, also several Buffaloes, of which there is great Plenty and they are very good Eating. Though they are a very heavy Beast they will out Run a Horse and Quite Tire him. *July 31st.* We Travelled over many Hills from which we had a very Pleasant Prospect of the Valleys which abounded with fine green Trees and abundance of Grapes and other Fruits, but which were not Ripe. From the Top of one of these Hills we perceived a great Smoke at a Distance from us, which we Imagined to be at the Camp of a Party of Spanish Horse which were sent out on Purpose to hinder us if possible from going to make this Treaty of Peace with the Indians and which has since been of so great Service to us, the Friendly Indians annoying the Spaniards very much. We encamped at Occomy [1] River where we found a Horse belonging to one of the Spaniards; We crossed the River and killed two Buffaloes of which there are abundance, We Seeing Several Herds of sixty or upwards in a Herd. We Camped at Ocmulgas [2] River where are three Mounts raised by the Indians over three of their Great Kings who were killed in the Wars. *August the 6th.* We came to Dollus Rivulet where we Encamped; In the Night came to us Capt. Wiggin, Mr. Gudell, and two of the Chief Indians, before they came to us they hooped which our Indians

---

[1] Oconee. [2] Ocmulgee.

Answered, then they came to our Camp and saluted the General in a very friendly Manner which he Returned. *August the 7th.* We set forward and on our way we found several strings of Cakes and Bags of Flower etca. which the Indians had hung up in Trees for our Refreshmt. *August the 8th.* We Encamped about two Miles from the Indian Town, The Indians sent Boys and Girls out of their Town with Fowls, Venison, Pompions, Potatoes, Water Melons, and Sundry other things. About ten of the Clock we set forward for the Indian Town and were met by the Indian King And some of their Chiefs, the King had English Colours in his hand. We Saluted them and they Returned our Salute, and then shaking Hands with the General and Company the King very gracefully taking him by the Arm led him towards the Town, and when we Came there they Brought us to Logs which they had placed for that purpose Covered with Bear Skins and desired us to sit down which when we had done The head Warriours of the Indians brought us black Drink in Conkshells which they presented to us and as we were drinking they kept Hooping and Hallowing as a Token of gladness in seeing us. This Drink is made of a Leaf called by the English Casena (and much Resembles the Leaf of Bohea Tea) It is very Plenty in this Country.[1] Afterwards we went to the Kings House or rather Hut where we Dined, at night we went to the Square to see the Indians dance, They dance round a large Fire by the beating of a Small Drum and Six Men singing; their Dress is very wild and frightfull their Faces painted with several sorts of Colours their Hair cut short (except three Locks one of wch hangs over their Forehead like a horses fore Top) they paint the Short Hair and stick it full of Feathers, they have Balls and rattles about their Waist and Several things in their Hands, Their Dancing is of divers Gestures and Turnings of their Bodies in a great many frightfull Postures. The

[1] The black drink was a tea made by boiling the leaves of the *Ilex cassine.* The southern Indians drank it on deliberative occasions, and especially at the Green-corn Dance, for its supposed purifying and mind-stimulating effects.

Women are mostly naked to the Waist wearing only one short Peticoat wch reaches from their Waist a little below their Knees, they are very nice in Smoothing and putting up their hair, it is So very long when untied that it reaches to the Calves of their Legs. Their Houses or Hutts are built with Stakes and plaistered with Clay Mixed with Moss which makes them very warm and Tite. They dress their Meat in Large pans made of Earth and not much unlike our Beehives in England. They do not make use of Mills To grind their Corn in, but in lieu thereof use a Mortar made out of the Stock of a Tree which they cut and burn hollow and then Pound their Corn thérein, and when its pounded sufficiently they seperate the husks from the Meal by sifting it thro' a Sieve made of Reeds or Canes. The Chief Business of the Women is Planting Corn and other things and minding the Business of the House, The Men Hunt and Kill Deer, Turkeys, Geese, Buffaloes, Tygers, Bears, Panthers, Wolves and several other Beasts whose Skins they sell to the Traders for Powder Ball and what other Necessaries they want. *August the 12th.* We set out from this Town which belonged to the Couettaus [1] to go to a Town of the Causettasu [2]; As we drew near the Town the King came with English Colours in his Hand attended by his Chief Men, We saluted them and they returned the Salute; The King and his Chief Men conducted the General to their Square where he dined and after Dinner the General went to Captain Wiggins House where he lay that Night. *August the 17th.* The Indians went into the Square to Dance and some of the English Danced with them which pleased them very well. *August the 21st.* His Excellency General Oglethorpe went to the Square to give the Indians the Presents he had Caused to be brought for them, and to Establish that Peace with them which has since been so Beneficial to the English; He also settled the Trade between the Indians and the Traders. *August the*

[1] Kawita, a Lower Creek town on the Chattahoochee River in Russell County, Alabama.

[2] Kashita, a Lower Creek town on the Chattahoochee River, two or three miles below Kawita.

25th. The General set out from the Indian Nations on his Way home. *Septr. 12th.* The General arrived at ffort Augusta,[1] the Fort saluted the General with nine Guns, the General staid at the Captn of the Forts House. *Septr. 6th.* Several of the Cherokee Indians came to the General who Received them with all Tenderness. *Septr. 8th.* The General went to the Carolina Fort which saluted him with 15 Guns, at Night came down the Cherokee Indians and Saluted the Fort which Returned them 9 Guns. *Septr. 10th.* The Cherokee's came to settle a Peace with the General. *Septr. the 13th.* This day arrived advices to the General of a Declaration of War with Spain, at noon the General gave the Cherokee Indians their Presents they took their leave of him and returned very well Satisfied. *Septr. 16th.* The General set out from Fort Augusta and about Seven or Eight Miles from thence we stoped at a Fort belonging to Carolina which saluted the General with 15 Guns, the General staid and Dined there, this Fort is situate on a Hill and Commands two rivers; near the Fort are about one hundred Houses.[2] *Septr. 17th.* We set out from this Fort and as we were going down the River we met a Trading Boat going to Fort Augusta, the People on board her told us the Negroes in Carolina had raised up in Arms and killed about forty White People. We went to the Uchee Town and from thence to Fort Prince George [3] where we found thirty men come from Purysburg [4] to Strengthen the Fort. *Septr. 20th.* A Negroe came to the General and told him that what was said of the Negroes Rising in Carolinia was True and that they had marched to Stono Bridge where they had Murthered two Storekeepers Cut their Heads off and Set them on the Stairs Robbed the stores of what they wanted and went on

[1] Fort Augusta was on the site of the present city of Augusta, Georgia, and was at this time primarily an Indian trading post.

[2] This was Fort Moore, on the east bank of the Savannah, six miles below Fort Augusta.

[3] Palachocolas Fort, about sixty-four miles above Savannah.

[4] A Swiss settlement in South Carolina, twenty-two miles above Savannah.

killing what Men, Women and Children they met, Burning of Houses and Committing other Outrages, and that One hundred Planters who had assembled themselves together pursued them and found them in an open Field where they were Dancing being most of them drunk with the Liquors they found in the Stores, As soon as they saw their Masters they all made off as fast as they Could to a Thicket of Woods excepting One Negroe fellow who came up to his Master his Master asked him if he wanted to kill him the Negroe answered he did at the same time Snapping a Pistoll at him but it mist fire and his Master shot him thro' the Head about fifty of these Villains attempted to go home but were taken by the Planters who Cutt off their heads and set them up at every Mile Post they came to.[1] *Septr. 23d.* The General set out for Savannah and arrived *the 24th. Octor. 5th.* Tomo Cha Chi Mico or King of Yamacrau died greatly Lamented by all his People.[2] *Octor. 6th.* He was buried in the Square facing the Church at Savannah. *Novr. 5th.* The General set out for Frederica and arrived *the 8th.* Thus ended our Profitable Voyage to the Indian Nations which has been attended with the Success desired, the Friendly Indians annoying the Spaniards very much taking them Prisoners under the very Walls of the Castle of St. Augustine and Especially At the late Invasion when the Spaniards advanced within a Mile of Frederica where they signalized their Bravery and the Love they bore to the English even facing Danger itself by taking and killing every Spaniard they Came near, besides many other Fatigues and Dangers they underwent which will appear in the Sequel of this Story.

After our arrival at Frederica[3] on *the 14th of November*

[1] This was the Stono Slave Insurrection in which about sixty lives were lost.

[2] Tomo-chi-chi was chief of the Yamacraw Indians whose habitat was on the banks of the Savannah in the vicinity of Savannah.

[3] Frederica was a fortified settlement on Saint Simon's Island at the mouth of the Altamaha. It was founded by Oglethorpe in 1736 as a bulwark against the Spaniards.

advices came to the General that the Spaniards had been upon the Island of Amelia and had killed two of the Trustees'[1] Servts and Cut of their Heads, but was so terrified for fear of the English coming upon them that they Ran away leaving a Hatchet and Knife behind them. *Novr. 17th.* His Excellency General Oglethorpe being designed for the Island of Amelia ordered me to attend him which I accordingly did. We arrived at Amelia about Eleven at Night. Early next morning the General gave orders to surround the Island by Water and he himself would march through the Body of the Island with the Men divided into Small parties wch He accordingly did and Continued so doing till Night but could discover nothing but their Tracts and one of their War Sticks which they had droped in Haste. About Ten at Night the General set out for Frederica and having a fine Gale of Wind arrived at Six next Morning *Novr. 23d* Helaspelle and Tooanahowi (Nephew to Tomo Cha Chi aforementioned) with Several other Indians Set out for St. Augustine vowing to have Revenge for the two Men killed on Amelia. *Novr. 27th.* The Spaniards came a Second time on the Island of Amelia and fired at the very Centinels, the Friendly Indians were then there, but they were so Numerous the Indians Durst not attack them.

December the 3d. His Excellcy General Oglethorpe set out for the Spanish Look out to observe the motions of the Spaniards and see what preparations they were making, taking a body of two hundred men with him; but they discovered us before they could Land and fled to Augustine leaving us the House built for a Look out. We marched along the Beach and came within 25 Miles of the Town of St. Augustine, where we discovered a Party of Don Pedro's[2] Horse with some Indians and Negroes but as soon as they saw us they made the Utmost speed to the Town of St. Augustine and our Indians pursued them till they came to

[1] Georgia was founded as a proprietary province, and its proprietors constituted a board of trustees.

[2] Don Diego Spinola, who was commander of Fort Diego, Florida.

Diego Fort,[1] in the Pursuit they killed one Negroe as he was going into Diego Fort and brought his Scalp to the Genl. Who rewarded them very well. Afterwards we went to Frederica where we remained till *the first January* [when] The General Set out with a Body of 180 Men. We arrived at Talbot Island *Janry 3d* and went from thence to St. George's [2] from whence we saw a Sloop off of the Spanish Look out on St. Juan's Beach, the General endeavour'd to get to her in his Cutter but the Wind blew so fresh it obliged us to return back. The General went to the Spanish Look out and Set me and two more on shore there with orders to make a Fire, that the Sloop might see the Mouth of the River, soon after the General came and took us with him to St. Georges. *Janry 5th.* The Sloop came over St. Juans Bar and Anchored in the River and the Capt. came ashore and offered his Service to the General to assist him taking the two Forts up the River which the General accepted of. *Janry the 6th.* The Sloop and Boats came to sail having a fair Wind and went up the River St. Juan about four in the afternoon we Landed on a Point of Land distant about five Miles from the Fort San Francisco de Pupo.[3] The Indians went out on discovery but could see nobody so we set forward again and Came to an Anchor close under a Point of Land near the two Forts, here we landed the Indians on the south side of the River to way lay the Path to St. Augustine and to bring Intelligence of what Discoveries they should make, here we lay all night. Early next morning the General went in his Boat to See if he could meet with any of our Indians he soon met with one of them who told him all was Quiet and that we were not discovered and that his Comrades had way

[1] Fort Diego was on a rise of ground known as Diego Plains, about five miles from the east bank of the St. Johns River and twenty-five miles west by north of St. Augustine.

[2] This was Fort St. George which Oglethorpe had built at the mouth of the St. Johns. Opposite it was the Spanish outpost, or look-out of St. John.

[3] Fort San Francisco de Pupo, or St. Francis, was on the west bank of the St. Johns River, about eighteen miles west by north of St. Augustine.

layed the Path to St. Augustine, hereupon the General returned to the Sloop and Boats and ordered them to weigh
their Anchors and stand for the Forts which they did and on
our way we met some of our Indians in a Canoe who told
us the Spaniards at Picolato Fort [1] had discovered us and
were fled and our Indians had set fire to their Fort. The
Spaniards at San Francisco de Pupo seeing some of our
Indians took them for Spanish Indians and man'd a Launch
in order to Fetch them over and when they had got about
half way over the River they discovered our Boats and Returned for their Fort in greater Hast than they set out.
The General ordered the Men and Cannon to be Landed
under Shelter of a Point of Woods wch was within a Mile of
the Fort. As Soon as we had Landed we marched in the
Woods till we Came within Musquet Shot of the Fort where
we raised a Battery for our Cannon in the mean time keeping
them employed with our Small Arms, the firing Continued
very hot on both sides 'till such time we had finished our
Battery from Which we began to play upon the Fort, the
Fire from the Fort seeming to abate the General sent a
Drum to Summon them to Surrender the Fort to the English
which if they did they should have good Quarters, their
Answer was "take us if you can." Whereupon our Cannon
began to Play a second time upon the Fort very briskly and
every Shot taking Place soon obliged them to alter their
Tone and Cry for Quarters, which upon their surrendering
up the Fort was imediately granted. In this Fort was one
Serjt. and a Command of Ten men with one Indian, 7 Peices
of Cannon Ammunition Provision and several other Stores.
Janry the 8th. The General gave orders for repairing this
Fort raising Parapets and Pallisading it all Round, We also
mounted three more Cannon besides the Seven Peices which
were in the Fort before, also leaving a Detachment of 50
Men with Ammunition and Provision. *Janry 9th.* The
General ordered a Detachment of 30 Men of the Regiment
and a Party of Indians to go on the other side of the River and

[1] Fort Picolata was on the east bank of the St. Johns, a little
below Fort San Francisco de Pupo.

see if they could discover any Spaniards, they accordingly went and Discovered a Party of Spanish horse being about 20 or 30 in Number who as soon as they saw the English approach fled. Our Indians pursued but could not come up with any of them. *Janry 11th.* The General set out for St. Simons Island and on his Passage rec[eiv]ed advice that his Majesty's Ship the Flamborough was arrived in Jekyll Sound and that seven more ships of War were on their Passage to assist at the Siege of St. Augustine. *Janry the 17th.* The General arrived at St. Simons and *the 19th* got to Frederica. *January the 28th.* Came a Boat from San Francisco de Pupo with advice that the Detachment of the Regiment had taken three Spaniards with Letters from St. Mark's to St. Augustine.

May the 3d. The General set out for the siege of St. Augustine with a Body of 600 Men also giving me orders to attend him. We [had] also 150 Indians of Different Nations the Main Body of them being to follow us as Soon as possible with provisions and other Stores. *May the 8th.* At night we landed at the Spanish Look-out on the Florida side of St. Juan's River [and] here we lay very quiet 'till about four o' th' Clock the next morning, then we sent out a party of about 50 Indians on the Scout who returned at night with a Spanish Negroe who they had taken Prisoner they also pursued six other Spaniards as far as the Fort from which the Spaniards fired several Cannon shot at them but did no Execution, this day arrived two sloops and four Schooners from Charlestown with provisions and men for the Siege. *May the 10th.* The men being landed we proceeded in order To attack a Fort about twenty three Miles distance from St. Augustine. *May the 11th.* We came within shot of the Fort Diego which began to fire at us but did us no hurt. *May 12th.* We attacked the Fort wth a very hot Fire on the South side they also Continued a brisk fire of their Cannon at us, about 12 o' th' Clock we summoned the Garrison to Surrender the Fort and they should have good Quarters to which they Consented and Delivered the Fort up in which we found 13 Peices of Cannon with Small Arms Ammunition and Provisions also a

Garrison of 48 Men likewise Horses and abundance of Cattle which we drove up and killed for the Use of the Army. The Indians also took one of Don Pedro's Horsemen who was going Express to St. Augustine. The English and Indians so harrassed the Spaniards that they were afraid to appear without the Walls of St. Augustine. *May the 13th.* We marcht to St. Juan's River where we found Colonel Vanderdusen [1] and part of the Carolina Regiment also Lieutt. Colonel Cook from St. Simons. *May the 18th.* The General came from Diego he had marcht within two Miles of St. Augustine where were a party of Spaniards being about 400 Men and a Troop of Horse drawn up in a Line Just before the Town but when they discovered the English they imediately fled into the Town leaving several Horses which we took. *June the 5th.* The General went with a Body of 800 Men along the Sea Beach to See if the Spaniards would venture out and hazard a Battle. He marched as far as Moosa a Small Fort about $2\frac{1}{2}$ Mile Distant from St. Augustine and found it Deserted by the Spaniards who on their discovering our Troops fled to St. Augustine. We displayed Six Stand of English Colours on the Ramparts to try if we could Provoke the Spaniards to come out and give us Battle but all would not do, so we set Fire to the Fort and returned to Diego, struck the Tents and put them on board the Vessels in order to go to St. Augustine Barr. *June the 11th.* Came up with the Men of War who lay off The Barr of St. Augustine to assist at the Siege. *June the 12th.* The General landed on the Island of St. Eustatia over against the Castle of St. Augustine [and] the Captains of the Men of War landed 400 Men at the same time, a Party of our Indians came up with a party of Spanish Horsemen and killed four. *June 13th.* Capt. Warren went on board a Large Schooner to go over Augustine Barr and ordered the Faulcon Sloop and another Sloop to follow him, when they came to the Bar there was not Water Enough for the Schooner to go over so he was

[1] Alexander Vander Dussen, colonel of the regiment which South Carolina had sent to assist Oglethorpe in his operations against St. Augustine.

obliged to stay till next morning but the Faulcon Sloop got in over the Bar that night, the same day we took a Fort near the Castle and hoised our Colours there. *June 14th.* The Schooner got over the Bar and anchored under the side of a Hill within a mile of the Castle from whence they fired very smartly at us but none of their Balls took Place, the next day I went on shore on the Island of St. Eustatia where I was taken sick and Continued so during the whole time of the Siege afterwards, and at the breaking up of the Siege was sent sick to Frederica. Thus far and to this time I was Constantly with his Excellency General Oglethorpe, being in most or all the Places of Action 'till the day of my being taken Sick.

August 15th, 1741. General Oglethorpe preparing to Cruize on the Spanish Privateers that sculk'd along shore from Saint Augustine ordered me to attend him. He set out on board the St. Philip Guard Sloop, the Schooner Norfolk and Sloop Faulcon in Company and about 200 Men on board. *August the 17th.* We went over St. Simons Bar and *the 19th* parted Company with the Sloop Falcon she having sprung her Boltsprit. *August the 21st.* We discovered two Vessels at Anchor off the Bar of St. Augustine it being quite Calm we got out our Boat And towed towards them and the Wind freshning We came up with them apace and soon perceived that one was the Spanish Privateer Sloop of Saint Augustine and the other an English Ship that was her prize. We concluded to let the St. Philip sloop bear down upon the Spanish Privateer give her a Broadside and board her and that the Schooner Norfolk should do the like ; as soon as we came pretty well towards them the Spanish Sloop gave us a broadside which we returned and the Schooner did the like, as to the Ship she had a Launch full of Men ahead towing her over the Bar, and the Sloop after two or three broadsides slipt her Cable and ran over the Bar after the Ship, our Sloop during the Action having got pretty well in with the Bar, the Water was So Shallow we was obliged to wear her for fear of getting amongst the Breakers which broke very high, giving the Spanish Sloop several broadsides as we went and a Volley of Small Arms. Several Spanish Galleys which lay within the Bar fired very hotly at us but they were so far within the Harbour their Shot all fell short of us, night coming on we stood to the southward but it falling Calm we came to an Anchor and in the Morning went off the Bar again and lay too for the Spanish Sloop and Galleys to come out but they chose to lay snugg in their Harbour rather than run the Hazard of a Battle. We then tackt and stood for the Matanzas Bar but could discover nothing there So Stood to the Northward. *Augt. 24th.* The Schooner Norfolk sprung her Mainmast and we sent our Carpenter on board her and by 12 o' th' Clock made her fit for sailing. *Augt. 25th.* We made St. Simons Bar and having a fair wind got in at night and the General went to Frederica.

December 14th 1741. His Excellency General Oglethorpe preparing for another Cruize on the Spaniards I also was ordered with him, he set out on board the Guard Schooner Walker having 130 Men on board and the Guard Sloop St. Philips having the like number of Men on board, the same time set out a party of the Couettau Indians (being 40 in Number) to war against the Spaniards. This Cruize we not only thought of annoying the Spanish Privateers but also to destroy a new Fort they were building at the Matanzas. *Decr. 15th.* We went over the Bar of St. Simons and stood to the Southward. *Decr. 16th.* The Guard Schooner sprung her Main mast which obliged us to put into St. Simons, the General went on board the Guard sloop St. Phillip and said he would go to the Matanzas Ordering the Captain of the Schooner to make what Dispatch he could after him. *Decr. 19th.* The Schooner being refitted we saild over the Bar of St. Simons and *the 20th* about noon having a fine Breeze of Wind came off of the Bar of St. Augustine and had sight of the Castle which fired two Guns and we answered them with two false fires. We saw several vessels in the Harbour and two half Galleys seemed to stand for us but did not dare venture too far not even so far as the Bar. So we stood for the Bar of the Matanzas hoping to meet with the Guard Sloop St. Phillip but could see nothing of her, in the night we stood to the Northward as farr as St. Juan's River when the Wind began to freshen and blew so hard it obliged us to stand for the Offing and keep as much to Seaward as we could. The Wind Still continued to Freshen 'till at last it blew a meer storm. We having two six pounders in the head of the Schooner and she being something by the Head before, it caused her to pitch very much being Sometimes under water and strained her very hard which obliged us to throw the two Six pounders overboard. At Midnight the storm encreased to such a Degree that she would not lye too, when a Sea came in to Windward upon her Deck in such a manner that she taking a Lee roll having her Guns to Leeward laid her under Water as far as the Combings of her Hatchway and had not the men been very Brisk in heaving the Leeward Guns overboard I beleive we should never have righted her, our Boltsprit being gone by the Board, our Mainsail split and foresail all gone to peices also the fore Shrouds, but after the Guns Chests etca. were over board the Vessell righted to the unspeakable Joy of every one on board. It is most Certain we could not have Remained in the Posture we were without the Vessels sinking very soon, she leaking very much and the Pumps both stopped with Sand with which she was Ballast, here we lay at the Mercy of the Wind and Sea till *the 23d* at night, our Anchor which was [1] threw overboard (after our Boltsprit was Carried away) brought us up and we reckoned ourselves on Cape Canoveral shoals about two o' th' Clock in the Morning we stood for the offing. *The 26th* We had an Observation and found ourselves 36 Miles to the Southward of St. Simons Bar. *Decr. 28th.* We saw a Sail to the So[uth]ward of us there being little wind we came to Sail and sent our Boat ahead to discover what she was, they found her to be a New York Sloop bound for Frederica, the Wind springing up in the Evening We and the New York Sloop went into Jekyll Sound. *Decr. 29th.* The Guard Sloop St. Philip arrived having the General on board and a ship from Bristol in Company which they found

[1] We.

in Distress at Sea and after having releived her Convoyed her into this Port to the great Joy of everybody on board her who expected every Moment to be lost or to fall into the Hands of the Enemy.

May the 29th, 1742. Came Intelligence to his Excellency General Oglethorpe from the Rangers Camp at the White Post on the Main, that Lieutt Scroggs had discovered some Spanish Indians. Whereupon the General ordered me over (with two Horses to assist) that if Possible we could come up with any of them and take them. We accordingly went out and one of our men discovered a Spanish Indian sitting upon a Stump whereupon he fired at him and wounded him but the Indian made his Escape from him. We continued Scouting about for him Several days but could discover none of them, we found several of the places where they had Camped, and where they had pulled the Palmettoes up by the Roots to eat, but they finding themselves discovered had taken the Rout to St. Augustine without being able to Carry any prisoners or Intelligence.

June 22d, 1742. Intelligence came to his Excellency General Oglethorpe that several Sail of Spanish Vessels were seen off Fort William [1] and Cumberland the former of which Places they had attempted but were repulsed by the Guard Schooner Walker, The General imediately upon receiving these advices mounted his Horse and rode to St. Simons. *June 24th.* The Spanish Galleys being off of Cumberland Island The General went on board his Cutter taking me with him and ordered me to take my Bridle Saddle etca. with me, we went to the South End of Jekyll Island the General ordered a Detachment of the Regiment to go on board one of the Scout boats and follow him, there was another Scout Boat having a Detachment of the Regiment on board in Company. We were in all three Boats, the Genl. stood over the sound for Cumberland, when the Spanish Fleet (being 13 Sail) saw our three Boats going across the Sound, they

---

[1] Fort William was at the south end of Cumberland Island, where it commanded the entrance to St. Marys River.

stood for us and having the Wind and a strong Tide with them soon came so near us that a Smart Engagement ensued, We fired very hotly at them and they at us. The Scout Boat where Lieutent Sterling and Ens[ig]n Chamberlain was kept up with us and fired very hotly at the Spaniards. The other Scout Boat with Lieutt. Tolson on board and a Detachment of the Regiment went off and made her Escape up the River in the Main. The General and the other Boats fought Their way through the Spaniards and got to St. Andrews [1] from whence he drew off the Garrison Stores etca. and reinforced Fort William. *June the 25th.* The General went on board the Guard Schooner Walker and returned to St. Simons to the great Joy of all the People who imagined he was Cut off. I continued here with the other Rangers Scouting along St. Simons beach watching the Motions of the Spaniards, when I and two of Captain Jones's Rangers had orders to Swim over the fourth Creek and make a Fire at the fifth Creek (in attempting which one Burns had been drowned two Days before) We accordingly striped ourselves leaving our Horses with the Party of Rangers who were to secure our Retreat. We swam over the fourth Creek taking our Arms with us and made a Fire at the fifth Creek according to our orders and returned, the Spanish Fleet lying then close under the Shore and the place where we made the Fire being within Shot of them. *July the 5th.* The Spanish fleet having a Fair and fresh Gale of Wind with a strong Tide of Flood under foot came into the Harbour, as they came in one after another I sat on my horse up to the Saddle in Water and kept loading and firing my Peice at them, when I was ordered with another Ranger having some Indians with us to go into the wood right agst where the Spanish Fleet came to an Anchor and Shew ourselves and bring an Account if they Attempted to Land. As soon as they discovered us the Galleys fired several of their nine pounders at us. I continued going to and fro along the Beach observing their Motions till Eleven o' th' Clock at night, then I was ordered

[1] Fort St. Andrews, on the northeast coast of Cumberland Island.

to follow the General up to the Battery where his Excellency and Captain Carr stood 'till the Great Guns and Mortars were Naild or Burst. The Regiment having marcht to Frederica to Secure that place the Spanish Fleet being at the Mouth of that River and Seem'd as if they designed to attack Frederica by Water. About 12 o' th' Clock the General ordered the Union Flag which was at the Battery to be struck I having the honour of bringing it to Frederica. As I was coming up I found a sick man upon the Road whom I took upon my horse and brought safe to Town. *July the 7th.* Five Rangers were ordered out upon the Scout to discover what Motions the Enemy were making and bring what horses they could meet with to Town, and William Small, Ranger of Capt. Jones's Troop, was Shot through the Leg and thigh and his horse killed under him. The 'other four Returned with this Intelligence to the General, his Excellency imediately mounted his Horse followed by the Rangers Highland Company and Indians, his timely presence and Care gave us all such Courage and Activity that we killed Chased and put to flight this Body of Spaniards and Yamasee Indians. I was close by the General when he took Salvador Roman, a Spanish Grenadier, Prisoner. In our pursuit Lieutt. Robt. Scroggs of the Troop of English Rangers took Prisoner Captain Sebastian Sanchez for which and other Services he is since made Captain of the said Troop. We pursued the Spaniards half way down to St. Simons where we were ordered to halt, soon after came up to our Assistance 1 Captain 2 Lieutenants and 2 Ensigns with a Detachment of the Regiment, His Excellency posting the Detachment of the Regiment on one side of the Road and the Highland Company and Rangers on the other side with a Savannah or Meadow in the Front of them that they might be ready to give the Onset to the Spaniards if they should attempt to march towards Frederica again.

The Spaniards hearing of the Fate their first Party met with sent out another of 300 Men under the Command of Don Antonio Barbara Captain of a Company of Grenadiers; about three o' th' Clock in the afternoon the Spaniards advanced up to the Place where we were Posted and some of them being Come within our Lines a Sharp Fire continued on all hands and betwixt both parties for some time. The Spaniards fell in great Numbers amongst which was Several Officers and also that Famous Captain of Grenadiers; the Number of the Spaniards was so great and their Fire so brisk, that some Platoons of ours gave way and were Retiring in Confusion but the timely presence of the General prevented their Retiring far. He imediately ordered them to Rally, riding himself up to the Place where he found Lieutt Sutherland and Lieutt Charles Mackay with the Highlanders and Rangers had Entirely defeated the Spaniards. We lost not one Man in the two Attacks but one Mr. Maclane a Highland Gentleman who running very hard in pursuit of the Enemy spoiled the Circulation of his Blood and died Soon after he was brought to Town. The Spaniards after this never ventured out beyond their out Centinels who were also Fortified. I having been often out by order observing their Motions and within Musquet shot of them, The Rangers and Indians were always so near them that nine Spaniards were shot in their Camp as they were Eating. *July 15th.* The Spaniards in great Confusion Quit St. Simons and go on board their Vessels and some go to Sea and Some within Land to St. Andrews. The General followed them and Landed a Man on Cumberland Island with a Letter for the Commanding Officer at Fort William in sight of fourteen Sail of Vessels belonging to the Spanish Fleet who lay in the Sound at the Same time. The man got Safe to Fort William and told them the Spaniards were drove off of St. Simons Island which put new Life as it were into the People.

The General having received advices by Captn Gibson Commander of the Beauford Galley that there was ten sail of Spanish Vessels in St. Juans River [on] *July the 18th* he set out in his Cutter for the said River to Discover what strength they were of, also ordering me to attend him. We arrived in St. Juans River and Landed on the Florida side, here we found a Camp the Enemy had made and Several huts and houses of Palmetto also two Cedar Crosses. His

Excellency dined in one of the Houses then burnt their Camp and Carried the Crosses with him to Fort William. *July the 24th.* The General went out of Amelia Inlet in the Guard Schooner Walker and Joyned Capt. Francklyn in his Majestys Ship the Rose and the other Men of War and Vessells fitted out by Carolina and Georgia. [As] we Cruized off of the Bar of St. Augustine [and] the half Galleys appeared within the Bar, Capt. Hardy [1] had orders from the Commadore to attack them with the Small Craft but not to go over the Bar. With him the General went in one of his own Scout Boats a Voluntier. I also went in the Same Boat. We had one Man killed and two Wounded and the Boats Boom carried away by one of their nine pounders. Some of the Spanish half Galleys were disabled. The General was very desirous to go over the Barr but Captain Hardy had positive orders to the Contrary, and night Coming on which obliged us to Return to the Fleet. The next day the Fleet sailed for the Matanzas. The General went in his Boat to sound the Bar, in order to destroy a new Fort the Spaniards have began there and is not yet finished. The Swell was so great it was impossible to Land them. We found $3\frac{1}{2}$ fathom Water within less than Cannon Shot of the Fort. We returned to the Fleet hoping they would have Landed as soon as the swell was Fallen. The Sky looked very wild and seemed to threaten a hard Gale therefore Capt. Francklyn acquainted the General it was necessary to go off the Coast and Disperse the Fleet which was accordingly Done, Capt. Franklyn and the Carolina Fleet going to Charles Town, Capt. Hardy Continued cruizeing, Capt. Hamar conducted the Genl. and Georgia Craft off of the Bar where we arrived *the 4th September.*

[1] Charles Hardy, commander of the South Carolina fleet.

JOURNAL OF ANTOINE BONNEFOY, 1741-1742

INTRODUCTION

ANTOINE BONNEFOY seems to have left no other record of himself than this *Journal*, and interest in this centers in the Cherokee treatment of him as a prisoner and in his "Pierre Albert" who was instrumental in enabling him to escape. Since Colonel Chicken's visit in 1726 the English traders from Charleston had carried to the Cherokees the germs of smallpox, which in 1738 proved fatal to nearly one half their number. They complained that they had been poisoned, and some of their towns began dealing with the French. Oglethorpe met a delegation of them at Augusta in September, 1739, on his return from the Creek assembly at Kawita, and in a measure healed the breach.

The French, however, were no less active than the English. In 1736 they engaged Christian Priber, a German Jesuit, to alienate the Cherokees from the English. Priber, a man of culture who spoke Latin, French, Spanish, German, and English, took up his residence at Tellico, donned Cherokee dress, adopted the Cherokee manner of living, learned to speak their language, rendered himself generally useful, and won confidence and esteem. When thus strongly intrenched, he began to inspire hatred of the English and love of the French. He brought about the coronation of a Cherokee chief as king of the "Cherokee Confederacy," secured for himself the office of royal secretary, and projected the establishment of an unbridled communistic society at Kashita, in the Creek country. Learning of his activities, the authorities of South Carolina demanded his surrender, but the Cherokees refused to give him up. In 1743, however, while he was passing through the Upper Creek country on his way to Mobile, he was captured by some traders and taken to Frederica, Georgia, where he died after a brief confinement in the barracks. Priber was none other than Bonnefoy's "Pierre Albert" who was sorry for the French prisoners, who spoke English and French "quite fluently," who "wrote German, Latin, English, and French with equal correctness," who was wanted by the Governor of Carolina, and for whose communistic project the prisoners "agreed to feign enthusiasm" as a means of promoting their plan of escape.

A manuscript copy of Bonnefoy's journal (French) is in the Archives Nationales, Paris : Colonies F. 3 : 24, ff. 361–371. The translation which is here printed is by Dr. J. Franklin Jameson.

JOURNAL OF ANTOINE BONNEFOY, 1741-1742

Journal of Antoine Bonnefoy, containing the circumstances of his captivity among the Cherokee Indians, from his departure from New Orleans in August, 1741, in the pirogue of the Sieur Chauvin dit Joyeuse, of whom he was an engagé, till his arrival among the Allibamous.

THE convoy destined for the Illinois, composed of three bateaux and . . . pirogues, of the year 1741, was commanded by the Sieur De Villers, officer. The enrolment, including officers and traders, of this convoy was of 28 men in each bateau and eight or nine in each of the pirogues. This convoy set out from New Orleans *the 22d of August 1741.* The pirogue in which I was, followed the convoy till within sight of the River Ouabache,[1] where we arrived *the 14th of November*, at evening, and passed the night at that place.

On the 15th the convoy set out again as usual at daybreak, and our boat went in its usual order till seven o'clock, when the commander caused the bateaux to cross the river and signalled to follow him. The Sieur Marin, voyageur, whose pirogue was in front of us, asked Legras (the Sieur Joyeuse having been sent from the Arkansas to the Illinois by land had given the command of this boat to one Legras) if he was not in favor of continuing on our course without crossing the river. Unwisely, being agreed, we continued on our route in company. An hour after having left the bateaux, we perceived at the entrance to a little bayou, a

[1] By interchange of names, the Ouabache (Wabash) River appears on maps of this period as a tributary of the Mississippi, namely the Ohio, while the name Ohio River is given to its tributary, the Wabash.

quarter of a league from the mouth of the Wabash, a number of pirogues tied to the shore. We examined their appearance and took them for Illinois and Missouris. The savages from these pirogues, who were on the land and of whom we did not perceive a single one, had disembarked 20 fathoms above their boats. The pirogue of the Sieur Marin, which we had formerly followed, was at this time behind ours. There were eight men of us in each. Under these circumstances, and under the impression that the savages were Illinois or Missouris, we came around the bayou and the boats, up to the place of ambush, where a first discharge of muskets from the savages instantly killed our skipper and two of our oarsmen, and wounded two men in the other boat, which, being behind, had time to make off and was saved. The savages directed so heavy a fire upon our boat that we were obliged to lie down flat, to escape certain death. Immediately 20 of these savages got into their boats to hasten after the pirogue of the Sieur Marin, who escaped from them.

A moment afterward, these same pirogues came and surrounded us, The shore was lined with the other savages, who were aiming at us. The surprise, and the death of our skipper and of two of our oarsmen, having put us out of condition to defend ourselves, we surrendered at discretion, to the number of four Frenchmen and one negro, and were seized, each by one of the savages, who made him his slave. Brought to the land, we were tied separately, each with a slave's collar around the neck and the arms merely, without however depriving us of freedom to eat and to pergailler when in the sequel we were ordered to do so.

This action took place in sight of the bateaux, which had become distant only to the extent of the breadth of the river. The commander contented himself with hoisting his flag on his bateau, without giving us any aid. We however remained all day in the same place. The savages who had taken possession of us proved to be Cherakis,[1] instead of

---

[1] Cherokees.

Chicachas [1] as we had thought at the time of the firing. The convoy entertained the same opinion, following the information given them at New Orleans.

When we had been bound with these collars the savages, having found in our boat what had been intended for our breakfast, brought it to us to eat, and gave us to understand by signs that no harm should come to us, and that we should be even as themselves. They then unloaded our boat, and distributed the goods equally among the 80 men of the party, with the exception of the iron and three kegs of rum, which they left in the boat, having filled all their kettles and even three barrels in which the powder had been — after having divided up the latter. I observed that these savages were careful not to spoil the goods they could not take away. They passed the day of *the 15th* in packing their merchandise, till night, when they embarked in 22 boats, with two, three, four, or five men in each according to its size. My companions in misfortune, and I, followed our masters, bound in the manner I have described. The party took up its course, paddling without making the least noise, along the River Ouabache [2] till six o'clock the next morning, then rested about two hours, during which time they broiled some meat they had found in our pirogue when we were captured. They gave us (as they always did) a portion equal to theirs, after which they resumed their paddles, and gave us each one, after having made us each drink, as with the first meal, the evening before, a cup of rum. I bathed a wound I had received in the knee, from a musket-shot in that first discharge; after which I was not further troubled by it. It was not so with the negro, whose wounds began from that day to become worse. We embarked again, as I have just said, and continued down the Ouabache [3] to the River of the Cherakis, [4] which leads up to the village of those savages and falls into the former river thirteen leagues from its junction with the River St.

[1] Chickasaws.
[2] Up the Ohio.
[3] Up the Ohio River.
[4] Tennessee River.

Louis or Missipi. When evening had come the savages landed at the mouth of the river, and passed the night there, and made stocks to keep us in safety. In these my three comrades were set, who were: Joseph Rivard, son of the Sieur Rivard of Bayou St. Jean,[1] Pierre Coussot, son of Coussot the pilot at the Belaxy[2] in 1719, Guillaume Potier, half-breed, son of Potier, habitant of the Illinois, and Legras's negro. The savage to whom I belonged did not wish that I should be put in the stocks. The next day we entered into their river, which they did not leave till the third of February, marching and hunting on alternate days, till we were four days by land from their first village.

The 20th of December my savage took off my slave's collar. Rivard and Potier kept theirs a fortnight, and Coussot a month. They were not put in the stocks except the first four days, and then only during the night. At the beginning of January we were adopted by men of prominence in the party. I was adopted as brother by a savage who bought me of my master, which he did by promising him a quantity of merchandise, and giving me what at that time I needed, such as bed-coverings, shirts, and mittens, and from that time I had the same treatment as himself. My companions were adopted by other savages, either as nephews or as cousins, and treated in the same manner by their liberators and all their families.

The same day on which my collar was taken off, the negro, whose wounds had grown worse, was set at liberty, and the head man of the party told him to return to the French, but not knowing where to go, he followed the pirogues for two days. On the third, which was *the 23rd of December*, the savages, tired of seeing him, gave him over to the young people, who killed him and took his scalp.

On January 10 or 11 our party met a troop of savages, Chicachas. They, recognizing each other as friends, negotiated, and made several exchanges of merchandise and

---

[1] A trading post on the Bayou Saint John at the south side of Lake Pontchartrain. [2] Biloxi.

slaves, smoked together, and prepared to continue on their routes as we had begun. In the course of this river, which I estimate as 450 leagues from the Ouabache to the first village of our savages, there are three waterfalls. The first is situated about half way up. The portage is about one-quarter of a league. The second is eight days' journey further up. The portage amounts to a good league. At this place the river is two leagues broad, and rolls its waters like a cascade, a league long, in the shape of a hill, like that of the portage which we were obliged to make. The third, at which we arrived on *the first of February*, has a portage of only about 100 paces. The river at this place is extremely rapid, and generally is so, more and more, from this upper-most fall to the place where we left it, *February 3*, to make the rest of our journey by land. The savage who had adopted me gave me, before setting out upon the march, a gun, some powder, and some bullets. The pirogues having been unloaded, each savage carried, as well as ourselves, his pack of booty. We immediately set out on the march, and on the seventh arrived in sight of the first village, which was called Chateauké and Talekoa,[1] which are two different councils, though the cabins are mingled together indistinguishably. At the first sight of our savages, all the men ran out to the place where we then were, for the ceremony customary among this nation. Our clothes were taken off, and a stock was made for each of us, without, however, putting us in it; they merely put on us our slave's-collar. Then the savages, putting in each one's hand a white stick and a rattle, told us that we must sing, which we did for the space of more than three hours, at different times, singing both French and Indian songs, after which they gave us to eat of all that the women had brought from the village, bread of different sorts, sagamité (corn porridge), buffalo meat, bear meat, rabbit, sweet potatoes, and grau-mons.[2] We passed the night at this place. The next day,

---

[1] Tellico, a Cherokee town on the Tellico River near its junction with the Little Tennessee.　　　　　　　[2] Grapes (?).

February 8, in the morning, the savages having *mataché* themselves according to their custom, *matacherent* our whole bodies, having left us nothing but our breeches, made the entry into their village in the order of a troop of infantry, marching four in each rank, half of them in front of us, who were placed two and two after being tied together, and having our collars dragging. The rest of the savages made the rear guard in the order of the prisoners (?). They made us march in this order, singing, and having, as we had had the evening before, a white stick and a rattle in our hands, to the chief square of the village and march three or four times around a great tree which is in the middle of that place. Then they buried at the foot of the tree a parcel of hair from each one of us, which the savages had preserved for that purpose from the time when they cut our hair off. After this march was finished they brought us into the council-house, where we were each obliged to sing four songs. Then the savages who had adopted us came and took away our collars. I followed my adopted brother who, on entering into his cabin, washed me, then, after he had told me that the way was free before me, I ate with him, and there I remained two months, dressed and treated like himself, without other occupation than to go hunting twice with him. We were absent thirteen days the first time and nine days the last.

At the time when we arrived in the village there were three English traders there, who each had a store-house in the village where I was, and two servants of theirs. There was also a German, who said in French that he was very sorry for the misfortune which had come upon us, but that it would perhaps prove to be our happiness, which he proposed to show us in the sequel.

I also found in the same village a son of André Crespe and also Jean Arlois of Bordeaux, who both had gone up the river in 1740 in the boat of the Sieur Turpin, who was defeated five leagues from the River Ouabache along with the boat of Liberge and Pettit. The party of Cheraké savages which defeated these boats was 70 men. The same party defeated five Canadian voyageurs in the Oua-bache the same year, and killed 25 out of 28, having two men killed and one wounded. The action has been differently related by the three Canadians who escaped. We found also a negro and a negress who formerly belonged to the widow Saussier, and having been sold in 1739 to a Canadian, deserted when on the Ouabache, on their way to Canada, and were captured by a troop of Cheraquis who brought them to the same village where I found them.

February 12, Rivard and Coussot followed, to a village five leagues from that where I lived, the two savages who had ransomed and adopted them. Cussot deserted from there 15 days after, and was lost six days in the woods, into which he had retreated because of a panic he had at the village where he was, and to which he did not return again.

The savage who adopts a captive promises a quantity of merchandise to the one to whom he belongs at the moment when he buys him. This merchandise is collected from all the family of the one who makes the purchase, and is delivered in an assembly of all the relatives, each one of whom brings what he is to give and delivers it, piece by piece, to him who sold the slave, and at the receipt of each piece he makes the rounds of the assembly, constantly carrying what has been given to him, it being forbidden to lay down any piece on the ground, for then it would belong to whoever touched it first. The collection of my ranson was made on *the 9th* and *10th* and the ceremony on *the 11th*.[1]

The 13th, the ceremony of our enfranchisement having been made on the preceding day, I had occasion to ask the German, who was called Pierre Albert, who had accosted us on the day of our arrival, and who was lodging in the cabin of my adopted brother, what he wished me to understand. I prayed him to explain to me what was this alleged happiness which he promised us. Guillaume Potier and Jean Arlut were present. He replied that it would take time to explain to us what he had to say to us, addressing himself

---

[1] This paragraph is written in the margin of the manuscript.

to all three; that he thought we ought to join his society; that he would admit us to an establishment, in France, of a republic, for which he had been working for twenty years; that the form of the government should be that of a general society of those composing it, in which, beyond the fact that legality should be perfectly observed, as well as liberty, each would find what he needed, whether for subsistence, or the other needs of life; that each should contribute to the good of the society, as he could. I told him, as did my two comrades, that we were disposed to join him as soon as he should have shown us some security respecting his establishment.

The next day we got together again and I began to ask him where he had learned French, which he spoke quite fluently. He told me that, being of a good family, he had been instructed in all that a man ought to know; that after having completed his studies, he had learned English and French; that he spoke these two languages with a little difficulty so far as the pronunciation was concerned, but that he wrote German, Latin, English and French with equal correctness; that for twenty years he had been working to put into execution the plan about which he had talked to us; that seven or eight years before he had been obliged to flee from his country, where they wished to arrest him for having desired to put his project into execution; that he had gone over to England, and from there to Carolina, and had also been obliged to depart thence for the same reason, 18 months after having arrived there; that having found among the Cherakis a sure refuge he had been working there for four years upon the establishment which he had been planning for twenty; that the Governor of Carolina having discovered the place of his retreat had sent a commissioner to demand him of the savages there, but that then he was adopted into the nation, and that the savages, rejecting the presents of the English, had refused to give him up; that he had 100 English traders belonging to his society who had just set out for Carolina, whence they were to return the next autumn, after having got together a considerable number of recruits, men and women, of all conditions and occupations, and the things necessary for laying the first foundations of his republic, under the name of the Kingdom of Paradise; that then he would buy us from the savages, of whom a large number were already instructed in the form of his republic and determined to join it; that the nation in general urged him to establish himself upon their lands, but that he was determined to locate himself half way between them and the Alibamons,[1] where the lands appeared to him of better quality than those of the Cherakis, and there he would be disposed to open a trade with the English and French; that in his republic there would be no superiority; that all should be equal there; that he would take the superintendence of it only for the honor of establishing it; that otherwise his condition would not be different from that of the others; that the lodging, furniture and clothing should be equal and uniform as well as the life; that all goods should be held in common, and that each should work according to his talents for the good of the republic; that the women should live there with the same freedom as the men; that there should be no marriage contract, and that they should be free to change husbands every day; that the children who should be born should belong to the republic, and be cared for and instructed in all things that their genius might be capable of acquiring; that the law of nature should be established for the sole law, and that transgressions should be punished by their contrast, as in the case of the *taillon*.[2]

Note. The individual was to have as his only property a chest of books and paper and ink.[3]

My comrades and I planned our flight, and agreed together to feign enthusiasm for the execution of the project of Pierre Albert, who had the confidence of the savages, and they left us at liberty with him. I noticed even, on different occasions, that he urged them to live peaceably

[1] Alibamu, or Alabama Indians.
[2] A feudal tax supplementary to the taille.
[3] This note is in the margin of the manuscript.

and to ask peace from the French. The savage with whom I lived, who was one of the principal men of the nation, and the other chiefs, sometimes asked me in what manner they could appease the French and bring them to their place to trade. I told them that it would be necessary for them to send a calumet of peace to the nearest post; that I supposed that would be the post of the Alibamons.[1] They told me that they had already been there, but that they feared the savages of those regions,[2] with whom they were not on good terms; that they did not wish to have any new war — in this entering into the peaceful spirit of Pierre Albert.

I told them, with regard to the trade into which they wished to bring the French, that our Limbourgs[3] and guns, being better than those of the English, would cost them twice as many furs as they now paid, but at the same time our merchandise was much more durable; that a pound of our powder had twice as much effect as a pound of the English. This they seemed quite to understand. They even had in mind to send a calumet of peace at the time when I escaped.

Note. They know inches and measures and have steel-yards which Pierre has made them.[4]

While Pierre Albert and I were working toward peace the three English traders were daily instigating the savages to continue to make war upon us. They were themselves working to enlist parties; which I saw them doing some days before my flight. After having had their drum beaten by one of their negroes who was a drummer, and enlisted 70 men, they distributed among them, from their store-houses, the munitions necessary for going to the Ouata-mons,[5] as well against the savages as against the voyageurs of Canada. Of the 52 villages which compose the nation

---

[1] Alabama Fort, or Fort Toulouse, at the confluence of the Coosa and Tallapoosa rivers.

[2] Creeks and Choctaws.

[3] Limbourg was a kind of French cloth.

[4] This note is in the margin of the manuscript.

[5] Weas.

of the Cherakis, only the eight which are along the river are our enemies. The other villages remain neutral, either because of their remoteness or their spirit of peace. Carolina is 15 days' journey by land from the village where I was, Virginia 20, and the Alibamonts 10 to the south, reckoning to the first village, Conchasbekas,[1] which is three days' journey from the French Fort Toulouse.

A fortnight after we had arrived among the Cherakis I saw in the village where I was 15 Natchés, four of whom came into our cabin. They told me that they were going hunting among the Chicachas, to seek 15 of their men who were still there; that on their return they were to have a village of 75 men. I asked them if there were still some among the Ouyachitas. They told me that those who had been there were almost all taken captive, but that the rest had rejoined them.

The 29th of April a day on which the savages had given themselves up to a debauch, was that which we chose for our escape. We had got together a sufficient amount of ammunition. We went out from the village at nine o'clock in the evening. Jean Arlas had his gun. Coussot was not armed, not having been able to take his from the cabin where he was. Guillaume Potier, who was in our plot, having got drunk with the savages, was not in condition to go with us, and we could not wait longer for him without risk of being discovered. We marched until daylight, going to find two pirogues that were in a little river six leagues from the village. In one of these we embarked, but were obliged to abandon it after an hour and a half of progress. We found the river barred by a great tree which did not leave enough space to send the boat under it, but on the other hand, was too high, and the boat too heavy, to admit of passing it over, which we made many ineffectual

---

[1] The identity of this place has not been established; but about this time there was in the Upper Creek country — N. by E. of Fort Toulouse — a village named by the French Conchaques, whose inhabitants spoke a dialect almost identical with the Alabamas.

attempts to do. In this extremity we were obliged to take a false course on *the 30th of April* and *1st* and *2nd of May* to the north and northwest, and found ourselves at evening on the banks of the river, which we crossed. We put ourselves ten leagues from the village, and continued our false route in the same direction on *the 3d, 4th* and *5th.* It was now five days that we had fasted, not having dared to shoot. We killed a calf and the next day a cow. We rested on *the 6th* and *7th,* when, after having held a little council on the course we ought to take for our safety, I was determined that we should make our march along the river, where we planned to make a raft to take us to the place where the savages had left their boats when they carried us into slavery. Our plan was to take ourselves to the Illinois by the same route on which they had taken us. We arrived on *the 11th* on the banks of the river, made a raft of canes, upon which we loaded our meat and our ammunition, which we lashed to the raft in the same parcel with Jean Arlas's gun, keeping mine for need. We proceeded seven or eight leagues further north than we had been, had passed the place where the pirogues were, and were surprised to find ourselves at the first waterfall. We struggled to get to the shore, and reached a great tree which was six fathoms from the bank. Our raft fell foul of it. All the forward part sunk about six feet. Arlas and Coussot, who were on the forward part, cast their arms about the tree. Then the raft raised and freed itself, and carried me along without my being able to stop it and passed the fall without breaking up. The current was so great that, though I was near the land, it was impossible for me to stop the raft until a league and a half below, where I expected my comrades would come and find me. I fired several shots to let them know where I was during the three days that I remained there waiting for them, without result. This made me think that they were lost. My gun, my powder horn, and my pouch were lost with my comrades, but I recovered the gun of Arlas with our ammunition, and a little meat upon which I lived for four days. On *the 15th,* not having seen any mark or heard any signal on the part of my comrades, I pushed off, and went down stream for two days and a half. On the third day, which was *the 17th* of the month, I landed on the side of the Alibamons, and took my way southward over a hilly country for nine days and a half. On *the 27th* of May I arrived at the first Alibamon village, Conchabaka, by a beaten path which I encountered on the seventh day of my march, which led me to the end of the river of the Allibamons, on the other side of which is the Indian village, which, however, I could not see. I fired my gun three times at a venture, and the savages replied, firing one. Immediately after I perceived many people on the bank of the stream, several men to whom I signalled to come and bring me over the river. They questioned me much, taking me for an enemy, and fearing that I had come to lay a snare for them and to take from them some scalps, as had happened to them a short time before. I spoke to them in French and in Mobillian, which, after two hours of questions, caused them to make up their minds who I might be and where I came from. One of these savages crossed up above me without my seeing him, and after having discovered me and seen that I was alone and a Frenchman, he took me across to his village. They gave me to eat, which I did with avidity, for I had fasted five days, my gun having failed me at need every time that I had occasion to use it.

After I had eaten, the savage, in whose house I was, took me into the council house. When I was there a council was held respecting me, though I did not know it. All the people of the village having taken their arms surrounded the cabin. The chief of the village was absent, and it was proposed to give me to the English. There were then in that village six Englishmen from Carolina and a detachment of about 15 Chicachas who were there to escort the English to their village. The English and the Chicachas wished to prove to the Conchabekas that it was for their interest to give me up to the English. The greater part of the village were of that opinion, but he who brought me over opposed it in such way that he prevailed, saying that I belonged to him; that none of them had been brave enough to go and seek me when I called them; he would dispose of me, and would take me, as I had requested him, to the chief of the French among the Alibamons, whose friend he wished to be. During the time that I was in the council-house, the English came and gave me their hands, inquiring in the Chicachas language respecting my adventures, and how I had been able to come where I was. I told them in the Mobilian language, which they understood, that having been taken by the Cherakis in December, I had escaped from their villages a month before, and that I had been compelled, after having lost my two comrades, who had escaped with me, to take my flight in the direction of the Alibamons, being no longer in a state to proceed to the Illinois, as had been our first plan. They took me to their store-houses, where they gave me to eat, and wished to engage me to follow them to Carolina, which I refused to do, and returned to the cabin of my savage. Then the 15 Chicachas came to see me, and asked me the same questions as the English had just asked. They then asked why the French did not give them peace, saying that the Chactas [1] vexed them continually. To all this I replied that they ought not to expect peace until they had driven the English from their villages; that moreover it could not be true that they wished peace, since they struck at us every day. They assured me that with the exception of a party of young people, which had acted contrary to the consent of the nation, the last year at Pointe Coupée,[2] they were a people who had struck no blow; that I could see clearly that those which had been ascribed to them had been inflicted by the Cherakis. I told them that in that case it would be necessary to make known to the Great French Chief the dispositions which they wished me to understand that their nation entertained: First, by driving out all Englishmen,

[1] Choctaws.
[2] A French settlement on the lower Mississippi.

and secondly by settling the Natchéz in the environs of the Rivière à Margot upon the Missisipy, and breaking forever with the English, because as long as they received them they would engage the Indians always in some enterprise against us. To this they agreed. I smoked with them the same day, and the next, which was *the 28th of May.*

The 29th, in the morning, I set out upon the march, escorted by two savages, to go to the post of the French, where I arrived on *the first of June,* which was the last day of my captivity. Monsieur Derneville, captain, commanded at this post, who, though I had served under him not long before my journey, did not recognize me until after I had been named to him, so much was I disfigured.

He gave a present to the savages who had served me so well, and I told him the adventures of my journey, as stated in the present journal.

JOURNAL OF DE BEAUCHAMPS' JOURNEY TO THE CHOCTAWS, 1746

INTRODUCTION

THE Choctaw Indians in De Beauchamps' time occupied most of the territory from the Tombigbee River westward to the Mississippi and on account of their number, upwards of ten thousand, were among the most powerful of the southern tribes. A number of them having been sold into slavery by the South Carolinians, they were, immediately after the founding of Mobile, in 1702, easily persuaded to abandon the English and ally themselves with the French. They continued united in their adherence to the French until 1735 when, at the "pressing engagement of a prime magistrate" of South Carolina, James Adair of Charleston undertook to open a trade with them. Adair at that time was near the beginning of his forty years of experience as a trader among the southern red men, from which he wrote *The History of the American Indians*. He gained an audience with Red Shoe, a Machiavellian chief, at an opportune moment of his resentment toward an offending Frenchman, satisfied him that whisky and ammunition could be had from the English at lower prices than from the French, and from that day until the end of the French-English conflict in America the Choctaws were divided into English and French factions.

In March, 1746, while the French party were gone to Mobile to receive their presents, Red Shoe was busy attempting to bring about peace between the Choctaws and the Chickasaws, who were adherents of the English. The chiefs of the French party returning in time to defeat his efforts, Red Shoe, in a fit of anger, ordered the assassination of Chevalier de Verbois and two other Frenchmen, and it was for the purpose of exacting satisfaction for this act that

De Beauchamps undertook the mission of which the journal here printed is an account.

Little is known of De Beauchamps except what may be learned from his journal. A manuscript copy of this is in the Archives Nationales, Paris: Colonies F 3 : 24, ff. 422–445. The translation from the French which is here printed is by Mr. Waldo Gifford Leland.

JOURNAL OF DE BEAUCHAMPS' JOURNEY TO THE CHOCTAWS, 1746

Louisiana. The 28th August 1746.
Journal of the Journey of Monsieur De Beauchamps, Chevalier of the Military Order of St. Louis, Major of Mobile, to the Tchactas,[1] in execution of the Orders of Monsieur De Vaudreüil, Governor of the province of Louisiana, of the 28th August 1746, for the purpose of inducing that nation to make amends for the assassination of three of our Frenchmen — a gentleman cadet,[2] a soldier, and a trader — committed the 14th August, 1746, by order of Ymatahatchitou,[3] medal chief of that nation, who has thrown over the French in favor of the English hoping to procure greater favors from the latter.

September the 16th at eight o'clock of the morning I departed from Mobille by canoe, accompanied by Messieurs Grandelle, Lieutenant of Swiss; Péchou De Verbois, gentleman cadet; Roucere, King's Interpreter; A French corporal; Two French soldiers and two Swiss; A Spaniard to lead the horses loaded with goods; A savage and a negro belonging to Monsieur de Beauchamps.

I set out by water, with the goods and the outfits of the horses, for the Mobilliens [4] whence after the arrival of the horses, I was to set forth over land, by the Tchactas road.

We arrived at my habitation [5] towards three o'clock of the afternoon and remained there until *the 17th*. I de-

---

[1] Choctaw Indians. [2] Chevalier de Verbois.
[3] Ymatahatchitou was known to the English as Red Shoe.
[4] The Mobilians, a branch of the Choctaw tribe, dwelt in the Indian town of Mobile at the head of Mobile Bay.
[5] De Beauchamps owned and resided on Twenty-One Mile Bluff, the first highland above the French town of Mobile.

parted thence at four o'clock of the afternoon and passed the night at the place of one Myot, a settler. *The 18th* we set out at day-break and between 7 and 8 o'clock of the morning we reached the Mobilliens who awaited us and who were playing a game of ball by way of fitting themselves for following us. Upon my arrival they sang the calumet and an hour afterwards the horses, destined for this expedition, arrived, having left Mobille on *the 15th*. I learned that there were 4 Tchactas, newly arrived, who said that the rebel Imatahatchitou had many partisans throughout their nations, adding that he did not seem satisfied as yet, with having caused the assassination of the three Frenchmen, and that he made no more of that affair than if he had killed the wood rats which ate their hens; that for that matter they [the victims] were traders and so of little account; that he would readily console himself if he had caused the death of a chief of some consequence, and would not have regretted dying afterwards.

Thereupon I delivered to them a discourse on this matter and told them that I had long known that that rogue sought only to bring trouble upon the nation by impoverishing it — men, women and children. The savages, who feared lest some accident befall me and my companions, implored me, with insistence, not to go beyond their villages, urging that my presence, far from advancing our affairs, could only serve to hinder them and to embitter feelings. [They said] that the nation, which seemed well disposed towards giving us satisfaction, must be left to act of itself, and that my presence might be a check on those who are the best disposed toward us. Seeing that they could not turn me aside from undertaking this journey they told me that I, as well as my people, ran great risks, whereupon I replied that I did not fear to go among a nation that was allied to us and that I had known for 28 years, and that, as I had never done it aught but good I could not persuade myself that it desired to do me ill. [I told them] that their arguments would not prevent me from proceeding on my journey, that, for that matter, I was not counting on going among enemies, but, on the contrary, among our allies, there to establish peace and union, so that they might live as in the past; that I feared nothing for my life when it was a question of rendering my service to my country [and] that I would sacrifice it right willingly; [I said] that I was not going to the Tchactas to disseminate discord but to restore everything to order after that they should have made white the ground that some of evil purpose had reddened; that not for a moment did I doubt that that nation would give us satisfaction, even as we ourselves, six years before, had done by it. Finally the chief of this village, the chief of the Manibâ, and the red chief of the Chicachas,[1] seconded by the chief of the Youany [2] did all in their power to turn me aside from continuing my journey.

M. De Bonville who arrived from Tombekbé on the morning of *the 19th* was present at all the harangues, and told me that the rebel Yamatahatchitou, had gone to the Tchicachas to beg of the English that they send as much merchandise as they could to the Tchactas in his dependency, but the letter of M. Hazeur might, [he said], contain some details which he did not remember, or which he did not know. This determined me to dispatch a post for the more prompt conveyance of M. De Bonville, and to receive the latest orders of Monsr. De Louboey,[3] to whom I transmitted all the discourses which the savages had held forth. I even sent the interpreter in the pirogue that he might bring back to me the reply and that he might himself render an account of what he had heard from the savages. *The 25th* the Sieur Roucere arrived with the reply of Mr. De Louboey who informed me that nothing should delay my journey [and] that M. Hazeur did not write him of anything in particular except that the rebel had gone to the Chicachas. We had learned the contrary from a Youany savage who

[1] Chickasaw Indians.

[2] There was a Choctaw town of Yowani on the Chickasawhay River near the north border of Wayne County, Mississippi.

[3] De Louboey (Lubois) seems to have been in command of Fort Condé at Mobile.

had arrived the preceding day at eleven o'clock of the morning — and I had so observed in my letter to M. De Louboey. Immediately the latest orders received I made all preparations for the departure.

The 22d I set out towards noon with my companions and 14 horses — six saddle and eight pack — [and] 57 savages as porters, escort, and guides. I arrived happily *the 26th* at the first Chactas village, without any misadventure but with much trouble and effort on account of the pack-horses. We found the roads fairly good and we came through without rain, which saved us much hurt. The savages of this village received us exceeding well and displayed abundance of friendship for us.

I found the chief very ill with a kind of dysentery. They brought us to eat, both me and those of my following [and] after the first compliments they asked of me the object of my journey, being greatly surprised to see a chief, such as I, in their country.

I replied that I bore a message from their father, and that, if curiosity led them to learn the circumstance of it, those who deported themselves well could come with me to the Chicachas when I purposed to hold an assembly, and that I would make known to them, in the same time as to the others, that which the Taskânamgouchy accepted.

The 27th, in the morning, we set ourselves en route for the Chicâchas, where we did not arrive until *the 28th* in the afternoon. Before reaching the village the Srs. Chambly and Larouve came to meet me and said that the Reverend Father Baudoüin [1] was in good health and awaited me with impatience. I repaired at once to his dwelling where I found a large number of savages who were waiting for me and who received me, in appearance, with an evidence of friendship. The first compliments over, on the one side and on the other, I told them that being a little weary, I would not talk to them today, as I had need of a little repose, but that on the morrow, at 8 o'clock of the morning

[1] Michel Baudouin, for eighteen years a missionary to the Choctaws.

I would bring them the message of M. De Vaudreuil, their father. This appeared to please them and we departed, whereupon I conferred with the Reverend Father Baudoüin as to the object of my mission.

The 29th, in the morning, all the Chicachas and the others repaired to the assembly that had been appointed [and] I addressed them in these terms : That they must be surprised, or rather rejoiced to see me among them; that, having learned that there was discord in a nation which I had always loved, and which had on different occasions, given proofs of its attachment to the French, I came bearing the message of M. De Vaudreuil, their father, who exhorted them never to quit his band; that they saw perfectly that the rebel only sought to degrade his nation and to make it wretched; that the assassination of our three Frenchmen, which he had caused to be committed, was a more than sufficient proof of this, since the wretch had aimed at the life of our people only to the end of empoverishing them [the savages], their women, and their children. What would become of you, said I to them, if we abandon you; what resource will you have ? If this nation does not make amends, by giving up a head for a head, you force us to abandon you. To whom will you have recourse ? To the English ? It is beyond all possibility for them to supply you with the fourth part of your necessities, [and] thus your women and your children will die of want. Whereas, upon giving up three heads, following the agreements made with your elders, M. De Vaudreuil, your father will forget that which has passed, and I, who am an object of your ingratitude, shall be overjoyed, before leaving you, to have restored the peace and union which have so long reigned between us. We ask of you nothing but what is just, seeing that in 1740 M. De Vaudreuil rendered justice to you on account of a man and a woman whom some Frenchmen had killed, and on that occasion you all promised to do the same by the French should the Tchactas commit any act of that sort. I well realize, I said to them, that it is not for the Chicachaé to render this justice, but what I required of them was to support my words when the Tchactas, to whom I had given notice of my arrival, should be assembeld.

Then I read to them the intent of the instructions of M. De Veaudreuil and made them feel the weight which they should attach to that message — which tended only to their welfare and to that of their families. [I told them] that they should recall their first estate, that if today they are Men it is to the French alone to whom they are under obligation, they [the French] having put arms into their hands that they might defend themselves against the nations which were oppressing them and making slaves of them. This signal service has made them respected of the other nations, and has even made them, so to speak, the arbiters of their neighbors, both because of their numbers and because of the warriors which our munitions and our arms have formed; [I said] that in default of that satisfaction [which we demanded], we could not allow any traders in their nation, for fear lest a like accident should again occur, wherefore the good would suffer for the guilty, [we] not being able to know their inmost hearts so as [to dare] to risk further Frenchmen among them. [I told them] that the English moreover, knew the Tchactas of old, that they would not trust them, [and that] they are too wise to commit themselves to an ungrateful nation which treats its benefactors in that fashion. I touched on the spots where they are the most sensitive in repeating what I knew [of them] 28 years ago, and [in pointing out] what the Tchactas were then. After this discourse, in which nothing was overlooked in order to convince them of the necessity of giving us satisfaction, and of the evil which would follow for the nation if they refused, Mongoulacha mingo, demanded permission to speak and with anger and animosity delivered himself of the following discourse.

I do not think, he said to me, that the Tchactas are giving heads for those of your Frenchmen; that as for the head of the rebel Ymatahatchitou it was useless to count upon it. (I had taken care not to designate the heads which we demanded); that he had long known that we sought the ruin of the red men. That, said he, is how the French are, and to support his evil words, he cited to me [the case of] a chief of his race at the Thoméz,[1] whom M. De Bienville,[2] in the early days of the old fort[3] of Mobile, had sent to the islands to die; and [he said] that he [Bienville] had had this man taken by force. This seditious discourse would have produced a very bad effect if I had not had the means of turning against him the trick he had made use of in order to prejudice the minds of the savages, for the lying rogue of whom he spoke had only been sent to the islands upon the demand of the Thoméz. This was confirmed by an Ymonguolacha who dwelt there when the man in question had been sent to Havannah, [and furthermore] M. De Chateauguay[4] had since seen the man, at the house of a priest, and had asked him if he would not be glad to see again his kinsfolk, whereupon he replied that being a Christian he thought no more of the red men and esteemed himself happy to have quit them. The chief, who was not looking for this counter, was disconcerted for a moment. He began again to inveigh against us with unbearable reproaches adding that he well knew that he would never return to favor with us, since he had rejected our words; that, the savages having told him that the medal chiefs were deprived of their authority, which was conferred upon the Red chiefs, he had been led to cut off his medal and to throw it into a creek; that since then he had been told that [such an act] was as if he had killed ten Frenchmen; that he was convinced that sooner or later he would be put to death for that mistake; that furthermore he did not trouble himself on account of my threats to

---

[1] The Tohomes, or Thomez, Indians — who spoke the Choctaw dialect and were closely associated with the Mobilians — had a settlement on the west bank of the Tombigbee, a few miles above the Indian town of Mobile.

[2] Jean Baptiste Lemoyne, Sieur de Bienville, who in conjunction with his brother, Pierre Lemoyne, Sieur d'Iberville, founded Mobile. [3] Fort Louis.

[4] Sieur Lemoyne de Chateaugué, a brother of Bienville.

abandon them; that he had no great obligations to us since he had kept nothing of what had been given him, that the garments he wore came from M. Diron [1] who had sold [them] to him for a slave. Then he addressed his people and said that since the French were abandoning them they would have to take up again the bow and the arrow, that furthermore he was not going to seek the English but that he would remain at home [and be] poor. He followed with numerous extravagances, — which revealed to me his evil heart expressing itself in open hostility. I ordered him to desist, which he did not do until the second summons. It is true that a bottle of brandy which the red chief of his village had given him to drink, the morning of this assembly, contributed not a little to making him vomit forth his indecencies and his insolence. He even said that if he had come to Mobille at the time of the [presentation of] gifts and M. De Vaudreüil had rejected him he would have said and done more; he even wanted to spring upon me after [I] had imposed silence upon him, [but] this he denied, afterwards, when he was in cold blood. I told him that had he been daring enough to do such a thing I should have killed him, or had him killed on the spot. Finally he quitted the assembly without taking leave of anyone and went off home like a madman to tear down the French flag, which he had hoisted as soon as he saw mine at the Reverend Father Baudoüin's, and which, until then, he had left [flying].

Mingo houma Tchitou of this village spoke, after him, and said that I ought not to be surprised at what his chief had just said to me, that he had warned M. De Louboey of it before coming [here], and [that he had warned] us ourselves at the Mobilliens. He added that he had said that the nation must be left to act of itself, that it was not yet inclined to accord us justice, that it was necessary to have patience, [and] that he hoped we would have reason to be satisfied in the end. In short his harangue was only a

---

[1] Diron d'Artaguiette, author of the second journal of this volume, and at one time commandant of Fort Condé.

repetition of what he had said to M. De Louboey and to me before my departure from the Mobilliens; he only made me see that, in spite of all the fine promises which he had made me on the way, he was no more inclined to our interests than his chief, covering himself with the mantle of cowardice, saying that he was afraid and did not know which side to take.

The Captain of the same village arose and spoke with moderation. [He] said that the Tchactas were free to go to seek the English, that for himself he would never quit the hand of the French, that the evil deed of Ymatahatchitou was going to make them all wretched, that they would see themselves forced to take again their ancient weapons (that is the bow and the arrow), a sorry resource, said he to his people, for those who have a family to nourish and to support, and all the more so as we have [*i.e.* they had] completely lost the use of them; that as for himself we ought to be assured of his attachment, that he had given us convincing proof of it in the wounds which he still bears and which he had received in our service. After this discourse the assembly broke up.

The 30th I despatched a courrier to M. De Louboey to inform him that I had arrived with my men, among that nation, in good health and without accident. I detailed to him how dissatisfied I was with the harangues which the Chicachaé had made to me and for which I was not prepared by the demonstrations of friendship which they had evidenced to me the day before.

The same day I despatched a courrier to the Couchas[1] to notify Allibamon maingo [sic], the medal chief, and his people that I had arrived and [to direct him] to give notice of it throughout all the Eastern district, telling him that if he judged my presence necessary in those parts he had only to let me know [and] I would leave on the instant to repair thither. I profited by the same occasion to despatch the

[1] The Couchas or Conchas were Choctaws inhabiting the town of Coucha or Concha in the northeast district of the Choctaw country.

letters with which I was intrusted for Mr. Hazeur, to Tombekbé,[1] where he is in command, informing him of my arrival. I told him that I had demanded three heads, indiscriminately, for the three Frenchmen whom the rebel had had assassinated, and that he should conform himself thereto.

The 1st of October the courier whom the Reverend Father Baudoüin had sent to Mobille to carry news from the Tchaktas to M. De Louboey arrived with the reply to the letters of the Reverend Father. I received one from M. De Louboey together with a copy of the one from M. Leseur,[2] commandant at the Allibamons, whereby I saw with pleasure that the Abékas,[3] very far from giving support to the rebel Ymatahatchitou, — as he had intended in sending to them three pieces from the scalps of our Frenchmen — had, on the contrary, regarded the treachery with horror; they placed the fragments in a white skin and took them to the captain of the Pakamans [4] who enveloped them in a second [skin] and then carried them to M. Lesueur, assuring him that the Abékas, Talapouches,[5] and Allibamonts [6] detested with all their hearts the odious acts of the Tchactas; that if that nation refused to give us prompt satisfaction, they would even permit all [their men] to go there to persuade them to it; that they would utterly refrain from aiding such an ungrateful nation. After having learned this news I reassembled the savages in order that I might impart it

[1] Fort Tombecbé, on the west bank of the Tombigbee River about twenty miles above its confluence with the Black Warrior.

[2] Le Sueur, commandant of Fort Toulouse.

[3] Upper Creek Indians inhabiting the region of the Coosa River above Hatchet Creek.

[4] There is doubt as to the identity of these Indians but it seems likely that they were Upper Creeks inhabiting the town of Pakan-Tallahassee on Hatchet Creek about eighteen miles from its junction with the Coosa.

[5] The Tallapoosas were Upper Creeks inhabiting the region of the Tallapoosa River.

[6] The Alibamas inhabited the region at and below the confluence of the Coosa and Tallapoosa.

to them. After I had related everything to them in detail I observed that the people who had comported themselves in that fashion were savages who had the English among them, but that, — as the Tchactas are great liars [and] so might imagine that I wished to avail myself of the same privilege in order to engage them to give us satisfaction, — the Red man who had just delivered to me the letters was going to relate everything to them that he had learned from the Apalâches savage who had brought this news from the Allibamonts, since, being a red man like themselves, they would have perhaps more faith in him, [but] that they ought nevertheless to be persuaded that a man like myself was incapable of imposing upon them.

I ordered the one armed man who had brought this news, and who is a notable of the village, to speak. He arose and under five heads reported with much circumstance all that the Apalache had told him, adding that peace had been made both on the upper river and in the region of the Ouäbache [1] Choüanons [2] and Chêraquis; that twelve Choü-anons had come to cement it also with all the nations of the Allibamonts, Talapouches, Abékas, Caoüitas,[3] Cachetas,[4] etc., and that this spring there were to come a hundred [Chouanons] to settle at the Allibamonts with the people of their village who settled there ten years ago. He added furthermore, that peace reigned throughout all the nations, that all the roads were white, that those people could go everywhere and that the Tchactas were the only ones who had reddened the ground. This discourse, in harmony with mine, did not fail to disconcert somewhat the chief of the village as well as all those who had yielded in the first assembly.

Nevertheless the chief repeated, being sober, the same nonsense that he had addressed to us, being drunk; but

[1] Wabash. [2] Shawnee.

[3] Kawitas, Lower Creeks inhabiting the town of Kawita on the Chattahoochee River.

[4] Kasihtas, Lower Creeks inhabiting the town of Kasihta on the Chattahoochee River a little below Kawita.

with more gentleness I spoke to him about the flag which he had taken down and told him that the flag was not for himself alone but for all the village and that he must raise it again or else I would have it taken away from him. He had it put back and left it until after my departure. The Captain, with an aged notable, Ytémongoulache, spoke strongly in our behalf. The red chief, still disconcerted, spoke not a word.

The Taskanangoutchy of the Ÿouanis thereupon delivered his discourse, strongly in our favor, saying that nothing was more just than the demand which I made upon them; that it was meet that prompt satisfaction should be given us so that I might conciliate them in spirit and re-establish peace and union among the Tchactas; that as for himself, being *inoulacta*, he would never give vent to evil speech, nor would he receive the English, even though they came with many wares; that he would hold to the French whose hand he had taken from the days of tender youth, as had all those of his race. This speech over, each one went his way. The same day the messenger whom I had despatched to the Couchas and to the Ayé paté goula to announce my arrival, arrived at eight o'clock of the evening and told me that he had not found Allibamon Mingo, he having gone to his desert, which is far removed from the village, but that Toupâou mastabé, the captain, had been rejoiced to learn of my arrival [and] was going to notify his great chief to repair hither with the notables; that he [Toupaou mastabé] was grateful to me for not having gone beyond this village, by reason of the risks which I and my men would have run in going to see them, for the heart of the red men was bad and had some accident befallen me it would have occasioned a war among them, for they would not have suffered me to be insulted, either while on the way or in their villages. The messenger told me that they begged me not to pass beyond this village, that I would expose them to being massacred by the Tchactas, their own faction being the weaker, [and] that they would come at once to see me to receive the messages of the great chiefs of the French, their fathers.

The 2d October I despatched a courier to the six villages of the dependency of the Chicachaé and Ougoulasalaya, to notify them of my arrival, and [to tell them] to come to receive the message which I bore them from M. De Vaudreüil, their father.

The same day I despatched a notable to Tombekbé to carry letters to M. Hazeur in which I informed him that in view of the circumstances, and of the attachment of the three nations of the Allibamonts, Abékas, and Talapouches, it was no longer desirable to demand three heads, indiscriminately, but that, on the contrary, we must fix upon the head of the rebel Ymatahatchitou. I told him that if the deputies of the Allibamons arrived, he should receive them well — since they were undertaking that move only with the view of engaging the Tchactas to give satisfaction to the French — and to send them on to me if that were possible.

The 3d of the said [month] Allibamont mingo, Toupaou mastabé, and Quikanabé Mingo, all three Couchas, accompanied by the Taskanangouchy and by the medicine man of the Bois Bleux, arrived. I talked to them on the same day and repeated to them the message of M. De Vaudreuil and what I had learned from the Allibamonts by the letter of M. Lesueur, as I had done at the preceding assembly, adding only in speaking to Allibamonts Mingo, that having learned that he had comported himself perfectly in this affair, I addressed directly to him the words of his father, as he was the only great chief to whom I could have recourse for support of my own, [and] that I begged him to tell me, without concealment, if what his father and I demanded, was not just. To this the chief, after rising and making two circles — one of which indicated the settlement of the French, and the other, larger, enclosed the Tchactas nations — made reply. He commenced his discourse in these terms : That I ought not in the least to doubt his attachment for us ; that it was not his fault that this evil affair was not already ended, for he had represented all the consequences of it to the nation and particularly to the people of his village and dependency; that he perfectly remembered his first estate; that it was not necessary to spare people who had long sought only the loss and ruin of the Tchactas nation, and who had just capped the climax with their crimes; that all the red men must see clearly that all the promises of Ymatahatchitou were vain and chimerical; that he regarded all those projects as impossible; that as for him, his will was good but that he could not give us the satisfaction which we justly demanded, fearing to set all the nation against him; that if he were seconded he would do it with a good heart, but that his village, and that of the Chicachaé, which are united from of old, could not give this satisfaction, however great their desire, without running the risk of being cut to pieces by the rest of the nation; that it was necessary to await the chiefs of the region of the west who are the most concerned in this affair, since the Frenchmen who were assassinated lived in their villages; that it would be seen what they think of it; that he would use all his influence to engage them to do justice by us and would speak to them outright and boldly to bring them to it. In short this chief spoke with all the eloquence possible on the side of our interests, often repeating that if the Tchactas lost the French they must needs look upon themselves as dead, since their women and their children would not only be naked as in the past but would die of destitution and hunger.

Toupaoü mastabé, captain of the same village, next spoke [but] not in the way I had expected. His discourse contained nothing but tricky terms, ambiguities, and fear; he brought forth as many difficulties for [the settling of] this affair as though I had demanded of him things that were unjust. Such an harangue from a man whom I thought wholly devoted to the French surprised me extremely. His discourse was very long, stupid, and tiresome; he repeated from time to time his great deeds, but always refrained from saying anything satisfactory to us, except that he would always love the French, that he would not abandon them, but that he was afraid and could do nothing for them.

Quikanabé Mingo made no harangue at all; he contented himself with saying to me, after the assembly and before all who were in the chamber of the Reverend Father Baudoüin, that as soon as he had learned the sad news [of the assassination of the French] he had made ready to march to execute justice, that he had failed because no one had been willing to second him, that if there was a willingness to aid him he was entirely willing to start out again, nor did he fear to risk his life to avenge the French and to re-establish peace in the nation to the end that he might rescue it from the oppression of Ymatahatchitou and of the English, knowing furthermore that these latter are unable to supply their needs. [He said] that of this he spoke with knowledge since he had formerly been [one of] their captains and their partizans — [and] that but for M. De Beauchamps and the Reverend Father Baudoüin he might still be — but he had recognized his mistake and would always sacrifice himself for the French, his benefactors. He told me in private that he took this affair so much to heart that, although he did not promise me anything, I would perhaps hear of him; that he was returning at once to succor his children whom he had left dying; that he had already lost one but a few days before, for whom he was in mourning, that it had required nothing less than a message such as mine to have made him leave his hut where he was in tears.

The Taskanamgouchy of the Bois Bleux next spoke, and made a speech very much in our favor, saying that he had always been the destroyer of the English, and that if any of them came among the nation I might be assured that he would shoot them; that as soon as he had received the news of the act of Ymatahatchitou he had on the spot caused the alarm to be sounded and had gone, with sixty warriors of his village to the Yazoü of the East, the drum beating, counting upon all the Tchactas to take part in the affair, [but] not having found anyone to second him in that village nor in those roundabout he had been obliged to turn back. The chiefs told him, by way of reward for his good will, that he was crazy, that it was not yet time to avenge

us, and that there was too much of risk to run; that first
of all there must be taken the opinion of all the chiefs of
the nation, [and] that until then it was fitting to remain
quiet. The medicine man who had accompanied him said
nothing; he contented himself with applauding indiscriminately both the speeches of Allibamonts mingo and the
others.

I then spoke in private to Toupaoumastabé, captain [of
the] Couchas. It appeared by his reply that he was better
inclined toward us than he had appeared in his harangue;
he said, by way of excuse, that the Red men did not dare
to say in public what they thought, because Ymatahatchitou
had spies in the assemblies, but that he hoped nevertheless
that we would have grounds for satisfaction without loss of
time.

The 4th, in the afternoon, I received a reply to the first
news that I had sent to M. Hazeur, wherein he informed me,
that, jointly with me, he would demand indiscriminately
three heads of the murderers.

The same day Taskanamgouchyaclako, chief of the Yazoü,[1]
came to see me and spoke me very fair. He told me that
he was going to bear the message of M. De Vaudreuil, his
father, throughout all the region of the east and to engage
[the savages] to unite with Allibamont mingo the bearer of
the message, and to second him in securing the satisfaction
which I demanded of them; that if Choulkôoülactâ were
not dead those two great chiefs would have concerted to
render us justice, whether or no, but unhappily the latter
had died in a time when we had the most need of him, that
he had realized all the consequence of [the affair] and had
so declared, before dying, recommending to all his relations
and warriors never to leave the French.

The 1st, the chief of Oüny [2] with his second and a few

[1] The principal town of this name — a Choctaw town — was
on the site still known as Yazoo Old Town in Neshoba County,
Mississippi. There was another town of the same name farther east.

[2] There was a Choctaw town of Oony on a branch of the upper
Chickasawhay River in what is now Newton County, Mississippi.

warriors arrived and spoke to me right well, as did also his second. I had good grounds for being content with them, although [they are] neighbors of the rebel.

Oulissô Mingo of the Eaües noires spoke no ill, notwithstanding he was suspected of being in the interests of Ymatahatchitou. The same day arrived the courier from Mobille with letters for me and M. Hazeur.

The 16th at noon arrived the courier whom I had sent to Tombekbé [and] by whom I had had sent word to M. Hazeur, that, in consequence of the action of the Abékas and Allibamonts it was necessary to determine upon obtaining the head of the rebel, and no longer to demand three heads indiscriminately. M. Hazeur, to whom this news gave much pleasure, replied that he would second my views in all respects.

The same day I sent on to Tombekbé the letters which had come to me from Mobille. By the same occasion I informed the Commandant of the former post, as to the speeches, good and bad, which I had listened to but [said] that I did not discern any great attachment for us although I had every reason to be content with the fashion in which Allibamont mingo had declared himself, as well as Taskanamgouchy of the Bois bleux and some others; that I was awaiting the six Villages and the western party in order to sound their hearts, which would doubtless be as hardened as that of the chief of this village who had spoken much ill to us.

The said day, at ten o'clock of the morning the chiefs of the villages of the Cannes jaunes, Bouttouloucaÿ, Tala, Mâchoubaouenyà, Ceniâchâ, and Toussana,[1] arrived. I talked to them until three hours past midday after having explained to them, in the strongest terms, the message of M. De Vaudreüil, their father, and that which the men of the Allibamonts had done.

[1] These six villages were in the region of the upper waters of Chickasawhay River, within the limits of the present Newton and Jasper counties, Mississippi.

The chief of Tâla arose and spoke in these terms: that what I demanded of them was impossible; that I ought not to hope that they should deliver me any heads for those of the Frenchmen; that if he had known that it was for that that I had summoned him he would not have taken the trouble to come; that he had thought I was come to propose to them to make war upon the Chikachas, expecting that the goods which I had brought should be spread before them to engage them to receive my message; that they perceived well enough that the French meant to impoverish them; that he did not concern himself about that; that he would remain at home at his ease. It is to be remarked that this chief is of the race of Ymatahatchitou.

The chief of the Cannes jaunes, who is a young man, without authority, next spoke, saying neither good nor ill, except that he had several times warned the French to beware of the bad Tchactas, that they [the French] were not ignorant that there were many of ill will; that he had several times warned the Sr. Chambly as well as the others, of them.

The chief of Machoübâouenyä, who is of the race of the great chief of the nation, spoke very well, but his second, Mingo oumâ said nothing of any account.

Ymatahapouscouche, and Fanymingo Tchâha of the Ceniacha, spoke next and said that they did not see any likelihood that the red men could do us justice without running many risks and that they were not at all inclined to get themselves killed through love of us.

The chief of the Bouetouloucay spoke in the same tone. It even appeared that their discourses were shaped upon the understanding which they had reached among themselves while on the way. They added that if they were not furnished with munitions and if their arms were not repaired for them, they would, at the worst, but be obliged to resort to their former weapons, — meaning thereby the bow and the arrow. I impressed upon them that that was but a slender resource for people who had lost the use of them [the bow and arrow], to which they made no reply.

They contented themselves with saying to me that if they had wars with any nations they would defend themselves as they could — referring thus to the Allibamons because of what I had said about them.

Allibamont mingo, whom I had told to support my words, made a great and fine speech to them, to persuade them to join with him in obtaining for us the satisfaction which I demanded of them, in the name of their father; in order that I might re-establish peace and union among them and procure for them the means of supporting their women and their children, who would die of hunger, if their munitions and the repairing of their arms were cut off.

Then he recounted that, so far from finding support among the Abékas, as Ymatâhatchitou had made them hope, these latter had held his action in horror, upon seeing the pieces of French scalps which he had sent them, and instead of exhibiting them upon their huts, as he had sent word to them to do, they had kicked them aside and then had wrapped them in a white skin to take them to M. Lesueur at the Allibamonts. This chief told them further many other and very pertinent matters, in order to make them the better feel of what consequence it was for all the Tchactas nation to give us a prompt and ample satisfaction. He also told them of all the evil which might result [from failure to do so], whereupon the chief of Tousana responded that he, as well as the other chiefs, had very well heard what I had said to them; that it was needless for him to give himself the trouble to repeat it; that he did not regard him as of any consequence in this affair, and that he was not seeking his opinion as to what he should do; that he ought to content himself with drinking and eating with the French chiefs and [do] nothing else. This evil argument compelled Allibamont mingo to silence, in spite of the desire which he had to make them realize all the horror of the crime committed by the Tchactas, — especially Pouchimâtaha, chief of Tousana who had had the trader of his village assassinated.

Pouchimataha arose then, and said that he supposed that

the goods which I had brought were intended to engage them to go to war upon their enemies and ours, but that he saw, on the contrary, that they were for the purpose of getting them to support [me]; that he was not at all of that opinion; he added many other things, in the same tone and but little satisfying. The red chief of the Nâchoubaoüénya did likewise and endorsed what this last chief had recited. I told him that a man like myself did not go on the march without goods; that those which I had brought were intended for the subsistence of my warriors and for making presents to whom I saw fit; to which he dared not retort; no more than did Pouchimataha and the others. I broke up this assembly in telling them that I would render a faithful account to their father of the attachment for him and for all the French which they had displayed to me. They then set themselves to eating what the Chicachaé had prepared for them, [and] as soon as they had their bellies full they came to take my hand and quickly departed without saying anything more.

The chief of Toussanâ and the red chief of the Nachou-baoüenya remained and gave some signs of good will and attachment in the hope, without doubt, that I would make them a present by way of reward for the evil discourse they had held me; but their hopes were vain as were those of their company, whom I sent away with nothing.

Allibamont mingo, who had a violent attack of fever, by reason of having vehemently harangued for a part of the day, left on the morrow at daybreak to return home and bear the message of M. De Vaudreuil throughout all the district of the east and in his dependency, while going to mourn the death of Choulkooulacta (I learned that the rebel Ymatahatchitou had been there some days previously to weep over the grave of that chief) — ceremonies which are religiously observed among them. I gave the letters for M. Hazeur to Allibamont Mingo who charged himself with the safe delivery of them; among them was the copy of the letter of M. De Vaudreuil, who transmitted the news which the frigate *La Mutine* had brought him from France.

The 7th the great chief of the nation who had arrived in the morning with Ymatahamingo of the Ebitoupougoula, and the second of Tchichatalaya, spoke to me in excellent terms and said that he was very sensible to the perfidious act of Ymatahatchitou, but that he was old and unable to undertake anything; that even of late his hut had been shot at and [there had been shooting] in his deserts; that he was in great fear lest those of evil intentions should make an attempt upon his life after the measures that had just been taken, but that he would, with all his force, urge the nation to give us satisfaction in order to re-establish peace and union among the Tchactas that they might live together as heretofore; that as for himself personally he would never hold any other language than that of his father, but that he could not take any action, that he feared too much lest he himself be assassinated.

Ymatâha mingo, or the Monkey, said that as for him [if] I commanded him to make war upon the Chikachas he would set out upon the instant with his warriors, but that, when it came to fighting against his own nation he was too fearful and not at all so inclined, thus making an exhibit of cowardice, like the others.

I sounded this chief in private through the interpreter who reported that the savage was not willing to declare his intentions in public but that he would do his best to make us satisfied with him, without however promising anything positive; however, as he has great ambition perhaps he will attempt something [to gain] the promised reward.

The 9th the great chief and those who had accompanied him returned. They all assured me of their fidelity as well as of that of all the Ayépatégoulas. The great chief, before his departure, gave evidence of much displeasure at the evil language held by the Six Villages and by the [chief] of Toussana, and ordered Ápaninantcla of the Céniachas to tell them, from him, that they must come to make their excuses to me, both for their evil discourse and for the brusque fashion of their leaving, and that he would speak right roundly his mind to them in the assembly which was to be held for the scraping of the bones of the dead. In consequence the chief and the second of the village of Nachoubaouenya, came the day of my departure, to express their regret at having spoken ill as well as at having departed so brusquely; that they had acted thus without reflection, but that they came to make me their excuses, assuring me that they would never abandon the hand of the French.

The same day, in the afternoon, arrived the Ditémongoulacha chiefs, of the west, to whom I delivered the message of M. the governor and [told] what I had learned from the Allibamonts. They replied that my demand was just, but that although they realized all the consequences, they were not bold enough, nor strong enough to attack the party of Ymataha Tchitou which was still powerful; that they had taken upon themselves to avenge us, but that, finding themselves alone in this determination, they had not dared make the attempt for fear of not being sustained by the nation. [They said] that when the partizans of the rebel find themselves impoverished they will withdraw from him, and that then they will be able to give us the satisfaction which we demand; but that up to now he [Ymatahatchitou] had filled them [his partizans] with imaginings and the hope that they would shortly be enriched with goods, both from the English and from the Chikachas; that as for them they saw well enough that all those promises were vain and futile and that it was impossible for him to hold to all that he had promised them; that for their part we ought to feel assured that they would never abandon the hand of the French to take the hand of the English; that furthermore they would do all in their power to avenge the death of the man Petit, their trader, and that if they could not take vengeance upon the red men they would take it upon the English, should they be crazy enough to come among the nation. In short I was very well satisfied with the chief of this village and with the red chief, who nevertheless is of the race of the rebel.

Sonâkabétaska promised me further to avenge the death of the Sr. Deverbois at the next [ceremony] of scraping the bones of the dead, and to escape, thereupon, to New Orleans.

The same day, about evening there came to see me the red chief, brother of Allibamon mingo, and the white chief of the Eaux noires, chief of Oskéatchougma. I spoke to the former of what he must have learned from his brother as well as from the captain of his village. He replied that he had not seen his brother, but that the captain had recounted all to him; that as to what I demanded of them on behalf of M. De Vaudreüil their father, he regarded it as impossible; [he said] that the Couchas had even constructed a fort, as much for their own security as for that of the French, whose hand they did not wish to abandon; that he did not believe however that the party of Ymatahâtchitou could long hold together, as his people see no fulfillment of the promises he has made and is still making daily.

The white chief, who is a worthless fellow, told me that Ymatâhatchitou, seeing nothing coming of all that he expected from the English, Chikachas, and Abékas, began to repent him of having corrupted their lands, and that he [Ymatahatchitou] had said that if goods did not come in abundance before long, it would be necessary to satisfy the French by giving up the heads of three of the warriors who had committed the deed, and that as for himself, being gouty of the feet and feeble, he thought his warriors would pardon him and allow him to die his own death, which, by reason of his infirmities and of his age, would not be long delayed; for it would be shameful for him to die at the hands of his nation. The Abékas of the west, who are his partizans, having learned of this language replied that not having first given their word in favor of the murder, they would not consent to give their heads to whiten the land which he had made red; that it was far more just to give up his own head since it was only at his solicitation that the warriors had spoiled the roads [grattés (sic) les chemins] on the strength of the false promises which he had made them.

The 10th, Tichoumingo, of this village, who has been

about in the nation, arrived and told me that the Tchactas of the party of Ymatahatchitou, who had been to the Chikachas to sell their peltries, had returned without having sold a single one, there being no goods to be had among that nation except for ammunition; the Chikachas had told them that they did not have any [ammunition] for themselves, and that even if they had it would not be for the Tchactas, that they would carefully keep it for their own defense and for the subsistence of their families. The Tchactas, seeing such a scarcity were disconcerted by this misadventure and were obliged to bring back their peltries, much dissatisfied with their journey. This story, although doubtful at first sight, has been confirmed to me by other savages of that quarter.

The same day the Soulier Rouge of the Yanabé [1] came, about four hours after midday with his brother and a warrior of the same village. He told me that I must excuse his chief who would gladly have come to see me had not sickness prevented him. I spoke to this notable of the murder committed by order of Ymatahatchitou. At first he made me a reply modelled upon those of the others, and only told me that since his return from Mobille he had not gone outside of his hut, to which I retorted that that was not what he had promised to M. the governor when the latter had given him his present; that I saw with indignation that hardly out of sight of the house of their father all the promises they had made to him had faded away, or been drowned in the Baÿouygo; that, from hearing them talk at that time I supposed that the Chikachas were even now all dead, but that I saw, with chagrin, that all those who had so highly vaunted themselves, had not only done nothing for us, but on the contrary they were, it seemed to me all of like mind with those who had committed this horrible deed, to say nothing of having tacitly consented to it, since they had remained so quiet after the assurances they had given their father that they would die in behalf of the French.

[1] Ayanabi, a Choctaw town about one hundred miles west of Fort Tombechbé.

The 11th arrived one Gaspard, trader at the Couchats, from Tombekbé with a letter from M. Hazeur who sent me the letter from M. Lesueur, Commandant at the Alliba-monts, respecting the letter which M. De Louboey had sent me, in the first place, by the one-armed man of this village, relating to the scalps sent by Ÿmatahatchitou to the Abé-coutchy Abékas.[1]

M. Hazeur informed me, in his letter of the 9th that Paémingo of the Castachas [2] had been to see him and had spoken to him at first in unbefitting terms, saying that he had just exposed his life in the service of the French from whom there was no reward forthcoming, nor any trade in peltries, since the French were no longer willing to trade with the Tchactas until we should have had satisfaction for the three Frenchmen killed by their brethren. This worthy harangued with vehemence on other scores, constantly referring to the chief of Boukfouka,[3] and said that the Tchactas of that quarter did not appear disposed to accord the satisfaction which we demanded of the entire nation; he complained that they did not make much of him, and then reported what he had done, but recently, for the French — risking his life and those of his warriors in their service: [namely] that having prowled a long time about the Chikachas villages, without finding any one off in some lonely place, he found himself compelled — in order not to return empty handed — to go into the village where he had killed a young man who had fallen on the doorstep of his hut; that he had not been able to take his scalp on account of the risk that he would have run; that [this] being known of the French he had thought that he and his warriors would have been given cause for satisfaction; that, coming to see a French chief he had brought some

---

[1] Abéka or Abihka Indians inhabiting the town of Abikudshi on Tallassee Creek, about five miles from its junction with the Coosa River.

[2] A Choctaw town about three miles southwest of the old Choctaw town of Yazoo.

[3] A Choctaw town on one of the head streams of Pearl River.

peltries and he hoped that, in consideration of his deed, they would not refuse [to trade with] him; that if they would not trade the worst that he could do would be to gamble for them with a few red men like himself. M. Hazeur, in reply to his first proposition said that he did not have the gift of divining whether he had taken a scalp or no; that as for the peltries he had not looked in his pack to see whether he had any to trade; after which he told him that not only would he pay him for the scalp, in consideration of his zeal and attachment, but that he would also trade with him for his skins, although that was forbidden, for he did not want to send him away ashamed after he had performed such a fine deed and had run so many risks in our service. Thereupon this party chief was mollified and conferred at length with M. Hazeur, with regard to the satisfaction which we demanded, and promised to do his utmost to procure it for us. [He said] that he was going to join with Taskaoûmingo of the Bouksoukâ [sic], Pouchymâtaha of Toussana, [and] Illetaskâ of the Ÿmougoulachâ so that they might all together persuade Tatoulimataha, elder brother of Ymataha Tchitou, to give us this satisfaction; he being of the race of the rebel it was fitting, in order to avoid the consequences, that he should be the one to perform the act.

The same day the brother of Paémingo, mentioned above, arrived towards seven o'clock of the evening with a letter which M. Hazeur had given him for me, dated the 7th, wherein he conveyed the same information as in the letter of the 9th, which had been delivered to me by the man Gaspard.

The Soulier Rouge, of the Ÿanabé, spoke next, saying that he was ashamed to appear before the French chief after the disgraceful thing that had come to pass in the nation, but that he saw no way of making amends because of the fear in which they stood of kindling a civil war among the Tchactas; that I should be assured that he would always cherish our interests with warmth, [but] that he did not feel that he himself was brave enough to make an attempt upon the life of Ymatahatchitou, who was well guarded, and that furthermore he was not of his race.

To which I replied that it was far more shameful for me to have come among a nation which I supposed entirely devoted to our interests, because of the benefits which their ancestors had received, and which they [themselves] would still receive daily; that I saw with astonished surprise that all those great warriors, captains, red chiefs, and notables, did not dare to undertake anything against a man who sought only their undoing, and to disunite them in causing them to lose the moiety of the French, and to make them wretched; that if, however, they did not give satisfaction to their father, in reparation of the offense committed by Ymatahatchitou, I doubted not, that upon my return, M. De Vaudreuil, perceiving the lack of zeal for the execution of his orders, would at once cease all commerce with a nation so ingrate. I further said several very strong things, recalling to them all that we had done for them and in the strongest terms. This brought about a change in this party chief, who appeared much touched by the feeling reproaches, which with justice, I had just addressed to him. He told me that he could not express himself in public, that there were too many spies, but that he would tell me his sentiment in private.

I learned then that Tamatlé mingo, war chief of the Couchatÿs Allibamonts [1] was to arrive on the morrow with his son, a Tchactas [who had] settled among them, and [the] nephew of the Soulier Rouge above mentioned, together with some Tchactas who accompanied him. M. Hazeur had told me, in his letter of the 9th that he was sending them to me.

The brother of Paémingo of the Castachas, who had brought me the letter of M. Hazeur of the 7th, gave me an account of his brothers raid on the Chikachas, in which he himself had taken part, and set forth, with much discourse,

---

[1] The Koasati, Alabamas inhabiting a village near the confluence of the Coosa and Tallapoosa rivers.

their services to the French, as is reported above in the paragraph dealing with the letter of the 9th.

I replied to him that I was well satisfied with the conduct of his brother; that I should render an account of it to M. the governor, who would without doubt recognize that mark of attachment; that it was glorious for him to have carried out his word, [but] that it was not the same with *all* the captains, red chiefs, and other notables of that nation, who, vying with each other, had assured M. De Vaudreuil, at Mobile, in the strongest terms, that, immediately upon their arrival [*i.e.*, return] each one would arouse his party to go against the Chikachas, their enemies and ours; but that, hardly had they lost sight of his house, as well as of the good reception and the good cheer which he had tendered them, than all those mighty and fine promises had gone up in smoke and that, instead of keeping the word which they had given their father, the most of them had remained asleep in their huts; others had gone to the Chikachas to trade, instead of to make war, and to learn at the same time the thoughts of the English so that they might know the truth of the words which Ymâtahatchitou had spoken to them, both as to goods and ammunition and as to the storehouses which they [the English] were, or which they are to establish in that nation, and [that they might learn] when this would be accomplished.

[I continued by saying] that Paémingo then, was the only one who had held to the word which, in leaving, he had given to his father, [and] that I went so far as to hope that he would not stop [halfway] in such a good course, but that he would do his utmost to obtain for us the satisfaction which we demand of the Tchactas, so that it might be possible to re-establish among them a peace, which, in all appearance, has been troubled only with the consent of all the captains, red chiefs, and other notables of the nation, who had given no proofs of their zeal and fidelity in our service. This sharp reproach, vehemently uttered, astonished the Soulier Rouge of the Yánabé to such a point, that he asked a second time to speak in private, saying that he would demand nothing better than to satisfy the French and to reestablish the [supply of] munitions and goods, in order to ward off the misery to which we were going to reduce them; [and] that further, if they did not do us justice, they would be despised by the other nations who would rightly regard them as ungrateful and faithless.

The 12th Tamatlémingo of the Allibamonts, his son, and a Tchactas of the Yanabé [who] is settled among them, arrived in company with the Souliers Rouges [sic] of Tombekbé, and Rassétaou mastabé of the Couchas; the Chikachaé people received them with, in appearance, a demonstration of friendship. After they had rested a little and had had to eat, the savages were assembled together and I spoke to Tamatlémingo and told him to set forth to all the savages of the assembly, in which there were several Tchactas of different villages, the subject of his journey and to conceal nothing from them.

Thereupon he commenced his address with much gentleness and calmness saying that he did not know well the Tchactas language but that he would express himself as best he could. He began by saying that he was surprised that the Tchactas had not yet rendered us justice in the matter of the three Frenchmen who had been assassinated among them, [but] that without doubt they did not realize the seriousness of it. It is amazing, said he, that, receiving daily benefits from the French you should have been carried to this extreme; do not count in the least upon the English, your hopes would be ill founded; so there are only the Chikachas who can have abused you in that way in order to make you wretched and to avenge themselves upon you at their pleasure, cutting you off from all aid from the French as well as from the English; that they ought to know that these latter were not people to give them any presents, as did the French; that at the very most they might be able to trade their skins to them if they took them to the Chicakas [but] that as for ammunition they were not able to furnish four of their villages with it; that they knew, on their own account how it was, being neighbors of the English; that without the French whom they have among them they would lack absolutely for ammunition unless they wanted to load their guns with limbourg [1] and other articles of merchandise; in that case, said he, perhaps the English could furnish them a little; that they should rest assured of what he said to them, although the Tchactas of evil intentions made him pass for a liar; that, indeed, he had not come to bring them a message, but only, on behalf of M. Leseur as well as of the Allibamonts, Talapouches, Abékas, Caoüytas and other nations of his district, to see if justice had been rendered us; that if the Tchactas doubted what he told them they could send some of their spies with him to the Allibamons, to report back to them what the nations of those quarters think of them. He added that he was surprised that the Tchactas should hearken to Ymatahatchitou, in preference to the French from whom they received so many daily benefits; that the trader who was at the Chikâchas, and whom he mentioned by name, was nothing but a thief, who would not dare to return home; that he was surprised that the Tchactas should have confidence in a man of that character, [to the extent of] abandoning a certainty. Then he recounted what had taken place upon the occasion of the [incident of the] pieces of scalp which Ymatahatchitou had sent by a Tchactas to the Abécouchÿs Abékas, his story conforming to what M. Le Sueur had told me, and, said, moreover that all the nations today found themselves reunited at the fire of the French, and that there were only the Tchactas, like a little circle (which he illustrated by joining his thumb to his forefinger) who would be miserable, because of their mistakes; that the Chaouanons had come to them [i.e. the Allibamonts] saying that they had just made peace with the Chéraquis, that M. De Bertet,[2] commandant at the Illinois, had whitened the land of all the northern quarter, and that they come to them for the same purpose — which [overture] the Allibamonts and others

[1] A kind of French cloth much in demand among the Indians.
[2] Chevalier de Bertel or Bertet was commandant in the Illinois country in 1742–1749.

have accepted. The twelve Chaoüanons returned satisfied with [the result of] their mission, and promised M. Lesueur that this spring a hundred of them would come to settle down under the fort. He told them again that the Englishman gave no presents at all to the red men, that he gave nothing except for skins and that the inhabitants of the village where he dwelt were obliged to furnish him with provisions. In short this chief spared no effort and said all that he could to appeal to the Tchactas. Perceiving how little movement they made I said to him that their hearts were harder than steel.

The captain of the Chikachaé, after the speech of Tamatlémingo, made a little speech to the assembly, presenting to it a bow and some arrows and saying that he had just tried his ancient arms but that he could no longer make use of them, having lost the art; hoping thereby to touch his auditors and make them realize how wretched they would be should we abandon them.

The young Tchactas, nephew of the Soulier Rouge of the Yanabé, [who had] come with Tamatlémingo then spoke very well in our behalf, pointing out to his uncle that time was precious and that he ought to profit by it in giving us satisfaction; that it was useless for the Tchactas to think that the English could supply their necessities or that they would come among them; that he knew only too well the effects remembering the disobliging manners of that nation towards him in former times; furthermore the English traded not at all or but very little in ammunition, which had led the Allibamonts, Talapouches, Abékas and Caouylas to cherish and regard the French infinitely more than the English, who ever sowed evil words among the nations for the purpose of troubling them; whereas the words of the French were always the same, that is to say, white and beneficent for the red men; and he assured [them] that all that Tamatlémingo had said was true. This discourse publicly uttered by a Tchactas made a very good effect.

The Soulier Rouge of the Yânabé then forbade the Chikachaé to share their munitions with the other Tchactas in order that the latter might the more speedily come to want; that as for himself, he would never leave the French and would carefully avoid the English, except to kill them if they came among the nation; [and] that he would always, with pleasure, carry out the will of M. De Vaudreuil his father. He then spoke to me in private and asked if no one had volunteered to kill Ymatahatchitou; I told him No, not wishing to let him know who had given me their word [to do so]. I said to him that he was young and full of ambition and that he ought to persuade Paémingo of the Castachas, Taskaoüamingo, captain of the Boukfoukâ, [the Captain] of Toussana, and Illétaska of the Ymongoulachas to have that act of reparation done by Tâtoulimatâha, elder brother of Ymatâhâtchitou, in order to avoid the consequences. He replied that he did not wish to have the captain of Boukfoukâ co-operate with him, that he was too ambitious, — which did not displease me as I had learned that he had given his consent to the death of the Frenchmen — but that he would gladly join with Paémingo, regarding [however] the others as suspects. He asked me if the one who should kill Ymatâhatchitou would be given the medal, which I promised him, together with the present of [the position of] Captain [for the second] and [for] the third, the present of [the position of] village chief, as well as a reward for the warriors, whereupon he replied that that business could be accomplished in a fortnight after my arrival at Mobille not being willing to attempt anything while I should be among them, or on the road, for fear lest some accident might befall me or my men. At eleven o'clock of the evening he came to ask me if I would give him two pieces of limbourg in addition to what I had promised him. I replied that I would, and even more if it were necessary; [I said] that the message of his father, and my message would remain with the Reverend Father Baudoüin in my absence, as well as at Tombekbé. He requested of me a great secrecy in this affair; I told him that I would observe it most religiously but that I could not dispense with communicating the matter to Mrs. De Vaudreuil and

Louboey. Tell them, said he, but let them speak of it to no one.[1]

The 12th the courier, whom I had despatched to M. De Louboey the first of this month to notify him of my arrival at the Tchactas (indicating to him the small satisfaction I had had from the speeches which the Chikachaés had made me), arrived with the reply to my letter and brought me another letter for Tombekbé.

The 13th Tatoulimatâhá arrived with the former chief of Tchanké.[2] After I had told him the object of my journey, as [I had told] the others, he replied that as for him, he would never make an attempt upon the life of his brother; that, aside from that, he was always inclined toward the French and would not abandon them; that his brother's faction was too strong [for him] to dare risk killing him; that even were he promised a storehouse full of wares he would not do it; that if others than he wished to undertake it, they should take care that it did not come to his knowledge, because he could not avoid going over to his [brother's] faction if he [*i.e.* his brother] should be killed; that, in spite of that, he could not approve of the wicked deed which his brother had had committed against the French; that he knew, from of old, that his heart was evil, and he had many times blamed him for it. Nevertheless, if he [his brother] should pass on to the Abekas or the Talapouches, we would be free to have him [his brother] killed, and not only would he [himself] not say a word, but he would be rejoiced. It is useless, said he, to think of having him killed by his [own] nation. He added that if his brother had committed that evil deed it was only because of desperation at seeing how he had been treated, formerly, at Tombékbé, together with

[1] Ymatahatchitou, or Red Shoe, was not killed until the summer of 1748 after the more influential chiefs of the nation had decided that he should be sacrificed as a means of restoring peace between the warring factions, and even then his death was of no avail, for the English by means of bribes had a younger brother placed at the head of their faction and the war was continued.

[2] Chunkey, a Choctaw town in the neighborhood of the "Six Villages."

the ill treatment he had received, both in his own person and in the persons of his wives. He even asked if it was by order of M. the governor that there were sent chiefs and other Frenchmen, who were in the nation, to employ insulting terms towards them and their wives. That we ought to know that that caused much hard feeling and that the red men killed each other for such things. He added that his brother had seen with indignation the little importance that we made of him; that it even seemed that a trader had been placed with Pouchimatahâ at Toussana, only for the purpose of emphasizing it; [all of] which had determined him the more promptly to commit that folly; that it was true that the English had demanded but one French head for an Englishman who had been killed by the Tchactas of the village of the Bois Bleux; that the warriors had exceeded his order, which made matters worse. He also said that the partisans of his brother hoped that the English would have supplied them with goods and munitions in abundance, but that they already realized that their hopes were vain and futile; that an Abékas of the west who had been to the Chikachas to trade his skins, had returned from there much dissatisfied, without having brought back either goods or munitions; that the Chikachas had told him that they did not have any for themselves [and] that even if they had they would not trade with him and that he could carry back his skins, which he was obliged regretfully to do. Upon his return he had displayed his dissatisfaction to Ymatahatchitou, who was much surprised [and] told him to have patience until the English convoy should arrive, when they would have everything in abundance. That is the way that man feeds them with imagination, while we are unable to obtain anything with the reality, either through our presents or through trade.

I sounded this Captain in private: he replied to me that it was true that in the beginning, [upon the occasion] of the death of the Frenchmen, he had given the Reverend Father Baudoüin some hope that he would avenge us, but that to-day, whatever attachment he might have for us he would not dare to undertake such an affair. And he said to me nothing more.

The former chief of Tchanké spoke well, in the evening, for us; and [spoke] ill in the morning.

The 14th Tamatlémingo, with his men, took leave of me and promised to hasten to the Allibamonts to deliver the letter, with which I had charged him, to M. Lesueur, whom I directed, as soon as he should have received it, to send to the Abékas to prevent the English from taking any extra merchandise to the Chikachas, so that these latter should not be able to trade anything to the Tchactas, and to spare neither effort nor goods to keep them [the Tchactas] away from those parts, that being the surest method of forcing them, in spite of themselves, to give us satisfaction, thus putting us in a position to reform many of the rascals of that faithless nation who indirectly have been accomplices in the affair of Ymatahatchitou.

Tamatlémingo, to whom I confided my thought, appreciated fully the importance of it, and promised to make all possible diligence [saying] that on the day after his arrival he would take the orders of M. Lesueur to go to the Abékas where he would act in conformity with my intentions. I also wrote by him to M. Hazeur and told him that I was leaving with some hope of [securing] vengeance; that I had set everything in motion for the attainment of our ends; that I was leaving to Providence, to the Reverend Father Baudoüin, and to him to do the rest; and above all that he should not delay Tamatlémingo [explaining the reasons], but that, on the contrary, he should urge him to make great diligence; that he should trade no more munitions to the Tchactas; the Reverend Father Baudoüin will act in the same way, on his side.

The 14th after having taken leave of the Reverend Father Baudoüin, recommending him to appeal strongly to those who seemed well inclined toward us, and to bring it to pass that the promised reward should not fall to the race of the rebel, so that we might be in a position to degrade it [the race] later, I was about to mount my horse when I was told that some chiefs of the district of the east were arriving in the village. I waited for them until ten o'clock, [but] seeing that they did not come I told the Reverend Father to announce to them the message of M. the governor, to make them a small present as I had done to those who came to see me, and to take the medal of Choubkoôulacta if they brought it, and to send it to me. I mounted my horse that I might join my men who had left that morning for the Yoüanys, ten leagues distant, where I arrived in the evening. They received me with affability and assured me of their fidelity.

The 15th, in the morning, I left for the River of Baka-tanné, which I reached by evening, by roundabout and difficult roads in order to avoid surprises, the savages of our escort fearing much for us, which led them to make us take an indirect route.[1]

The 16th at daybreak the Taskanangouchy of the Youânis joined me, with letters from M. Hazeur and one from the Reverend Father Baudoüin, who sent me the medal of Choulkoualacta, telling me that Uatachimingo [and] Thiououlacta had come to see me and to assure me of the fidelity of all the district of the east, that they had handed over the medal to him, which he sent me, that he was even sorry that I had not seen them, because I would have been as satisfied with them as I had reason for being dissatisfied with the Oügou lafalaÿa and with the six villages ; but that he had not left them in ignorance of anything as regarded the object of my journey, and that they had all promised to act accordingly.

The 17th and *the 18th* we continued our journey without any misadventures. We had rain day and night and were obliged to cross several ravines and creeks with unbelievable troubles and fatigues.

The 19th we set out early in the morning. We had much bad weather and were obliged to cross still further ravines and creeks which were much more difficult and

---

[1] *Fausser la route.*

troublesome than [those of] the two preceeding days, since we were in water up to the belly. I was even obliged to leave two of my horses three leagues from here, they not being able to hold themselves up any longer. In spite of all that my people came back in good health. I arrived at Mobille towards one hour after midday. I dismounted at the house of M. De Louboey, where I recounted to him, in few words, the success of my journey, to tell him more when I should have changed, being all drenched. That, then is the fruit of the journey which I have made with pleasure for the service of the King and of the Country.

May God bless my work

Signed   DE BEAUCHAMPS.

JOURNAL OF CAPTAIN PHINEAS STEVENS' JOURNEY TO CANADA, 1752

INTRODUCTION

PHINEAS STEVENS and three younger brothers were with their father in a meadow near Rutland, Massachusetts, when, the 14th of August, 1723, they were surprised by five Indians. The father escaped, two brothers were killed, Phineas and the other brother, Isaac, were taken prisoners. Phineas was a youth in his eighteenth year; Isaac, a child of four. The Indians resolved to kill the child, but Phineas saved his life by making them understand that he would carry him on his back. They were taken to Canada, but were soon ransomed. In 1740 Stevens removed to the frontier town Number Four (now Charlestown, New Hampshire) of which he was one of three principal founders, and here, in 1747, with a garrison of only thirty men he successfully defended a wooden fort against a war party of three hundred or more French and Indians under Boucher de Niverville. Throughout the third Intercolonial War he was frequently commissioned by Governor Shirley to command volunteers for the defense of the frontier.

Peace having been concluded, Shirley sent him to Canada in 1749 to recover whatever prisoners were held there either by the French or by the Indians, and in 1752 Acting Governor Phips sent him thither on a second mission for the same purpose. While on each of these missions he kept a journal. That kept on the first mission was published in 1837 in the *Collections* of the New Hampshire Historical Society, Vol. V. That kept on the second mission is the one here printed. It is especially valued for its record of the ransom of John Stark, the hero of Bennington, for "an Indian poney . . . for which we paid 515 livres." The original journal was found on one occasion "at the bottom of an old churn in a garret in Charlestown." It was subsequently removed to the State House at Montpelier, Vermont, but was there destroyed by fire in January, 1857. A copy of it, however, has been preserved in the Library of Congress.

JOURNAL OF CAPTAIN PHINEAS STEVENS'
JOURNEY TO CANADA, 1752

Instructions to Capt: Phineas Stevens and Mr. Nathaniel Wheelwright, appointed to proceed to Canada, to negotiate the restoration of the Captives belonging to this Province, now remaining in the hands of the French or Indians there.

You are hereby directed with all convenient speed to proceed to Albany, and there furnishing yourselves with a suitable Guide and Guides and other Assistance necessary for your convenient and safe Travel, to go direct to the Fort at Crown Point, and upon your arrival there apply yourselves to the Commanding Officer of that Garrison, and after shewing him your Passport and acquainting him with your general business, request of him to give Orders for your Speedy and Safe Conveyance to the Governour or Commander in Chief of the Province of Canada.[1]

And upon your arrival at the place of Residence of the said Commander-in-Chief, immediately wait on him, and deliver my Letter to him shew him your Passport, and take his time for receiving his Answer to my demand of his delivering up, without Ransom, the Captives in the hands of the French or Indians; which you are to urge as far as you shall find necessary, or Convenient.

But if you find he cannot be prevailed with to release the Captives without Ransom, you must treat with him about their release upon the easiest and most reasonable Terms that may be obtained.

You must use all the advantages you may have of getting a knowledge of the several Prisoners, whether English or

[1] Charles Lemoyne, Baron de Longueuil, was Governor of Canada from February to July, 1752.

Indians belonging to this Province, now remaining in that
Country, with their respective Circumstances and Condition, and if it should be pretended that any of them are
unwilling to return you must endeavour, if it be possible to
come at a Speech with them, and use your best endeavours
to prevail upon them to return with you, with the leave of
the Governour or Commander-in-Chief.

You are hereby impowered and directed to draw upon
the Province Treasurer, for such sum or sums as you may
find necessary, as well for the Ransome of the Prisoners, as
for the Charge of their Travel and other Contingencies that
may require it, or use such other way or method of supply-
ing your Credit as you may find most suitable.

When your business is finished and you have received the
Governour of Canada's Despatches for this Government,
take back your English Passport and get one from the
French Governour for your safe conduct home.

You must keep a Journal of your Proceedings, and also
an Account of the Articles of Expense of the Publick money
put into your hands, and lay the same before me and the
Council, at your return.

Cambg [1] April the 15th 1752.

S. Phips.[2]

[Cambrg N.E., April 14. 1752.

Sir,[3]

This comes to your Excellency by Captain Phineas
Stevens, who was employed by Governour Shirley, before
his departure for Great Britain, to carry Dispatches to you.

The Affair Captain Stevens was then engaged in (viz. to
procure the recovery and return of our Captives in the
hands of the French and Indians) being not yet fully effected,
I have sent him together with Mr. Nathaniel Wheelwright,

---

[1] Cambridge, Massachusetts.
[2] Spencer Phips was Acting Governor of Massachusetts in
1749-1753.
[3] The Governor of Canada.

with these my Letters to you: And with Directions to do every thing necessary on the part of this Government, for the Deliverance of the rest of our Captives, still remaining in any part of the Government of Canada.

You will therefore please to receive these Gentlemen in the Character of Messengers from this Government, for transacting the Affair abovementioned, and give them all the assistance necessary to make their Business successfull, that so, (if it be possible) there may not remain one single subject of This His Majesty's Government, either English or Indian under their miserable Captivity.

And I am the rather moved to urge this Business with freedom and importunity, by reason of the solicitous care our respective Masters have expressed to have this matter completely effected; as you will see by the inclosed Copy of his Most Christian Majesty's Order to your Excellency (which I suppose you have received,) the Counterpart of which I have also received from his Britannick Majesty, my most Gracious Master; and I have so completely fulfilled the Directions contained therein, as that I am well assured that there is not one single Person, French or Indian, Subject of his Most Catholick Majesty, or in alliance with him, under Captivity, in any part of this Government.

I must in a particular manner repeat my pressing Demands for the restoration of any of those Indians, (now surviving) the Subjects of this his Majesty's Government, who were taken upon the Sea, being on a Whaling Voyage, or any other Indians belonging to this Province, some of whom it has been reported are treated as Slaves, tho' in this Province they live in as much freedom as the English themselves.

It seems highly unjust and contrary to the Form of the Articles of Peace, always stipulated between the Powers of Europe, that this Government should be put to any charge for the Ransom of Prisoners of War, after a Peace concluded; and I am confident that no one instance can be produced of any Ransom being paid by the French Government or private persons for the release of their Prisoners or that their Release was ever denied them under pretence of their being in the hands of the Indians: And therefore I must once more urge my Demand that all the Prisoners belonging to this Government may be discharged without Ransom.

I have [*remainder of this letter missing*]

April 27, 1752. I set out from No. 4.[1] for Canada, my son Samuel with me; came two miles below Fort Turner; and lodged at Caleb Hows.

April 28th. Hired said How with two horses (for which I paid him two dollars) came to Deerfield. Lodged at Col. Hinsdell's.

April 29th. To Hatfield, where I met with Mr. Wheelwright, and returned with him to Deerfield the same day, where we remained, preparing for our journey till

May 4th then set out and came at Francis Taylor's, 12 miles, and lodged a[2] 1 dollar.

May 5th. To Fort Massachusetts,[3] accompanied by Capt. Moses.

May 6th. After making a present to the soldiers of one dollar, we set out, accompanied by Capt. Williamson, till noon; then took our leave of him, and came to Albany. Same day had an account of three soldiers being drowned in the morning of the said day, belonging to the fort at Albany.

May 7th we spent in visiting and consulting with some of the chief men in the place how to proceed in our Journey to Canada.

May 8th. We agreed with an Indian to assist with his son in our journey; and also engaged Mr. Sanders[4] (the mayor of the city) to provide all things needful for our journey.

May 9th. We sent a man to Skanately[5] to buy a canoe, for a suitable one was not to be found in Albany.

[1] Now Charlestown, New Hampshire.
[2] For.
[3] Fort Massachusetts was near the site of the present town of Adams, Massachusetts.
[4] Robert Sanders was Mayor of Albany in 1750–1754.
[5] Skaneateles, N. Y.

May 10th. Lords Day — exceeding dry sermon.

May 11th. The two Indians came from Stockbridge, in order to go with us.

May 12th. Fixed our canoe, and set all things in readiness for our journey.

May 13th. I set out from Albany, with Heywood, and Samuel; and the two Indians came with our canoe and lading 16 miles, and lodged at Jacob Foot's, a Dutchman.

May 14th. I hired the said Dutchman to carry our baggage in a wagon to Stillwater, 6 miles. I with the two Indians came up the swift water in the canoe. Then took the lading and came to Saratogue [1] and lodged [having travelled] 24 miles this day. Mr. Wheelwright came on horseback this day from Albany, and lodged at Saratogue.

May 15th. I came with the canoe three miles above Lydies'es,[2] and lodged at the foot of the falls. Mr. Wheelwright lodged at Lydies'es. It rained at night.

May 16th. Col. Lydies joined Mr. Wheelwright and met the canoe (at the place where we take our departure from Hulstines [or Hulstions] river)[3] with five horses which assisted us in carrying our baggage. We came this day half way over the carrying place, and lodged by the branch of Wood creek. It rained hard at night.

May 17th. We came to the Lake St. Sacrement [4] about noon, with all our bagg[ag]e. Col. Lydies, with the two Indians with him, turned back. After we had mended our canoe, we embarked, and came eight miles, and camped on the west side of the lake. Showery weather.

May 18th. Came over said lake. Lodged at the canoeing place from said lake to the drowned land.

May 19th. Carried our baggage over the carrying place; then embarked, and came to the French settlements, three

---

[1] Old Saratoga; now Schuylerville.

[2] John Henry Lydius, who had built Fort Lydius to protect his settlement at the Falls of the Hudson. This fort was destroyed by the French and Indians in 1745 and ten years later the historic Fort Edward was erected on the same site.

[3] Hudson River. [4] Lake George.

miles south of Crown Point. Lodged in a French house. A very stormy day. Wind at head, and rain.

May 20th. The storm continued at North East and rained. We came to Crown Point at two o'clock afternoon. The commandant received us kindly.

May 21st. It stormed. We remained at the Fort.

May 22d. The storm somewhat abated. We set off from the Fort at six afternoon in a large batteau accompanied by a French officer and five soldiers; came about two miles, and lodged on the east side of the lake [1] in a French house.

N.B. The commandant of the Fort fitted us out with all things necessary for our journey.

May 23d. Set out very early in the morning. Cloudy and some rain; but not much wind. Came about thirty miles; the wind freshened up at northeast. We put into the mouth of a river, on the west side of the lake; at which place there is a fine pine plain. After we had refreshed ourselves, we embarked and came twelve miles, and lodged on an island.

May 24th. Lords day. The wind blew up at south. We hoisted sail at day light. The wind continued in our favor till afternoon, which brought us in sight of Fort La Motte; then turned into the northeast. We then took down our sail, and rowed till four afternoon, which brought us to the south end of the above said island,[2] in sight of a number of French houses; but the wind so very high, and having a large bay to cross, we turned to the west shore. A little before night the wind fell: We crossed the bay three miles to a French house and lodged.

May 25th. Set forward early in the morning. Came fifteen miles, and stopped at a French house on the east side, just above an Island. Below [3] said Island it is called Chamblee River.[4] Here we refreshed ourselves, etc. Then

---

[1] Lake Champlain.   [2] Isle La Motte.

[3] *I.e.* north of.

[4] That part of the Richelieu or Sorel River above the Falls was at this time known as the Chambly River.

embarked, and came eighteen miles to St. Johns fort.[1] Immediately upon our arrival the officer of the fort sent an express to La Prarie for horses and carts to convey our baggage from hence.

May 26th. About ten in the morning the two carts came. After dinner loaded our things into the carts and came off. The officer, Mr. Wheelwright, and myself rode on horses sent for that purpose. Came to La Prarie a little before night. It rained most of the way.

May 27th. A large batteau and a number of hands was made ready, which brought us to Montreal. We arrived at the Governor's about ten in the forenoon. After he had read our passport, letters, etc., we retired to Madam Carols where we took up our lodgings; then returned to the Governor's, and dined. After this we visited the commissioners and several other gentlemen.

May 28th and so [continued doing] till *the*

30th [which] we spent in making the best inquiries we could where our prisoners were, etc.

May 31st. The Sabbath day. It rained at night.

June the 1st. We dined with the Governor, and at night supped with an officer. This day a schooner arrived from Quebec, and we have a hint as if she brings news of a large army's being about to go to Jebuctoo[2] and also that a mutiny has happened amongst the soldiers at Quebec.

June 2d. Had the news of the Indians killing and taking four of our people.

June 3d. Dined with the Commissary.

June 4th. Mr. Linglauesne and his wife came to visit us.

June 5th. Nothing remarkable.

June 6th. Mr. Wheelwright and I wrote a letter to Governor Phips, and several other letters for New England.

June 7th. Sabbath day. Very hot weather.

June 8th. Mr. Wheelwright went to Connewago with a number of French gentlemen.

[1] Fort Saint John was at the head of the falls of the Richelieu River.

[2] Chebucto, now Halifax, Nova Scotia.

June 9th. Had further news of more mischief being done on our people, and that three prisoners were brought to Crown Point.

June 10th. Paid a visit to the Governor, who told us he had no intelligence of any prisoner being brought to Crown Point. At night we supped at Mr. St. Luke Laurens. This day three men and a woman obtained a pass from the Governor and set out for New England themselves. Said the[y] belonged to the Province of Pennsylvania.

June 11th. Nothing remarkable.

June 12th. I visited French's sisters. This day were told by John Tasble that the mischief the Indians had done on the English was at White River, and that there was six in company. Two made their escape; two killed; and two taken prisoners. At night was taken with a terrible purging.

June 13th. I kept house with the same distemper.

June 14th. Sabbath day. Two small schooners arrived at Montreal from Quebec, loaded with flour; which might certainly denote a very great scarcity; for the most of the supply for that place are in time of plenty carried from hence. This day dined at Madam Lestushes Supped at a gentleman's house near the same place.

June 15th. Lewse, a Frenchman, (who lately came from Albany,) came to visit us. Gave an account of two negroes being taken at a place called Canterbury one [1] Merrimac River; one of which he saw at Crown Point, bought by the Commissary of said Fort, for 400 Livres. The other made his escape the fortnight after he was taken. He also informed us he saw nine Indians set off from thence for war, who told him they designed for some of the English settlements, for if they must fight the English they would not go so far. They look upon them to be all one people.

June 16th. It thundered and rained a small matter in the morning. Mr. Wheelwright set off for Quebec about 12 o'clock, with Mr. Deplace, the high Sheriff. We have

[1] On.

repeated accounts of the Dureedweer Indians doing [evil] upon the French traders in the westward, which puts the merchants in Montreal into a consternation. There is nothing can hurt this country so much as to distress their trade in those parts; for their income from thence seems to be the dependance of the whole country. Vast numbers are employed in that business. We are told that 200 large birch canoes and batteaux are gone up the river this spring — some five, and some six men each; so that upwards of a thousand men are already gone upon that business. Their method of carrying on the trade is for the chief traders of factors to remain in that country for three or four years, and have supplies sent them yearly. Tis said some of these traders go 3000 miles; but their supplies are not sent so far — they go no farther than some of the French forts that are kept in those parts—viz—those westward parts. So these ramblers are obliged to return once a year to said forts for a new supply. Could our people be so well spirited in time of war as to go and destroy those forts, it must in a short time so impoverish Canada that it must fall an easy prey into our hands.

June 17th. A soldier was shot to death for deserting from some of the French forts in the westward. This day I received a letter from Mr. Hardwick, a prisoner at St. Francois, taken from Chebucto.[1]

June 18th. It thundered and rained a small matter, but the drought is very great. The wheat in this country suffers very much. There is intelligence from Quebec that several vessels are arrived there from France laden with flour and pork.

June 19th. I received a letter from the missionary of St. Francis and another from the abovementioned woman. A number of Indians came to town to night. Tis said they have brought two scalps, and two prisoners; but it wants confirmation.

June 20th. I went round the town to look for a good

---

[1] Now Halifax, Nova Scotia.

gun. The scalps abovementioned were brought from the westward, and tis said are Indian's scalps.

June 21st. Sabbath day. Hot and dry.

June 22d. A number of the chiefs of the St. Francois Indians came to Montreal, and showed me the respect as to come the same day and pay me a visit.

June 23d. After dinner the Governor sent for me to appear before him and his council to receive a message from the St. Francois Indians. I accordingly did and after their spokesman had made his speech, he delivered me a large belt of wampum, which he said I must deliver with his message to the Governor at Boston. The same day I gave my old Indian father a hat, price 10 Livres — he being one of the chiefs abovementioned.

June 24th. I sent a letter to one of the Jesuits at St. Francois by an Indian.

June 25th. I had a hint from an Indian as if a belt of wampum was come into this country from some of the Six Nations in order for a treaty with some or all the tribes of Indians here. There is numbers of the former tribes of Indians coming to Montreal every few days. The drought is now very extraordinary. The wheat in this country, tis thought, has received so much damage already that a crop cannot be expected this year, and as they had but a very small crop last year, the calamity of this country must certainly in a little time be very great.

June 26th. Something likely for rain, but very hot and dry.

June 27th. A small matter of rain fell in the morning; in the afternoon windy and dry. The great probability of a scarcity casts a sadness in all faces. In the evening it clouded up and bid fair for rain, but broke away with but a small sprinkling.

June 28th. Sabbath day, and kept as a day of rejoicing with them for the birth of a young prince born in France, they have lately had news of.[1] They went in procession

---

[1] Louis, duc de Bourgogne, born September 13, 1751, eldest son of the Dauphin, eldest grandson of Louis XV., and heir to the throne. Louis XVI. was his younger brother.

and fired all their cannon, viz. 33 in number. A black cloud came up at night, but no rain.

June 29th. I paid my respects to the Governor. He informed me of a great difficulty at Chebucto, but did not let me know what it was about.

June 30th. Four large birch canoes containing nine or ten Indians each came to Montreal. Tis said those Indians' place of abode is 1800 miles from hence. There came also a batteau with nine or ten Frenchmen to town from a French fort west of our English governments, 900 miles from hence. They brought with them an Englishman, who deserted from some of our Indian traders from Philadelphia. His name is Jonathan Lafavour. There came also four canoes of Indians from Albany.

July 1st. A large number of Indians came to town from Becanco[ur] an Indian town on the south side the Great River near the Three Rivers. This day a number of women came to the Commissary for bread, and upon his refusing to let them have any, one of them took him by the throat. Exceeding hot and dry weather.

July 2d. I received a letter from Mr. Wheelwright at Quebec informing of his speedy arrival at Montreal. The weather is yet exceeding hot.

July 3d. Mr. Wheelwright returned to Montreal from Quebec; brought with him two men taken at New Medows last summer. Great numbers of Indians are daily coming to town to receive their presents from their fathers, as they term it.

July 4th. Two of the Ottawa Indians, being almost drunk, fell out to such a degree that one stabbed the other with his knife so that he expired in a few minutes. An old Indian that sit by and see the action ordered a lad of about 14 or 15 years of age (being a near relation of him that was stabbed) to charge his gun and be ready to kill the other as soon as the first was dead. The boy accordingly did with deliberation. The French people that were by told the murderer to make his escape. He moved off slowly. The boy stood with his gun in his hand till his kinsman was quite gone; and as soon as he see him fetch his last breath, he went after the other with as much calmness as he was in pursuit of some game. When the murderer saw the lad after him he endeavored to hide himself; but the boy was so lucky as to see him lie down in a place of wheat. The boy went as near as he thought convenient, and then first gave him a mortal wound; but he retained so much strength that he rose up and pursued the boy but not far. The old Indian that gave the boy his orders seeing that he was not killed outright ran with his knife and gave him several stabs, so that he died immediately — so that in half an hour's time they were both dead. This was transacted just without the wall of Montreal.

July 5th. Sunday. Two prisoners were brought to town from St. Francoes, viz. Seth Webb and Amos Eastman. We bought them at 300 Livres each, and ten livres each for the charge of bringing them to Montreal.[1]

July 6th. I received a letter from the missionary of St. Franscoes.

July 7th. Mrs. Honor Hancok, a prisoner taken from Jebucto was brought to Montreal; which we bought at 300 livres, and 30 livres for the charge of bringing her.

July 8th. Mr. Wheelwright and I went to visit a captive girl named Elizabeth Cody. She lived at the hospital south of the town.

July 9th. A great number of the St. Franscoes Indians came to Montreal. Brought with them some of our captive boys. There came up a smart thunder shower at night, and for about half an hour it rained hard, so that the water run in brooks in the streets.

July 10th. Mr. Wheelwright and I paid our respects to the Governor, in the morning. [In the] Afternoon I bought two guns, price 65 livres, 10 sous, each; of which Mr.

[1] In *Documents Relative to the Colonial History of the State of New York*, Vol. X, pp. 252–254, is a copy of what purports to be minutes of conference of Stevens with the St. Francis Indians held this day — July 5, 1752 — in the presence of the Baron de Longueuil. For some of the captives named below, see C. Alice Baker, *True Stories of New England Captives*, pp. 335–348.

Wheelwright paid 66 livres, 15 sous. The heat increases very much.

July 11th. An exceedingly hot day. Being by the river side I see the French people dig ice out of the bank, which was hove up in the winter and covered by the bank falling down upon it. They use this ice to preserve their fresh meat.

July 12th. Sabbath day. Hot and dry. Clouds of smoke are rising in all parts of this country — a surprising sight at this time of year.

July 13th. Mr. Wheelwright and my self went before the Governor with a Dutch girl taken in the war, named Elizabeth Cody, and an English boy named Solomon Metchel, 12 years old taken about one year ago. Upon their refusing to go home the Governor would not give them up. The same day John Starks [1] was brought to Montreal by his Indian Master. He was taken a hunting this spring. He is given us for an Indian poney in his place, for which we paid 515 livres.

July 14th. We took our leave of the Governor and the rest of the chief Officers and made all things ready for our return to New England.

July 15th. We set out from Montreal for New England. Brought with us eight prisoners, viz: two taken from Jebucto, Thomas Stanard and Honor Hancock; two men from New Hampshire, Amos Estmon and John Stark, taken a hunting; Joseph Fortner, taken west of Pennsylvania; from the Massachusetts Edmund Hinckley, Samuel Lambart, and Seth Webb. We came this day to Laperary.[2] It rained a smart shower as we crossed the river, and some in the night.

July 16th. Set out from thence — came to St. Johns. Our baggage was brought in carts. An officer is sent with us, who has orders to conduct us to the first English land. We remained till 5 afternoon, then set out with a batteau and a birch canoe. Came 18 miles and lodged.

July 17th. Embarked very early in the morning. Came

[1] John Stark, the hero of the Battle of Bennington (August 16, 1777).   [2] La Prairie.

about 45 miles. Met several canoes from Albany. It rained some showers.

July 12th. Sabbath day. Two small barks arrived from Quebec. I this day saw a man in prison. [He said] His name was Johnson and that he had an uncle in Boston, named George Johnson, and a kinsman one Wm. Johnson. His father, he says, lives in Edinburgh in Scotland, and is a man of note. Look back for the 12th day and then add this above.

July 18th. Embarked early in the morning — wind at head and some rain. We came to the mouth of Otter creek and turned ashore to lodge; but the small flies were so plenty that we could not sleep. We embarked again about 2 at night — wind at northeast and some hard showers of rain. We hoisted sail and came to Crown Point about sunrise. I would note that my old Indian master came in the canoe with me and that the quarter part of the St. Fransioes Indians have left their town for want of protection, and are on the road to the Dutch Settlements. We remained at Crown Point all day, being Sabbath day. The wind blew hard all the day, but we could not prevail with the Indians, being none here but of the St. Fransioes tribe. The negro which the Commissary of the fort bought of the Indian taken at Canterbury, we cannot get for the same money we suppose he bought him for. The gentleman declares he gave 600 livres for him. We have been informed he gave but 400 — the captain's lady told us she was offered him for that money.

July 20th. The Indians we had engaged to go with us to Lydies's failing us and not coming, obliged us to remain at the fort all day. Just at night agreed with two other Indians so that Mr. Wheelwright and five of our people set off at sunset. I with the rest lodged at the fort.

July 21st. I, with the people left with me, set out from Crown Point at ten in the morning, accompanied by an officer and ten soldiers, who brought us in two log canoes. We came all night up the drowned land. Arrived at the landing place at the west end of the great bay west of the mouth of wood creek. At 8 the next morning we slept and refreshed ourselves till two afternoon; then bound up our packs and set forward. Came about one mile and passed by a family of Indians. Came 7 miles and camped.

July 23d. In the mo[r]ning I missed my sword which I had left at the place where we first took up our packs. Sent two men back : they found it with the Indians abovementioned. We came this day to Col. Lydis's. Met with Mr. Wheelwright (who came by the way of the lake St. Sacrement.[1]) He was obliged to leave the canoe and loading on the carrying place. The Indians leaving him, he came to Lydeses for help.

July 24th. I went with Lydieses son with three horses to assist in getting our things to Hutson's River. I hired two Mohawks to carry the canoe. Brought our things to the river and returned to Lydyes at night met great numbers of the St. Francois Indians coming to Albany with beaver.

July 25th. Came from Lydyeses to Saratogue. Lodged at Mr. Killians. The two Mohawks that brought our canoe over the carrying came thus far with us for which we paid them six dollars.

July 26th. Sabbath day. Mr. Wheelwright and his man came on horseback to Albany. I with the canoe and the rest of our people came within 10 miles of Albany. I paid 3 dollars for the carrying our things by the bad water.

July 27th. Came to Albany about 12 o'clock. Remained there the rest of the day.

July 28th. I remained at Albany upon the desire of a number of the St. Francois Indians, who this day had a sort of treaty with the Dutch Traders. They met at 10 forenoon — [They] made a small speech to the Dutch, in which they manifest a great desire for peace; then delivered a belt of wampum and a pack of beaver. The Dutch desired their attendance at 3 afternoon. They accordingly met, when the Dutch made their speech, in which they gave them free liberty to come and trade without molesta-

---

[1] Lake George.

tion, and [told them] that the road was open. Then [the Dutch] made them a present of a belt of wampum, and two pieces of   2 kegs of rum, tobacco, etc. The Indians received them thankfully.

July 29th. I set out from Albany with my son. Came to the first Dutch house on Hoosack river, and lodged. Wm. Heywood and the seven prisoners who came off the day before lodged at Fort Massachusetts.

July 30th. I came to Capt. Rice's where I overtook the above said men. Here we all lodged.

July 31st. Came to Deerfield and lodged.

August 1st. I sent an express to Boston with the letters that came from Canada; and four of the prisoners went down the country road for home, three of which belonged to the eastward, the others to Jebucto. I came with the rest of the people to Northfield.

August 2d. Lords day. Went to meeting. After meeting came to Hinsdell's Fort [1] with my son and Joseph Fortner. The two Hampshire men set off for Wenchester.[2]

August 3d. Came with my son to No. 2. Left Fortner with Col. Hinsdell. Wm. Heywood remains at Northfield to hunt for his horse, that left him at the carrying place.

August 4th. Came to No. 4. Found my family all well, my wheat all reaped, etc.

August 5th and *6th.* My people finished reaping my oats.

August 7th. I begun to   them.

August 8th. A paper was drew up, and signed for me to go to New Hampshire, etc.

August 9th. Lords day.

August 10th. A day of rain. I prepared for my Journey.

August 11th. I set out for Portsmouth. Came to Col. Hinsdells fort.

August 12th. Stopped the greater part of day at said fort to get my linen washed. Came to Northfield at night.

---

[1] Hinsdels Fort was near the west bank of the Connecticut River, a little above what is now the northern boundary of Massachusetts. A few miles N. by E. of it was Fort Dummer.

[2] Winchester.

August 13th. [Came] to Deerfield to get my clothes. Returned the same day to Winchester, where I met Capt. Hubard. We lodged at Major Willards.

August 14th. We came to   and lodged at Col. Berrys house. It rained the most of the day.

August 15th. [Came] to Luneinburge.

August 16th. Lords day.

August 17th. Hubard and I, in company with Mr. Bellows came to Col. Blanchard at Dunstable and lodged.

August 18th. After dinner I set out from thence and came to Chester and lodged at Capt. Dalford's.

August 19th. Said Capt. set out with me and came to Portsmouth. I remained there till *the*

24th. In which time I lodged a proposition with the Governor and counsel for the township No. 4. I came from Portsmouth to Ipswich, and lodged at Mr. Rogers'.

August 25th. Came to Boston by the way of Cambridge and Roxbury.

August 26th. At Boston I lodged with Mr. Lyman.

27. I set out from Boston. Came as far as Marlborough.

August 28th. [Came] to Rutland.

August 29th. At Rutland.

August 30th. Lords day.

August 31st. Came from Rutland to Hardwicke.

Sept. 1st. Came to Hatfield.

Sept. 2nd. [Came] to Deerfield. Bought a trunk of Madam Hinsdell, in which I put my clothes and sent them to Northfield. The next day, which, according to act of Parliament,[1] is *the*

14th. I came to Col. Hinsdells fort. It rained some

Sept. 15th. I came to Killbruns at No. 3, and lodged.

Sept. 16th. [Came] home to No. 4.[2]

Sept. 17th. Lords day. From the

[1] By the Act of Parliament here referred to eleven days were omitted in the record of time so that the day after September 2, 1752, was recorded as September 14, 1752.

[2] There is a note in the margin as follows: Joseph Woods moved out of the fort this week.

18th to the *23d* exceeding dry weather. The Great River is thought to be as low as has been known these many years past. Some of our people are gone down to Deerfield and Hatfield this week, viz. Dr. Hastings and wife, Joseph Willards and Hastings wives. Thos. Putnam and Isaac Parker went with a canoe for salt, etc. I this week begun to fall timber for a house.

Sept. 24th. Sabbath day.

Sept. 25th. I sawed timber for clapboards etc. A great supply of rain at night. The water in puddles the next morning.

Sept. 26th. It rained part of the day.

Sept. 27th. A hard frost at night.

Sept. 28th. I began to make a road at the south end of my house lot. Ebr. Putnam and his brother Larence set out upon a journey.

Sept. 29th. I finished the above said road. The whole cost me seven days work.

Sept. 30th. It rained hard afternoon.

October 1st. Lords day. Stephen Farnsworth had an ox killed by the fall of a tree.

Oct. 2d. Wright had a barrel rum brought to the fort. I bought a three acre lot of Joseph Woods.

Oct. 3d. Elijah Grout left me and set out for home.

Oct. 4th. I fell timber, etc.

Oct. 5th. I begun to hew timber for my house.

Oct. 6th. I gathered my corn.

Oct. 7th. I carted my corn.

Oct. 8th. Sabbath day. It rained hard all day.

Oct. 9th. The storm continued.

Oct. 10th. At husking. Pleasant weather, but clouded up at night, and bid fair for more rain.

Oct. 11th. It rained the most of the day.

Oct. 12th. I finished husking my corn.

Oct. 13th. It rained part of the day. It is now a very wet season.

Oct. 14th. Lieut. Bellows came to No. 4.

Oct. 15th. Sabbath day.

Oct. 16th. I fell timber, etc.

Oct. 17th. Stephen Davis came to town.

Oct. 18th. I hewed timber with six scoope. The boat came to the falls with salt, rum, etc.

Oct. 19th. Hewed timber with 8 schooars.

Oct. 20th. Hewed with 6 do. Doct. Hastings and wife returned home. Ruth Parker came home.

Oct. 21st. Hewed with six hands.

Oct. 22d. Sabbath day.

Oct. 23d. Hewed with six do. Our people are yet busy at harvesting.

Oct. 24th. Five hands at hewing.

Oct. 25th. Five do. This day two barrels [of] rum [were] brought to the fort.

Oct. 26th. It rained hard the most of the day.

Oct. 27th. Four hands schooring. Drew part timber off.

Oct. 28th. I finished hewing in the forenoon Three at schooring. Afternoon the carpenters went home.

Oct. 29th. Sabbath day.

Oct. 30st. I drew my hay out of the great meadow. Our cattle are now all let into said meadow.

Oct. 31st. There fell a small snow in the morning about 2 inches deep, but all went off before night.

Nov. 1st., 2d., and *3d.* I drew timber for my house etc. Fine pleasant weather. We are now set out for

Nov. 4th. Fine weather.

Nov. 5th. Sabbath day, very warm for the season. I have a cow calf.

Nov. 6th. Drew timber, etc.

Nov. 7th. Davis came in the morning, father Perry with him. Began to frame my house the same day.

Nov. 8th. At framing. Deacon Addams and family came to No. 4.

Nov. 9th. At framing. Lieut. Johnson's wife brought abed of a daughter.

Nov. 10th. At framing. This day a number of men from Woodstock came to No. 4.

Nov. 11th. Forenoon it rained — obliged us to lie by. Afternoon at raising. Begun to raise the sides of the house.

Nov. 12th. Lords day. Our people begin to assemble together for the worship of God.

Nov. 13th. At framing. The lower part of the house is almost up.

Nov. 14th. At framing. A small snow fell at night.

Nov. 15th. I begun to raise my house.

Nov. 16th. I finished. Wheeler and old Mr. Putnam raised the same day. Davis and Jeremy went home.

Nov. 17th and *18th.* Nothing worth notice.

Nov. 19th. Lords day.

Nov. 20th. I sent my son Enos down to Hatfield in company with several others. A stormy day.

Nov. 21st. The storm continued.

Nov. 22d. I worked at my cellar.

August 10th 1752

Cash borrowed of John Hastings Jr 14 Spanish Dollars
      of Caleb Wright   Do. 2
      of Moses Wheeler   1 do.

After I returned home I paid John Hastings one dollar, and allowed Wright for his on my bond against him.

Nov. 23d. I went to No. 3 to help Lieut. Bellows raise his house and a barn. A small snow fell at night.

Nov. 24th. We finished raising the above buildings and returned home. Cold for the season.

A Short Description of the City of Montreal in Canada

Viz: Its built on the south side of the great island called the Island of Montreal. This island is said to be fifteen leagues in length and   in breadth, called the most healthful part of their country, mostly inhabited by tenants put on by the priests and nuns; for they own the greater part of the land. The city is about $\frac{3}{4}$ of a mile in length, and about 100 rods wide in the widest place. It stands on the side of St. Lawrence's river, encompassed round with a wall 16 or 18 feet high. The wall on the river side stands about three rods from highwater mark. The town lies upon a descent of land, so that from the water side to the upper part, or northwestwardly side of [the] town, is up hill, but not very steep.

There is but two streets that go through the length of the town, and so about nine or ten cross streets. This town contains about four hundred dwelling houses, besides public buildings. There is five chapels or churches, viz: one for the barefoot friars; one for the close nuns, to which joins the hospital; one do. for the holy sisters, and one for the Jesuits; and one which is called the great church, where the priests say mass. There is one more just without the walls on the south side joining to the Kings Hospital.

N.B. The walls of the city are not so wide at the north end as at the south; for at the north are but about thirty rods wide. Here is the battery, on a rise of land which commands all the city.

DIARY OF A JOURNEY OF MORAVIANS FROM
BETHLEHEM, PENNSYLVANIA, TO BETHABARA
IN WACHOVIA, NORTH CAROLINA, 1753

INTRODUCTION

THE Moravians made their first settlement in America, in 1735, on the lower Savannah River, where Count Zinzendorf had obtained from the Georgia Trustees a grant of five hundred acres. Rather than bear arms against the Spaniards they removed to Pennsylvania in 1738–1740 and settled Bethlehem and Nazareth. Here by their industry and sobriety they won the good opinion of Thomas Penn, the proprietor, and with his assistance the Moravians procured, in 1749, an Act of Parliament expressly designed to encourage their immigration to the British colonies in America, there to enjoy full liberty of conscience, exemption from military service for reasonable compensation, and permission to make a solemn affirmation instead of taking an oath.

Under the new conditions the Moravians immediately set about to acquire a large tract of land in America on which to build a central town with administrative offices, and with trades, industries, and schools, the town to be also a center from which to carry on missionary work among the Indians, and the remainder of the tract to be sold to and occupied by Moravian farmers. Land was cheaper in North Carolina than in any of the colonies to the northward. Lord Granville, President of the Privy Council, was proprietor of the northern portion of that colony, and he made a liberal offer. Augustus Gottlieb Spangenberg, a bishop in the Moravian Church and superintendent of Moravian affairs in Pennsylvania, was commissioned to select a suitable site. With five of the brethren, all on horseback, he set out from Bethlehem the 25th of August, 1752. The party reached Edenton, North Carolina, the 10th of September and was there joined by Lord Granville's agent and surveyor-general. Weeks of hardship followed, but late in December a site was selected in the region of the head waters of the Yadkin, and here a tract of 98,985 acres was surveyed and named Wachovia. Bishop Spangenberg returned to Bethlehem, and in August, 1753 Lord Granville deeded the tract to the agent of the Church for £500 and a yearly rent of three shillings per hundred acres.

The next step was to establish a settlement, and to this end a party of twelve single men set out from Bethlehem the 8th of October with six horses and a wagon loaded with their effects. The party consisted of Rev. Bernhard Adam Grube, the first minister of the new settlement; Jacob Loesch, business manager; Hans Martin Kalberlahn, physician; Henrich Feldhausen, carpenter; Erich Ingepretsen, carpenter; Hans Petersen, tailor; Jacob Lunge, gardener; Herman Loesch, farmer; Christopher Merkli, baker; Friedrich Jacob Pfeil, shoemaker and tanner; Jacob Beroth, farmer; and Johannes Lischer, farmer. Brethren Gottlob Koenigsderfer, Nathaniel Seidel, and Joseph Haberland accompanied them, but these three soon returned to Bethlehem. The road which they traveled the greater part of the distance was that from the Yadkin River to Philadelphia by way of the Shenandoah Valley, a road which at the time was in the making as the result of a general movement of Germans from Pennsylvania to the "back parts" of Maryland, Virginia, and North Carolina.

It is the account of their journey that is given in this *Diary* which was written by one of the party, most likely by Brother Grube. The original document is preserved in the Archives of the Moravian Church at Winston-Salem, North Carolina; the translation which is here printed is by Miss Adelaide L. Fries, the Archivist.

DIARY OF A JOURNEY OF MORAVIANS FROM BETHLEHEM, PENNSYLVANIA, TO BETHABARA IN WACHOVIA, NORTH CAROLINA, 1753

Travel Diary of the First Company of Single Brethren Going to North Carolina. 1753

At the evening service ("Singstunde") we were prepared for our journey, received the blessing from our dear Brother, and finally partook together of the "Cup of blessing." The next morning, that is

Oct. 8, 1753, we rose early and made ready for our start, our dear Br. Christian Seidel [1] holding morning prayer for us. And so with a feeling of blessing and contentment we set out from our beloved Bethlehem, — the Brn. Grube, Jac. Lösch, Feldhausen, Erich Ingepretsen, Petersen, Lunge, Hermanus Lösch, Markli, Pfeil, Beroth, Lischer, Kalberlahn and Joseph Haberland, the last named to accompany us only to the Susquehannah. Our "Chor Jünger" [2] Br. Gottlob, Hoffman, Eberhard, and several other Brethren went with us for a few miles, and when we had taken tender leave of each other we went our way humbly happy over the goodness that the Lamb of God had shown to us poor mortals in His congregation. The Brethren Gottlob and Nathanael followed us in a few hours, and in the evening we met at the Missellimer Mill and remained there over night, — the people were fairly civil in their entertainment of us though hitherto they have refused to let Brethren stop there. On the way we picked up several pieces of our

[1] Christian Seidel was a Moravian missionary to the Indians.
[2] Superintendent or Leader of the Choir, — *i.e.* the Choir of unmarried men, "Choir" being a division of the congregation, not a group of singers. A. L. Fries.

baggage which had been left by our wagon when it stuck fast and had to be unloaded before it could be pulled out.

Oct. 9. We arose very early to continue our journey, the Brn. Grube and Kalberlahn going a little in advance. A man came to them inquiring whether any one in the party knew how to let blood, saying that a poor servant lay sick at Uly Hui who had heard of us and begged that we would come to him; we therefore went and Br. Kalberlahn bled him, for which he was very thankful, and the people declared themselves as being friendly toward us. At noon we reached the house of Br. Jac. Müller; he was not at home but his son took us across the Tulpehokke [1] in a canoe, it almost upset but our little boatman held it steady. Soon we reached Heidelberg Schoolhouse, and found Br. and Sr. Müller [2] well and glad to see us again and to have us to a meal. There were other Brethren there working on a new hall who rejoiced to greet us once more. Toward evening we reached the home of Br. and Sr. G. Lösch, who gave us hearty welcome; we found there Br. Christ. Rauch who had arrived shortly before us. The Brn. Merk and Ziegler, who had preceded us thus far with the wagon, related their experiences by the way, that it had taken them four days to reach Tulpehokke, and that they had been obliged to abandon part of the baggage, because it had rained a great deal and the road was very muddy. Before we retired Br. Nathanael conducted a "Singstunde," and then we laid ourselves down, as it were, in the arms of Jesus.

Oct. 10. Br. Gottlob held morning prayers. Then we had a conference about our wagon, which is several inches too wide, and therefore does not keep in the beaten track. We finally unloaded it and took it to the blacksmith's shop. The damp articles we dried in the sun. Mother Lösch prepared the necessary provisions for our trip. Br. Rauch

[1] Tulpehocken Creek.
[2] Joseph Mueller, Herman Loesch, and John Merk were members of the exploring party who accompanied Bishop Spangenberg to North Carolina in 1752.

took leave of us and returned to his home in Quittopehill. Br. Beroth crossed the Susquehannah to see his father once more, rejoining us at the river. Br. Nathanael wrote a note to Br. Pader, who is now in York on the Catores,[1] telling him of our journey to Carolina. In the evening when our wagon was ready, having been made three inches narrower, we repacked it by moonlight so that we might make an early start nest morning. Some Brethren from Tonigal, on their way to visit in Bethlehem, arrived at the house; there was hardly room enough for everybody, but Br. and Sr. Lösch rejoiced to have so many Brethren under their roof. Br. Gottlob held a sweet "Singstunde."

Oct. 11. We rose early and prepared for our journey. We gave letters to the Tonigal Brn. to be taken to Bethlehem. Father Lösch lent us his wagon to be used until we were across the Susquehannah, and Mother Lösch supplied us bountifully with bread and meat. Then we bade farewell to these dear people, thanking them heartily for all their trouble and care on our account; they both wept like children, realizing that now for a while they could not see their two sons, Jac. and Herm. At noon we reached our school-house in Quittopehill, and stopped there for lunch. The Brn. Neuser and Engel welcomed us heartily and we were glad to see them. Br. Peter Kucher fed our horses and rejoiced to see us once more. Several Brn. called on Johann Tanneberger, who was much pleased to have a visit from Bethlehem Brethren. When we started again the Brn. Neuser and Engel accompanied us as far as Xander's, which we reached by evening. As we drove over the mill-race bridge it broke in, and it was truly a wonder that our horses and wagon were not thrown into the water; we thanked our Heavenly Father for the escape and for the help of our companions, of which we had great need. Br. Xander was not at home, but his wife and daughter gave us good care. Br. Neuser and Br. Engel went home this evening. Br. Gottlob held a sweet "Singstunde," and spoke

---

[1] Codorus Creek.

on the text "Walk as the children of light," referring feelingly to the blessing and joy that can come into the life of a child of God; and then we went peacefully to rest.

Oct. 12. We rose at four and after morning prayers had breakfast at five and set out at six o'clock. Several young men who love the Brethren accompanied us a little way and were pleasant and cheery. We had traveled eight miles when suddenly a thick tree fell across our team, giving us a fright; however, the trunk fell just between the horses so that neither the horses nor the man who rode one of them were hurt, though a bush on the other side of the road was crushed. This was indeed a marked instance of the protection of our Father, and we thanked Him earnestly and besought His continued care. To-day we shot several fawns, partridges and squirrels. In the evening we made our first camp in the forest, one mile from the Susquehannah, by a creek. All busied themselves collecting wood and building a fire. Br. Erich undertook the cooking, and after we had eaten we spread our blankets and lay down to rest. We also considered whether we should not take Father Lösch's wagon with us, for it was evident that we could hardly make the trip with only our heavily loaded wagon, but as we had not discussed it with Father Lösch we decided that we could not do it. We set our first nightwatch, — Br. Nathanael took the first two hours, and was followed by Br. Grube, and he by Br. Lösch, and in the future three or four Brethren will watch each night. At midnight a drunken Irishman came and laid himself by our fire, but did not disturb us. Br. Gottlob hung his hammock between two trees and rested well in it.

Oct. 13. After eating some broth we set out on our journey. The Brn. Grube and Lösch went ahead to the Susquehannah at Harrison's Ferry [1] to see about our crossing. Br. Grube found an opportunity to send a letter by a Trader to the Brethren in Shomoko. The Susquehannah was so low that the Ferry-boat could not run, so we decided

[1] Harris' Ferry, now Harrisburg, Pennsylvania.

330

to drive across. The Brn. got into the wagons and on the horses and we crossed safely. The Susquehannah is one mile wide here. Br. Beroth and his father soon joined us and brought a letter from Br. Pader, regretting that he could not come to see us and sending affectionate farewell. Two miles beyond the Susquehannah we loaded on our wagon all that had been in Br. Lösch's wagon, since that must now return home. It had been the intention that our beloved Br. Gottlob should here also bid us farewell, but he decided that he and Br. Haberland would go all the way to North Carolina with us, and all hearts rejoiced that we were to have our "Jünger" so much longer with us. Br. Gottlob and Br. Nathanael wrote letters to Bethlehem, and entrusted them to Br. Merk, and then the wagon started back, taking Br. Merk and the little Joseph Müller and G. Lösch. The latter wept sorely at parting from his two brothers, and we were all touched. Then we took up our further way. Beroth's father, who was much pleased that he had seen the first Carolina company, bade us farewell and returned to his home. It is counted 30 miles from here to Yorck on the Catores. The work became rather heavy for the horses and the Brethren had to help push, but we had a good road which was a great blessing. Some miles from the Susquehannah we stopped for the noon hour by an inn, where there is good water. The people thought Br. Gottlob was a Clergyman. We went on; it began to rain, but the shower did not last long. Five miles from the inn we came to a creek; and eight miles beyond to another. We put up our tent for the first time, as a heavy storm came on, and were fairly dry under it and the Brethren slept a little. The storm passing we started again at midnight, and drove several miles to the next stream. We passed a little town called Carl Isles,[1] which contains about 60 houses and is chiefly inhabited by Irishmen.

Oct. 14. Sunday. About four in the morning we set up our tent, going four miles beyond Carl Isles so as not to be

---

[1] Carlisle, nineteen miles W.S.W. of Harrisburg.

too near the Irish Presbyterians. We lay down and slept well for some hours. After breakfast the Brethren shaved, and then we rested under our tent. At noon we dined on pork and dumplings. In the afternoon we were visited by the people from Jersey who were recently in Bethlehem, and they told us about our road. They had broken their wagon crossing the Susquehannah, and were thereby detained several days. They were very friendly, and wished they could stay with us. Toward evening we went three miles further to Widow Tennant's Tavern, and spent the night by the creek. People who were staying at the Tavern came to see what kind of folks we were. We asked them about our road and they were quite polite to us. One of them was born in Silesia, and as a boy lived in the Herrnhut Orphanage; another was the son of the Commissioner of Sakana, and lives in Friedrichstown, Va. We slept to-night without a tent and were quite comfortable.

Oct. 15. We started at 2:30 A.M. had moonlight and a good road; and it was 80 miles to Friedrichstown. On the twelve miles to Shippestown,[1] — a little town, — we found no water. We had a little work done on our wagon, as the pole had been injured. The smith charged a big price and his work did little good. We saw the Blue Mts. some 8 to 10 miles to our right, and had unusually fine weather. We stopped for noon eight miles further on by the Kanikatschik,[2] which is no larger here than the Manakis at Bethlehem. A couple of miles beyond we stopped for the night by Corrnell Chimpersen's mill, where we had good water. Br. Nathanael held the evening service.

Oct. 16. Br. Grube conducted morning prayers, and we set out at 4 A.M. On the way we bought 10 bushels of oats, and after driving five miles had breakfast by a creek where Irish people live. Two miles further we found good water, also three miles beyond, where a house stands back a little on the left. One mile more brought us to a Tavern. We

---

[1] Shippensburg, twenty-two miles W.S.W. of Carlisle.
[2] Conococheague Creek.

could again see the Blue Mts. quite plainly. In another mile we reached a German inn, where we bought some hay and spent the noon hour. Two miles from the inn we passed the boundary between Pennsylvania and Maryland, it is said that Maryland is here only six miles wide. From the Susquehannah here the residents are chiefly Irish, and they have good lands, but one can buy little or nothing from them. Two and a half miles further we came to an old Swiss, where we bought some hay. He was very friendly and asked that we come to see him again. One mile beyond we bought some kraut from a German named Fende Kra, which tasted very good to us. We went on and camped for the night two miles from the Patomik,[1] putting up our tent by a creek. The man on whose land we were came to see us, was very friendly, and took supper with us. He said that he knew the Brn. Rose and Nyberg well, and that some years earlier they had preached in his house here. He was a Swede by birth. Br. Gottlob held the evening service, then we lay down around our cheerful fire, and Br. Gottlob in his hammock, which he had swung between two stakes.

Oct. 17. We started at five o'clock and had two miles to go to the Patomik which we reached at daybreak. Br. Jac. Lösch rode in first to find the ford which makes a decided curve between the banks. We crossed safely but it was very difficult to drive out at the other end and we had a great deal of trouble to get up the bank. The river is here about as wide as the Lecha at Bethlehem, but in flood it runs far over the high banks, and flows swiftly, — toward the south-east. Half a mile from the river is a plantation, and four miles further a Tavern; the road was stony. Four miles further we found good water, and a Tavern; four miles beyond the Tavern we stopped for noon by a creek near a mill which stood on the left of the road. Three miles further was a spring, and after driving four miles more we put up our tent by a creek. For supper we cooked

---

[1] Potomac.

chicken, which tasted very good. Br. Nathanael conducted evening prayer.

Oct. 18. We rose at three; Br. Nathanael held morning prayer. Br. Gottlob reminded us that this was the birthday of our beloved Johannes.[1] The Brn. Gottlob, Haberland and J. Lösch went ahead to Friedrichtown to order various things. We soon followed them with the wagon, having one mile to go to Robert Kornike's mill, and eleven more to Friedrichstown, for seven of which we found no water. We breakfasted by a creek, and two miles beyond found water again. At noon we passed through Friedrichstown,[2] which consists of about sixty houses rather badly built. One mile beyond Friedrichstown we stopped for lunch near a mill, and bought some bread and corn. The Brn. Gottlob and Haberland rejoined us there. We then drove on, soon came to water again, and had four miles to Jost Haid's mill, setting up our tent just beyond. Br. Jac. Lösch rejoined us there; he had been to several plantations to buy bread and oats but had been able to get little. We turned our horses out to graze in a meadow as we had no feed for them; the Brn. Lischer and Merkli stayed with them during the night. Br. Gottlob held evening prayers, and we spoke of our dear Johannes, sang several sweet verses of blessing in his behalf, thanked the Lord for his call of grace, and prayed that we might have him among us for a long time yet. Then we lay peacefully down to rest under our tent.

Oct. 19. We rose about six but had not slept much having been disturbed by the smoke. One mile beyond our camping place we stopped to bake bread, and about nine o'clock started on again. Several of the Brn. went ahead two and a half miles to Neuschwanger, a German, who lives half a mile to the left of the road. There is a straight track cut from his house to the main road. The Brn. procured bread and hay and brought it to the main road, where the

---

[1] Bishop Johannes von Watteville.
[2] Now Winchester, Virginia.

rest waited with the wagon. On the plantation Br. Haberland unexpectedly met a man who knew him, — a man who
some years ago in London carried the love-feast bread to
Bloomsbury. The man was very happy, and told the other
Brn. that when he saw Br. Haberland it seemed as if he
were in heaven. He told us all about himself, and that he
had three years still to serve,[1] and he would be most happy
to see other of the Brethren. We went five miles further
and came to Baumann's mill, where we bought several
bushels of oats, but we had to wait several hours while it
was thrashed. Some Germans visited us and we enquired
about the way, but they gave us little comfort, saying that
beyond Augusti Court House [2] the road was so bad that it
was doubtful whether we could travel it. It was five miles
from Baumann's to Justice Funk's mill, and it was after
dark and rather late when we reached there. The outlook
was unpromising for a camp for it was pitch dark, and no
wood near; but we set up the tent on the mill creek in a
pleasant place under a large tree, all went to work to collect
wood for the fire, and in a few minutes all was ready. Some
people came to see us and wondered much at us. On the
way we had lost a sack of oats, so a couple of the Brn. took
a lantern and went back and found it. Otherwise we had
a good trip to-day; we could plainly see the Blue Mountains
on our right. Some high mountains were directly in front
of us. Br. Nathanael held the evening service, and then
we went to sleep.

Oct. 20. Very early the Brn. brought in our horses from
pasture. Br. Grube waked the other Brn. by singing a few
verses, and after eating our broth we set out about five
o'clock. There was a considerable hill just ahead and we
had to push hard to help get the wagon up, and reached the
top before daybreak. We heard that from here we would
see no house for 20 miles, but that we would find water

[1] Probably three of the five years which the man was bound to
serve in return for payment of his passage from England to
America.

[2] Now Staunton, Augusta County, Virginia.

every three or four miles. Several Brn. went hunting, but returned empty handed. Six miles to the left we saw high mountains, which ran toward the south-west. Our course, however, was mostly south by west, the land apparently barren and grown up in pine trees. We drove twelve miles this morning, and stopped for noon by a creek. In this neighborhood, one mile to the left of the road, there lives a man named Jac. Müller where one can always buy oats. Then the road goes up-hill for a while, and when we reached the summit we crossed the "Narrow Passage," which is so narrow that two wagons cannot pass, and there are very deep valleys on each side. In the valley on the left flows Stone Creek, and another creek in that on the right. The road goes about south on the ridge. We traveled eight miles this afternoon, and put up our tent near the Shanidore [1] Creek, which is about again as wide as the Manakis, but dangerous in high water, and difficult then to cross. We had a pretty camping place to-night, and felt happy, and thankful to the Lord for bringing us safely so far. Br. Nathanael held evening prayers.

Oct. 21. We drove five miles and crossed the Shanidore,[2] then camped on the bank for Sunday. The Brn. Jac. Lösch and Kalberlahn were bled, as they were not feeling very well. We turned our horses into the woods. In the afternoon we cooked something good and had a pleasant little tea together. An Englishman came by and drank a cup of tea with us and was very grateful for it. The Brn. Petersen and Herm. Lösch went ten miles off to an Englishman, to help him thrash oats tomorrow. It was very warm to-day, and we and our horses enjoyed the rest. In the evening just as we were about to retire two Germans came up, who had been into the upper part of Virginia to take up land; they spent the night with us. They come from near Yorck on the Catores, and know Br. Philipp Meurer.

Oct. 22. We set out again at five o'clock. Br. Jac.

[1] The North Fork of the Shenandoah.
[2] Shenandoah.

DIARY OF THE MORAVIANS

Lösch went to the plantation where the Brn. are thrashing oats. The South Mountains were about three miles to our left, and looked as high as the Blue Mountains on the road to Gnadenhütten. There are a good many plantations in this neighborhood, but most of them hilly. We stopped for noon by a creek. The Brn. returned bringing eleven bushels of oats. It was warm and sultry weather and we found no water in the eleven miles between our last night camp, and this place. It is 200 miles from here to Williamsburg, the capital of Virginia. We went a mile and a half further to a tavern keeper named Severe and inquired about our way, but could get no definite information. Three and a half miles beyond the road forked. The Brn. Gottlob and Nathanael took the left-hand road and found a woman who told them about it; they returned and we took the right-hand road, but found no water for ten miles, it grew late, and we had to drive five miles into the night to find a stopping place. We had to climb two hills where every one had to help push or we could not have made it, for our horses were quite exhausted. Two Brn. had to keep a little ahead to seek out the road; and so we came at last to Thom. Harris' plantation, where we bought food for our horses, and set up our tent a little way from the house. The people were friendly and assisted the travelers gladly.

Oct. 23. We started at daybreak. We bought a bottle of milk to use at our noon lunch, but the bottle broke and we lost it all. Two miles from camp we bought some meat; had six miles to North River,[1] where we stopped for noon; this creek is half as large as the Lecha, but is impassible at high water, and there is no canoe near. Our meat and dumplings tasted good and refreshed us. This afternoon our way for a while was directly south. At three miles we came to a creek, in two more to a run, and one mile further we came to a spring, we went two miles further and camped for the night by a creek, not far from a plantation. Br. Nathanael held evening prayers, and then we slept in the care of Jesus.

[1] A tributary to the South Fork of the Shenandoah.

337

Oct. 24. At 2 : 30 A.M. our broth was ready, and at three we were on our way. One mile from camp we found good water, the same one mile further. Two more miles brought us to Middle Branch,[1] a fairly large creek, with a bank difficult to climb that gave us much trouble. Most of the Brn. crossed on a fallen tree, Br. Kalberlahn fell in but did not hurt himself. It was not yet day when we crossed the creek. One mile beyond was a creek, and then one mile to Robert Bohk, who has a pretty plantation and good water. There we bought some hay and chaff and the people were very polite. Three miles further we came to Augusti Court House, a little village of twenty houses, surrounded with hills. This whole section is settled by Irish and English. The road forks here, — that to the right goes to Carolina. Immediately beyond Augusti Court House the bad road began, it was up hill and down and we had constantly to push the wagon or hold it back by ropes that we fastened in the rear. There was no lack of water, which we found every couple of miles, and we put up our tent eight miles from Augusti Court House by a spring and an old tumble-down house. Br. Jac. Lösch went to several plantations to buy food for our horses, but the people had none, though they were friendly and regretted that they could not help us. Br. Gottlob conducted the evening service, and as this was Br. Lunge's birthday we sang some verses for him, and enjoyed the evening with him. Then we laid ourselves down in the arms of Jesus.

Oct. 25. Half a mile from camp the road forked, we took the left, but had no water for five miles. Then one mile further we took breakfast by a creek; drove six miles, and stopped for noon at a pretty spring. We met two Seventh Day Adventists, who had been to Carolina and were returning to Pennsylvania, they gave us information about our way. Br. Nathanael was somewhat ill. On the left we saw great mountains and sometimes came quite near them. Our road runs constantly south-west. In the

---

[1] Another tributary to the South Fork of the Shenandoah.

evening we set up our tent on a hill, and had to carry the water some distance. Br. Gottlob went half a mile ahead to a Free Negro, who is the only smith in these parts, to have his horse shod. The negro and his wife, who was a Scotch woman, were very friendly to Br. Gottlob, and told him that they had recently come hither from Lancaster, that they had often heard Br. Nyberg [1] preach, and also the Brn. in Philadelphia, and that they were now reading the "Berliner Reden." They were very glad to see Brethren, and happy to serve us. During the night the woman baked bread for us, invited Br. Gottlob and Br. Nathanael to breakfast, and begged that as they returned they would not pass them by but stop and speak to them, for they loved people who spoke of the Saviour. The negro understood German well. The Brn. Hermanus and Lunge went to neighboring plantations to buy food for the horses. It rained almost all night, but we kept fairly dry in our tent.

Oct. 26. We rose rather late on account of the rainy weather. A couple of the Brn. took breakfast with the negro, who felt very important at entertaining two ministers. We had bad hills to-day and as soon as we were at the top of one we had to hang on the break-rope, and even then it was dangerous going down. In spite of the hills this is a fertile section, with few stones and a rich black soil; it is settled mostly by English and Irish. The Brn. Gottlob and Nathanael went ahead, and spent the night a mile and a half beyond the North Branch of James River with Mr. Brikstone, a well-to-do man who a few years ago moved here from Canistoge,[2] and knows the Brethren well. The rest of the Brn. with the wagon, spent the night half a mile from the Branch, which they could not cross on account of the high water. It began to rain and continued almost all night, and as our tent was on a hill the water ran through it and we were all soaked through and through. Br. Grube held the evening service.

[1] Laurentius Thorstansen Nyberg.
[2] Conestoga, Pennsylvania.

Oct. 27. We rose early to dry our clothes, and the sky cleared. We were very thankful to the Saviour for giving us good weather again; it was badly needed for without it we could hardly have gone forward, for our wagon is very heavily loaded, and the ascent of the hills is almost more than we can manage. We had two miles of bad road, up hill and down. Then we reached the house where the Brn. Gottlob and Nathanael had spent the night, and were well served at a reasonable price. This is a pretty, fruitful neighborhood; in the distance one sees the encircling high mountains. This morning for the second time we had to take off half our load, in order to climb the hill, for it was so slippery that the horses could not keep their feet in pulling but fell constantly to their knees. Our noon rest was at Buffler Creek,[1] which is half as wide as the Lecha, but in flood runs far over the banks. Br. Lösch shot the first turkey, which we ate for supper. Passing over the creek we came immediately to a long high hill, which took us an hour to climb, and we all had to push on the wagon. But we had fine pleasant weather, and from the top there was a beautiful view of the great mountains, and the valleys on either side of us. We drove some miles along the ridge. At two and a half miles we found a foot-path leading to the left, and as we had heard that there was a spring a short way down in the valley and we were very thirsty some of the Brn. went for water which greatly refreshed us. Br. Hermanus followed this path to a plantation to try to buy feed for our horses but could get none. Then he went to another man, named Illison, where he purchased several bushels of corn, and stayed over night. Our road was bad, always up and down hills. In the evening we set up our tent eight miles from Buffler Creek, by a stream, made a good fire and rested from our labors which today have been rather trying. Br. Nathanael held the evening service, and we were all so tired that we dispensed with the night-watch.

Oct. 28. We rose early to continue our journey. One

---

[1] Buffalo Creek.

of our horses was sick. After a mile and a half we bought corn at a house. One mile further we came to a small creek, and two miles beyond approached the Blue Mountains. We stopped for noon by a large, beautiful spring, six miles from our night-camp. Br. Hermanus rejoined us, bringing several bushels of corn. Our afternoon road was stony and bad, and we constantly had to steady the wagon with ropes to keep it from overturning. Four times we crossed a bad, stony creek, and the banks were so high that it was difficult to pull out. The South and Blue Mountains here approach within two miles of each other; we turned to the right to the Blue Mountains. Towards evening we saw Jeams [1] River; the road to it ran down so very steep a hill that we fastened a small tree to the back of our wagon. locked the wheels, and the brethren held back by the tree with all their might, but even then the wagon went down so fast that most of the brethren lost their footing ; no harm was done, and we thanked the Lord that He had so graciously protected us, for it looked dangerous and we thought at times that it could not possibly be done without accident, but in spite of stump and stone we got down safely. We made our camp near the River, and rested well after the fatigue of the day, for the road had all been bad and yet, we had made sixteen miles. A man visited us, and asked whether we had come down the steep hill; he expressed surprise at our success, and said we need not have come that way, but might have turned to the right toward the Blue Mountains and have followed a good road around through a valley. Br. Gottlob held evening prayer.

Oct. 29. We rose at five, having had a rather cold night with frost for the first time on this trip. We drove half a mile to the River, and found two roads, the one to the right going one mile further to Lunis Ferry,[2] that to the left fording the river. A couple of the Brethren rode through to see what kind of a crossing it was, for there were many

[1] James. [2] Looney's Ferry, across the Fluvanna River.

rocks and stones in the stream. Fortunately for us all the rivers and creeks are low just now, otherwise we could make little progress, for even the smallest creeks rise so in rainy weather that the horses would have to swim. From the Buffler Creek here we crossed streams every two or three miles. We crossed Jeams River safely, and thanked our Father in heaven that He had helped us through so many difficulties. We then had two miles of good road, crossed a creek, and came to a house where we spent most of the day, taking time to bake bread and to kill a hog that we bought. We were visited by the Mr. Illison from whom Br. Hermanus recently bought corn, and he asked that the Brethren would shoe his horse, which was done. He said that he would soon go to Philadelphia, and offered to attend to anything we wished done there. The Brn. Gottlob and Nathanael wrote letters to our friends in Bethlehem, addressing them to the care of Sam. Powell in Philadelphia, and we were glad of the opportunity of sending our Bethlehem friends some account of our journey. This evening we went about four miles further over a rather bad road. On the way we got some bread that we had had baked at Lunis' Mill. We crossed a large creek, and set up our tent two miles from the Mill near a stream, but immediately had to change our position because the wind blew the smoke into the tent. It also began to rain. We turned our horses loose in the woods. The Brn. Petersen and Merkli, who had remained behind to finish baking the bread, came late in the night, and had had to swim the creek at Lunis' Mill, which is quite deep.

Oct. 30. The weather was bad, it rained and snowed, but we kept fairly dry under our tent. Our horses had strayed off and it took several of the Brethren nearly all day to find them, and we were glad when we had them back, for we had heard that in this neighborhood horses were often stolen, and that might have happened to ours. As the Brethren came in cold and wet through and through we had a cup of tea all round, and enjoyed it together. We changed the position of the tent on account of the smoke.

Br. Gottlob held the evening service. We for the first time tried baking bread in the ashes.

Oct. 31. We rose very early and prepared to continue our journey. Immediately we had to climb a considerable hill, which was very hard on our horses for the ground was frozen and covered with snow. One mile brought us to a small creek, and another to a larger one, near which was a plantation. Then came more hills, and from the top a beautiful view, the Blue and South Mountains forming a pretty oval, their summits all covered with snow. The farther we went the more snow we found, and travel was difficult. Two miles to the left was a plantation and some of the Brethren went thither to drink milk. Near at hand was a small creek, then the road rose again. After a mile and a half we came to another creek not far from a planta-tion; this would be a good place to camp as there is good water and wood. One mile further we came to a very bad piece of road, so sloping that we could hardly keep the wagon from slipping over the edge down the mountain, and had to use the tackle frequently. Then we began to descend, and in a half mile came to a small creek; we drove a bit up its valley, and took our noon rest there. One of our horses was sick, we gave him something that helped. After going a mile and a half further we passed over some bad hills, and by a fence, and came to Joseph Macdonald's house. Two years ago he came here from Manakesie [1] in Maryland, and before that he used to attend the preaching of the Brethren; he was friendly and told us about our best road without waiting to be asked. Half a mile from his house the road forks, the right hand going to New River. We took the left, came to another creek, and five miles further on camped for the night. Towards evening we met an old man whom Br. Nathanael engaged in conversation, and as we passed near his fence we asked him to sell us some turnips, but he was so good as to make us a present of a nice quantity, and gave an invitation that any of our

[1] Monocacy.

people passing this way should visit him. He had heard perhaps a hundred lies about the Brethren, — that we were "bearded people," [1] that we enjoined celibacy,[1] etc. — and now learning the truth the old man rejoiced, and took a friendly leave of us. His name is Müller. Another of our horses was sick and we bled him.

Nov. 1. With earliest dawn we were again on our journey, but again had to bleed a horse. The change in food is largely responsible for the illness of our horses. At one and a half miles we found water, there was a small creek half a mile beyond, and one mile further another, near which was an old plantation, and the road forked, we going to the left. A quarter of a mile more brought us to the road leading to the left up the hills to Warrik, and to a stone house of which we had heard and where we expected to buy provisions, but we could get little. The people count it nine miles from here to Runoke.[2] The road was narrow and we often did not see how we were to get through, indeed without our axes we would have been in a bad fix. We also had to work the road itself so that we could pass. We met three men from Warrik who had been to Carolina and were returning home. They said the road was very bad, and we would probably not be able to buy any provisions on the way. Br. Nathanael wrote a note to Br. Christ. Rauch, and sent it by these men. Two miles further we came to a little creek, and in two miles more to another which was full of stones, and we had much difficulty in getting up the bank. Another mile brought us to a large Buffalo Lick, where formerly many buffalo gathered because the marsh was rich in salt. Not far from there we came to a plantation where there is good water. We went about half a mile further, and then our road, — a rather narrow one, — turned to the left. That to the right is much better and leads to Grain Brayer.[3] We stopped for noon by a creek, and had to drive through a large marsh. Br. Lösch, who had gone

---

[1] Certain sects in Pennsylvania held these tenets, and the Moravians were sometimes confused with them. A. L. F.
[2] Roanoke. [3] Greenbrier.

ahead to see if he could buy some corn, rejoined the party. About four o'clock we reached the Runoke, and had to wait for the corn, which was not yet shelled. Several of the Brethren went to the nearest plantation to help the people shell the corn, and two of them thrashed oats. It grew so late that we had to stay here all night. Mr. Evens, a miller who lives across the river, came to us and gave advice about the care of our sick horses, we tried his plan and it helped them. We thought today much about our brethren in Heidelberg, and wished they could know that the Saviour had brought us well and content so far. We made twelve miles today.

Nov. 2. We rose early, having slept little because the smoke troubled us all night. At day-break we crossed the Runoke, which was very low, and not quite so large as the Lecha, but full of slippery stones; and in high water it runs half a mile over the banks. We had much difficulty in getting our sick horses across. A quarter of a mile beyond we came to Evens' mill, where our road turned to the left and became very narrow. A mile further we came to a steep hill, and the road sloped badly. We soon stuck in a ditch, and were in danger of breaking our axle. In another mile a rather high hill rose before us, and we had to unload half our things and carry them up on our backs, and even then we could hardly get the wagon up. The going down was also steep, we locked two wheels, hung a tree on behind, and all the brethren held back by it; and so we crossed this hill safely. Then we had a mile and a half of good road, and stopped for lunch by a creek. It looked much like rain and there was a large hill before us. We asked a man that we met whether we could get across the hill today and he said "Yes, some one lived on the top, and we could spend the night there." We believed him and drove to the foot of the hill, crossing a large creek. Then we tried to climb the hill but it was impossible, the hill beging too steep. So we decided to unload and carry the things up the hill. The Brn. Lischer and Pfeil stayed with the wagon, and the rest of us made the ascent. Half way up it began to rain and was hard on us and our horses, but we hoped on the top to find the house of which the man had told us. The time seemed long to us and when we reached the summit neither house nor water was to be found. There was nothing to do but go on down the mountain in the darkness and heavy rain. At last in the valley we found a little creek, having been two and a half hours in crossing the hill. There we made camp as best we might, having much trouble to get a fire, for it was raining heavily and everything was wet. We set up the tent and lay close together on the wet bedding, and rested a little. Toward morning it cleared and was very cold.

Nov. 3. At dawn we went back across the hill to get the other things and the wagon. The Brn. Gottlob, Nathanael, and Kalberlahn, stayed with the tent. The Brethren who had remained in the wagon had also had a cold night, and we were glad to see each other again. We loaded our horses and took most of the things to the top of the hill, made a fire, and Br. Haberland stayed while the rest went back for the wagon. Although it was almost empty it was all we could do to push and pull it up, but in half an hour we were at the top. Loading our belongings we traveled a little way upward along the ridge; then came the descent and we locked the wheels, hung a tree on behind, and all held back by it, and so we came safely down to our tent, and rejoiced that the Saviour had so helped us. Although there were a couple of steep, sloping hills before us, yet we crossed them before night, and set up our tent by a creek, turning our horses into the woods. We were all very tired and sleepy and let the angels be our guard during the night.

Nov. 4. We had an almost untrodden road, and had to cut a number of trees out of the way. Our wagon stuck fast in a mud-hole, and it took two hours to get it out. The tackle did us good service. One mile beyond we found water, then had four miles of good road to a creek, where we stopped for noon. In the afternoon we crossed Maggedi Creek,[1] near which lives Benjamin Reh, an old man of

---

[1] Maggotty Creek, a branch of Blackwater River.

about 90 years, and his wife who is nearly a hundred. Both are quite bright and active, gave us milk to drink, and were very friendly. Near this house is a deep muddy place, then we climbed a steep hill to the Warrik Road, which leads in a western direction and is fairly good. At two miles we crossed a small creek, and three miles beyond set up our tent by a large creek. Here we had to guard our horses carefully for we had heard that there were people about who would lead them off. We cooked dumplings this evening and they tasted good, and after prayers we lay ourselves peacefully to rest.

Nov. 5. We rose early and went on our way. Had several miles of good road along the ridge. When we had driven five miles we came to the home of Mr. Robert Kohl, Justice of the Peace, from whom we bought some corn. He is a pleasant man, and expressed regrets that he did not know we were coming, for he would gladly have met us and led us by a better and nearer way so that we could have escaped the hills and mountains. The road was indeed not entirely cleared, but there were so many of us that we could have gotten through with little trouble. He said he would see to it that this road was opened at once. Two Brethren stayed here to help shell some bushels of corn that we bought. We had again some bad places to drive up. At half a mile was a small creek, and another half mile brought us to Black Water,[1] a large creek with very steep banks. In one mile we again came to a small creek, and in two miles more to another where we stopped for the noon rest. There were some muddy places here but we got through safely. Then the road turned to the left up the mountain but we missed it and came more to the right to an old mill-race at Ringfros Mill, kept to the left of it and turned up the mountain again and regained our proper road. At one mile we came to a small creek and marshy place; then to three more creeks at half mile intervals. One mile further on the left was a new plantation,

---

[1] Blackwater River, a fork of the Roanoke.

and half a mile beyond we had to drive through a bad swamp and creek. One mile further we reached the home of Robert Johnsen, and bought some hay from him. He went half a mile with us to show us the way across the creek, and a pleasant place in which to pitch our tent. Our course today was west and south-west, and we made 16 miles; the road was fairly good apart from the marshy places and the steep banks of the streams. It is 25 miles from here to Smith's River.

Nov. 6. We took up our journey; Br. Hermanus remained behind to thrash oats for Mr. Johnsen. We had to drive through many muddy places and the wagon was often in danger of sticking fast. We had much work cutting out the road, which was so narrow that we could hardly get through, our long wagon could scarcely turn and twist along it, and we often had to use the tackle to get the wheels out of the holes. Two miles from camp we passed through a fence, had a great deal of marshy land, and drove perhaps thirty times across a creek that wound through the swamp. Br. Hermanus rejoined us bringing several bushels of oats which he had thrashed. Mr. Johnsen, a Welshman, had spoken freely with Br. Hermanus, had first asked him how he had come to join the Moravians, and when Br. Hermanus had told him he began to relate his own story for the last few years. At one time he had become very uneasy and could hardly bear the distress of his heart; then he had turned with all his misery to the Saviour, and He had let him feel the power of His blood and that had given him peace, and so it was with him to this day. And if at any time his heart was not quite right with God he turned again to the Saviour, and all was well. It was the same with his wife and eldest son. He had spoken of this only to those in whom he felt and saw the same spirit, for the World understands as little of such things as a horse, and therefore he kept silence. For nine years he had not heard a sermon; and he begged that when one of us should pass this way again he would stop with him. We all rejoiced when Br. Hermanus told us this, and were glad that also in this dark

wilderness the Saviour had His people, who loved Him. At
night we set up our tent in the swamp; in spite of all our
labor and toil today we made only ten miles. Br. Gottlob
held evening prayers, and then we lay down to rest.

Nov. 7. At daybreak we started again and soon were
out of the swamp, then immediately had a hill to climb that
went down very steeply on the farther side. At the foot
we crossed a medium-sized creek, then came another hill,
and we had a hard time getting up for the ground was so
slippery that the horses could not keep their feet. The
road was good for one mile, then it led again into a swamp,
several times crossing a creek. Our wagon was somewhat
injured, for the banks of one creek were so steep and high
that in going down the back of the wagon was strained and
a board in the body broke. We soon mended it, and spent
the noon rest by this creek. Br. Lösch went ahead to look
over the road. We came at once to a very steep little hill,
and then there was a long ascent. From the top we saw
the Pilot Mountain in North Carolina, and rejoiced to think
that we would soon see the boundary of Carolina and set
foot in our own dear land. We drove one mile along the
ridge, then there was a very steep descent. At the foot we
crossed a large creek with very steep banks, and finally
came to Smith's River, driving a mile through beautiful
lowlands where there were many grapes, which tasted very
good to us. Br. Gottlob rode ahead to spy out the road.
We came to a hill, thought we could cross it yet this evening, but on trying found it impossible for the ascent was too
steep. Br. Gottlob came back and said it would not be
possible to pull the wagon up fully loaded; so we set up
our tent at the foot of the hill near the river. Several of
the Brethren took the horses half a mile away to a meadow,
and spent the night there. We had a comfortable, peaceful
night.

Nov. 8. At daybreak we prepared again for our journey,
and carried half our goods to the top of the hill, and even
then had much toil and trouble before we got the wagon up,
for it was very steep. On the summit we reloaded our

goods for the descent. In the valley we crossed a small creek and were scarcely over that when we came to a second hill and had to unload again and carry almost everything to the top, for this was the steepest hill we had yet crossed. We were all glad when we were over it. Going down we locked two wheels, hung a tree on behind, and made the descent safely. People had told us that this hill was most dangerous, and that we would scarcely be able to cross it, for Margan Bryand, the first to travel this way, had to take the wheels off his wagon and carry it piecemeal to the top, and had been three months on the journey from the Shanidore to the Etkin.[1] At the foot of the hill we crossed a large creek with high banks; it runs into Smith's River close by. We came to a plantation, and the people were kind, and without question showed us the right road, which one mile from here turns to the left, and is less traveled than the one going straight ahead. One mile beyond we came to a rather large creek with such high banks that we hardly knew how to get over it, but with labor and toil we accomplished it safely. We drove two miles further before camping, but the road was very bad, and we stuck fast several times. We set up our tent by a plantation; and today in spite of all our efforts we have advanced only seven miles. It began to rain, and we were all rather damp when we lay down.

Nov. 9. Most of the Brethren rose very early; they could not sleep on account of the heavy rain, the water running under us so that we lay in it and could not escape it. The river had risen two feet during the night, and we saw that it was impossible to cross. We had numerous visits from the people living near, who were greatly surprised at our long wagon, and that so many unmarried men were traveling together. They asked about our Minister; and on this whole journey Br. Gottlob has won the affection of the people, who would gladly have had him baptise their children. Toward noon the rain stopped and we hoped for

[1] Yadkin River.

better weather, but it began again harder than ever, and we could hardly keep a little fire burning. We changed the position of our tent and dug a ditch around it to lead off the water, but the rain beat through the tent so that in a short time everything was most unpleasantly wet, and we were up most of the night.

Nov. 10. It began to clear a little. The river, however, was still higher, and we spent most of the day drying our blankets, mending, and darning our stockings. We also bought some bushels of corn and some meat from our neighbors, who were glad that we had to stay here so long, and that it meant money for them. In the afternoon we held a little Lovefeast, and rested our souls in the loving sacrifice of Jesus, wishing for our beloved Brethren in Bethlehem that they and we might live ever close to Him. Br. Nathanael conducted evening prayers, and then we lay ourselves down to rest.

Nov. 11. Several Brethren went early to the river to see whether we could cross and found it had fallen two feet. We had a man show us the ford, and one of us rode through on our gray horse, then we ventured it, and crossed safely. The banks were fairly easy to climb. We drove through a swamp, stuck quite a while in a hole, and had much difficulty in getting out. Mr. Hikki, who lives half a mile from here and who has a store, came to meet us and was very friendly. It was a bad bit of road to his house where we bought some provisions. (This will be the nearest place where we can buy salt.) A couple of miles from there we met a man from North Carolina, who lives near our land. He told us that it is generally known that we will soon arrive, that he had heard that we had two Ministers with us, which was a good thing, for the people lived like wild men, never hearing of God or His Word. He was also glad that we had a Doctor in the company. Two and a half miles beyond Hikki's we stopped for noon at a creek, where there is good pasturage, the road thither being fairly good. Then again it led through marshy places and over steep hills, with water every half or quarter mile, often accompanied by deep mud. We set up our tent by a creek, and made only eight miles today, although we hurried all we could. We were glad for the pleasantly warm weather. For supper we cooked Virginia potatoes,[1] which tasted good. Br. Nathanael held evening prayers, and then we went peacefully to rest.

Nov. 12. We rose very early, and about 3 A.M. ate our pumpkin broth. Then the road led on through thick and thin, and often up steep hills where we had to push with all our strength. A boggy place, fully 100 paces long, we avoided by cutting a new road on the left across the hill, which was a great help. We came to a creek called Horse Pasture which is about as large as the Manakis; it had been very high within the last few days, but had fallen again. Here we had one of the worst banks we had seen, and people had told us some way back that we would hardly be able to cross; but our grubbing hoes and shovels did us good service and we made it safely. Near this creek is a new plantation, and they call it fully twelve miles from here to Smith's River. We went on four miles, and stopped for noon at Adam Loving's plantation, where we bought ten bushels of corn, and the people were very friendly. The men showed us the ford through the first branch of the Meho[2] River, which is not much wider than the Manakis at Bethlehem, but has such steep banks that it took us two hours to cross. It is a great blessing that the water has fallen since the last rain, for otherwise we might have been detained a long time. Three miles beyond we reached the main branch of the Meho, which is about as large as the Lecha at Gnadenhütten. The approach was fairly easy but the other side much worse, and we worked into the night before we could make the bank passable, and even then we had trouble enough to get out. We spent the night there, and as we had little wood we all gathered around one fire, sleeping for the last time on Virginian soil. We made 13 miles today. A man who lives not far from here

[1] Sweet potatoes.   [2] Mayo.

came to us, asking about Valentin Fuhrer, and whether he still lives in Bethlehem; he knew him well, for 15 years ago he lived near Fuhrer's father on North River.

Nov. 13. We rose at three o'clock, for it began to rain, and we hastened on our journey, but lost our way, going too far to the right. At dawn we crossed the boundary of North Carolina, where the road crosses a creek two miles from our last camp. Br. Haberland lost his hat trying to cross on a tree that lay across the stream, but he found it again when it grew lighter. The road was fair, apart from some steep hills, and we had water every mile or two. We stopped for noon on a little mountain seven miles from the Meho; near by runs a creek with a high fall. In the afternoon we had some hills so steep that we could hardly climb them; also bad banks to some of the creeks. Toward evening it began to rain and we hurried as fast as we could to reach Ten River [1]; but it grew so dark that we had to stop three miles from it at a creek. We made a fire and cooked a little food; then it began to clear with the north-west wind. At midnight we started again, in order to cross Ten River. One Brother went ahead of the wagon with a torch of pine-wood to light the way, and at 2 A.M. we reached Ten River, and as it had not rained any more we thought it would not rise and we might spend the rest of the night on its bank before crossing. It was cold and we had little wood to burn. We were all very tired, having come 25 miles today from the Meho River. Our hearts today have been with our Brethren, and each of us in spirit has drawn near the nail-torn hands and pierced heart of our "Chief Elder." [2]

Nov. 14. We went very early to see whether we could cross the river, but it had risen two feet, and was running rapidly. So we had to wait, and meanwhile worked on the approach which was very steep. Some Brethren went hunting, but came back empty-handed. The man who lives near the river came and invited the Brn. Gottlob and

[1] Dan River.
[2] On Nov. 13 the Moravian Church makes special acknowledgment of Jesus Christ as its "Chief Elder." A. L. F.

Nathanael to his house and they accepted. He insisted that Br. Gottlob should baptise his child, but Br. Nathanael asked that he be excused, as he spoke little English, and could not do it at any rate. The man was not satisfied, and said he did not care how it was baptised, just so it was done now. Br. Jacob Lösch crossed the river in the canoe, and went on eleven miles to Mr. Altem to order provisions.

Nov. 15. Several Brethren went hunting, but secured nothing. The Brn. Gottlob and Nathanael crossed the river in the canoe with the Brn. Haberland and Hermanus Lösch, swimming their horses across with them. They plan to go today to Mr. Altem, who is well acquainted with our land, and have him go with them tomorrow to look over the property, and find a place where we can stay until we select the best place for our settlement. Br. Grube stayed with the other brethren by the river which was still too high. In the evening we were visited by a German lad, who lived on the Etkin, and had been to Smith's River for 11 quarts of salt, for which he had paid 50 cents. Br. Grube held evening prayers.

Nov. 16. We rose early to ford the river. The bank was so steep that we hung a tree behind the wagon, fastening it in such a way that we could quickly release it when the wagon reached the water. The current was very swift, and the lead horses were carried down a bit with it. The water just missed running into the wagon, but we came safely to the other bank, which however we could not climb, but had to take half the things out of the wagon, and tie ropes to the axle on which we could pull, helping our horses, which were quite stiff, and so we brought our ark again to dry land. Half a mile beyond we drove through a wide swamp, then up a long hill. We stopped at noon by a creek near a plantation. At four o'clock we reached Mr. Altem's, ten miles from our last night's camp, having had just about the worst road of our whole journey. We rejoiced that the Lord had helped us so far. Toward evening the Brethren Gottlob, Nathanael, Lösch, etc. rejoined us, having looked about a little; six miles from the edge of our land they found a little house, which a German [1] built last year and then abandoned. We set up our tent by Mr. Altem's house. Br. Gottlob, Br. Nathanael, and the others who were on the trip through our land today took supper with Mr. Altem. We retired early, being quite worn out.

Nov. 17. We rose early having had a cold night; it looked much like snow. Some of the Brethren went ahead with axes and grubbing hoes to clear the road and cut down the steep banks of the creeks. One mile from Altem's we crossed Down Forck [2] Creek, and came to the new road leading across our land to the Etkin. On the right hand side of the creek is a plantation, and the people gave us two sacks of pumpkins and offered us a wagon-full more free of charge. Two miles from our land we crossed Buffler Creek. One mile from our land we stopped for the noon rest. The Brn. Gottlob and Nathanael had gone ahead to the next plantation, which adjoins our land, and the people presented them with a couple of bushels of turnips. At last, at half past twelve, we reached the boundary of our land, whereat we all rejoiced; and there we were met and tenderly welcomed by Br. Gottlob and Br. Nathanael. It touched us, and we thanked our Saviour that He had so graciously led us hither, and had helped us through all the hard places, for no matter how dangerous it looked, nor how little we saw how we could win through, everything always went better than seemed possible. We wished that the dear ones in Bethlehem, now gathered in the Sabbath Lovefeast,[3] could know that we, in less than six weeks, had safely reached our land. We drove three miles further on the new road, then turned to the left and cut a way for two and a half miles to the little house that the Brethren found yesterday. We reached it in the evening and at once took possession of it, finding it large enough that we could all lie

[1] Hans Wagner. [2] Town Fork.
[3] The Moravians of that day often set apart Saturday afternoon as a preparation for Sunday, — hence "Sabbath" and the Lovefeast. A. L. F.

down around the walls.[1] We at once made preparation for a little Lovefeast, and rejoiced heartily with one another. Br. Gottlob began the singing with the little verse; —

> We hold arrival Lovefeast here,
>   In Carolina land,
> A company of Brethren true,
>   A little Pilgrim-Band,
> Called by the Lord to be of those
>   Who through the whole world go,
> To bear Him witness everywhere,
>   And nought but Jesus know.

The texts for the day were strikingly appropriate; — "I know where thou dwellest," — even in a desert place. "Be ye of the same mind one with another." While we held our Lovefeast the wolves howled loudly, but all was well with us, and our hearts were full of thanksgiving to the Saviour Who had so graciously guided and led us. Then we laid ourselves down to rest, and Br. Gottlob hung his hammock above our heads.

[1] On the site of this house, in Bethabara, or Old Town, a monument was erected in 1806 bearing the inscription: *Wachovia settlement, begun the 17th November, 1753.*

MINUTES OF MR. HAMBURGH'S JOURNAL, 1763

INTRODUCTION

To attempt to introduce the *Minutes of Mr. Hamburgh's Journal* is like attempting to introduce a stranger, for the *Minutes* are shrouded in obscurity. Who was Mr. Hamburgh? Where is the journal of his travels from Detroit to Chicago and the Mississippi River by way of Lakes Huron and Michigan and the Illinois River, in the year in which Pontiac directed the Indian uprising against the English? Who wrote these *Minutes* from his journal? These are questions to which neither contemporary nor later records seem to have an answer. A copy of the *Minutes* has been preserved for years in the Library of Congress, but there is no record of its acquisition.

Was the man in question a trader? and was his name Hambough instead of Hamburgh? Parkman, in his *Conspiracy of Pontiac*, quotes from a letter of June 19, 1763, by Richard Winston, a trader at Saint Joseph's, to his fellow-traders at Detroit, which reads in part as follows: "I have only to inform you that by the blessings of God and the help of M. Louison Chevalie, I escaped being killed when the unfortunate garrison was massacred, Mr. Hambough and me being hid in the house of the said Chevalie for 4 days and nights. Mr. Hambough is brought by the Savages to the Illinois, likewise Mr. Chim. Unfortunate me remains here Captive with the Savages."

MINUTES OF MR. HAMBURGH'S JOURNAL, 1763

Minutes of Mr. Hamburgh's Journal who travilled this Contry in the year 1763

DETROIT so called by the French Signifying a Strait [is] Situated on the River whereby Lake Huron Emptieth it Self into Lake Erie. From Detroit up the River to Lake St. Clair is nine miles, a Small Lake not above 15 Leagues in Circumference. From this Lake it is 60 miles up the River Huron [1] to Lake Huron. Several of Chiproy [2] Nations Are Settled on this River. The Country is Low and Rich Soil there. Hunting Ground is none of the best. From the Entrance of Lake Huron the french call it 300 miles to Mishlymackena [3] and it is Recorded a Good Passage to goe it with Battoes in 10 or 12 days. About half way is an Indian Town they Call them the Sequena [4] Indians — on Account of the bay of that name on which their town is Situated. They are chiefly of the Ottowa Tribe. The Bay of Saquena Is about 24 or thirty miles in Length and they generally Cross it in Canooes or Battoes from point to point about 12 Miles without Seeing the Indian Town. You have good landing place[s] for Battoes all a Long the South side of this Lake.[5] Mishlymackana So Called By the Indians from Lake Mishymack Or Great Lake, Lies on the Entrance of this Lake. . . . Seperated from Lake Huron no Otherwise but by some Islands And the Oposite Point which forms [a] Strait about 9 miles across. The Country about Mishyly-mackana is Sandy Pine Wood, and Hunting [is] Very Scarce. The Indians who Live here are of the Ottowa Tribe. Their

---

[1] Saint Clair River.   [2] Chippewa.   [3] Michilimackinac.
[4] Saginaw.   [5] Lake Huron.

Town is about 30 miles from the fort and is Called By the french Arbre-de-Chroche.[1] In Summer Time they Live Partly upon fish which are very Good and Plenty at this Place and in the Winter their chief Hunting Place is about the great River and Tiakanamasso, Large River, which falls in the south side of Lake Mishlymacana about 50 or 60 Leagues from their town. This place is Likewise Remarcable for making the best and Largest Birch Canooes, one of which Will Carry about 6000 Weight. From this place the french Call it 300 miles To the River St. Joseph. You have good Landing Places and Rivers for Battoes to goe in from 13 to 15 Leagues Distance, Hunting is Scarce all along here About. . .

To goe from Misshlymackana to the Green bay you cross from the fort [2] to the Opposite Point As mentioned Before. You Proceed on the north side Mishlymakana, a very Dangerous Shore Being full of Banks which Extend themselves at Some Places for 2 or 3 miles into the Lake. There is scarcely any Rivers to goe in with Battoes and the shore [is] very straight, you Pass numbers of Islands on one of which are some Indian Cabbins of the Oottnottmy [3] Tribe. The bay is 30 miles in length And the fort Lies on the further End of the Lake. They have Great Plenty of all kinds of wild foul here. The distance is 60 Leagues from Mishlymackana — from the green bay the french Call it 300 miles to St. Joseph River, the shore is Very dangerous all along this side the Lake, few rivers that will aford you a Harbour in Bad Weather so that you are oblige[d] to Hall up your Boat upon the Beach — About halfe way is Mishlymackana [4] River, [there] is a sand Running along the Entrance of it which makes it difficult To Enter In Bad Weather — The Breakers Being very high. There is an Indian town at about one mile from the Entrance. On it is inhabited By Part of the

[1] Arbre Croche, on Little Traverse Bay, at the site of the present Harbor Springs. The Jesuits established a mission here in 1741.

[2] Fort Michilimackinac or Mackinac.

[3] Pottawatomie. [4] Milwaukee.

Sackys[1] And some mixture Of Battowamys,[2] and Ottowas. The next remarkable River is Chycacoo,[3] here is an Indian town Called by the name of the River Chose. At the Entrance of it [it is] inhabited By the same nations as Millymaky.[4] Here the Country Begins Again to Be very Pleasant, good soil, and Hunting very Plenty : Such as Buffiloes, Deer, Bears, and it is 30 Leagues to the River St. Joseph, Good Shore all along and rivers for shelters from storms. 9 miles up this River, the Chykocoo, the french used to make a Carrying Place into an other River for about 3 miles which falls into the river Illinois and is deep Enough for Large Battoes to goe or up or down. From the Entrance of St. Josephs River it is 20 Leagues up to the fort, the River is Crooked And in summer time it is shallow in some places. Fort St. Joseph Lies on the East Side of the river and On Indian on the oposite Side shore the Chief of the Pottowany tribe Resides. The Country in Levil, good Soil, And Hunting Exceeding Plenty : Such as Elks, Deer, Bears, Raccoons, Bevers, Otters, Turkeys, and other kind of wild fouls in great Plenty. . . . from Detroit the french cal'd 300 miles to St. Joseph by Land, the first 30 Miles are very swampy and Exceeding bad Traveling, But the Rest of the Road is Very Pleasant, the Country is Quite Levil, Intermixed with several Rivers and Creeks which in Summer time You may all Pass on horse Back, in Freshets you must make Rafts ; You Pass three Small Indian Towns all of the Pottowamy tribe — Severall small Lakes and Pleasant Hunting all the Way — Fort St. Joseph Lies on the River of the same name at 20 Leagues Distant from where it Enters into Lake Mishacony. 6 miles above the fort is a carrying Place aBout four Miles long into the Kykaggy River Which is But Very small in its Beginning Like Wood Creek ; Running Exceeding Crooked for a Bout 30 Miles When it inlarges and Deepens. About 120 Miles Down this River Lies an Indian town Consisting of about 20 Families of the Masco-

[1] Sac Indians.
[2] Pottawatomie Indians.
[3] Chicago River.
[4] Milwaukee.

tain [1] Tribe and about 60 Miles further falls In the Chykacoo
River and is Called afterwards Ilinois River. The Chief
Hunting ground of the Battowaymes is along this River
for about 200 Miles Down to a Place Called Le Rocher —
The greatest Plenty they have here is Racoons, Otters,
Some Bever, Elks and Dear, and Buffilows in ABundance;
about 300 Miles from St. Joseph is a french fort of Very
Little Importance. There was an Officer And 5 men Sta-
tioned there when i Past it In the year 1763 — from this fort
or Port Called Epec; it is 300 [miles] down the River Where
it falls Into the Missisippi And would be Navagable for Large
Sloops to Come up this far. All a Long Down this River the
Country is Exceeding Pleasant And Levil and for the most
Part Consisting of Large Plains Which Extend themselves
as the french Informed me for several Hundreds of Miles,
the Plains are Well stocked With Buffelows And Deer
Especially Along the River as they Run through it. The
Country all Along Down Produces Plenty of mulberry Trees
and the Nut Called Bacane [2] — There is Several Rivers falls
into it where off I know no name. One of them Runs
Through the Saacks Country towards the Green Bay. This
River Ilinois Enlarges Greatly Below this fort, And is nigh
as Large at the Mouth as the Missippi — Receive it at 60
Miles above the First french settlement Called the Canos
there is A small fort and about 70 or 80 Families; it Lies
upon a small River at about One mile Distant from the
Missippi. From here it is 45 miles To Fort Chartre,[3] A
stone fort Neatly Built And fortified for small Arms With
good Barracks for Officers and Soldiers, Sufficient for 500
[men]. It is Situated not 400 Yards from the Missippi with a
Dry Ditch About; there is about 100 french families Living
near it. Here Resideth the Commandeth Of all the Ilenois
Settlement, Who Receives His orders from the Governor Of
New Orleans. There is Two Indian [villages] Not Halfe A
mile from it Close upon the Missippi, Called Beory [4] and

[1] Mascouten.   [2] Pecan.
[3] Fort Chartres, on the east bank of the Missippi, about
twenty miles above the mouth of the Kaskaskia.   [4] Peoria.

The other Metschy [1] Containing Both of them ABout 300 Warriors. From this Place to the next Settlement is ABout 18 Miles — There is a small fort and about 150 families Liveing By it. The Town is called Aveas. The Indians who Live Heare Calls themselves Cascaskys.[2] It is situated Upon a Small river. At 9 miles Distant from the Missippi there is two small french towns, Besides those Mentioned Above, Of about 20 families Each, this is all the french have on the East Side the Missippi. They have another Village on the other side opposite Aveas Called Misere, Consisting of about 50 families which is all which Remaineth to the french after the Last treaty of Peace. The Hole Settlement is Called the Ilenois On Account of the Indians who Have Settled themselves Heare after they Had Been Driven away from the River Illenois By other nations, so you must not confound this Settlement which Lies on the East side of Missippi with the River Illenois. This settlement produces Plenty of Wheat Barley, Tobacco and some Cotton, and it Has Extensive Indian trade; it Produces Some fruit: Applies, Pears, Quinses, and Peaches. The land is low And the Missippi Gennerally over flows in June; the Excessive Heat that followeth afterwards occasioneth the fevers to Be Very frequent. In August and September they Have great Plenty of Wild fowl in the Swamps.

[1] Matchinkoa.   [2] Kaskaskias.

JOURNAL OF AN OFFICER WHO TRAVELLED IN
AMERICA AND THE WEST INDIES IN 1764
AND 1765

INTRODUCTION

THE author of this journal was an officer of the Sixty-sixth Regiment of Foot which was stationed in the West Indies. Lord Adam Gordon, son of Alexander, second Duke of Gordon, was Colonel of that regiment in 1763–1775. The *Officer* left Charleston the middle of March and proceeded northward through North Carolina. He says: "Mr. Dobbs, the Governor of North Carolina, died whilst I was there, and is succeeded by Colonel Wm. Tryon." On April 1, 1765, Tryon wrote the Board of Trade: "I seize this opportunity . . . to acquaint your Lordships, Governor Dobbs died at Brunswick the 28th of last month. I was escorting Lord Adam Gordon thro' part of this Province, when the news of this event reached me."[1] Again, on the 26th of May, 1765, Tryon wrote the Secretary at War recommending the appointment of one Robert Howe as commander of Fort Johnston and added: "Lord Adam Gordon, who did me the honour of passing a few days with me in his tour thro' America, will speak to the character of this gentleman."[2] The *Officer* left Montreal for Quebec "about the end of July 1765." The Newport *Mercury* of September 2, 1765, printed a news item from Quebec (July 25, 1765), announcing the arrival there of "the right hon. Lord Adam Gordon, Col. of the 66th regiment of foot, and member of parliament for Aberdeen, accompanied by Commodore Loring;" and the Massachusetts *Gazette* of September 19, 1765, printed a news item from Quebec telling of Lord Adam Gordon's departure the 2d of August. Sir William Johnson, to whom the *Officer* paid a visit on his way from Albany to Niagara Falls and another on his return from Canada, wrote the Board of Trade the 28th of September, 1765: "My son now accompanys Lord Adam Gordon to see England. . . . Lord Adam has made an extensive Tour thro' this Country,

---

[1] *Colonial Records of North Carolina*, Vol. VI, p. 1320.
[2] *Ibid.* Vol. VII, p. 40.

and has made many remarks and observations worthy attention."[1] From his second visit to Sir William the *Officer* proceeded to Boston, and the Massachusetts *Gazette* of September 19, 1765, contains an account of the reception of Lord Adam Gordon, "a Member of the British Parliament, now making the Tour of America" by the Selectmen of Boston during which they requested him to use his influence in favor of Massachusetts in the Stamp Act controversy. The *Officer* embarked at New York for England the 14th of October, while the Stamp Act Congress was in session. The New York *Mercury* of October 7, 1765, contains this announcement: "On Monday last came to Town, the Hon. Lord Adam Gordon, after a Tour thro' his Majesty's American Islands, and Colonies on the Continent; and we hear intends to go for England by the next Packet. Anderson, in his *Scottish Nation*, states that Colonel Adam Gordon returned to England in 1765 "and having been intrusted by the heads of the colonies with a statement of their grievances, on the 20th of November of that year he had a long conference with the secretaries of state on the subject." The Pennsylvania *Gazette* of February 13, 1766, contains a London news item announcing the arrival of Lord Adam Gordon and stating that on the 20th of November, 1765 he had "a conference with His Majesty's Secretaries of state, when it is said his Lordship informed them of the present state of North America, and of the uneasiness of the people on account of the new stamp act." The identification with our anonymous journalist seems fairly complete.

Lord Adam Gordon was the fourth son of the second Duke of Gordon, and was born about 1726. He was M.P. for Aberdeenshire from 1754 to 1768, and for Kincardineshire from 1774 to 1788, was commander of the forces in Scotland from 1782 to 1798, and died in 1801. A copy of the Journal — in other than the author's hand — has been preserved among the King's Manuscripts in the British Museum 213, ff. 1–69. The Library of Congress has a transcript of this copy.

[1] *Documents Relative to the Colonial History of the State of New York*, edited by E. B. O'Callaghan, Vol. VII, p. 766.

JOURNAL OF AN OFFICER WHO TRAVELLED IN AMERICA AND THE WEST INDIES IN 1764 AND 1765

Journal of an Officer in the West Indies who travelled over a part of the West Indies, and of North America, in the Course of 1764 and 1765

WE left London *on Tuesday the 10th of April 1764,* and arrived the same night at Portsmouth, without meeting with any thing extraordinary, unless it was, that we remarked that neither the Attendance or accommodation was near so good as it is either on the great North Road or on the Road to Bath, or many other Roads in England. The Fountain Inn, the best at Portsmouth, is both extravagant and dirty — and if you except the Publick Docks, Stores etca., etca. which belong to the Naval Department there, and the Fortifications which are accounted the best in England, there is nothing else worth a Travellers notice. The Country for some Miles round the Town, is flat and Morassy, and not at all pleasant — nor is it reckoned a healthy Situation. Near it, at Gosport, is a new Hospital for Sailors, worth visiting. — *On Thursday the 12th of April* we Embarked in a small Boat for Cowes, in the Isle of Wight, but it falling little Wind, we put in at Ryde, a very pretty little Village on the opposite Shore, and proceeded to Newport, the principal Town of the Island, where we found ourselves much better than at Portsmouth. It is a very agreeable little Town, almost in the Center of one of the best peopled, and best wooded Countries you could wish to see. The ancient Castle of Carrisbrook, stands within a Mile of Newport: there is in it a very remarkable deep Well, and in Carrisbrook street, a small Spring, from whence you may have Water, as good as at Bristol, to Carry to Sea. I have now some of it in my possession since 1758, which was thrice on the Coast of France that Summer, and is at this hour as good, and as Sweet as at first, owing to its being put into New Bottles.

On Sunday the 15th the Weather came moderate, and the Wind fair to carry us out. About Noon we went on Horseback to Cowes, embark'd, passed the Needles, and came to an Anchor off Yarmouth, and next day, about Noon, took our leave of the Needles. In the Channel we found it very Squally, and the wind variable 'till *the 30th*, when it came fair, we then took our Departure from the Lizard. The Weather proving much milder we left off Fires in the Cabbin, and proceeded very agreeably along the Coasts of Spain, Portugal and Africa, 'till *the 29th* at noon when we made Porto Santo, an Island twelve Leagues short of Madeira ; *the 30th* at night, we anchored in the Road of Funchal, at about half a Miles distance, and landed there next morning early, the Weather continuing to grow warmer, and the Air more serene. Whether it proceeded from the Squalls we had met in the Channel, or that things appear worse at a distance than when present, I could not perceive any material disagreeable difference in crossing the Bay of Biscay, from what I had felt at Sea in other places — but had it been otherways, the pleasure we felt in our approach to the Island of Madeira (which increased beyond description as we advanced and could distinguish the uncommonly beautifull Landscapes with accuracy) would have more than compensated for the fatigues of our Voyage.

Perhaps some short account of an Island, so happily situated, may not be altogether disagreeable. — It is supposed to be in circumference   Miles,[1] and to contain from one hundred to one Hundred and twenty Thousand Souls, of which they reckon upwards of Thirty Thousand Men fit to bear Arms. The Port and Town of Funchal is the best, and Capital Town of the Island. — here is fixed the Seat of Government, Civil, Military, and Ecclesiastical, and

---

[1] Madeira has a coast line of about eighty-five miles.

from this Port alone 20,000 pipes of Madeira Wine are exported at an average annually, and as the demand increases, so does the Cultivation of the Grape, which in some extraordinary years amounts to 30,000 pipes. The Island lies in the Latitude 32 deg. 31 Min., Longitude [west from] Greenwich nearly 1 hour and 6 Min: variation Com[p]ass and is commonly computed to be in length about 18 Leagues, and in breadth about 8 Leagues.[1] — The whole is one Immense Mountain, the Sides and hollow places of which are cultivated in Vineyards, as is the Coast in most parts round the Island for a League up from High Water mark.

With regard to the merit of this Climate, by observations from Farenheits' Barometer, the Mercury has not, for many years been lower than Fifty six, nor higher than Seventy eight, except with a Levant wind, and from what I saw and could hear, it would appear that there is no Tree, Shrub, or Plant, that is yet discovered in the habitable Globe, but would be easily propagated there.

The fertility and goodness of the Soil is very uncommon; It produces everything almost Spontaneously, for the Inhabitants there can scarce be said to use art. — Grapes are the only Staple and it is supposed at this day in 1764, there is not above one tenth part of the whole Island Cultivated.

The Situation of Funchal is extremely agreeable and Romantick, — it is built along a curv'd Beech, at the extremity of which are two indifferent Forts, two advanced Bastions in the length, and a bad Wall connecting the whole. It is singular that so high a Surf runs there that no Quay or landing place has ever been attempted, and it is very doubtful if any such could be made effectual, altho there is reason to believe that for about the Sum of one hundred thousand pounds Sterling well managed, a Work might be made to join the Loo Rock at the Westernmost end of the Beech to another Rock on Shore, which would constitute a Safe Port and Retreat for Shiping in most Winds.

[1] Madeira is only thirty-two miles long and twelve miles broad.

Something of this Sort is extremely wanted, because when the Wind is high, either from the No[rth] or So[uth] it is not possible for Ships to ride it out. The Water is deep close in Shore, and a very large Vessel may come too within fifty yards of high Water mark, which seldom rises above seven feet. — The Town itself is ill laid out, and not well built, neither is it so well kept as it might be, when one considers that from the rising grounds which surround it, they might have every Street overflow'd once or twice a Day.

The principal Buildings are the great Church, the Castle where the Governour resides, which (besides a Strong Wall towards the Land side, has a tolerable platform and Battery to the Sea) the Bishops house, and the Custom house, adjoining to which is the Exchange. Some of the Natives and some of the British Merchants residing here, have very convenient houses which are roomy and cool, but it appears uncommon to us that they have few sash Windows, and never live in the lower Story, which is generally made use of as Storehouses. Their best appartments are up one pair of Stairs, and over those, in many of their houses, is their dinning Parlour and Kitchen, which is in general the only Fireplace. Each house however has a kind of Balcony, open on one or more Sides, to which in warm weather The[y] retire, — some of them are very high, and they give them the name of Mirandas. The very Gardens in Town are full of Grapes, and the best of them have Walks covered with Vines, and some of them with the Alexandrian laurel, and other Shrubs, which shade you, and render the air cool and pleasant, to those who either walk, or Sit under them. Almost every Man of any fortune, has a Villa at some little distance, and many of them in sight, these they call Quintas and the appearance they make, being all Whitened and interspersed with Vineyards, Figtrees, and Groves of sweet Chesnuts, much used by the Peasants, is perfectly Romantick and Chinese.

The ground on which the Town Stands, rises to the land side all round, so that the Streets and Lanes, which are ill pav'd, and Steep, render walking disagreeable to Strangers, the Roads are everywhere bad and rocky, and on every hand impassable almost for any thing but a Horse or Mule, which they use to bring in their Wine, each carrying two little Barrels slung across, eight of which go to a Hogshead and Sixteen to a Ton.

The people in general are middlesized, Strong, and well made, mostly black hair, black eyes, and fine teeth! the Men are proud, and Ceremonious to a degree extremely forbidding to us. — the Women of the best sort, come seldom abroad, have little or no education, and in general seem more to resemble the first or upper Servant than the Mistress of the Family. — They live much in distinct and distant appartments, and by Report, if a Lady and Gentleman, can fall on a way to meet, it is the fault of the Gentleman if he is not happy, since it is a maxim with the Ladies there, that an opportunity is never to be lost.

The British and Natives do not mix much together, but it would be highly unjust to omit acknowleding the attention, politeness and good breeding, which the present Governour and Captain General Don Jos: de Saa, shew to every British Subject, a Country he much esteems, and honours.

About the distance of three Miles towards the higher part of the Mountain stands a Chapel and an adjoining building, which they call the Church of our Lady of the Mountain. — It stands fifteen hundred feet higher than the Surface of the Sea, of perpendicular height, and commands an extensive view of the Town, the Bay, and the Country towards the East and West Side, and behind it you see the Mountains rising still more Sharp and sudden; in short it is worth a Travellers notice, but I would advise him if not very fond of Walking to use a Mule.

The Church itself is nothing very extraordinary, nor are the Churches in general in Madeira, either singular in their outward or inward Ornaments. — The Jesuits is the handsomest I saw, and their Convent is capable of containing many brethren, it is at present empty, and the Garden quite neglected, the finest trees of various kinds, I saw on the

Island, were in it, and it is capable of much improvement. — Upon the whole did this charming Island belong in property, either to the British or the Dutch, I Should suppose it in a few years to become the most envied Spot in the World, since with art and little Industry, it is capable of every improvement.

I discerned during a Weeks stay, about eight, or more sorts, of very valuable and large growing Timber trees totally unknown in Britain, the wood of them varying much from each other, and many of them evergreens, and as they grow best towards the highest, and hilly part of the Island, I am in hopes they may be introduced into Britain.

Doctor Thomas Hebberden, a Gentleman not more famous for his Skill in Physick, Mathematicks and Botany, than for the pleasure he takes in communicating to others his knowledge, and the love he has in doing good to the whole and to every individual, has been kind enough to promise to send me seeds, plants, and Specimens of all the indigenous timber trees growing on this Island, which I am hopefull may prove useful to our Country Men, lovers of improvement and exotick knowledge in times to come.

We left Madeira with regret, after passing a Week there most agreeably, and in less than four and twenty hours fell in with a fine fair Breeze which wafted us pleasantly thro' the Ocean.

Water all over the Island is excellent, and in great abundance, besides Grapes, they have Oranges, Lemons, Ananas,[1] Peaches, Nectarines, Apricoks,[2] Plumbs, Pomegranates, Mulberrys, Pears, Apples, and many other Fruits, and all the Kitchen stuff we ate, had a remarkable rich flavor. — Their chief Commerce is with Britain, and the British Colonies : they also send a few Vessels yearly to the Brazils, but I leave you to Judge of their industry, by mentioning one circumstance, which much surprised me, — they bring most of the Lime they use in this Island from Lisbon, and some from England, altho the Island of Porto Santo, within twelve

---

[1] Bananas. [2] Apricots.

Leagues of Madeira, produces good Lime Stone in abundance. — They grow some Wheat, and other grain, but are mostly supplyed from Britain, and North America with Flower, particularly when the Crop of Chesnuts fail, which the poorer sort, gather and dry in a manner to preserve them good for many months, and use as the Irish do Potatoes, instead of Bread.

On Monday the 7th of May we went on board the Polly, and Sailed that evening with the Land Breeze, but it coming calm in the night, we did not lose sight of Madeira all Tuesday, *on Wednesday the 9th* we fell in with the Trade Winds, which blows at that season of the year from N. E. to S. E. and having fine moderate weather, proceeded on our Course without meeting with any occurrence worth mentioning 'till *the 10th of May*, when we made the Island of Antigua.

On the 31st in the Afternoon, we came to an Anchor in Parham Bay, and came on Shore that evening, at Parham Town, from whence we walked up to a Seat of Valentine Morris Esqr. called Crabbs, about half a Mile from the Town.

The Island of Antigua, appeared green and pleasant, the coast on that side much varied and broke by the Islands and Capes running into the Sea. — Long Island on the Left as you enter Parham Harbour is very beautiful and well cultivated, having two or more Sugar Works, and Wind Mills upon it.

As much of Antigua as I saw, is pleasant, the want of Springs and Rivers, is in some degree compensated by, the pains they have taken in making for each House, one or more large Cisterns (or Tancks) which are Terrassed over, and catch all the rain Water that falls on the Houses, by Conduits and Pipes well adapted for that end. But the want of Water to cool the Stills used in the making of Rum, is much felt by the poor Negroes, who carry it on their heads, in large Vessells and sometimes from a considerable distance.

Almost all the people of fashion live on their Estates in the Country, and are all more or less engaged in making of Sugar and Rum. — There are several large properties in the hands of Familys residing in Britain, who let them out to Managers, that pay them a certain agreed annual rent on the Exchange, and these Gentlemen generally make themselves great fortunes.

St. Johns is the principal Town, and the Seat of Government. It is regularly laid out, and well calculated to receive all the cool Breezes both from the Sea and Land. The Court House, Council room, and Assembly room, are grand and well contrived, over against them is a good Guard house and a Magazine well supplied with small Arms, and some Cannon. The New Barracks are spacious, well situated and well contrived, the[y] stand Airy, have a large Garden, two noble Cisterns, a handsome Area before them, and every conveniency one would wish, unless that they are not sufficiently inclosed. They contain one Compeat[1] Regimt and are said to have cost the Island in all, near Ten Thousand pounds Sterling.

The present Governour Mr. Thomas,[2] is a very well bred sensible man, and lives very genteely at his own house in the Country.

Upon the whole it is a very happy Island, the Society is good, and they have no disputes, but live all well together, in good harmony. I never met with more Civilities, during a Weeks stay, or left a place with more regret.

Besides the Governour, there are on the Island, Warners, Brebners, Hallydays, Maxwells, Grants, and many other of Note — all good people.

We hired a little Sloop for Twelve pounds Currency, and Sailed for St. Christophers, *on Tuesday evening the 5th June*, after having passed the King's Birthday at St. Johns, very joyously, with much Company and the Officers of the 38th and 68th Regiments — and *on Thursday the 7th*, I met with the Cornwal, Captain Mc Kenzie,[3] who had the 66th (my Regiment) on board.

The Island of St. Kitts is well watered, and has a much richer Soil than Antigua; It is also well wooded and has

[1] Complete.
[2] George Thomas, governor of Antigua from 1753 to 1766.
[3] Alexander McKenzie.

also three good roads for Ships. — Basseterre, Old Road, and Sandy Point. — At Old Road, all the Men of War touch and Water. — Mr. and Mrs. Walter Pringle, and the Baillies, and Mr. Smith (of Eton) live there, and are very hospitable and agreeable people.

We Sailed from Old Road on Saturday, after taking in some water, and coasted pleasantly by St. Eustatia,[1] Porto Rico, and Domingo,[2] making the rock of Alta Vella, and so on, due West or a little to the Southward of West, 'till we arrived in sight of Jamaica, which happened *on the 13th June 1764.*

On Monday the 18th day of June early in the forenoon, we came to an Anchor in Port Royal road, where we found Rear Admiral Sir Wm. Burnabys Flag flying, and several of His Majesty's Ships of War.

It is the Rendezvous of the Fleet, and at Port Royal is a Store house, Magazine, Hospital etca., etca. for the Navy, much frequented in all times. In coming into Port Royal Harbour, you Sail close under the Grand Battery, and very near where the old Town stood, before the great Earthquake, Hurricane, and Fire, which happened there in the years 1692, and 1701, after which the remaining Inhabitants removed to Kingston across the Bay some Miles, which is now the most trading, and only very considerable Town in the Island. It is large and very well Inhabited, the Streets spacious, and regularly laid out, cutting one another at right Angles, — And in the upper part of the Town, called the Savannah, are many Sumptuous houses, with Gardens, and Offices in proportion. It would [be] very warm here, but for the Sea Breezes, which commonly set in about 10, — A.M. — and last 'till near 4 oClock P.M.

From Kingston to Spanish Town, where the Governour in Chief resides, and their Council, and Assembly meet, is Seventeen Miles by Land, Turnpike road all the way, thro' a Sandy Country. — About half way, you pass a little River, at a Bridge, near Mr. Wallins, a pretty place.

The Governours House is large and roomy, and [on] one side

[1] Saint Eustatius. [2] Santo Domingo.

of the Square or grand place — facing it stands the Court and Assembly house, with a Guard room near it. — The whole of this is a confused poor Town, Situated on the Rio Cobre and supported alone by the concourse of people, whom business with the Government brings to it. Here is no Sea Breeze, but towards the evening the Land Breeze makes the Air Cooler. The afternoons and Nights here are more intolerably warm, than I felt them in any other part of Jamaica. — I lived with Governour Littelton [1] and his Lady and Family, than whom nobody could be more polite, friendly or agreeable. — I attended him also to his Farm, (Penn) and to his Mountain, which is cool and pleasant, the Road to it all along the River is most enchantingly Romantick, and the three last Miles, which are thro' the Mountains, and a Horse road only, is very much out of the Common run, and [un]like anything I ever saw in Britain, being entirely covered with a variety of Wood and Underwood not known in Europe.

From Kingston I had occasion to visit the Quarters of my Regiment, for which end I went on Horseback over Wag Water (acqua alta) Mountains, to St. Georges Parish at Anotta Bay, a handsome and very commodious Barrack, on the North side of the Island, where it is most narrow; — from that I visited St. Anns, St. James's, Westmorland, Hanover, St. Elizabeths, Vére, Clarendon, and St. Dorothys, returning to Spanish town (St. Jago de la Vega) and Kingston, from whence I made the Windward Tour, taking in St. Davids, St. Thomas in the East, and Portland Parishes, which almost compleated the Tour of the Island, the middle part of which is very Mountainous, tho' Interspersed with many fine Vallies, and feeding and breeding grounds — the Sugar Plantations are more frequent in the Lands that occupy seven or ten Miles of the Coast, and are extremely rich, altho' the expence of Stock, and of Wear and Tear, is much greater than what attends any other kind of Estate, particularly when Negroes are at a high price.

[1] William Henry Lyttelton, governor of Jamaica 1762-1766, previously governor of South Carolina, and afterward Lord Lyttelton.

With regard to the Country it is not easily described, as it is so much varied, and the greater part of the high grounds remain still uncleared. — It is well watered by Rivers, and has more fine Harbours than almost any other Island of its Size in the World. — Of these Port Royal, Port Antonio, Lucea, and Morant Bay are the best. — Men of War also come frequently too at Savannah La Mar and Bluefield Bay, at which last place they generally water, and frequently Rendezvous in time of War.

The Forts of which, the Chief are, Fort Charles at Port Royal, Fort Augusta at Mosquito point, Rock Fort, Fort George at Port Antonio, a Fort at Savannah La Mar, and one at Lucea, are in general bad, and much out of repair, with scarce any good Artillery. — The Barracks in general insufficient, and ill contrived, tho mostly in good Situations; the Country from a variety of causes, is not enough attentive to these matters; altho' it appears they have already over built themselves, as they wished and calculated as if they should always have two compleat Corps, on the Old high Establishment of 1000 Men each, and indeed that Number seems not more than sufficient to secure them from Intestine rebellions and Insurrections of their Negroes, who are daily increasing beyond the proportion of white people, the last being supposed not to exceed in all 25,000 Souls, and the Slaves and Mulattoes not under 160,000. —

The Gentlemen of property residing on the Island, are in general extremely civil and remarkably hospitable to Strangers — I have reason to know it, as I was at so many of their houses in the Country and in Town, where they live elegantly and well, and are able to entertain their Guests in every respect better than people of the same property can do in Europe, particularly where one stays all night. —

There are few Horses or Carriages to be hired, and the Inns in general are poor places, and of bad Entertainment, owing entirely to that hospitality which takes universally — in so much that every Gentleman you visit, offers you his Carriage or Horses, to convey you, wherever you please to go. — The Horses are generally small and are best when bred from a Spanish or English Stallion and a Creole Mare.

N.B. They seldom put any Shoes on such, but almost all the New England Horses, which are here in much Vogue, on account of their easy Gait, are Shod as in Britain.

I cannot say I much admire the Creole Women, either for beauty or Conversation. — amongst the Blacks and Mulattoes, I have seen some wonderfully well made, and with very agreeable features, tho' often attended with one Circumstance, very disgusting to new Comers.

At the Bath, in the Parish of St. Thomas in the East is a very remarkable hot Spring — It seems warmer than the Water at Bristol, and I was obliged to let it stand some time in the glass, before I was able to drink it, — it is good in many disorders, particularly Rheumatick Complaints. — At same place is a Bath tolerably well frequented, the distance from the Village to the Spaw is about two good measured Miles, a good Horse road, and at every Quarter of a Mile, is a Shed or covering of the Palmeto leaf, for Shelter to Invalids against rain, which in Jamaica, and particularly in that neighbourhood, is frequent and very heavy, resembling Water poured from a Bucket more than any European Shower I ever was in. —

This Island produces many of the Conveniencies and more of the Luxuries of Life — but the generality of its Inhabitants look upon themselves there as passengers only, for which reason, all their attention is bestowed on their Plantations of Canes, from whence Sugar, Rum and Molasses are produced — these are the Staple Commodities, to this may be added Coffee, Pimento (allspice) some Ginger and some Cotton.

Their Mutton is tolerably good, Beef is rare and dear, Poultry dear, and Pork excellent. — Wild Pidgeons good, Fish a variety, but particularly Turtle, seldom more than a Bitt (sixpence) a pound, — besides these, their land Turtle and black Crabs, are delicious. — Upon the whole, I found every thing in Jamaica much misrepresented, as well in regard to the Climate and Country as to the Inhabitants.

Of all their fruits I prefer the Shaddock and Orange.

Citrons and Limes grow in every Hedge; nothing can exceed the beauty and variety of their Woods, but there is scarce any thing deserving the name of Garden in the Island. — At Mr. John Ripleys near Kingston, I saw eight Acres of land under Pine Apple, which he sells there at a Bitt apiece, or three for two Bitts. — He has also a great quantity of Bees, some, which he calls Spanish Bees, have no Stings. He is making a tryal of Madeira Grapes, but I much doubt his Success.

Some years ago, during the Administration of Admiral Knowles as Governour,[1] there was an attempt made to alter the chief Seat of Government, and all the Judicatories from Spanish-Town to Kingston — this set the whole by the ears, and since that time there have always subsisted disputes and Factions in their Assembly, in which will always be a few aspiring and Hot headed Men, desirous of Conducting. — At present Mr. Lyttelton by his prudence in siding with no party, and Governing by no faction, has almost got over the opposition he met with in carrying on the King's business, which no Man can have more at heart.

On Sunday evening the 5th of August I embarked on board the Tartar, Sir John Lindesay Commander, in Port Royal road. — We Set Sail early on Monday, and after making the great Kaymana and the Capes of Corientees and Cape Antonio, on the West end of Cuba, we kept a Cross the Gulph of Florida falling in with the Tortuga Bank, and the Bay of Apalachy. — On this Bank we catched much good Fish of sorts not known in Europe, and some Dolphins. — *On Sunday evening the 19th of August*, we took in a Pilot, and came to an Anchor within the Points, and beyond the Castle on Rosa Island, and on Monday afternoon came to an Anchor about two Miles off of Pensacola Fort and Village, in five fathom Water. —

The Fort is an Oblong Square with a double Stockade and a very narrow Ditch dug in the Sand. Four Bastions are in-

[1] Sir Charles Knowles was Governor of Jamaica in 1752–1756.

tended. — The Governour's is the only tolerable House in the place. — It is covered with Shingles, and has a Balcony both ways up one pair of Stairs. — All the other Houses are on the ground, and covered with Palmeto Leaves. — It is a very poor place, the Soil a deep white Sand for many Miles round.

The Garrison is supplied with very good and Wholesome water, from a little River which surrounds the place at some distance. — The Space between the Town and River is mostly cleared of Wood, but no farther. —

The Pitch Pine grows all round in great quantities, but not very near each other, at every here and there one finds a Cedar Swamp, and under the large trees is much Brush of Candleberry, Myrtle, and Shrub Oak.

The Harbour of Pensacola, or rather the Bay is magnificent, and might contain any Fleet, was it not for want of Water at the Bar, at present nothing beyond a Fifty Gun Ship would get over, but was a Squadron for North America ever to be built, flatter and more after the Dutch Model, it might obviate this difficulty. — At present there appears scarce a probability of improving such desert Sands, yet it is difficult to Say how the Spanish Trade may operate, since it will be more commodiously carried on here, than at any Port belonging to Great Britain, particularly after that the Crown of Spain shall be in possession of all the East of Missisipi and New Orleans. — To the Westward of the Harbour lies English point, Point Pedro, and beyond that a fine River, navigable for small Craft many Miles — on the Coast of this, I perceived a greater variety of trees and Shrubs, amongst which I found both the Magnolias, a Sweet Bay, two kinds of Mapples, two kinds of Cedars, and an infinity of Candleberry Myrtle, with some other sorts resembling our Oaks, Beeches and Cedars. — The Ibex here is not large, but like Underwood, the Pines however are the principal produce of the whole, and next to them the Cedar is in the greatest plenty. Holly is very scarce. — I have seen but one Plant.

An Island called Santa Rosa forms the Mouth of the Harbour, and on it stands a trifling little Fort, where is commonly a Serjeants Guard with a Flag Staff, to give notice to the Fort of Pensacola, when any Vessel is coming in, it is customary for him to fire one Gun, and hoist his Colours.

This Island has no Springs, and in bad Weather the little Garrison in it, has been distressed both for fresh Water and provisions.

Pensacola is by all accounts a most healthy Situation, scarce any have died there since our having it, but some who came ill from the Havannah.

A[t] Mobile at this Season, everybody is ill, several have died, and in the Regiment Quarter'd there, they have but one Officer able to do Duty.

It may not be improper in this place to take notice of a great neglect at home.

In East Florida and the Illinois are supposed to be fifteen hundred Men, consisting of three Battalions, at present the 22d, 34th and 35th, and yet they are so incomplete, that I am certain in the three, it would not be possible at this time to collect more than five hundred Men for Service. Some of the Regiments are Commanded by a Captain, and in all of them the proportion of Absent Officers is too great, in a Country as yet so little reconciled to our Constitution and Government.

At Pensacola they have no fresh Meat, but what is brought from the Country about Mobile and the Missisipi, and it would be of the greatest consequence to Florida, that a Land communication between these two Forts should be compleated, which would not be very expensive or difficult, the whole distance not exceeding Seventy Miles, thro' a Country not very thick of underwood, or a great many rivers intervening. One or two small Posts will be needfull, if this Plan should be followed, near the Rivers of greatest Note, which may be Garrisoned one from Pensacola and another from Mobile. I Should suppose a strong house to contain one Company of Men, and its Officers, at each of the two Posts, would be a sufficient force, and they might be relieved every five or Six Weeks.

It may be worth considering in some time hence, how far

the Rivers running into Pensacola Bay, may or may not have a communication with those which run at the back of West Florida and Georgia, by which means a safe communication for Goods and Passengers might be not improperly established, between Pensacola, Augustine, Savannah, and East Florida.

The heat here is much less intense than at Jamaica or the Leeward Islands, for there comes almost a daily breeze from the Sea, and the Nights (even in the Dog-day season) are very pleasant. — The Officers complain much of Cold in the Winter Months, and Easterly Winds which are very cutting. The Houses too are all framed of Wood, and covered with Palmeto leaves, the Sides either plaster or bark of trees, and Scarce a Chimney to be seen, so it is no wonder they are cold.

Fish I never saw in more abundance, or better, indeed it is the Chief sustenance of the Garrison; they have got some Hogs, Goats, and Poultry, but nothing can be trusted out of the Stockade, since the Indians, who come frequently to them, make a custom of stealing every thing that will eat, or be usefull. A propos — these all ride, and generally bring down more Horses than they require, those they barter for Rum in different quantities, and as the Horses are all Stolen from the back lands and Traders in Georgia and Carolina, they sell them cheap, that is from two to four Gallons of Rum a piece. — but Caveat Emptor! for if you do not keep him in the Fort, or a close house, 'till they are gone away with their presents and purchases, you will lose him the night after you buy him, and the Indian will sell him again to the first bidder he meets. They bring down a few Deer and other Skins, but not in quantities, and now and then they bring in some Venison, which is seldom good.

In the Winter Months the Deer come down nearer the Coasts, at which time the Bears, Wolves, and Foxes are also in great Numbers and often troublesome. — Allegators here are very numerous; I saw several, and was present at the killing a large one, which lay with its head out of cover on the Beach — we all passed it at first, and thought it was dead, but one of the Company touching it on the head, it yawned, and just then it received several Shot and bullets before it died, It might measure twelve feet or more.

During my stay at Pensacola, there came many Indians, in particular the Wolf King, two other Kings, and several Head men of Tribes. — The Wolf seemed a Sensible Old Man, said he might be a hundred years old, and that the fatigues he had undergone in going down to the Colonies in Georgia and Carolina, had effected him and made him look as old as he did.

He professed great friendship for the British, and kept a Strict rein over the Indians in his Company, they were called about 300, and encamped or lay in the Bushes in a Wood by a Brook, within less than half a Mile of the Fort. — They are a hardy well made Set of people, calculated seemingly to bear fatigue, their features are manly and expressive, and with the advantages of European Education and Address, would equal them in many particulars. — They early rub themselves over with grease and some juice of an Herb, which renders their faces and bodies of a dunn copper tint — they pluck all the hair off their beards, and value high foreheads, — what hair remains they plait or braid behind wearing a variety of things mixt with it, such as Strings, Shells, and feathers; some wear pieces of Metal and Shells to their Ears, which are almost always cut or Slit in uncommon Shapes, others have rings in the gristle of the Nose, and others large broad Bracelets round their Arms and Wrists. — The young Children that attend them down go naked, their Squaws and themselves are fond of having their faces painted with vermillion and black, in strange manners — when they come down it is always on Horse back, and when they return they carry their Kegs of Rum, which they call Taffy, upon their own backs, on Horse-back, as well as much of the other presents, the most usual of which are as follows. Rum, Fire Arms, Flints, Powder and ball, Knives, Razors, Blankets, Shirts of all sorts, Beads, looking-glasses, and many other trifles; for these and such like they barter Skins — mostly Deer Skins.

George Johnstone Esqr. was Governour when I was at

Pensacola in 1764. — Salary £1200 Ster'g and £300 more for purchasing and maintaining a Schooner for the uses of the Province.

On the 12th of October 1764, I left the Tartar at anchor near Rose Island and Sailed in a small Schooner, along with Mr. John Steward[1] (Superintendant for His Majesty's Indian affairs) to the Southward for Mobile, and came to an Anchor off of the point that Evening within the Bar — next day we made Sail up the Bay, the River Poisson being to Starboard, and the Isle Dauphine, or Massacre, being on our Larboard Quarter, rather a Stern. We had a good Pilot, one Jerome Matulicht, a Sclavonian, who resides between Mobile and Orleans, and is a very sensible fellow. On that part of the Bar of Mobile which we traversed, were all breakers, and not more than eight feet water, but on the best passage you have fourteen feet water. After you have crossed the Bar, which is not to be risked without a Pilot, you may carry up with you Sixteen feet water, keeping the middle of the Channel, until you come within two, or two and half Leagues of the Town. — Round the Point Mobile there is good holding ground for small Craft, and if you follow that up, you enter into a Bay called St. Andrew's Bay, leading up the River Poisson, which ends in a Swamp, lying in the Road between Pensacola and Mobile. — On passing over St. Andrew's Bay and River, you come to point of Land called Mallet point, from which place, quite up there occurs nothing very remarkable, 'till you meet the great Alibama River, which in its course divides the Creek, and Chactaw Nations. On the Western Shore of the Bay of Mobile you meet first the River au Pouilles, then the River au Chevreuils, and lastly the River au Chiens, two Leagues below the Town. The Fort, formerly Fort Conde, stands on the Western bank of Tombecby[2] River, which is called Mobile River, for the space of twelve Leagues upwards, and all the Land which lies between the said River, and the Alibama is held common, between the Creeks and Chactaws,

[1] Captain John Stuart.   [2] Tombigbee.

altho' the last pretend, that the Creeks should not pass the Alibama river.

When you get within two, or two and a half Leagues of Mobile, the Water becomes shallow, unless you keep up on the East or Alibama Side, where you may ascend above the Town, round a Swamp, and then come down to Mobile, by a Channel, called the Spanish Channel.

The Fort is on an Unwholesome Situation, altho' it stands rather higher than the Town. — It is a Quarre of Brick, having a bad dry Ditch, a covered way Stockaded, and an unfinished Glacis. It is Casemated and has bad Barracks on three Sides, which may contain about three hundred Men. Upon the whole, it is Strong enough to resist all Indian Attacks. The Town consists mostly of Straggling houses, built of Wood, or Wood and Brick; the Streets are well laid out, but in the Summer and Autumn, almost everybody is ill of Fevers, Fluxes and Agues; Bark is much Administered and Seldom fails. The Water in and near the Town is bad and often brackish the Natives who remain, fetch what water they drink, at three Miles distance, and in general stand out better, than the Garrison, and New Settlers. — I have reason to believe that such Situations, as are either totally on the Salt water, or totally on the fresh water, are the most healthy, and that such as are between both, are seldom free from Diseases, particularly in the fall.

The Land round Mobile, tho' light, is certainly better than about Pensacola, and from what I have seen in South Carolina, I should think it very proper for the growth of Indigo; at present it will produce most of the American and many European fruits and roots. I ate here some excellent white Figgs, and Saw Vines and Mulberry trees in abundance. The Pines are the Same as about Pensacola, but better grown, in their Rivers too, they have Mullet and other fish in plenty, but all the Channels at hand, are so full of Logs, Stumps, and trees, that it is not possible to hawl a Seine, and if you catch fish on the Alibama Side, in warm weather, they will Stink before you can bring them to Market. I was told the land on the East of the Bay, exceeds the other, and is very tolerably planted, and Inhabited by French. In October 1764, when I was at Mobile, the Garrison which consisted of two Regiments, was so ill, and Weak, as scarce to be able between them to furnish a Subalterns Guard. Few Guns were mounted, and those that were, were Iron Ship Guns. All the Platforms, Casemates, and Mens Barracks, wanted repair, and there were within the Fort no Appartments for Officers, or place for Stores.

In returning from Mobile to Pensacola, you Steer down the Bay, to the point of Mobile, eleven Leagues due South, from that to point Lagune, four Leagues East and by North, thence to Point la Croix, East and North, Northerly, three Leagues, then to Point Perdido, sam[e] Course three Leagues, and from that to the Flag Staff on St. Rosa Island, four Leagues East and by North. The Bar at the Mouth of the River Perdido, has not more than four and a half feet water on it, at low water, and having a prodigious Surff, cannot be attempted but by very small Craft — indeed. — As the Wind may be, there is very good Anchoring for small Vessels, either within or without the Point of Mobile, and when the Wind is from the Northward, small Vessels, may lay safe, close in, under the East end of Isle Dauphin ; from the Point cross the Bay to said Island is about three Leagues, in some parts of which you have no more than Six feet Water, and the Island bears from Point Mobile almost due West.

The Soil of this Island is a Sand, but produces Wild Indigo, and China Oranges ; I found on it both the Magniolas, the Persimoin Plumb, a variety of Oaks, Pines, Cedars, Plantanes and Maple, — Fish and water Fowl in plenty, in due season, but no Deer. I returned to Pensacola *the 26th of October*, and Embarked on board the Packet-boat, Lesslie Groves Esqr. Commander, *on the 1st Novr.* for Augustine. —

N.B. Was Saluted at leaving Mobile and Pensacola, by the Forts and Ships with 15 Guns, and Convoy'd over the Bar by Sir John Lindsey, and Captain Lockyer of His Majesty's Ships Tartar and Nautilus.

On the 5th and 6th Novr. we had hazy weather and heavy Squals on Shore, in so much, that we with great Risk and difficulty were able to weather the Banks, running off from Cape St. Blaize.[1] — I never Saw a greater Sea. — *On the 7th* the weather mended, and we kept on our Course, Steering South and by East for the Tortuga Island, and *on the 9th* about noon we made it, it bearing then from us East, or East and by South, about four Miles distance, fourteen fathom Water. We then Steered for the other Tortuga, laid down in some Charts, but said not to exist in others; We never made it, but on the following day, discovered some high lands in Cuba, which then bore from us South East, about eight Leagues distance, we kept off in the Night, and stood in Shore by daylight — It appeared much wooded, and the Inland very high. — On the Tortuga Bank, we caught abundance of excellent Red rock Cod, and Several Dolphins, with bait of the Sucking Fish. — *On Sunday the 11th* Cuba bore right ahead, five Leagues. We Stood in and found ourselves off of a Creek Called Aruca, about eight Leagues to the Eastward of the Havannah; Stood in and off Shore, Steering due West, and on that evening, about Six, came to an Anchor off of the Moro[2]; about a hundred yards off it bore E. S. E. — We sent our Letters on Shore, but were not Suffered to Land.

Monsr. Le Conde de Ricla, the Spanish Governour, wrote me a very polite Letter, excusing the necessity he was under, to conform himself to the repeated Orders of his Court, and sent me some Wine etca. — But Monsr. O'Reilly, and Father Butler of Ireland were not so Civil. All the part of Cuba I saw, to the Eastward of the Havannah, is high, and much wooded, the Harbour seems capacious, and the Town and Works round it, seem all to be commanded by the Moro-Castle, which appears extremely inaccessible, by reason of its great height above the Water to any attacks of Shipping; I saw many people at Work, and was told, they were employed, in repairing the Old, and constructing the New Works of the Moro, four or five thousand people daily. — After taking on board some Water etca. we Weighed about five *Monday evening the 12th*, Steering for the high land,

[1] San Blas.   [2] Morro Castle.

called the Matanzas, from which all Ships, going thro' the Bahama Streights, chuse (if possible) to take their departure, in order, to get well into the Gulph Stream, and to avoid falling in with Cape Florida, or the Shoals and Rocks, which lie off of it, and are called the Martyres. To a person who has not seen it, it is scarce possible to conceive an Idea, of the Strength and velocity of the Current, you meet here, which runs ever to the Northward, and in that degree, that altho' the Wind should be right ahead, the Stream will nevertheless hurry you thro', in a most amazing Manner.

From the Matanzas you hold a Northerly Course, and you can scarce go amiss, when once you get into mid-channel. In 22 Deg's 20 Mins N. Latitude, off the Florida Coast lies a dangerous Shoal, which runs out some Leagues from the Main land; It is called Cape Canaverall, — there is a small Channel for Coasting Vessels, between the Main and it, and I am told the Spanish Coasters used it, as well as a Channel between the Keys and the Cape of Florida. — But neither of these passes are to be risked in a Vessel of any draught of Water, or without a Pilot. In Latitude 28 deg. and 30 Min. lies the North end of the great Bahama Bank, and beyond that Latitude the Current will hustle you both to the Eastward and Northward, Surprizingly. In Latitude 30 you will have Soundings many Leagues off Shore, but will not be able to make the land clear, 'till you get into eight or nine fathom Water. It will then be distant from you some two Leagues, or two and a half, and you will be easily sensible of the Change of colour in the water, which on this Coast becomes ever whiter and more muddy as you approach the Land. — All the Coast, at, and about Augustine, appears flat, and White sand, much the same as in West Florida. Trees are seen Inland, and little worth notice besides occurs.

Our passage was a disagreeable one, owing to a very short high Sea; however as we got to the Northward, we had better weather, and *on the 19th of Novemr* we made the Land right ahead and Stood in. — By an observation at noon, we found ourselves in 30 Deg. 6 Min. North Latitude, consequently to the Northward of our Port, which by the most accurate

390

observations hitherto made, lies in 29 deg. 53 Min. North Latitude.

About noon we came to an Anchor off [St.] Augustine Bar, in about five fathom Water: the Island on which the Town stands, as well as the Island on which the Light house is built, being then in sight: the Pilot boat, and a very ill calculated, insufficient boat she is, came off, and carried us in over the Bar and Breakers. I[n] this short passage, I apprehend, we ran more risk of being lost, than in any former part of our Voyage — Many boats and lives have been lost there, and I never intend passing it again, unless upon actual Service. There is another passage called the Swatch, almost as dangerous as over the Bar.

Augustine has all the appearance of a place that will thrive, altho' the Bar is an insurmountable obstacle to its being a place of Exportation: for at the best of Tide, you can bring with you but twelve feet of water, yet, when once in the Harbour, you are safe, and have deep water. — But large Ships lying at Anchor, off the Bar, or plying off and on, run risk of being blown on Shore, or on the Breakers which are terrible, and what is worst, it shall happen in blowing weather, that for days, and Weeks, no boat or small Vessel, can venture, either to go out or in over the Bar. As soon as the projected road from the Province of Georgia to Augustine is compleated, most people will come that way, to Augustine from Savannah, Charlestown, and all the Northern Provinces.

It may not be improper here to take notice, that the River St. Mary's which divides Georgia from East Florida, may in time became a usefull Port to both Provinces. —

The mouth of this river by a very exact observation, lies in 30 deg. 47 Min. N. Latitude, and has at the deepest seven fathom water at entering: but you may carry into the river's mouth four fathom and three fathom water, for fifty Miles up at high water.

The distance between the South point of Cumberland Island, and the North point of Emilia,[1] which forms the

---

[1] Amelia Island.

Entrance, is about one Mile. Upon the whole, this River, tho' little known and less frequented, may justly be esteemed one of the safest Bars, and Entrances on all the Coast, from Cape Florida, to the Capes of Virginia.

The Land on both Banks of this very remarkable river, is mostly Pine-Barren, with here and there some trifling Swamps, and several fine Bluffs; particularly on the Florida Shore of it; which remarks when duly considered and weighed, may some future day, deserve a more narrow and closer view and attention, and will therefore plead my excuse for saying so much on the Subject. On the opposite side of East Florida, and about half distance from St. Mark's, to the Cape of Florida, lies the Bay of Tampa, which is sometimes called Bahia del Spiritu Santo: It is supposed to have Water to carry in any Ship in the World, and safe space within to contain any Fleet. — but as an exact Survey of it is now actually taking, by orders from home, I will say no more of it, only to remark, the Utility it may prove to be of, in any future War with Spain — in cutting off all communication between La Vera Crux,[1] and Cuba, as from the nature of the Trade Winds in the Gulph of Mexico, all Ships on that passage, must come almost within sight of said Harbour, or Bay, as it is more properly called.

The Land for thirty Miles round this Bay, is claimed by John Gordon Esqr., as a Spanish purchase: two considerable Rivers empty themselves into it, the heads of which (some imagine) actually [connect] with the Rivers that fall into the Sea, near Augustine, but most people allow, that with a very moderate expence, a water communication, could be made so, as to have inland Navigation across that part of East Florida, lying in a Line from Augustine to the Bay of Apalachy, or near it.

The Fort at Augustine is a Quarré, smaller but better finished than the Fort at Mobile: It is built of Stone, which soft at first Quarrying, grows hard in the weather and is extremely white. It is Casemated all round the four sides, and can Mount from Seventy to Eighty pieces of Cannon.

[1] Vera Cruz, Mexico.

At present no more than Twenty are Mounted, it is neatly executed, but on too small a Scale, tho' Strong on account of the great difficulty of approaching it, owing to the Swampy land and very Shoal water, that almost Surrounds it.

Governour Grant [1] has fitted up the House and formed his Establishment, his Council and Courts. Many Gentlemen of worth and Substance, from Carolina and Georgia, are in terms to Settle in this Province, and intend to plant Indigo, Rice and Cotton, all which, it is presumed must answer well. Towards the Cape, and on the South Keys, grow abundance of Mahogony, live Oak, and other Timber, valuable in Ship-building, and other uses; the Rivers, Bays, and Coasts abound in Fish, more and in greater variety than in Europe, the Inhabitants of Providence [2] catch Turtle there every year, and Supply themselves, and the adjacent Continent with it, as they do Europe with Mahogony, cut on the above named Keys. Two hundred Bermudians have intentions to Settle themselves towards the Cape next fall and more of them will follow, since they are assisted, and enabled, by a generous and publick Spirited donation, of five pounds Ster'g to each Settler, Woman and Child, by John Savage Esqr. of Charlestown, who means to lay out for this purpose, not less than five thousand pounds Sterling.

The Soil, in and near Augustine is light, and Sandy, yet it produces every species of Garden Stuff known in Britain, when sown in due season. — When I was there in November, we had Pease, Beans, Sallad, Oranges, Limes, Critons and Lemons, the Gardens of every house in Town are full of them, and also produce Grapes, Figs (two Crops) Peaches and Pomgranates. I am assured the Avocada Pear, the Plantane, and other West India fruits, have come to perfection there: from whence one may suppose it not impracticable (particularly towards the Cape, where there is richer land and more Sun) to raise Sugar, Coffee, Pimento, and all the West India productions.

---

[1] James Grant was governor of East Florida in 1763–1771.
[2] *I.e.*, of New Providence (or Nassau) in the Bahamas.

The Town of Augustine has several good houses in it, the Streets are not ill laid out, but too narrow (a Spanish Mode). It is remarkably healthy, perhaps the most so of any Town in America; the Climate in Winter is pleasant, beyond the Idea of any man who has never been out of Europe; the Spaniards lived in it to a remarkable old age, healthy and chearful; our Sick Soldiers from the Havannah, almost all did well, and continue to look well in Augustine, and altho' surrounded with water, meadow and Marsh, fevers and Agues are scarce known. It is enclosed by a bad line, and a sort of Ditch, the line was planted with the Palmeto Royal, but its best defence is the great difficulty to bring up any Artillery against it, for the reasons already given. After all, from what I have seen of it, and heard of it, was I ever to apply for any land in America, it should be in this Province, which has many of the advantages, and none of the disagreeable Circumstances, that too visibly must occur, in planting and Settling the adjacent Province of West Florida.

On Thursday the 28th of November, I crossed the Swatch, and got on board the Packet, and *on the 2d of Decemr* after rather a tedious passage we came into Tiby [1] road, which is the Entrance into Savannah River, passed three Miles higher up, and came to an Anchor off of Cockspur Fort, on the right hand going up.

The Province of Georgia, extends from St. Mary's to the East bank of the Savannah river, the Northern Stream of which divides it from South Carolina. It was Settled originally by Oglethorpe in 1738,[2] and was vested in the hands of several t[r]ustees, however that plan failed, and for a little more than twelve years, it has been a Royal Government, since which alteration, it has annually increased, and in a great proportion too, — so late as the year 1761, the Rice exported from this Province, did not exceed five thousand Barrels, in 1763 it amounted to 12000, and is annually increasing, — in this same year they exported, commodities to the amount of £50.000 Sterling.

[1] Tybee. [2] 1733.

The Capital Town called Savannah, is extremely well laid out, and the buildings in it are increasing in Number, and Size. — It stands on a bluff fifty feet above the Surface of the River, about fifteen Miles from the Mouth at Tiby Lighthouse, about   Miles [1] below Purisburg [2] and near three hundred Miles, below Augusta, to which place Savannah river is Navigable for large Boats. — By Land the distance is near half as much.

Within twelve miles of Savannah, the Governour [3] carried me to visit the Orphan house,[4] which is a large Substantial commodious Building, erected by Contributions collected from the charitable and benevolent, by the Revd. Mr. George Whitfield, and supported to this period in the same manner. Several Orphans have been reared and educated here, and put out to different Masters. — Upwards of £12.000 Sterg has by the Books, been collected, expended, and most exactly accounted for, by the said Revd. Gentleman, who has contributed a Sum, little short of £3.000, of his own towards it, and is now about conveying and punctually vesting it (together with all the land, Negroes, Stock etca. amounting to an annual fund of near £500, a year Sterg) in the hands of Trustees, to be named by Royal Charter, for a College to educate youth, which disinterested plan, is justly much applauded, by the Governour, and Province of Georgia, as tending very much to the advantage of that Province, and all other His Majesty's Southern Dominions, where no place for Education of that kind has yet been attempted.

The produce of Silk does well here, but will still stand in need of the aiding hand of Parliament — the annual quantity, at an average of three years past, made and sent to Britain, has been about 1000 pounds weight, and is likely rather to increase than diminish. Mulberry trees grow in great perfection, as well as other European productions, except Apples. — I saw a Cabbage from one root, which produced many heads, and spread over a Circumference of thirty

[1] Twenty-two miles. [2] Purrysburg, South Carolina.
[3] James Wright was governor of Georgia in 1760–1782.
[4] Bethesda, on a bluff near the seashore.

feet. — It has stood and Seeded three years. The same Garden produced a Potatoe, which weighed ten pounds and three Quarters.

The Governour and Council live all in love and unanimity and there is all the probability in the world, to judge from the face of the land, the multitude and depth, as well as the long course of their Rivers, their inShore Navigation, and the Security derived to them from the addition of the two new Southern Provinces,[1] as well as their own Industry and Application, that Georgia will become one of the richest, and most considerable Provinces in British America, and that in a very few years, provided peace continues. The Soil about Savannah is light and Sandy, which is troublesome in windy weather, the Tide land on both sides the river, is mostly Cypress Swamp, and the fittest for Rice, and all other productions that can exist, since, when properly banked in, and drained, you need have no dependance on Seasons, but either overflow or keep dry your fields, just as you please.

N.B. Some land of this nature in South Carolina has produced Rice for forty years successively, and has improved every year as well in the quality as quantity of the grain, without any manure.

On the Carolina side of Savannah River, in one Stretch there lies near 40.000 Acres of such Swamp land, as yet mostly to clear, and on the Georgia side, a large proportion of the same land, tho' not quite so much. — The Exports from Georgia are, Rice, Indigo, Pitch, Tar, Turpentine, Hides, Deer Skins, Lumber, Timber of most kinds, and for most purposes, and raw Silk. I am told Sunbury is a thriving place, and a tolerable Harbour and Bar, a forty Gun Ship can come up above Tiby and lie Safe.

James Wright Esqr. was Governour of Georgia in February 1765 when I was there, a very worthy Gentleman and much respected by the Province, and by every body who has the happyness of knowing him.

The Currency of both Floridas, and Georgia is Sterling money.

[1] The Floridas.

I arrived at Charlestown, the Metropolis of South Carolina, *on the 8th Decemr. 1764,* having landed at Beaufort in Port Royal Island, some days before from Savannah river, which divides it from Georgia, as an imaginary Line does this Province from North Carolina.

It is of all the Southern Provinces the most considerable, on account of the Number of Inhabitants, the quantity and the variety of its productions and Exports, and the good condition of its Inhabitants. There seems in general to be but two Classes of people — the planters who are the proprietors, and the Merchants who purchase and Ship the produce.

Rice and Indigo are the two grand Staples of this Province, of which very great quantities are annually made and Exported to Europe and elsewhere. — It has been augmenting annually in Numbers, wealth and Industry, since the Crown purchas'd out the Lords proprietors, and as none of its Exports or productions, interfere with those of the Mother Country, it will be prudent in her to give this Province all possible encouragement.

Almost every family of Note have a Town residence, to which they repair on publick occasions, and generally for the three Sickly months in the fall, it being a certainty, that the Town of Charles Town, is at present the most healt[h]y spot in the Province; fevers and other disorders are both less frequent in it, and less virulent in their Symptoms; this is attributed to the Air being mended by the Number of Fires in Town, as much as to its cool Situation, on a point, at the junction of the two navigable Streams, called Ashley and Cowper [1] Rivers.

The Inhabitants are courteous, polite and affable, the most hospitable and attentive to Strangers, of any I have yet seen in America, very clever in business, and almost all of them, first or last, have made a trip to the Mother-Country. It is the fashion indeed to Send home all their Children for education, and if it was not owing to the nature of their Estates in this Province, which they keep all in their

[1] Cooper.

own hands, and require the immediate overlooking of the Proprietor, I am of opinion the most opulent planters, would prefer a home life. It is in general believed, that they are more attached to the Mother Country, than those Provinces which lie more to the Northward, and which having hardly any Staple Commodities of their own growth, except Lumber, Stock and Horses, depend mostly on Smuggling Molasses and other Contraband Commodities.

The Town of Charlestown is very pleasantly Seated, at the conflux of two pretty rivers, from which all the Country product is brought down, and in return all imported goods are sent up the Country. — The Streets are Straight, broad and Airy, the Churches are handsome; The other places of Worship are commodious, and many of the houses belonging to Individuals, are large and handsome, having all the conveniencies one sees at home. — There is a Law against building houses of Wood, which like other Laws in other Countries no body observes, however, the most considerable buildings are of Brick, the others of Cypress and yellow Pine. The houses now are about fifteen hundred, but increase annually in a very surprizing manner.

Their Bar, which is very intricate, seems their only defence, for tho' they have a Fort below the Town, and a kind of earthen Rampart, with some Tabby works, round particular parts of Charlestown, yet it would not be tenible, against attacks of Shipping, or from the land, and therefore must fall a prey to any Enemy, the moment we lose our Superiority at Sea. — A Forty Gun Ship has been in, but small Frigates and Sloops are generally employed on that Station.

The Town of Beaufort, Situated on Port Royal Island and Sound, has more depth of water on its Bar, but being on an Island there is a difficulty of bringing down the exportable Commodities, which will for ever prevent its Rivalling Charlestown, in wealth or grandeur.

On the Northern part of South Carolina, Stands George-Town, a pretty little Town near Wynyaw river,[1] and not far

---

[1] Georgetown is at the head of Winyah Bay.

from Pedee, Black river and Wakama,[1] which river, I should think, would make a more Sure and Commodious boundary, between the two Carolinas, than any limits they now have.

The back Country towards the Cherokee Mounts and Nation, is all healthy and fertile land, producing large Oak, and other deciduous timber, and is finely watered, without much Sand or Pine-barren, but is not yet fully peopled; — In general what part of South Carolina is planted, is counted unhealthy, owing to the Rice-dams and Swamps, which as they occasion a great quantity of Stagnated water in Summer, never fails to increase the Number of Insects, and to produce fall fevers and Agues, dry gripes and other disorders, which are often fatal to the lower set of people, as well White as Black. —

Within these two or three last years, a pretty considerable quantity of Flax and Hemp, has been raised by the Germans and other back Settlers, which, as well as the produce of a considerable part of North Carolina, comes down to Charlestown in Waggons, drawn with four Horses, two abreast — perhaps at the distance of three hundred Miles — this would appear extraordinary at home, but it must be remember'd that they live at no more expence when travelling than they would at home, since the[y] lie in the woods all night, make a good fire to dress their Bacon, and turn their Horses loose near them, 'till day light, after which they proceed on their Journey, and carry back in Return what goods they stand in need of themselves, or for their neighbours in the back Settlements.

It is pretty singular to remark, that the Number of White Inhabitants, fit to bear Arms in one of their back Counties, called Craven County, — does, — at present exceed what was the Number of fighting Men, in all the Province Seven years ago, — from this — I conclude that the farther you go back from the Sea Board in America, the more fertile the land is, and the more healthy the Climate, for there the people

---

[1] Waccamaw.

increase and breed, and rear up more Children than towards the Pine barren and Sandy Shores.

The Tide Swamp land in these Southern Provinces is by much the most valuable, since, when they are properly banked in, and your trunks and dams in perfect good order, by a judicious use of these advantages, it is alternately equally capable and fit to produce the two great Staple Commodities — Vizt Rice and Indigo, the first requiring an uncommon degree of moisture or Water, and the last, dry and rich land, altho' the light land very near the Shore, will fetch very Surprizing Crops of Indigo, for two or three years, but it must then be thrown out, and left to time to recover its fertility.

Poultry and Pork, particularly Hams are excellent here. — Beef and Mutton middling, and Fish very rare and dear; the general drink of the better people is Punch and Madeira Wine, and many prefer Grog and Toddy. — All the poor, and many of the Rich, eat Rice for Bread, and give it even a preference; they use it in their Cakes, called Journey Cakes and boiled, or else boiled Indian corn, which they call Hominy, and of this they have two sorts, the great and small — the last I think the best.

Upon the whole, this is undoubtedly one of the most opulent, and most increasing Colonies in America, and bids fair to exceed all the others, if it advances in the like proportion as it has done for forty years past. —

The unhappy differences which have Subsisted for some years past, between the Governour and the Commons — House of Assembly, and are not yet set to rights, have been the means of this Country not standing so well at home, as otherways they would have done, and as they really deserve to do.

The Country from Pedee river to Brunswick in North Carolina, is altogether a Pine-barren, as indeed is most of that Province that lies on the Sea Board, but up Cape Fear River, after it divides into the North East and North West Rivers, the land grows better, and when properly cleared and Cultivated, will produce all manner of Grain in plenty and perfection.

About twelve miles below Brunswick lies Fort Johnston, a tolerable little Quarré, built of Tabby, and mounting about thirty pieces of Cannon 18 and 9 pounders, — the best of the Water lies near this Fort, tho' there is another Channel for small Vessels. — The Bar is not a bad one, and has on it about 19 feet, or better at high water.

About fifteen Miles above Brunswick, on the forks of the River lies the Town of Wilmington, a very pretty Situation, but the Land about is very poor — near it is a good Saw-Mill, and a very commodious Creek. — The Country from Wilmington to New-Bern is very indifferent, but about New Bern, on the conflux of the Nuse and the Trent, the land is better, and if the Seat of Government Should ever happen to be established there, as it probably may, from its being nearly Central, it will become a place of Note very soon, and will outvie any other Town in North Carolina.

From that to Tar River, Ronoak River and Halifax, the Country mends, as one goes back, near the last place at Occaneechy neck there is an excellent tract of land, on it is the Seat of Mr. Jones,[1] a good House, and a pretty place, from that you have but a few miles to the Virginia Line.

The Province of North Carolina abounds in White Inhabitants, they are said to be upwards of 42.000 Men fit to bear Arms, and live mostly in the back Country. They grow but very little Rice or Indigo, raise a good deal of Wheat and other grain, and export more Naval Stores, Pitch and Tar than any other Province, also some Deer Skins, and other Furs, but they are much divided among themselves.

Mr. Dobbs[2] their Governour died whilst I was there, and is Succeeded by Colonel Wm. Tryon, a very worthy Gentleman, very agreeable to the Province, and equal in every respect to the Charge His Majesty has reposed on him.

I left Charlestown *the Middle of March 1765*, and proceeded on to North Carolina, thro' a very bad Country, from Wakama River to Brunswick, full of Pine-barren and Sand, the back called long Bay is pleasant enough, to a

[1] Willie Jones, a political leader in the American Revolution.
[2] Arthur Dobbs was Governor of North Carolina in 1754–1765.

Stranger, the Accommodation for Travellers is but very middling, and for Horses very bad, 'till you reach Cape Fear River.

Brunswick does not seem very thriving, altho' the late and the present Governour, have mostly made it their residence.

Wilmington is a larger and more populous Town than Brunswick, it lies up the same River 15 Miles, which, close to it, forks, and runs in both divisions, for two hundred Miles up and more—On these Branches I saw some good provision Land, and Some Swamp, which if well managed, would bring Rice, but the Rice produced in that Province falls Short of that in South Carolina, being less heavy in equal quantities; hetherto [1] the Settlers have gone more upon Naval Stores than raising Crops, and in that and cutting Lumber and Staves, consist most of there sure Trade. Here, in the back-lands, they raise Hemp, Flax, Wheat, Corn and Pease, and are extremely Populous in Whites, who come out poor and earn with hard labour, their bread and Clothing.

It is far behind the neighbouring Provinces in Industry and application. — My Lord Granville is proprietor, of more than one half of the best of the Province, and tho' it is but an unprofitable Estate to his Lordship, it affects the whole, and is the means of Differences and Disputes, which hurt the whole. [2]

Mr. Dobbs and the Assembly could not agree for some years past, but I [have] reason to believe that Mr. Tryon the present Lieutenant Governour, by his prudence and coolness, and by siding with no party, but doing the King's business, and consulting the good of the Whole, and moving the Assembly to Newburn, the most Central Town, will greatly recon-

---

[1] Hitherto.

[2] Richard, Earl Granville, great-great-grandson of Sir George Carteret, who was one of the original proprietors of Carolina. When the other proprietors sold their shares to the Crown in 1729, Granville's father refused to do so and was subsequently given his share in land.

cile the heats and Animosities, which have long subsisted, between the Northern and Southern Interests of this Province.

The Land from Newburn to Halifax is better, and you cross Tar River, and Several Creeks before you come to Ronoak on which is Halifax, a pretty neat small place and was thriving before Tobacco fell, but is now falling off.

After you cross James River the land mends, and is good all the way to Williamsburgh, which is the Seat of Government,[1] and much resembles a good Country Town in England : here is a very handsome Statehouse, commodious for all the Courts, and both the Houses of Council and Assembly — a very large and handsome College [2] — probably Eighty Students, a foundation of Mr. Boyle's for the education of Six Indian boys.[3] — One Mr. Horrox [4] is President, and there are two other Masters.

There are many good Houses in Town, where the Courts meet twice a year, in April and October, and continue for 24 days together, except Sundays. — The Governour and Council are Judges in all Causes.

The people are well bred, polite, and extremely civil to Strangers. — The Governour's House is handsome and commodious, and he himself very happy, and the people so in him.[5]

There are two other Courts of Oyer and Terminer, at which the Council also attend, there[6] powers are greater than those of any other Province, and they have no Chief Justice.

The principal Rivers of this Province, beginning to the Southward, are James, York, Rappahanock, and Potomack, which divides from Maryland. — These fork, and form several large and Navigable rivers, which go up the Country, some

[1] Of Virginia.
[2] The College of William and Mary.
[3] The Indian School, a branch of the College, was founded by Robert Boyle.
[4] Rev. James Horrocks was president of William and Mary in 1764–1772.
[5] Francis Fauquier, lieutenant-governor of Virginia in 1758–1768.   [6] Their.

of them two hundred, and some of them more [than two hundred] Miles.

I am well assured by Gentlemen, whose veracity I can depend upon, that the back Country of Virginia, particularly towards Lord Fairfax's [1] property, is as fine, and rich land, as any in the world, producing all kinds of grain and grass in perfection, and great abundance, being also extremely temperate as to Climate, and having scarce any Musquitos, or other troublesome Insects.

The Soil of the lower part of Virginia is light, tho' often a whitish clay at bottom, producing the best Tobacco in the World, and many other useful Crops. — From the high Duty on that Commodity, its value is fallen, and many people are going upon Hemp, which it is hoped may succeed, if the Bounty is continued.

This Province was the first Settled of any on the Continent, it has always been a Loyal one. — The first Settlers were many of them younger Brothers of good Families, in England, who for different motives chose to quit home in search of better fortune, their descendants, who possess the greatest land properties in the Province, have intermarried, and have had always a much greater connection with, and dependance on the Mother Country, than any other Province, the nature of their Situation being such from the commodiousness and Number of Navigable rivers and Creeks, that they may Export to, and import from, home everything they raise or want, from within a few miles of their own houses, and cheaper than any neighbouring province could supply them. They have almost always lived in good harmony with their Governours, and with one another; they each live at their own Seats, and are seldom at Williamsburgh, but when the publick business requires their attendance, or that their own private affairs call them there, scarce any of the topping people have [a] house there of their own, but in the Country they live on their Estates handsomely, and plentifully,

[1] Thomas Fairfax, whose estate, comprising nearly one fourth of Virginia, lay for the most part between the Rappahannock and the Potomac.

raising all they require, and depending for nothing on the Market.

Money is at present a scarce Commodity, all goes to England, and I am much at a loss to find out how they will find Specie, to pay the Duties last imposed on them by the Parliament.[1] I have had an opportunity to see a good deal of the Country, and many of the first people in the Province and I must Say they far exceed in good sense, affability, and ease, any set of men I have yet fallen in with, either in the West Indies, or on the Continent, this in some degree may be owing to there being most of them educated at home, but cannot be altogether the cause, since there are amongst them many Gentlemen, and almost all the Ladies, who have never been out of their own Province, and yet are as sensible, conver[s]able and accomplished people, as one would wish to meet with.

Upon the whole, was [it] the case to live in America, this Province, in point of Company and Climate, would be my choice in preference to any, I have yet seen; the Country in general is more cleared of wood, the houses are larger, better and more commodious than those to the Southward, their Breed of Horses extremely good, and in particular those they run in their Carriages, which are mostly from thorough bred Horses and country Mares, — they all drive Six horses, and travel generally from 8 to 9 Miles an hour — going frequently Sixty Miles to dinner — you may conclude from this their Roads are extremely good — they live in such good agreement, that the Ferries, which would retard in another Country, rather accelerate their meeting here, for they assist one another, and all Strangers with their Equipages in so easy and kind a manner, as must deeply touch a person of any feeling and convince them that in this Country, Hospitality is every where practised.

Their provisions of every kind is good, their Rivers supply them with a variety of Fish, particularly Crabs and Oysters, — their pastures afford them excellent Beef and Mutton, and their Woods are Stocked with Venison, Game and Hogs.

[1] The Stamp Act is here referred to.

Poultry is as good as in South Carolina, and their Madeira Wine excellent, almost in every house; Punch and small Beer brewed from Molasses is also in use, but their Cyder far exceeds any Cyder I ever tasted at home — It is genuine and unadulterated, and will keep good to the age of twelve years and more. —

The Women make excellent Wives, and are in general great Breeders. — It is much the fashion to Marry young and what is remarkable in a Stay I have made of near a Month in the Province — I have not heard of one unhappy couple.

The Numbers of Inhabitants in Virginia, are supposed to be not fewer than 444.000 — of near equal proportions of Whites and Blacks, the Mulatoes are much less frequently met with here, than in the more Southern Latitudes, and their Slaves in general are more handsome, and better Clothed than any I [have] seen elsewhere; — the generality of those born in the Province, are brought young to Church and Christen'd, and most Parishes have one, two or three very decent Churches in them, built of Brick and Sashed, in which, established Clergymen of the Church of England, officiate alternately.

Norfolk is the Port of most traffick in Virginia, it contains above four hundred houses, has depth of Water for a Forty Gun Ship, or more, and conveniencies of every kind for heaving down, and fitting out large Vessels, also a very fine Rope-Walk. There is a passage Boat from Hampton to Norfolk, but the pleasantest Situation [on] one of them I ever saw, was York, on the beautiful River of that name, which commands a full view of the River down towards the Bay of Chesepeak, and a pretty land view across to Glo[u]cester Town and County, which contains some of the best lowlands in the Province. The timber resembles that in the Southern Provinces, but I apprehend there are none of the great Magniolas,[1] northwards of Carolina.

Tulip trees are in great quantities, some I [have] seen [are] not less than twenty feet round, and Ninety high, the

[1] Magnolias.

Dogwood flourishes here, and is covered with beautiful white flowers in April, the Woods are full of a more beautiful kind of HoneySuckle than ours, but not near so fragrant. — In the back Country there are Mines of Lead and Iron, which if properly wrought, and duly encouraged from home, would turn out well. — All manner of European fruits, roots and Garden Stuff do well here, and many of the productions of warmer Countries. — Altho' Oranges cannot stand the Nipping frosts, and cold land Winds, that blow during the Winter Months, their Springs are incertain, and weather very changeable, which produces in Spring and fall, fevers and Agues, which the Natives themselves are very liable to : — In general, I think it a more healthy Country than South Carolina, and in every respect a more pleasant one. —

Mr. Fauquier was Lieutenant Governour in 1765, when I was there, and Sir Jeffery Amherst Governour,[1] the Salary from home 2000£ Sterling, and the perquisites not much less — perhaps —1500£. — N.B. a very good House and Garden in Williamsburgh.

The quantity of Tobacco, exported at an Average, of Ten Years past from Virginia, is supposed to be from Fifty to Sixty thousand Hogsheads annually, at about a thousand neat pounds per Hogshead.

About the beginning of May I crossed Potomack from Colonel Philip Lees[2] to Cedar point, — about forty Miles from its entrance into the Bay of Chesepeak. — This River divides Maryland from Virginia, and is one of the largest and most considerable in these parts, being Navigable for Frigates as far up as Alexandria, a place noted in this Country, by being that, where General Braddock disembarked his unfortunate little Army ; — The land on both Banks of this River, is in general good and Strong, producing Tobacco and most sorts of European grain, — I observed scarce any Pines

[1] Sir Jeffrey Amherst, governor in 1763–1768, never visited the province.
[2] Philip Ludwell Lee (1727–1775) of Stratford in Westmoreland County, eldest brother of Richard Henry and Arthur Lee. He was at this time a member of the Council of Virginia.

on it, and the timber I did see, began to decrease both in Size and Number, owing to the more ancient occupancy of Virginia and Maryland. The Country from Potowmack to Annapolis, the Capital of Maryland, is extremely pleasant and very open for America, it is a light black mould, which with good Husbandry would last for ever. It is as uneven as many Counties in England, and better wooded than most of them, tolerably watered, but not so much so, as Virginia, nor are the people in general so opulent, altho' the publick are in better circumstances, their paper Credit being all Sunk, and a Balance at home in their favour.

Lord Baltimore[1] is proprietor of all this very delightful Province, but has never visited it. — the Roman Catholick Religion is tolerated here, and its professor[s] are very Numerous, and some of them very easy in Circumstances. —

Annapolis is charmingly Situated, on a Peninsula falling different ways to the Water, which nearly surrounds it. The Town is built in an irregular form, the Streets generally running diagonally, and ending on the Town-house, others on a house which was built for a Governour, in Governour Bladen's time, but never was finished, — the plan of this, was an excellent one, and the Situation of it most Elegant, Standing on an agreeable rising ground, in a beautiful Lawn, commanding the view of the Town, the River Severn, the Bay, and all the Creeks running into it, — nothing could be better chose, nor better executed as far as they went, but upon some unhappy difference between the Governour and Province, the whole was Stopped — the timbers and Roof, tho' ready, never closed in or Shingled — and from the Weather and Moisture, is now become so much damaged, as never again to be in a condition, to be repaired or finished.[2]

The State House, and House of Council and Assembly, stands also on a little hill in the Town, but it, as well as the Church, the Publick School, and their other publick Works, are going fast to decay. The present Governour Horatio

---

[1] Frederick Calvert, sixth Lord Baltimore, proprietor 1751–1773.
[2] Thomas Bladen was governor in 1742–1748. The house was subsequently completed for the college hall of St. John's College.

Sharpe Esqr. has a house in town, but resides much at a little place he is now building, at about 6 or 7 Miles up Severn River, which here falls into Annapolis Bay, forming the Peninsula on which the Town stands. — The views all round this place are agreeable and uncommonly Romantick — the Banks all Bluff, and such intersections and doublings of wood and Water, as form the most pleasant and variegated Landscape. Kent Island is seen about 12 Miles distant, which is the common passage over the Bay to the North-ward, from this you have another Short Ferry, which brings you on the Mainland, which is here called the Eastern Shore, others go up this Side, and cross two narrow Ferries above, going along the Western Shore, and most people when the Wind serves, embark at Annapolis and Sail up to Rock-hall, leaving Kent Island to the Left, which is a Navigation of 25 Miles, but cuts off more than 30 Miles of your land road to Philadelphia.

Mr. Middleton keeps a good House, and is provided with good Boats, for Men, Horses and Carriages.

The principal Staple of Maryland is Tobacco and Indian Corn, — they are beginning to have Meadows and Hay, their Number of Whites are wonderfully encreased, and said to be towards 60.000. The Country in general is more healthy than those to the Southward, and the Gentlemen of fortune are polite and hospitable and their Women counted handsome; they are inclosed by Virginia, which makes them backward in contributing anything to the publick exigencies in times of danger and difficulty. I cannot but lament the Government's being Proprietary, seeing such great and insurmountable difficultys do daily result from it.

Marlboro [1] is a pretty little Country Village, Situated on a Creek, and having a great deal of open land round it, capable of much improvement. London Town stands on the West side of South river, is also a pleasant Village, about four miles short [2] of Annapolis; I am told the back Country is still more pleasant and fruitful, but time did not admit of my Seeing

[1] Upper Marlboro.   [2] Southwest.

it. — The face of the Country much resembles Europe in general.

From Annapolis you cross Chesepeak Bay to Kent-Island, about 12 Miles, this Island is flat and fruitful, as is the remaining part of Maryland we traversed. — The Channel between Kent Island and the Main, to the Eastward of it, is narrow, and the Country is very pleasant all the way to Chester, or Newtown [1] on Chester, which, tho' small is well Inhabited, — about half way or rather more from Chester to Newcastle on Delawar, runs the boundary Line dividing Maryland from Pensylvania, this has been long matter of Litigation and is not yet finally adjusted, tho' I was informed the Commissioners are now engaged in bringing it to an Issue. — Newcastle is pleasantly situated, but has no trade — the Men of War generally Winter there, the River being narrow at that place, and commands the passage up to Philadelphia; — It is the Capital of the four [2] associated Counties annexed to Pensylvania, but which have an Assembly, and Laws of their own, which in many particulars differ both with their neighbours in Pensylvania and Maryland.

The Country from this Town to the great and Noble City of Philadelphia, is extremely pleasant, well Inhabited, fruitful, and full of Orchards, — you Cross Christines, a ferry over a River running into Delawar, which is deep, and safe riding in all weathers to Chester, from that to Skuylkill ferry, between which river and Delawar the City stands — the Country is Charming, the Ferry boats are the most convenient, and best served of any I ever Saw, you may drive in your Carriage and Six without getting out or Unharnessing one Horse, which is a great saving of time to Travellers.

The City of Philadelphia is perhaps one of the wonders of the World, if you consider its Size, the Number of Inhabitants, the regularity of its Streets, their great breadth and length, their cutting one another all at right Angles, their Spacious publick and private buildings, Quays and

---

[1] Now Chestertown.

[2] The three counties now comprised in the State of Delaware.

Docks, the Magnificence and diversity of places of Worship (for here all Religions who profess the Name of Christ, are tolerated equally) the plenty of provisions brought to Market, and the Industry of all its Inhabitants, one will not hesitate to Call it the first Town in America, but one that bids fair to rival almost any in Europe. It is not an hundred years since the first tree was cut where the City now Stands, and at this time it consists of more than three thousand Six hundred Houses. — It is daily encreasing, and I doubt not in time, will reach all the way, from River to River, — the great and foreseeing Founder of it, Mr. Penn having wisely laid out the Space so far, which is daily taking and filling. — I must not pass over two foundations here, which do them much honour; their College for education of youth,[1] and their Hospital for the reception of all Sick persons whatever, including Lunaticks, which is supported by the benefactions of the Charitable and well disposed Subscribers.

Doctor Smith[2] is at the Head of the College, a very eminent Divine; — the propriety of Language here surprized me much, the English tongue being spoken by all ranks, in a degree of purity and perfection, surpassing any, but the polite part of London.

There are several large Towns and Villages, well inhabited and very industrious, particularly Lancaster and Bristol, but everybody of Note has a residence in Town, which is all built of Brick, and well paved, with flat foot walks in each side the Streets, the Germans in this Province, are not under Sixty Thousand, and there are White Men enough fit to bear Arms, and able to repulse all Indians [that] could molest them, was their Spirit equal to their Numbers. — With regard to their Farming, you may judge, when I was told, they have not less than twenty thousand Waggons, which at four horses each, would on an emergency make a boby[3] of 80.000 Horse. — All this Province and the Jerseys, bear much the face of Europe, and I have no manner of

---

[1] Now the University of Pennsylvania.
[2] William Smith.   [3] Body.

doubt, whenever Providence shall think fit to enable America, to Stand alone, that Philadelphia from its Central Situation, and other very obvious reasons, must become the Metropolis of it.

The Quakers here bear the great Sway in Government, which is clogged and incumbered, and I cannot help wishing that this, and every other Proprietary Government in America was reannexed to the Crown, and Governed by Royal Governours, whose Salaries ought to be permanent, and independent on the fickle will, and fancy of those they are sent to Superintend; 'till this most desireable end shall take place — America will never cordially unite, or be induced to act warmly and effectually, either towards their own defence, or to such other purposes, as may equally tend to their own, and to the Honour and advantage of Great Britain.

Every body in Philadelphia deals more or less in trade — here they build Ships, and export Timber of all sorts, and for all purposes, many timber Frames for the West India Planters houses are Ship't from thence, their Intercourse with Jamaica, and all the Leeward and Windward Caribbee Islands, being very considerable. — Grain, Hay, Biscuit, Beef, Pork, Shingles, Lumber and Malt Liquor, are their Chief exports; they live handsomely, and are all going in a degree into home Spun Woollens and Linnens, which seems to be the natural consequence of restraining that branch of Trade, by which alone they got Specie, enabling them to make remittances for British Manufactories.

The Governour of the Province is named by the Proprietor Penns, and approved by the King — his Birth is an uneasy one, as by his Instructions he has it not in his power to comply with many very unreasonable requests of his Assembly, who in Return generally tack his provincial Salary, to some Bill, which they are confident, he neither can or will pass.

In 1765, John Penn was Governour, an Excellent young man but parties ran so high between the Quakers and Presbyterians, to whom the other Sects United, as being all too weak, it made things quite disagreeable; to this the two

Parties, for, and against a change of Government added Combustible matter—and occasioned many inconveniencies, both to the Publick and Individuals, which a more Stable and permanent Form of Government would obviate.

The River Delawar divides Pensylvania from West Jersey. — I crossed it at Trent-town,[1] a pretty Country place, and proceeded to Princetown, where is Seated a very large and Spacious College, well managed, with a Sensible Clever Master, and Appartments for more than one hundred Students. — It is Called Jersey College, or Nassau Hall.[2] — All the Country, from this to Brunswick, where you cross a River of that Name, and so to Elizabeth town, is Verdant and beautiful, tho' not so rich as Pensylvania, — at Elizabeth town I took boat, and landed at New York, about Sixteen Miles; I took a ride up the River, from Elizabeth town called Passaick, for twenty two Miles, and in my life I never saw, a more beautiful Country, its Banks are all clear, and houses at every 500 yards, on both sides of it, the falls of this River are remarkable, the whole falls into a Cleft, which seems as if formed by some Earthquake, near 70 feet high,— soon after which, it turns a Mill, and has over it a pretty long wooden Bridge, becoming in a few miles lower, Navigable for small Craft quite into the Bay, — at the mouth of this, and dividing it from Hankhawsack[3] river, rises a remarkable high Hill, covered with wood, called Snake hill, and all along the West side of Passaick, are an infinity of salt Hay meadows, which turn to good Account, as Manure or fodder to the poor — they carry it many Miles, spread it over their grass grounds as litter, or as dung, and often Plough it in, after which it brings good Grain, and White Clover in quantities, it is remarkable it will not fatten either Cattle or Horses, but it will keep them well up, in the State they are in, when it is first given them, 'tis here of an Inestimable Value for dung and other uses, and conveyed both by Land and Water many Miles.

[1] Trenton. [2] Now Princeton University.
[3] Hackensack.

This Channel divides [the] Jerseys from Staten Island, and runs up as far as Perth-Amboy — the principal Town of East Jersey, as Burlington on Delawar, over against Bristol, is of West Jersey; I could not find there was any thing very material to be seen at either of these Towns, where Assemblys and Courts are held alternately, and their Governour frequently has a residence at each place.

The Jerseys in general is a pleasant, open and well cultivated Country, producing Grain, Grass and Cyder in great abundance. It is often called the Garden of America, and its appearance very much resembles England, the Soil is not rich, but is kindly, and it is counted extremely healthful — the North, or Hudsons river, divides it from New York Government, till it meets the New York Line, 20 Miles above that Town at Corbett's point.

The Establishment for their Governour and Officers of Justice, is here very trifling, and consequently they will never, whilst on the present footing, be filled by men of great Character or reputation, in their respective professions.

New York Province was originally peopled by the Hollanders, but was given up to Britain, about one hundred years since, from which period it has enjoyed, uninterruped peace and happiness. At present two thirds of the Inhabitants, as well in the Province as in the Town, are Descended of the Dutch and Germans, who have flocked over to this and the Adjacent Province of Pensylvania in Incredible Numbers, and make many of them excellent Settlers, particularly the Germans, who can live upon less, and are more Industrious, than any Britons.

The City of New York has long been held at home, the first in America, tho' it neither comes up to Philadelphia in Beauty, regularity, Size, or the Number of its Inhabitants, and houses of the last; there are under three thousand at this time, about 300 Stores, 12 Churches and places of Worship and perhaps 20,000 Inhabitants, — here are more Negroes than in any Northern province, and by being the Seat of Government, Civil and Military, and the place to which all the money for the Exigencies of America is sent from Britain, — is rich — the Situation of it is cool, being on a point formed by Hudson's river, which runs up many Miles, and is Navigable above Albany, and by East River or Sound, which dividing the Main from Long Island, runs towards Boston and Rhode Island, and forms an Inland navigation safe and very commodious for many Miles. Over against the Town to the Eastward lies a part of Long Island, which has been long peopled; the Soil of it is naturally light and Sandy, and almost wore out, yet the old Inhabitants are loth to quit this hold, on account of its remarkable healthiness and pleasantness, there is scarce a possibility of distinguishing it from England : by Situation as an Island, it is much like the Isle of Wight, a ridge of high lands runs quite thro' it, lengthways, on the South side of which being very gravelly, I am apt to believe good Wine might be produced.

The Land in the Neighbourhood of York, is naturally as bad as can be and as full of Stones, but the great Demand for all Stock and nec[e]ssaries, as well for themselves as the Shipping, renders it worth while to Improve all that is within reach of the Town, or within reach of the Banks of either of the two rivers on which it Stands.

The Fort[1] is not Strong, one platform mounts a great many heavy Cannon, — the Governours house and Garden is within the Fort, and are handsome and convenient, — the Streets are not regular nor Wide, but standing on a descent, on three sides are washed by every rain, which makes it clean and wholesome. People here, live to a good Old age, and very Comfortably, did they chuse to be contented. It is hoped they will soon come to better temper, after Taxes become more familiar to them.

Albany by Water is   Miles up Hudson's River, and is perhaps the pleasantest Soil in the World — there Sloops are excellent, and built on purpose for that Trade, never going to Sea. — about half way, or not quite so much, the river runs thro' a high Ridge of Mountains, which they call

[1] Fort George.

the Highlands, nothing can more delight an European traveller, as it differs so much in grandeur, and natural Magnificence, from any Scene he is acquainted with — the Rocky
Steep hills, are all covered with wood to the Summit, and in
some places the Water falls over them beautifully. After you
pass these narrows, the Scene grows more Cultivated, and
all the way up, at small distances, you meet Settlements
on each hand, mostly Dutch and Germans. — This River has
many Islands and Head lands, and altho' in the Map its
course, appears very Streight, yet the turns and breaks in it,
are Infinite and vary the Scene most agreeably, at every two
or three miles distance. Stone for building and Lime Stone
every where abound. At a little distance back from the
River, the Soil grows deeper and the Settlements are more
Numerous; At a place Called Sopus,[1] they breed the best
draught and Saddle Horses, and all along its course the
people live plentifully and pleasantly. In Spring tides a
Vessel drawing nine feet, may go up to Albany, and in common tides, one drawing about Six. — The land about it is
as good as you could desire, 'till you get up the hill going to
Schenectady to which place being 20 Miles, it is all a Sandy
Pine-barren. — There is an old Stone Fort at Albany and a
Stockade, also a large Hospital, Barracks and Store houses
for a considerable Number of Men, but being built of Wood,
and in a hurry, they are like every other publick Work in
America, — going fast to ruin.

The people of Albany are mostly descended of low Dutch,
and carry down with them, the true and Characteristick
marks of their Native Country, Vizt an unwearied attention
to their own personal and particular Interests, and an abhor-
rence to all superiour powers. — I have been told it was
found necessary in 1765 to Send a Captains Command
there, to prevent the entire and total Destruction, of all the
buildings and Stores belonging to the King, which was but
too well effected before their arrival.

In the last War it was a place of consequence the Rendez-

[1] Esopus.

vous and Head Quarters, from whence all orders were Issued and Expeditions fitted out, as well against Canada, as against the French on the Lakes, to all of which places it lies convenient, by means of the water communication of Hudson's river and the Mohawk river, leading to Fort Stanwix.

The Town itself is dull and ill built, having the Gavel[1] end of their houses all to the Streets, which are very dirty and crooked, and confined by the rising grounds, close behind the Town.

The land along the Banks of the river, is excellent and well improved. — One Mr. P. Schuyler[2] has a good house near it, lately built in a better Stile, than I have generally seen in America. — The Family of Rantzlaar[3] has possession of this tract for many Miles. The first view you have of Schenectady, the Mohawk river, and the Country on its Banks, is remarkably pleasing, after travelling so far over a Waste. The Streets of Schenectady are Spacious, the River is there very beautiful and the Soil excellent, — the land here and all the way up the Mohawk river, is planted, and Sells very high. From this to Fort Johnson, up the said river is 18 Miles, it is a narrow vale or Strath of excellent Soil, hemm'd in on both sides with high grounds, uncultivated, and covered with a variety of Timber, but exceedingly pleasant to the Eye, and cut by a thousand little Brooks, descending rapidly from above. It much resembles Westmoreland, or the Banks of Tay, above Perth — From this, off the river, about 14 Miles back, Sir Wm. Johnson[4] has made a New Settlement, and has built himself a very comfortable house,[5] having a good Garden and Field, all cleared in an Absolute Forrest. Here the Land is excellent, and produces without Manure, all sorts of grain — The timber here is an immense Size, Hemlock, Spruce, Sugar Maple, Elm, Ash two kinds, Beech and some white Pine, and Balm of Gilead Fir. — At this place he is generally crowded with Indians, mostly of the Five Nations, who are generally our

[1] Gable.   [2] Philip John Schuyler.   [3] Van Rensselaer.
[4] Superintendent of Indian Affairs for the Northern District.
[5] Johnson Hall, on the site of the present city of Johnstown.

friends, when properly used. — These are the Mohawks, Oneidas, Onondagas, Cayugas, and Seneccas, these last are counted the bravest and most enterprizing Tribe of all the Northern Indians, the[y] Claim an Immense tract of Country, and exact Subordination and respect thro' fear from almost all their neighbouring Tribes. — They are not the best affected to the British, and are so treacherous, as to require a constant attention over them.

I passed some Days at Sir Wm. Johnson's, but no consideration Should tempt me to lead his life. — I suppose custom may in some degree, have reconciled him to it, but I know no other man equal to so disagreeable a Duty.

A few miles above Fort Johnson, on the opposite [side] of the Mohawk river, Stands Fort Hunter, an Indian Settlement or Castle, as they generally call it, belonging to the Mohawks, which Tribe is the most Civilized of all the five Nations; Some ten miles further up the river, and on Sir Wm.'s Side, is, at a little distance back a German Settlement, called Stone Arabie,[1] consisting of one hundred families. It has two places of Worship, Lutheran and Calvanist, their land is perfectly cleared, nothing can be prettier; indeed all the lowlands on this Mohawk river are so, from Schenectady to some small distance above the German flatts, which Vale is as rich, fertile, and peopled, as any on the Thames, the high lands on both sides of this Vale are varied delightfully, and will no doubt when Cleared, become of great Value, at present, the timber and Stock of young Cattle and Horses, they maintain in Summer, make their possession only desireable.

From a little above the German flatts, quite to Fort Stanwix the Country is all wood, except one plain ten Miles Short of the Fort, called Oriske[2] fields, and that is in dispute. Seven Indian Huts were on it, when I passed it in June 1765. It seems capable of every Improvement, the River is Navigable quite up and the Soil to judge from the Timber, is as excellent as any in the World.

Fort Stanwix is built nearly at equal distance, between

[1] Stone Arabia.   [2] Oriskany.

the Navigable part of the Mohawk river and Wood Creek, and here are kept all the Carriages, Horses and Oxen, used in the transporting over land, the Boats and goods going from one Water to the other. The Posts from Fort Stanwix to Schenectady, down the Mohawk, are Fort Skuyler, Fort Harkeman,[1] Fort Hendrick, Fort Hunter and Fort Johnston. In time of War we generally had a Non-Commissioned Officer, at each, to forward Orders or Letters, and to Assist in the Conveyance up of Stores and of Ammunition, which come all from Albany and York. — In time of War they were Stockaded, and are now going to decay, which is shamefull. The Roads up this communication, are almost impassable, and the Bridges broke down and Rotten.

The ground where Fort Stanwix is built, is all cleared from river to river, about a Mile round the place. — It is a Quarré of Logg Work, all going to ruin so fast, that I firmly believe in three years it will be all down. — It is calculated for a good many Guns, but had only 18 Mounted when I was there in June 1765. The Casemates are not tight or Wholesome, and the Barracks are not well Contrived. It would seem that a Fort mounting Artillery here would be unnecessary, since our acquisition of Canada, but a Strong Post against Indians, must always be kept up, upon Account of Supporting this very necessary Communication, of covering the people Employed on it, and protecting Traders and others, who have occasion to come that way with goods, as also to find Horses and Carriages, to Convey the goods and Boats, across to Wood Creek and back. — The Batteaus are Slung on a long Carriage with four Wheels, and often came all the way from Schenectady, to the Fort on Ontario at the mouth of the Onondaga river, returning the same way. These Boats loaded will draw a foot and a half Water, and are carried over the little falls of the Mohawk, for a Mile or more, in the manner above Described. I have heard, the Carriage at these last, as well as at the carrying place at Stanwix might be removed by means of Canals and Sluices,

[1] Fort Herkimer.

but am not certain of the fact. All the land on the Mohawk is counted good, and Sells very high, it wants nothing but Industry, and Inhabitants to make it a rich, pleasant and Independent Country. From Schenetady to Fort Stanwix, is by land about 100 Miles, and more by water: during the last War, our Troops, Baggage and all heavy Stores, attending General Amherst to St. Lawrence, went this way and so on to Lake Ontario.

One Mile from the Fort begins Wood Creek, which after receiving several Brooks into it, and running upwards of 20 Miles, aided by three Sluices and Dams at the head of it, falls into Oneida Lake, being at most seasons Navigable for Batteaus and small Craft — The land is mixed and not equal in any respect to that on the Mohawk river, being much of it a Pine-barren, — and at Fort Oneida, or Royal Block house, quite light and Sandy.

This is a Small Stockaded Post, for a Subaltern and thirty Men, Situated where Wood-Creek enters the Lake, and the first now occupied, from Stanwix to Lake Ontario.

There were Several little Redoubts on Wood-Creek, in one of those called Fort-Bull, an Officer and all his Detachment, were Surprized and Scalped by the Indians in 1756. — From Royal-block-house to Fort Bruinton,[1] where we have another Subaltern and Stockaded post, is counted about 30 Miles by Water, this is Situated soon after Onondaga River leaves Oneida Lake, which, running a Course of near 50 Miles, emptys it self into Lake Ontario at Old Oswego. — The Land all along this very beautiful river, is Indian and in a State of nature. — Many other Rivers enter it as it descends, particularly the Senecca, or Cayuga river, at Trois Rivieres, Navigable for Canoes, and going up into the Country bearing their name.

The Onondaga falls — a trifling portage — are 12 Miles Short of Lake Ontario, but you pass many Refts and Rapids on your way to them, — At this place we have another little Subalterns Post, where this great river falls over a Rock,

[1] Fort Brewerton.

from 12 to 18 feet high, and afterwards runs all its Course thence to the Lake with a very quick and Rapid current, in so much that your Batteau descends without Oars in an Amazing Short space, — On a point where the river Onondago enters Lake Ontario, Stands our New Fort bearing that name — a neat Pentagon but never finished, much preferable however in point of Situation to the old Fort, we had facing it on the other Side the river called Oswego. — Like other American Forts, it is fast verging to decay, being of Wood and Sods, it might mount Seventy pieces of Cannon, but has now about thirty Mounted. The harbour lying on the Oswego Side is not the best, but ten feet water on the Bar, and very narrow. — At this place in the Winter Months, are laid up all the King's Vessels on this Lake, from Novemr to April, and here they have hitherto built them, except a small Sloop built at Niagara.

There are four Vessels belong[ing] to Lake Ontario, which may be about 250 Miles in length. — These Vessels are chiefly employed in bringing Stores and Provisions from Oswegatchee,[1] and Fort William Augustus, Situated high on St. Lawrence river, to Fort Ontario, and Niagara, — from which last place they are conveyed up Niagara river to the lower landing, in Batteaus, and from that overland about 8 miles, to little Niagara, from whence they are reshipped, in other Schooners belonging to Lake Erie, and dispersed at all our other Posts on the upper Lakes, as far as Detroit and Michelimachinack.

The falls at Onondago, already mentioned, are Extreamly beautiful, and the Navigation of that river, for the last 20 Miles, down to Ontario, owing to the Number and diversity of the Islands and Banks, is uncommonly pleasing. — I must not omit here the Striking appearance of Lake Ontario, which does not Shew itself, till you are very near it, and after so long a continuance in the Woods, gives the weary Traveller no other Idea than that of the Main Ocean, — for at Fort Ontario, the Lake is so broad, that you can discover no land beyond it.

[1] Now Ogdensburg.

At this Fort, not above one third of the Works are finished, and such as are — are all going into disrepair, insomuch that if something is not speedily done, the money already laid out will be totally thrown away, and the place will no longer be in a State of defence, even against Indians. — In 1765, there were but two Companies of the 46th — Howes [1] — in Garrison there, a force in all degrees inadequate to a post of so much Importance, from that too, are two trifling detachments up the river, all which might be instantly cut off by the neighbouring Seneccas, the bravest and most treacherous Indians of all the Six Nations, against whom we can never be enough on our Guard. — It is a Pentagon. The Barracks are pretty and the Works tolerably well laid out, but on too small a Scale, — the Casemates are insufficient, very damp and very unwholesome, there is a rising ground from which the Fort might be attacked, and a hollow which would be of great consequence to an enemy, in facilitating their approaches under its cover, and out of reach of any of our Guns.

Commodore Loring.[2] a Post Captain in His Majesty's Navy, Superintends the Navigation on these Lakes, and the Lakes of Champlain etca. and acquits himself well of that disagreeable Duty; he is very polite and attentive, as are All the Gentlemen Commanding Vessels under him in his Department; the accounts and Expences of which, passes all thro' the hands of the Commander in Chief in America, and are by him transmitted home annually, as a Contingent Expence.

The Surf in this and the other Lakes is Surprizingly great, in an on Shore Wind, the[y] are Suddenly agitated and soon laid, but are as dangerous as any Sea, to which, both in Colour and motion, they bear the nearest resemblance.

Schooners are best adapted for this Navigation from 100 to 200 Tons burthen, these have some Small Guns and plenty of small Arms, and being now all built with close Quarters, are proof against Indian attacks, or being boarded. The

---

[1] Sir William Howe was made colonel of the 46th regiment of foot in 1764.

[2] Joshua Loring was made a post captain in 1757.

Indians of all the Nations, inhabiting the Countries round the Lakes, are extreamly intimidated by our Vessels, they have often attempted to Surprize and destroy them, but have never Succeeded. — to me it appears, we are not Strong enough in this Department, and that some Stricter regulations are Still wanting: as well as places of Shelter in Winter Months and squally weather, which is very frequent here, into which our Vessels might retire a l'abris du Vent, and [be] covered from Attacks from the Shore, If such places were Established, in proper situations on those Lakes, Docks might [be] Erected and Vessels of all Sorts, as well for private Trade as public Service, might be easily and Cheaply constructed, in a part of the World, where Oaak, and all Ship timber every where abounds, and where there is Nothing but Inhabitants and Industry wanting, to make it a flourishing and delightful Province, to this we may add, that if something of this sort is not soon done, the Expence will be greatly Inhanced, since the nature of these Lake[s] is such, that they are not navigable with any degree of Safety during the Winter Months, as well from the weather, as from the Quantities of Ice, from which it will [be] even difficult to protect Shipping in Port, without a good deal of Expence and attention.

Upon the Whole, as these Lakes are at this hour Unsurveyed, their Coast unknown, as well as the Shoals, Islands, and Rocks unnoticed, it is not any matter of Surprize to me, that so many of our Vessels there have been lost and destroyed, but that any of them should have escaped. At present we have three Armed Vessels on Lake Ontario, and as many on Lake Erie and the upper Lakes — From Fort Ontario to Niagara, by Water is about 160 Miles, the water is deep, as it is mostly in this Lake, some parts not being Sounded with one hundred fathom. From Niagara to the head of the Lake is about thirty Miles. — The Nation of Seneccas live round this Fort, and all along the South side of the Lake, as do the Missesagues,[1] and Chippeways, on the opposite Northern Shore.

[1] Missesauga Indians.

The Fort of Niagara, which was built by the French, and taken by us in 1759, by Sir Wm. Johnson, is situated on a point of land, formed by the junction of the river bearing its name, and Lake Ontario; from the bank of the river to the Bank of the Lake, runs a pretty regular Work, consisting of a Tenaille, a Ravelin, two Lunettes, a bad Ditch, a covered way, and a good Glacis, the Stockade is totally gone and rotten, having been constructed in a hurry and with perishable Materials, and the defences towards the Water are ill laid out, of Earth and Sodds: it is true our Engineers have ever since we had it, been patching it up, but as fast as one bit is done, another falls down, so that it seems to be a Work without end, and without answering any good purpose whatever, — more Surprizing, when the best clay for Bricks in the World is at hand, and very good Stone and Lime may be had by water carriage, at a trifling distance, on all Sides of this Fort.

When I consider, the very particular Importance of Niagara, from its commanding the Chain of Communication by water from St. Lawrence, and from New York, to all the back Indian Country, I am Surprized, Government does not more Seriously attend to it, and put it in a respectable Situation: by this Navigation all our upper Settlements on the Lakes to the Illinois, and even to the Missisipi, may, and must be supplied; a very thorough Communication and Trade, with all the Western Indians, may be maintained and Improved, and our Superiority on the Lakes established, without risk or doubt, and yet it is neglected! — the Works are failing daily, the Barracks for the Men and Officers going into disrepair, and never were sufficient; No Shelter yet erected for the Vessels in Harbour, the place itself is neither equal to resist the attack of Regulars or of Indians, — the Garrison too weak, even had it no out Detachments, and lastly no Government, or person of any Authority, to bridle the Cursed race of Traders, or treat or Settle with the numerous and warlike Tribes of Indians, who repair hither with Skins, in order to supply themselves with those Luxuries the[y] get from us, and cannot now do well without; all these considerations call out for more attention from home, and convince me that it would be for the good of the Publick to give the charge and Government, of what I may now be allowed to call back America, to some man of Sense and Service, who should reside in it, and be Impowered to act, as Circumstances should require.

In *July 1765* the Garrison consisted of 110 Men fit for Duty.

About 13 Miles above Niagara, are the famous Falls, which are almost as difficult to describe, as to represent their heighth — the breadth and quantity of water, falling over a Rock 134 feet high, astonish and pleas[e] you, they greatly more than answered any Ideas I had formed of them, and I doubt much if in any part of the known World, there is any thing of the kind, so Magnificently Stupenduous.

The river where it falls is about 600 feet broad, but the constant Stream occasioned by the fall, prevents your clearly discrying the Immense heighth, the Water for Several Miles below is too Strong to be Navigated, even by small boats, and for a little way above, it is not Safe from the Suction and Refts and Rapids. It divides its Stream a little above the falls, forming an Island of small extent, which, but just Separates, the great and smaller falls, this, even would appear great and tremenduous in any other place, except when you see them both together. I often visited these falls in June 1765, and every time, I beheld them with more Astonishment and Satisfaction. About two little Miles above the falls, we have a very neat little Stockaded post on the Shore called little Niagara, here the Vessels from Lake Erie etca. disembark their goods, which are put into Waggons, or Wains, drawn each by four Oxen and so conveyed over the carrying place, about 8 Miles down to the lower landing, where we have another post, to protect and cover the Batteaus, which at this place take on board the goods, and are carried down the Stream to the Fort of Niagara, and so over the Lake to the river St. Lawrence etca., etca. From a rising ground about half way, across this portage, and abreast of the great falls, you have a most extensive and commanding prospect, all over the flat Country, quite to the Lakes and

over it, — this they call Mount Pleasant, and at a pass on it, extreamly narrow and well Chosen, a party of our people was attacked by the Seneccas in 1763, and cut off, Lieutt. Campbell Commanding Officer was killed, and the few that escaped their Inhuman fury were forced to throw themselves down the Precipice into the river, where some were drowned, Some had their Brains dashed out, and not above five or Six escaped.

The River above the falls, almost immediately extends its breadth, receiving into it several Streams, on both sides, which forms many Islands. — The Chippewaw [1] and Senecca [2] Creeks, are two of the most remarkable, running each up into the Countries, inhabited by these Nations. — Of the Islands, Navy Island, and Grand Isle, are the only ones of any Note, on the first of these we have a landing, and at this place have been built, all the Vessels for Erie, and the upper Lakes. Commodore Loring assures me, that nothing can better answer that purpose, having in its Neighbourhood plenty of Timber for Ship-building, and being well Sheltered and Situated in every respect. — Off this Island our Vessels often lie, for want of a place of Security on Lake Erie, which is the more necessary, that when a Vessel of any burthen, has got below the Rapids, two Miles short of the Lake Erie, they cannot be hauled up said rapids, without more Assistance of Men than the Troops in that Neighbourhood can well Spare. On the Shore just where the River Issues from Lake Erie, and on the North side we have another Stockaded post — Called Erie — the distance from this to little Niagara is 20 Miles, and from this to the mouth of Detroit river is Computed about 100 Leagues, and Six Leagues more to the Town and Fort, on Said river.

Lake Erie is much Shallower than Ontario, and more liable to Squalls and bad wheather, but has better Anchorage, the Water too is more thick and less wholesome. — In my Life I never drank better, than in the Middle of Lake Ontario. The Soil about Fort Erie, is rich and good, as

[1] Chippewa River.   [2] Tonawanda Creek.

indeed is all the land on both Sides the river, between the
said two Lakes, that is as far as to produce excellent Timber,
which when cleared, white Clover succeeds in great plenty,
and you see a Soil, which will, with Cultivation produce all
European grain and Herbage; this holds equally to Grand
Isle, which is covered with a variety of Timber, fit for most
purposes. — It is about 18 Miles long and Six broad, and
granted by the Indian Nations in Congress, July 1764,
together with all the Islands in the river, from Lake Erie to
Lake Ontario, to Sir Wm. Johnston Baro[ne]t. — The Indians
at this time granted to the King for ever, the carrying place
at the falls, and a quantity of land on each Side the river
from Lake to Lake.

All this Land is now covered with wood, very Improveable
to the falls, but from them to the lower landing, the Channel
is narrow and rapid, the Banks are Steep, Rocky and Romantick, in some places perpendicular, and in others hollowed
out by the Stream and Current, so that they are (in that
Space) almost Inaccessible, and yet, bare as they are of Soil,
are crowded with a variety of Trees and Shrubs, — most
delightful to the Eye, amongst which are some Cedars and
Pines. — All the other parts of the Land on the river, and the
Islands in it, and most of the land near the Lakes, is covered
with most excellent Timber — Vizt — Oaks, a variety,
Hiccarys, Maples, Ash of two kinds, Elms, Beech, Birch,
Lime and Sassafras. On the Chippewaw Creek, is White, or
New England Pine in abundance, but you will observe that
the Land, where Pine grows all over America, is almost
always light and Sandy, and where the other kinds above
named grow, with a variety of Trees I am ignorant of — You
are almost certain of a good Loamy or mixed Soil, which when
cleared and drained, will immediately produce white clover
very thick, and Sweet, and the farther you penetrate back
from the Coast, I have ever in America found, the Soil the
fatter, and the Timber of all kinds to be of a greater Size,
altho' in all parts of it I have visited, you meet every here
and there, with a Strip of poor land, covered with pines and
underwood. Before I leave these Lakes, I must Say they

abound in good Fish, and of a variety, not unlike, but yet not the same, with ours in Europe. Below the falls they [1] Salmon, above them, white fish in plenty, and of a good Size; A Seine is a good Companion, and the best resource to the poor Soldiers, who works harder here, than any where, and Suffers more than he ought, owing to the Mistaken Œconomy of those who advised obliging the Soldiers to pay for their Salt provisions, which too often are not the best in the World, and which may easily be proved, to be considerably a greater Expence to the Government, than to have continued to them their provisions, as the Men now must be punctually paid for all kinds of Work, which formerly they did with good will and cheerfullness, without any additional pay.

I left Niagara in the Schooner Brunswick — Captain Speers, — Commodore Loring on board, on *the 5th of July*, Steering for the Northern Shore for Caderaqui,[2] which may be about 70 Leagues distance, Lying East North East, the Navigation is good, 'till you get amongst the Islands, which are many, and all covered with wood. The French at this place, had a pretty little Stone Quarré, which Commanded the River bearing that Name: Their Fort was called Fort Frontenac, and up the river close under this Fort, they had a Safe and Commodious harbour for all their Lake Vessels; You bring into it from two and a half to three fathom Water, the best Channel lies to the Starboard as you go in. It seems a pity we should have dismantled it so much, as it abounds with Hay, Stone and Lime-Stone, is a Safe road, [with] plenty of Fish and Timber for Ship-building not very distant; besides which, I understand it would be a great Saving of expence, Risk and time, if the Batteaus from Montreal, which at this time bring up the Stores and Provisions for all the upper Posts, only as far as Oswegatchee, could bring them and Lodge them there, as they always did in the French time. The Navigation from Frontenac to Oswegatchee being very Unsafe and Rocky, for loaded Ves-

[1] There are. [2] Now Kingston, Ontario.

sels, and extremely incertain, on account of the Shoals and Currents : whereas from Frontenac, across to Fort Ontario or Niagara, it may be run in 24 hours, or less, without much Risk, so that one good Vessel would do all the business on said Lake, instead of three now employed, and I hold it that the expence attending the other two Vessels, must considerably exceed that of bringing in Canada Batteaus, the Provisions from Oswegatchee to Frontenac, about 30 Leagues, not to mention the advantage of a safe harbour at all times to the King's Vessels on Lake Ontario. I do believe fifteen hundred pounds would reinstate this Port, as Timber, Stone and Lime-Stone are contiguous, and nothing but Labour requisite. It lies among the Missesagues, who are, and have been always our friends, and I believe they would be pleased to have us again amongst them.

From Frontenac to Oswegatchee, where we have a small Post is about 35 Leagues, thro' an infinite variety and Number of Islands of all Sizes,[1] in some places the Channel is very narrow, and difficult to hit, on account of the Sunken Rocks and Shoals — in one place not more than two fathoms. — As you descend, it becomes more rapid, and when you enter the last narrows, about Seven Leagues Short of Oswegatchee, the Current is extremely strong, running not less than three and a half knots an hour. — Nothing can please more, or appear more Romantick, than this passage from Caderaqui, the Islands and Keys are almost all of them covered with Pine, and some other Brush, growing almost out of the Rocks, for Scarce any mould can be observed : the wood is Scraggy and Stunted, and will never arrive at any Size for use. — As you descend, the Coasts of the main land begins to mend, and at Oswegatchee the land is good and produces well, — from Oswegatchee to Fort William Augustus, is about two Leagues : here it was the French endeavoured to interrupt our progress, by fortifying hastily a small Island, lying nearly in the middle of the river, however, all the Batteaus of the Army passed it, and left it to the right with scarce

[1] Thousand Islands.

any loss of Men, yet Mr. Amherst [1] did not chuse to leave it behind him, so he attacked it from three different Batteries, two from Islands and one from the Main land, and carried it in Six days, after opening ground. The Works are Mouldering, having never been good, nor do I think in prudence it ought to be repaired, as it can never be of use to us, to have a Fort in that place. From this we took Batteaus, and in about Six Miles, arrived at the first dangerous Rapid, called le long saut. The distance from Fort William Augustus to Montreal, is about 30 Leagues, in which space you have about Seven or Eight of those rapids to pass, all of them bad, and not to be attempted without a Skilful Pilot, but with one who knows the Channels, and can keep her head to the Water, there is not much risk. I did not get out at any of them 'till we arrived at La Chine, nine Short miles from Montreal, where we Slept the second night. There are two remarkable broad parts in this passage, the first Lake St. Francis, the other Lake St. Louis; here the water is very smooth, with little current to be discovered, and at the bottom of each, are two of the great rapids. On St. Francis is a little Village of Christian Indians called St. Regist,[2] where a Jesuit and one French family reside. They have all of them tolerable houses, and live by cultivating land on the Neighbouring Islands, and by Fishing and Shooting. Here Salmon and other good Fish abounds. The Banks of this river all the way from Oswegatchee, seem good and capable of improvement, but are little inhabited, 'till you come down as far as it is met by a branch of the great or Outtaawaw river,[3] over against Isle Perrot, there, and above the point of Cedars, you have houses at every four or five hundred yards along the river, all the way to Montreal on the left side, and a few on the right as you descend, which has the most agreeable effect you can conceive.

Isle Perrot is altogether cultivated and well Inhabited,

[1] Jeffrey Amherst, who in 1758 was made a major-general and took command of the expedition against Canada.
[2] St. Regis. [3] Ottawa River.

between it and Isle Jesus and Isle Marie, now Montreal, runs up the chief Channel of the great river, which is one way to Michelimackinac and the upper Lakes. On this Route, you have 36 Portages, yet it was much frequented by the French Traders, and is now used by some of Ours. — Over against La Chine, Stands a pretty considerable Village of Catholick Indians, about 300 fighting Men — The French call it St. Louis, and they call it themselves Chanawaga,[1] from a Country of that Name on the Mohawk river, from whence they migrated. It [is] surrounded with a Wall and Stockade, has a handsome Church, and good Corn Mills belonging to the Indians, any Canadians who live thereabouts, being obliged to pay them Rent, or some trifling acknowledgement, for the Lands they hold of them.

The Canadians are a Robust, hardy, clean made set of people, accustomed from their tenderst years to cold and fatigue, they resemble greatly their Indian neighbours, as well in looks and complexion, as in their manners and Laziness. It is true the Country is good, and the Climate most healthful; a Working man, by labouring hard one day, may well support himself and his family for a Week, which, together with some natural Inconve[n]iencies, may in a degree excuse their want of Industry. They have generally Six or Seven Months of Frost and Snow, during which time their ground can produce but little, or nothing, as soon as these are past, they plough and Sow, and in less than four Months their harvest begins and is all got into their Barns. Their Stock must all be Stall fed, and are sometimes obliged to be housed all Winter. They grow about Montreal excellent Wheat, Corn and Barley, Pease and all manner of Kitchen Stuff in abundance. I do not think the water of the river so good as in Lake Ontario, altho' they have Springs and pump water[2] enough. Montreal, originally Ville St. Marie, stands on an Island of its name, which may be about Leagues long[3] and three broad, there is plenty of Meadow

---

[1] Caughnawaga.   [2] Well water.
[3] Montreal Island is about thirty-two miles long.

pasture all round it, and within a little distance, perhaps two Miles, is an Hill, from whence you have a very beautiful and extensive prospect of the river, the Islands in it, and all the adjoining Country, — the face of it, is much like a good part of Europe, and less wooded than most parts of Inhabited America. — The Town may have about 600 Houses, the Streets are narrow, it runs along the river, and is three times as long as it is broad; the Jesuits and Recollects have each an Establishment in it; There are also three Nuneries in it and several Churches. The best built part of it, was burnt down in May 1765 — upwards of a 100 houses in a few hours were destroyed, and had not the Wind, which was very high, most providentially come about, the whole City might have Shared the same fate. The Military were of infinite use on the occasion, the people have never had the precaution to have one Fire-Engine, altho' they have suffered three different times, in less than an hundred years.

Most of the Noblesse of Canada, have residencies here, and altho' Quebec has been, and must always be the Key of Canada, and the Seat of Government, yet from its Situation and Communication by Water, with all the back Countries and Lakes, Montreal must always be a place of consequence, tho' not a place of Strength, there is a good Stone and Lime Wall, with some Embrazures and loop-holes, all round it, which is quite Sufficient to protect it from Indian insults and attacks. — The house of the Jesuits, will make at a very moderate expence, an Excellent Barrack to contain twelve or fourteen Companies, which number ought always to be there, and is sufficient.

The whole Island of Montreal, and other lands dispersed in the Province of Canada, hold[1] and belong to the Communauté de St. Sulpice in old France, and bring them an Income, not under four thousand pounds Sterling per Year.

The Women here affect dress very much, and resemble in their manners, conversation and behaviour, those of their Mother Country — such as Stile themselves Noblesse scarce

[1] Are held by.

hold any correspondence but with one another, despising all the others, and calling them des Bourgeois. They are in general rather pretty than handsome, very clever and entertaining, but not mindful of their family matters, to which they have not been accustomed, and therefore as well as on account of their Religion, to which they are exceedingly bigotted, they never can make good Wives for English Officers, altho' the Experiment has been lately tried, and they seem to have no objection to such connections. The people in general, and even the most sensible of them, are prodigiously fond of their ancient manner of Government, and have not yet found out, the advantages attending a free Inquest by Juries. Time only can open their Eyes in this matter, and many others, where the Scale will always appear to a cool and Sensible Man, to be of our Side.

The rivers supply them well with Fish and their Markets has [1] Butchers meat good in its kind and in Season. I am told that in December they lay in their Stock for Winter, consisting of Meat and Poultry and Fish these are laid in a Cellar to freeze, and keep good with ease and without putrefaction, 'till the end of April or Middle of May, when the Frost Subsides and Spring recommences.

Of the French Inhabitants and Officers, Several of whom had gone home on the conquest of Canada by the English, are returned to it, others have Sold their properties to British Subjects, and all have taken the Oaths of Allegiance, and will, I think in the succeeding generation become useful Subjects, both in Peace and War, if properly moulded by those, who by their Superiour Stations and good example make [2] take the lead in a point of so much essential consequence to Great Britain and America. In 1765, Major General R. Burton,[3] commanded at Montreal as Brigadier General, he was equally well respected and loved by the Troops and by the Inhabitants, as every honest man will in Command, who does his Duty in a Gentleman like manner, and has determination and good breeding.

[1] Have. [2] May.
[3] Ralph Burton, who was made a major-general in July, 1762.

About the end of *July 1765*, I left Montreal to go to Quebec by Water, the Passage is Sixty Leagues, and the Country on each side the river, for the greatest part of the Way, is very much Inhabited, having a parish Church, at the distance of every eight or nine Miles, many times they are placed opposite to one another, and have a very agreeable effect.

The Channel of this river is in many places, narrow and difficult, yet capable with good Pilotage, to admit of Twenty Gun Ships, as high almost as Montreal; The Country from Montreal to the plains of Maskindngi[1] is all cultivated, but these being liable to be overflowed in the Springs and the falls, are used only as Hay meadows, they are of a considerable extent, and Interspersed with woods, Creeks, and Marshes, however the Hay is excellent, and in great Quantities most years, they house it all in Barns, built on the Spot, and elevated above the high flood mark, and they convey it to their habitations, either up or down the river, in Summer in Boats, in Winter on Sleads, (a kind of Vehicle every where used in Canada, during the Seven Winter months) these are drawn generally by one Horse, and in them the Ladies and Gentlemen go avisiting, both in Town and Country, during the continuance of the Snow; they travel 60 Miles a day over rivers, Lakes, and Morasses, and thro' Woods which for the rest of the year, are totally inaccessible; they are both open and covered, and when they are made large to hold four people in them like the body of a Coach, they put more Horses to them, according to the weight to be drawn. In this Season every thing of heavy carriage is transported, as Timber, Stone, Iron Ore, Grain, etca., etca.

The Banks of the St. Lawrence is more thickly Inhabited than of any River I ever Saw, and I am told whilst it was in possession of France, they could by Signal, and communication of a kind of Cannon, from Parish to Parish, and by Flags and Signals, which every Captain of Militia had

---

[1] Maskinonge.

at his door, on a long Pole, like a May Pole, convey an Alarm, all the way from Montreal to Quebec, in a very Short time, an advantage attending their method of settling, which in our Provinces was never thought of. Lake St. Pierre lies above Trois Rivieres; — in this Lake are many wooded and well Inhabited Islands, and a variety of Channels, Rocks and Shoals, — The water is here least deep, as being more expanded, and near the upper end of it the River Sorrell, which conveys down the Waters of Lake Champlain and Lake George, falls into the River St. Lawrence. The Town of Trois Riviere,[1] as well as Montreal and Quebec, stands on the North West Bank of this Noble River, — The Situation of it is grand and Pleasant, it has a Parish Church and King's or Governour's House, a Convent of Recollets, a Nunnery of Urselines, and some few other good private houses. In the French time, Trois Riviers and Montreal, were two distinct Governments, Subject, as well as that of the Illinois, to the Supreme controul of the Governour General of Canada. All these places are healthy, the land about Trois Rivieres is light and Sandy, like an English heath, with Pitch Pines at great distances, and a few other Trees and bushes, but open enough to hunt with hounds. From this I went to the Iron Works or Forges, nine Miles back, and Situated on a Brook which runs into the river of Trois Rivieres, the Source of which lies towards Hudsons Bay, and is Inhabited by Indian Tribes of different Nations. About eight and twenty years ago, these Works were set on foot, on the French King's account, several Workmen were sent out from France, of which a few are still remaining. As much Iron was made as supplied Canada, also afforded a considerable overplus, which was annually Ship't off at Quebec, and esteemed equal, if not superiour to any Swedish, or other European Iron, particularly on account of its toughness, and not Snapping. The Ore is about Nine Miles off, and some of it nearer, but on the opposite side of the river, they used to dig it in Summer, and bring it down to the

[1] Three Rivers.

Smelting house in Sleas[1] in Winter over the Snow. The Works were roomy and compleat, their Supply of water was large, and constant, and the Iron made much in esteem amongst themselves and in Europe, at present, all is going to ru[i]n, the Works are Stopped, and if not resumed, the former expence in building Mills and Engines will be totally thrown away and of no future use; these now would do much good, and save great outlay to any Company of Adventurers from Britain, or elsewhere, who might chuse to take a Lease of them and Work them. It may not be improper here to remark, that in good policy all Iron Works, we have in America, Should be encouraged by the Mother-Country, both on Account of Saving our money from going to the Northern Countries of Europe, and that, without Iron or some such heavy commodity, it will be impossible for large Ships to load safely with Hemp and Flax, two of the great Staples, with which North America will in a few years be well enabled to furnish, not only Great Britain and Ireland, but all her own Internal demands for Cordage etca., etca. Trois Rivieres is just half way from Montreal to Quebec, Vizt 30 Leagues, — from Trois Rivieres 'till you get with[in] four Leagues of Quebec, the Banks are beautifully cultivated, and form a most rich and striking view; as you get nearer Quebec, they become every where steep and Rocky, and altho' altogether covered with Brush and Underwood, are uncommonly romantick and pleasing: the Channel from Trois Rivieres, is in some places exceeding difficult, and not to be attempted without a Skilful Pilot, notwithstanding which difficulties, in 1760 General Murray's[2] Army, with some Frigates under Captain Deane and all the Transports got up it, to Isle St. Therese, which lies about 10 or 12 Miles below Montreal, without any Material loss,

---

[1] Sleighs.

[2] James Murray, who was left in command of Quebec after the French surrendered that city to the English in 1759, and who defended it against an attack by the French in 1760. He was appointed governor of Quebec in October, 1760, and was governor of Canada in 1763–1766.

the French Army attending them on each side the river as they advanced; at low Water, one would think it impossible any vessel could get up, so full of Rocks does this River appear. Above the Rapids of Richelieu the Tide is scarce perceptible, altho' it swells the water, all the way up to Trois Rivieres, or even as far as the point du Lac, which forms the lowest end of Lake St. Pierre. The pass of De Chambeau is at Richelieu, from whence our Vessels were fired at, from an occasional Fort, thrown up round the Church; this seems a Commanding pass on the river, and might be very useful Should there ever be a necessity to Interrupt its free Navigation again. Just at Quebec, the River St. Lawrence is more narrow than any where from Frontenac to its Mouth, being not more than eleven hundred yards over, and from this it was our Batteries demolished all the low Town, the Chateau St. Louis, the Cathedral, the Bishops house, and almost every good house, in even the upper Town.

This famous City is Situated on a Commanding point of Land, formed by the influx of the River St. Charles, into that of St. Lawrence, the highest part of the upper Town, called Cape Diamond commands all round, and with a good Citadel which it undoubtedly ought to have, would be immensely Strong: there is a vacant space betwixt that and the Town, which shelves down towards the low Town, at the back of which, the rock in most places, is almost perpendicular and very high, on the edge of this precipice, hanging over the low Town, stands the King's House, called Chateau St. Louis. No Situation can be better chosen, or more grand, for it commands the view of the Bason, which is capable of Containing any Fleet, the Low Town and the road before it towards the river St. Lawrence, where Ships come to an Anchor, besides all the Cote de Lauzon, the Point Levi, the Isle of Orleans, and part of the Banks of Montmorrency. It is much demolished, as are the Cathedral, and Episcopal Palace, which stands a little lower, yet has almost as Commanding a prospect. In good policy, these Buildings, should all be repaired, as is already almost every house in the lower Town, and many in the Upper. The Jesuits have here a Noble College, built round a Square, and a good Garden; it would make an exceeding good Barrack, for a Regiment, including Officers. The Recollets have also a house and Garden, as have the Seminary for the Education of youth, which is large and Spacious, and is now refitting. Their Garden is one of the best, and their Establishment must ever be useful; there are two Convents for Women in Town, and another very large Establishment called the General Hospital, for Sick and wounded of both Sexes, which is about a Mile and a half out of Town, on the River St. Charles, has a good deal of land in property, and will always be Serviceable. These Ladies had[1] great attention to our Sick and wounded Officers and Soldiers, and deserve the Royal protection.

The Country on every Side of Quebec, is Strong and well worth Seeing for a Soldier — the Works are badly constructed, and may be Enfiladed from beyond the river St. Charles, they would require a Numerous Army to defend them, and an open communication with the Sea. It always has [been] and alway[s] must be esteemed the Key of Canada, which now seems to be a natural part of our American Empire, and ever should have been thought so, nor Should we upon any account, ever part with it. A Stranger going to Quebec, ought carefully to visit the Cove de Foulon, where the gallant General Wolfe[2] heroically Landed, and the Height of Abraham where he gloriously fell; the Isle of Orleans where he first disembarked the Troops and the heights of Montmorrency and Point Levi, where he Established his Posts, and from whence he Battered and Bombarded the Town, and from which he fired on the French Army in their Lines, which ran along the Coast, from the Tete du Pont, on the river St. Charles, to the falls on the Montmorrency. He will also visit the Post of Repentigni, above said falls, and the Banks of St. Charles for a League

[1] Paid.
[2] General James Wolfe, who was in command of the English forces which captured Quebec in September, 1759.

above the Town, — the Ride from the Town by Saint Bruit, St. Foix, the two Lorettos and Charlesburgh, returning by the Bridge, or rather Ferry on Charles river, is as fine as any in America : the View is bounded by a Ridge of Mountains, distant and little known, but all covered with Wood.

Quebec in time of Peace is well supplied with all provisions, Fish and flesh, and is I think, one of the most agreeable Quarters in America : indeed I would prefer Canada, for Society and conversation, to any Province I have yet seen ; the people are good humoured, sensible, very polite, and fond of Strangers, they are gay and not giddy, and brave, without boasting of being so : their Women in general know a good deal, and are both handsome and agreeable. Upon the whole, when one thinks of an hundred Thousand Souls, in Canada, all of whom, must now be Supplied from Great Britain, a large extent of Country, the best of which is still to people and Cultivate, and these a hardy race, born to Arms and to fatigue, I, for one, must always esteem Canada, a most Essential acquisition to America, and not less so to Britain, provided She is sensible enough to see, and improve the advantages, which this Colony may be of to both.

The river St. Lawrence is Navigable for Twenty Gun Ships 160 Leagues up to Montreal, and for Batteaus up to the Lakes.

Some Thoughts relative to Canada, as It appeared affected in 1764

THE people of this Province in general (100.000 Souls) seem not at all dissatisfied with their new Masters, but having ever since their existence been governed by a Military power, are extremely averse to our Forms of Civil Government, and very desirous (one and all) to be continued on their old footing. — There may be several Causes assigned for this.

1st. All the Noblesse in the Province are descended from

Officers sent out at different periods from France. They have always had Commands, and in all times of danger or Alarm, were accustomed to turn out at the head of their people, which people, from their earliest Infancy were hardily brought up to Arms, to Scour the Woods, and Mount the Rivers, to Shoot and to fish, by which means many of them procured their Subsistance, never chusing to Cultivate more land than was barely necessary.

2dly. The Priests, most of whom are from France, have a great ascendancy over all the Canadians, particularly the lower sort, and to do them justice they do not seem to have made bad use of their Authority, for before our Arrival in Canada, there scarce ever was heard of a Murder, a Theft or a Bankruptcy : the Ideas of the Roman Catholick Religion are much more connected with, and calculated for the French plan of Government than ours, and they would certainly preserve more respect to themselves by continuing on the old plan.

3dly. The Canadians have always been taught a great degree of deference and respect for their Superiours, which is not yet worn out, and we see that where custom has made that the case and the people are protected, they feel just as gay and well pleased, as in Countries, where every one is on a footing of equality.

Upon the whole I think they were too suddenly adopted into our Government, at a time [when] there was no proper people of our Religion and Language to be made Magistrates, and before the Natives could have any Idea of our Laws and Forms of Justice, which are ever prolix and very expensive. In former days all their Suits were determined in a short time and at scarce any expence, at present the case is diametrically opposite, and therefore it is no wonder they complain of the Change.

4thly. The British Inhabitants as yet settled in Canada, are the Scum of the Earth, — they give themselves airs of importance as Justices of Peace and Magistrates, whilst they instil nothing but Licentiousness and Faction into the minds of the Inhabitants, who are innocently made to believe things that are false and groundless, and from want of knowing what our Constitution is, and judging only from the bad behaviour of such fellows as are set over them, they are with great reason apt to think ill of such people, and to condemn the whole System.

I should think it would much tend to the good of the Province to do something to gain the good will and attachment of the Noblesse or better sort, — to lower the influence of the Priests, and to establish Funds in the Province to defray Its ordinary expences, Civil and Military, perhaps without any expence to the Mother Country, already too much Saddled. To attain these good purposes, I would by act of Parliament vest all the Religious property of Canada unalienably in the King; — I would give pensions to all the Supernumerary Priests during their lives, and Settle fixed Salaries upon all the Parish Priests, Masters and Professors in the two Seminaries of Quebec and Montreal. I would confine the Number of Female Convents and Nuns, and give to each House an adequate annual income in money. I would vest in the King all Tythes etca. I would considerably add to the plan of education in each Seminary, and I would have one Academy for the Province of Trois Rivieres, where the Masters should teach in English and French, in which Languages, I would oblige all Priests after such a term of years to preach alternately. When this was settled, I would throw into this Fund, all other the King's revenues in the Province, whether Customs, Stamps etca. I would have a Brigade of Militia, not under 3000 in three Battalions, the Governour for the time being perpetual Colonel in Chief. In this as Officers I would Commission indiscriminately French and English according to their property and birth, each taking the Oath of Allegiance only. I would give them Rank equal with our Provincial Troops, and some retainer like half pay, this would infallibly gain the affections of the better sort and would be a useful nursery in a future War, either against Spain, or any of our own Provinces that might wish to shake off their dependance on Britain. Any young Canadian Officer, who should turn Protestant and distinguish himself, I would take into the Regulars Service, chiefly into Regiments going home. These Militia should meet and Muster so many times a year at Quebec, Trois Rivieres and Montreal. — I would have them double Officered in the French manner, and if possible liable to Martial Law: the men should be of a certain age, and should serve for a stated term, but upon marriage should be entitled to his discharge and a piece of land, except in times of actual danger and Alarm. The Officers and Men should have full pay when on Duty out of the Province, and be treated as Troupes des Colonies. I would have an open and free toleration of all Christian Religions, throughout Canada and the two Floridas, and all the back Country. Barracks to be built, furnished and repaired. — In short all Establishments, Civil, Religious and Military to be provided for from these Funds, subject always to the controul of the Governour and Council, and finally with an appeal to the King in Council. — If there should be any overplus let it be laid out in publick uses, Viz. in constructing Goals and Bridges, cutting and repairing high Roads and Canals, paving Streets, and establishing Posts and Post-houses.

In what relates to Montreal, I have forgot to mention the Messieurs De Saint Sulpice, who are proprietors of the Island of Montreal, and many other Lands and Mills to the amount of near 4000£ a year Sterling.

The Number of Houses in Montreal, from Six to Seven hundred before the Fire, and about the Same at Quebec.

I left Montreal in *August 1765,* and crossed over to La Prairie, which stands on the opposite Shore of St. Lawrence, and about nine Miles higher up the river, from this to St. John's on the river Richelieu or Sorell is fifteen Miles by land; from St. John's to the Isle au Noix, on the same river is fifteen Miles, from that to Crown Point is Ninety Miles, and from Crown Point to Ticonderoga, is fifteen Miles all by Water. The Shore from over against Montreal to La Prairie is well Settled and Cultivated, but poor land:

from that across to St. John's, the land is richer, and a good deal of Wood and Meadow: At St. John's there are some Settlements, and here the Provision Vessels of Lake Champlain, take in the Stores for the Troops, which are all Supplied from Montreal and St. Lawrence. These provisions may either go overland from La Prairie to St. Johns, or by Water up the Sorrell. Chamblé, a small Post and Fort, lies on the Sorrell, lower than St. John and on the same Side. I am told there is not there anything much worth seeing, and therefore I did not visit it: from St. John's as you ascend, their is scarce a Settlement, 'till you come to the Isle au Noix, a place pretty remarkable, as having been very strongly fortified, and naturally very inaccessible. It stopped the progress of the British Arms 'till the year when Mr. Amherst by coming down and Mr. Murray by coming up St. Lawrence each with an Army, so much engaged the French attention in these Quarters, that it obliged them to Abandon this Strong Post to Colonel Haviland,[1] who had spent some time and Ammunition before it to no purpose. It is at present neglected, and the Works mouldering away. It is the property of Colonel Christie, who lets it at 25£ a year rent, and it produces good Wheat and Clover. This place is so Morassy, that all the Shells that fell, sunk in and never appeared again, and could not have been carried, but by the French abandoning of it.

On both Sides of Lake Champlain, the land is but middling, as well as on the Islands, some of which are large and well Wooded. — Crown Point is finely Situated on a promontory running out into the Lake, the river au Sud going to Ticonderoga, bounding it on one Side, and the Bay on t'other. The Fort is of Wood, built in a most masterly manner. It has five Bastions, Mounts 105 Guns, and has Casemates for 4000 Men, and to hold Provisions de Guerre et de Bouche for four months. It has cost much money

---

[1] William Haviland, who came to America in 1757 as lieutenant-colonel of the 27th regiment of foot and was in command of about 3,400 men when, in 1760, he besieged the French post at Isle aux Noix.

and trouble, and as the Wood Work is beginning to give, if it is not taken in time, it will in a year or two more, be in as bad a State, as the other American Forts I have seen. It becomes less an object, since Canada is ours, but must always Command these Lakes. Scarce any Guns are Mounted, the Ditch is all cut or blown in a Lime Stone Rock, but is not finished, nor the Glacis, nor is any out Work of any Sort, except three fortified redoubts with Cannon.

Sir Jeffery Amherst has very properly given them good bounds round the Fort from Water to Water; Within the Fort are good Stone Barracks for Men and Officers, which, if they were finished, would conveniently contain 500 Men. The Situation of the Fort seems to be well chosen, altho' one face of the Pentagon is enfiladed, from across the River at not much more than five hundred feet distance. — It would not take less than 20.000£ Sterling to finish properly this Fort. From this to Ticonderoga the Lake grows narrow, and this the French called Riviere Sud, as leading to the South Bay, — the land on either side is but middling, distance 16 Miles. Ticonderoga Stands on an eminence on the point formed by the river from Lake George which at this place falls into Lake Champlain. The works are ruinous — it is a Quarré, all of Wood and some bad Casemates, it is much Commanded by the High ground behind it, along which from the river to the Lake Monsr De Montcalm constructed his famous Lines, which we attacked Unsuccessfully in 1758; — they are a Short mile distant from the Fort, were immensely strong, having three or four Batteries, all five Loggs high, and as well laid out for defence as the nature of the ground could admit of. At some small distance from the Fort, nearer the Lake, we have a fortified redoubt, which Commands the Harbour, where all the Lake Vessels are laid up in Winter, and some of them have been built. About a Mile beyond the Lines is the famous Saw Mills, where we have now a Bridge Established, and a Blockhouse to Cover the Mills, — here the Troops retreated after their Repulse — $1\frac{1}{2}$ Mile farther is the landing place on

Lake-George, and a Block-house — near to this General Abercrombie's Army landed, and here they re-imbarked, and not far from it the Gallant Lord Howe [1] was killed. Colonel Roger Townshend was Shot the year after by a Random Shot from the Fort, as he stood within the French Lines then abandoned, in order to reconnoitre the Situation of the place.

The Country all Around Lake George is Mountainous, and Rocky, bearing bad Wood, and Scarce a Hut but one, about 12 Miles from the Landing on the right Side as you ascend the Lake. It is called Sabbath day point. 24 Miles further you arrive at the upper end or head of the Lake, which in all is 36 Miles long — the Banks are Inaccessible, the timber seems fit only of [2] Charcoal or Pot-ash, but the Water and Fish are remarkably fine. I could perceive no Brooks or Rivulets running into it 'till we got to Fort George, near which are two little Streams : they say it is altogether supplied by Springs in its own Bottom, and for that reason it is always longer of being frozen over, than any Neighbouring Lake or River. — Upon the whole, I would advise a Stranger to visit Lake George, and Lake Champlain, before he visits Ontario or Erie, because if he does not, the former will appear greatly to a Disadvantage.

When you land at the Upper end, you find a Small Stockade Fort, tumbling down and not tenible, built in a hurry after we took back possession of that ground, on which stood Old Fort William Henry, which the French burnt and Abandon'd. A little above this (and now Called Fort George) we have a Compleat Bastion built of Stone, the Casemates of Wood ; It mounts ten Guns, and was a part of a Quarré begun, but postponed, I think Judiciously, after it was determined to have a respectable Fort at Crown Point, besides, it was, and always must be commanded by rising grounds on three sides. Very near this Spot, was General Deiskaw [3] defeated by Sir Wm. Johnston in 1755,

---

[1] Brigadier-General Viscount Howe, who was second in command in the expedition of 1758 against Ticonderoga and Crown Point.
[2] For. [3] Ludwig August Dieskau.

and some provincials he then had here, and here General Abercromby intrenched his Army, after his return from Ticonderoga in 1758.

From this place to Fort Edward is 15 Miles, — It may not be amiss to remark in this place, that before the last War with the French, we scarce ever had any Post, higher than Fort Edward, and seldom or ever Interfered on Lake George, which was then all French Indian hunting Country. The Country, from Lake George to Fort Edward, on Hudson's River, is mixed, some light and some good Oak land, and is now beginning to Settle, the Army during the first years of the last War, having cleared a great part of it, which is nearest Fort Edward, where you fall in with Hudson's river is much the best. The Fort is in a Meadow, close on the river, commanded on three Sides, but as it is too bad to keep together, for more than one Winter more — it is scarce worth saying more of it, it was a Quarre of Logg Work, all in ruin, there are about 24 Guns, most of which are falling into the Casemates, on which they are placed.

The Meadow round the Fort, and an Island over against it in the River is all cleared and looks Extreamly pleasant. Just above the Fort is a Ford, and over against it there is a Block-house, which Commands the Fort and every place within it : half a Mile below this, there is a Ferry and Schau, very commodious for Passengers : from this to Saratoga, all down the said Hudsons river, the Country is very rich and pleasing and peopling very fast. — Saratoga [1] is 14 Miles lower in a fertile Vale, on a Creek which gives it that name, which there enters Hudsons river. On this Creek Philip Schuyler Esqr. of Albany, has two good Saw Mills and a very pretty little house. On this Land he produces Hemp, from Six to Ten Feet high, and for two Crops running. From Saratoga to Still Water is 12 Miles, still descending Hudsons river, all peopling and Clearing very fast, in so much, that tho' in the beginning of last War, all

---

[1] This town subsequently became known as Old Saratoga to distinguish it from Saratoga Springs.

was abandon'd from Fort Edward, to within three Miles of Albany, and cut off by the Indians in the French Interest, I will venture to say, that will never again happen. The distance from Still Water to Albany is 24 Miles, still down Hudsons river. — Having a mind to visit the falls of the Mohawk river, Called the Cahoes, I turned short, about half way to the Right, and crossing, Saw Mohawk river, at Loudoun's Ferry. I went down a Mile to see them; here the fall extends quite across and is pretty, but I must confess had in it nothing Striking, after having seen those at Niagara, which it is Impossible once to see, and ever to lose the Idea of. From this I crossed the Country to Schenectady alread[y] described. From Schenectady I made another visit to Sir Wm. Johnson, a Gentleman of much worth and undoubted merit with respect to his King and Country. Should any thing happen to Sir Wm. I know of no body equal to the Important Post he fills, with dignity to himself and much Utility and Advantage to Britain and America.

The Country all along the Mohawk river is beautiful and well Inhabited, as far, and a little above the German flatts already mentioned.

From Schenectady to Albany, it is all a Pine-Barren, the River banks at, and near the Town are fertile and Verdant, the Country is Hilly, and Soil light and Sandy, all the way to Kinderhook, producing Pine and some Oak, the Road pretty good, — from this to   it is Stoney, and rather Mountainous, with good Oak and Chesnut Timber, the Country very hilly and not thick Settled, bad roads. Four Miles farther, you cross a very Steep and high Hill, after which you have a tolerably good road to Barrington,[1] a pretty Scattering Country Village, Situated amongst rocks and Hills covered with Brush and Pines: from this th[r]o' Sheffield to Canaan,[2] you pass thro' a delightful Vale, well planted and thickly Inhabited, with Orchards to every house, which are here Warm and well built, the Men well clad, and the

---

[1] Great Barrington, Mass.   [2] Canaan, Conn.

TRAVELS IN THE AMERICAN COLONIES

Women remarkably tydy and handsome, from Canaan to
Norfolk, the Country is Romantick and young peopled, the
Roads but middling, being not above Twenty Years Settled;
— from this you travel 14 Miles thro' the green Woods,
the worst road I have seen in America; this is a Newcut,
and not a habitation all the way, tho' I am told there will
soon be Several. After you pass this Forest, of Noble
Chesnuts and other Trees, but no Oaks, you fall in on a
pretty little River,[1] at [a] place called New Hartford, which
you descend all the way to Simsbury a pleasant little Village;
Twenty Miles short of Hartford the Capital of Connecticut.
All this Country is fully Settled, and is just like England.

Hartford is a Large Scattering Town, on a Small River,[2]
which, as well as that [at] Simsbury falls into Connecticut
River. — It has two handsome Meetings,[3] on a *Platform* of
their own, the people are uncommonly Stiff, and formal, and
as Industrious as in any one Province. — Here they build
Vessels, for the Lumber Trade to the West Indies, from 100
to 150 Tons, and float them down in Freshes, in. Spring and
Fall. — The Number of Inhabitants, in Connecticut, are
supposed about 100.000, and their Militia Roll about 30.000,
that is from 16 to 60 years of Age. — All the Country to
Endfield,[4] thro' Windsor, is fully Inhabited, and all along
the Connecticut River, up and down, fine rich Meadows
and Fields. — The Post Road goes up from Hartford to
Springfield on the river, but if you leave it at Enfield, and
take to the Right thro' the Woods, you save eight or ten
Miles, and travel a better Road, to a place called Birts, —
from this to Kingston or Palmer, you go thro' a very pleasant
Country, which continues so all the way to Leicester; you
often meet the view of the Chicabee River, in twenty years,
this part of the World, will not fall short of the most beautiful part of England.

To Worcester the Soil and Views continue most striking
and agreeable, — this is one of the best built, and prettiest

[1] Farmington River.   [2] Park River.
[3] Churches or meeting-houses.   [4] Enfield, Mass.

448

Inland little Towns I remember to have seen in America. It is fine land all the way to Shrewsbury, and good Road, from this all the way to Boston, it is populous and pleasant, the best Road is to quit the Post road, three Miles East of Shrewsbury, and fall again into it, a Mile West of West-Town. On this Road you meet with Houses and Villages all the way to Boston, which stands on a Peninsula, with a narrow neck or Causeway, which is the only access by land to it. It has been Settled about an hundred years 1616 [1] — next to Virginia — has in it 2.100 houses, many of which are better, more Spacious, and more Commodious, than those I saw, either at Philadelphia or New York, — they all have Gardens, and within it, is a Common and a Mall, and two remarkable rising grounds called the Beacon-Hill, and the Fort-Hill, — from these you Command all the Town, the Harbour, the Castle, the river Charles, and all the Country, and I doubt much, if there is in the World, a finer, or more Variegated prospect. The Main Street is two Miles long, leading from the Gate all the way to the Ferry, which plies over Charles river to Charlestown, a very pretty Village, rather Older than Boston and very well served, — the Number of Inhabitants in Town, are supposed to be about 23.000, — in the Province of Massachusets 35.000,[2] and about 10.000 fit to bear Arms, but this Calculation is rather high. — This is more like an English Old Town than any in America, — the Language and manner of the people, very much resemble the old Country, and all the Neighbouring lands and Villages, carry with them the same Idea. — The better kind of people in and near the Town, seem well bred and Sensible. They lament their present Plan of Government, which throws too much weight into the popular Scale, and they know by Experience the bad Consequences, attending that Circumstance. When the Stamp Duty was first laid by Act of Parliament in 1765, the first and most flagrant acts of Opposition to it, and of a

[1] 1630.
[2] The population of Massachusetts at this time was estimated as high as 350,000, and that is probably the figure here intended.

Riotous and Licentious Spirit in the Mob, broke out here, and were fatal to the House and property of their Lieutt. Governour Mr. Hutchinson.[1] After all it would appear, as if nothing but a thorough alteration of their Charter and form of Government, giving to His Majesty the Nomination of Councellors as well as Governour, and putting it together on the footing of a Royal Government would operate effectually; for without some such Change, and an Adoption of Spirited Measures, and an Adequate degree of force, to Co-operate with, and to Support Civil Government and Laws, that ancient rugged Spirit of Levelling, early Imported from home, and too successfully nursed, and Cherished, will, in the four New England Governments never be got the better of. Palliavites[2] may be applied, and the danger postponed, but the Malady is Radical, and will be cured more easily now than in aftertimes, particularly whilst we have Peace in Europe.

The Entrance of Boston Harbour, is Nine Miles off; It has but one considerable Channel for large Ships, and that is in many places crooked and very narrow; About three Miles below the Town stands Castle William on an Island. It is a very small Quarré without Works much exceeding the Fort. Shirley's Battery of Forty pounders might damage any Ships considerably, before they could bring their Broadsides to bear, but otherways it is not Strong. I am told Sixty Gun Ships have been quite up to the Town, and some say there are five fathoms in the worst of the Channel, which may be totally blocked up, by Sinking one Vessel across it. The Harbour is full of Islands, Bays and Shoals: there is on one Island almost opposite to the Fort, called Shirley Island, a Church and small Town, and a Blockhouse and Battery on another. — The Fort might mount 140 Guns, the Barracks there might contain a Thousand, or twelve hundred Men. On the Whole, what is there, is in better repair and more Compleatly furnished, than any Provincial Fortification, I have yet seen in America.

[1] Thomas Hutchinson.   [2] Palliatives.

Altho' the face of the Country is very rough and Stoney, about Boston, and some Miles round, yet it is a most healthy climate, and kindly Soil, producing every European Grain and Root in plenty and perfection, besides Indian Corn. — I never Saw such Quantities of Apple and Pear Trees, all the Roads are lined with them, — the poorest Farmer, or rather proprietor, has one or more Orchards, and Cyder is their common Drink, altho' they grow good Barley, and that Hops grow there, every where, with little trouble or Culture, more large and high, than any I remember in Surry.

The Men here, resemble much the people of Old England, from whence most of them are Sprung. I was rather sur- prized to find here, and not amongst the Richest, the re- spectable Names of Howard, Wentworth, Pelham, Pierpoint, Dudley, Carey, Russel, Temple and many others of less note and Ambiguity; but the levelling principle here, every where Operates strongly, and takes the lead, every body has property, and every body knows it.

The Women here, and at Rhode-Island, are Accounted the most beautiful of any, on the Continent, and I am apt to believe it is so. At a Ball of Seventy Ladies, I saw about one half handsome ones; perhaps one reason is, that every Girl who has a pretty face and good Clothes, is free to come, and is well received at Publick places there, where there is no Sort of distinction of persons.[1]

---

[1] During Lord Adam Gordon's visit to Boston a committee appointed in town meeting (Sept. 12, 1765) waited upon him, and James Otis, the chairman, addressed him as follows:

"MY LORD,

"I have the Honour with the Gentlemen present to be a Com- mittee from the Town of Boston, the Metropolis of his Majesty's ancient and loyal Province of Massachusetts-Bay, to wait on your Lordship in the Name of the Town, to congratulate you on your safe arrival, to express their ardent Wishes for your Prosperity, and humbly to request your kind Representations and Influence in Favor of this Town and Province, as your Lord- ship's Wisdom and Justice shall direct; particularly with Re-

Cyder is so plenty, as to Sell at a Dollar a Barrel, Cask included — 34 Gallons.

The Country from Boston to Providence 45 Miles, is mostly rough and Stoney, but there is a fine plain near Providence, called Sea-Conck-plain,[1] and a beautiful river called Patucket, on the West side of which, and within a Mile is a Spermaceti Work, for Candles, which cost about one Shilling and Sixpence per pound. Providence is a large Town, built on the Banks of the River, and having several good Houses in it, Here and at Newport, they hold their General Courts for Rhode Island, which is the smalest province in America, containing about Forty thousand Whites and Five thousand Negroes. The Harbour of Newport is good and deep enough for any Ships to come in.

gard to the new Parliamentary Regulations that so nearly affect the Rights and Privileges, as well as the Trade and Commerce of his Majesty's American Dominions, and which have created such universal Uneasiness among his Majesty's most loyal Subjects on this Continent."

To which, or rather to the vote in town meeting on the preceding day, Lord Adam replied:

"Gentlemen, —

"I find myself very sensibly obliged to you for this Mark of your Attention, and for the Honor you have done me, by your unanimous Address of Yesterday; for which, and your good Wishes, expressed in it, I beg leave to return you my best Thanks.

"I have had much Satisfaction in the Tour I have made in British America, and am extremely sorry to understand, there should at this Time, subsist any Uneasiness among his Majesty's good Subjects there; more particularly, in the ancient and loyal Province and Town of Boston.

"What little Influence I may be supposed to have, shall ever be chearfully employed, where the Interests of Great Britain and America are concerned, which to me seem inseparable: Having ever been of Opinion that any Man, who could wish to see a Distinction or endeavour to create a Difference between them, must be an Enemy to both. . . .

"Ad. Gordon."

Massachusetts Gazette, Sept. 19, 1765.

[1] Seekonk.

From Newport to York[1] is a good Navigation, thro' the Sound about 200 Miles. — The Narrows towards York is very pleasant, 'till you come to a place called Hell-gate, where you must have a Pilot, and chuse your time or Tide, else it is not to be risked. Near this, and a little lower, is Morisania, the Seat of Lewis Morris Esqr. and the prittiest and best conditioned Farm in America. — It is Nine Miles from York, Consists of 2050 Acres, for which he has been Offered 22.000 pounds Sterling. It has a bad House on it.

From York harbour to Sandy-hook, is about Ten Leagues, after you pass the Narrows, which are formed by two points, of Long Island and Staten Island; — You meet with Sand Banks, which render it necessary to take in a Pilot, he generally leaves you about the Light-house, on Sandy-hook, after which you have no Stop, but Nantucket-Shoals, about twenty five Leagues off, and bearing from the Hook, East half Southerly.

Behind the Hook when at Sea, you make the High-land of never Sink, which in very clear weather, is seen, at least ten Leagues off, and appears at first like an Island. On Sounding all hereabouts, one may Catch good Sea Bass, and black Fish in plenty, with ground Bait.

I embarked at New York, on *the 14th of October 1765*, On Board the Harriet Packet, Captain Robinson for Falmouth.

[1] *I.e.,* New York.

JOURNAL OF CAPTAIN HARRY GORDON, 1766

INTRODUCTION

CAPTAIN GORDON records in this journal an account of a journey which he undertook as Chief Engineer of the Western Department in North America. He received his instructions in New York, the 9th of May, 1766, from General Thomas Gage, Commander-in-Chief of the English forces in America, proceeded to Philadelphia four days later, and thence to Pittsburg, where he embarked the 18th of June in company with Ensign Thomas Hutchins, Assistant Engineer and subsequently Geographer-General of the United Colonies; George Croghan, a deputy superintendent of Indian affairs under Sir William Johnson, and the most influential of white men among the Indians of the Ohio and Illinois country; George Morgan of the Indian trading house of Baynton, Wharton, and Morgan at Philadelphia; about one hundred Indians of the Six Nations; and a large party of Delaware and Shawnee Indians. The mission of Croghan, who was also under instructions from General Gage,[1] was to attach the Indians to the English interest. The mission of Gordon was to look over the matter of defense and propose means of securing to the English the Indian trade in the territory from which the French had been expelled by the fourth intercolonial war.[2]

---

[1] For a copy of the instructions see C. A. Hanna, *The Wilderness Trail*, Vol. II, pp. 38–39.

[2] The 11th of November, 1766, General Gage wrote from New York to the Earl of Shelburne: "An Engineer was sent in the Spring down the Ohio to the Ilinois with Orders to proceed down the Mississippi to New Orleans, and to return to this Place by the way of Mobile and Pensacola: I expect that his Report will enable me to send your Lordship ample Information of all those affairs with respect to the Indian Trade in general, I find great Quan-

Harry Gordon was a captain in the 60th Regiment. The best commentary on his Journal is in the letter by General Gage accompanying its transmission to the Earl of Shelburne, which is in part as follows:

New York, Febry 22d 1767.

"My Lord,

"I have the honour to transmit your Lordship a Copy of a Journal made out by Captain Gordon, Chief Engineer of North America, in his Progress down the Ohio to the Ilinois, down the Mississippi to New-Orleans, and from thence to Mobile and Pensacola. It contains chiefly a Description of the Country he passed through, with the Distances and Latitude of Places taken, I believe with more Accuracy than has ever been done by any other Person, And your Lordship will also find in it some Account of the Trade of the Mississippi and Settlements made upon that River.

"That Trade will go with the Stream is a Maxim found to be true, from all accounts that have been received of the Indian Trade carried on in the vast Tract of Country which lies on the Back of the British Colonies; and that the Peltry acquired there, is carried to the Sea either by the River St. Lawrence or River Mississippi, as the Trade is Situated on the Lakes, inland Rivers, and Streams, whose Waters communicate respectively with those two immense Rivers. The part which goes down the St. Lawrence, we may recon will be transported to Great-Britain, but I apprehend what goes down the Mississippi will never enter British Ports: And I imagine that nothing but a Prospect of a Superior Profit or Force, will turn the Channel of the Trade contrary to the above Maxim.

"The Traders on the Branches of the Mississippi, will never be tempted to bring their Peltry into the British Provinces whilst they get high Prices for their Skins at

titys of Skins and Furrs are procured, but the Traders, particularly those upon the Lakes shew little Regard to the Regulations that have been made, to oblige them to traffick only at the Forts; which they avoid, and rove at Pleasure."

New-Orleans, or can ship them from thence immediately for foreign Markets in foreign Bottoms, Nothing then but Force can oblige our own Traders to bring the Produce of their Trade in those Parts into our Provinces to be exported to Great Britain, or prevent foreign Traders from intruding upon the Territorys ceded to His Majesty.

"The only Method to effect this, would be to put in Execution what is proposed in Captain Gordon's Journal vizt: To erect Posts on the Rivers Ohio and Ilinois near their Junction with the Mississippi, in order to prevent all Furrs and Skins from coming into that River from the Eastern Branches, and to prevent foreign Merchandise being smuggled into His Majesty's Territorys by means of the Ilinois and the Ohio. I must confess upon Reflection, that I have strong Doubts after all whether such Posts would effectually answer all the Purposes expected from them, for tho' the Vigilance of the Officers might be very great, it seems no difficult Matter for Traders to pass the Posts unobserved in the Night, or by Collusion with Indians, whom we could not seize without a Quarrell, they might get by unmolested at all Times.

"Captain Gordon's Journal gives an Account of Fort Chartres, with his Opinion of the only use he conceives it to be of: I must own Myself to have been of the same Opinion from the first Account I received of it's Situation. It does maintain a kind of Superiority over the Indians in that Country, keep up an Interest with them, and is a Check upon His Majesty's New Subjects there, whom I apprehend will not be the most faithful Subjects, whilst their former Countrymen are settled so near them, as the opposite Shores of the River.

"As Fort Chartres will certainly be destroyed very soon without a possibility of preserving it; other Posts must be built if it is Judged proper to maintain the Country of the Illinois in his Majestys Possession. And in such Case, it would be Advisable to erect them on the Situations mentioned, and take every Precaution to confine the Trade to the East of the Mississippi, as far as shall be in our Power.

"The Accounts I have received from the lower parts of the Mississippi on the Subject of Trade are of the same Nature, respecting the Peltry being carried to New Orleans, and of their being smuggled into that Place from the parts of West-Florida; That they are conveyed from Mobile along the Coast into Lake Ponchartrain, and likewise by the River of Pearls which falls into said Lake, which they cross to a Place called the Bayoue of St. John where a French Detachment is constantly posted, and within a very short way of New-Orleans. I am likewise informed, which is confirmed by Captain Gordon, that the French cross over to the East side of Lake Ponchartrain, where they make great Quantities of Pitch and Tar, with which they carry on a very good Trade with La Vera Cruz. A Detachment from Mobile posted on some Advantageous Spot in Lake Ponchartrain, might in great Measure defeat such Proceedings.

"The Spaniards are not yet settled in their New Acquisition, Your Lordship is informed how their new Subjects are already disgusted with a Spanish Government, we may wait with Patience for some time in observing their Conduct and the System they shall adopt in Carrying on their Affairs. They have no experience in Indian Management or Commerce, and perhaps Mismanagement in these Particulars may give us an Advantage, we can't otherwise expect, for the Post of New-Orleans will always give them a Natural Superiority over us. . . .

"But with respect to the Carrying on of Commerce with the Indians, the present method pursued, particularly in the Northern District, of suffering no Trade but at the Posts only, approved of by most People at first from it's good Appearance, is found upon Tryal not to Answer. It would be a good Plan if it could be executed universally, but the Posts cannot be multiplied to the Degree necessary to compleat it. From hence the Traders complain that they are prevented from getting the Quantitys of Furrs, they could procure from Nations who live at a great Distance from the Posts, were they not restrained from going to them; which gives the French Traders an advantage

INTRODUCTION

over them who go and reside amongst such Tribes, and by their Intrigues do a great deal of Mischief. It is also so contrary to the old Custom of Trade, and no People more Attached to Customs than the Indians, and they find so much more Trouble than formerly to procure their Necessarys, that the Indians are in general very averse to the Plan; are desirous that all Traders should come amongst them, and encourage them to act contrary to their Regulations.

"It may be difficult to fix the exact Boundarys of Trade to each Province respectively, or to prevent the Traders from one Province, when in the Deserts, from rambling into the Precincts Allotted to others. But it's certainly very Necessary that the whole should be Subject to some general Rules and Restrictions. I am of Opinion, That the Price of all Goods should be fixed, for every part of the Country, that no Trader should trade without a License, and a very small Fee taken for such License: That the Traders should give Security for their good Behavior and observation of all Rules and Restrictions, That tho' Licensed in one Province they may be brought to Punishment in all, for any Frauds or Misdemeanors, or in any shape breaking the Condition of their Bonds by which they obtain their Licenses. That every Trader should be obliged to return with his Peltry to that Province from whence he received his License, and make Returns of the Quantity and Nature of the Peltry he brings with him. This Method may in some Measure prevent their going down the Mississippi; Returns should also be made of the Quantity and Nature of the Goods they carry out. That the Indian Commissarys should be so stationed, that every Nation may be able to lay their Complaints before some of these Commissarys, who should be empowered to do them Justice in the Case of Misusage or fraudulent Dealings on the part of the Traders; transmitting the Names of such People to the respective Governors that they may meet with proper Punishment. The Indians should be made acquainted with all the Rules and Restrictions particularly with the Prices fixed for the Goods, and warned to trade with none but the Licensed Traders. This

I conceive will give them a high Notion of His Majesty's Regard for them, by the Care they will see that is taken to prevent their being abused or defrauded.

"I have taken the Liberty to offer Your Lordship My Sentiments on this Material Point, and tho' sensible of the Difficulties of exacting a Strict Observance of any Rules, from a Set of People, who for the most part, are near as wild as the Country they go in, or the People they deal with, and by far more vicious and wicked, yet by due Care and Attention in His Majesty's Governors and the Indian Agents and Commissarys, I think much good may be done. The above Reflections are also calculated upon the Plan adopted, of laying every part of the Trade open to all Adventurers. I have only further to add at present on this Subject, if such a Plan coincide with our Principles of Government, that of all the Systems of Indian Commerce which have come within My Knowledge, I have found none equal to that adopted by the French; which a long Experience proved to be a good one. The whole Country was divided into Districts and sold, upon Condition of paying yearly Revenues to the Crown, to certain Traders or Companys of Traders; who enjoyed exclusive Rights of Trade in their respective Districts. It was the Policy as it became the Interest of all, to treat the Indians well and conciliate their affections. If they were ill used, they would go to the Neighbouring District for their Necessarys. If those of one District intruded upon the Territorys of others, Government was not troubled but the Persons aggrieved were re-dressed by Law. And the whole Business of Indian Commerce was transacted greatly to the Benefit of the Crown, to the general Satisfaction of the Savages, without Trouble or Expense to Government, and the Trade flourished Exceedingly. . . .   "THOS. GAGE."

The official copy of this journal has been preserved in the Public Record Office, London; C. O. 5: 85, pp. 123-140, and there is one transcript of this in the Library of Congress and another in the Canadian Archives, at Ottawa. There is also a copy among the Hutchins Manuscripts in the Library of the Historical Society of Pennsylvania; in that copy Captain Gordon begins his account with the receipt of his instructions and passes briefly over his journey from New York to Pittsburg. Portions of the Journal have been published in Thomas Pownall's *Topographical Description of . . . North America* (1776), in the *Journal* of the Illinois State Historical Society (July, 1909), in C. A. Hanna's *Wilderness Trail* (1911), and in the *Collections* of the Missouri Historical Society (1911).

JOURNAL OF CAPTAIN HARRY GORDON, 1766

THE 18th of June,[1] Mr. Croghan having finished his Business with the Indians, the Batteau's being fitted, and having Engaged the Sufficient Number of Batteau-Men; We embarked on the Ohio at One P. M.; By the Rains that fell this and the preceding day the River Ohio had risen between Two and Three Feet, so that the largest Batteau's of the Merchants that were sent under our Escort which consisted of Indians, never touched altho' 7 Tons Burthen.

The 19th We arrived at the Mingo Town,[2] which by our Reckoning is 71 Miles below Fort Pitt[3]; The Country

---

[1] In the Hutchins copy of the journal this entry is preceded by the following: "Having received His Excellency, the Commander in Chief's, Orders and Instructions the 9th of May, I preceded to Philadelphia with Ensign Hutchins, Assist. Engineer, the 13 of same Mon[th]. Having purchased at that Place the necessary Store[s] for our further Journey and hired Carriage for them to Fort Pitt, we left Philadelphia the 23d, and got [to] the Ohio the 14th June, having been delayed by Sickn[ess] several Days on the Road; of which I acquainted Mr. Croghan, Depy. Indian Agent, by Express, as I had Orders to accompany Him.

"I found the Road over the Allegheny Mountains extremely bad, and will be most probably impassable for Carriages by next Summer.

"The Fort at Ligonier, near the western Foot of the Mountains, is much Shattered, by the Timbers and Stockades being almost rotten. The Country near the Fort is very fine, healthy, and Soil rich, producing plentifully all Kinds of Grain, Hemp, or Flax. There are some Inhabitants now, and many more would assemble there was any Right of Possession or Property secured to them.

"I described to the Commander in Chief the Condition of Fort Pitt by Letter 16th of June."

[2] Mingo Town was inhabited by Indians of the Six Nations who separated from their tribesmen about 1750.

[3] Now Pittsburg.

between broken, with very high Ridges, the Valleys Narrow, and the Course of the River plunged from many high Grounds which compose it's Banks; At this Village, Indian business detained us a Day, but altho' the Rains abated the 19th in the Morning, the River rose for several Days, and run so Rapid as to carry us with moderate Rowing from 6 to 7 Miles per hour. *The 23d* we came to the Mouth of the Muskingum before Noon, observed and found the Latitude to be 39° 19', The Muskingum is a very large River 250 Yards Wide at it's Confluence with the Ohio; It is said to be Navigable 150 Miles upwards for Batteau's, and runs thro' a pleasant Country, as that near it's Junction appeared to be. Many small Creeks and Streams run into the main River, a Mark of the Lands near it being plentifully watered; Our Indians killed several Buffaloe, between the Mingo Town and the Muskingum; We first met with a herd of this kind of Animal, about 100 Miles below Fort Pitt, but they are not so Common, untill we pass the Scioto; At this Place we arrived *the 29th June* 366 Miles below Fort Pitt, the Navigation we found Uninterrupted to our largest Batteaus: The Flood Indeed was with Us, but at any Time there will be no Obstacle from the Mingo Town, which is 71 Miles from Fort Pitt, nor much from the Big beaver Creek.[1]

The River Ohio from 50 Miles above Muskingum to Scioto, is most beautifull, a Number of Islands are to be seen of different Sizes, but all covered with the tallest of Timber; The long Reaches, among which is one of 16 Miles and a ½, inclosed with the finest Trees of different kinds of various Verdures and Leaves of the largest Sorts, Afford a noble and Enchanting prospect. The Rivers Hockhocking [2] and Canawha [3] fall into the Ohio in this Space, besides others of a Smaller Size: Up the big Canawha,[4] the Northern Indians penetrate into the Cherokee Nations, and is a large fine Stream by report, Navigable 100 Miles, towards the Southward.

[1] Beaver River.
[2] Now called Hocking.
[3] Little Kanawha.
[4] Great Kanawha.

The Country is Every where pleasant, in the bends of the Rivers course are large level Spots of the richest Land, and on the whole is remarkably healthy, by the Accounts of Traders who have been some time with the Indians hunting in those Parts; One Remark of this Nature, may serve for the whole Tract of the Globe, Comprehended between the Western Skirts of the Allagheny Mountains, beginning at the Post of Ligonier, thence bearing S. Westerly to the distance of 500 Miles Opposite the Ohio Falls, then Crossing them Northerly to the Heads of the Rivers that Empty into the Ohio; Thence East along the Ridge that separates the Lakes and Ohio Streams,[1] to French Creek, which is Opposite the Post of Ligonier Northerly; This may be from proper knowledge Affirmed, that it is the healthiest, (as no Sort of Chronicle disorder ever Prevails in it) most pleasant, and most Commodious Spot of the Earth known to European People Supposing a State of Nature.

We remained near the Scioto untill *the 8th July*, Observed and found the Latitude 38° 22'. The greatest part of the Shawnese Nation were Assembled here at the desire of Mr. Croghan; Matters being Settled with them (altho' with Difficulty) We pursued our Route *the 8th July, the 16th* We Encamped opposite the great Lick,[2] and next day I went with a Party of Indians and Batteau-Men to view this much talked of Place. The beaten Roads from all Quarters to it easily Conducted us, they resemble those to an Inland Village where Cattle go to and fro a large Common. The Pasturage near it seems of the finest kind, mixed with Grass and Herbage, and well watered. On our Arrival at the Lick, which is 5 Miles distance South of the River, We discovered laying about many large bones, some of which [were] the Exact Patterns of Elephants Tusks, and others of different parts of a large Animal. The Extent of the Muddy part of the Lick is $\frac{3}{4}$ of an Acre. This Mud being

[1] This ridge crosses the state of Ohio from the northern part of Darke County E. N. E. to Trumbull County.

[2] Big Bone Lick, in Boone County, Kentucky, about twenty miles southwest of Cincinnati.

of a Salt Quality is greedily lick'd by Buffaloe, Elk, and Deer, who come from distant parts, in great Numbers for this purpose. We picked up several of the bones, some out of the Mud, others off the firm ground, Returned, proceeded next day, and arrived at the falls *19th July*.

The Ohio Continues to be Narrow the whole distance from Fort Pitt to within 100 Miles of the Falls,[1] it's breadth seldom Exceeds 500 Yards, and is Confined by rising grounds, which causes many Windings, altho' the reaches are sometimes from 2 to 4 Miles long: The longest of them and most beautifull, are (as has been said) above Scioto. The River, 100 Miles above the Falls, widens to 700 Yards in many Places, a Number of Islands Appear, the grounds diminish generaly in height, and the Country is not so much broken. Some few of the banks are overflowed in high Freshes, but this is but Seldom, and there is hardly any Place from Fort Pitt to the Falls, where a good Road may not be made along the banks, and Horses be Employed in drawing up Bilanders against the Stream, which is gentle if no Rain Flood is in the River. The height of the Banks permits their being Every where inhabited, nor do they Seem Subjected to crumble much away. The little and big Mineami Rivers [2] fall in below the Scioto, on the N. Side, and the Licking Creek [3] and Kentucke, on the S. side. There are many good Encampments on the Islands and a very remarkable Safe one opposite the Big Lick.

The Flood that Accompanied us many Days, left us at Scioto, and we found the Water at the Falls, low. The Falls ought not to be called so, as the Stream on the North Side has no sudden pitch, but only runs rapid over the ledge of a flat Limestone Rock, which the Author of Nature has put there, to keep up the Waters of the Ohio; And to be the cause of that beautifull Stillness of the Rivers course above it. That this Bed or Dam should not wear, it is made almost flat and smooth to resist less the current, which would

---

[1] The Falls of the Ohio are at Louisville.
[2] Little Miami and Great Miami.   [3] Gunpowder.

sooner get the better of greater resistance, but as it is still Subject to wear, there is made Enough of it, being two Miles wide, and it's length into the Country on each side, as covered with soil, Unknown. Mr. Morgan [1] unloaded one Third, and with the Assistance of the Indians, who knew the Channel best, and were usefull and willing, got his Boats safe down the Rapid on the North side. The Carrying Place is $\frac{3}{4}$ of a Mile on this side, and half as much on the S. E. This last is Safer for those that are Unacquainted, but more tedious, as during part of the Summer and fall they must drag their Boats over the flat Rock. Had we Continued with the Flood we should have had no Carrying at all. The Companys Boats that passed in April were not Sensible of any Falls, neither knew the Place where they are. In the course of Communication, a Serjeants Post will be necessary and usefull here, the Situation of it will be marked in the Plan. The Water was reckoned low at the Falls, it could not be otherwise, as since the Rain that fell at Fort Pitt where we set out, we have only had two Small gusts of about an Hours Continuance Each. The heats of the Day have been by no means intolerable, and the Coolness of the Nights have required a thick Blanket for Covering in our Tents. Notwithstanding of our Distance from the Fort being 682 Miles our Latitude is not much Southerly. At the Falls we make it 38° 8'. Another Observation before I leave this Place, which is that the Westerly, and South West Winds, generaly blow up the River, and will Assist that Navigation. Several pieces of Spar and Oar were brought in by Our Indians while we remained here.

We left the Falls *the 23d* and Encamped *the 31st* on a large Island,[2] Opposite the Mouth of the Wabash, which we make $317\frac{1}{2}$ Miles below the Falls. From the Falls to about half this Distance the Country is very Hilly, the course of the River very winding and Narrow, and but very few Spots of level land on the sides of the river. The Hills are mostly Stoney and Steep; but from the great herds of Buffaloe, we

---

[1] George Morgan. [2] Wabash Island.

observed on the Beaches of the Islands and River, into which they come for Air and Coolness in the Middle of the Day, it may be Imagined good Pasturage is not very Distant. 837 Miles below Fort Pitt, we leave the Ridgey ground behind, the Country grows flatt, and the River whose Bed widens, is often divided by Islands. The Navigation is good from the Falls; But where the low Country begins, Attention must be had to keep the principal Channel, which is in general to the right coming down. The Wabash is maskt by a large Island round which Boats may go most times of the Year. The End of the Fork of the two Rivers is narrow and Overflowed, 1½ Miles upwards it is higher ground. The Party of Indians we had two days sent before to View the Country joined us, and reported they could only discover Tracts of some small hunting or War Parties but none of any Number together. The herds of Buffaloe are hereabouts Extraordinary large and frequent to be seen. The River Wabash at it's Confluence is 306 Yards Wide, and Issues in with a Considerable quantity of Water of a Muddy kind. It is Navigable between 3 and 400 Miles upwards, but should be used by small Boats, as those of the Companys sent up it were obliged to be lightned in order to proceed; Indeed the dryness of the Weather had caused a lowness of Water in both Rivers. Observed the Latitude at Wabash 37° 41'. The Country between the course of this River, and that of the Mississippi is in general Flat, Open, and of a Rich Luxuriant Soil; That on the Banks of the Ohio is level and in many Places Overflowed hereabouts.

The 2d we left the Wabash in the Evening, next Morning we halted near the Saline or Salt Run, of which any Quantity of good Salt may be made. From this Place the Deputies from the Northern Nations, were Sent across the Country by Mr. Croghan to the Ilinois, to acquaint the Commandant and Indian People there of our Arrival in those parts.

The 6th in the Morning We halted at Fort Massaic [1]

[1] Fort Massac.

formerly a French Post 120 Miles below the Mouth of the Wabash, and 11 below that of the Cherokee River;[1] The Country 25 Miles from the Wabash begins again to be Mountainous, being the N. W. End of the Apalachian Mountains, which entirely terminate a small Distance from the River, Northerly; They are here between 50 and 60 Miles across, and are Scarpt Rocky Precipices, below them no more high lands are to be seen to Westward as far as those that Border the Mexican Provinces. The reason of the French's sending a Garrison to this Place, was to be a Check on the Cherokee Parties that came down the River of that Name, which is Navigable for Canoes from their upper Towns, and who harrassed Extremely the French Traders intending to go among the Wabash and Shawnes [2] Nations; The Situation of this Fort is a good one; Jetting with a Point a little into the River, the Reach of which up and down it discovers to a Considerable distance; a Garrison here will protect the Traders that come down the Ohio, untill they have accounts from the Ilinois; It will prevent those of the French going up the Ohio or among the Wabash Indians. Hunters from this Post may be sent amongst the Buffaloe, any Quantity of whose Beef they can procure in proper Season, and the Salt may be got from the abovementioned Saline at an easy rate to cure it, for the use of the Troops at the Ilinois, and in the other Posts on the Mississippi. The Situation is a good one, no where Commanded from, nor can the Retreat of the Garrison (a Consideration in the Indian Countries) ever be cut off; The River being, from the Entrance of that called the Cherokee, from 7 to 800 Yards wide. It will in a political light hold the Ballance between the Cherokee and Wabash Indians, as it favors the Entrance of the former, across the Ohio into the latters Country, and covers their Retreat from it, and there is no proper Spot for a Post nearer the Cherokee River above, or the Mississippi below, but this, as the grounds on the Banks of the Ohio, begin to be very low; The Current

[1] Tennessee River.   [2] Shawnee.

of the River towards the Mississippi is very still, and may be easily ascended if affairs are any way doubtfull, at or near the Ilinois.

7th. We got to the Fork of the Ohio in Latitude 36° 43′, about 40 Miles below Massaic, we took a Survey of the River in coming down, our bearings and Distances from the method we imagined, and carefully pursued, have a considerable right to be Exact, and have been Corrected with Observations on the Latitude that are to be depended on. The gentle Ohio is pushed back by the impetuous Stream of the Mississippi, whose muddy white water is to be seen above 200 Yards up the former; We examined the ground for several Miles within the Fork, it is an Aggregation of Mud and Dirt, interspersed with Marsh, and some Ponds of Water, and is in the high times of the Mississippi Overflowed, which is the case with the other sides of both Rivers.

9th and *10th* repaired the Boats, and fitted them strongly with every thing in our Power, to Encounter the Stream of the Mississippi, which we thought hardly possible, having been so long used to the much gentler one of the Pleasant Ohio.

11th August having been Joined by a Party of the 34th Regiment from Fort Chartres,[1] We began to Ascend the Mississippi, whose Rapid Stream has broke thro' the Country, and divided it every where into a Number of Islands; The low lands on each side continue 8 Leagues upwards, when it becomes broken, and small Ridges Appear for the rest of the Way to Kaskaskies.[2] There are many Islands in this distance some of which [are] entirely of Rock; That called by the French La Tour, which it much resembles, is 6 Leagues below the Kaskaskies River. The distance of this River from the Forks is 31 Leagues.

The Mississippi's principal Stream is from 5 to 700 Yards wide, but it is scarcely ever to be seen together, and some small parts are above a Mile distant from one another; The principal Stream likewise often Shifts, and the deep

[1] Fort Chartres was on the east bank of the Mississippi about twenty-four miles above the mouth of the Kaskaskia.
[2] Kaskaskia River.

Channels also which makes the Pilotage of the River Extremely difficult, and boats often get aground in ascending, chiefly when Endeavoring to avoid the rapid Current.

The 19th we got in the Morning to the small River of the Kaskaskias 80 Yards Wide at the Mouth, but deep 5 Feet, which it carries up to the Village, and is said to be Navigable 50 Leagues farther. A Detachment of 1 Officer and 30 Men are Quartered here, where We arrived the same Day, distant from the Mouth of the River of that Name 2 Leagues; The high Grounds mentioned, Skirt along the South side of the Kaskaskias River, come opposite the Village, and continue along Northerly, in a Chain nearly paralell to the East Bank of the Mississippi, at the Distance from it of 2 to 3 Miles; This Space between, mostly is Level, Open, and of the richest kind of Soil, in which the Inhabitants of the Ilinois raise their Grain etca. The Kaskaskia Village is on the Plain, it consists of 80 houses well built mostly of Stone, with Gardens, and large Lots to Each, whose Inhabitants live generaly well, and some of them have large Stocks of Cattle and Hogs. There was a New Fort begun by the French of Logs, opposite the Village on the rising ground, t'other side the River but entirely Commanded it. Ens[ign] Hutchins I sent by Water to Compleat the Survey to Fort Chartres; That I might [see] the Country, I went by Land.

The Road to Fort Chartres is along the Plain, passing in some Places near the Chain of Rocky heights above mentioned; The distance to the Fort is 18 Miles; The Road passes thro' the Village of the Kaskaskia Indians of 15 Cabbins, and afterwards thro' a French one Called Prairie de Roche, in which are 14 Families; This last is distant 3 Miles from Fort Chartres; Between is the Village called Le Etablisment, mostly deserted, and the Inhabitants gone to Misere [1] on the bank of the River, a little higher than Kaskaskias.

The 20th. Arrived at Fort Chartres, where I found a well

---

[1] Misère, misery, the popular nickname for Ste. Geneviève, on the Missouri side of the Mississippi.

imagined, and finished Fort of 4 Bastions of Stone Masonry, designed defensible against Musquetry; The Barracks are also of Masonry, Commodious and Elegant; This place is large enough to contain 400 Men, but may defend itself with a third of the Number against Indians, if care is taken to mow the Weeds near it, which grow to 10 and 11 Feet height and very rank; It is now in danger of being undermined by the Mississippi, whose Eastern Border is already within 26 Yards of the point of the S. W. Bastion. The Bank I found Thirty Feet high, Sandy with small gravel (very uncommon Soil for the banks of this river, that are mostly Mud or fat Clay) and perpendicular, so that the crumbling Occasioned by frost, would demolish in a little Time this small Space befor[e] the Bastion. When we took possession of this Fort, the River was above 100 Yards distance, and before that, the French who foresaw its Approach, had Expended much Labour and Money to try to prevent it. They Fascined and piled the Banks, but the torrent soon got Passage behind them; Had they brought the banks to a large Slope, retired those of a gravelly kind, so as to have an Eddy on them in Flood time, drove a Number of Button Wood Short Stakes in the Slope, which immediately take Root, and got together floating Trees, and anything Else of that kind the Floods bring down, made those fast at the Point where the Stream divides to come by the Fort, and round the Island opposite to it; This last might have averted the Strength of the Current towards the Western Bank, and by Stopping the Rubbish that comes along with the Floods, have formed a Bar at the Point; The gravelly Banks would not have resisted the Flood, an Eddy would have laid upon them, nor there have been any Resistance to the Current at Bottom, whose Effect would have thereby been diminished. Upon these principles I gave Instructions to Lieut. Pittman [1] Assistt. Engineer at this

[1] Lieutenant, after Captain, Philip Pittman was the author of the book, *The Present State of the European Settlements on the Mississippi* (London, 1770; repr., Cleveland, 1906), important for its excellent maps.

Post to proceed. The ruin of the Fort was Inevitable next Spring, without doing something, but a part at least may be saved, at a Small Expense, to lodge the Garrison till other Measures are resolved on. The Sickly State of the Troops did not allow of getting any Number to work during my Stay, nor was the Water low Enough or the heats abated to make much work, otherwise Adviseable.

This being the case I proceeded *the 28th* to view the Country upwards. Our own Boatmen being Sickly and much fatigued, I went by Land, Accompanied with Lieut. Pittman and Ens[ig]n Hutchins, to Kyahokie[1] 45 Miles distant from the Fort, and the uppermost Settlement on our Side. In the Route we pass Le Petit Village 5 Miles from the Fort, a place formerly Inhabited by 12 Familys, now only by one since our Possession. The Abandoned houses are most of them well built and left in good Order, the Grounds are favorable near the Village for Grain, particularly Wheat; and Extensive cleared Land, Sufficient for the labor of 100 to Cultivate. We turn off here to the Eastward, and in 2 Miles come on the high Ground, where We keep on till within 3 Miles of Kyahokia, when We Returned to the Plain to get to that Village. Here are 43 Familys of French who live well, and so might three times the Number, as there is a great Quantity of Arable clear land of the best soil near it; There is likewise 20 Cabbins [of the] Peiori[2] Indians left here, the rest and best part are moved to the French side, 2 Miles below Pain Court.[3] It is reckoned the Wheat thrives better here than at Kaskaskias, owing probably to it's being more Northerly by almost a Degree. At this Place We Endeavored to hire 3 Men and a Canoe, as we said to View the Missouri, but our Intention was as far as the Ilinois River. We could not prevail by Intreaty or Money to get such a Number, or even a Canoe to go with us. An Invitation came from Mr. St. Ange,[4] the French

---

[1] Cahokia, near the mouth of Cahokia Creek, and a little below the site of the present East Saint Louis.

[2] Peoria.   [3] Saint Louis.

[4] Saint Ange de Bellerive.

Commandant in the Ilinois, to go to Pain Court with promise to be Assisted in our progress upwards. We went to Pain Court *the 30th* where we Stayed next day, were civilly treated by Mr. St. Ange, and the other Gentlemen, but thro' a little Jealousy, were disappointed in going Upwards, and returned to Kyahokia *the 31st* in the Evening.

The Village of Pain Court is pleasantly Situated on a high ground which forms the West Bank of the Mississippi, it is 3 Miles higher up than Kyahokia, has already 50 Familys Supported Chiefly from thence, and seems to flourish very quick. At this place Mr. Le Chef the principal Indian Trader resides, who takes so good Measures, that the whole Trade of the Missouri, that of the Mississippi Northwards, and that of the Nations near La Baye,[1] Michigan, and St. Joseph's, by the Ilinois River is entirely brought to him. He appears to be sensible, Clever, and has been very well Educated; is very Active, and will give us some trouble before we get the parts of this Trade that belong to us, out of his Hands.

We found it Impracticable to go further upwards, without waiting for a Boat from the Fort, which would have been a long time a coming, and otherwise might have given Jealousies that would have Occasioned greater Disappointment, as Mr. le Clef is readily Served by the Indians, He has planted within 2 Miles of him: We returned to Fort Chartres *the 2d of Septr.* by the same Route we came.

Some Days were Employed in Visiting and directing Lieut. Pittman in the Work He was to Set about, and Composing Instructions regarding his Viewing the Country towards the Ilinois River, and likewise that on the other hand to the Ohio, and the old Post of Massiac. I found Myself no longer usefull at Fort Chartres and returned to Kaskaskias *the 6th.*

The next day viewed the Country round this Village, in order to fix a Situation for the principal Post, in case of the

[1] Green Bay, Wisconsin.

Demolition of Fort Chartres by the Current of the Mississippi, which most probably will happen in three Years time, perhaps in less; Viewed that part to the Northward of the small River, as also along the Bank of the great one upwards to search for a Rising Ground, and a Shelter for Craft, which now lays at the Village, thro' want of such at the Fort; We discovered nothing to purpose. The afternoon We crossed the small River, and a Foot, with much Fatigue, Visited the Situation of the Fort begun by the French as mentioned already. We found it a very good one accessible only on the East Side; the West by which we went up [is] narrow, Steep and Easily defended. It Commands the Town, and the River Below, overlooks the plain towards the Mississippi which does not seem 3 Miles across in a Straight line, and has a fair chance of being a healthy Spot, at least an Airy one, as it is high placed, on dry ground, and near good Water.

Our Possession of the Ilinois is only usefull at present in one respect, it Shews the Indian Nations our Superiority over the French, to whom, they can thence perceive we give Law; This is dearly bought by the Expence it is to us, and the Inconvenience of Supporting it. The French carry on the Trade all round us by Land and by Water; *1st* up the Mississippi, and to the Lakes by the Ouisconsing,[1] Foxes,[2] Chicagou,[3] and Ilinois Rivers; *2dly* up the Ohio to the Wabash Indians, and even the small Quantity of Skins or Furs that the Kaskaskias and Peiori's (who are on our Side) get by hunting is Carried under our Nose to Misere and Pain Court. A Garrison at the Ilinois River, and a Post at La Baye, will partly prevent the first; and one at Massiac will, as has been said, Stop their Intercourse with the People on the Wabash, who consist of Several Nations. Coop'd up at Fort Chartres only, We make a foolish figure, hardly have the Dominion of the Country, or as much Credit with the Inhabitants as induce them to give us

[1] Wisconsin.
[2] Fox River of Wisconsin and Fox River of Wisconsin and Illinois.   [3] Chicago.

any thing for Money, while our Neighbors have plenty on trust.[1]

8th Septr. We were prepared to descend the Mississippi, but that Night I was seized with a Fever, which continued

[1] The 15th of July, 1766, General Gage wrote Secretary Conway: "Advices from the Illinois mention an illicit Trade, whereby French Goods are Smuggled up the Ohio and to the Lakes, and the Peltry of those Countrys carried down the Mississippi to New Orleans; where Skins and Furs bear a Price of ten Pence Pr Pound higher, than at any British Market. The best Means, Seemingly, to prevent this Trade, carried on by Collusion between some of His Majesty's New Subjects from Canada, Detroit, and other Places, and the French Traders, would be, to pass a Law to Seize and confiscate all Furrs and Skins going down the Ohio below the Ouabache, or down the Ilinois River below the Rock, as well as all Skins and Furrs from the Ilinois Country or above it, which shall be found on the Mississippi below the Mouth of the Ohio, or carrying over to the west Side of the Mississippi. All foreign Goods found on the East Side of Said River, I presume are confiscable. It would be necessary to put such Laws in Force, that Posts should be erected on the most convenient Spots near the Junction of the Ohio and Ilinois Rivers with the Mississippi. It is not easy at present to ascertain whether the Ilinois would answer such Expence; It is reported from Philadelphia, that the Traders from that Province have sent Goods thither amounting, with Costs of Transportation, to £50,000 but it remains to be informed, what Returns they will get from thence: I would observe however, from the Plan adopted to support and extend the Furr Trade by Means of Forts and Posts in the Indian Country, that the Ilinois seems from it's Situation the most proper Place to Secure the whole Country Eastward of it to the British Traders, and to prevent the French gaining the Peltry from the Nations inhabiting the Lakes, and other parts of His Majesty's Territorys where fine Furrs are produced.

"The last Letters from the Ilinois are of the 28th of April by which I am informed, that a great deal of the Bank between Fort Chartres and the River had fallen, and it was apprehended that it would continue falling to the Fort before the End of Summer. From all Accounts the River gains so considerably upon the Banks every year, that Fort Chartres must soon tumble; nor can I find there is any Possibility to prevent it, by means of Facines or Pickets, or taking any other Precautions. The Situation of the Fort is bad on many Accounts, but the Construction of it the best of any yet built in the Indian Country."

with Unremitting Violence until *the 16th* at Night; *17th* being much better, I pursued my Route down the Mississippi *the 18th* tho' but in a weakly state of Body.[1]

Lieut. Pittman had made a Plan of the River in coming up, which upon Examining We found to be Exacter than anything We could do, in tumbling down this rapid Torrent. We therefore Continued to descend the River until we came to the Natches. To give an Idea of the Mississippi at this Season when the Water is low, One must suppose a large hollow in which You are, and a low Country into which You must descend. Where you are, on one side, is a Bank from 25 to 30 Feet high, where very often, you see and hear great Pieces of Mud or Clay, on which are growing Trees, tumbling into the Torrent; Round You is the Stream from 3 to 5 Knots an Hour in which are huge Trees in the Current, fast to the Bottom, but bent by the impetuous Stream, and some of them only bobbing up their heads, when their own Elasticity gets the better of the Strength with which the Water bends them down; On the other hand is a large Beach of Mud, Spread over some times with Sand, in which one or more Spots are seen covered with Trees; Before You is a quick descent of Country appearing much under You. This You see divided sometimes with Sandy Beaches and at others with Streams of Water interspersed with a Thousand Logs, and thro' which to direct your Course, is a very great uncertainty. When you Land, and with much difficulty Scramble up the Banks of falling Mud, You find traces of the Floods and Stuff that hinders your going far, or You find yourself on Muddy Sands, where you may wander among Pieces of broken Land for a Mile at least, without reaching the firm ground, indeed it has little Title to be

---

[1] For a letter by Croghan dated at Fort Chartres, Sept. 10th, 1766, and giving an account of his conference with the Indians at that place, see Hanna, Vol. II, pp. 49 and 50. Regarding himself Croghan wrote: "I have been so ill this fortnight past that I have not been able to write. . . . As I am so reduced in Sickness, I shall be obliged to go round by New Orleans, as I'm not able to ride a Cross the Country to Fort Pitt."

called so anywhere to the Westward, as there is no height to be seen nor any sort of Soil to tread on but Soft Mud, or among canes. On the Eastern bank there are the following high Lands after we passed the Ohio and before we reached the Natchez. Vizt. Mine au Fer,[1] those on Artaguet and Margot Rivers, that on the Yazous [2]; The Small and great Gulf where Stone is to be seen [3]: These are the only habitable Grounds above the Natchez.

It may be thought next to Impossible to Navigate against this Stream, yet Such is the force of Oars, that large Boats of 20 Tons are brought by them to the Ilinois in 70 Odd days, which is in some parts 500 Leagues by Water from New Orleans, when the River is low. At that Season there are many large Bends, along the inward side of these, the Boats get on as there the Current is not at all strong; when the River is high and [has] Overflowed it's Banks, the distance is lessened, and the Water does not run with such Rapidity as when lower and Narrower. In those high times there must be Tracks of Country Thirty Miles wide, overflowed. Those Boats go to the Ilinois twice a Year, and are not half loaded in their Return. Was there any produce there worth Sending to Market, they could fetch it at no great Cost. They bring however Lead, the produce of a Mine on the French Side; but it comes in but small Quantitys, they have not Skill in working of it, neither have sufficient Numbers of hands to carry it on. The Boats in time of Floods, which happen only in May and June, go down to New Orleans from the Ilinois in 14 or 16 Days.

The 6th October We visited the Fort at the Natchez, a Detachment of Sixty Men of the 21st Regimt, had come up to this Place Six Days before. They found the Fort in a repairable State; The Parapet made of Cypress hewn Timber,

---

[1] Near the present site of Memphis. The Rivière à Margot was either the Nonaconnah River or Indian Creek, or, if some old maps are to be trusted, the Coldwater then running northward into the Mississippi. [2] Yazoo.

[3] The "Petit Gouffre" was near Rodney in Jefferson County, Mississippi; the other at Grand Gulf in Claiborne County.

was only deficient in one Side of Five, which is it's Figure; Several of the Walls of the Houses and some of the Roofs were Entire, and the Bridge tho' not very sound, Served by being a little supported. It was lucky this condition was such, had it been otherwise, the want of either Artifices, Materials, or Tools, would have put the Detachment to great Inconvenience. The Situation of this Place is high and Pleasant, Commanding a Prospect of a very large and handsome Country, in many Places Cleared, diversified with gentle risings, which are covered with Grass, and other Herbs of a fine Verdure. It is $\frac{3}{4}$ of a Mile from the River, and cannot Command the Craft that lays under the Bank, a lookout for a Serjeants or Corporals Guard must be built for that Purpose.

The Natchez was among the first Settled Spots in Louisiana; The Soil is good on the highest Grounds, black and light, and properly Exposed for the growth of the Vine. Indigo will prosper on the flat Parts, or even on the ridges for some time; The Number of Mulberries, and the Climate are favorable for Silk, and Tobacco would be a. mere Drug there. The Place from the goodness of the Water, and Soil, must have good Air. It is in Latitude 32° 25', yet the Winters Cold is Considerable. The Distance from New Orleans is 94 Leagues, and 50 of them above their highest Settlement at Point Coupée,[1] (the few Banditti at Arkansas, don't deserve the name of Settlement) which most probably will be the highest for many Years. This is a proper distance to Attack from, but not Easily to be Attacked up such a Stream. The common Communication to the Natchez is up the Mississippi, but it may be supported down the Ohio, and a Force sent from thence, that will be truly formidable to our Neighbors below; Such is the Natchez. It's only Disadvantage is a Port to the Sea, the free Navigation of the Mississippi is a Joke, no Vessel will come to Ibbeville[2] from Sea, it was once done and found merely

[1] Pointe Coupée was, and is, on the west bank of the Mississippi, a few miles below the mouth of Red River.

[2] *I.e.* no vessel will come up the Mississippi to the mouth of the Iberville.

Possible at the King's Expence. Neither is there any Restriction by the Treaty from Building what Forts they Please at the Bar or on the River, as will certainly be done when the Spaniards get the Dominion.[1] In time of War they probably will make use of these Forts to keep us out of the Mississippi, which may be possible to do, as Vessels must Warp up to New Orleans.

The 8th We passed the River Rouge,[2] 50 Leagues up it the French have a Fort at Natchitoche. The Spanish Governor[3] went up to Visit this Post, as it is the nearest Place to Mexico, and not very distant from the out Posts of the Spaniards.

The 9th We went a Shore on the French Settlement of Point Coupee. It Consists of 110 Families, who live much at Ease; Their produce is at present only Tobacco and Corn, they likewise cut Some Lumber. They are not Strong Enough in Negroes to Attempt making Indigo, which is the only Reason they don't, Their Situation is low, and [they] are obliged to have Levée's of Earth to keep off the Floods: These People are much displeased at the Approach of Spanish Government. There is here a small ruinous Stockade Fort with 1 Officer and 10 Men in it.

The 10th in the Morning we Visited Fort Bute[4] which is 12 Leagues below Point Coupée; This is a Square with half Bastions (they had better been whole ones) of bad Stock-

---

[1] Though Louisiana was assigned to Spain by the treaties of 1763, Spanish occupation of Louisiana did not begin till March 1766, when a governor arrived, but without power to rule.

[2] Red River.

[3] Don Antonio de Ulloa, who, though without power to rule, went about at once upon a general inspection of posts.

[4] Fort Bute was at the junction of the Mississippi and the Iberville, the latter being an overflow stream of the Mississippi and connecting it in time of high water with Amité River and Lakes Maurepas and Pontchartrain. At other seasons goods were carried from the Amité to Fort Bute along the path following the winding course of the Iberville, a distance of ten or twelve miles. There was at this time a project for connecting the Mississippi with the Amité by a canal twelve feet in both width and depth.

ades. There are Huts in the inside for Officers and Men, for 100 in Number. The Intention of this Post is to cover our Communication to the Mississippi by Ponchartrain and Maurepas Lakes, and thro' the Gully or Ditch of the Ibbeville, when there is any Water in it which is only the case, when the Floods come down the river. The Bed of this was now 24 Feet under that of the Ibbeville. We Endeavored to View the clearing of this last, but were only able to go along it for 3 Miles, on account of the Rankness of the Weeds, thro' which there is no Path. The Bottom of the Ditch in that Space was pretty clear, only some Logs cut up, that are not cleared away. Had there been any Craft at the other End, I would have Endeavored to penetrate to it, and Viewed the Obstructions between the Amit,[1] and Lake Maurepas. Those are now the principal, and by Mr. Robertson Engineer's Report of them, they will require a great deal of Labor to remove; It is now to determine, whether that is to be done, or continue at the option of the French or Spaniards, for our Communication by Boats up the Mississippi; while they indulge us, they make us Pay for it, as I fancy the Expence of Our Equipments at New Orleans will Confirm.

The 13th we were within 2 Miles of New Orleans, we did not make this Day above 10 Miles, with all our Strength of Oars, of which we rowed 8, our People having mostly recovered, so Strong the Easterly Wind blew. The Colony of New Orleans is inhabited 20 Leagues above the Town on each Side the River, which is to within 10 Leagues of the Ibbeville. A little below this last place, the Mississippi Stream is less Rapid, the River Widens, the Banks are lower, and the whole appears more pleasant. The upper Settlers of the Colony are just Planted, consisting of Poor Acadians for the most part. But 40 Miles above the Town, You See well Built Houses, many Negroes, and Several Indigo Works in good Order. Of this last there is a Quantity made, and is Reckoned good of it's kind. The Plantations continue

[1] Amité.

JOURNAL OF CAPTAIN HARRY GORDON

well Improved towards the Town, whither We arrived *the 14th* in the Morning. There are no Nations of Indians below the Ilinois on the Mississippi, 'till You come to the Arkansas, they live up the Branches of the Arkansa River near the French Post, which is Half way to New Orleans. They consist of 150 Men. The Mississippi in Floods runs round the Island formed by the two Branches of this River. The Next Nation of Indians, is the Tonicàs [1] below the Natchez, a small Nation of about 30 Men; Then the Oumas [2] and Alibamous of about 150 both: The last has settled here lately, having withdrawn from the River of that Name, when we took Possession of West Florida.

Neither the French nor Spanish Governor were in Town; [3] The great aversion the Inhabitants had Shewed to be under the Spanish Dominion, and their Remonstrances against the Ordinances he Published, had Chagrined him so much, as to be the principal Reason of his Stay so long at the Balise.[4]

New Orleans is but a small Town, not many good Houses in it, but in general healthy and the Inhabitants well looked; It's principal Staple is the Trade for Furrs and Skins from the Ilinois, their want of Negroes keep back the Indigo making: They have Attempted Sugar, and there are now Five Plantations that produce it, but they do not make it turn out to great Account. There is only a Stockade round the Place with a large Banquet, their Dependance for the Defence is the Difficulty of Approach, that up the River is tedious and easily opposed, particularly at the Detour d'Anglois, and there is only 12 Feet Water on the Bar. The Military Force at this Place is at present Small, not above eighty Spaniards remain of those brought with their Governor; He, it was said, Expected 1000 Men, 300 of which would be Sent to the Ilinois, whether that Reinforcement was to Come from Old Spain or the Havannah, I could not learn with Certainty.

[1] Tunica. [2] Huma Indians.
[3] The French governor was the Sieur d'Aubry.
[4] Balize, at the bar near the mouth of the Mississippi.

483

Our Boat and Baggage being carried to the Bayoue de St. Jean,[1] for which we Paid 20 Dollars for the Boat alone, and is only 2 Miles distance; We left New Orleans *the 15th* in the Evening, and lay that night at the Bayoue. To this Place the Trade from Mobile comes,[2] and all manner of Smugling: There are Three Schooners, constantly ply[ing] between the East Side of Lake Ponchartrain, and here, Employed in bringing Tar. There is a good Harbour for Craft here.

The 16th in the Afternoon We went along the Bayoue, which is 2 Leagues long, and only Twenty Five Feet wide in many Places; It is deep enough but the Windings are so Short sometimes, that a Schooner has Difficulty to turn; The Grounds on Each side were under Water Except in three or four Places where Rice had been cut off, and in general the Country is Overflowed, between Lake Ponchartrain and the Mississippi, to within 2 Miles of the last; this particularly in high Easterly Winds, which was now the cause of the Waters Height. At Dusk we passed the Blockhouse at the Opening into Lake Ponchartrain, in which was a Serjeant and 12 Men, French and Spaniards, and some small Cannon Mounted; We continued Rowing till 11 o'clock and rested. Next Day by Noon we were across the Lake, the Wind in our Teeth. That afternoon we went down the Regolets which is the Communication between the Lake and the Sea; It is 2½ Leagues long and deep from 4 to 5 Fathom. In Crossing the Lake, We saw several Smokes on the East Side, which we were told by our Pilot was as many Tar Kilns; Part of the Produce we saw unloading at the Bayoue; We continued Coasting along until *the 25th* when we reached Isle Dauphine, the Wind contrary the whole Way; We Landed several Times, but were always carried or went in a Canoe, the Coast being so flat as seldom to permit Our Boat that only drew 27 Inches of

[1] Bayou of Saint John.
[2] This trade route passed along the Gulf Coast, up the channel to Lake Pontchartrain, and across that lake to the Bayou of Saint John.

Water to come near the Shore, one Place Excepted, which was during the Storm on the 22d when the Ferret a little way without us lost her Masts : We Landed several Times, and Saw the Shore the whole way, it is covered with Pines, and in general barren Land, but good for Pasturage. The few Inhabitants being only Six on this Tract of Country, that is near 100 Miles in Length, have Numbers of Black Cattle; Any Quantity of Tar or Turpentine may be easily made; One Crips, employs a dozen of Negroes on this Commodity, which he sends to New Orleans, to a good account. There are a Number of Cattle on Isle Dauphine, the only Stock [that] can live on it, its Soil is like that of the Coast already described.

The 26th. We Entered Mobile Bay and got to the Fort *the 28th* which is 160 Miles Distance from New Orleans; The Soil on the West Side the Bay, is better than that on the Coast, it will fetch Corn and Cotton, Garden Stuff and Excellent Pasturage. An Inhabitant called Rochon, has by Repute above 1000 Head of black Cattle, he has likewise a Number of Negroes, who he chuses chiefly to Employ on the Tar and Lumber Way.

There are Several good Houses near the Fort at Mobile; This is a Square with 4 Bastions, built of Brick in the Way of Revetment, with a Counterscarp of Brick and Glacis; The Barracks in the Fort are so low, that they are deprived of air, and are mere Ovens in the Summer time, from the Reflexion of the Sun. 60 Men will defend the Fort against Indians; The Navigation up the Bay, Ten Leagues long, is not to be attempted by Strangers, and it is only capable of Receiving Small Sloops; There are a great many King's Houses outside the Fort, that will be of but little Use, if a larger Garrison than the above is not kept there; Two Rivers run into the Bay from the Chactaw Countries, but I am informed most of the Trade of that Nation is carried by French Traders across Lake Ponchartrain, and up the Bayoue to New Orleans.

The 30th. Sailed for Pensacola, whither we arrived only *the 4th of November*, altho' the Distance is but 13 Leagues between the Bars; I should have gone much sooner in my Boat that I left at Mobile. We carried $3\frac{1}{4}$ Fathom over the Bar.

Pensacola Bay is a very good Roadsted, yet 2 Brigs, and 4 Schooners and Sloops, were drove from their Anchors and Wrecked, [in] the Storm of 22d last Month, altho' the Height of the Gale [was] off the Nighest Shore.

On Entring the Fort I was Astonished to see the poor Huts that are in it; but much more so when viewing the Condition of them, and that of the *Poor Soldiers* who inhabit here. Their Barracks are covered with Bark on the Sides and Roof, which naturely Shrivels in a short time by the heat of the Sun, which was the case now. The Firmament appeared thro' the Top and on all sides, The Men were walking About like Ghosts on a damp Sandy Floor, that is near a Foot under the Level. They were repairing the Roofs, but this has been the Bane of Cost, and but a short Time serving as a Cover never to keep out the Rain from those large Buildings; Some of the Officers Huts were Similar, only the difference of a few Boards laid over the sand to tread on, others of the Officers were well enough Lodged, but this the fewest part; The Hospital has only the distinction of always being first Covered, and the Provision Stores that of being the last. The Destruction of the best Regiments is thus accounted for, without the Climate, which yet I am apt to believe also does its Part.

It is high Time to fix the Necessary Garrison for this place, and as soon as that is done, to Erect proper Barracks for them. The Rooms should be raised at least 5 Feet above the Ground, there will be more and better Air, and I am Convinced be Healthier. In the furnishing of them, Attention Should be had in those Parts to prevent the Men from being Tormented in their Beds by the Muskitos, being open to them as they now are, Exposes them like the Beasts of the Field, to the Sting of these Venomous Insect or Fly, only there is not so many out of Doors, as Inside, nor do the Beasts Eat Salt Meat, as the Soldiers are obliged to live on, and therefore not so much Inflamed by their Poison.

The underparts of the Barracks, may serve for Stores of Different kinds. After this it ought to be considered in what manner the whole is to be inclosed; The Stockades round it at present, are and will be, totally rotten by next Year.

While We remained here I viewed along with Brigadier Taylor,[1] the Country adjoining the Town, in order to fix on proper Situations for 3 Blockhouses demanded by the Governor, for the Protection of the Town from the Creek Indians; These were accordingly fixed, and as the Situation of 2 of them will probably be Healthy, if Executed, They will be Convenient for Hospitals, when the Creek Alarm passes.

Having given the Acting Brigadier all the Intelligence demanded of me, and taken the proper Inspection and Informations at this Place, and a Vessel being ready to sail, that was to touch at the Havannah, [St.] Augustine, and Georgia, with the Approbation of the Brigadier Mr. Hutchins and I Embarked *the 12th*. *The 17th* in the Morning we were off the Havannah, but the Wind blowing fresh at N. N. W. we could not land with our Boat, and the Master of the Vessel having been threatened to be fired into, from the Moro,[2] the last Time he was at the Place a few Months ago, would not go in with the Vessel This Day we were off and on Sometimes within ¾ of a Mile of the Moro I could Discover very plainly the ground of the Cavannas, and all that from the Moro, to where our Encampment was, that the Artillery and Stores were Landed at.

The Moro itself is Compleatly repaired, several Casemated Cannon added towards the Sea. The Piece of Rock by favor of which the Assault was given[3] is blown level with the Bottom of the Ditch. The Counterscarp and Covered Way in good order, and considerably Raised; and a Re-

---

[1] Colonel William Taylor was acting brigadier-general in charge of the southern department.   [2] Morro Castle.

[3] The reference is to the action of July 30, 1762, in which the British regular and colonial troops, then besieging Havana, took the Morro Castle by storm.

doubt as before, in the Point towards the Sea with 4 Embrasures; A Counter guard or Fleche now making before the left, or Bastion next the Town. There is a very large Work Erected on the Cavannas, which by the Centry places on the Angles, I take to be a Horn Work, with a double Branch towards the Ground before the Moro. This Work is very nigh Compleat; The Bastions of the Town are raised Considerable, and a large New Work raised on Mount Jesus, the Form of which being at a greater Distance, I could not Ascertain. The Punto and North Gates are Compleatly repaired.

The 28th, 29th, and part of the 30th in the Latitude of Augustine, but the Wind did not permit us to Visit that Garrison, of likewise a Battalion; which altho' not in His Excellency's Instructions, should gladly have seen. Probably such a Dimunition of Numbers may Safely be made of Troops and Staff in these Floridas, as will defray the Expence of Accommodating them that Remain.

The 30th being very Short of Provisions, and the Wind just permitting to lay a Course for Charlestown, we steered for that Place, whither we arrived with some Difficulty *the 6th December.*

A TABLE SHOWING THE DISTANCES OF THE REMARKABLE PLACES ON THE OHIO, AND MISSISSIPPI RIVERS

	Miles		Miles
From Fort Pitt to Logs Town	18½	From Fort Chartres, to Cascasquia River . . .	24
Big Beaver Creek . .	29¼	Ohio	114½
Little . . Do.	42	Mine au Fer	129½
Yellow Creek	52	River Dartaguet . . .	236¼
Mingo Town	71½	River Margot	300¾
Long Reach	123¼	River St. Francois . . .	371¼
End of Do.	138	River Arcansas . . .	479¼
Muskingum River . .	161	River Yazous	637½
Little Kanhawa River .	172¾	Grand Gouffie	684
Hockhoking River . .	186	The Natches	729
Big Kanhawa River . .	266¼	Au Roche D'Avion . .	772½
Guyandot River . . .	308	River Rouge	783
Big Sandy Creek . . .	321	Center of Tonicas Village	811½

JOURNAL OF CAPTAIN HARRY GORDON

*A TABLE SHOWING THE DISTANCES OF THE REMARKABLE
PLACES ON THE OHIO, AND MISSISSIPPI RIVERS*
(CONTINUED)

	MILES		MILES
From Fort Pitt to Scioto River	366	From Fort Chartres to Beginning of Settlement of Point Coupee	813
Big Buffaloe Lick	390	The Fort	828
Little Mineami River	492¼	End of the Settlement	832½
Licking Creek	500¼	Center of les ecors du lait	835½
Great Mineami River	527	River Ibbeville	867
Where Elephants Bones are	560¼	Village of the Oumas	903¼
Kentucke River	604	Beginning of German Settlements	918¼
The Falls	682	The Fort	930½
Beginning of the low Country	837¾	End of Settlements	941
Large River on East Side	902¼	New Orleans	963½
Ouabache River	999¼		
Big Rock	1042		
Shawanoe River	1094¾		
Cherokee River	1107¾		
Fort Massiac	1118¾		
Mouth of Ohio	1164		

[Signed] HARRY GORDON.

Endorsed Captn Gordons Journal 1766 In Majr Genl Gage's (No. 5) of the 22d Febry 1767.

JOURNAL OF DAVID TAITT'S TRAVELS FROM
PENSACOLA, WEST FLORIDA, TO AND
THROUGH THE COUNTRY OF THE UPPER
AND THE LOWER CREEKS, 1772

INTRODUCTION

CAPTAIN JOHN STUART, Superintendent of Indian affairs
for the Southern District from 1762 to the close of the
Colonial era, experienced in that office some of his greatest
difficulties with the Creek Indians. The traders had promoted drunkenness and insolence among them. They
were habitually at war with the Choctaws. They were
frequently robbing and murdering white people. They
resorted to Pensacola in great numbers for provisions and
other presents. In November, 1771, Captain Stuart, with the
advice of Governor Peter Chester of West Florida, attempted
to negotiate with the chiefs of the nation for a strip of land
extending thirty-five miles up the Scambia River and four
miles back on each side, the alleged purpose being the
growing of rice and corn where it could be purchased for
the Indians at reduced prices. But the chiefs who came to
Pensacola in response to summons for this purpose alleged
upon their arrival that they were "without authority to
transact the business they came upon."

To bring the Creeks to a willingness to cede that land,
to promote peaceful relations among the Indians and between the Indians and whites, and to inquire into the relations between the Creeks and the Spaniards, Stuart sent
David Taitt on the mission of which his journal is an account.
In a letter to Hillsborough, dated Jan. 6, 1772, regarding
these affairs Stuart added: "As Taitt is a good surveyor and
a man of prudence, he will answer the purpose of observing
the disposition of the Indians and obtaining some knowledge of their intrigues with the Spaniards and the western
tribes as well as giving a more perfect idea of the geography
of the country in which all the printed maps are shamefully
defective."

After Taitt's return Stuart wrote to Hillsborough, June 13, 1772 : "The Upper Creeks in a general meeting refused to cede the lands which was asked of them upon the River Scambia, which Mr. Taitt attributes to the machinations of the traders, who grossly insulted him in the presence of all the Indian chiefs upon a supposition that he was to oppose the cession of land in their favor. Indeed the most dangerous consequences may be justly apprehended from their licentious behaviour." The 19th of July he wrote again to Hillsborough : "I . . . submit to your Lordship Mr. Taitt's journal of his journey through and proceedings in the Upper and Lower Nations as well as copies of his letters to me from thence; by which the licentious behavior of the traders as well as the temper of the Indians will appear to your Lordship. In the present situation of affairs I think it necessary to send Mr. Taitt again to the nation. His presence will be some restraint upon the white people there and by this means the necessary information relating to the views and machinations of the Indians can be obtained."

Taitt continued to serve as Stuart's deputy and in October, 1772, the Governor and Council of Georgia appointed him a justice of the peace in the Creek country to preserve order among the traders and other white persons and to report all persons trading with the Indians without a license. During the War of Independence Commissioners of the Continental Congress urged the Creeks to turn out Taitt, telling them he had done nothing but create disturbances among them, but Taitt kept the Creeks loyal to the British and led them in arms against the Americans. In 1777 he was engaged in litigation for the recovery of losses sustained in taking up seven negro slaves in the Creek country who had escaped from their masters in Georgia.

An original copy of his journal is preserved in the Public Record Office, London : C. O. 5, 73, pp. 551–617, and a transcript of this is in the Library of Congress.

INTRODUCTION

Instructions to Mr. David Taitt

MOBILE 20 January 1772.

I think it necessary for the Good of His Majestys Service in the Department entrusted to my Management to be very attentive to the Transactions of the Upper and Lower Creek Indians; particularly as I have received Credible Information, that Messengers have lately been in said Nations from the Great Western Confederacy of whose Business it is of importance to the Public Tranquility of the Southern Provinces, that I do endeavour to learn and acquire full Information. I therefore have determined to send you as a person well qualified and in whom I repose full Confidence, and you are to proceed as soon as possible with the Inclosed Letters to the Chiefs of the Tallipousses, Abekas, and Alibamons to the Upper Creek Nation and at your arrival in any of the Villages of said Nation you will apply to Mr. Joseph Cornal the King's Interpreter for said District who will be aiding and assisting to you in Conveening the Chiefs and Headmen together at some Convenient Place to whom you will Cause my Talks or Letters to be read and Interpreted, and you will Carefully and particularly take down in writing their Answers as well as any other Message or Talk they may have to send me.

You will by all prudent and proper Means without exciting the Jealousy of the Indians Endeavour to Learn the Business of the Northern Messengers as well as their disposition towards us and any Connection they may have formed or be about to form with any other Nation of Indians.

You will in a Particular Manner address Yourself to Emistisiguo and the Second Man of the Little Tallassies upon your arrival in The Nation, whose Advice and Countenance will be of great service to you.

After having delivered the Letters and Talks, and made the Enquiries Recommended, You will proceed to the Coweta Town, and after summoning all the principal Chiefs, You [wi]ll Explain to them the Letters for them which you Receive Herewith, and Endeavor in all your Power to Promote the Business therein Recommended.

As I have Received Information that there has been for some time past an Intercourse and Correspondence between the Lower Creeks and Spaniards, at the Havannah you are to use every prudent means possible to acquire Information of this Correspondence and the Views of the Spaniards and Indians and for this Purpose you will apply to Captain Aleck Great Medal Chief, Talleaché also Great Medal Chief and the Pumpkin King.

You are, if it is possible to be Effected without giving Umbrage or Raising Jealousy in the Indians, [to] Ride thro' all the Indian Villages of the Upper as well as the Lower Creek Nation, and take particular Notice of their Situation and make such observations as may enable you to draw a Plan of the Country and of the Rivers etca. You will take particular Notice of the Behavior of the Traders and their Method of Traffick and upon the whole be Particular in every usefull Observation of all which keep a Diary or Journal to be delivered to me when the Service you are going upon shall be performed.

After you have executed the above Instructions you will proceed to Charlestown and Report to me which I expect will be in the Month of May next, and you will be allowed after the Rate of Fifteen Shilling's sterling p[er] day for your Trouble and all Expences.

You will be very Particular in your Remarks upon the Rivers the Depths and Courses and the distances of the Roads and every Information which may enable you to lay down the situation of the Country of the Villages and of the Roads, you shall Travel as well from Pensacola to the Nation as from thence to Charlestown.

If Mr. Cornall be necessarily Employed and prevented from accompanying you to the Lower Creeks, you must apply to Some Able Person to undertake that Service in Case Stephen Forrest should not be upon the Spot and you will agree with such Person for a Certain Sum for which you will give an Order upon me.   [No signature.]

JOURNAL OF DAVID TAITT'S TRAVELS FROM PENSACOLA, WEST FLORIDA, TO AND THROUGH THE COUNTRY OF THE UPPER AND THE LOWER CREEKS, 1772

JANRY 30TH 1772. I left Pensacola about five OClock this afternoon and went to the six mile Creek, where a Mr. Cameron and two hirelings (who came to Pensacola with Mr. Joseph Cornal his Majestys Interpretor for the Upper Creeks) were Encamped, about 12 Mr. Cornal came out of Pensacola and rested at this place all Night.

Janry 31st. I sett out this Morning in Company with the four persons before mentioned to the dividing paths going to Mobile and the Upper Creek Nation, and from thence took the bearings and distance of the Creek path which runs mostly North and by West along the south side of the Conica or Scambia [1] River, in the Evening we Encamped at a Cane branch about 26 Miles from Pensacola.

Febry 1st. I sett out this Morning four minutes before Eight and took the Course and distance of the path untill ½ past two when we Encamped at a Cane branch, we travelled about Nineteen Miles this Day mostly North west and by west Crossing Several little runs and bogey branch's of the Scambia River; about seven OClock at night it began to rain and Continued to rain very hard all night.

Febry 2d. We set out this morning fourteen minutes after Eight and Continued our Course NW b[y] W about Eight miles, and then NNE Nine Miles and Sixty Eight Chains further, Crosing severall small Creeks and bogey runs, which fall into Scambia River, it Continued raining all this Day.

[1] The Escambia of Florida and the Conecuh of Alabama.

Febry 3d. This morning we had some snow and a very hard frost, we set out Seven minutes after Eight and Arrived at the little Scambia [1] or Weoka Twenty minutes past ten being six miles and sixty Chains NE from last Camp; the River was greatly swelled with the rains that fell the two preceeding days, which Obliged the people to Carry over the baggage and provision[s] on their backs; walking on a logg that lay three feet under water and aCross the Channells of the River. The River is divided into 2 Channells by a small Island about fifty yards Long and thirty yards broad, each Channell being forty feet broad, and Six feet and a half water in them at this time; but in dry Seasons the river is fordable at the South East End of the Island; on Each Side this River is a low Swampy thicket allmost two hundred yards broad and very difficult to pass through in wet weather, after Crossing the River we Travelled about $\frac{3}{4}$ mile N b[y] W to a little run where we Encamped about half past one and in the Evening Mr. Cornel Shote a Large buck, the Land from Pensacola to this place is all a pine barren, and in Severall places a brown Gravley Soil, With a number of little Creeks and Cane branches which cross the path and fall into the River Scambia.

Febry 4th. We set out this Morning twenty Minutes past nine, the Horses having strayed off in the Night detained us latter than usual, we went along the path NNE one mile and a Quarter, where we came up with Mr. Cornall who went off before us and had Shote another buck; here we Stoped at the side of a run (being the same where we were Encamped last night) to Dry the venison and wait for an Observation which I took at twelve OClock and found to be in Latitude 31° 14 minutes North; being 43 miles to the Northward of Pensacola Answering to 49$\frac{3}{4}$ English Statue miles, we stayed at this place all night.

Febry 5th. We sett out this morning two Minutes after Eight and took the Course and distance of the path untill fourteen minutes past two when we Encamped at a Cane

---

[1] Now the Escambia of Alabama.

branch Runing NW b[y] W into Weoka or Little Scambia. We went this Day mostly North and be [1] East 18 miles along a Ridge between the branches of the Weoka and Scambia River. This Day Mr. Cornall shote two young bucks and brought the Hanches to Camp leaving the body in the woods.

Febry 6th. We set out this Morning Nine Minutes past Eight and Travelled till Twenty Nine Minutes past three mostly NNE Twenty three Miles Twenty Chains, to a Cane branch Runing NW b[y] N into Coosa River, This Day we passed through some Oak and Hickory Land of a Light Sandy Soil; In the Evening Mr. Cornall shot a Turkey hen and brought to Camp.

Febry 7th. We sett out this Morning fifteen Minutes past Eight and Travelled Mostly NNE Twenty one Miles and a half to a small branch of Coosa River; where we Encamped in a strong Clay ground having very little mould on its surface. The path in this Days March is on a Ridge between the branches of Scambia and Coosa [2] Rivers, and mostley thro a pine barren.

Febry 8th. We set out this Morning a quarter before Eight and Travelled North East Twenty Eight Miles, and three Quarters between the branches of Coosa and Scambia Rivers and mostley Pine Barren.

Febry 9th. Last Night three horses strayed off and Could not be found till Eleven OClock this forenoon; when I sent off the packhorses, but stayed with Mr. Cornall and Observed in Latitude 31 degrees 54 Minutes North. I then set out and Travelled NE near Twelve miles to a hill where a hurricane has broke down and blown up by the Roots, great Numbers of Large Oak Trees; for the disstance of a mile and a half in a strong Clay ground. We Travelled on, Six miles further, NE to a small run, going into a branch of Coosa River. About a mile from last Camp we left the pine barren; and four miles from this Crosed the last

[1] By.
[2] Now the Alabama up to the junction of the Coosa and Tallapoosa.

branch of Scambia which this path Crosses; the ground here is of a very Strong Red Clay having about three Inches of black Mould on its Surface.

Febry 10th. We set out this Morning ten Minutes before Eight, and went NNE Thirteen miles and a Quarter to a riseing ground Clear of Trees or brush wood, for the disstance of $\frac{1}{4}$ mile in length, from East to West, and half a Quarter from North to South. Here I Observed in Latitude 32 Degrees 3 minutes North, after taking this Observation I went about NE b[y] E Eight miles to a Large Creek [1] forty feet broad and Nine feet two Inches deep; runing NNW into Coosa River; here we were obliged to Unpack the Horses and Swime them over; we walked upon a Log that lay aCross the Creek, and then went NE b[y] N Three miles and a half to another Large Creek 30 feet broad and Nine feet Deep, runing NNE into Coosa River; we were Obliged to Swime our horses here also, one of the Packhorsemen fell from the Log Laying aCross the River and lost two Kegs of Rum which he was Carrying on his Shoulder; but was taken out himself by another man who went to his assistance, we Encamped on the North East side of the Creek in a Large Cane Swamp and Continued here all this night.

Febry 11th. The Creek having fell Considerabley since last night the man went in Search of his Rum and found it (about $\frac{1}{4}$ mile from the place it was Lost) hanging to a Raft of Wood under water, we then went on our Journey NNE about Eleven Miles to a Large Creek Called Cathoma Runing WNW into Coosa River, and is about 50 feet broad and fifteen feet Deep at present, but is fordable in Dry Seasons, between this Creek and last Camp we passed thro several little Savannahs entirely Clear of Trees or underwood in the Middle, and Surrounded with rows of trees between Each Savannah making a very pleasant prospects for a Considerable distance and appearing more like the works of Art than of Nature, about a mile from Cathoma

---

[1] Big Swamp Creek.

Creek, on the South west side of it, we met some Shawnees, and one McFall a Virginia man, going out to hunt Deer. We went NNE about six miles further to the side of a Clear Savannah where we Encamped all this Night. Mr. Cornall the Interpreter having got Drunk with the Indians which we met set out for the Nation by himself and left us without any guide.

Febry 12th. I sett out this morning with the three people that remained with me, and went mostley NNE Thirteen Miles to the Coolamie Old Town [1] on the south side of the Tallapuse River. It was with a good deal of difficulty that we Could find out the proper fording place, as the River was Considerably Swelled with the late rains, and overflowed several places where the principal path Crosses. We however at last arrived at a James Germanys plantation whoes Negroes Carryed over my baggage etca. in a Canoe and Swame the Horses over the Tallapuse River which is about 200 yards aCross and about Twenty feet Deep at this time but is fordable in the Summer Season; after geting every thing over, I set out for the Tuckabatchie Town,[2] about 16 miles North from this and on the North West side of the same River, and arrived there at ten OClock at Night.

Tuckabatchie 13th Febry 1772.

I went this Day and viewed this Town which Stands upon a point of Land on the North west side of the River, the Town, or village is Scattered along the banks of the River for the space of three Miles round Each side of the point; which is from ¼ to 2 miles broad and nearley Cut off from the main by a Creek Called Wallhatchie which falls into the Tallapuse River about two miles and a half

---

[1] Kulumi, an Upper Creek town on the south bank of the Tallapoosa River, about ten miles northeast of the present city of Montgomery, Alabama.

[2] Tuckabatchi, on the Tallapoosa River between the present town of Tallassee and the mouth of Wallahatchee Creek.

below the point. The Land here is in Several places Sixty feet above the Common Surface of the River, but was Overflowed about two years ago and did Considerable damage to several villages and plantations. On the sides of this River the soil is of a Dark brown Colour, and produces Indian Corn Extreemly well; and would answer for any kind of European Grain; in the Spring all the fields are Covered over with Strawberries and wild Onions but the good Lands do not Extend above two miles back from the side of the River in any place Excepting at some particular points; in this Town are about 120 Gun men and two Traders. On the South East side of the River round the point of Tuckabatchie stands the great Tallassie Village which formerly Contained about one hundred men but now not above thirty the rest having settled two other villages one at the distance of Eight the other Twenty five miles from the Tallassies.

Tuckabatchie 14th Febry 1772.

I went this morning to the Town hot House where was only a few Old Men sitting and smoking Tobacco. When I went in the men present came a[nd] shook hands with me and offered me their Tobacco to smoke, afterwards they presented me with a Calabash filled with black drink made from the leaves of Casina which they parch in an Earthen pot till they are of a Dark brown Colour, they then put water upon them and boil it up till it is very Strong. They afterwards put a Strainer made of Split Canes into the pot and so take the drink out of the Strenner [1] with a Calabash, entirely free from any leaves, they cool it in a Large Earthen bowle by heaving it up with gourds or Callabashes till they raise a froth on the Top as Strong as that on porter, when it is Cool enough they fill some gourds with [it] and Carry it into the hot house in winter or Square in Summer, and present it to the head man or King of the Town first and likewise to any Stranger that is present two or three

[1] Strainer

men Singing while the others Drink. As soon as they have done Singing, they Receive the Callabashes from head man and Stranger and Exchange them that they may drink together, then it is handed all round to every person present without the Ceremoney of Singing or Exchanging Cups. The Square is formed by four houses about forty feet in Length and ten wide. Open in front and devided into three different Cabins each. The seats are made of Canes Split and worked together raised about three feet off the Ground; and half the width of the House, the back half being raised above the other about one foot; these Cabins serve for beds as well as seats in Summer. The hot house is generally built at the north west Corner of the Square having the door fronting the South East. The one in this Town is a Square building about 30 feet diameter rounded a little at the Corners; the walls are about four feet high; from these walls the roof rises about twelve feet, terminating in a point at top. The door is the only Opening in this house for they have no window nor funnell for the smoke to go out at, there is a small entry about ten feet long built at the out side of the door and turned a little round the side of the house to keep out the Cold and prevent the wind blowing the fire about the House; they make a Circle of pitch pine Split small; or in lieu of the pitch pine they use small dry Canes, leaving a small space of the Circle Open where the fire is lighted, still keeping some person Employed to add pitch pine or Canes to one part of the Circle while the fire Consumes the other. In this house the Indians Consult about the affairs of their Nation in the Winter Season and in their Square in Summer.

Tuckabatchie 15th Febry 1772.

I went this Morning to the Hot house and Stayed there about two hours Smoking and drinking black drink in the usual Manner, and about twelve OClock I went aCross the River to the great Tallassie Town which Stands on a fine plain along the bank of the River, and Surrounded by Little hills which begin to rise about half a mile from the River; in the Tallassies and Tuckabatchie there is about one hundred and fifty Cattle. While I was at the Tallassies the Dog Lieut. of the Ottesey [1] Town came to me, and wanted to give up a Commission which he had Received from Capt. Stuart [2] at last Meeting at Pensacola. He said that his Uncle wanted to have the Commission given to his son which Caused severall disputes between them and as he Received it from Captn. Stuart he desired that I would take it for him again as he did not Like to be at variance with his Uncle. I desired him to keep it till I Could have an Opportunity of Seeing his Uncle, in the Evening I went back to the Tuckabatchies.

Tuckabatchie 16th Febry 1772.

This day I went down to the River side under the bank on the south side of the point and Observed for the Latitude of this Town which I found to be in 32 Degrees 26 minutes North Latd.

Febry 17th. This Morning I went to Survey part of the River round this Town taking a Mr. Cameron with me to watch the Indians while I took the Course of the River and made the necessary Remarks, which I did partly from a small Mount near the Interpretors house, this mount as well as Severall others is of a Circuler form being about one hundred feet diameter at bottom rising about 20 feet Sloaping towards the top till it is about 50 feet diameter. This mount has lost great part of the North side by the River, these Mounts are Artificial but the Indians cannot give any Account of the Reasons of their being made. I was prevented going up the side of the River so far as I intented [3] having met with a party of Indians who were all very drunk they were accompanyed by one Francis Lewis, who was in the Same Condition as themselves, this Lewis who is a hire-

---

[1] Atasi; on the Tallapoosa, opposite present Sistrunk, Ala.

[2] John Stuart, Superintendent of Indian Affairs for the Southern District. [3] Intended.

ling to Mr. George Galphin at Silver bluff,[1] According to his usual Custom had met with the Indians (last night as they came into Town with their Skins from hunting) and Supplyed them plentifully with rum on purpose to get what skins they had brought in, and deprive the other Trader of any part of them. This man makes it a Common practice to give Rum to his wench for to purchase back the goods from the Indians, which he has before sold or Trusted them with, so that he is Obliged to fitt them out a Second time on Credit, which greatly increases their Debts to his Employer, but is a great profit to himself as the Skins that he purchases with Rum or goods bought with it he Claims as his own; this I have been informed is a common practice with hirelings in this Country.

Tuckabatchie 18th Febry 1772.

I went this Day with Mr. Cornall to the Ottesey Town about five Miles down this River and on the South side of it, here I met with the Dog Lieut. but as soon as his Uncle saw me come into the Town, he went and hid himself being ashamed of the dispute between them. I desired the Lieut. to Keep the Commission as he is the only good man that can be depended upon in this Town; in the Evening I returned to Tuckabatchie where a young man who I had sent two Days ago with a Message to Emistisiguo and 2d Man of the Little Tallassies was Returned with a Message from the later desiring me to stay where I was untill Emistisiguo returned from the Upper Towns, when they would come and see me.

Febry 19th.

This Morning a Mr. Vanden Velden, a Clerk belonging to a Mr. Mackay of Augusta,[2] came from the Little Tallas-

---

[1] Silver Bluff, S. C., on the left bank of the Savannah about twenty-five miles below Augusta, Ga., was the seat of the trading-post of George Galphin who has been styled " a merchant prince of the Georgia forest."

[2] Mackay's trading house was a half-mile west of Augusta.

sies[1] with a Message from Emistisiguo for me wherein he said that when he had any talks to deliver to his Father Captn. Stuart he went and delivered them himself and if I had any from his father to him, he Expected that I should go to him, this Message being very different from what I Received from the 2d man last night, I supposed it to be Mr. Veldens own as he seems to be a man that loves to hear himself speak and would wish to be thought of Consequence amongst the Indians. I desired him to acquaint Emistisiguo that I should be at the little Tallassies in two Days.

Febry 20th.

This Morning I sent to the half way house about twenty five Miles from this, for the King of the great Tallassies desiring him to come in to his Town that I might Talk to him there before that I went to the Little Tallassies as there was so much rain last night which Swelled the Creeks so much that I Could not Cross them to Day.

Tuckabatchie 21st Febry 1772.

This Morning I went to Cross the River at the great Tallassies but Could not get a Canoe and was told that the Tallassie King was not come into the Town. I returned to the Square in this Town and after black drink sent a man for my horses that I might go to the little Tallassies in the Morning.

Little Tallassie 22d Febry.

I sett out in Company with the Interpretor for this place which lays about west north west Twenty five miles from Tuckabatchie; about two Miles from the Interpreters house in Tuckabatchie Came to a Creek Called Wallhatchie which was so much Swelled with the late rain that we Could not Cross it; but were Obliged to go Round almost to its head. I took the Course and distance of the path as we went along till I arrived at this place which is a small village on the

[1] Little Tallassie stood near present Wetumpka, Ala.

East side of Coosa River about ten Miles above its Confluence with the Tallapuse River. I went to a house of Mr.
Mackays where I was met by the 2d man of this Town and
Mr. Velden, Mr. Mackays Clerk, who Intertained me very
well with some fresh pork and fowles, but in the Evening
when the grog begun to Operate in his brain he was Exceeding Troublesome in his discourse which was Chiefly about
the Indians, afirming that he Could make them as Obedient
and Submissive as any Civillized Nation in the world; and
that only in the Space of Six Months; without any Expence
to government, a thing impossible to be done. The 2d
Man Observed that Mr. Velden talked a great deal too much
and that he wrote all his own talks for he never gave any
other person Opportunity to Speak, this Evening the 2d
Man Sent a Run[n]er for Emistisiguo who lives about four
Miles from this, but he did not come this Night.

Little Tallassies 23d Febry 1772.

This Morning the Messenger Returned from Emistisiguo
desiring me to go to the Hickory Ground about four Miles
Lower down this River; the 2d man and Mr. Cornal went
with me and when we Arrived there Emistisiguo who was
sitting in the Square rose from his seat and took me by the
hand telling me that he had Caused his Square to be sweept
Clean to Receive me and that it was now white as well as
his heart. After the usual Ceremoney of Smoking Tobacco
and drinking black drink I informed Emistisiguo that I had
brought some talks from His father Captain Stuart, for
him and the other Headmen of the Upper Creeks. He
Observed that several Talks had met together in the nation
at this time and hoped that the Day would Come when he
shou'd hear them all, but he was now going to war and at
his Return would appt a meeting for that purpose, he said
that there was a Talk from the Merchants of August[a] which
one of their Traders had brought into the nation, desiring
the Creeks to Confirm the Lands granted by the Cherokees
to their Traders, and promising them a very good Trade if

they agreed to their demands, viz a Blanket which is Commonly sold for six pound of drest deer skins they would sell for a buck skin in the Hair; this he said was just like a man telling a fine storey to his Children to make them Merry at Night but in the Morning would be foregot. He said that one of his people had lately been to the westward of Mississippi and Observed some French people there very poor for something to Cover themselves with and what little Necessaries they had were Obliged to purchase them from the English in the same manner as Indians, viz with Skins. He desired to know the Reason of their poverty and likewise said that there was some Indians near these people who had only a little Moss to Cover their nakedness. He then made a Complaint against a James Lesslie, a Trader in the Abicouchies,[1] who he says had given him a very great affront some time ago. The manner of it was this, Emistisiguo being in the Town house in the Abicouches was Complaining to his people that the Traders had got a good Many Cattle in the Country Contrary to the Govr. of Georgia's promise, to him, and said that as the Govr. had given him Liberty to Kill any Cattle brought into his nation by the Traders without his Consent he wou'd not foreget the talk. Lesslie asked him who or what is the Governor? he is no King for we white people have but one King but in this nation we Obey non[e] but the Merchants that Supply us with goods. Emistisiguo said that he was always told that the Governors were great beloved men, and desired that I should ask Lesslie his Reasons for despiseing them and Affronting him before his own people; which I promised to do at first meeting when they were both present. About two OClock I went to Emistisiguo's House where he had Caused Dinner to be provided for me and the people with me, after Dinner I desired that he and the 2d man might go with me to the Coolamies, a village about 12 miles from the Hickory Ground on the Tallapuse River, this I did on pretence of giving them a private letter from Captain

[1] The Abikudshi, or Abacoochees, dwelt in a town on Tallassee Creek about five miles from its junction with the Coosa River.

Stuart; but on purpose to remove any Susspicion that might arise from my going to the different Towns to make the Survey which I intend; Emistisiguo Excused himself as he was going to war in a few Days and must prepare for that purpose but desired the 2d man to go with me. He then desired that I would give him a letter desiring the Inhabitants about Mobile and Tansa [1] Rivers to use him and his people well in case he should be Obliged to go that way and be in want of any thing; this I promised to give him, telling him not to let his people take any Indian Slaves or Kill any Cattle or Steal horses from the plantations which he promised to Observe, in the Evening I set out with the 2d man and the Interpretor for the Coolamies where we Arrived after Dark and Stayed at a James Germanys, a Trader in this village. The Indians in this Town were all very Drunk but not any way Troublesome to me this Night.

Tuckabatchie 24th Febry 1772.

This Morning a little before Day Messrs. Germany and Cornall and 2d Man of the Little Tallassies went with me into the Coolamie Square, where the Indians were at black Drink. The Head men Received me after their usual manner by Shakeing hands, Exchanging Tobacco and giving black drink, and after Day Light they fired a Cow horn in the Square. I then sent to the Mucklasses [2] for some of the Head men of that Town and some white men who were Idleing about, against whome Complaints were made by the Indians at last meeting at Pensacola; about ten OClock the Wolf King and a John Adam Tapley came from the Mucklasses; after the Wolf had rested himself a little, He made a Complaint against a John Pigg, a Trader in the Coolamies, accuseing him with haveing stole two horses from him. Pigg denied the Charge but accused one Aaron Whey, a Hireling of Mr. Richard Browns in the Coosadas,

[1] Tensas.
[2] The Mucklasses had a settlement on the Tallapoosa River, three miles below Kulumi.

who lived at Piggs house, when he stole one of the horses, the other horse the Wolf King had sent with a James Gray, about two Years ago to Pensacola to Carrey some presents from the Governor which the Wolf King had sent for. Gray sold the Horse to Captain Edward Crafton of the 31st Regt. for Seven Guineas, and told the Wolf King that his horse had Cut one of his feet almost off by some broken bottles in the Streets but gave him two three Gallon Keggs of Rum for him; some time after the horse Returned to the Mucklasses when the Wolf King took him again into possession, but Pigg hired a person to steal him, and Carryed him down towards Augusta and there sold him, and sent the wolf King a Kegg of Mixed Rum. I told the wolf King that I should make Whey Return the horse which was in his possession but as he had Received pay for the other already and the horse being gon[e], I Could not get him restored. I Expected he would be satisfyed. Immediately after the Wolf King had don[e], a head man from the Fushatchies,[1] a small village about $\frac{3}{4}$ mile further up the River, came and Complained against John Pigg for Stealing four horses from his Nephew, about three years ago. Pigg Acknowledged himself guilty and Accused three others with being Concern'd with him. I Ordered Pigg to pay the Indian immediatly for his horses, but he pleaded his unability and beged that the others might be Obliged to pay a part as they Received part of the proceeds. I acquainted the Indian that I should Oblige them that had stol[e]n his horses to pay him for them at which he was very well satisfyed. I then acquainted the Head men what bussiness I was come upon into their Nation and desired their Attendance when a meeting should be Called, which they promised to do. About twelve OClock I left the Square and went with the Wolf King and 2d Man of the Little Tallassies to Mr. Germaneys where we dined, after which the wolf said that he wanted to Speak to me in favour of the Traders who had got plantations in the Nation. I desired him to wait untill the meeting when all the Headmen

---

[1] Fusihatchi.

would be present which would be the properest time for that subject. I then took leave of him and the 2d Man and set out with the Interpretor for the Tuckabatchies where we arrived before Dark. When we entered the Town an Old Man told the Interpretor that there was a meeting apointed by the Morter, Gun Merchant and Paya Lucko, to be at the OakChoys[1] in fifteen Days.

Tuckabatchie 25th Febry 1772.

This Day I Received a Letter from the Morter with fourteen pieces of cane for a meeting to be at the OakChoys, and desireing me to send him a small drink by the return of the Messenger and if I had any talks for them this would be a very good Opportunity at their Meeting, the Messenger haveing returned last night I Could not send any Answer.

Tuckabatchie 26th Febry 1772.

This Morning I sent Emistisiguo the Letter which I had promised him, Likewise desireing him to stay untill the Meeting with the Morter and Gun Merchant was over, as I thought his presence Necessary at this time.

Tuckabatchie 27th Febry 1772.

I went this Morning to the Square to black drink and after breakfast went with a Mr. Cameron and Surveyed the River as far as the great fall which is about a mile and half above the Uppermost part of this Town. The fall is about one hundred feet high over Rocks which devid[e] the River into three Channels when the River is high and two when Low. Below this fall there is Several little falls and Rapides for the Space of a mile and half so that a boat cannot go further up then the Uppermost part of the Town. I Caused Mr. Cameron to watch while I took the Course and distance of the River etca.

[1] Okchayi, an Upper Creek town on Oktchayi (now Kialaga) Creek in the southeastern part of Coosa County, Alabama.

Tuckabatchie 28th Febry 1772.

This forenoon a Richard Baillie, a hireling Trading for Mr. Mackay in the Ottesey Town, came here from Pensacola where he and some others had been to purchase Rum with Skins. This practice is Carryed on by several hirelings to the great damage of their Employers as they Carry off the Skins which they have purchased with goods and barter them at Pensacola for Rum, with which they purchase more Skins or the Horses which are Stolen from Indian Traders, and from the different provinces, but for fear of being detected in this practice themselves they give the Rum to their Wenches who purchases these things as their own property, thereby depriveing the Merchant of his just Right and preventing any Recovery of Stolen horses except [by] paying them a very good price for them. William Simory, another hireling for Mr. Mackay in the Hochlawella Town, came here; this man is accused with telling the Indians that the white people was going to war with them this Spring; and that the Trade would be stoped, that Captain Stuart had been Sailing round their Land making Observations of their Country; and by and by will send Troops to their Country to take their wives and Chilldren. For a proof of what he had said, he and the traders for some time past, had been Ordered to Carry very little Amunition amongst them; this every trader knew, tho no one would tell them of it but himself, for he was a Dead man altho yet alive amongst them; as he had been formerly a Soldier to the great King and run away from him and would now live and die amongst them. When he came to me he behaved in a very insolent manner, Riding up to me in a very threatening posture. I made him dismount from his horse and Ordered him to atend at the Meeting at the OakChoys, there to Answer before the Traders and Indians, to what was aledged against him, which he promised to do. This Evening Messrs. Brown and Velden came here, the latter brought me a letter from Emistisiguo acquainting me that he was going to war next Day; and that the 2d man of the little Tallassies would be with me soon [1] Days before the Meeting with the letters which they had brought from Pensacola.

Tuckabatchie 29th Febry 1772.

I went this Morning with Messrs. Brown, Velden, and Cornall, the Interpretor, over to the Great Tallassies where the King of the Town and head men were in the Square at black drink. After the usual Ceremoneys, one of the Headmen said to the Interpretor that the Reasons of Calling a meeting by the Morter and head men of the Upper Creeks, was on Account of a Letter from the Merchants at Augusta demanding lands for the payment of their Debts; which Caused a great Murmering Amongst them. After black Drink one of the head men intertained us at his house with some bears meat for breakfast, in the Evening Mr. Velden set out for the Lower Creeks, and Mr. Brown for Coosada.

Tuckabatchie 1st March 1772.

This Evening the 2d Man came here from the Little Tallassies and Acquainted me that Emistisiguo was gon[e] to war and had left the Letters (which he brought from Pensacola) with his Speaker to Carry to OakChoys to the meeting. At night we were alarmed by some drunken Indians threatening to Kill a white Man, and promised to pay the Interpretors house a visit for that purpose, which Obliged him and the 2d man to go to Sleep at a Corn house, a little distance from his house. I however went to bed as usual, but about ten OClock the fellow who had been before threatning was setting out to pay us a visit and luckily tumbled over the threshold of the Door, and two of his Companions Entering at same time, one of them struck him with his heel in the Stomach which nearly deprived him of life and prevented him paying us the disagreable Compliment which he intended.

[1] Some.

Tuckabatchie 2d March 1772.

I went this Morning to the Great Tallassies with 2d man and the Interpretor. The Tallassie King and 2d man had a great deal of talk about the meeting apointed by the Morter etca but Could not persuade the former to go to it as he seemed doubtfull of some bad Talks being amongst them. After black drink I went with the Tallassie King, 2d man and Interpretor to James McQueens, a Trader in the Tallassies, where we dined and Stayed most part of the Day on Account of the Indians being Drunk at the Tuckabatchies. In the Evening I went over and was again desired not to Sleep at the Interpretors, as the Indians still threatened to Kill some person there. I was informed that Francis Lewis a Trader and one McFall had been drinking with them untill one of them flashed his gun at McFall and would afterwards have Killed him had not some Women put him into a Canoe and Carried him over the River to the Tallassies. As non[e] of them had been about the Interpreters house to Day I desired to Sleep here this night also. The Interpretors Wench then said that I was like a person Unacquainted with padling a Canoe but after being overset once or twice will take better Care in futture. The 2d man then said that he would sleep in the room with me and when any person came to trouble us he would desire them to burn the house with us both but we were not disturbed this Night.

Tuckabatchie 3d March 1772.

This Morning the 2d man and Interpretor went over to the Tallassies to black drink, where the 2d man Ordered the Interpretor to send to the Head men of the Towns on the Tallapuse River and desire them to attend at the Meeting which the Morter had Called, and there hear the Talks which I had for them. The Interpretor accordingly did. I sent for Frances Lewis and acquainted him that If the Indians were Troublesom hereafter I should send them to his house and Order them to take every Kegg of Rum which they Could find and not allow them to pay for it. He said that he had not any left and promised that non[e] of them should be made drunk by him during my stay in this Town.

Tuckabatchie 4th March 1772.

I went this Morning to the Hot House with the 2d man of Little Tallassies, where we had black drink and afterwards bears meat and Callavances drest in Oil, after which the 2d man spoke to the head men and Warriors of this Town saying that he Supposed they wondered at his not Comeing into there Square before this time, but when he came into their Town he saw them all drunk and not only so, but threatening to Kill the white people for which Reason he should not have come now had not I brought him. He said that it was with the white peoples Rum which they got Drunk with, and if they brought non[e] amo[ng]st them they would not be satisfyed, and they Could not live without the white people altho the white people could without them and Even these young people who wanted most to make war with the white people would be the first to draw back when their Nation stood most in Need of them. He said that he Supposed that there was not a man amongst them but would like to have a blanket to Cover them and likewise a flap for their wives and if they had Children would like to see them Cloathed. He Observed that they were already at war with the Choctaws and thought these Sufficient without falling out with the white people.

Tuckabatchie 5th March 1772.

I sent this Morning for my horses to go to OakChoys but they Could not be found which prevented my going this Day. In the Evening the Horses were found.

Cailedgee [1] 6th March 1772.

I set out this Morning with the 2d man of the little Tallassie and the Captain of the Hochlawella Town, and the

[1] Kailardshi.

Interpretor, from Tuckabatchie for this place which lays NNW Twenty five Miles from the former. This village is Scattered along the sides of the Oachoy [1] Creek for the Space of Eight miles, south towards its Confluence with the Tallapuse River. There are about Seventy Gun Men in this Town and Plantations and one Trader. At the Traders house I met with Charles who had brought the Letters from Emistisiguo with the white wing pipes and Tobacco etca, which he Received at Pensacola last meeting there. As soon as I arrived at the traders a young Indian came and desired me to stay with them this night and go to their hot house to black drink as their people were going off to war next Day. He went to the Hot house and some time after sent another to Acquaint me that black drink was ready. I went with the Interpretor and Trader etca to the hot house, and after the usual Ceremoney of Smoking Tobacco and drinking black drink we were intertained with the Warriours and Women danceing Round the fire in the middle of the house, till about ten OClock when I left them and went to the Traders house where I stayed all night. While I was in the hot house I Caused the Interpretor to speak to one of the head men who was not going to war and desired him to Attend at the meeting at the OakChoys, which the Indian promised to do.

The road from Tuckabatchie to this place is pretty good for space of twelve miles, being over a pine barren. It afterwards goes over Several little broken hills covered with Sharp Stones, very Troubles[o]m[e] for horses to pass, as far as a Creek Called Chinahatchie,[2] about 20 feet wide and one foot deep at present, being a flat Rockey bottom. The Oak-Choy Creek, on which this village stands, is very Serpentine and runs nearley South into the Tallapuse River. This Creek is 40 feet wide and 2 feet deep but not Navigable for Canoes on Account of Severall Rocks and little falls which Cross it.

[1] Kialaga.   [2] Cedar Creek.

OakChoys 7th March 1772.

I went this Morning to the Cailedgee hot house to black drink and Stayed there till ten OClock, at which time I set out for the OakChoys, three Miles North of Cailedgee and on the north East side of the same Creek. As soon as I arrived the Gun Mercht, or Mico Lucko, sent for me to the square to drink black drink where I stayed about two hours and then went to the Traders. In the Evening the Gun Merchant came and Invited me to the Square to black drink. This Night the men danced three or four times Round the fire in the hot house, and then the women danced the Snake dance, the leader haveing her legs Covered with Turpin shells which is filled with small stones on purpose to make a noise. In this dance there is two men sitting on a Seat with their backs to the fire and fronting the Women. As they come Round the men ratle a small Callabash in their hands singing all the while the women are danceing round. This dance lasted about two hours, when I left the house; but the Indians stayed all night.

OakChoys 8th March 1772.

This being the Day appointed for the meeting of the head men, but the Morter and several others not being come no business Could be done. In the afternoon I went about three mile further up the Creek to see a Ball play between the Men of this Town and these of the fish Pond, a village belonging to this laying about Seven Miles North East on a Creek Called Elkhatchie, which falls into the Oakfuskee River above that Town. In the Evening I returned to this place where Paya Lucko was Arrived from Oakfuskee.

OakChoys 9th March 1772.

I waited all this day for the Morter but he did not come.

OakChoys 10th March 1772.

This day the Morter and other head men came and Likewise severall Traders and hirelings. This Evening the In-

517

terpretor spoke to Paya Lucko, about giving Satisfaction for the white man that was Killed in the Hillabies, and likewise Concerning some Indians threatening his life, for demanding Satisfaction for the last that was Killed. Paya Lucko said that it was part of the bussines of this meeting to settle every thing of that Kind and as he was one of the heads of the family who lost the last man for Satisfaction, every thing should now be settled so that he need not be any more affraid of his life on that Account.

OakChoys 11th March 1772.

This Morning after the headmen had finished their private bussines the Morter desired that I would let them hear the Talks which I had from their Father for them. The Gun Mercht at same time enquired of the Traders for a letter which the Merchts at Augusta had sent into the Nation, but the Traders denyed knowing any thing of such a letter. I delivered the Letters which Emistisiguo brought from Pensacola in Novr. last and these which I had from Captain Stuart [1] about the lands on Scambia, which the Chiefs promised to answer next Day.

[1] With his instructions Taitt received two letters to the Upper Creeks. One of these was as follows:

20th January 1772.

To the Great and Small Medal Chiefs and all the Head men and Leaders of the Abekas, Tallepusses and Alibamons in the Upper Creek Nation.

FRIENDS AND BROTHERS,

This will probably meet you at your return from Hunting and will be delivered by a beloved man who I send to be present at your meeting, where you will consider of and answer the Message sent you by Emistisiguo and your other Chiefs who were at Pensacola, who no Doubt have acquainted you of our Talks when there, and which I hope will prove agreeable. The Bearer Mr. Taitt will immediately send off an Express, to Acquaint me with your Determination with Respect to the Scambia or Conica Lands.

As the Parties going to War who cross over to our Settlements on the West side of Mobile Bay have for some time past made it a practice to rob and plunder the Plantations, and Kill poor

OakChoys *12 March 1772*.

This Morning I went to the hot house where Mico Lucko brought in a white Skin with some Tobacco and a Red pipe

Peoples Cattle, by which many Families have been greatly distressed I send the Bearer of this to Speak with the Chiefs of the Lower Towns, and to see if a stop can be put to such proceedings, for all the Parties who have committed such Violences came from the Lower Towns, and as you know that such Insults are inconsistent with the Peace and Friendship which ought to subsist between you and your white Brethren, I hope you will Join me in endeavoring to prevent and stop them and that you will send a Messenger and a Talk with this Beloved man to the Cowetas and Lower Towns concerning these Robberies.

When Mr. Cornal Arrived here he found the great Leader and other Chiefs of the Chickasaws with me. Their Talks are good as they always have been they acquainted me of Several Messages sent to them by the Northern Indians thro' your nation. They also desired me to acquaint you that as you and the Chactaws are both their Friends, they hope you will not carry on the War against each other through their Towns, but find another Road to your Enemies. That if your parties should at any time be Hungry and in Want of provisions they will be glad to Treat you as Friends and supply your Wants, but they will not suffer either you or the Chactaws to carry Prisoners thro' their Towns, they will not meddle with Scalps but they will set the Prisoners taken by their Nation at Liberty if they are carried into their Towns.

I recommend to you to pay Attention to the Talks of Paya Mattaha, he is a Warrior of great Experience and Judgment, and you may be sure he will always Give you good advice, he is a Red man and loves the Red People, and for their sake holds me fast by the hand for he knows that I am the Father and Friend of Red men.

I add no more at present but referr you to my former Talk to which I expect a favourable answer.

I am
Your Friend and Brother
signed J. S.

The other letter from Stuart was in part as follows:

Jan. 20, 1772.
To the Great Chiefs of the Upper Creek Nation:
. . . "You acted like Good and just Men in giving satisfaction for the two White Men Killed on the Mobille or Chactaw Road.

519

rolled up in the skin which was sent from the Quarpas [1] or Arkansaws (a small nation on the west side of Mississippi) with a peace talk to the Chickasaws and from thence to this place. The Morter gave me some of the Tobacco to smoke with them while Mico Lucko delivered the talk to the Headmen and Warriours but as the Interpretors went out of the house before this was given I Could not learn what it was. After this bussines was over, the Morter, Mico Lucko, and Stocklitea, or white Lieut., gave me an Answer to the Letters which I had delivered to them Yesterday but desired me not to demand Satisfaction publickley, but promised to give it as soon as they Could get an Opportunity to do it, as they Could not Kill any person publickley. In this Town and villages belonging to it is about 70 Gun

You also promised Satisfaction for a man Killed at the Hillabies, but this you have failed in, and the Murtherer still Lives. Two men have since been Killed upon the Occonies: so that there are three Murthers unsatisfied by you. You say you lost a man at Augusta last year, and that he was beaten by a white man in such a manner as to cause his Death. Governor Wright acquaints you in his Talk that his Death was Owing to Drunkenness and the oversetting of a Canoe by Accident; the case is not Clear, however supposing that you are Right and that it ought to pass in Satisfaction for one of the three Deaths which you Owe; Mr. Cornal says that a Party who had stolen Horses from the Inhabitants of Little River was pursued by the owners, and that one Man of yours was killed. This practice of Robbing the Settlements has often been complained of: and amongst all Nations killing a man in defence of a Persons Just property is allowed of. However upon the present Occasion should the Death of this Robber be allowed to pass as further satisfaction even then you would still be indebted for one Murther unattoned for. Your Justice will point out what is to be done and what we expect. . . .

"I have often told you that no Talks about Land should be Listened to except what should come from me. I also told you in my former Talks and to your Warriors at Pensacola that the Lands Ceded to the Traders by the Cherokees was without my knowledge and without any Orders from the King. I had received no Orders to ask those Lands of the Cherokees — I have none to ask them of or take them from You. . . ."

[1] Quapaws.

Men and one Trader. In the Evening I went to Cailedgee where I stayed all night.

Tuckabatchie 13th March 1772.

This Morning I set out from Cailedgee with the Interpretor, 2d man of the little Tallassies, and Hochlawella Captain. At Cailedgee I was Obliged to purchase a horse from the Trader, having delivered one to the Hochlawella Captain, and which I bought at Mobile, but was stolen about three years ago by one Colbert, a Trader, in the Chickasaws when he passed thro the Abicouches to that Nation. In the Evening we Arrived at this place.

Tuckabatchie 14th March 1772.

This Day the 2d man Returned to the little Tallassies and the Captain to Hochlawella.

Tuckabatchie 15th March 1772.

This Day I wrote a Letter to Captain Stuart with the Indians Answer to him about the Scambia Lands, and In the Evening a McFall, whom I had Engaged to go to Pensacola with them, came here for that purpose.

Tuckabatchie 16th March 1772.

This Morning I sent off McFall with the letters for Pensacola and in the afternoon the Ottesey Captain (who had been appointed by the Headmen to go with the beaver Tooth King of the great Tallassies, to the Lower Creeks, when I should go there) came here, and acquainted me that he Could not go to the Lower Creeks, as he must go to war on Account of his Nephew whose life was in danger from having Killed an Indian in Rum drinking a little time ago.[1]

[1] On this day Taitt wrote the following letter to Stuart:

TUCKABATCHIE, 16 March 1772.

SIR:

I arrived in this Nation the 12th of Last Month and on the 14th sent a Messenger to the little Tallassies for Emistisiguo and the 2nd man; the 2nd man sent an answer by the Messenger

Tuckabatchie 17th March 1772.

This Morning I sent my Servant to the white ground with a pack horse for McFall to take to Pensacola.

that Emistisiguo was gone to the Upper Towns and as soon as he had returned they would come and see me; the Day after I had Received this Answer a Mr. Vanden Velden a Cracked brained dutchman, Clerk to Mr. Mackay came from the little Tallassies with a message from the big fellow: wherein he said that when he had a Talk to Deliver to you He went with it himself and if I had any Talk from You he Expected the same Compliment paid to him and that he was going to war in a few days.

I looked upon this Message to be Velden's own as he was very Solicitous to know my Business here; on Account of some Talks which the Merchants in Augusta has sent to the Upper and Lower Towns; about the Lands which the Cherokees gave to their Traders; this man is Employed in Rideing about the nation with an Interpreter; On the 22nd I went to the little Tallassies where I met the 2nd man with whom I went next morning to the Hickory ground about four miles Lower down the Coosa River where the big fellow lives; I stayed with him most part of the day but could not give him your Talk on Account of the people present. He Acquainted me that he was going to war in four days and as soon as he returned he would appoint a meeting of all the Upper Creeks, he likewise desired that I would give him a letter desiring the Inhabitants on Mobile River to use him Civilly in Case he should have Occasion to go that way; in the evening I set out with Mr. Cornell and 2nd man and went to the Coollimies a Small Town upon the Tallapuse River about Twelve miles distant from the Hickory ground; at and near this Town lives most of the Idle people and Hunters which Complaints were made against at last meeting at Pensacola, which was the reason of the 2nd mans Comeing here to speak to them, Next Morning The Wolf King and a head man Called The Setter came to this Town and made a Complaint against one John Pigg a Trader for Stealing five Horses, Pigg acknowledged to be concerned with four other persons in Stealing four of the horses. I ordered him to restore the horses that was in any of their possessions and to pay for what might have been sold or lost by him and his accomplices; As I have no authority to punish ofenders of this kind I cannot oblige them to punish Indians unless they please, but shall do all I can to persuade them as Indians will certainly make reprizals if they cannot get their own, in the evening the 2nd man returned to the little Tallassies as did Mr. Cornell and self to this Town. On the 25th I received a letter from the Morter

JOURNAL OF DAVID TAITT

Tuckabatchie 18th March 1772.

This Day the Indians in this Town being all very drunk, I went over to the Tallassies where I stayed most part of for a meeting to be at the Oak Choys the eight[h] of this Month, the Morter had heard of my being here after he had appointed the meeting; therefore desired if I had any Talks to give them that I would come there as he expected the lower Creeks; I sent a Messenger to Emistisiguo with a letter desireing him to stay till this meeting was over before he went to War. He sent for answer that I now had an opportunity of delivering Talks which I had brought from you without giving myself much Trouble or waiting long for his return which was uncertain. He was now pursuing Steps in the same manner as white people who never begin a work and leave it half finished. He was going after a single life at which he would be satisfied. He likewise Observed that the fighter was not yet come that when he Came and they went to run the line the Weather would be very hote so that a great allowance of Rum must be given them such as Six Hogsheads three or four would not do; He said there would be Copers and White people present at the meeting and no doubt but his Intentions would be oposed but said he should have every thing if he returned alive.

On the 1st Inst. the 2nd man came here and acquainted me that Esmistisiguo was gon[e] to war and had left the Talks etca which he brought from Pensacola with his speaker and desired that they might be first read at the meeting; I set out on the 6th with Mr. Cornell the 2nd man and Captain Tanahopaya of Hochtawella Town for the Oak Choys, we waited there four days before the Morter came; on the 11th Inst. after they had settled the Business which they met upon which was in regard of giving Satisfaction to pacify those families who had lost their Relations; the Gun Merchant acquainted me that they had finished their bussiness that the path was Clear and the White people might now pass and repass in safety, The Morter then desired that if I had any Talks I might read them. [At the] same time the Gun Merchants asked the traders for the paper from Augusta but they denied knowing anything about it, I delivered your letter which Emistisiguo brought and then Governor Chesters about the Scambia or Conica Lands as likewise what I brought from you excepting the one for satisfaction as the Morter and Gun Merchants assured me that that bussiness was already agreed upon and that they did not want it made publick for fear of the Offenders being too much upon their guard or make their escape, On the 12th I received the answers which is here enclosed.

the Day and in the Evening I sent for the beaver Tooth King, and desired him to go to the Lower Creeks and deliver the Message which he had Received at last meeting; as I

The whole Chiefs of the Abeckas or upper towns were present, five of the Tallapusses and two Alibamons but none of the lower Creeks, You will plainly observe by these answers that the Nation is divided one part against another which is caused by a jelousy subsisting between the Abeckas and Tallapusses in regard of the respect that has been of late showed to Emistisiguo, who unfortunately is of a Slave race; but I suppose when he and the fighter comes in, the scale may turn as the Tallapusses and Alibamons seem inclined to give up the Land that you have asked from them, on the other hand the Merchants and Traders in this Nation does all in their power to make every measure you propose prove abortive; the Interpreter seems to know very few head men above the Town in which he lives, although in my opinion those in the Upper Towns carry the greatest authority I have not as yet been able to compleat the Bussiness which I came upon in this nation as I found the Indians in such a Situation by the Idle speeches of some unworthy hirelings to whom the Merchants in Augusta had made known some of their Intentions that if I had been observed in doing the smallest matter I must have run a very great risk for what the Indians does not understand themselves the Traders will assist them and you know the Indians jelous disposition; I hope to complete every thing before the Express returns which I shall wait for in this Nation, as I have no authority to make any demands of Land from the lower Creeks.

Mr. Mackays Clerk has been gone to them some time to try what he can do for the Merchants; their meeting in the upper Creeks is proposed to be on the 10th April and in the Lower on the 20th of same month, Mr. Golphin [George Galphin] has taken upon himself to get the Consent of the Lower Creeks, and they are to ask for some more Land than what the Cherokees gave to pay the Debts due by the Creeks and the traders, and in case of a Refusal to stop sending any Goods amongst them this summer which some of the Traders has already acquainted the Indians with, some of the Merchants letters I have seen, and particularly one to Mr. Cornell from a Mr. Greerson [Grierson] in Augusta acquainting him with their letter which they had sent into the Nation by a Mr. Rea a Trader in a small Village belonging to the Oakfuskies, whose speech the white Lieutenant delivers; Mr. Greerson first desires Mr. Cornell to give them all the assistance in his power withall threatening him with the heavy debt which hangs over his head

Could not go untill that I heard from Captain Stuart, I likewise desired him to enquire if Stephen Forest was come

then promising the forgiveness of all his debts besides pecuniary Emolument in case he succeeds, this Mr. Greerson says is the conditions on which Mr. Forester is to go to the lower Towns; whether Cornell may take the bait I cannot tell he has already refused to go to the Lower Towns because I told him that I would not allow him to give out the Merchants talk, after he had promised Mr. Rea; I should not have Exposed Mr. Greerson's letter till I had the pleasure of seeing you had not his brother advised some of the head men whom I had asked to the meeting not to go, telling them that I was not a beloved man but some runaway he took care not to make his appearance after that he found that I had heard his talk. The traders in this Nation excepting a very few are Composed of Deserters, Horse thieves, half breeds and Negroes. They all trade without any Licenses or permits; the Merchants fits out some Traders with goods on their own acct. and others they hire to trade in opposition to the Traders; these hirelings fits out others which they find Ideling about the Nation so that in some Towns there is three or four Stores where one would be Sufficient, all Trade without any Regulations whatsoever and undersell one another to that degree that goods are sold at first cost or rather given away. Some indeed will give a Kegg of Rum to every fellow that will sell his Skins to them. Some of these hirelings after getting a few Skins with the Goods which the Merchant has entrusted him with, Carrys them to Pensacola where they Barter them with the Merchants for Rum; with it they buy the Horses which the Indians steal from the Settlements of the Different Provinces. Unless there is a Stop put to sending Rum in such large quantities amongst these Indians no man will be safe amongst them for after one trader has made them Drunk he will send them to his Neighbour to break his Doors and plunder him which has been attempted to be done in this Town since my comeing here, one Francis Lewis a Hireling of Mr. Golphins had near thirty Keggs in his house at my Arrival which has keep't this Town Continually Drunk, there is many others in the Nation of the same stamp as this man, Some Carries on no other trade than buying of Horses with Rum; These men I think should be sent to some other place as the Indians are Continually Complaining against them.

There was a talk from the Quapas with a White Skin, a pipe and some Tobacco delivered to the head men at this Meeting; about Thirteen Chickasaws were at the Abicouchies lately want-

up from Augusta. He promised to set out in a few Days, and at same time said that when he was going to the Meeting to settle in this Nation: the Head man of that Town gave them leave to settle the Ground they formerly Possessed on Condition of their Continuing in this Land, they returned to their own lands and it is uncertain whether they come back. There has been Complaints made to me by the Head men of some Towns on this River against their having to many Traders, particularly the Captn of Hocktawella Complains of having three Traders in his Town where there is only about Seventy Gun men. He says that when the last Trader came there which is about two months ago the head men advised him not to open his Goods but go somewhere else, but their advise was to no purpose, he says that the Young Fellows will have the Goods when they are brought amongst them and will never be able to pay for them.

I have made the Observations recommended by you in respect to the Country from Pensacola to this place and likewise taken the Latitudes of Different places; about two miles N b[y] E from Crossing little Scambia I observed in Latitude 31.14. This Town is in Latitude 32.36 and is the farthest any Boat or Canoe can go by this River on account of falls which begin at the upper end of the Town and at 1½ miles above the Town is one about one hundred feet high. My Quadrant is now of no use the Sun being got too far to the Northward for observing by Land.

The King of this Town desires that you will be so good as [to] send a small drink by the Bearer, as he says by the time that he returnes Emistisiguo will be come in and we shall have more talks which will be more agreeable to you than these you now receive; I was obliged to give a kegg of Rum in lieu of the wine which was promised in the talk that Esmistisiguo carried.

The bearer is McFall who[m] the Complaints was made against for hunting; he has delivered himself up and promises not to hunt any more. As to Horse Stealing I do not find that ever he has brought any into this part, if you have any Letters to send I shall be obliged to you to dispatch him as soon as possible, any bussiness you think proper to entrust me with while in this nation shall be punctually executed by giving me proper Authority. One of the lower Creeks killed a man down at the Ogeechie some time agoe. I hear that Mr. Habersham had desired Mr. Golphin to send and demand Satisfaction. Whether it has been done or not I cannot say but the murderer still lives.

I remain with the greatest Esteem,
Sir your Most Obedt and most hum[ble] S[ervan]t

(Signed)   DAVID TAITT.

ing at OakChoys he Called at the Upper Euffallas [1] where he saw a Trader named Thomas Greerson,[2] who desired him not to go to any meeting, telling him that I was not a beloved man but some runaway who wanted to Oppose them in their Land affair by saying that I had Letters for the Indians. The beaver Tooth King answered Greeson saying that he knew that the white people had Laws to punish any person that offered to Commit such things as he had mentioned, and he had already seen me and was sure that Greeson durst not tell me so, but he would the first time he saw me, this he had told all the head men at OakChoys while I was there; but I being a little bussie then did not rememb[e]r it.

Tuckabatchie 19th March 1772.

This Morning I intended to go to the Upper Towns but it begun to rain about six, and Continued so all morning. In the forenoon I Recd a letter from James Germaney, a Trader in the Coolamies, informing me that he Could get proof of William Simorys being guilty of high Treason, and likewise of his Stirring up the Indians by Speaking disrespectfully of the Governors and Superintendant of Indian affairs. This Day I heard from the Lower Creeks by two Eutchies [3] who informed me that the man who Killed the white man at Ogechee, had been Killed by his own people in the Geehaws.

Tuckabatchie 20th March 1772.

I sent this Morning for my horses to go to Survey the Upper Towns but they had strayed off in the night and Could not be found till late in the afternoon which prevented me going this Day.

[1] Upper Eufaula was situated on Eufaula Creek a few miles south of the present town of Talladega, Talladega County, Alabama.

[2] Thomas Grierson.

[3] The Eutchies, or Uchees, had a settlement on the west bank of the Chattahoochee River at or near the mouth of Big Uchee Creek in Russell County, Alabama.

Cailedgee 21st March 1772.

I sett out this Morning with my servant to Survey the road etca to this place, the Interpretor refuseing to go on pretence that he did not know the road. I however proceeded to take the Course and distance of the roads and Creeks etca, my servant who is a Spaniard and has resided in this Country several years knowing the roads to the different Towns. I stayed at this Town all this Night.

Oakfuskee 22d March 1772.

This Morning I went to the Square in the Cailedgees where the Indians had prepered black drink for me. After I had drank some with them I went to the OakChoys taking the bearings and distance of the path etca. I stayed in this Square with Mico Lucko some time, Smoking; and drinking black drink and then sett out for the Euffallas [1] about Eight miles East by South from the OakChoys and on the North west side of the Oakfuskee or Tallapuse River. The road from OakChoy to Euffalla is over Several little Stoney hills very bad for horses traveling. The Euffalla Town is Situated on a low point of land surrounded by high barren hills on the west side and by the river on the East. I rested here about two hours and then set out for Oakfuskee about five miles NNW of Eufalla and on a point on the west side of same River. This Town some years ago was the Largest in the Upper Creeks, Containing three hundred Gun men, but now not above thirty, the Inhabitants having Scattered about the Hunting grounds on Account of Plantations. I stayed at this Town all night.

Oakfuskee 23d March 1772.

This Morning I went to the Square in this Town, with one of the headmen Commonly Called Wills friend. He sent for Paya Lucko desiring him to come to the Square, but he declined coming on Acct. of some dispute amongst them-

[1] Eufaula, on the Tallapoosa River, in Tallapoosa County; not to be confused with Upper Eufaula.

selves; but after black drink he came to meet me at the
Traders where Wills Friend had Caused some fowles to be
prepered for breakfast. Paya Lucko behaved very Civilly;
and seemed willing that I should stay some Days in his
town; but Observed that at present they had but very
little to Intertain me with. About Eleven OClock I set out
for a small village Called Elkhatchie,[1] about four miles NNW
from Oakfuskee, situated at the mouth of a Creek of the
same name, runing ENE into Oakfuskee River. The Creek
is about 30 yards wide and 12 ft. Deep at this village, which
Consists of four or five houses, but about half a mile up the
Creek is fordable. After Crossing in a Canoe I went to Secuspoga, another village of the Oakfuskee Indians about five
Miles NNE from Elkhatchie, and on a point on west side of
Oakfuskee River. This village stands on a level piece of
ground about half a mile broad bounded by hills on the west
side. There is about forty five Gun men in it and one Trader,
named Robert French, a hireling of Messrs. Campbell and
Son in Charlestown. From this Trader I received a Large
Silver medal, and Commission which the Morter had given
to him about Eighteen Months ago, desiring him to Carry
it to Mr. Mackay at Augusta and give it to him for Captn.
Stuart. This French had done but Mr. Mackay refused to
accept of it, and desired him to Give it to the Morter again
when he returned to the Nation; but the Morter would
not take it, saying that the promises made to him when
he Received it at Pensacola were not fullfilled. I reproved
Mr. French for keeping it so long without acquainting
the Interpretor or bringing it to me at last meeting.
The Interpretor he said he never shou'd have acquainted
any thing about it, but intended to have brought to me at
the meeting but had forgot it untill he had got to the fish
pond (about seven mile from OakChoys) where he returned
from without Seeing me. In the Evening I went to the
Square where Paya Lucko's Son came from Oakfuskee and
acquainted the headmen that the Little Tallassie people

[1] Island Home, Ala.

had brought in a Chactaw prisoner and burned him in that Town.

Hillabies 24th March 1772.

This Morning I went to black drink in the Square at Socuspoga, where I stayed till ten OClock and then set out for this place. Paya Lucko's son went with me on pretence of being my guide but I suppose this piece of kindnes was the Effect of jealousey and not intended as any Service to me. I made him ride on before, and keept my Servant between him and me, thereby preventing him from seeing me take Observations of the Course of the path and Creeks as we past. This Town is about ten Miles NNW from Socuspoga, on the branches of a Creek Called Yallafattee,[1] which falls into the Oakfuskee River. Above Socuspoga there is Several little villages or plantations Scattered about the branches of this Creek, which is Confined between high hills on Each side having very little planting Land Excepting what is about the sides of the Creek. In this Town and villages are about one hundred gun Men, one Trader, and one Indian factor. This Evening I went with Mr. Scot, the Trader, to the hot house where was only a few Young Men, the rest being all gon to war against the Chactaws. Amongst the Young Men that are here is the one who Killed Mr. Scots Servant some time ago, and for whom Satisfaction has been promised. At Night I went to Mr. Scots house where I stayed this night.

Hillabies 25th March 1772.

I stayed at this Town all this Day and Surveyed the different branches of the Creek etca.

Natchie[s] 26th March 1772.

This Morning I set out from the Hillabies, Mr. Scot accompanying me to the little OakChoys, a small village about three miles WSW from the Hillabies, and on a branch

[1] Hillabee Creek.

of Yallafattee Creek wh[ich] joins the other branch at the west End of the Hillabies. In this village lives the Morter and about twenty OakChoy people. I went to the Morters Summer house where the people were at black drink, but the Morter had been gon[e] a hunting for some Days. After drinking some black drink etca I set out for the Natchies, a small village of the remnant of a people of that name who were drove from the Mississippi by the French.[1] This village is about Twenty seven Miles NW of the Hillabies and on the south side of a Creek Called Clanahumgey [2] which falls into the Coosa River about nine miles west north west from this. About Eight miles South East from this I Crosed over a high hill very steep and Covered over with Sharp Stones; this hill which Continues nearly South west towards the Coosa River is part of the great mountains which devide the Northern and Southern part of America. From the Top of this hill is a very beautifull prospect over the Tops of hills all round this. I Arrived at this Town abt five OClock in the afternoon and went to a Traders house where I stayed all this Night.

Natchie[s] 27th March 1772.

I went this morning to black drink to the Square where I was very kindley Received by the head men of the Town who told me to look on myself as being amongst my friends and not to be affraid of any thing, for their fire was the same as Charlestown fire and they never had Spilt the blood of any white Man; after that I had Smoked Tobacco and drinked black drink with them they desired that I might Stay in their Town all day as they were building a hot house and Should have a dance in the Evening which they wanted me to see. In the Evening I went to the Square where thirteen Chickasaws had joined the Natchies and Creeks for the dance, (these Chickasaws are making a Settlement

---

[1] The Natchez Indians were driven from their home, near the site of the present city of Natchez, Miss., by the French in 1730.
[2] Tallassee Creek in Talladega County.

on the side of a Creek Called Caimullga [1] about 15 miles north from this, and falling into the Coosa River at the Chickasaw Trading path, about a mile above Clamahumgey) The women being dressed like Warriours with bows, hatchets, and other weapons in their hands, came into the Square and danced round the fire, the pole Cat dance, two men Singing and ratling their Callabashes all the time. In this Town is about thirty gun Men, Natchies and Creeks and one Trader.

Abicouches 28th March 1772.

This Morning I left the Natchies and came to this place which is about three miles NW b[y] N from the former and on the North side of same Creek. As soon as I Came into the Town I went to the hot house where Machbichemalla, Commonly Called Mcbeans friend, and Effatiskiniha, or Mackays friend, wellcomed me to their Town telling me that I was amongst my friends on the west side of the great hill who never had spilt the blood of any white man but had always held them fast by the hand, and they looked [upon] their fire and [that of] the Natchies [as] the same as [the] Charlestown fire. Effatiskiniha said that most of the old people were dead and he was the only one left in his Town to protect the white people, which he would do as Long as he lived, and said that there was men growing up amongst them which he hoped would protect [them] when he was gon[e]. I told him that I had heard that he and his people had always behaved very well to the white people and desired to know if he thought any thing deficient on our side. He said that he Supposed I was now tired with my journey, and would not at present say any more, but would meet me in the Evening. I desired him to send for the head man of Tallassiehatchie, a small village about three miles further down this Creek, that I might enquire of him the reasons for his people breaking their Traders doors, and Turning him out of their town, which he promised me to do. I likewise sent

[1] This settlement was at or near the site of the present town of Kymulga on Talladega Creek in Talladega County, Alabama.

for Mr. Cuzens, a Trader in the Natchies, to Interpret between me and the Indians. In the Evening Mr. Cuzens and the head man of Tallassiehatchie came and went with me to the hot house where, after the Ceremoney of drinking black drink and Smoking with the head man of Tallassiehatchie, I asked him about the affair of John Bell, his Trader. He said that his Young people had broke Bells doors and destroyed his household utensils such as pots, bowles etca and Spoiled all his victuals, because he would not give them such a good Trade as the people of the puckantallahassie did, which sold Stroud and duffle Blankets at Six pound leather each and every thing else in proportion, and took their buck Skins at five pounds and doe at three. But as for his part he was the man that brought a white man to his Town as he was very poor for one before he got him and is now poor since he left them. He said that he was a very good white man and not any wise Cross so that he loved him very much, but did not desire him to stay after his people had used [him] so very Ill nor did he desire him to go back as something bad might happen for which he should blame himself if he desired him to stay. As the men were dancing and making a noise round the fire in [the] hot house, I went out into the Square with Mr. Cuzens, Mckays and Mcbeans friends etca, Mackeys friend acquainted me that he had a small favour to ask of his father Captain Stuart which in the first place was a Stand of Colours to Show that he was an English Man and a friend to the white people, next a bag of powder and two bags of ball, some flints, and a box of paint, as they were often very poor for these things, being much Exposed to their Enemy by being the outside Town of their Nation, and their Traders being often Robed of their horses etca before they Could Cross the great hill. He likewise Observed that there was not a great Coat in the Town. Mcbeans friend desired me to acquaint Captain Stuart that he was the man who talked to him at Augusta about the Chactaw war as [1] some things

---

[1] And.

in private, and when I should mention that, Captain Stuart would remember who he was. This man was the first that Killed a Chactaw and brought prisoners into this Town. He says that he made war on purpose to keep his Young people from falling out with the English and as soon as his Nation makes peace with the Chactaws he will Spoil it again as he knows they must be at war with some body. In this Town is about forty five Gun men and two Traders.

Abicouchie 29th March 1772.

I went this Day to Tallassiehatchie about three Miles west North west from this and on the South side of Clanahumgey Creek. I stayed some little time with the head men viewing the Creek and village, and went to the mouth of Caimullga Creek where it joins the Coosa River about half a mile above the Coosa Old Town and two Miles west North west from Tallassiehatchie. On East side of Coosa River is very good Level Land for a Considerable distance up, and on the East side of the River, between Caimullga and Clanahumgey, is a fine Tract of Land where the Coosa Old Town formerly Stood but now mostly grown over with small Oaks. Some people from Tallassiehatchie are now building house[s] and making plantations where the old Town formerly stood. In the Evening I returned to this place where I stayed all night.

Wakokays [1] *30th March 1772.*

I set out this morning from Abicouchie and after Crosing part of the large mountains Arrived at this village which is thirty Miles SSE of Abicouchie and Situated on a branch of hatchet Creek,[2] Surrounded by high barren hills very Rockey. There is plantations Scattered along the sides of the Creek for Eight or ten Miles down towards Puckantallahassie.[3] This Creek, which falls into the Coosa River about 18 miles South west of this, is about 60 feet broad in

---

[1] Wakokayi. [2] Ponchishatchee or Hatchet Creek.
[3] Pakan-Tallahassee.

most places but not navigable, being full of Rocks and Shoals. In this Town etca. is about one hundred Gun men and two Traders, who Keep four Trading house in the Town and plantations.

Wakokays 31st March 1772.

This Morning it rained very hard which prevented me from going to Puckantallahassie, the people belonging to this Town are mostly gon to war so that I Could not see any of the head men.

Weoka 1st April 1772.

I set out this Morning from Wakokays having one Campbell, a Trader in the Puckantallahassie, for my guide to that place, which is about fourteen Miles South west from the former and on the west side of hatchet Creek. The path goes mostly along side of the Creek and Croses it several times keeping along the tops of very Steep hills. When I Arrived at puckantallahassie I was met at the Traders house by four Old men being all that were in the Town, Devals Landlord and the rest being gon[e] to war. This Town is within four miles of Coosa River; and has twenty Gun men and two Trading houses in it. From thence I set out for Weoka, a small village Situated on a Creek of the same name about Twelve Miles South East be East from the Puckantallahassie. The road (Except the first four miles from thence being very hilly) is very good being mostly thro an Open pine barren. I arrived at night at a house belonging to Mr. Greerson where I stayed all this Night.

Coosada 2d April 1772.

I sett out this morning from the Weokas which is a small village Surrounded by hills having very little low land for planting Excepting a narrow Stripe along the sides of the Creek where it is Situate upon. I took the Course and distance of the path to the little Tallassies which is about 13 miles South be East from the former, the path going thro a level pine barren. From the Tallassies I went to the Hickory ground and in my way thither met with a young Indian going to Tuckabatchie. I desired him to send the Interpretor to meet me at Coosada to morrow, I then went into the Square where Emistisiguo and his Warriours who had returned last night, were sitting. As I had no Interpretor I Could not have any Conversation with him. I however drank some black drink and eat some bears paws etca. and then set out for this place which [is] Situated in the forks of the Coosa and Tallapuse Rivers about a Quarter of a mile below the Old French fort.[1] In this Town is forty Alibamons and one Trader.

Coosada 3d April 1772.

I sent my Servant this morning to the white ground, a village about Eight miles up the Tallapuse river, to Enquire if McFall had returned from Pensacola, my servant returned and told me that he arrived last night and was gon this Morning to Tuckabatchie. In the afternoon I went with Mr. Brown, a Trader in this Town, and Surveyed part of the Rivers Coosa and Alibama below this Town.

Coosada 4th April 1772.

I went this Morning to Wetunkey, a small village about one mile ESE from this, up the Tallapuse River, where Emistisiguo and the fighter, viz, Toopoya and Several other headmen were present at the building of a new hot house. In this village after black drink I went to a Thomas Mosleys, a Trader in this Town, where Emistisiguo came likewise. I desired a Jacob Monthack to Enquire of Emistisiguo where he and his people had been and what he had done since he went to war, he said that he was amongst the settlements at Tansa and at Monsr Badons Opposite Mobile and some of his people had been there, but did not see any Enemy. He said that the Inhabitants used him very well giving what provisions he Stood in need of, but after he left the

---

[1] Fort Toulouse, or Alabama Fort, erected in 1714.

settlements some of his people were in want and had Killed one beeve, and he sent the marks of it to Tansa by a white man, but the Coolamie people having Seperated from him had Killed three Cattle and Stole three horses, which he was very Sorry for, and promised to get the horses again and Carry them down to their owners. In the Evening I went again to Wetunkey Square where men and women were all danceing, about Nine OClock I Received the Letters which McFall brought from Pensacola. Emistisiguo being gon[e] I desired Toopoya to send for the 2d man to Come here on the morning that we might appoint a meeting to give Captn Stuarts Talks to them. I then Returned to Coosada where the Interpretor was Arrived.

Tuckabatchie 5th April 1772.

This Morning I went with Mr. Brown and the Interpretor to Wetunkey where Emistisiguo desired to hear the Talks from Pensacola, saying that there was now a good many head men present. I acquainted him that the Talks were for the head of the whole Nation and that I Could not read them to a part, but when the 2d man came they might appoint a Day to meet at the Oak Choys. After black drink I went to Coosada where I stayed about two hours and then returned to Wetunkey where the 2d man came. We then Appointed a meeting to be at OakChoys in Eleven Days from this. Emistisiguo made Eleven pieces of Cane which I sent with a letter to the gun Merchant desiring him to send to all the Towns above him. About two OClock I set out for this place in Company with Messrs. Brown, Mosley and Cornal; at the white ground I met McFall who says that about one hundred miles from this nation he was Robed by 113 Chactaws, some of them held him fast to the ground while others took the Cock off his riffle and Sixteen Carrots of Tobacco and some Sugar etca. but did not take any rum. From the white ground I went to the fushatchies [1] about two miles further up the river; here the Indians pre-

---

[1] Fusihatchi.

pared black drink and desired me to stay and drink with them. I went to their Square where they hoisted an Old ragged Jack on a pole telling me that they had no better Collours to adorn their Square with. After drinking with them I set out for this place where I arrived about nine at night.

Tuckabatchie 6th April 1772.

I sent a letter by one Perkens to Stephen Forest at the Eutchies, Ordering him to Call a meeting of the Lower Creeks on the 23d Inst. Mr. Cornal acquainted me with the Answer which the Lower Creeks sent to the upper in regard of Satisfaction etca. which I wrote down. The Made [1] Dog of this Town is very bussie preparing Physick and Causing the people to dance every night on purpose to bring back to life their fire Maker who was killed six months ago by the Chactaws and by them Skined, but his wife who is Sisster to the Mad Dog perswades the people that he comes to her sometimes in the night and that he keeps about the Square and hot house and will soon make his Appearance in publick if they make the Physick strong Enough, and take proper care. To Day the King of the Town, being tired with fasting, eat some victuals, which spoild the Physick, and prevented the fire maker coming this night but the Mad Dog desired that the people might attend every night in the Square, untill the fire maker did come which he assured them would be soon.

Tuckabatchie 7th April 1772.

It rained very hard all day which prevented me from going to make any Observations.

Tuckabatchie 8th April 1772.

This Morning Messrs. Brown and Mosley went to the Coosadas, the former having agreed to send me a man for a guide to go along the river side from this place to Wetunkey.

[1] Mad.

Tuckabatchie 9th April 1772.

This Day the beaver Tooth King and Mad Dog of this Town came and Smoked, and Talked with me Concerning the Traders having Cattle amongst them. The mad Dog is very much against it, and says they were poor before the white people came amongst them, and they will remain poor, and if the Traders were not poor they would not come amongst them, therefore if they do like not their method of living they may return to their own Country again. I desired the Mad Dog to go to the meeting and there speak any thing which he had to say before his own people which he promised to do.

Tuckabatchie 10th April 1772.

This Day McFall brought me some thing which he had left in the woods after being Robed. In the Evening I went to the Square where both Sexes were dancing round a fire, the Mad Dog stood up and said that he was uncertain as to the time when the fire Maker would come, but said that it might be three or four nights, and Ordered them all to attend untill he came. The mad Dog is a very Artfull fellow and is trying to impose on the Credulity of his people on purpose to free his Sisster from her widow hood, who by their Laws must remain a widow four years.

Tuckabatchie 11th April 1772.

This Morning one Howard, a half breed, came from the Geehaws and Complained against one Hugh Simpson, a Trader in the Tallassies, for Stealing a horse from him some Days ago. This Howard is the person that held the Murderer untill two others Stabed him with their knives in the sides. I went this forenoon to the Great Tallassies to make some Observations on the Town and Creeks etca. In the Evening Lave, a hireling of Mr. Browns at Coosada, came to be my guide by the river side to Wetunkey.

Tuckabatchie 12th April 1772.

This Morning I went down the south side of the Talla-puse River, and Surveyed as far as the Otteseys, about five miles SSW from this and on the South side of the River. The Town stands on a fine plain Close by the bank of the River; there is about Sixty gun men and two Traders in it at present. I Crossed the River a little above the Town, and went up the North side of it to this place having my Servant who is a Spaniard for my guide. This Day a Thos Jones came here from Pensacola, and says that he had letters from Mr. Charles Stuart [1] for me, but was met about fifty Miles from the Nation by Nine Chactaws who Robed him of his horse, gun, Cloaths, provision and Money, and tore the Letters in pieces. Their leader had a small Medal and spoke a little English; he took Jones Blanket and hat from him and throwed him down an Old Soldiers blanket and hat.

Coolamies 13th April 1772.

I set out this Morning with Lave for my guide and took the bearings and distance of the path and river as far as the Hochlawella, and from thence to this place, where I stayed at Mr. Germaneys all night.

Coosadas 14th April 1772.

I went this Morning to the Coolamie Square to black Drink where John Pigg came, and informed me of three Negro men, which were brought into this nation about three years ago by some men from Mississippi, and [that] there was a Mr. Weldren who had been formerly in the Chactaw nation but then resided at Wetunkey who wrote a letter in the name of Lieut. Govr. Durnford [2] Offering a reward for apprehending the men and Negroes on which the men run off and the Negroes were taken by Mr. Richard Brown and

[1] Charles Stuart was a Deputy Superintendent of Indian Affairs for the Southern District.
[2] Elias Durnford, governor of West Florida 1769–1770.

Thos. Mosley and by them Carryed down to Silver bluff
and Sold to Mr. George Galphin as their Own property for
six hundred pounds South Carolina Currency and Eight
horses; this James Germaney Likewise declared to be true.
The head men of this Town were so much ashamed of the
behavour of their people in Stealings horses etca. from the
Settlements that they went out of the Square without speaking to me. I went to Mr. Germaneys to Breakfast and then
set out with him to the Mucklasses, a small village three
miles farther down the River, where the wolf King lives,
to whoes house I went and after Smoking with him, he said
that he wanted to send to Pensacola for a little Rum and
some other little things from the Governor and beged that I
wou'd write a letter for him, which I promised to do provided that he would go with me to the Meeting at OakChoy
and get the Land granted which Captn Stuart and the Govr.
of Pensacola had asked from them. He said that for his
part he would give his Consent and was sure all the Tallapuses would do the same, but he was not able to Ride so
far as the OakChoys but would send his Nephew. He then
beged that John Pigg might not be allowed to remain in
the Nation as he had no goods and was a very great horse
thief, having already stole one from him and was affraid
that he would Steal every one that he had; he likewise had
told the Indians that I was come to Spy their land before
the white people made war with them. I desired Mr. Germaney to send Pigg to me in the Morning, and then set out
for this place taking the Course and distance etca.

Coosada 15th April 1772.

I went this morning to the Tuskigie [1] Square to black
drink. The Square is about a Quarter of a mile above this
Town on the south side of Coosa River, and near the Old
French fort. The Inhabitants of the Tuskigees are a remnant of Northen Indians and speak a different Language from
the Creeks; there is but twenty five gun men and one In-

---

[1] Tuskegee.

dian factor in the Town. After black drink Emistisiguo and Toopoya came to me at this place and likewise John Pigg from the Coolamies. I then asked Emistisiguo and Toopoya, (having Jacob Moniack for Interpretor,) if they would Suffer Pigg to be taken and sent to Pensacola as they knew what Complaints had been made against him both by their own people and the Traders. Emistisiguo said that he looked upon me as having the same power as if Captain Stuart was present, and that I might do what I thought proper for they knew Pigg to be a bad man. I then sent for Pigg and Told him what was alledged against him and then took him prisoner, [at the] same time Offering him his Liberty to go to Silver bluff upon his finding Security for his appearance at Augusta to Answer to what he was accused of; after some time Messrs. Brown and Mosley were Security and gave their Obligation for his appearance.

OakChoys 16th April 1772.

I set out from Coosadas about one oClock, with Toopoya and a white man for a guide and arrived here in the Evening.

OakChoys 17th April 1772.

This Morning I sent to the little OakChoys for the Morter and in the Evening the Messenger returned and told me that the Morter would be here to morrow morning. This afternoon the Interpretor and the beaver Tooth King came from Tuckabatchie but did not bring the Mad Dog with them, he being affraid to leave his women after the Tricks he and them has been playing.

OakChoys 18th April 1772.

This morning the Morter came and after black drink I delivered Captain Stuarts Letters to the Chiefs who assembled at the Gun Merchants house for that purpose. They promised to give me an Answer next Day about the Land but Could say nothing about the Slave as it was the Lower Euffalla people who Murdered him. I Ordered Mr.

Cornall to go with me in the Evening to the fish pond about seven miles off, this he refused thinking it no part of his duty as Interpretor. After I had delivered the Letters which I had for the Indians, Mr. Thomas Graham, one of the traders, desired leave for the Interpretor to deliver a Letter from the Merchts at Augusta to the Upper Creek Indians. This I told Mr. Graham was Contrary to any regulations made by the Government, who did not allow any person, or body of them, to treat with Indians about Lands, Excepting the Superintendants appointed for that purpose; but if there was nothing in the Letter that interfered with the duty of the Superintendant or the Governors, I should have no Objection to let it be read, otherwise I would not allow it. He assured me that it was only to desire payment of their Debts. I then allowed Mr. Cornal to deliver it. The first part was telling the Indians that they had received a letter from them demanding Satisfaction for some of their people who had been Killed by some persons in Georgia. This they said was in the Governors power and not theirs to do. They then ask[ed] for the Lands above little River which the Cherokees gave to their Traders and likewise for the Lands on the East side of Okono [1] River, as far as the Lower Trading path, as a payment for the Debts which they owed their Traders, saying that it was not the Superintendant nor Governors that Supplyed them with goods and unless they gave them the Land they would not be able to Supply them, at same time asking [for] the Land in their own Names; which was read to the Indians.

Tuckabatchie 19th April 1772.

This Morning the Morter came to me at Nicolas Blacks house in the OakChoys; soon after the gun Merchant came and desired the Morter to go and Consult with them about the Answer which they were to give to day, but the Traders having given him three or four drams of rum, he refused to go. I then went into the Traders Store with the Morter

[1] Oconee.

and Gun Merchant, and made the Interpretor ask the first his reason for giving his Medal and Commission to the Trader in the Socuspoga. While the Morter was telling his reasons one Hugh Simpson (who Trades in the Great Tallassies as a hireling to Messrs. Campble and son in Charlestown) came into the Store and carryed out a Kegg of Rum. He then returned into the Store and after Staying some time said that he was going to Carry the Rum into the Square to the Indians. I Ordered [him] at his peril not to do it untill I had done with them. He returned again to the house and told me that I had no Right to speak to any Indians in private that the Rum was his and he would do as he pleased in this Country; he would not Obey any Governor Nor Superintendant nor any person but his employer, useing a great deal of very Abussive Language. Upon which I desired the Traders present to give me assistance to Secure Simpson. This they all refused; at same time Simpson said to Messrs. Graham and Greerson and several others, that they had set him on to Abuse me, and now they were affraid to speak themselves. The Gun Merchant said that I now saw the behavour of their Traders, which was as bad as any of their Young Men, and he wondered how they agreed so well together. I gave the Morter his Commission and Medal which he accepted off on Condition of geting a riffle and some Shells which he alledged had been Long promised him. I then went to the hot house where I Received an Answer to Captain Stuart['s] letter, and in the Evening I came to this place.

Tuckabatchie 20th April 1772.

This Morning I wrote a letter to Mr. Charles Stuart at Mobile acquainting him with the Indians Answer About the Scambia Lands, and sent it by Jacob Moniack who goes in ten Days for Mobile.

The Morter came to me this morning and made a Complaint against one Pretor, a hireling of Mr. Galphins, who had stole some horses from him, and likewise to get his riffle from Cornal which had been sent by him six months ago but had been broke in Carrying. The Morter received it from Cornal but desired that Captain Stuart might send him another, and Likewise the Shells which had been Long promised him.

LOWER CREEKS.

Chavacleyhatchie, or Half wayhouse 21st April 1772.

This Morning I set out from Tuckabatchie Leaving the Morter at the Interpreters waiting for the Return of Pretor, from Silver bluff, that he may get paid for the horses which Pretor Stole from him. I took the bearings and distance of the path to this place which is twenty five Miles ENE from the Tuckabatchie, situated on a Creek Called Chavucleyhatchie being the North branch of Nufabee Creek, which emptys itself into the Tallapuse River at the great Tallassies. In this village which belongs to the Tallassies are about 20 Gun Men and one Trader.

Geehaws[1] 22d April 1772.

I set out this morning from Chavucleyhatchie taking the Course and disstance of the path etca. to this place, which is nearley East about forty five Miles, about nine OClock I arrived at Mr. Raes Store where I Stayed all this Night.

Geehaws 23d April 1772.

This Morning Mr. Rae sent to the Eutchie Town (about three miles up the Chatahutchie river) for Stephen Forest, the Interpreter, who came to me about Eight OClock, when we went to the Square and Appointed a meeting to be at this place on the 26th Inst. Mr. Forest acquainted me that he had already given the Merchants Letter to the In-

---

[1] Geehaws, or rather Chehaw or Chiaha, was on the Chattahoochee River near the site of the present Columbus, Ga., and the crossing of the Lower Creek trail which traversed Georgia in a course W.S.W. from Augusta.

dians who had assembled together and insisted on hearing it; but that he had asked the Land in his Majesty's name and not for the Merchants.

Geehaws 24th April 1772.

This Morning I went to the Eutchies in Company with Messrs. Robert and James Rae and stayed about two hours at the Traders house, and then went to a Ball ground at the upper End of the worsitas where the Eutchie and Geehaw people were playing Ball. After Ball play, Tubahathee or white Cabin, invited me to his house to eat and in our way thither Shewed me the place where the Indian was Killed who had Murdered the white Man at Ogechee, there was a little piece of ground hoed over to Cover the blood.

Geehaws 25th April 1772.

I went this morning in Company with Mr. Robert Rae and Survey'd the point where this village Stands, which is a very fine level piece of ground from 30 to 60 feet above the common Surface of the River; but about two years ago was all overflowed by the rising of the River which did Considerable damage to the houses etca.

Geehaws 26th April 1772.

This forenoon I delivered Captain Stuarts letters [1] to the Indians that were met in this Square but neither the

---

[1] Taitt received from Stuart the following letter along with his instructions.

To the Great Chiefs and Leaders of the Lower Creek Nation.

MOBILE, 20th January 1772.

FRIENDS AND BROTHERS:
I send you this Talk by a Beloved man who I have desired to Smoke and Talk with you. I hope you will take him by the hand and Listen to him with Attention.

In the month of September last the white King of the Euphalies was at Pensacola, he and I talked together for I took him to be a man of Sense. I then sent you a Talk by him informing you of

JOURNAL OF DAVID TAITT

Euffalla nor Tamatly people, who had done the Murders and Robed the plantations did appear, so that I Could not Receive any Satisfactory Answer from these that were present.

the Robberies of some of your People, who under pretence of going to war have for some time past made it a practice to plunder our plantations and settlements to the Westward of Mobile Bay. I now again send the Bearer to speak with you upon the same Subject, hoping that you who are Governors of your nation will put a Stop to such Violent proceedings, which are inconsistent with Friendship. I hope you have not forgot the Treaty of Augusta entirely; you are the Chiefs who signed the Treaty. I therefore expect that you will stop such proceedings.

My Friends:

A Party of the Tomautley People some time ago carried away a Family of Indians Slaves, who belong to a Planter on Pascagaula River, the Man they Killed or Burnt, the Woman is still among them you can have no right to keep this Woman and Children. They were poor defenceless Slaves, could not be your Enemies being brought from a Country far to the Westward of the Mississippi where you never go to War. I wish to Know if you the Chiefs of the Nation suffer such proceedings. There is no honor in taking and Killing a poor Slave the property of your Friends. I hope you will send your Talk that the Woman and Children may be restored to their Master.

Friend and Brother Talleachie:

It is long since you and I talked together but one Day or other we shall possibly meet and renew old Talks. You know it was agreed upon that we should not Keep any thing a Secret from each other. I hear that there are many Talks between your Nation and the Spaniards, I hope you will communicate all you Know to the Beloved messenger who carries this. I likewise desire to Know the Messages sent in by the Shawnese and Western Indians, for I hear that you lately received Talks from them.

Brothers:

I have not forgot the old Talks at Augusta and I hope you remember them also, we then agreed to keep the path Clear and free from thorns and bad weeds, and that you and I should Join in Endeavours to keep it Straight and white. I hope you are of the same mind still, and that you will send me a good Talk by the Bearer which I will accept of and hold Fast for the Good of the Red as well as of the white People.

I am

Your Friend and Brother

Signed J: S:

Geehaws 27th April 1772.

This Day I went in Company with Messrs. Robert and James Rae to the Hitchitas, a village about three miles SSW from this, and on the East side of Chatahutchie River. The village is situated on the bank of the River and Surrounded by hills on the East; at the distance of half a mile there is about Ninety Gun men, and two white Traders and three Indian factors in the village.

Cowetas 28th April 1772.

I set out this morning and took the Course and distance from the Geehaws to the Eutchies [1] where I met the Interpreter, and then went with him to ClayCatskee, a village about six miles further up, on the west side of the River. Here I met with Scutchabe, the Young Lieut. of the Cowetas, to whoes house I went, and after Smoking etca. he informed me that his son with some others had been Over at Havannah about a Year ago, where they were very kindly received and Intertained, but he did not think that the Spanish Governor had taken so much Notice of his son, as of the others, although he had sent his Commission with him. He says that his son brought over two Keggs of Rum, one Kegg of wine, Some Snuff, and some other little triffles, and the Governor desired he, viz, the Lieut. might go to Havannah as he wanted much to see him there. He says that he had held the french, English and Spaniards by the hand at the same time, and when the latter was at St. Augustine and St. Marks, he Received presents from them, which he says were of little value, and not equal to what he receives from the English; but as the Spanish Govr. had such a desire to see him he intended going to Havannah this Summer, Although he had been informed that the sea is very Mountanious making the boat go from the Top of a high hill into a very Deep valley with great Swiftnes; but as some of their Women had gon[e] aCross these waters, he being a man

---

[1] See p. 527 n. above.

was not affraid; besides he was now Old and in case he should be drowned all his Troubles would then be over. He therefore determined to go and if he returns alive will let Captain Stuart know every thing that passes between him and the Governor, and will hide nothing from his Father. He says that there is always vessels fishing and Cutting Lumber amongst the Keys about Cape Florida where he will go and meet with one to Carry him over.

From ClayCatskee I went to the Little Cowetas and in the Evening came to this place after taking the Course and distance of the path and Creeks etca. In ClayCatskee are Sixty Gun Men and three Indian factors; in the Cowetas, Little Cowetas, and Bigskin Creek, are two Hundred and twenty Gun men, two Traders and two Indian factors.

Geehaws 29th April 1772.

This Morning I went to the Coweta Square [1] where Scutchabee, Sempoyeffa, and some other head men were present. After drinking black drink with them I went with Scutchabee and Sempoyeffa to a half breed, named Abraham, at whose house we breakfasted on Coffee, Tea and fowles etca. After breakfast the Young Lieut. Ordered two young men to go to the Cherokees and bring two of their head men to the Cowetas about the Time of their busk or Green Corn dance (which will be about the begining of August) that they might Enquire of them whether they had given the Land above little River to the white people or not. Sempoyeffa said that if his sons had not been gon[e] to war he would have accompanyed me in the Canoe to Tamatley, but as he Expected them in soon, he Could not be absent. About twelve OClock we set out for the Cussitas, a village about five miles down the River from the Coweta and one the East side.[2] As soon as I had Crosed the River and Entering into the Cussita Kings yard, he Caused a Cow horn to be fired,

[1] Or Kawita, a town a little below the falls of the Chattahoochee.

[2] In present Chattahoochee County, Georgia.

and one when I went into his house where I Smoked and eat with him, and then went to his Square where his beloved men and Warriours were present. After Smoking with them I went with the head warriour to his house on the Top of a high hill and from thence viewed the Town which Stands on a fine plain Extending along the side of the River and about half a mile back, is bounded by high hills. The flood two years ago overflowed all this Town, but at present the banks are fifty feet above the Surface of the water. In the Cussita is one Hundred gun Men and two Traders.

Geehaws 30th April 1772.

I went this Morning to the Worsita Square (adjoining this Town) in Company with a Mr. Scot from the Hillabies.[1] After Staying a little in the Square, Salegee with the Interpreter and a John Miller, a Trader from the Eutchies, came into the Square. Miller read a Letter from Mr. Galphin being an Answer to one which the Indians had sent him after Killing the Murderer at this Town. Mr. Galphin tells them that they did very Right in giving Satisfaction and that he had sent their Letter to the Governor of Savannah; he likewise Says that he had turned some of his Cattle over Ogeechee on the Indian Land, but was now hunting them up to put on his own again, the Grass being now grown up after being burnt at the time of puting his Cattle over Ogeechee. Mr. Galphin had desired Stephen Forest to ask for a piece of Land on the west side of Ogechee for his Chilldren and their Mother to live upon, this the Indians with some dificulty granted upon Condition that only one white man should remain on the plantation to take care of the Negroes. This Afternoon the Interpreter went to the Oakmulgeys to purchase a Canoe for me to go to Tamatley and in the Evening he returned and acquainted me that he had purchased a new one.

[1] Near present Ashland, in Clay County, Alabama.

Geehaws 1st May 1772.

I went this Morning to the Eutchies Square and after some Conversation with the headmen I found that they were not guilty of Robing the plantations along shore as mentioned in Captain Stuarts letter to them, as they Never go that way but they blamed the Euffalla and Okonay people for it. After I left the Square I went to a Mr. Millers where I met with some Geehaw people who desired me not to go down the River in a Canoe as they alledged there was some dangerous Whirlpools in the river which they said would sink the Canoe; in the afternoon I returned to the Geehaws.

Geehaws May 2d 1772.

Earley this Morning Taleachey came to me and told me of the danger of the River and seemed very Much against my going to Tamatley.[1] I went with him to the Square and after he had Smoked with me he went to the head war Cabin where he Called two warriours to him and talked very much against my going to Tamatley by water. When the Interpreter came into the Square they acquainted me that the Land where the Euffalla people had Killed the Slave and burned the House was theirs, and not belonging to the English, being on the south side of yellow water bay, and not where the Yamasee Indians formerly lived; they also denyed knowing any thing of the grant given to Stephen Forest of two miles Square on the bay of St. Rosa. In the afternoon Taleachey and Salegee came to me and proposed to send two head men to Tamatley for the slaves, and insisted on my not going, alledging the danger of the River and badnes of the people there. In the Evening Mr. Richard Brown came here with John Pigg in his way to Augusta.

Geehaws 3d May 1772.

This Morning I went to the Worsita Square where I agreed with Taleachey and Salegee to send two head men

[1] In Russell County, Alabama.

to Tamatley for the Slaves. They wanted me to send for Emistisiguo and another head Man from the Upper Creeks to know of them what Lands were given on the south side of Pensacola bay in 1765; this I did not agree to, as I was Certain that Emistisiguo would not come. In the afternoon I went to the Eutchies to see a ball play which Ended in favour of the Geehaw people who played against the Eutchies.

Geehaws May 4th 1772.

I went this Morning with the Interpreter to the Square but the Head men who were appointed to go to Tamatley did not come; they afterward came to me at Mr. Raes where I agreed with them about going and gave them a letter to one Burges, a Trader there, desiring him to assist them in geting the Slaves and likewise a White woman, who Causes great disturbance amongst the Indians and Traders, by telling the first that the goods are sent amongst them by the King, and the Traders deceive them by Selling the goods whereas they are intended to be given to them.

Topahatkee, one of the men Appointed to go Tamatley, acquainted the other head men present that he was at the Congress at Pensacola in 1765 and remembered the boundary that was then Settled, and declared that the plantation where the Euffalla people had Killed the boy was within the line granted to the white people.[1]

[1] On this day Taitt wrote Stuart:

Sir:

I received your letter and Talk of the 25 March which I delivered on the 16th April at the Oak Choys to the Upper Creeks Emistisiguo and the fighter were present but I received much the [same] answer as before only they agreed to give leave to people at Pensacola to plant on the lands as far as the Spanish Cowpen as Land lent, and the Islands in the Coosa River if the Governour would accept of them; Emistisiguo was as much against giving any Lands as any man present, but said that he would go and run the line when the Mulberries were red, they have agreed to let what Cattle the Traders have in this nation Remain alive, but no more to be brought amongst them and no plantations to be made by the Traders, they would give me no answer about the

Geehaws 5th May 1772.

This Morning Topahatkee came and acquainted me that he Could not go to Tamatley to Day, the Creeks being greatly swelled with the rains which fell last night and this Morning.

Geehaws 6th May 1772.

This afternoon Topahatkee and Chimhuchi set out for Tamatley; in the Evening Mr. Richard Brown set out for Silver bluff in South Carolina. I sent a letter by him to Capt. Stuart.

Geehaws 7th May 1772.

Last night and this Day it Continued raining so that the River Rose about four feet.

Geehaws 8th May 1772.

This afternoon John Miller, Trader in the Eutchies, came and acquainted me that he should set out to morrow for Silver bluff.

Boy which was killed, as that was done by the people of the lower Eufallas, the Abeckas desired that no more than ten Keggs of Rum might be brought to each Town by their Traders and the Tallapuses desired only four, as some of their men had been lately killed in Rum drinking and others greatly burnt. After I sent the Express to Pensacola and went to the Upper Towns I received the Morters Commission and Medal from a Robert French to whom the Morter gave it near two years ago, Saying that you had throwed him away in not Sending him the rifle and Black drink Cups you had promised him, I could not see him when I went to his Village as he was gone ahunting, but at the Meeting I talked to him about it, when he gave me the same reason as he had done to the Trader. I however got him to accept of his Commission etca. again on promising him what you had done should be performed. The riffle he has since got from Cornal [is] in very bad order so that he expects another in its place, he came to the Tuckabatchie the day after the last meeting where he received his riffle from Cornal I also gave him a Stroud Blanket flap and Boots and a Shirt on purpose to satisfy him, I cam[e] down here the 22d last month and delivered your Talk on the 26th but could obtain no Satisfactory answer as neither the Eufalla nor Tamatly people were present, the Eufalla people

Geehaws 9th May 1772.

This Day Stephen Forest came and acquainted me that he Should go from the Eutchies to the Pallachocolas[1] to morrow and there wait the return of the Messengers from Tamatley.

Geehaws 10th May 1772.

In the afternoon I went with my servant and Surveyed the path from the Eutchie Creek about six Miles from this place, having left it undon[e] on the first night which I Came here.

Pallachocola 11th May 1772.

This Morning Benjamin Stedham, the Trader in this Town, sent a Servant with a packhorse to the Geehaws to Carry my baggage to this place and in the afternoon I sett

say that they have done no wrong as the house they burnt was on their own land but this I shall talk to them about in a few days when I go to their Town, I intended to come down the River to Tamatley and had prepared a Canoe for that purpose by permission of the Indians here, since they have raised many objections aledging that there is several dangerous whirlpools in the rivers and the people there are a set of runagadoes from every Town in the Nation, but I believe their care of me arrises more from Jelousy than any other thing, This day I shall send two head men from this Town to Tamately for the two Slaves which are alive, although the Boy is sold to a Trader there, the Man and Girl they murdered at the place where they took them. I expect the Messenger will be back in ten days when I shall set out for Augusta. I have sent down a John Pigg a Trader in care of Mr. Brown to Mr. Golphins, when I have the pleasure of seeing you at Charleston I shall let you know the reason of it which I believe you will be satisfied with. . . .

I am with greatest respect
Sir Your Most Obedt humble Servt
(signed) DAVID TAITT.

Geehaws 4th May 1722.

P.S. I just now received a Letter from Emistisiguo wherein he says that the Northward Indians had sent a white Skin with Red Borders into the Cherokees that they were for war but he did not believe their talk.

[1] Or Apalachicola, nearly opposite Columbus, Georgia.

554

out with my Servant and took the Course and distance of the River and path from the Geehaws, which lays six miles NNE from this.

Pallachocola 12th May 1772.

This afternoon Salegee came from the Geehaws to go with me in the morning to the Lower Euffallas.[1]

Lower Euffalla 13th May 1772.

This Morning I set out from the Pallchocolas with Messrs. Stedham and Forest, and Salegee, for this place, which is about twenty three miles South from the other and on the west side of Chatahutchie River. When I arrived at the Town Edward Hains, the Trader, acquainted me that the Indians were all very drunk, the Coosa Kings brother having brought five Keggs of Rum from Pensacola, to buy horses and Corn etca. to Carry to his people at Chacta-hatchie River; soon after the Indians came to the Traders house, they were all very drunk but behaved very well for some time, but while the White King and some other Chiefs were Smoking and talking with me on a Cornhouse Scaffold, a young fellow run against one of the Traders doors and broke it in pieces by a thrust with his foot. He turned to the store and broke it likewise. Some other Indians then took him away and prevented any more mischief being done at this time. At night Messrs. Stedham and Forest went with me to the pine barren about 300 yards from Town where we Encamped and Stayed all this night, as did Like-wise the Trader and his family; about twelve OClock at night the Indians returned to the Traders house and broke his doors again but Carryed no goods off.

Pallachocola 14th May 1772.

This morning I sent Mr. Forest for the White King of the Lower Euffallas and Tomachichi, the Leader of the party who Killed Mr. Comyns's boy and Robed the plantation in

[1] In Henry County, Alabama.

Pensacola bay, but when they came they were so much in Liquor that they were unfitt to do any kind of bussines. I therefore desired them to come to this place to morrow which they promised to do. I left Salegee on pretence of Staying for them but on purpose to get the Course and distance of the path along the River side thro the different villages between the Euffalla and this Town.

Pallachocola 15th May 1772.

I went this morning with Mr. Stedham to the Square to black drink, the Interpreter being Indissposed with a fever, could not go with me. In the afternoon Monjoy, and another head man came here from the Swaglehutchie. Monjoy Showed me a Commission which his father, Tomeche, Received from Governor Midleton in the year 1726. They stayed here all night waiting for Salegee with the head men from the Lower Euflallas, but they did not arrive this night.

Pallachocola 16th May 1772.

This Day Monjoy and the other headman Returned to the Swaglehatchies and in the Evening Salegee came from the Lower Euffallas and acquainted me that the white King and Tomachichi would come here tomorrow.

Pallachocola 17th May 1772.

This Day a John Dun with his wife and Servant boy came here on their way to Pensacola from Sundburry [1] in Georgia and in the Evening Tomachichi and the white King arrived from the Lower Euffallas.

Pallachocola 18th May 1772.

I went this Morning to the Square where I read Captain Stuarts Letter to the Euffalla head men, Salegee, and some of the Headmen of this Town. Tomachichi, who headed

---

[1] Sunbury.

the party that Killed the boy and plundered the plantation, gave me an answer to the Talk, and promised to take better Care for the futter,[1] and agreed to go and run the line to prevent any more Mistakes happening, as they alledged that the house was without the boundary. After that I had received an Answer in the Square, the white King and Tomachichi came to me at the Traders house and desired a letter to Mr. Charles Stuart which they promised to deliver to him when they went to run the line, and promised to give more land then what they had agreed to at the Congress in 1765 on purpose to regain their Honnor, which they said they had lost by Killing a Slave boy.

Pallachocola 19th May 1772.

This Morning John Dun with his wife and boy set out from this place for the Tuckabatchies, in their way to Pensacola. I sent a Letter by Dun, to be forewarded by Mr. Cornal, the Interpreter, to Mr. Charles Stuart at Mobile, acquainting him with the Answer which Tomachichi gave me for his Killing Mr. Comyns's Slave boy. I went this forenoon to view the point where the Pallachocola Town formerly stood about a mile and half below this, but Could not get an Opertunity to Survey any part of it on Account of ten or Twelve Eutchie Women who where gathering Strawberries all over the Old Town.

Pallachocola 20th May 1772.

This Morning Salegee came to me from the Geehaws and said that his daughter loved a little paceing horse of mine, and had sent a little Stallion by him to give me in Exchange; this I exused myself from doing by telling him that I was going a long Journey in a few Days which the Stallion would not be able to perform but gave him a Shirt and some Ribbon for his Trouble in going to Euffalla with me.

[1] Future.

Pallachocola 22d May 1772.

This morning the Coweta people Returned from War and brought a Chactaw Scalp into their Town.

Pallachocola 22d May 1772.

I went this morning to the Old Pallachocola Town below this, and Surveyed it and the River round the point where the Town stood. About one OClock Chimhuchi and Topahatkee, whom I had sent to Tamatley, returned with the Slave wench which I sent them for. Her Husband and daughter were Killed when first taken, and the boy sold to John Meally, a Trader, who has since sold him to Mr. Galphin at Silver bluff. The white woman run off with an Indian who is her husband, so that they Could not find her.

Chimhutchi informed me that when he went first to Tamatley and Demanded the Slave two of their head men, viz the Tallassee and Ochissis Kings, raised a Quarrel amongst the people, and asked him how he Could think of asking any Satisfaction for the white people, as they Supposed that he and the Upper Creeks must have heard what had passed between some of the Tamatley people and some Spaniards at Talagachapeapapea, or Pea Creek (on the west side of Cape Florida). Lately the Tamatley people Carryed one of their Women, who speaks Spanish, with them, to be Interpreter between the Spaniards and them; the former told them that the Kings of England and Spain had laid a Considerable wager whereby the former was to Kill all the Indians of this nation in a Certain time, which if he did perform was to be paid the wager by the King of Spain and in case of failure was to pay him the wager. They likewise said that the time was now at hand that they had agreed upon to decide the wager, and the English would fall upon them soon. Chimhutchie perswaded them that what the Spaniard told them Could not be true, upon which they gave him the Slave wench and sent me a letter desiring a pass to go to war against the Chactaws by Water.

Pallachocola 23d May 1772.

This Morning I sent an Indian to the Euffalla for the white King, desiring him to come here on purpose to Carry the Slave wench to Pensacola with him. I likewise sent Mr. Forest to the Coweta to see if he could learn any thing more from Scutchabee about the Spaniards. In the Evening the Indian whom I had sent to the white King, arrived and told me that he would be here tomorrow.

Pallachocola 24th May 1772.

I went this Morning to the Square to black drink, where Mr. Forest came from the Coweta about Eight OClock. He had seen Scutchabee, who informed him that a Shawnee or Savannah, who had been lately at New Orleans, came to him with a Message from thence, wherein he told him that he, viz Scutchabee, would be sent for to [attend] a meeting at the Red bluff Opposite Mobile, where he Supposed some French beloved man would be present, and he would likewise be sent for to [attend] a meeting with some Spaniards to be [held] at the Mouth of Appalachacola River, or somewhere there abouts. This he was desired by the Shawnee to eat down into his belley and keep Secret untill the time came, as no person was to be acquainted with it but him. He desired the Interpreter to do the same, and Told him that he should hear every thing about it when next he came into the Nation, and said that he looked upon him a's one of themselves and beged of him not to speak of it to any person whatsoever. He desired to be Remembered to his Friend and father, Captain Stuart, and said that he had once promised him a pair of Arm plates but Supposed that he had forgot them, and desired that he might be put in Mind again. In the Evening the white King came from the Euffallas.

Pallachocola 25th May 1772.

This Morning I agreed with the white King to pay him a Sad[d]le for Carrying the Slave wench to pensacola with him, and gave him a Letter for Governor Chester and one for Mr. Charles Stuart.

May 26th 1772.

I went this Morning to the Pallachocola Square to black Drink where most of the head[s] of the Town were present. I informed them that I was going off this Day for Augusta, and desired that if they had any talks to send to Captain Stuart, that they would now acquaint me with them. They said that I had been in their Town but a Short time but had seen Nothing aMiss in their behavour to me, they were but a poor people and had but very little to Intertain me with as they Could wish, but any thing which they had to spare I was wellcome to, and Likewise to Stay in their Town as long as I pleased. They desired me to acquaint Captain Stuart that they had used me well and desired that the Trade might not be stoped. They were now planting their Corn and as soon as that was over they would go and hunt to pay their debts. After black drink I set out with Mr. Forest and my Servant to the Worsitas, where I went to the Square where Salegee and some others were at black drink. We Stayed with them untill our horses and baggage were got aCross the Chatahutchie River, and about Eleven OClock proceeded on our Journey, taking the Course and distance of the path as we went along; at a Branch of a Creek (which joins the River opposite the Eutchie) Called the twelve mile branch, we came up to one Howarth, a half breed Indian who was waiting for us on purpose to go to Charles Town to see his Father. We proceeded on to another Branch of this Creek where we Encamped all night.

Flint River Spring 27th May 1772.

This Day we Travelled mostly NE to this place which is ten miles to westward of Flint River. We met with two Indians with four horses Loaded with Rum etca. from Augusta.

JOURNAL OF DAVID TAITT

May 28th 1772.

About Eight oClock this morning we Crosed Flint River, which is about 200 feet aCross and very Rockey; at present the water is low so that we rode over it, but it often rises twenty feet above its present Surface, which Obliges the Traders to Carry leather Canoes along with them. The River runs nearly SE and joins the Chatahutchie River about one Hundred miles below this path; these two Rivers make the Appalachacola River. I proceeded from this river taking the Course and distance of the Path which goes mostley ENE this Day.

May 29th 1772.

We set out this morning taking the Course and distance of the path etca. to the Oakmullgey[1] River, which is the western branch of the Altamaha. The River at present is not above three feet Deep and 100 feet wide at Crosing, having a firm gravelly bottom, but is Seldom fordable except in very Dry Seasons; it runs mostly SE till it joins the Okono[2] River. I Stayed at the East side of the River waiting for an Observation to assertain the Latitude, but the Day turned very Dark and Cloudy which prevented one. After two OClock we proceeded on our Journey taking the Course and Distance etca.

May 30th 1772.

About Eleven OClock this Morning we came to the Okono River where a Robert Tool and James McQueen (two Traders from the Cowetas) with their Packhorses, were just going to set out. McQueen stayed and Sent me over a Canoe to Carry my baggage etca; here we were Obliged to swime the Horses, the River being twenty feet Deep at the Landing and about 50 yards wide. About half a mile above this there is a place Sometimes fordable. I Stayed on the East side of the River to rest my horses and view the land

[1] Ocmulgee. [2] Oconee.

where the Old Okono Town formerly stood, and then proceeded to Little buffloe Creek where Messrs. Tool and McQueen were Encamped. They informed me that William Simory and three others had passed by them on their way to the Upper Creek Nation, having a few horses Loaded with salt, Amunition, and Rum, but turned out of the path on hearing of me being behind, as they were Conscious of their own bad behaviour while in the Nation.

May 31st 1772.

Having lost four horses in the night detained me till near one OClock this Day before I Could find them to set out with; after finding them I proceeded to Ogeehee where I found a Israel Folesum with his wife and six Chilldren Encamped. He had thirty three head of Cattle with him, and some horses which he intended going to Pensacola with; but meeting with some traders at the Okono River, they advised him to turn back, telling him that the Indians would Kill his Cattle and Steal his horses etca., upon which information he was returning back and intended to go to Mississippi by the way of Holston River.

June 1st 1772.

Sett out this morning from Ogechee taking the Course and distance of the path to Briar Creek, where we rested the horses etca. and proceeded to Sandy run where we Encamped this night; in the afternoon while I was taking the Course of the path my Horse started forward and broke my Compass in pieces with one of his feet, but I luckily having another Compass did not prevent me from proceeding in the Survey.

Augusta 2d June 1772.

I set out this morning from Sandy run with Howarth and my Servant (Mr. Forest turning off to his plantation at Mcbean River) and Arrived in Augusta about two OClock after Taking the Course and distance of the path etca.

JOURNAL OF DAVID TAITT

Augusta 3d June 1772.

This Day I went and viewed the Town and plantations at Augusta, which Extends about five miles along the west side of Savannah River.

Augusta 4th June 1772.

This being His Majestys Birth Day, I went to see the Malitia of this place Reviewed by their Officers. The men made a very Sorry Appearance, some having Old rusty firelocks, others Riffles, and some being well Clothed and Others with Osnaburgh Shirts and Trousers; they fired platoons as ununiformly as their Acuttrements and dress. After the Review I went to Drink his Majestys health with the officers, where a Mr. Greersons, who is Captain of this banditto, came to me to make an Appologey for his brothers behavour in the Creek nation, alledging that it was a passionate Zeal for Obtaining the grant of Lands from the Indians that prompt[ed] him to so undecent behavour, as he Supposed that I was come there on purpose to prevent the Indians making any Cession of Lands to them.

Augusta 5th June 1772.

Rested all Day at this place.

Silver Bluff, South Carolina, 6th June 1772.

I Crosed Savannah River at the Lower End of Augusta and took the bearings and distance of the path to this place; a Mr. McLean accompanied me as far as this and returned in the Evening to Augusta.

Silver Bluff 7th June 1772.

This Day being Sunday I Stayed at this place.

June 8th 1772.

I sett out this morning with Howarth and my Servant, having a man from Mr. Galphin for my guide, and took the bearings and distance of the path etca. as far as a Mr. Youngs plantation, about thirty miles to Eastward of Silver bluff, the road from thence to this plantation being very bad and difficult for a Stranger to find.

June 9th 1772.

Sett out this morning from Mr. Youngs Plantation taking the Course and distance of the path etca to Crane Savannah where I mistooke the path and went too much to the Northward which Obliged me to go to a plantation on a Branch of SaltCatcher Creek where I Stayed all night.

June 10th 1772.

Sett out this morning taking the Course and distance etca to Georges hill about one mile and a half NE from SaltCatcher Bridge, where I was Obliged to stay all night, one of Howarths Horses having tired was not able to go any further; the River at SaltCatcher bridge is 250 feet aCross runing SE b S.

June 11th 1772.

Sett out from Georges Hill taking the Course and distance etca. about four miles from it. I left the horse that tired last night at a Doctor Days and then proceeded to Jacksons borrough where I Stoped at a Mrs. Colliet's to dine and feed my horses; after dinner I set [out] from Jacksons borrough and Travelled Eleven miles when all my horses tired so that I was Obliged to walk them at a very Slow pace for six miles further where I Called at a plantation belonging to a Mr. Smith, where I told him the Situation I was in with respect to my horses, and desired him to let them Stay at his plantation all night. But without ever giving himself the Trouble to get from his Chair, he told me that he had not any provision or food for my horses, and said that there was a Tavern about a mile further which was the properest place for to put up. I then set out and walked my horses three miles before I came to the Tavern, and when I lighted off my horse the Landlord informed me that his house was already full and that he had nothing to give my horses, without I would trust them in an Open pasture. He informed me that there was another Tavern about a mile further at next bridge. I then proceeded aCross the bridge and along a Marsh to next Tavern which was shut up, it being now between Nine and ten OClock at night, I went about 2 miles further where [I] met with an Open field where I put my horses to feed, and Stayed here all night.

Charlestown South Carolina 12th June.

I sett out this morning at four OClock, about four miles to the westward of Ashley ferry, and Arrived here about nine OClock. It Continued to rain all this Morning which prevented me from taking any Survey of the path etca.

David Taitt.

DR. JOHN BERKENHOUT'S EXCURSION FROM
NEW YORK TO PHILADELPHIA, 1778

INTRODUCTION

Dr. John Berkenhout was born at Leeds, Yorkshire, England, about 1730. His father, who was a merchant and a native of Holland, sent him to Germany to fit himself for a commercial career, but he became interested chiefly in politics, literature, and science. After a brief service in the Prussian army he held the post of captain in the twenty-fourth English regiment of foot during the Seven Years' War from 1756 to 1760. In the latter year he entered Edinburgh University to study medicine. He subsequently proceeded to the University of Leyden and there received the degree of doctor of physic in May, 1765. He wrote *Clavis Anglica Linguæ Botanicæ Linnæi* (1762), *Pharmacopæia Medici* (1766), and became famous with the publication of *Outlines of the Natural History of Great Britain* (1769–1771) and *Biographia Literaria, or a Biographical History of Literature, containing the lives of English, Scotch, and Irish authors, from the dawn of letters in these kingdoms to the present time, chronologically and classically arranged* (1777).

In the spring of 1778 the British ministry sent Dr. Berkenhout and John Temple to America to promote in some secret way the work of the Commission — consisting of Sir Henry Clinton, the Earl of Carlisle, William Eden, and George Johnstone — for restoring peace.

Berkenhout and Temple set out from London the 20th of April. They arrived at Portsmouth the following day. There they were detained more than four weeks before obtaining passage to New York. The storeship *Lioness*, on which they were to sail, arrived at Spithead the 11th of May, but they wanted the whole ward-room for themselves, Mrs. Temple, and servants, besides room for Temple's coach and a vast amount of baggage. This would have necessitated turning out from the ward-room the ship's officers and other gentlemen for whom the captain had been ordered to provide passage, and leaving behind a shipment of hats which the heads of the navy insisted should be taken. The captain refused to furnish the accommodations which Temple and the doctor demanded. The admiral in command of the port was appealed to, but he informed Temple that the ward-room or cabin belonged to the captain, "that the King could take the ship from him, but could not take his Cabbin." Lord George Germain and finally Lord North were communicated with, and the latest record regarding the situation contains a suggestion by Lord North that Temple give up his coach and unnecessary baggage and that the captain yield to the "pressing necessity" of accommodating Temple and Dr. Berkenhout.

Dr. Berkenhout had become acquainted with Dr. Arthur Lee in England. On his way from New York to Philadelphia the doctor made application to General Maxwell for a pass beyond the American lines. The general, on the 25th of August, wrote Richard Henry Lee, brother of Arthur Lee, regarding the matter and Lee replied four days later: "I do recollect that when my brother practiced physic in Virginia about ten or eleven years ago, I then heard him sometimes mention a Doctor Berkenhout who had written a pharmacopia which he esteemed, and that he had an acquaintance with and regard for the Doctor — Beyond this my knowledge of Doctor Berkenhout or his concerns extends not. . . . I have laid your letter before Congress, and their sense seems to be, that you use your discretion in cases similar to that of Doctor Berkenhout, governing yourself by the nature of the circumstances." [1] The doctor states in his journal that he received the pass the 24th of August, which was the day before the general wrote Lee.

Soon after his arrival in Philadelphia the doctor inquired of

[1] *The Letters of Richard Henry Lee*, edited by J. C. Ballagh, Vol. I, p. 432.

INTRODUCTION

Lee if he had received a letter from his brother concerning
him, and having stated that "his intention in coming to
America was to provide a settlement for his family in a land
of liberty, and to find a place where he could practice physick
to advantage," he asked Lee's advice on these matters.

When Dr. Berkenhout had been in Philadelphia six days,
John Dunlap published in his *Pennsylvania Packet* of September 3 the following notice: "A correspondent observes,
that in the *Packet* of the 16th of July last, there is an article
under the London head of April 21, advising, that Dr.
Berkenhout and John Temple, Esq. had the day before set
out from London to Portsmouth, to embark for America,
supposed to be sent on a private embassy to Congress —
and that [in] an article in the *Packet* of the 13th of August,
there is an account of the arrival of those gentlemen at
New-York, and hopes that the Congress will disappoint
them of their base intention, (for they can have no other)
of getting among the good people of these States, in order
to sow dissensions among them." [1]

This notice led to Berkenhout's arrest, search, and impris-
onment the same day by order of the Supreme Executive
Council of Pennsylvania. Among his papers was found the
following letter which he acknowledged intending to send to
Richard Henry Lee:

"SIR:
"The important business in which you are engaged will
not permit you to favour me with as much of your conversation as I am inclined to wish for, I presume therefore, to
trouble you with the following reflexions on paper; they
appear to me of consequence sufficient to deserve a moment's
attention.

"America will most assuredly never relinquish the independence she hath so nobly acquired; this Independence
the Commissioners have no power to grant; it is therefore,
evident that no treaty of pacification can possibly com-
mence. Reflecting on this situation of affairs; most ardently

[1] Ballagh, *Letters of Lee*, Vol. I, p. 459.

solicitous to prevent the further effusion of blood, and impatient to behold the peaceful establishment of this delightful asylum of liberty, I presume to offer myself a voluntary negotiator between the two contending powers. You start at my presumption, but I am sure your candour will suffer me to proceed. If I were to return immediately to England, I am confident that I could command the eager attention of the Ministry; that I could convince them of a thousand errors into which they have been led, relative to the general disposition of the People of America, the Power of the State, the inflexibility and sagacity obvious in every department, and many other particulars, sufficient to convince Great Britain that every idea of subjugating America is futile and ridiculous.

"This information I might give the British Ministry, without any countenance or assistance from Congress or any of its members; but to render my success indisputable, I could wish that I might be enabled to delineate the outlines of such a Treaty of peace and commerce as America would probably approve; I say probably approve, because I do not expect that Congress will give me the least degree of authority. I would presume to request a mere sketch or outline of essential Articles on a slip of Paper, not signed, and intended only to assist my memory." [1]

After confinement for eleven days Dr. Berkenhout was released on condition that he should return immediately to New York. He was soon back in England, where he was awarded a pension for his services and was again busy with his pen, writing *Lucubrations on Ways and Means* (1780), which contained suggestions regarding taxation that were in part followed by Lord North and subsequently by Pitt; *Essay on the Bite of a Mad Dog* (1783); *Symptomatology* (1784); and *Letters on Education to a Son at the University* (1790). If his purpose in America was to create dissensions, he was not without success, for he was the means of widen-

---

[1] *Minutes* of the Supreme Executive Council of Pennsylvania, Vol. XI, pp. 569–570.

ing the breach between Silas Deane and the Lees, Deane charging the Lees with treasonable connections with him.

A manuscript of his journal has been preserved among the Sackville Manuscripts, which have descended from Lord George Germain to Colonel Sackville George Stopford Sackville, to whom the Society is indebted for permission to copy and print the document.

JOURNAL OF AN EXCURSION FROM NEW YORK TO PHILADELPHIA IN THE YEAR 1778

SUNDAY, the 24th of August, with a pass from Sir Henry Clinton, I embarked in a Sloop, with a flag of truce, and landed the same evening at Elizabeth-town, in the province of New Jersey. The rebel-troops extremly ragged. General Maxwell,[1] after some hesitation, gave me a pass.

25th. After dinner sat out for Brunswick, where I arrived late in the evening. A dismal town, but pleasantly situated.

26th. Travelled with three intelligent Americans. Dined at Prince-town, remarkable for its fine College, which is now an Hospital. Slept at Trenton on the Delaware. When General How was stopt by this river, in his march to Philadelphia, it was not fordable; but by means of pontoons, or rafts, it might have been passed with great facility. It is so narrow, that the opposite bank might have been effectually scowered by his cannon. Washington at[2] not, at that time, 3000 men able to bear arms. The Quaker, who then acted as Quarter-master general,[3] affirms that, the morning when the British army was expected to pass the Delaware, being at breakfast with Washington, the General said, with a sigh, "Well, 'tis a noble cause lost! For my own part, I will retire to the banks of the Ohio, where I hope, the English will not think it worth their while to molest me." The same morning he wrote

[1] Brigadier-General William Maxwell, who had been stationed at Elizabethtown to watch the British and the American loyalists.
[2] Had.
[3] Thomas Mifflin, the leader of the Conway Cabal that proposed to have Washington superseded by General Horatio Gates.

to Congress, that his next letter would probably inform them of his having disbanded his army. This I was told by Matlack,[1] secretary to the Executive Counsel of Pensylvania. When Lord Cornwallis, with the flower of the British Army, lay at Trenton, with Washington in his front, a small rivulet between them, and the Delaware in Washingtons rear; that General had not more than 1500 men. He escaped in the night, leaving fifty men to keep up the fires in his camp, and, by a very extraordinary march, was, before morning, in Cornwallis's rear at Princetown, where he surprized a part of the British army. — Recollecting that when people in England were astonished at General Howe's retreat from the Delaware, when he was almost in sight of Philadelphia, Washingtons impregnable intrenchments was the only reason assigned for the retrogade march and subsequent circumnavigation of the British Army; I travelled in hourly expectation of being obstructed by these formidable intrenchments, and was impatient to contemplate their construction: but how was I astonished to find, that no such intrenchments ever existed! How was I surprized, when convinced, from the concurrent testimony of a hundred witnesses, that Washingtons whole army scarce equalled General Howe's advanced Guard; that Washington had actually given up the Game, and that the British troops might have marched triumphantly into Philadelphia, without lett, hindrance, or molestation.

My arrival at Trenton also brought to my recollection the surprize of Colonel Roll,[2] with two Hessian regiments. I enquired of a very sensible inhabitant what was the cause of that disaster. He told me it was intirely owing to Roll's dispising his enemy, and disregarding all intelligence; he also rationally observed, that foreign troops ought not to have occupied an out-post, as they did not understand the language of the Country.

27th. Fell down the Delaware, in a Sloop to Philadelphia. Conversed with the passengers on board, and

[1] Timothy Matlack. [2] Johann Gottlieb Rall.

obtained a good deal of information concerning the disposition of the people in general. I sent General Maxwells pass, with a card, to Richard Henry Lee, one of the delegates for Virginia. He paid me a visit next day, accompanied by one of his colle[a]gues.[1] He afterwards introduced me to Adams, and to several other members of Congress, with whom I frequently conversed, Jointly and seperately. The subjects of our conversation were chiefly — The cause of their declaration of independance — Their treaty with France — Reasons why Britain ought immediately to make peace with America — State of the American Army — Cause of their success — Governor Johnstone's private letters; his political opinions and conduct etc.[2]

Septr. 3d. Having now conversed with many of the Congress, and with the inhabitants at large, during a whole week, I was this day honoured with a visit from Nichola [3] the Town-major, who had orders to seize my papers and to conduct me to the Executive Council. I attended him to the State-house. This sage Council interrogated me concerning my business at Philadelphia — Whether I was not sent by the British Ministry, or by the Commissioners? They said, they had received intelligence from Doctor Franklin of my voyage to America. My papers were perused with great attention, by two of their Members, and, before their contents were known, my commitment was signed.

This Executive Council was composed of men who, from their appearance and capacity, seemed such a club of tradesmen as commonly assemble at an Ale-house, in the borough of Southwark.

By virtue of this commitment, I was conducted to the New-Jail, and there delivered to the custody of a wretched fellow, whose aspect was sufficient to strike horror into the breast of a man of moderate resolution. During my con-

[1] Colonel Nathaniel Scudder of New Jersey.
[2] George Johnstone, governor of West Florida in 1763-1767; as a member of the British peace commission he wrote several letters of which his fellow commissioners disavowed all knowledge.
[3] Colonel Lewis Nicola.

finement, I was twice visited by a Doctor Rush,[1] whom I had formerly seen at Arthur Lee's chambers in London. He was lately a Member of Congress. Under an American mask of sympathetic feeling for my situation, with uncommon loquacious plausibility, he expected to make some important discovery concerning the nature of my commission. From this Doctor I learnt the purport of some of the secret articles of the treaty with France.

I was afterwards frequently visited by Matlack, Secretary to the Executive Council. His character is that of a deep, shrewd Fellow. He affected great openness, and ingenuous conversation. He said — "If I had anything to propose, I might safely speak to him, without reserve; if I wanted any information, he would frankly answer my questions; or, if there was any other person, any man of letters with whom I wished to converse, he should be immediately sent to me." In the last of these conversations, finding me rather less communicative than himself, and determining to try the effect of fear, he told me, that I must not be surprised, if still closer confinement should be thought necessary. He spoke with the Jailor privately. I was then seperated from the other English prisoners, and was ordered not to receive visits from any person whatsoever. Nevertheless I had orders, next morning, to prepare to quit the dominions of the united States at a moments warning.

Septr. 14th. Matlack called upon me about 12 o'Clock and requested me to sign the following paper: viz.

"I John Berkenhout Doctor of Physic, do declare upon my honour, that I will immediately proceed, by the usual rout, to Elizabeth-town in the State of New-Jersey, and from thence within the British lines, and that I will not, from this time, untill my arrival there, do, or say any thing which can, by any means, be construed, or understood to be injurious to the States of North America."

After I had signed this paper, Matlack requested that I would prepare to depart at two Oclock, at which time he

---

[1] Dr. Benjamin Rush.

returned and attended me to the Delaware, where I embarked on board a Sloop for Trenton. This Sloop was loaded with deals and Shingles for building Stables at Trenton for Washingtons Light-horse.

Matlack, previous to my departure, gave me a copy of the above paper, with the following pass.

"The above mentioned Doctor John Berkenhout is ordered to return to the City of New York after having been some days past confined in this city, by order of the supreme Executive Council of the Commonwealth of Pensylvania."

T. MATLACK.

Philadelphia Septr 14th 1778.
   To all concerned.

This Matlack I think, might be bribed, and I believe it not impossible to open a secret correspondance with him.

On my passage from Philadelphia to Trenton, whilst the Vessel lay at anchor, I went on shore, on the Pensylvania side of the river in quest of provisions. Accidentally meeting with one Smith a Quaker, he asked me to dinner. There dined with us a Colonel Penrose of the Jersey Militia, who had been in almost every skirmish during the Campaign of 1777. I obtained some information from this Colonel. They asked me if I knew anything of a Doctor Berkenhout, then under close confinement at Philadelphia? They said people were generally of opinion that he would be hanged.

I travelled from Trenton with three rebel officers: they were Irishmen; their names Quin, King and Power. Quin has a company; he formerly rode private in Ligoniers Horse.[1] These Gentlemen being neither remarkable for wisdom nor sobriety, told me all they knew concerning the former and present state of their army. They unanimously confirmed the accounts I had before received of Washingtons perpetual danger, the incredible distresses of his army and his constant inferiority in point of number. They assured

---

[1] The Black Horse, or 7th Dragoons, a regiment of which Field-Marshall Lord Ligonier (1690–1770) had originally been colonel.

me, that at one time last year, many of their officers were literally without shoes. On this road we passed a number of continental waggons (so they are called) with flower and Rum for Washingtons army. They have five thousand of these Waggons, the drivers of which, being taught the use of arms, act in the double capacity of Waggoners, or Soldiers as occasion may require.

On my return to Elizabeth town, I waited on General Maxwell with my pass. I sat with him near an hour. We drank *Grog*, and talked of General Howes campaigns. Some of his maneuvres, he said, were well enough; but that he was certainly too indolent and too ignorant for the command of such an army. He assured me that the British Army were preparing to evacuate New York, and added, "I knew we should have no more fighting after Howe refused to give us battle at Ches-nut Hill." This Maxwell always commands their light troops. By his language he must be a Scotchman, or from the North of Ireland. Before the rebellion he was a farmer in New Jersey. He wears an old thread-bare blue coat, and a still shabbier hat. In England, one would take him for an invalided corporal of Artillery.

Septr 19th. I came with a flag of truce to Staten Island, and thence to New York the same evening.

Reflexions

The Executive Council, by which I was examined consisted of seven or nine of the lowest, most contemptible fellows I ever saw assembled, except at the Robin Hood.

The members of the present Congress, are, in general, unpolished, illiterate, poor and of no character. Adams, and the two Lees of Virginia have most influence.

Washington is doubtless a man of some genius; but he owes his reputation chiefly to his opponent's want of abilities, or to something worse. Last winter Sir W. Howe commanded, at least, four times the number of the rebel army. If instead of remaining at Philadelphia he had marched

Southwards, so as to have covered Pensylvania, most of the inhabitants of that Province would have declared for legal Government, and would have elected a constitutional assembly. Washington must, in that case, have retreated Southward, in order to secure or destroy his magazines, and thus the provinces of New-York, New Jersey and Pensylvania, would have been effectually covered. Pensylvania alone would supply an army of 50,000 men, for any length of time, with every necessary of life. A great majority of the inhabitants are firmly attached to the king.

That it is impossible to compel Washington to fight, is a very palpable, and hath been a very fatal mistake. He might, with much more facility, escape in an open country. In America, the roads in which an army can possibly march are few, therefore knowing the situation of his magazines, it is always easy to know what rout he will take. I speak with some degree of confidence : I was bred a Soldier.

Most of the Americans with whom I conversed, on my Journey through the Jerseys and at Philadelphia, lamented their seperation from the Mother Country, disapproved the declaration of independance, and detested their French alliance.

The rebel army consists chiefly of Irish transports and of Officers from that country.

If the natives of America were tempted with British establishment and the friends of Government properly supported and secured, an army might soon be raised sufficient to destroy Washington in one campaign.

The Refugees which are now in England and at New York, a burthen to the Nation, might, with very little expence, be so situated as to assist Government in the present contest, and secure the future tranquility of America.

The paper currency of the Congress is now at four and five to one. A little perseverance on the part of Britain will soon reduce it to nothing. They want men, and they will soon want subsistance.

The Hessian troops are extremly disliked by the Americans. Most of Polaski's cavalry are Hessian deserters.

DR. JOHN BERKENHOUT'S EXCURSION

At Philadelphia there is not a single ship, or the least appearance of commerce, consequently wine and every other foreign article is extravagantly dear. The country people are by no means reconciled to paper money.

If Washington be ever defeated and resolutely pursued, his troops will disperse, and hide themselves in the woods. They are not as they have been represented, a respectable body of Yeomanry, fighting *pro aris et focis;* but a contemptible band of vagrants, deserters and thieves.

Gerard [1] is dissatisfyed. Franklin deceived him. That Machiaevel in craft and principle, assured him that the heads of the people were friends to France, and that the operations of the French fleet would be seconded by 80,000 men.

A pardon to all convicts would diminish Washingtons army. Commissions to his officers and the command of as many men as each Officer should bring over, with British and Irish establishment, would, I think, totally ruin his army.

The minority are egregiously mistaken in supposing that the Congress acknowledge any obligation for their opposition to Ministry. They echo their speeches; but they mention the Speakers with contempt.

In treating with America, nothing upon the great line of honour is to be expected. As Britain advances towards accommadation America will recede, in constant expectation of gaining still one point more. If Britain were so weak as to acknowledge their independance they have other claims which they would most impudently make, and which Britain, if she values her existance, must never grant.

The insolence of these demagogues, who rule America, is intirely founded on their opinion of Washington's superior talents. They are however jealous of his power, and are

[1] Conrad Alexander Gerard, who, as principal Secretary of the Council of State of France, negotiated on the part of the French Government the first treaties of alliance and commerce between France and the United States. About the middle of July, 1778, he had come to Philadelphia as the first minister of France to this country, and remained in that capacity until September, 1779.

so extreamly fearful of the people, that the authority of Congress is constantly exerted in suppressing every publication calculated to undeceive them.

Nothing would so effectually shake the resolution of the Congress, as unanimity in the British Parliament.

Whenever these people are resolutely opposed, the[y] will be found pusilanimous and contemptibly abject.

When Britain once resolves to conquer America, the business is done. Previous to this (pardon my presumption) I wish that Parliament would resolve, not to treat with Congress on any terms whatsoever.

TRAVEL DIARY OF BISHOP AND MRS. REICHEL
AND THEIR COMPANY FROM LITITZ, PENN-
SYLVANIA, TO SALEM IN WACHOVIA, NORTH
CAROLINA, 1780

INTRODUCTION

THE synod of the Moravian church, which was held at Barby, Saxony, in 1775, centralized the government of that body by making the minister of each congregation an agent or representative of the Unity's Elders' Conference and by restricting the membership of the church council, in which was vested the power to elect elders and trustees. The synod of Barby also formulated certain doctrines and pronounced them essential. To adjust the American branch of the church to these new enactments and "to give comfort and counsel to the Brethren" the Unity's Elders' Conference commissioned Bishop John Frederick Reichel. He procured a safe conduct from the British authorities; arrived at Bethlehem, Pennsylvania, in April, 1779; convened a conference of ministers at Lititz on the 5th of August, and subsequently visited almost all the scenes of the church's activity, North and South. This diary is an account of his journey from Lititz to Salem, and the one following is an account of his return over the same road, which traversed Virginia east of the Blue Ridge. The diarist of the return journey seems to have been Christian Heckewelder, who was largely instrumental in procuring from the legislature of North Carolina the Act of January, 1779, permitting an affirmation of allegiance and fidelity by the Moravians of that State to answer for an oath. Who wrote the diary of the journey to Salem may perhaps best be left to conjecture.

The diaries, in German, have been preserved among the archives of the Moravian church at Winston-Salem, North Carolina. The translation here printed is by Miss Adelaide L. Fries, Archivist.

TRAVEL DIARY OF BISHOP AND MRS. REICHEL AND THEIR COMPANY FROM LITITZ TO SALEM IN THE WACHAU (WACHOVIA) FROM MAY 22, TO JUNE 15, 1780

MAY 22. About nine o'clock in the morning, after an affectionate farewell to the dear Brethren in Lititz, we began our journey in the name of the Lord and under His guidance, rejoicing in the knowledge that the Brethren in Pennsylvania and the Wachau were praying for us. Our company consists of ten Brethren,[1] and four teamsters. The Brethren Simon Peter and Zahm accompanied us two miles. At noon we had our first meal in the woods, — a cold lunch. In the sixth hour we reached Anderson's Ferry,[2] where the Susquehannah is 1¼ miles wide. On the side from which we approached there is a high sandy bank, and the wheels of Conrad's wagon sank to the axle in the sand, and were freed only after one and a half hours of work with levers and extra horses. On the other side is a high stony ridge. We were so fortunate as to get our two wagons and three riding horses across within two hours, by means of two Flats, which are too small for a river of such considerable size; but frequently travellers are detained here for an entire day. Each crossing takes only ten minutes, and they race with each other. But they had to cross over and back three times, and the loading and unloading takes as much time as the crossing. Here they charge $56.00 for taking over a six-horse wagon, and $8.00 for a horse and rider; at Wright's Ferry,[3] where the Susquehannah is two

---

[1] Bishop and Mrs. Reichel, Br. and Sr. Jeppe Nielsen, the Single Brother Joh. Fr. Peter, Br. and Sr. Aust, Br. and Sr. Blum, and the Single Sister Mar. Magd. Reutz.

[2] Anderson's Ferry was about four miles above Wright's Ferry.

[3] Wright's Ferry ran between the present Columbia and Wrightsville.

miles wide, the charge is $90.00 for a six-horse wagon, and $12.00 for a horse and rider. Some two miles from the Susquehannah, on a creek called Susquehannah Creek, we made our first outdoor night-camp, in a pretty open space surrounded by tall trees. We admired the blue dome above us, set with sparkling diamonds, and quenched our thirst with wholesome tea, and satisfied our hunger with Lititz bread and meat. During the night some of us lay under a cloth stretched across three poles and pegged to the ground, but as the other tent was not to hand the rest lay under the roof that God had made, beside a big fire, for the night was cool. Br. Blum was our commissary, Br. Aust camp-master, and the Sisters Blum and Aust did the cooking. The others helped where they could. That we should have slept well this first time in our unaccustomed quarters was not to be expected, but as time wore on we wished for nothing better. Tob. Hirte visited us, and later served us in various ways.

The 23. After strengthening ourselves with coffee at breakfast we travelled to the top of the Susquehannah ridge, from whence a beautiful view of plantations, houses, fields, orchards and meadows, hills and valleys, extended all the way to Yorktown,[1] which we reached about eleven o'clock, receiving a hearty welcome from Br. and Sr. Neisser. Here we remained till three o'clock, to our mutual pleasure and joy. In parting Br. Neisser gave us the Daily Text as encouragement for our way; "The Lord will give grace and glory; no good thing will He withhold from them that walk uprightly," with which words we encouraged one another. Here our party was joined by a tanner named Doub, who had been visiting friends in Pensylvania and was returning to Carolina. We made 17 miles to-day, and camped for the night on a green hill close by a house. Here for the first time we were all in tents, and rested very well.

The 24. It was so cold a morning that we could scarcely keep warm at breakfast. We broke camp at six o'clock.

---

[1] York, York County, Pennsylvania.

This morning in a rough piece of woodland, Conrad's wagon in going down a hill ran into a tree, and crushed the left front wheel. We thanked the Saviour that the wagon and horses were not thrown to the ground, for it looked as if that might easily have happened. This accident detained us an hour until the wagon could be repaired. At 1 : 30 we reached Mc.Allister's (formerly Hannover's),[1] where we had a beautiful mid-day rest in a barn. We refreshed ourselves on the good beer to be obtained here. Toward evening we passed through Peter-Town,[2] and camped for the night two miles further on, on the Maryland line, near Stauffer, the brother of Sr. Cath. Stauffer of Bethlehem. That night, as we sat around our fire and held our evening service, in the darkness a wall seemed round about us, and the words came naturally to our minds, "I will be a wall round about you," Zech. 2, 5. And in the forest we seemed to see a city, with high castles and towers and houses, wrought out with finest architectural skill. To all the frogs added their night music.

The 25. The morning again was cool. It was after six o'clock when we broke camp. Danitown [3] is a little village with one solitary street, lying seven miles from our camp, at a point where the forests are sprinkled with pines. The road thither was full of people to-day, as it was the Catholic festival of Corpus Christi, and they were going to the Catholic Church in Danitown. On the way we passed the home of Adam Loesch, and spoke with him. He was planning to sell his house, and move to Holston River in Virginia, 400 miles from there. Beyond Danitown, which we had reached at 9 : 30, Hauser's wagon almost upset. Br. Reichel had alighted when to our pleasure we were met by Br. Schweisshaupt, and the two Brethren Weller and Kampf from Manakosy,[4] the road from the latter place here coming out into the main road to Friedrichstown.[5] They showed us the way to a pretty mid-day resting place on the large Fifer

---

[1] Now Hanover, Pennsylvania.   [2] Petersburg.
[3] Taneytown, Maryland.   [4] Monocacy, Maryland.
                    [5] Frederick, Maryland.

Creek,[1] over which there is a bridge now impassable. There we pleasantly conversed together, near the home of Gentleman Bruce, a cousin of our deceased Br. Steph. Bruce. Br. Schweisshaupt and the two Brn. from Manakosy, who were able to supply us with fresh provisions, accompanied us for two miles to the place where the road from Baltimore to Manakosy crosses the road to Carolina at right angles, then took friendly leave of us, commending us to the good guidance of our God. From there it is 9 miles to Manakosy, and about 50 miles to Baltimore. To-day we made 20 miles, and camped about 75 miles from Lititz and 8 from Friedrichstown, in a beautiful green spot. In the evening we again saw a wonderful scenic effect, — a round amphitheatre, with high arches and pillars. The nights began to be milder, and the heat of the day more oppressive.

The 26. At 7 : 30 we crossed the Manakosy, a stream half as large as the Lecha near Bethlehem, and at 9 : 30 reached Friedrichtown, where we stopped at the Inn of Mr. Grosh, Brother of the Groshes of Lititz, where we had a good meal. He has a pleasant English wife, who waited on us in a kind and courteous manner; she has many lively, attractive children, who speak only English. The old father is still bright and well. Here we met Br. and Sr. Kamp, of Manakosy (she was a Protzmann), and their five months old child who gave us much pleasure with his lively, pretty, good-natured ways. We also met Br. Schau, of Carolsmanor, who begged Br. and Sr. Reichel to visit Carolsmanor on their return trip; his family are very anxious to re-establish close connection with the Brethren. Br. Reichel visited Mr. William Ockel, an inn-keeper in the town and a friend of the Brethren, who offered to forward letters and attend to any commissions for the Brethren going to and from Carolina. We were annoyed by the unpleasant conversation of the misguided Hepner, who ran away from Lititz. Every word that he spoke was a lie, as we learned from Br. Kamp, who knew him in Manakosy and knew all his tricks. His

---

[1] Pine Creek.

wife, a Virginian, who had been in town barely eight days
when he married her, left him after seven months and returned to her own home. He is working in town. Friedrichtown has a pleasant location, a stream runs through it,
and it contains good houses. Congress-money still has good
value here, — 40 to 1, — many say 30 to 1; indeed there
is little silver in the town. It was necessary for us to exchange silver for Congress-money, as we were going into
Virginia where for the most part there is little money and
silver is little used, and Br. Blum, through Mr. William
Ockel, found a man who gave us 55 for 1. Then we resumed
our journey, and near Hiel's home, nine miles from Friedrichstown, met Br. Shau's wife, from Carolsmanor, who
repeated her husband's invitation; two miles further on
we made camp near Mr. Th. Noland's house, close to the
road which turns to the right from the Foart road towards
Noland's Ferry, which crosses the Patomoak two miles
from here. So far our journey had been very pleasant.
Now, however, the Virginia air brought storms. Here and
there in the woods we saw Virginia cabins, built of unhewn
logs and without windows. Kitchen, living room, bed room
and hall are all in one room into which one enters when
the house door opens. The chimney is built at the gable
end, of unhewn logs looking like trees, or it is omitted altogether. Everywhere we saw the negroes moving about;
one came in the evening to our tent, probably to see what
was worth stealing. Neither we nor the teamsters liked
the place, which was not convenient for a camp; but no
one knew of a better place, nor had courage to seek one,
for the sun had set when we reached there; yet all had a
presentiment of impending trouble.

The 27. The next morning, rising early, we found that
Br. Reichel's chest, containing all his books and papers, the
Deed to the Wachau, letters, and his and his wife's clothing,
had been stolen from the wagon, together with a flask of
rum, some food, and Hauser's sickles and clothing, which
filled us with consternation! This delayed our further
journey until about eight o'clock. Br. Aust rode back two

miles to tell Leonh. Heil, who keeps an inn. He returned
with him at once, and suggested writing out a description
of the stolen articles, which could be put into an advertisement, and posted up everywhere, and this was at once done.
He promised to do his best to find the stolen goods. Meanwhile Mr. Th. Noland had risen, and was informed of the
occurrence. He seemed much embarrassed and perplexed,
and said he feared the theft had been committed by some
of his negroes, and promised to try to find the guilty party ;
he rode two miles into the woods saying they had probably
hidden the things there, but soon returned saying he believed
the thieves had fled across the Patomako.[1] On this supposition Leonh. Heil went with us to the Patomoak, and
promised the ferrymen, who are also negroes, that they
should have a large fee if they would find the stolen property.
Later this man Heil took much more trouble for us in this
matter. *Note.* Mr. Th. Noland and his father and father-
in-law have 200 negroes in this neighborhood, on both
sides of the Patomoak, and this neighborhood is far-famed
for robbery and theft. Travellers should take care here.
The road on to the Patomoak was bad. Going down a steep
hill to a bridge over the Tuscaror Hauser's wagon almost
upset, which excited much alarm. About 9 o'clock we
reached the Patomoak, and as there was only one small
ferry boat it was 11 : 30 before we and the wagons and horses
were all across. The high water line on the southern side
of the Patomoak is the boundary between Maryland and
Virginia. It was very hot to-day, and there was a storm
in the afternoon. Sr. Reichel was not quite well these two
days. Our journey to-day was short, and we made our
night camp two miles from Louisburg.[2] This evening the
two Carolina riding horses ran away again two miles into
the woods. It took Br. Blum until eleven o'clock to find
and bring them back, and meanwhile his travelling coat,
which he had hung on a stump between the tents, was
stolen, as were also two bells, two towels, and the feed

[1] Potomac. [2] Leesburg.

591

sacks. We now keep watch all night, but the watchman could not prevent this theft, for the night was very dark, and the negroes, who had a free evening, were roaming everywhere. We have learned by sad experience that Virginia is full of thieves.

The 28. Tob. Hirte and Doub, who had remained behind for several days, rejoined us yesterday, and to-day Br. Reichel sent them back to Mr. Th. Noland, with instructions to look about, and to see what he would advise about the stolen goods, and especially whether he could not get back the papers. He gave them a letter to this effect to the said Noland. We made our noonday camp on the great Goes-Creek,[1] eight miles beyond Louisburg, and as it was Sunday we rested until four o'clock. The way here, and beyond, was very hilly and stony. We cooked with rice the hens we had bought in Louisburg, but the pot tipped over and we had to cook a second time. In the afternoon we made five miles more, and stopped for the night in an open place by a run.

The 29. In the morning we found that the two Carolina horses had run off through the woods towards home, and they fed themselves bountifully in a fine field of clover. The worst of it was that we suspected they had been stolen, which might easily happen to us in Virginia, where there is much horse-stealing, and we thought this the more because a man, whom we later learned to be only simple, had hung about eying our every movement as intently as though he were watching someone or were planning some roguery. As we thought that the quickest way to recover the horses would be to promise a reward to the rogue we did so, but the horses did not appear. Having spent till eight o'clock on the matter we then continued our journey, leaving Br. Blum to seek the horses, and with the help of three men, to whom he had to give over $100.00[2] for their trouble, he found them about mid-day in the aforesaid clover field, and brought them to us after we had camped for the night. At

[1] Goose Creek.   [2] Continental currency.

noon we had halted in the woods, one and a half miles from Redhouse. Redhouse is 25 miles from Louisburg, and 130 from Lititz, that is 195 from Bethlehem. We camped for the night eight miles beyond Redhouse. The ticks, whose acquaintance we had already made at the Susquehannah, now began to be very troublesome.

The 30. We soon reached Nevill's Tavern, which is ten miles from Redhouse, and six miles further passed through Germantown,[1] — when one is in the town one asks where the town is. To-day we made only fourteen miles partly on account of the hilly, rough, and marshy road, partly because Hauser's wagon broke several times and had to be repaired, and during the afternoon Conrad's wagon stuck in a deep hole, and it took four extra horses, that is ten in all, to pull and twist it out. Since we left the Patomoak it has thundered every day and especially this entire afternoon, and in the evening it began to rain and rained all night, so that tents and beds and clothes were all soaked.

The 31. It was very muddy and wet, but we made fair progress. About 8 : 30 we forded the Rapihannik,[2] as there is neither bridge nor ferry. After a heavy rainstorm we halted for our mid-day lunch. Then we went on through thunder and rain till we reached a new house, whose owner, Mr. Shelton, had gone on a trip to North Carolina. His wife, who had two sick children, gave friendly answer to our request, and showed us into a room where there were four beautiful double beds. We were glad to be under a roof, and to sleep in the dry. As a matter of precaution Br. and Sr. Blum stayed with the wagons, which drove a little further into the woods. We paid $1 : oo Cont. apiece for our night's lodging, and $1 : oo Cont. for a quart of milk. Sr. Reutz was thrown from her horse to-day, and while not seriously hurt she was afraid to ride again.

Jun. 1. It was only six miles to the Rapidan, but the water was so high from yesterday's heavy rain that we could

[1] Nevill's Tavern, Red House, and Germantown were on the Winchester and Fredericksburg road.
[2] Rappahannock.

go no further. We took advantage of the time and the good weather to dry our wet clothes and beds, for washing and cooking and other domestic tasks, and enjoyed being together in the woods.

The 2. We started at 5 : 30 A.M. and crossed the Rapidan safely. The water only came up to the wagon-beds to-day. Here the teamsters bought a good supply of feed for the horses, for we were approaching the section where the English prisoners were and knew we would be able to get little as the Commissary had bought it up for them. After crossing the Rapidan one follows the bank of the river for about four miles, and all kinds of beautiful trees are mingled together. If a town were laid out here and the land brought into a better state of cultivation this would be an unusually pretty section. In spite of the hills we made twenty miles to-day, which is much for us. Toward evening Tob. Hirte and Br. Hr. Stoehr caught up with us. Tob. Hirte had reclaimed a few pieces of Hauser's clothing from Th. Noland, but nothing more. Heil was continuing his kindly efforts in the matter. We camped for the night in a beautiful green spot. It rained a little during the night.

The 3. We started out at five o'clock and made twenty-three miles, which was our longest day's journey. It was very hot and oppressive, and in the afternoon we had a severe thunder-storm and heavy rain. About five o'clock, as Conrad was trying in vain to force his horses to pull the wagon over a particularly steep place, there was a flash of lightning and crack of thunder, and instantly the horses had the wagon over the bad place. Hauser's wagon was standing by a mudhole, and his horses shied, almost upsetting the wagon. We gave the Saviour childlike thanks that all turned out so well for us, and that the storm came no nearer, for not far behind us and on Stanton [1] River ahead of us the storm brought hail which beat the crops to the ground. We camped half a mile from Bird's Ordinary. (Ordinary is the Virginia name for an inn.)

[1] Roanoke River.

The 4. We wished to make an early start, but Conrad's horses had strayed off, and that detained us two hours, — it would have been longer had not Br. Stoehr found them and brought them to our camp. We shortened our mid-day rest because eight Continental wagons camped near us. Already on the 28th and 29th of May we had met a number of wagons, belonging with these, which had been to South Carolina with arms and ammunition and were now returning. Br. Hr. Stoehr took a letter from Br. Reichel to Br. Marshall and went ahead to announce our approach. We made about eighteen miles to-day, and camped for the night half a mile from Peyne's Tavern in a large uncultivated field in which a school-house stood. During the night the two Carolina horses started off, but were soon brought back.

The 5. This morning one of them had again gone to the woods, and had to be driven in. They knew they were nearing home, and were in a hurry. We had seven miles to go to reach the James River, which we crossed by means of a small ferry, getting over about eleven o'clock. To reach the ferry we had to drive down such a steep and badly washed hill that it was a wonder that the wagon did not turn over. On the other side of the river we lunched on a beautiful green height. In the afternoon we refreshed ourselves on the first ripe cherries. From two gentlemen, who came through Salem, we received certain information that Charlestown had been forced to surrender to the British, the report being confirmed by the stories of both sides.[1] This made a great stir in Verginia. From there on we saw many people fleeing from South and North Carolina, and the Virginians thought us queer creatures to be going to North Carolina. While we were camped six miles from Cumberland Court-House 100 Militiamen rode by, who had been drafted at Cumberland Court-House. A drunken fellow kept us a whole hour that evening telling us the circumstances of the capture of Charlestown. We were thankful when he finally departed without talking all night.

[1] Charleston surrendered the 12th of May.

The 6. We set out at five o'clock, and passed Cumberland Court-House. In the afternoon we went five or six miles out of our way, for the Appomatik [1] ford was impassable and the teamsters thought a side track to the right would lead to a bridge across that creek. It thundered and rained and grew to be dark night before we found a place where there was water and where we could camp. We were now in a section where there are few springs, and the soil is mostly sand, glittering with isinglass.

The 7. Starting about six o'clock we found the right way to the bridge over the Appomatik, which we crossed about 8 : 30. It is a small but deep stream, with steep banks which make fording impossible. From then till noon we travelled a miserable road over hills and valleys, and through a creek with steep banks, and saw large orchards along the way. In the afternoon, after we had passed the Academy, which had many broken window-panes, our track turned again into the main road. In the evening after we had set up our tents there came a thunder and rain storm. We were twenty-eight miles from Stanton River.

The 8. During the morning we met Mr. Shelton, in whose house we spent the night of May 31. We gave him news of his family, and he expressed his pleasure that we had lodged there. We crossed a bridge over the little Roanoke, a small but very deep stream, and passed Charlotte Court-House. We had rain until nearly noon when it cleared somewhat. But as we finished lunch there came a thunder storm with strong wind and pouring rain. We crept into and under the wagons and so protected ourselves from the rain. In the afternoon it was clear, and we crossed marshy ground on a corduroy road half a mile long, to drive over which would certainly be good medecine for a hypocondriac. We spent the night in a pretty open green spot, where we ate the first Journey-Cakes with a good appetite. It was a very cool night.

The 9. In the morning we crossed a bridge all full of

---

[1] Appomattox.

holes, and were grateful to the Saviour for our safety as we considered the very apparent danger. We also passed safely through the deep bottom as we neared Stanton River and across its ford whose steep approaches gave the teamsters much trouble. It took eight horses to pull Conrad's wagon out, and that with difficulty. On the farther bank we stopped at noon, and nine miles beyond made our night's camp.

The 10. The roads were very bad. Steep hills washed by the heavy rains alternated with deep bottoms and swampy places. Everything fell out of the wagons. Here we made a new arrangement. Br. and Sr. Neilsen and Br. and Sr. Aust rode double on two of the horses, and Sr. Reichel rode for the first time alone, the rest went afoot. We thanked the dear Lord that everything went through without accident, and that Sr. Nielsen was not hurt when she fell from her horse. Noon was spent at the high Bannister Bridge. We had trouble in getting water enough from a muddy spring. Our night camp was half a mile from Old Halifax, 100 miles from Salem.

The 11. When we were in Old Halifax we asked about this famous town and received the information, "You are in the very city." (This is only an application of an old story.) There are only a couple of houses here. Sr. Reichel had a headache to-day, but was better in the afternoon. At noon as she lay on a bed in the shade a hog jumped over her because the dog was after it, and that cured her. (This creature is far too familiar in Virginia, and must be forcibly driven away.) The heat was great, and we had storms every day. We made nineteen miles to-day, and camped by Lynch's Tavern.

The 12. Yesterday afternoon and this morning the road was so hilly, rough and washed by the rains, that we might well thank the Saviour that we had no accident. Br. Jeppe Nielsen was so weak to-day that he could not ride and had to stay in the wagon most of the time. Hauser was made happy by the arrival of his men, Jac. Stotz and Sam. Strubb of Bethanian, who came to help him, and as one of the wheel horses to Conrad's wagon was quite worn out one of theirs was put in its place. We stopped for noon at the Sandy River. Toward evening a heavy storm broke, and we were soaked.

The 13. A miserable road, ruts filled with sand by the rain, stony, hilly, and full of holes. Hauser nearly had a bad accident with his horses and wagon, for as they were going down a steep hill the breast chain broke and the near horse was thrown under the wheel; but the driver saw it in time and the horse escaped serious injury, being only scratched on crupper and one foot. The hand of the Lord protected us that we did not have a terrible misfortune. This morning we crossed the Carolina line, and our noon rest was for the first time on Carolina soil. Here we were joined by Mr. Habersham,[1] who had had Br. Wagner on his estate in Georgia, showing him much kindness during his illness; he had his lady and children with him and they were fleeing from South Carolina and the British. He conversed pleasantly with the Brn. Reichel and Nielsen, and rejoiced to hear from the latter that he had seen Br. Wagner in England and that he was doing well. Further on we met his loaded wagons and 150 negroes. In spite of the recent rains we passed safely over Smith's River and Matrimony Creek, and camped for the night one mile beyond the latter.

The 14. In the morning we came to within a short mile of the Meho[2] River. As we rested by a beautiful spring we were joined by a Presbyterian minister, who came hither from Virginia last spring, and who asked us all sorts of questions concerning our position on matters political, and after an earnest but discreet conversation bade us a friendly farewell. There is an outdoor pulpit here where he probably preaches. The semblance of a pulpit is built of logs and boards fastened between two trees; the benches are of

[1] In 1774 the Moravians established a mission on Joseph Habersham's estate in Georgia for the conversion of the negroes, and immediately following the surrender of Savannah to the British, on the 29th of December, 1778, Habersham removed his family to Virginia. [2] Mayo.

logs, resting on blocks. In this woodland church we made our mid-day camp. Now we became very eager to reach Salem, and our joy was great when two miles beyond the Meho we met the Brn. Marschall and Herbst, with the wagon of the Single Brethren and the teamsters Br. Broesing and Br. Hr. Stoehr, coming to assist our further journey. We thanked the Saviour with grateful hearts that He had brought us so far on our way, and we spent a happy evening in camp.

The 15. We rose early and took up our journey with joy, crossing the Dan River safely, and reaching the Brethren in Salem about six in the evening, thankful to the Saviour Who had guided and led us like children, and had given us to feel His peace and presence throughout the entire way. We were welcomed with trombones, which played "Euren Eingang segen Gott."

June 16. The wagons, which were left behind yesterday, arrived safely this morning. And so we are in Salem, in this town of the Lord's peace, — may He bless us and be with us in all we shall do for him. Amen!

TRAVEL DIARY OF BISHOP REICHEL, MRS.
REICHEL, AND CHRISTIAN HECKEWELDER
FROM SALEM TO LITITZ, 1780

EXTRACT FROM THE TRAVEL DIARY OF THE BELOVED BR. AND SR. REICHEL AND THE SINGLE BR. CHRIST. HECKEWELDER FROM SALEM TO LITITZ

AFTER Br. Reichel had conducted a tender and touching farewell service for the dear congregation in Salem on the evening of *Oct. 4, 1780*, closing with the church's blessing, we left

Oct. 5. At nine in the morning, the prayers of all the Brethren going with us from the town of peace — Salem. Br. and Sr. Marschall,[1] Sr. Neilsen, and a gratifying number of Brethren, went a little way with us, the Marschalls twelve miles to Sam. Waggoner's, where we took our first mid-day lunch, and then they bade us and we bade them an affectionate farewell. Br. Johan Krause, however, went on with us to our night camp, which we made a mile from Dan River, and gave us good help this first evening. This afternoon we were accompanied by a number of very ragged travelers who were going our way, but they finally left us. Mr. Moses Martin wanted to keep us over night, but it was early when we met him and we thought it better to go several miles further, so it was rather late when we set up our tent by a branch, and after enjoying our evening meal lay down to rest in the primeval forest for the first time on this journey.

The 6. At six we broke camp, and soon passed Dan River, where after a tender farewell Br. Krause left us to return home. The high bank of Dan River gave us much trouble, for though the wagon was lightly loaded it slipped back into the water three times, but by God's help we finally

[1] Frederick William von Marshall and his wife, who were at the head of the church in North Carolina. They attended the synod of Barby and returned from Europe with Bishop Reichel.

got out, and by mid-day we were at the Meho,[1] where we fed and lunched. This afternoon we met a number of travelers, including several wagons that were fleeing from the Indians. We camped on Matrimony Creek, and rested quietly.

The 7. Taking up our journey at 5 : 30 we thanked our kind Lord for our night's rest, and with united hearts and voices sang, — "Solt ich meinem Gott nicht singen," and this we did each day of our trip, after breaking camp and after Br. Reichel had read us the daily texts, and the names of those whose birthday it was. We soon crossed Smith's River, again meeting many families traveling, and seeing many of Mr. Habersham's camping places. We stopped at noon near Col. Perkin's, where the Col. himself visited us, and we camped for the night on a branch four miles beyond Sandy River, where Br. Heckewelder had camped two years earlier, and slept sweetly and quietly all night.

The 8. Early in the morning we passed through a hilly section; as our morning hymn we sang, "Wach auf, mein Herz, und singen." Soon we met two wagons from Jersey on their way to Rowan County, and the teamsters told us that the road from Redhouse to Halifax, (a distance of 200 miles,) swarmed with soldiers, going to Carolina; that they had been impressed, but had gotten away, and they said we would have the same fate; but we took no notice of that and went calmly on our way. As the floods in this section had ruined nearly all the fields fodder was very dear and hard to get. This afternoon we saw the sun for the first time on this journey, so far each day we had had mist and fine rain, but the sun shone so warm that we expected more rain to follow. At twilight we went through the miserable town of Old Halifax, and were thankful that we were not halted. We camped half a mile further on, where we were met by some acquaintances from the Forks of the Adkin,[2] who were returning thither, and by them we sent greetings to the dear Brethren in the Wachau. This night also we slept quietly and undisturbed.

[1] Mayo. [2] Yadkin.

The 9. Happily and thankfully we went on our way, and soon met wagons coming from Petersburg, whose owners told us that a French fleet with 7000 men and a number of cannon on board had run in to Southkey. At nine o'clock we passed the high and dangerous Bannister Bridge, and ate breakfast there; and stopped at noon eight miles beyond, near two brooks. Toward evening we reached Stanton [1] River, where we met soldiers going to Carolina, and it was quite dark before we got across. We camped half a mile further on and everything was quiet there and around us.

The 10. We broke camp about a quarter before six, and went on our way, were met with many requests for news, and complied by telling what we heard yesterday. This afternoon we had much trouble to find water, and drove until late before we could find a place to camp; stopped at last near a house but everything went wrong, and our chocolate fell into the fire twice. Toward evening, too, one of our horses got sick, but we had a horse-doctor see it, and he soon cured it. When all was once more in order we closed the day, thankful for our successful journey so far, and lay down to rest; but it was a cold night.

The 11. The first stage of this day's journey was to Prince Edward Courthouse, which was soon left behind, and then we went on to the Appomatick River which we reached about noon. It is only a little river some five rods wide and not deep, but is crossed by a ferry which has the advantage that when it is turned round the other end almost touches the other shore. It runs on a rope made of grapevines and hickory withes, and a child could manage the whole thing, but a grown negro is kept there by his master, who built the ferry, and had to dam up the water to run it, and one must pay $40.00 to cross with a wagon and four horses. We passed quitely by the numerous Ordinaries, or Taverns, which are in this section, and of which Wright's Ordinary is the best, and stopped for the night four miles

[1] Staunton.

this side of Cumberland Courthouse, but lost much time trying to find water which is scarce in this neighborhood.

The 12. It was early when we reached Smith's Shop, where a good honest man lives, and we bought a supply of oats. At noon we were nine miles from James River; the day had been rainy, but in the afternoon it began to rain in earnest, and this brought back Sr. Reichel's headache, which had troubled her several times already on this trip; Br. Reichel also had several attacks of diarrhea, which made the journey hard for him also. At four o'clock we passed James River, and went three miles further to a branch near a plantation, where we put up our tents. The owner of this plantation, so he said, had fodder stolen from his fields nearly every night, so early in the morning of

The 13 he came to us and accused us of having taken his corn, he was assured that we had not done so, that we had bought our fodder earlier and paid for it, and that we never did such things. He believed us, and returned contentedly to his house, and we entered happily on the eighth day of our journey. We paused for a little at nine o'clock to eat breakfast, and the younger Rothrock came by; he lives eight miles from Bethlehem and was on his way to Carolina, and after talking to him a while we sent greetings by him to the Brethren in the Wachau, asking him to tell them of our safe journey so far. At noon we were beyond Pains Ordinary, and after Sr. Reichel had taken a little coffee she at last lost her headache, which pleased us all. This afternoon we saw the first traces of the Army, said to be going from Virginia to North Carolina, for we met perhaps 100 militia-men, traveling however without organization. They asked whence we came, and when we answered, "From North Carolina," they thought we were refugees and said, "Turn back to your homes, we will soon recover your property." We thanked them politely but went on our way, telling them that the wagon would soon return. The weather, which had been rainy all day, cleared toward evening; we overtook the Jersey wagon which was in Salem recently and there purchased and laid in supplies; it left more than a week before us, and one of the men had been sick with fever the entire way. This night we camped four miles beyond Birds Ordinary, by Mr. Watson's Plantation, and after sharing our evening meal all slept calmly and comfortably.

The 14. In God's name we continued our journey, and soon met several families from the Forks of the Adkin traveling to Maryland, and had the pleasure of giving their poor hungry children some of our food, which their elders acknowledged with many thanks. In the afternoon a pleasant incident happened. A stocking had fallen from our wagon, and was found by two Virginia gentlemen, who followed us a couple of miles, riding quite out of their way, and after making sure that it belonged to us they gave it to us, which astonished us greatly, for it was an unusual example of Virginia custom. Late in the evening we passed Orange Courthouse, which was full of men as this had been Muster day, and we rejoiced that they let us pass quietly ; we camped half a mile beyond, near a Negro Quarter, whose inhabitants speedily visited us wishing to furnish us apples, blades, and milk, but we could not use the milk because it had been thickened with flour, and the blades might have been stolen and were at any rate not of the best, so we held off. In spite of the constant coming and going of the negroes the night passed safely, and they feared to disturb us on account of our good dog, constantly on the alert.

The 15, Sunday. The weather was very cloudy and dark, and for several nights the halo round the moon had prophesied rain, which we certainly had to-day. This morning we passed through the beautiful country along the Rapidann, where almost every kind of tree is to be seen, crossed the river about noon, and saw and spoke with our acquaintance and good friend, Mr. Marvin Moore, who knew us at once, inquired after Br. Joseph, Marshall, Etwein, and others, and would gladly have taken us in, but we hurried on, stopped one mile beyond for lunch and were caught in a heavy rain which forced us into the wagon and continued the entire afternoon, and finally obliged us to stop at Capt.

Bradley's, otherwise Dutch Coopers, where we were well cared for. Here we heard that Gen. Arnold, who had planned to betray Gen. Washington into the hands of the English had deserted to them.[1]

The 16. After breakfast we set out with clear weather, found the streams up but not too much to permit us to pass. In the afternoon by a house we met George Hamm, who since May has been away from home peddling here and there. We had a very bad stony road, especially in the place known as the Devil's Race Ground, where we saw rocks enough. About five o'clock we passed the place where Germantown once stood, but little of it is now to be seen; and four miles beyond, on a branch, we camped for the night, but so heavy a storm with a N.W. wind arose that we could hardly set up our tent, and we had to let it stand quite crooked. We committed ourselves to the protection of the guardian of Israel, who kept us safe body and soul, although at midnight the storm-wind blew so that we momentarily expected the tent to come down on our heads; however the wind lulled somewhat toward morning.

The 17. We breakfasted about 3:30 A.M. and went on with our journey, though it was so cold that we fastened the wagon cover closely, instead of looping it back as usual. At sunrise we passed Capt. Nevill's, and soon after the storm-wind rose again. We saw several families fleeing from Carolina to Maryland. On Goose Creek we set up our tent for the fourteenth and last time on this trip, and on account of the cold storm and the lack of fuel we found it chilly sleeping, but we rested calmly and undisturbed, for which

The 18 we thanked the Saviour in our morning prayers; we also sang several stanzas wishing a blessing on our dear Br. Johannes on this his 63rd birthday. The Daily Text impressed us: "Those whom He hath gathered out of the lands, from the east, and from the west, from the north, and from the south, they shall praise the Lord for His good-

[1] Benedict Arnold's plan to surrender West Point to the British was discovered the 23d of the preceding month by the capture of Major André at Tarrytown.

ness, and for His wonderful works to the children of men."
Ps. cvii, 3, 8. Soon after sunrise we passed through Leesburg, a pretty little town, and in the afternoon at three we
crossed the Potowmoak, and one mile further on Br. Reichel
inquired at Th. Nowlin's about the things stolen on the
journey south, but recovered little. Mr. Nowlin, they said,
had gone to Philadelphia, (but very likely he had only gone
out the back door when he saw us coming,) his wife appeared
to be honest and gave us, she said, all that they had recovered of the goods; and we left as soon as possible, so as
not to lose things a second time, since such incidents seemed
to be the custom of the place. Toward evening we reached
Leonh. Heil's, and he showed us the way to Mr. Johnson
at Carols Manor, where we arrived about eight, were welcomed and entertained. This man and Schau's family are
the only Brethren still living at Carols Manor, the rest have
moved away, some to the Wachau, the others elsewhere.
Br. Reichel spoke much with Mr. Johnson about the school-
house here, and the land belonging to it, both of which lie
practically abandoned, for Heil who lived there for a while
has let it go to ruin instead of taking care of it since the
Brethren moved away. They would like to have a Brother
here again as teacher, but they are too few and not able to
support him, much as they would like to do so.

The 19. We left this place to-day, having received much
kindness from Mr. Johnson, and made our way back into
our road, for it was impossible to get to the school-house in
the wagon; however we sent word to Br. Schau of the
arrival of Br. and Sr. Reichel. By nine o'clock we were
already in Friedrichstown,[1] and stayed several hours at the
home of Mr. Thomas Ogle, where we ate breakfast; he was
not at home, having gone to Manakosy to his sick mother,
but he came back just as Br. and Sr. Reichel were about to
leave, was very friendly, and promised his service in for-
warding our letters to Carolina. Br. Heckewelder hired a
horse and rode ahead to Manakosy to announce the approach

[1] Frederick, Md.

of the Reichels to Br. and Sr. Schweisshaupt, which came to pass that evening about six o'clock to the great joy of both sides. They rejoiced to find here letters and "Nachrichten" from Europe and Pennsylvania, which were being held here for them. This evening and

The 20, also, most of the Brethren called to welcome these dear Brethren, and rejoiced from their hearts to have them in their midst after so long a time of waiting. Br. Heckewelder went on business to Friedrichtown, returning in the evening to Br. and Sr. Wetter's, who live a mile and a half from the school-house, from whence the following day he went to Mr. Benj. Ogle and to the iron smelter.

The 21. To-day Br. and Sr. Reichel were busy with "Sprechen" with the members living here.

The 22, Sunday. The entire congregation, young and old, was at the school-house. At ten o'clock Br. Reichel preached on the Gospel for the day, the servant whose debt his lord remitted, applying it to Jesus' constant willingness to forgive our faults and sins, and that He so gave us example how we should treat our neighbors, forgiving them willingly and living among them in peace according to the mind of Jesus. "Kinderstunde" followed, and after that the "Viertelstunden" for the unmarried men and the unmarried women. Then the whole congregation had their harvest "Lovefeast," which had been postponed to welcome the Reichels; at this service Br. Reichel communicated greetings from the Unity's Elders' Conference, and also from Br. and Sr. Marschall who were here in Manakosy just one year ago. Then there was the "Society" meeting, in which Br. Reichel spoke plainly of the true and right spirit for a member of the "Society," and received several persons into the membership of the "Society." Then they called on Br. and Sr. Joh. Jac. Wetter at their home, as Sr. Wetter was unable to attend the services on account of a baby daughter, which

The 23, at ten o'clock in the morning, during "Kinderstunde," and with a keen sense of the presence of the children's Friend, was baptised by Br. Reichel. In the afternoon the communicant members had a Communion Lovefeast, at which Br. Reichel spoke earnestly to the housefathers and mothers concerning the training of their children, warning them not to be guilty of harm done their children but to guard them from opportunities of going astray, as becomes true members of the congregation and participants in the Holy Communion, also in view of the approaching celebration of the Lord's Supper he applied to this congregation the Daily Text; — "The Lord is nigh," — which they keenly felt. Then was the "Absolution," and immediately thereafter some thirty Communicants partook of the body and blood of our Lord in the Holy Communion, Br. Reichel leading the Liturgy. Then the congregation took tender leave of Br. and Sr. Reichel; and then we began to prepare for our further journey, all being in readiness by night. This evening the Reichels had many things to talk over with the Schweisshaupts so were very late getting to bed, and we had hardly fallen asleep when Peter Schneider waked us, — at 1:30 A.M., — thinking that it was almost day. We submitted and got up, ate breakfast for the last time with the Schweisshaupts, and prepared for our journey, but the morning was so dark that it was five o'clock before we actually set out. We took tender leave of Sr. Schweisshaupt, but Br. Schweisshaupt went with us to Tanitown,[1] and so we entered,

The 24, Oct. in the name of the Lord, upon our further journey, contentedly and cheerfully, and soon reached the home of Mr. Benj. Ogle, who came out to the wagon and took friendly leave of us. The Brn. Schweisshaupt and Heckewelder had riden ahead to Tanitown on business, the wagon reaching there about ten o'clock, and a couple of miles further on we stopped and had a cold lunch near the house of a good friend Carl Tehr, brother-in-law of Nal. Schleider. Here Br. Schweisshaupt bade us and we him a tender farewell, and he returned home. At 2 P.M. we passed through Peter Little's Town, where the David Lau now

[1] Taneytown.

lives who formerly lived in Stinking Quarter, and who is acquainted with the Brethren; however we did not stop long there but hurried on to our night's stopping place. A couple of miles from the town we met Br. Schaub on his return trip, who rejoiced us with letters and "Nachrichten" from Bethlehem and Lititz; he turned back with us to McAllister, and on the way told us all about our dear Brethren in Pennsylvania, from whom we shall now not long be separated. About four o'clock we reached McAllister and stopped with a Mr. Kellwick, recommended to us by Mr. Benj. Ogle of Manakosy, and we saw at once that he was a good inn-keeper and kept an orderly house, and he lodged and served us well. Br. Reichel opened the package of letters brought by Br. Schaub and found many satisfactory letters from Bethlehem and Lititz, while Br. Heckewelder was pleased to get one from his brother in Salem on the Ohio. Then we went peacefully to rest, and slept well until five o'clock in the morning, when our worthy host gave us breakfast, and at seven o'clock on

The 25, we took up our journey, happy and thankful for the good we had there enjoyed; and we refreshed ourselves with the beautiful Daily Text; "I will speak of the glorious honour of Thy majesty, and of Thy wondrous works," Ps. cxlv, 5.

> "O Wunder dem kein Wunder gleicht —
> Gott ward ein armer Mensch wie ich,
> Vergoss Sein Blut und starb für mich."

All day yesterday a woman walked in front of our wagon, on her way to Yorktown, today out of pity we took her into the wagon, and she seemed to be a decent person. We reached Yorktown about two o'clock and were most lovingly received by Br. and Sr. Neisser, and Br. Neisser at once gave us the latest news from Lititz and elsewhere, and we had a pleasant time together; toward evening Br. Neisser took Br. Heckewelder to call on Br. Dav. Tanneberger, who has come here from Lititz to set up a beautiful new organ for Mr. Fischer, and we enjoyed seeing this truly handsome work. This evening Br. Reichel gave Br. Heckewelder instruction for his journey, and he set out

The 26, early in the morning for Lititz, and at four in the afternoon he reached Lititz with the wagon, was greeted with surprise and heartily welcomed, and announced the arrival of Br. and Sr. Reichel in Yorktown, — which the Lititz Brethren had long desired to hear; he also at once delivered all letters that had been sent by him.

The 30, Oct. In the evening at eight o'clock Br. and Sr. Reichel also reached Lititz to the great joy of the entire congregation. Praise, glory and honor be unto Him from us poor sinners for this successful ending to our journey; Amen!

COLONEL WILLIAM FLEMING'S JOURNAL OF
TRAVELS IN KENTUCKY, 1779–1780

INTRODUCTION

COLONEL WILLIAM FLEMING was born of noble lineage at Jedburgh, Scotland, the 18th of February, 1729. He attended a school in Dumfries, studied surgery at the University of Edinburgh, and served in the British navy as a surgeon's mate until taken prisoner by Spaniards. Upon his release his health was so impaired that he resolved to remove to Virginia, where he arrived in August, 1755. The same month he joined Washington's regiment and acted as surgeon for the Virginia troops with the rank of ensign. He was made a lieutenant in 1760 and a captain in 1762. In Dunmore's War he raised a regiment in his county, Botetourt, and in command of this, at the Battle of Point Pleasant, he received a wound in the breast which disabled him from active military service during the War of Independence, although in 1776 the Committee of Safety made him lieutenant of his county. Colonel Fleming was a member of the Virginia Council in 1780–1781, and in the summer of 1781, as the only member of the Council in Richmond during the Cornwallis invasion, he was acting governor. He resigned his seat in the Council the 28th of September of this year, and his last important public service was rendered as a member of the Virginia convention which ratified the Federal constitution in June, 1788.

The victory of the Virginia troops in the Battle of Point Pleasant was an opening of the way to the settlement of Kentucky, then a western county of Virginia. In 1778 and 1779 George Rogers Clark put a stop to the British instigation of the Indians against the Americans of that section by capturing all the British posts in the Northwest except Detroit, and promoted immigration to Kentucky. The legislature of Virginia having taken notice that "great numbers of people have settled in the country upon the western waters, upon waste and unappropriated lands, for which they have been hitherto prevented from sueing out patents or obtaining legal titles by the king of Great Britain's proclamations or instructions to his governors, or by the late change of government and the present war's delay until now of the opening of a land office," passed an Act, in May, 1779, "for adjusting and settling titles of claimers to unpatented lands." [1] The execution of the Act was intrusted to a commission consisting of Colonel William Fleming, Edmund Lyne, James Barbour, and Colonel Stephen Trigg, who were appointed by the governor and council.

Colonel Fleming's journal is an account of his travels in Kentucky while in the discharge of his duties as head of the commission. The manuscript is among the papers of the Lyman Draper Collection in the library of the State Historical Society of Wisconsin. On the cover is a note by Mr. Draper which is in part as follows : " The within original Journal was found among the manuscript papers of the late Colo. Wm. Fleming, preserved by his daughter, Mrs. Dorothy Bratton, near Christiansburg, Virginia — from whom I obtained it, with other valuable papers in August 1844." The handwriting, too, of the manuscript has been pronounced by those familiar with Fleming letters to be Fleming's. A painstaking copy is among the Reuben T. Durrett Manuscripts in the library of the University of Chicago, and it is from the copy that the journal is here published, the original not having been located until this book was on the press.

[1] W. W. Hening, *Laws of Virginia*, Vol. X, pp. 35–50.

COL. WILLIAM FLEMING'S JOURNAL IN KENTUCKY FROM NOV. 10, 1779, TO MAY 27TH, 1780

1779 *Nov. 10*.[1] We kild the Buffalos [and] the Pack horses followed us for some miles but dropt behind when they came up with us and missed the horse they turned back to look for him but came no more up with us we marked[2] about three miles over short broken hills and then fell into a Buffalos path that run on a ridge dividing the waters of the Town from Chaplains fork[3] we went through some very good upland with water but too beachy. Our march this day [was] 10 miles.

Nov. 11. The 11th set out early [and] in 4 miles fell in on the Town Fork went through beach bottoms, on the river on each side, kild a Buffalo, crossed by the mouth of Bucheers[4] Creek shot an Elk a three Year old 4 feet high, so poor we could not use any of it. Kild a Buffalo Cow very fat, but so old her horns wrinkled from the top down. Our march about 8 miles went along a Buffalo path crossed the River several times went through some rich bottoms but subject to overflow, went up a sidling pass, high steep rocks remarkable near the surface and very fit for building, being in natural squares etc. fell in on Floyds Creek and

[1] The first part of this journal is lost. Lewis Collins, in his *History of Kentucky*, Vol. I, p. 20, states that the commissioners opened their session at St. Asaph's on the 13th of October, 1779.

[2] Marched.

[3] Town Fork, or the East Fork of Salt River which flows close to Harrodsburg, and Chaplin's Fork which is the West Fork of Salt River.

[4] Brashears' Creek, which joins the East Fork of Salt River a few miles above the site of the present town of Shepherdsville.

came to a settlement [1] where we dined and got some taffieo drink here we were informed that day week a young man was wounded and another taken prisoner on the path we came down, on inquiry we found Bucheers Creek was 25 miles from this place so that we had fell on the Town fork below it and what we imagined to be Bucheers Creek was a nameless Creek 12 miles from this, we came on to Bullets Creek 4 miles further over very level flat Oak land our march 16 miles.

Nov. 13. Bullets Creek [2] as it is cald is perhaps the best Salt Springs in the Country. The Earth is excavated for twelve or fo[u]rteen feet over an area of many acres. By digging from thence to any depth of feet, water boils up the deeper, the stronger, they have a trough that holds very near 1000 Gallons which they empty thrise in the 24 hours, they have 25 kittles belonging to the Commonwealth which they keep constantly boiling and filling them up as the water waistes from the trough first into kettles which they call fresh water kettles and then into others after this management for 24 hours they put the brine into a Cooler and let it stand till cold or near it and draw off the clear brine into the last boilers under which they keep up a brisk fire till they observe it begin to grain when they slacken the fire and keep them at a simmering boil till it grains they then put it to drain when drained they think it fit for use it is observed that the pits will some weeks fill with strong water and then decline when the present pits were first dug it was observed that every four or five days the pits flowed up and over the tops and then sunk that they continue to swell up now, but not so regularly nor so high — it is noticed that the brine increases in strength as the moon does in Age and so remarkable that it looses or gains half a bushel in the 24 hours making the trough thrise emptied that is near 3000 Gallons water boil[ed] down yields from three to 4 and 4$\frac{1}{2}$ bushels Salt. mostly 3 and $\frac{1}{2}$ bushels the dryer the

[1] Brashears' Station, now Shepherdsville.
[2] Bullit's Lick, discovered by Captain Thomas Bullit in 1773.

weather the better for making Salt these remarks I had from Cheneth the manager here was several flocks of Parrots flying about — I observed several Stones in a brown husk when broke the inside consisted of a multitude of irregular hexagonal Crystals some well defined — we set out for the Falls [1] three quarters of a mile from the lick on the road to the Flat Lick we went up some rising hills that had earth rich in salt peter.   Pine trees grew on the top of them the first Pine I met with in this Country we went through some fine level Oak Land but scarce of water met with none but at the Fish Pool 8 miles from the lick, that very bad — the sand round these springs seemed glazed or cased over with lead — four miles further we reached the Flat Lick the land round it good but low standing in water, we encamped two or three miles beyond the lick at a place so scarce of water that most of our horses strayed a great way in quest of water.

Nov. 14.   We went through some ponds and some good flat land and reached the falls in Six miles there is a great number of Cabbins here and a considerable number of Inhabitants the many of them were absent — there is a pond runs just beyond the Town the water of which drains through the earth and breaks out in the River bank which is the water used generally by the Inhabitants and is not wholesome the River when the Channel is coursed is $\frac{3}{4}$ of a mile broad but at this time the bed was dry for $\frac{2}{3}$ of the breadth which contributed to the sickliness of the Inhabitants there being a great number of them complaining of the fever and Ague and many of the Children dying the banks of the river are 40 or more feet high and an Iland [2] opposite the Town of about 50 acres which overflows almost entirely in freshets the bed of the River in some places is one continued Rock stone which may be raised in squares fit for building, interspersed is pieces of excellent coal and some of the Channel appears so mixed with a coaly substance that it seemed a vein of coal, cald the Cat head vein there are several other Ilands below the town the falls are about a

---

[1] The Falls of the Ohio at Louisville.   [2] Corn Island.

mile in length the Channel at present on the other side, there is a fall on this side 8 feet perpendicular so that it cannot be passed but when the River is full when there is no difficulty, great number of Geese Duck and Swan resort to the falls the land round the Town is not near so rich as about Harrodsburg and upwards, there is little Cane and that small about this place, but it will always be a place of importance — several people died whilst we were here the disorder they complained of was occasioned by a relaxation of the solids, from bilious Complaints which brings on such a Corruption of the fluids with a Visidness of the Juices that it degenerates and breaks out in cancerous eating soars I have seen the Maxillary and the glands about the throat and tongue both in Old and Young persons entirely destroyed some have Vomited corrupted bile as green as Verdigrease so that the whole of the disorders that at this time reign here is occasioned by bile — Capt. Doge arrived here with a recommendation to Col. Clark[1] as an Indian Agent from what I can discover of him he is a man that thinks he is of more importance than he really is, his conduct seems superficial the only thing to reccomend him is what he has suffered, whether justly or not time is to discover — Col. Clark continued here whilst we were here his plan of operation was to settle a number of people at the Iron Banks 30 miles below the Ohio on the Mississippi. All met with Capt. Henry Smith who was incamped on the Iland opposite to this. Nickl. Welch lodged in a hollow tree precipitally they had sold their possessions and settlement and came out after suffering many losses they were here and knew not where to go Welch proposed to go up with us Smith to fall in with Col. Rogers Clarks proposal of going to the Iron Banks. I rode out to Jno Floyds[2] incamped and got the lines of a survey run out for 1000 acres but as Mr. Douglass one of the surveyors rode one of my horses and came in the day after me they were turned out seperate

[1] George Rogers Clark.
[2] Captain John Floyd was the founder of Floyd's Station on the Middle Fork of Beargrass Creek, six miles south of the Falls.

and when the business was finished my horse was lost my boy had been taken ill with the fever and Ague and continued still sick.

Nov. 25. Left the Falls and came to Brashiers Station in our way back to Harrodsburg *the 26th* went up Salt and crossed it in six miles above the Station at the first Iland that had trees growing on it and where two men were fired on by Indians One taken the other wounded a few days before we got down. We went up Salt River for two miles on a Buffalo path up a Creek for 18 miles then crossed a Ridge and fell on another Creek went up it, passed several Cabbins, in about four miles above the mouth of the first Creek and several on the second Creek on *the 27th* which we passed and took a left hand draught went through good land. *The 28th* likewise went through considerable tracts of good land and fell on a Creek that emptied into Chaplains Fork of Salt River over bad beach knobs, it rained last night which was the first rain we have had since coming into this country this night there fell a snow and so dark on *the 29th* that was bad travelling and we made but a small journey. We lost three of our Company. One went after a Buffalo two took a different course we did not join before we got to Harrodsburg.

Dec. 1st. Encamped in a draught 15 or 16 miles from Harrodsburg [which] we reach[ed] *Dec. the 2nd.* Our Journey after we left Chaplains Fork was over steep short bushy hills and short knobs and very brushy. One of the Company discovered among these knobs a Salt Spring five or six miles from where we crossed Salt River which was three miles below Jas McAfees place.[1]

Dec. 3rd and 4th. Did a little business and adjourned to Elkhorn.[2] It continued excessive cold. Col. Barbour prepaired to leave us. *The 5th* a storm of snow fell and the Kentucky rose which made us alter our Appointment from Elk-

[1] James McAffee's Station, on the East Fork of Salt River, six or seven miles below Harrodsburg.

[2] Bryan's Station, on the south branch of the North Fork of the Elkhorn.

horn to Boonesborough [1] *the 6th* continued cold with snow. The Inhabitants avered they never knew so severe weather at that season the winter generally setting in about Christmas and continuing about 6 weeks. Col. Barbour set out *the 7th* the Storm abating and Kentucky still impassible we set out from Harrodsburg *the* 10*th* I left my horses and Jno Thompson at Henry Wilsons and got a mare from Jno Boyd to ride to Boonesborough got to George Clarks *the* 11*th* came to St Asaphs [2] — Racoons in great numbers on our Journey these animals live on shell fish as well as nuts etc.; and in great numbers on Salt River and Chaplains Fork [3] — we kild numbers of Deer, Buffalo Raccoons and turkeys on our way from Falls and saw bears — before they retire for the winter eat Lawrel which purges them and clears their intestines of all facis which conduces to the inactive state they continue in all Winter which kild in this state their intestines are always free from everything but some indigested Lawrel in the rectum for 4 or 5 inches which serves like a plug to the intestines [4] the Night of *the*

[1] On the west bank of the Kentucky River at the mouth of Otter Creek.

[2] Also known as Logan's Fort, about twenty miles S.S.E. of Harrodsburg.

[3] In Our Journey to and from the Falls I observed all the branches of the Rivers either dry or stagnant water in pools sometimes these pools in the beds of the Rivers would be half a mile in length — after which the Channel would be for a little way quite dry in such places we found great numbers of open shells large and Glisten[ing] in the inside like mother of pearl of the Mussel kind there was of the fish in these shells. I imagine that when the water decreases and leaves these shells fish dry the fish languishes and dies the shells are easily opened by animals that devour the fish amongst which I recon the Raccoon, as well as other beavers etc: having observed great many Raccoons in such places and their tracts innumerable on the sand. — Note in MS.

[4] Bears in the spring when they leave their winter dormitories are very uneasy till they get clear of this hardened indigested stuff and are observed to hunt after the blossoms of the Dogwood tree which they devour in great quantities this clears the intestines and purges them after which they soon turn poor, lean, rank and not fit to eat. — Note in MS.

9th I was much disturbed in my Sleep I Thought Mrs ⸺ was plunged into a deep river by her horse which overwhelmed them both. I rode in after them and got her out dead and stiff on my taking her to the bank, water run out from her mouth and she showed symptoms of life etc.

Dec. 11. It rained hard in the night, *the* 12th showery all day in the evening lightened and thundered in the night a violent storm of wind rain, and snow *the* 13th windy and cold 14th Cold and Cloudy with some snow the night excessive cold hard Frost. 15th Cloudy but fair. 16th left St Asaphs for Boonesborough crossed Dicks river [1] at Coburns place, went up Gilberts Creek [2] and down a small creek that emptied into Paint Lick Creek [3] lay one mile short of the creek and was greatly favoured [by] the weather though it was cloudy and threatened a fall yet it held up till the morning, we had no tent with us, it rained in the morning and froze as it fell our journey [took us] about 20 miles through large quantities of Good Land. 17th crossed Paint Lick Creek and Silver Creek,[4] came up Tates Creek,[5] the road verry bad, the Cane laped over with the snow and rain and made it almost impassible, there is good land on the head of Tates Creek, got to Boonesburg in the evening 20 miles from our encampment the weather very severe it snowed a little in the Night, 18th the weather severely cold and cloudy did a little buisness.

Dec 19th. Clear frosty and very cold — *20th* went on with business the Frost continues severe we were informed of one of Davis' Family being lost in Rockcastle the[y] encamped in a fork of a Creek the water rising and surrounding

[1] The West Fork of the Kentucky.

[2] An east branch of Dick's River; its mouth is E. by N. of the site of Logan's Fort.

[3] The headwaters of Paint Lick Creek, a south branch of the Kentucky, are separated only by a water parting from Gilbert Creek.

[4] Silver Creek is the first branch of the Kentucky above Paint Lick Creek.

[5] The mouth of Tate's Creek is about midway between the mouth of Silver Creek and Boonesborough.

them Davis tried to swim over but was drownded the water rising put out their fire and the rest of the family perished. And likewise that Capt Quirk had Negro boy drownded crossing Rock Castle. The river had rose considerably from Snow Rain and transient thaws towards their head, the Kentucky had been full of ice for two days but was closed up this Evening and frozen over.

Dec. 22. The morning of the 22nd, which was moderate Clear and Sunshine, we were informed from Harrodsburg that a party of Indians had passed, by their tracts, between Chaplains Fork and Salt River, their trace being discovered 15 miles from Harrodsburg. *The 23 and 24* went on with buisnes.

Dec. 25. Rested the 25th being Christmas day. The Frost still continuing I crossed the Kentucky on the Ice and found it one hundred yards over opposite to the Fort. We heard by a man from the falls, the party of Indians whose tracts had been discovered had kild a man and boy and taken two boys prisoners at the mouth of Floyds Creek near Bushiers Station and that the People had left the Salt works and taken their kettles away leaving the Pots or kettles belonging to the Publick. Sam. Henderson arrived with some of the Commisrs from Carolina having quitted running the boundary line on some disagreement with the Virginia Commissrs who continued to go on with the line. — People hourly arrived with accounts of the distresses of Families on the road.

Dec. 26th. Clear and moderate Mr. Henderson took the Lat. and made this place 37 degrees 48'.

Dec. 27. Morning over east trail snow and then rain 28th, 29th, and 30th did buisness *the 29th* it seemed to relent and thaw but continued very cold and in the night snowed we put our horses over the Kentucky on the Ice and *the 31st* left Boonesburg for Elkhorn. Boonesburg has 30 houses in it, stands in a bottom that is surrounded by hills on every side that commands it, the hills over the Kentucky opposite as indeed all along the River is very very steep and discovers the Rock at no great depth under the soil, from which hills, small Army can do execution in the

Fort which is a dirty place in winter like every other Station, there is a lick close to the post called by the Indians deep lick in which there is a spring which serves the people in common that smells and tastes strong of sulphur there is likewise a Salt Spring or two but water weak in it.   Our Journey to Bryants [1] on Elkhorn was done in 15 miles crossed Boone Creek and Howards Creek and passed through several tracts of fine land.   Bryants Station as it is called, formerly the property of Col. Preston and exchainged by him for the horse shoe on New River is an exceeding fine tract of land and a happy situation.   There is at present about 50 families all but four came here this last summer and fall — there is plenty of small cane as we came from Boonesburg and about this place.   The Cane is a long time before it runs to seed some say 7 years after which it dies and Spring[s] up from the seed it bears grain larger than Rye.   the time the seed lyes in the earth is uncertain it grows in rich moist earth, sometimes large spots of a hundred acres will run to seed at once, sometimes you will meet with stalks that seed in spots when the other stalks of a younger growth do not, the roots of cane will continue years in the earth without being destroyed if in a favourable earth neither too wet nor to dry.

The hump or that remarkable rising on the shoulders of a Buffalo is formed by the Spinal Processes of the nine first Vertebrae of the back gradually rising in hight from the ninth to the third.   The Second and first being some thing shorter than the third, and the process of the third rising sometimes in bulls to the length of Eighten Inches the ninth to 3 or four inches these spines cut off and dressed the meat is reconed the sweetest part of the Buffalo.   There was numbers of Paroquitos [2] flying about Boonsburg.   We heard this day that the people moving out to this Country had lost 500 cattle and as was my horse by the rising of the waters and that in general they were in the utmost dis-

[1] Bryan's Station, about six miles northeast of Lexington.
[2] Parrots, in the margin of the manuscript.

tress numbers of families not being able to get in were building huts on the road to winter in.

1780 Jan. 1. The Frost continue[d] but a clear sun shine day did no buisness the Cl[er]k making out list of claims on Elkhorn and Licking necessary before we can proceed. —

Jan. 2. A Snow fell last night continued Snowing this morning

Jan. 3 and all day the snow 12 Inches deep Cold and piercing did buisness. *The 4th, 5th and 6th* the cold continued intense, *7th* Do *the 8th* Col. Line taken suddenly ill was bled —

Jan. 9. The Weather continued in the day Clear and Freezing in the night is severely cold as ever I felt it in America the People at this place all sickly from colds the hardships they endured in the Journey and the Change of Air the most of the Settlers moving from S. Carolina two young men died yesterday. The frost had penetrated fourteen Inches into the ground as we found by the opening of the graves.

Jan. 10. In the night it snowed and continued snowing in the morning of the 10th so that it was five inches deep on the old snow continued to snow buisily all day.

Jan. 11. The 11th clear above head — laid in a Claim for George Hendrix Settlement and preemption on the head of E. Fork of Hustons Branch of the Licking — Continued to do, buisiness *the 12, 13, 14, 15, 16, 17, and 18th* when we adjourned to Col. Bowmans near Harrodsburg. The Frost still continues clear in the day and cold.

Jan. 19th. Set out for Harrodsburg and reached Lexington 6 miles from Bryants so excessive cold we were afraid of being frost bit the night violently cold, my horse was turned out by Robt Paterson who neglected to unstop the bell and could not be found when the other horses were brought up — the other Gentlemen went on to Mr. Tods where they were to wait till I got up to them. — they made fiddle strings of the Sinues of the spine of the buffalo and sewed their mockasins with them being very strong and when dried very easily divided into Small fibers — so that this Animal is of the greatest service, of the horns they make Combs etc. the flesh is their common food, the Skins tanned makes a good leather but a little spongier than some Cattle, the hair on the skin in May, June and July is short smooth and fine, in the winter the coat thickens turns wooly and Feby is at the best this they spin into yarn and work it into coarse clothes like wool, in the spring they shed this wooly coat — the Frost still continues my horse not yet found — *the 22nd* I had a strong fever, occassioned by lying verry cold, and was something better this day the most disordered is my head, having got my horse which cost me 73 Dollars to recover again having been put out of the way for the hopes of a reward I set out and reached Capt. Levi Tods [1] in 6 miles passed through some fine land.

Jan. 24. Set out next morning for Harrodsburg went through part of Genl Lewis land reached Kentucky River [2] in 15 miles which we passed on the Ice, the Rocks from the Channel to a great height cast a dismal appearance, the hills on the So[uth] side very high and difficult, in 10 miles further reached Harrodsburg this day so exceeding cold I had one of my toes bit with the frost and some of my fingers frozen.

Jan. 26. Did no buisness *the* 27, 28, *and* 29 Proceeded on Buisness.

Feby. 2 I was seized with the most violent pain in my back which continued, *the 4th* I was bled for it and took a dose of Laxative pills with Quicksilver being the only purgative I had, but did not intermit the buisness *the 4th* the pain was easier tho I was still obliged to have my back bolstered up when I was in Court, the pills not working me properly for want in proper convenience in working it off the pain returned *the 4th and 5th* but went on with the buisness when Col. Lyne could attend he being frequently indisposed.

[1] Todd's Station, southwest of Lexington and in a direct line to Harrodsburg.

[2] The road from Lexington to Harrodsburg crossed the Kentucky at its confluence with Dick's River.

Feb. 6. The Frost still continuing, the Kentucky was frozen near two feet thick of Ice but the night of the 6th it turned cloudy rained a little which turned to snow, in the morning the snow was two inches thick on the old snow the wind Easterly and continues to snow, the People in general sickly seized with pains in their head, back and breast attended with a loosesness in the beginning which continued with some through the whole course of the disorder voiding a green or black bilious matter, the blood taken was black and Vicid or highly imflamed with a tough buff skin, having no assistance many died in ten twelve or fourteen days from their being seized. *The 7th* very dark cold and Cloudy *the 8th and 9th* Clear and moderate the night of the 9th it rained and continued *the* 10*th* to rain gently the snow melted and the thaw continuing the earth began to uncover *the* 11*th* 12*th and* 13*th* the thaw continued gentle and pain shifted a little lower in my back to the Joint of the thigh and down my thigh at times verry violent so that I continued to have my back supported and bound when doing buisness, my toe that was frost bit frequently paind me, the blisters broke and the new skin tender — we found the buisness far from being overcontrary to our expectations we having settled Certificates since we came here for 250 Claims. — The Spring at this place is below the Fort and fed by ponds above the Fort so that the whole dirt and filth of the Fort, putrified flesh, dead dogs, horse, cow, hog excrements and human odour all wash into the spring which with the Ashes and sweepings of filthy Cabbins, the dirtiness of the people, steeping skins to dress and washing every sort of dirty rags and cloths in the spring perfectly poisons the water and makes the most filthy nauseous potation of the water imaginable and will certainly contribute to render the inhabitants of this place sickly.

Salmon says the Buffalo improperly can rais the Urus or Lorax [Aurochs ?] described by Cæsar. Till *the* 23 it froze at night and thawed in the day, when it rained in the night and snowed all day the wind N.W. *the* 24*th* it froze hard *the* 25*th* Do *the* 26*th* more moderate *the* 27*th* the Court having finished the buisness rose at nine Oclock in the Evening, having in the course of this buisness granted Certificates for 1,096,650 acres.

For preemption of 400 acres	135450	. . Claimers	339
For improvers etc. 1000 .	259000	. . Do	259
For settlements	202000	. .⎫	
For preemptions to settlement	500200	. .⎬ Do	505
		⎭	
In the whole Acres . . .	1096650	. . Do	1103
Omitted in the above . .	1400	. .	2
	1098050	. . . . . .	1105

Feb. 27. Imployed in getting the Certificates finished and the Lists for the Surveyor and Auditors. *The 29th* the same signed the Certificates for the Surveyor. It rained in the Evening and all night.

March 1. March the first it hailed and snowed by turns my horses that were brought down got out of the Fort in the night which prevented my leavening [1] this place this day, sent Thompson up to Col. Bowmans [2] after them.

March 3. My horses coming in I rode out to Col. Bowmans eight miles from Harrodsburg on Cane run I rode through some good land belonging to Richd Itogen. Col. Bowmans is pretty good land and has good water there was about twenty families here mostly from Roanoke, the people were mostly imployed in making sugar by boiling up the juice of the Sugar tree which is a species of the Maple tree, there is two sorts of sugar trees cald black and white, from the Colours of the bark, and it is thought the black yields the strongest water the trees are cut in sloping two or three inches so that the hole or box may hold half a pint a hole is bored sloaping through the bark and wood to the bottom of the cavity and a reed or quill put into it,

[1] Leaving.
[2] Bowman's Station, east of Harrodsburg, not far from Dick's River.

the Juice that runs into the cavity is carried clear of the tree and runs into vessels placed to receive it gutters are cut through the bark and part of the wood on the side of the tree sloping downwards to guide the Juice into the larger cavity or receptacle in the tree, the juice is boiled down till it acquires a consistance like syrup and sweetness resembling Honey in this state it is called Molasses, the boiling continued as the watery particles exhale it turns thicker and dries, the fire is then slacked and if they design it in powder they keep continually stirring it when it grains and produces a sugar equal to Muscovedo, if not stirred it forms into a cake of solid consistence. the time for tapping the trees is in the spring and fall, a clear frosty night succeeded by a sunshiny day, the trees bleed the best, when the buds swell on the tree, the Juice is roapy and the time of making sugar is over till the Autumn, after the fall of the leaves. — from this juice they make beer, and vinegar and I am persuaded may make spirits, as the sugar with a little careful management may be made equal if not superior to that extracted from the Cane. It takes a large quantity of Juice to a pound of sugar but how much I do not know. I have been informed that sugar has been made from the walnut tree in the same manner.[1]

March 7th. Rode up to St Asaphs from Col. Bowmans, I observed a species of the wood pecker which I had not met with before, the Cock and the hen they are larger than the large brown the cock had a bright red head with remarkable large tuft of feathers on the Crown so that it may be called the Peacock Wood pecker the body and wings White and black.[2] I met with a tall tree 60 or 70 feet in the

---

[1] I must think that the sugar of the Ancients that we do not know at present, and which is entirely lost to us, might have been the Juice of some such tree as this if not the very same for I do not imagine the sugar tree confined to America only, but may be found in the same latitudes elsewhere parallel to those it grows in here. — Note in Ms.

[2] One of these birds was shot by my servent, which I took to be the hen, the feathers on the throat and belly and part of the

body and two feet or three in diameter, which I did not observe before, the bark something like a Cheery tree the wood when cut a crimson red and cald by some Mahogany [1] the grains of the wood resemble the Mahogany some thing but vastly coarser, when dry the red colour vanishes and it appears a glistening white, the leaf I do not know but am informed it bears a pod a foot long containing beans of a flat round form in a sweet acrimonious visid Juice.[2] re-

wing and tail a shining black, it had nine stiff and strong feathers in the tail forked at the end, the middle one being six inches long from where the feathers begin the whole length being 7½ inches the others on each side shortened in length, its wings ten Inches long from the shoulder to the tip, 18 long feathers in the wing, the two first and longest black the 3rd tipd with white and each succeeding one more and more till the next to the back are white, both above and below, the front and fore part of the Crown black, from the junction of the upper and lower bill white feathers on each side, leaving a triangle of black feathers from the Eyes and back part of the Crown which is deep red, the white feathers run backwards as far as the white on the wings intermixed with black so that the bird from the head so far appears speckled, the red part of the crown appears triangular, its legs was an inch and a half long with four toes set forward and back two each way, armed with strong crooked claws, the two outer ones the longest and four inches in length the bill white and bony verry strong and firm at the point shaped like a wedge each ⅛ of an inch broad and from that a ridge runs both in the upper and lower so that each forms a triangle an inch and a quarter broad at the Junction of the upper and lower bills, which is three inches in length, the tongue is six inches in length. The Iris when dead of a bright Yellow so far it differs from any of the species I have seen, the mechanism of its parts being as usual in birds of this kind, it weighed upwards of 1 lb. — Note in MS.

[1] Coffee tree — Gymnocladus Canadensis. — Note in MS.

[2] This tree is a species of larch it grows in Spain and on the Barbary side near Siteran cald in Spain Algerzalea, Garosera, Carrobe, or Locust tree. The trunk from 1 to 2 feet diameter, the leaves a dark green, ten on a twigg, five on each side the fruit in shape of kidney beans one inch broad and nine or ten inches long they issue in clusters from the branches and body of the tree in a singular manner, the pods thick, mealy and of a sweet taste when dry they are given to horses and Cattle as providender. The Alcarobe in Africa, the pod resembles the

turned from Logans *the 8th the* 10*th* rode to Harrodsburg the night of the 7th it thundered and raind, the creeks were high the 8th the 12th it snowed, we had advice from Licking that a man was wounded near Ridles the 8th and that some people were kild at Boonsburg the same day Col. Calaway and Pemberton Rawlings on the 9th and two Negroes taken.

March 13. Finished examining the books and rectified several mistakes we found two claims entirely omitted in the list, made out for the survey and three in the list sent to the Register with some mistakes in the names and some in the quantities of Land. Joseph Lindsays Claim is likewise not taken notice of because not located.

The old English Version of the Psalms as in the liturgy is translated from the Septuagint the new version from the Hebrew original.

Kettlewels practical believer [1] with Allen on fa[i]th prefixed to it, is reccommended as the properest books for instructing a Family in the fundamentals of the Christian religion in as short evident and valid a manner as the subject will permit.

March 14. Monday night there was a smart white frost succeeded by a warm clear day, the sugar trees run plentifully but the Juice was of an Acid cast apt to ferment and with difficulty turn to sugar, from the Molasses state, the grains smaller clamy and a little Acid cast which showed the

English bean the inner substance is sweet and lodged hard small kernels the fruit is eaten by the common people and by all the Moors in the feast Ashorah but is especially preserved for their horses to whom it is food and Physic, as it both drenches and fattens them.

After drying some of the wood of this tree it appeared verry coarse grained wood, and porous, and not good for any fine work being as coarse as common Oak and of a disagreeable smell when green. — Note in MS.

[1] John Kettlewell, *The Practical Believer; or the Articles of the Apostles' Creed drawn out to form a true Christian's Heart and Practice.* For a list of books in Col. Fleming's library see *William and Mary College Quarterly*, January, 1898.

time for making the sugar was past. After the fibers of the
tree is hardened by the winter cold and the Juices thickened
the accumulation if any being very languid. The diameters of the vessels are contracted, the first juice or sap
that rises is thin and spirituous which by degrees moistens
the rigid fibers of the wood, thins the thickened sap, in the
vessels and being carried to the different parts and extremities of the twigs and branches swells the buds and by degrees
the embrio leaves etc. expand, as they grow in dimensions
it requires a more nutritive Juice to support them and add
timber to the tree in the Autumn after the Summers heat,
which exhales the thinner sap the encreasing cold constringes
the woody and more solid fibres, the thicker Juice either
stagnates or their motion is very slow, and not being able
to circulate in the vessels as formerly the leaves loose their
verdure, turn pale or Yellow and at last drop off, yet the
Vesels not being entirely stoped, their diameters only de-
creased, a thin Juice or sap circulates in them as in the Spring
which may be made into sugar, till the encreasing cold puts
a stop even to this secretion in the root, when the Juices
are altogether froze, as it is the property of liquours freezing
to expand in dementions and to overcome the greater resistance, the Juices in trees by freezing taking up a larger space
than before, act in some measure like wedges and split the
tree with a considerable noise, as we found travelling in this
Country during the extremity of the frost, we frequently
heard them crack like Pistols for this reason a hard frost
destroys the succeeding fruit, the proper vessels being this
way destroyed, or if verry intense kills the tree altogether.
We this day had a confirmation of Col. Calaways and
Pempertons being kild and scalped, and two negroes taken
prisoners they were making a flat [1] a mile and a half from
Boonsburg we were likewise informed that the Indians had
Attacked Ridles Station [2] on Friday the 10th without killing any person but drawing off the horses and killing all

[1] Flat-boat.
[2] Riddle's or Ruddle's Station, on the east bank of the South
Fork of the Licking, northeast of Lexington.

their Cattle and that the same day they kild Wm Bryant Junr [1] about two miles from Bryants Station on Elkhorn. — we likewise had intelligence that two families were cut off at Dunnings lick One Bard had gon down to manage the Salt Works on Col. Clarks Acct — this account came by one of the men who had escaped we were allarmed this night by two men who went out to hunt horses who imagined they had met with Indians and a man from this place being missing but it proved a false alarm, the man coming in, and being sometimes lost in a Cane brake, had frightened the others. I purchased a baggage horse from Thos Carland a bay at 250 . . 10 . . 0.

March 16. It snowed a little in the night and verry cold in the morning of *the* 17th — which was very cold, a woman died here and was buried *the* 18th continued cold and in the night it snowed and covered the Ground.

March 19. Continued cold, tho the snow soon melted, had letters by Capt Roberts under Majr Slaughter which informed me of the hardness of the frost in the Settlements, and the excessive high price of provisions, that Corn was 40 shl a b. pork 10 shl per pound we have experienced the dreadful effects of the rise of provisions here Corn being 100 dollars per Bushel and meat so scarce we could not be supplied before the buisness was finished Salt was at 500 Dollars a bushel.

March 20. Last night it was cold and froze hard, the effects of the severe winter was now sensibly felt, the earth for so long a time being covered with snow and the water entirely froze, the Cane almost all kiled, the Hogs that were in the Country suffered greatly, being frozen to death, in their beds, the deer likewise not being able to get either water or food, were found dead in great numbers, tirkies [2] dropt dead of[f] their roosts and even the Buffalos died starved to death, the vast increase of people, near three thousand that came into this Country with the prodigious

---

[1] William Bryan, Jr. See R. T. Durrett, *Bryant's Station*, p. 44.   [2] Turkeys.

losses they had in their cattle and horses, on their Journey, and the severity of the winter after they got here killing such numbers, all contributed to raise the necessaries of life to a most extravagant price.

Yesterday I had a copy of the Act passed last session of Assembly [1] continuing the powers of the Commissioners for two months longer, as we had finished all the Buisness of the People in the Country I had great reluctance to be detained longer here but considering that a great number of People that were expected down the River Ohio from Pitsburg being detained by the Frost, and that there must be a number of Claimrs [2] in near 3000 persons that designed to come into this Country from that Quarter, as Asserted to the Commissioners in a letter from one Briscoe I determined to wait till we could take in those Claims or at least till Mr. Trigg [3] should return from the Falls whither he had gone after finishing the buisness before us at Harrodsburg — we had information that a man was kild betwixt Mr. Floyds and the Falls The People every where were buised in pulling Nettles which had been rotted like hemp by the frost and snow and yields a good Strong bark, the Nettles growing very tall and strong, when broke and spun makes a strong thread when wove makes a strong coarse cloth, but harsher than hemp. I have been told by Hunters that the Westerly and No Westerly Winds blow three parts of the year and that in Cloudy weather when the Sun did not appear to steer their course by they used to be directed by the motion of the Clouds depending on their driving to the Eastward and Southerly and were never mistaken they likewise asserted that all their storms and foul weather came from the No and Westward and their clear dry weather when the wind was Easterly and to the So this is contrary to what we experience to the Estd of the Alegany Mountains where the Southerly and Easterly winds bring foul Cloudy dirty weather and the No Westerly winds Clear and Cold.

[1] Virginia Legislative Assembly.   [2] Claimers.
[3] Stephen Trigg, one of the Commissioners.

There is a great extent of Level Marshy watery Country from the Lakes that lye to the westward [1] of Kentucky Country over the Ohio and great quantities of snowfall there in the Autumn and Winter months which as the Westerly [2] winds are most prevalent in that quarter, either drives it in snow or rain. Clouds [are driven] to the Eastward till these Clouds are intercepted by that continued high range of Mountains to the No of Virginia and in some parts of Virginia known by the Alleghana, in this Country the Cumberland, and G. Evans in his Analysis [of] the Osiota Mountains [says that] there storm clouds [being] thus intercepted by the Mountains the wind that rushes over their tops [is] divested of the watery clouds and continuing its course to the E[ast]-ward drives the clouds with its current, clears the sky and carrying many nitrous particles makes the weather Clear cold and dry. For this reason too the Ely [3] and Soly [4] winds divested of their watery and snow clouds by these Mountains blow clear and warm, whereas these winds are charged with clouds from the Sea coast which they let fall, in Showers etc. to the Eastward of these Mountains. The Cumberland Mountain is a continuation of the Alleghana Mountain. running in a pretty direct course from the NoEly to SoWly and altho several Rivers run through it both to the Nowd and Sowd yet it only affords them a passage running often into perpendicule[r] rocks of a great hight on both sides of the river not even allowing in many a passage for footmen between the rock and river, it is therefore a mistake in tracing the course of these mountains by the head of the different water courses, as it would confound several very different ranges of Mountains together. I likewise observed that [the] true Allegany is accompanied by a parallel ridge, the Lawrel, with [5] is either more or less visible in its whole course.

The appearance of the Country as to its risings, sinkings, and levels is entirely formed by the rock below the Surface

---

[1] Northward.   [2] Northwesterly.   [3] Easterly.
     [4] Southerly.   [5] Which.

which every where extends through this Country at the depth of from one to twelve or more feet and never above 18 or 20 but in general to the surface 3 or 4 feet deep frequently the rock appears on the Surface. There is generally a rich soil on the top under which a greasy clay of different colours and sometimes mixed with Sand frequently impregnated with Nitrous Vitriole, Sulphurious or Saline particles.[1] Under this is a shelly rock in layers loose and easily raised in flags of different sizes, I observed before in the channel of Salt River, this loose layer of rock gives free passage to water betwixt the strata, how deep this sort of rock goes I can not Assert but from what I observed in the Channel of the Kentucky, Salt River, Chaplains fork, of Salt River etc. : the bottom of the river where the water either stands or runs is a bed of Solid rock and when the water rises [to] the height of these layers of Rock it finds its way through them and runs dispersed under ground, this accounts for the nature of the Springs in this Country if they can be called so being only the river water running under ground amongst or betwixt these Strata of Rock and appear again either in Sink holes immediately vanishing or bursting out and running some way sink again as is [2] frequently happens to considerable streams which run for miles that disappears altogether, this likewise accounts for little fish appearing on opening the rock and earth where has [3] sunk in springs to

---

[1] The soil every where in this Country is surprizingly shallow as appears from the trees every where blown up by the Roots. The roots of each tree is matted like hazel with scarce earth enough to cover it and as they cannot penetrate in depth they spread in distance insinuating betwixt the loose rock and when overturned always bringing up flags of the rock with it. The richest soil is reckoned the black, the timber black Walnut, Cherry, Honey Locust etc. I have observed the richest soil to bear the shortest timber and to be the shallowest in the mold. I would therefore prefer a good timbered tract tho not quite so rich, to a richer tho worse timbered tract as there is a great probability of the ground being lasting not so subject to drought and where Springs of their being constant. — Note in MS.
[2] It.   [3] They have.

recover water; for this reason too we may account for the large quantity of Corn which delights in a moist soil growing so plentifully here on dry uplands as it appears to be, as well as the beach Sycamore and other growth delighting in a moist soil, and for the sudden rise and fall of the water courses. Below these layers of stone is a solid rock the depth unknown for this reason we may account for the great scarcity of Springs I do not remember to have seen one real gravelly Spring in the Country except one, for their drying up as well as the rivers in the summer and fall and for the river and branches so suddenly rising and falling on a rain or thaw of snow there is a descent from the head of Dicks River to near the Ohio, the Channels of the rivers lye verry low from the bottom of the Channels to the tops of the banks two or three hundred feet or more in perpendicular height, which when you have ascended the Country seems to go off levels the rivers are prodigiously crooked making many turns and windings and having worked their channels by washing away the earth and loose rocks makes the appearance of many knobs or short hills very steep and high. The most of the stone is a soft limestone of a blew or gray colour interspersed with veins of a soft white crystaline substance the stone clear of this feels soft and soapy to the touch, it easily burns to lime there is likewise free stone and grit fit for grindstones and Millestones. Flint and Crystals in some places, Iron ore and between Green River and Salt River lead. Bear fat is preserved sweet and pure by putting in a bunch of the Slippery Elem bark into it when rendering, hunters that preserve a great quantity of bears oil and take every method to get the largest quantity and sweet let the fat lye till it is quite tender and not fit to eat shave off the rough outer bark and take the slippery Clammy bark tye it up in a bunch and put it along with the fat in rendering when rendered strain it and the oil is pure and free from any bad scent. and will keep for a long time, it likewise preserves and sweetens hogs lard and I suppose would do the same with butter however it would be worth while to make a tryal.

March 17. Went to Harrodsburg found myself much indisposed got my horse shod and returned *the* 18th and 20th got bled 12 oz. the pain in my head and breast was a little relieved the blood was solid like liver and black as tarr the symptons returning with violence my head paining me greatly through my temples, above my eyebrows along the Sutures of my head and the hind part my eyes seemed so full and tense in the sockets that I could not turn them, I was bled *the 22nd* being determined to let the Vein breath till I found an abatement of the Symptons or an alteration in the Colour of the blood this did not happen till three pints or 24 oz. was in the basin and I was giddy I lost too much blood I was subject to slight twitches of and great faintness and weakness the blood would leave the extremities my fingers would turn pale white and have all the Appearance of a Corps a noise like the rustling of waters was constantly in my ears and my memory failed me the blood now taken was covered all over with a seemingly putrid gelly the surface of this was tough like parchment under which the gelly was half an inch thick the remaining substance was solid and firm like the blood taken away at first. I was now no longer at a loss to account for the different disorders I had observed for cancerous like ulcers in the throat and glands and for the different symptons in the fevers I had lived for a constancy on poor dried Buffalo bull beef cured in the smaok [1] without salt and dressed by boiling it in water or stewing it without any addition but a piece of Indian hoe cake which made my breakfast and the same for dinner — it was owing to this coarse food that I had such a thick vicid and black blood.

April 1. Had Letters from home by Nichls Belt all well.

April 4th. Were informed that three men were kild and scapled at Levi Todds Station the 27th.

Went up to Logans came down on Thursday Evening, on Friday all my horses missing. Left a double blanket with Mrs. Logan when there.

[1] Smoke.

April 6th. John Marston came up with Letters from Clark from the Falls he says there was a number of boats came down the Ohio that they brought provisions down the River so that Corn fell from 150 Dollars the bushel to 40. The Indians attacked all the boats that came down, they took one Capt. Bonnalds a Gentleman from Maryland and his family in the long reach the 28th March, there was 25 people on the boat. One Capt. Stull was the first man killed, they kild a man in another boat Col. Clark proposes establishing a post at the mouth of the Ohio which as soon as done he proposes going against the Shawnese in his rout to Detroit his principle object. I wrote to him by Capt. Roberts strongly reccomending it to him, if compatible with his other Operations the 17th March to which he has not yet returned an answer. — There was a man killed on Beargrass the 20th March Wm Akens was kild between Floyds and the Falls the beginning of April.

April 10th. Capt. Pawling came to Col. Bowmans and brought Letters from home informing me that the Military warrants were sent down by Capt Todd who had not returned and my preemption Certificates by James Brown who had Returned, he likewise informed me that two or three Canoes from Watago [1] who had designed to go down the Holstein in Compy with Col. Donalson but the small pox breaking out amongst them they kept behind Donalsons coming opposite to Chickamaga they landed and the Indians left their Town the Cannoes going past that place the next day a white man came to the bank and caled to them that if they wanted corn they should come on shoar that the Indians had plenty and would supply them, they accordingly going on shoar without their Arms the Indians murthered the whole being 30 men, women and children.

April 11th. My horses which were missing since tewsday last were brought in this day having left their walks and were making off. I observed the sugar tree in blossom

---

[1] Watauga, the name of two or more Cherokee towns : one on Watauga River, another on the Little Tennessee.

it bears a Yellow Campanulated or cup like Blossom in which rises about six or eight Stamina with the seed vessel on the top the cup is on an a Stilus an Inch long about 20 of these Campanulated Blossoms rises from the bottom of a Capsul composed of large hairy leaves and two rows of lesser leaves at the end of each twigg 4 or 5 of these capsules rising from the end of each twigg.

Nettles grow every where so plentifully in this Country that I look upon them to be the cause why horses seldom will stay here in the spring in the finest food they generally go off in May when the Nettles have acquired sufficient strength to sting their noses and lips are so severely stung by Nettles that it perfectly distracts them and forces them to range in pasture that is free from Nettles. This Evening two men came over from Lexington and informed us that one Nourse was kild there the third instant they had shot him in the thigh and taken him off 8 miles towards Licking before they kild him. They likewise reported that Majr Harrod had lost a brother that in coming down the River had gone on shore to hunt after some tools that was hid, that after he landed the people that were floating down the River in the boat heard 4 or 5 guns fired they waited at an Iland for him but he never came up with them.

April 16. Left Col. Bowmans for St Asaphs, lodged at Fishers *the 17th* reached St Asaphs *the 18th* went on Business received a Letter and Preemption Warrant by Campbel we heard of a man and a negro being part of a larger Compy from the falls being kild and scalped Eight miles from Jas McAfees.

April 19. This morning [I was] informed that two men from King and Queen on their return were scalped on Rockcastle my horses missing yesterday — got *the 20th* — entered into a Bargain with Mr. Douglass for Terrys preemption and settlement and passed Bonds.

April 21. Col. Logan [1] came home and brought in the preemption warrant for the Certificate purchased of Col.

[1] Benjamin Logan.

Bowman Assignee of James Ross and likewise intelligence that two men that went hunting on Muddy Creek a branch of Kentucky above Boonsburg was kild last Monday. We likewise heard that the same day a man was knocked down by an Indian at Levi Todds Station but the people in the Fort firing on the Enemy the man escaped.

April 23. Col. Knox arrived and brot out my Military warrant for 2200 Acres 2000 in my own right and 200 as Assignee of Thos Lovelle. Received several Letters intimating that a Combination of People were formed at the Falls to seize the Commissioners books and burn them received Letters from Col. Clark requesting me to fall on some plan to furnish him with £20000. I proposed as the only way to borrow money from thee people etc. and spoke to some People about it, heard that 4 men were kild on Cumberland that the Indians had taken off a number of horses from some people that had landed at the Mouth of Limestone, and by Col. Abm Bowman that his brother Isaac in his passage from the Illinois which he left in the winter for ,the falls, was cut off, with his party except two who made their escape he had not been heard of since.

April 24. Received from Col. Logan two military warrants of Capt. Christian of 50 acres each Assigned to him which I delivered to Mr. Terry.

April 26. Finished the buisness my horses missing.

April 27. Advertized 30 dollars for each. Heard of my two bays Col. Logan followed them and got them near Whitlys going off.

April 28. Rode down to Wilsons Station[1] left Thompson to hunt after the Roan entered my military warrants upon Green River on Panther Creek.

April 30. Rode to Harrodsburg heard a man was kild and another wounded on tewsday last at Squire Boones Station on Brashiers Creek Thompson came home from Col. Bowmans without having found the roan horse I sent him

[1] Wilson's Station was on a branch of Salt River two miles northwest of Harrodsburg.

back with the horse I rode to Col. Bowmans. Col. Logan brought my horse down.

May 2. Rode out to Col. Bowmans. By letter was informed that Isaac Bowmans boat coming round from the Illinois was attacked in the Ohio in the Night two men that were on shore kild at their fire a third made his escape and wrote from Cumberland River that he got on board another boat they had passed that there was three men on board I. Bowmans boat and that he heard several guns fired when he was making his escape that when they went to the place they found no signs of the boat but the remains of the two men that were kild. As the method for taking in the State Warrants was settled that all the warrants of the first date should be drawn for to settle the priority of entry each Claimer to make his entries according to the number drawn to his name and the drawings to be made on the 4th inst. I returned to Wilsons Station where the office is kept on Thirsday morning About one oclock the numbers for Warrants of the first date were drawn my Fortune turned up No 24 there was 300 Tickets. when the first was finished tickets for the warrants of other dates were drawn till the whole was finished. The Commissioner[s] closed the buisness of the district by signing the Registers and Surveyors lists and passing receipt for the Money they received.

May 5. The Surveyors put up an Advertisement that he [1] could not take in any locations before Monday next. I returned to Col. Bowmans after breakfast and examined the Lists to see that no mistake had been made and find that we have issued the last setting certificates as follows.

Acres

	Acres
To 400 Acres. Claimers since 1778	4400
Improvers before 1778	163000
Settlements and Preemptions	68600
To 223 Claimers granted Certificates for in the whole acres	236000

So that the general account stands as follows.

[1] They.

		ACRES
The first Sitting to 340 Claimers for Settt[1] since 1778		135850
To the Second Sittg 11 Do Do . . .		4400
Total No 351 of Claimers to 400 acres		140250
Preemption		
The first sitting to 260 for improvements before 1778		260000
The last Do 163 Do		163000
Total No 423 of Claimers for improvement		423000
The first sitting to 505 for settt and preempn before		
1778		702200
The last sitting to 49 Do		68600
Total No 554 for Sett and preempn. . .		770800

Total number of Claims 1328 Total number of Acres 1334050
Certificates granted by the Commissrs for Kentucky
district agreeable to an Act of Genl Assembly for asser-
taining the Claims to unpatented land etc.

To 351 Claimers of 400 acre preemptions since 1778	140250
To 423 Do of 1000 acres preemption for Impr before	
1778	423000
To 554 Do Settt and preempn before 1778 . . .	770800
1328 Total of Claimers Total of acres granted	1334050

May 7. This morning Stephen Trig came past Col.
Bowmans on his way home contrary to his intention when
I parted with him at the Office, then he designed to stay
till his buisness was finished, so that I was not prepared
to go with him. Yesterday we were informed that 7 Indians were discovered on Salt River near the upper McAfees.
The Inhabitants of this place catched numbers of fish yesterday and today all Cat fish except a black perch such as
in Roanoke.

May 8. Went to the Surveyors Office, but the Warrants
taken in on Thursday Last not being in order as the drawing was done with Confusion, by the plan they took in no
Locations till the ninth and then verry slowly. Numbers
of people being wearied out went away, there being no pro-

---

[1] Settlement.

visions to be purchased. *The Tenth* made my Locations and returned to Col. Bowmans. This day news came from Grants Station on Elkhorn that on Saturday the 6th the Indians had kild a woman and two men were fired on [at] the Fort but retreated with fifteen horses being pursued by a party were overtaken by them in Eight Miles when they took one prisoner that had been wounded at the Fort and brought him in he died that night but would give them no Answer to any questions Asked but that there was great numbers of Indians this side of Ohio and frequently desired our People to kill him.

May 11th. The most of the Party I designed to go in with having gon up to Logans and Whilleys [1] I prepared to set out this morning and rode up.

May 12th. Left Logans in my way home in Compy with Col. Garret from the Stafford County Capt. Pawling and Others. Overlooked Capt. I[r]win from Bedford and Cal[d]-well from Charlot in all about 20 incamped on a run a branch of Dicks River, three miles from Englishes. [2]

May 13. A Young man came into us that had been lost twelve days in his way from St. Asaphs to Pitmans Station on Green River. He was in a wretched condition subsisting on herbs during that time. We went the New road to Scags Creek and went through some good land on a branch of Dicks River came up with a Compy of fifteen men went down a long branch of Scaggs Creek that runs into it at the 3rd foarding. Crossed Rockcastle went up the river three miles and encamped on Raccoon Creek three miles above the mouth.

May 14th. Left Camp after 7 o'clock A.M. in about 1½ Miles passed the Graves of a Family that perished in the Winter they had encamped on a little rising the waters of the Creek breaking over the Banks surrounded them, it raining hard, extinguished their fire. The Husband en-

[1] William Whitley. Whitley's Station was about five miles southeast of Logan's Fort.

[2] English's Station, on the south branch of upper Dick's River, southeast of Whitley's Station.

deavoured to swim over to get fire from People not far from them but was lost in the Attempt his wife and some children perished in the Night with the extremity of the Weather. We passed the rock I took notice of the way out, and observed a long continued ridge in full Foliage while the trees on the hills we crossed had scarce any and but small leaves. In Sept. in my way out I noticed the same Ridge the leaves turned Yellow when the leaves on the other hills retained their Verdure, from which I Judge there is a mineral contained in the Mountain it lyes from the above Rocks N. and E. and is a long Ridge and about two miles or upwards from them. We passed the Hazel Patch when[1] the Boonsburg road comes in to St. Asaphs this day we crossed some hills and Swamps and encamped on a Ridge by a Spring half a mile from the place where two men were killed and a Negro taken prisoner this Spring. The place where the Indians attacked was fit for the purpose a narrow passage on a ridge with a draught on each side prevented Assistance had there been any at hand from surrounding the Enemy.

May 15. Crossed several Ridges to camp. 6 [miles back] we crossed Stock Creek.

May 16. Went up Richland Creek Stinking Creek passed Flat Lick[2] and encamped a mile from it.

The distance from Ligans[3] we made as follows.

To Inglisses[4] 15 miles. The head of Scaggs Creek 7.

To Rockcastle 20. To Hazel Patch 10. To Lawrel River 12.

To the head of Raccon Creek. To Stock Creek 8.

Richland Creek 7. Stinking Creek 8. Flat Lick 2. Cumberland Foard 8. Cumberland Gap 15. 113 miles.[5]

---

[1] Where.

[2] Flat Lick was on the east bank of Stinking Creek and near the confluence of that stream and the Cumberland.

[3] Logan's Fort. [4] English's Station.

[5] The road indicated by the above was "The Road from the Old Settlements in Virginia to Kentucke thro' the great Wilderness." It ran nearly direct in a southeasterly direction from Harrodsburg to Cumberland Gap.

At noon this day three men and a negro came in to us who belonged to a party of 12 from Lexington that were defeated about five miles before us, we marched in silence and pritty good order to the place and found John and Robert Davis from Amherst lying scalped and much mangled on the road. There was two war Clubs left on the head of one was the figure of a Lizard cut which I supposed belonged to the Spring Lizard of Chickamaga it appeared to me there was two parties out. One of 17 and one of 18 Indians we buried the Corps as well as we could and pursuing our Journey crossed Cumberland Mountains and encamped half a mile short of Walkers Creek. The Morning Cloudy with smart showers another man from the Lexington party came in, on the Road halted two miles short of Martins Cabbin in Powells Valley, rained all the afternoon we encamped on the bank of a Creek a Mile Short of Coxes place. Martins Cabbin 18 miles from Our Last encampment. Coxes 8 miles from Martins.

May 18th. This Morning put Our Arms in Order and went on. The People at Coxes had left their houses shut up but we saw some Cattle and dogs halted at the Glade Spring 8 miles from Coxes we passed a Ridge that a Stout Creek run through, one of our Party rode along the Channel of the Water below this natural bridge the road goes over we came to Scots at Christians Plantation and were informed that Messrs Todd and Trigg lay there on Saturday night and that on Sunday the Indians kild a man belonging to Coxes Station which made the People move to that Place : and that two men of the Lexington party had got there that day, we went up a big run, crossed Wallins Ridge which was verry Steep and Slippery as it rained on us, we encamped at the foot of it four miles from Scots. Two of the Lexington party came up with us.

May 19th. We went up a bad run and bad road all the days march, passed a verry bad and Slippery hill as bad as any of the Mountains passed Flats Lick where the road comes in from the Rye Cove, the road down Stock Creek verry bad and long, crossed Clinch which was rising so deep some of the horses were swimming in the midle of the River a swarm of Flies settled on my horses head and set him a plunging however I got safe over. We halted when we got over the River, then crossed several steep hills stoney road and Miry places a fresh Indian Tract was discovered, which brought our company into a litle Order encamped two miles from Moccasin.

May 20th. Gap. After our horses were got up we proceeded on our Journey went through the Gap crossed the No Fork of Holstein [1] River passed the Block house and halted three miles from it. Our company begun now to disperse. We went on and encamped at the head of Reedy Creek, I got my baggage put into Irwin and Caldwells Waggon, they having brought out a waggon with them this far on their way to Kentucky.

May 21st. Went to Col. Shelbys [2] 6 miles from our last Camping place, rested there that day paid Jno Cox 595 Dollars for cald in Money I had take[n] down for him.

May 22. Breakfast at Bakers some days before a party of Indians attacked a house on Nonachucky [3] had two of their party killed. Our People were relieved by some people that came up to their Assistance. A man was either killed or taken Prisoner in Carters Valley. halted at Grays three miles from Shelbys and was overtaken by a party who left Kentucky some days after we did and who met with Wimer one of the Lexington party at Martins Cabbin Powells Valley, when the party was attacked he quit his horse with a design to fight them but seeing his companions dispersed he was obliged to run and was fired at by an Indian. Wimer soon after falling by stepping into a hole the Indian thinking he had shot him run up to Wimer with his tomahawk and knife without his gun, Wimer recovering himself presented his gun at the Indian who stopt short in Amaze and standing motionless was shot down. Wimer then ran off and blun-

---

[1] Holston.

[2] Colonel Isaac Shelby, whose home at this time was close to the southern border of Virginia, and at or near the present Bristol, Tennessee.   [3] Nolachucky.

dering a second time fell in a hollow place, the Indians loosing his tract he loaded his gun and observing an Indian running toward him shot at him with a zest 50 yards and thinking he wounded him in the belly he was no longer pursued and made his Escape he discovered another party of fifteen whom he avoided, and got to where Skeggs Party overtook him, inable to go further from his Legg and knee being much swelled. Tomlins the only person missing of this Party got in wounded in both his Arms. Capt. Pawling coming up who had gone back for my sadlebags which I had left we went to Mr. Cummins 15 miles from Col. Shelbys he informed us that the Indians had attacked a Fort on Nonachucky and lost three after which they went to the house mentioned above.

May 23. Continued our Journey left the Court house on our right, passed George Finleys and fell into the road a mile below Capt. Daisurs went to Col. Wm. Campbells 23 Miles from Mr. Cummins.

May 24. Halted below the Magazine Spring passed Davis where I got a Gun of Capt. Christian he had sent out last Fall when he designed to go to Kentucky. I had picked up a Blanket of his at the Block house we passed Catarines and went to Capt. Stephens a mile down the River.

May 25. Went on our way dined at Wm Sawyers and reached Mr. Triggs at Mahanaim 37 miles from Stephens.

May 26. Crossed New River lodged at Mrs. Madisons.

May 27. Reached home, my horses got home in the Morning having sent them on the day before. I found my Family well and in health after nine months Absence.

Laus Die.

Warrant for 1000 acres on the waters of Goose, Beargrass Creeks beginning at a Sugar tree, Ash, Elm and Buck Eye on the side of a hill corner to Wm Christians land, thence N. 53° E. 400 poles Crossing the Creek to a Sugar tree thence So. 37° E. 400 poles crossing the Creek to two sugar trees on Col. Christians land and along the same crossing the Creek twice N. 37° W. 400 poles to the beginning.

Settlement and preemption Assigt of Jas. Ross On the head waters of a Smaller branch that empties into the Ohio near the upper end of the 3 Iland thence with Griffins East line to the branches of Harrods Creek for quantity.

The Buffalo lick in No 2 is a water lick at the foot of a hill betwixt the lick and the Creek on the So. side of the Lick. George Hendrix Settlement and Preemption upon an East Branch of Hustons Fork of Licking Creek including two of Credentons Cabbins and a marked tree with R. S. upon the West side of the 3rd Branch about three miles from the head. laid on State Warrants on the preemption beginning with   Towns upper lines on the sd Creek and running up both sides of the Creek including a tree marked R. S. on the West side of sd Creek and two of Credentons Cabbins.

April[1] *28.* Entered with the Surveyor of Kentucky 1000 [acres] by virtue of a Military War[ran]t on the waters of a branch of Panther Creek, emptying on the West side of the sd Creek above a Buffalo Lick branch, the lick lying about $\frac{3}{4}$ of a mile from Panther Creek the sd Land lying Northerly from the sd Lick about four miles including the Forks of the sd first mentioned Branch about 13 miles from the mouth of Panther Creek and running up both side[s] for quantity.

May 29. 200 acres Ass[ignmen]t of Jno. Lovell to include the Buffalo Lick in the above Location extending Northerly towards the above Location.

500 [acres], part of a Military Wart of one thousand due the sd Fleming lying about Pitmans Station Six Miles on a Spring branch that runs into Pitmans Creek of a branch of G. River to include two springs and a sink on both sides of the branches and running down to Pitmans Creek for quantity. This entery withdrawn and Joined to the follg:

500 acres part of a military Warrant for one thousand [acres] on the E. side of Panther Creek twelve miles from the mouth to include a spring marked E. H. L. H. with a small improvement. 500 acres N/3 withdrawn and laid on the Above round it.

[1] May.

Preemption on Beargarss of 1000 Acres Beginning at a Sugar tree Ash and Elm and Buckeye on the side of a hill corner to Wm Christians land thence N. 53 E. 400 poles crossing the Creek to a Sugar tree thence S. 37 E. 400 poles to an Ash and sugar tree thence So. 53 W. 400 poles crossing the Creek to two sugar trees on Col. Christians line and along the same crossing the Creek twice N. 37° W. 400 poles to the beginning.

Preemption and Settlement on a small E branch of Hustons Fork of Licking including two of Credentons Cabbins also a marked tree with R. S. on the west side of the said branch about three miles from the head.

Location of a Military Warrant. At the mouth of Panther Creek on both sides including a Cypress Spring on Green River just above the mouth of Panther Creek marked one Large White Oak a little below the Spring L. H. A Location on Little Mountain Creek a branch of Hinkstons Fork on the So. side below Wm Calks improvement One and a half miles on a small fork of the sd Creek on the West side and running up the branch for Compliment. The Waters of Licking this taken

Dollins best Pocket Telescope with a Stand.

1779 Nov. 2 Sent in by Col. David Robinson a Claim prov[ed] in before the Court of Kentucky to lands, as Surveyors mate to the Old Virginia Regt likewise Thos Lovels claim as a drummer in the sd Regt assigned to me, and sent a duplicate of these Claims for 20050 Acres by Col. Barbour.

Received by Mr. Wallances conveyance three Warrants from the treasury of One Thousand Acres each these Warrants left in my Portmantle with Henry Wilson at Fort Liberty.

1780 Jan. 4 Obtained a Certificate of preemption for One Thousand Acres of land for improving in 1775 located on Beargrass Joining Wm Christians the Commissioners Certificate I sent in by Capt. Craig a duplicate by Capt. Owen the 11th Feby 1780.

Jan. 13. Obtained a Settlement and preemption for Geo. Hendrix on a West Fork of Hustons branch of Licking.

14000 Acres.

Purchased a preemption of 1000 Acres from Henry Bauchman heir at Law to Jacob Bauchman for £200.

Sold the above to Jacob Mors for £500.

Purchased a preemption and Settlement at 10000 from James Ross by Col. Bowmans for which I gave Col. Jno Bowman my Bond. — Memorandum to get Col. Bowmans truss for the right side it take 3 feet three inches to measure round him.

Preemption on Beargrass	1000
On Eighteen Mile Creek	1400
Hendrix Licking	400
Lovets Military Claim	50
My own	2000
State Warrant	1500
	6350

Memorandum to get Col. Bowman's Salmon's Gography from Col. Prestons.

For Col. Floyd a 7 or 8 or 12 or 15 yds to be sent to Col. Bowmans Care.

Land Surveyed in Kentucky by Military

Warrants before 1779	206050
Certificates granted by the Commissrs	1096650
	1302700
Treasury Warrants of the 15th Feb.	1122992
Do to April 1st	802804
	1925796

At Wintleys Station

Women and Children	54
Men	22
	76

At St Asaphs

Women and Children	74
Men	25
Blacks	20
	119

Clarks
    Men 10
    Women and Children . . . . <u>23</u>

                                        33

Dougharlys
    Men 5
    Women and Children . . . . <u>16</u>

                                        21

Harrodsburg 400

Counterfit 30 Dollars July 22d 1776
    Do   40   April 11 1778.
Memorandum.
    To enter a Salt Lick 56 miles E. from Big glue licks on licking on the first Large Creek that empties into B. Sandy Creek about 30 miles from the mouth of Sandy. 100 Acres between Col. Lunn and Wm Fleming the expences to be equally born and Capt Linn to direct the survey L   In the Fork of 18 mile Creek three or four miles above the mouth of the Creek empties into the Ohio at the upper end of 18 mile Iland.
Certificates granted by the Commissrs in Kentucky . . . . 1334050 acres
Surveyed in Kentucky before 1779 by Military Warrants 206050
Warrants of the 15 October taken in 1779 . 1122992
Do to Apr 1st 1780 taken in by the Survey <u>802804</u>
                                   3465896

COLONEL WILLIAM FLEMING'S JOURNAL OF TRAVELS IN KENTUCKY IN 1783

INTRODUCTION

THE General Assembly of Virginia, on the 21st of June, 1781, passed a resolution providing for the appointment of a commission "to call to account all officers, agents, commissaries, quartermasters, and contractors, who have been or are in service in the Western country . . . and report to the governor." In the following November, a few weeks after his resignation from the council because of a rheumatic complaint, Colonel Fleming received a letter which prompted him to write Governor Nelson: "I am very sensible Government has great reason to apprehend impositions and fraud in almost every department in that Country (Western), chiefly owing to persons imployed in behalf of the State, who are at too great distance from the notice of their superiours, to be immediately caled to account for their misconduct, turn their views too much to their private interest — Great sums have been advanced for provisions, great quantities have been purchased, and great quantities by negligence have been lost — Capt: Todd, who will deliver this to your Excellency, informs me, only half of the horses purchased and paid for by the State in this quarter, on account of General Clark have been delivered. I hope the Commissioners appointed to settle and adjust these accounts, will have sufficient powers given them to discriminate the guilty from the innocent — that the latter may not suffer for the faults of the former." [1]

Colonel Fleming expressed the fear that his right arm which was rendered almost useless by "a severe rheumatic complaint" would not permit him to make the journey and he foresaw the need of a military escort for protection from

[1] *Calendar of Virginia State Papers*, Vol. II, p. 598.

the Indians, but as finally constituted the members of the commission were : Colonel William Fleming, Colonel Samuel McDowell, Caleb Wallace, and Colonel Thomas Marshall, father of Chief Justice Marshall. The manuscript of the journal is among the papers of the Lyman Draper Collection in the library of the State Historical Society of Wisconsin and there is a copy among the Reuben T. Durrett Manuscripts in the library of the University of Chicago.

COLONEL WILLIAM FLEMING'S JOURNAL IN KENTUCKY FROM JAN. 4TH TO APRIL 22ND, 1783

KENTUCKY *1783*. *Jany. 4th.* Left Mrs. Triggs [1] in Compy with Mr. Wallace [2] Our Ser[van]ts and baggage the day Cloudy with snow and cold, went to Harrodsburg where we were to meet an escort of 25 men ordered by the Commanding Officer of Lincoln County and there met Col. McDowal,[3] the Secretary, Genl Clark, Mr. Shannon and some others waited for the Escort meeting and one of the Serts coming in who had gon[e] by Col. Bowmans to deliver some letters etc. 27 s for James Smith, from Bowmans [4] he had taken the road to Henry Wilsons and detained us so long that we could not get further than McAfees [5] station which was deserted, the people having suffered greatly by the Indians last summer having several people killed and the place attacked briskly by a large party of Indians. In this place we lodged all night which was stormy with snow, we were Joined by some of the escort and some who took the Opportunity of the Compy going to Jefferson County.

Jany. 5th. Set out in the morning very cloudy, cold, snowing and threatening a Storm, crossed Salt River,[6] and Chaplains Forks, came on Simpsons run where at a spring

[1] Colonel Stephen Trigg, who had served with Fleming on the former commission, founded Trigg's Station, four miles northeast of Harrodsburg, in 1780. He was killed in the battle of Blue Licks, August 19, 1782.

[2] Caleb Wallace, one of the commissioners.

[3] Colonel John McDowell, Secretary of the Commission.

[4] Colonel Abram Bowman, founder of Bowman's Station, six miles east of Harrodsburg.

[5] McAfee's Station on the East Fork of Salt River, about seven miles from Harrodsburg, was settled by the McAfee brothers in 1779.

[6] East Fork of Salt River, Chaplin's Fork being the West Fork.

branch Genl Clark collected some petrified Cockles, it was so cold I could not light as the Compy rode briskly on those I fot[1] were sea cockles, some wholy petrified, others half petrified some single shells, others the whole cockles, some few of the Clam kind, some sheels[2] seemed broke and dented in by the pressure of foreign bodies from above, and cemented by the petrifying matter, they seemed either to be real Antedeluvians, or to have lain there since that part of this country was possessed by the sea, as these was real marine shells, in four or five miles we got to Kinslows[3] station which was entirely destroyed by the Enemy last summer about this[4] time of Col. Todds[5] defeat at Licking, excepting two dirty huts in which we could not lodge, we therefore encamped in a field the night very windy and cold and next morning, *Jan.* 6, in five miles we reached Cox Station, 32 miles from Harrodsburg; as the next day was Court day we determined to rest having buisness with the Militia Officers and Sherriff of the County we encamped in an old field.

Jany. 7th. A fine moderate day. Did our buisness with Col. Cox Col. of the County and gave the Sherriff summons' for such Persons as we were informed would throw light on the mismanagement of the public Stores etc.: — We eat with Col Cox, and got some corn from him paying 1 shl each meal and 3 shl busl for the corn. Here Mr. Jno. May desired me to give him any warrants I had to locate and he would locate it for me having only a 400 acre w[arran]t I gave it him, — spoke to Capt. Oldham to survey James Speeds entry round Manslick, sent up Archd Woods entry on the Beachfork to Thomas Woods at Wilsons by — Boyd and wrote him to get it surveyed as soon as possible as I could not take any further trouble on me about it — wrote to Hub. Taylor conserning my entries on Panther

---

[1] Found.   [2] Shells.

[3] Kincheloe's Station, on Simpson's Creek, a branch of Salt River.   [4] The.

[5] Colonel John Todd, who was defeated in the battle of Blue Licks, August 19, 1782.

Creek, that as he had kept the locations so long I expected [he] would survey them but if he declined to do it on Acct of any agreement with Mr. Lee on Mr. Masons acct that I had wrote to Col: Abm Bowman and Col. Knox to show the plans and to get one of his deputies to survey them, — We were Joined by some more of Our Escort and now were an Ensign and Seventeen privates instead of 25 promised.

Jany. 8th. The Eighth we set out for Louisville at the Falls of Ohio. a fine moderate day in 13 miles down the Creek over some indifferent land. We left the Creek[1] and went down Salt River 3 miles crossing at an Iland, where a boy had been taken and one kiled 2 days before I crossed at the same place in 79 — We left Salt river and Crossed Floyds Fork and Fern Creek, travelling through poor indiferent green cherry land. Floyds fork empties into Salt river, Fern Creek is lost in ponds and low flat land a back of the Falls — the land altered for the better as we came to sd branch of Bear grass. We passed Popes or Sullivans upper Station near dark and went to Col. Floyds 2½ miles from thence, going past the lower dutch Station or Hoglens, where the greatest part of our escort st[o]pped having parted with Gl Clark [2] and the rest of the Company at Popes except Mr. Daniel the Att Gl[3] As Col. Floyd was not at home we went to Louisville *the 9th* and discharged the Escort, drawing for them four days meat and flower and three bushl Corn, we found the place almost deserted of Inhabitants, the few left depending chiefly on the Garrsion, neither being provided with Corn or Forriage or other necessaries for the entertainment of travellers, nor Cane near the place. We found this place by no means proper to do buisness in, the Garrison barely having a sufficiency of provisions, that is bad Flower and beef, not being able to purchase any on the Credit of the State, they are supplied with Whiskey from Fort Pitt at 20 shl or 24 shl per Gallon and at this time they had it in great plenty.

---

[1] Simpson's Creek.   [2] General George Rogers Clark.
[3] Attorney General.

morning of the 10th

Jany. 10th. In the Afternoon three boats hove in sight, with 2000 Galls. One Family came down as setlers and several passengers Majr Harrods wife, the Majr [1] having left the boats at Licking Majr and Capt. Moseby with others ? Capt. Phill : Barbour was here 4 or 5 days before our arrival. Col. Floyd came in the Forenoon, we determined to move our quarters, either to Capt. Sullivans or Beargrass. at Gl Clarks desire we gave him our Oppinion in writing about the Posts he was ordered to erect at the mouth of Kentucky, Licking, and Limestone in which we advised him to set about the Post at Kentucky directly, as only one could be undertaken at once. In the Afternoon a signal was made on the other shore and there the Glass discovered five or Six men, boats were ordered to bring them over but we could not stay to know who they were, it drawing towards night, and being in hast to get from so disagreable a place where many of the men etc. were in Liquor, and our horses kept upon the Fort starving, spoke with Mr. Harrod who informed me, on their way from Kentucky they had rested themselves a day and two nights at Bellmonts and that the family were all well, got to Col. Floyds at night.

Jany. 11th. Finding no vacant house in that Station went over to the upper dutch Station but did not succeed. On our return to Col. Floyds we met with Capt. Sullivans who had been recommended to us as a proper person to lodge with. Gl Clark had spoken to him, and he expected the Commissn but he insisted on having ⅘ shl day for each, boys as well as others, for victualling only, which would have swelled our Account so high and seemed so extravagant that we were determined to return to Lincoln, but by Col. Floyds influence we got a Cabbin in the Dutch Station, and was victualled by Handberry and got Corn from Col. Floyds — and *the 13th* being Monday moved the[nce] and proceeded to buisness — *14th* Do. *The 15th*

[1] James Harrod.

being the day appointed for the return of the Summons to appear we prepared to go to Louisville — when we reached Fort Nelson at the Falls we found no Evidences, and determined to return to N : Holland. I was informed that the Frenchmen that came over were from St. Vincent [1] and Kaskaskias, that one of them was clerk to the Court at Kaskas[kia].[2] Mr. Carbono, on my enquiring for them Gl Clark, told me they were gon to Beargrass, that Affairs were in confusion in the Illinois, that they were at a loss who were to direct them, that they came in about this and were designed to go to Congress if the State of Virgi[ni]a had left them to themselves. I expressed myself several times to Genl Clark that I wanted to see the   I could not help them being they were sedulously kept out of the way, as the General hinted they came chiefly to him Capt. George returned from the Chickesaws in the Eavening but did not give us any information of his transactions but in general terms said all was well and that there was peace. We expected to see or know something more next day after he had rested, but was disappointed. We lodged in the Fort the night excessive cold.

Jany. 16th. We rode down to the lower end of the Falls rode into Rock Iland and several others, where we picked up many petrified substances. Walnut in different degrees of petrefaction, Buffalo dung turned to a perfect stone, Goose dung turned to stone, some partly petrified whilst some of the same remained in its natural state, petrified roots of trees and a petrified Buffalo horn which unfortunately broke in three pieces seperating it from the rock,[3]

[1] An English name temporarily substituted for the French Vincennes.

[2] A French settlement on the Kaskaskia River in Illinois.

[3] On examing this petrified horn I observed that the bottom part of it, for it was seperated from the bony substance in their side, was filled with a clayee matter hardened to stone, that the lip or solid part of the horn was perfectly petrified throughout and had the appearance of a Stalactites, that the lower part next the head was likewise entirely petrified, and that the longitudinal fibers, that formerly made part of the substance of the

petrified shells etc. I observed in the rocks in general that they had striate running in paralel lines through their whole substance and shooting out from their surfaces not well defined trochilee an inch in diameter two, three, or four inches in length with fine perpendicular rings on the surface circular and the joints rather confused than properly defined. The flat rocks that every where cover the bottom of the Ohio are formed by the sand and Clay that is left by the water, and the petrifying or stone cement insinuating between the particles hardning by degrees forms at last a solid stony flag which as it dries cracks in irregular squares of various thickness from 4 Inches to 18, 20, 24 Inches etc : thickness and fastning any thing lying on their surfaces or that is buried in them when in a soft state, is at length petrified with the rock; the Buffalo dung on the surface of the rock above the surface was as hard as what was below the surface so was the goose dung etc. : — I was informed the Oionn [1] or Illinois nut grows near the Falls and above Beargrass it is a species of the Hickory [or] the cotton tree neither of which I saw.

Jany. 17th. We returned to the Fort after riding a considerable time in the river. I spoke to Capt. George and told him the Commissrs requested of him an Invoice of the goods he purchased from Capt. Barbour. He informed me he had none and seemed to evade it which made me suspect Barbour had been tampering with him. Before we left Fort Nelson near the Eavening I went to see

horn, very plainly appeared, where the circular exterior fibers had been worn off, and the circles on the surface near the foot common in horns were compleat — in short there was not the least reason to dispute its being a horn compleatlly petrified, and a Buffaloes from its form and size — and that it grew on the right side of the head, it was Eight inches in a straight line from the Tip to the Butt in length, at the most 6¼ Inches in Circumference, and ½ at the tip, there was a small part of the lip so incorporated with the rock that it could not be separated which I judged to [be] half an inch in length — I picked up several pieces of pure coal. — Note in MS.

[1] Pecan.

George and found the [1] laid up in bed asleep, did not wake
him. — The Frenchmen were kept out of sight, — and we
set out for New Holland [2] — riding briskly my horse went
below a beach tree a limb of which hurt my left Eye and
Ear which bled a little but smarted a good deal — when we
got home we understood Col. Marshall [3] had passed in his
way to Louisville and found some Evidences attending that
was summoned. As we advertised that we should do buisness at this Place when we were at Fort Nelson and Gl
Clark not being come we could not proceed in their examination till all parties were present which at farthest will be on
Monday. The Inhabitants tan leather with beach tree
bark they likewise find sugar tree bark will answer, — Blue
Ash a spieces of the White Ash and called so from the bark
tinging water of that colour, grows to be a large tree as does
the Prickly ash, the White Ash and the Cotton tree. — The
soil after crossing Salt River alters much from what it is in
Lincoln and Fayelle [4] in general being mixed with Sand and
of a lighter colour, and much more inclined to Beach, and
few inhabitants of Louisville having moved from their
former situation higher up the river, and being supplied
with water from the well in Fort Nelson or making use of
the River water, say they are much healthier and not subjected to the Phagadencie Cancerous ulcers and malignant
fevers so general when I was there in 1779. The water then
used was streams breaking out in the river banks fed from
Ponds at some distance from the place, the water was highly
impregnated with noxious particles I imagine of the Arseni-
cal kind, either before it left the pond or in its passage
through the earth to the River. The well in the Fort is
supplied from the river, it is dug to the level of the bed of
the Ohio, the water filters through two strata of sand and
Pebles and rises and sinks in the well as the River rises and

[1] Him.
[2] New Holland, or Low Dutch Station, was on the west bank of
Beargrass Creek, a few miles S. by E. of the Falls.
[3] Colonel Thomas Marshall, one of the commissioners.
[4] Fayette.

falls, is   feet deep. Genl Clark, Mr. Daniel AttG,[1]
and a party came up from Fort Nelson and got a house adjoining fitted up, we drew 100 lbs flower at the Fort and
got corn for our horses from Col. Floyds.

Jany. 20th. Col. Marshall came from Lexington and
joined us to proceed on Buisness — We entered on Gl
Clarks papers and books and took several depositions relative thereto. Some hunters that had gone out this morning from the Station returned in the Night and reported
that fifteen miles from this on the trace to Boons station
they were fired on by five or Six Indians and that one of
their party was shot, Mr. Glahan, a young man that lived
at this place — the 19th in the Evening I went over to Col.
Floyds to see his eldest son, in a warm fever, and had some
talk with Jno. May about my land. He said that he had
spoke to Wilson who married Wid[o]w Pendergrass not to
let Kendrix Preemption interfere with my warr[an]t ajoining
— returned Monday morning —

Jany. 21st. Entered on Capt. Georges and Barbour affair.
George denied his having wrote to the executive that the
bell[2] he drew was to be paid in paper currency and is to
produce his letter tomorrow, several depositions were taken
concerning his conduct whilst at Fort Jefferson — a party
went out to bury the dead and returned at night. Our
servants could only get six of our horses two of mine and
one of Mr. Wallaces being missing.

Jany. 22nd. Took in deposition on various cases.

Jany. 23rd. Capt. George had not got his papers necessary to warrant us enter on C. Barbours buisness, he went
to the Falls, we were employed in taking depositions etc.
received a petition from the Reg[imen]t complaining that
many of them had not got their County money, were in ar-
rears for their pay and Clothing, desired Gl Clark to direct the
Capt. to make out his lists of for defi[ci]ency of Clothing etc.
We had information that two men were killed at the mouth
of Salt River the 21st continued to do buisness this week

---

[1] Attorney general.   [2] Bill.

the 29th went over to Col. Floyds and out with Mr. Jno. May, continued to do buisness taking depositions and getting what light we could in it till *Saturday the 8th Febry.* Col. McDowel [1] being determined to go up to Lincoln I was very anxious to get Capt. Barbours affair determined before he went as I perceived it went on best [2] slowly *10th* determined Capt. Barbours affair and settled it at 758811 lbs 6⅔ post cost and allowing him 2¼ advance for the Cargo delivered at Fort Jefferson made in all 24661.24 lbs 6 sh 8D instead of 237325 Dollars clear. Col. McDowal went up to Lincoln went over to Col. Floyds to get him to make a survey at the mouth of Harrods Creek. It rained and we put it off till next day, we rode to the mouth of Goose Creek but could find no beginning of Col. Byrds land, we then went up the river to Harrods Creek and began from McKinzies corner running down the river. It was then dark, we lay on Goose Creek next morning, run McKinzies lower line and compleated the Settlement survey of 400 acres, then run the 1000 acre warrant survey which nearly joined Spangliss line, Terrys Settlement and McKinzies lower line, one continued cane break; having finished, in our return viewed my preemption of 1000 acres joining Col. Christians land with which I am well pleased — returned to New Holland and went on with the buisness till Sunday morning.

Feby. 23rd. We were alarmed by the signal of two guns from the Falls, the usual signal being 1, 2 or 3 discharged from a six pounder according to alarm to be given. In two houres after the report was heard an Express arrived with intelligence that the Enemy had taken all the horses at the Falls and swam them over the Ohio below the Falls that Lt Clark and 25 men were dispatched across the River after them but returned and found the Enemy had taken of the most of the horses from Popes Station — continued to do buisness till *the 28th* we set out on our return for Lincoln, lodged in a Bottom which old Mr. Christian located. There is some good land and a pritty situation

---

[1] Samuel McDowell, one of the commissioners. [2] But.

for building on. We could not cross Salt River lower on Account of the back water from the Ohio, crossed a creek at the head of the Bottom and then Salt River, went to Col. Coxes got corn for our horses and crossed Chaplains fork, lodged to [1] miles from Coxs —

Mar. 1. The next day crossed the Beach Fork, came to Harrodsburg, and in the evening went to Mrs. Triggs. *Monday the 2d* went to Harrodsburg to the Gen. Court which adjourned to the low dutch station 4 *and 5th* at court, *the 6th* met the trustees for the seminary of learning at Mr. Madisons, agreed on proposals to be laid before the Assembly, returned at night to Mrs. Triggs, and *the 7th* rode to Col. Bowmans to do buisness. Saturday night rode to Mrs. Triggs.

Mar. 10th. Went over to Lexington to finish the Buisness which we did on tuesday and Wednesday, and designed to return on Thursday. On Wednesday Evening a man that had been at Harrodsburg came in, he was fired at by Indians half way from the River, his horse was wounded in the Neck, he made his escape. A party was ordered out on thursday which detained us that day and we finished the whole buisness, paid Col. Marshall, for two surveys which Col. Boon is to make for me that the plots might not be detained in the Office, *Friday the 14th* returned. 15th rode to Mr. Mays and paid him his fees for Survey etc. of the settlement I purchased from Douglass, a warrant adjoining, and my preemption, — we were informed that the Indians had taken the horses from Sulivans old Station and kild one man and wounded another on Salt River after we left Beargrass. Met Col. Floyds at Mr. Mays and paid him for the corn I had for my horses, likewise gave him three half Goona's' for expences of their carriers etc. : in making my surveys — I went to Mr. James Speeds on Saturday Evening and got an obligation for his making me a right to the half of Six hundred acres, a location I gave him around Col. Todds entry on Manstun for allowing him to half of

[1] Two.

my interest in the Agreement with Col. Todd, returned on *Sunday, the 16th*.

Mar. 17th. Went to Col. Bowmans and continued doing buisness till *Saturday the 22*. In the course of this week I received letters from Mr. Fleming etc. by Capt. Madison, we were informed one Mouns and another were kiled on Rockcastle, two men kild on Cumberland, and Col. Daniel Smith wounded, small parties of Indians were seen in different skirts of the settlement, many chased by them. Col. Jno. Montgomery and two or three others were pursued coming from Beards town,[1] and alarms were given at some of the stations — we fixed on *the 4th of April* to set out from Col. Logans, on our return and dispatched Advertisements to that purpose — Got Col. Jno. Bowmans and Col. Abm. Bowmans depositions proving Joh. Ross assignment of a Settlement and preemption claim to 1400 acres of land taken before Col. Benjm Logan — took in all the Claim but had not time to enter into a consideration of them, we broke up on Saturday night, on Sunday bundled up the papers. All Saturday and Sunday it rained verry hard and raised cane run so that my Sert could not Cross it with my horses. Thursday, Friday and Saturday it thundered very loud and longer than I ever observed it before. Monday continued to rain, the Rivers and Runs exceeding high, which determined the Party to post pone setting out till Wednesday, *the 9th* employed in getting my load and Sadles etc. in order for the Journey.

April 3. The express that Col. Legras Maj. Boscroon and Capt. Frolier etc. were come to the Falls dispatched the letters to Col. McDowell to stop him he being on his way to Col. Logans. *Saturday the 5th* rode to Col. Harrods. *Sunday 6th* returned to Mrs. Triggs from Jno. Smiths where I lodged verry ill, took a smart purge, received a letter from Harrodsburg informing the Illinois Gentlemen were come up. I wrote them to ride up to St. Asaphs where we would take in their claims, was informed that a prisoner was taken at Sturgis Station on Friday week and on last

---

[1] Bardstown.

Sunday two Indians were shot of a raft crossing Floyds Fork. *Monday the 7th* being better left Mrs. Triggs, in my way lodged at Saml Givens and on *the 8th* got to Col. Logans where I met Col. Legres, Maj. Bowman, Capt. Frolier May, Williams and Mr. Henry from St. Vincent were joined by Col. Marshall and Mr. Wallace in the Evening here we were informed that a party of Indians had taken horses from a Station near Coxs were pursued overtaken at the Ohio and two of them Killed, the horses except one recovered, a number of Rafts discovered near Estells Station. One Lane, a Surveyor, kild above Boonsborough, *the 10th* a man was kild on the road from Harrodsburg to Coxes on the Beach Fork in this week several people were pursued and fired on in various quarters horses taken from Gilberts Creek. *On Saturday 7th* Genl Clark and Mr. Daniels came up and informed us that Col. Floyds: One of his Brothers and another person going to the Salt works were fired on by Indians, Col. Floyd Mortally wounded, his Brother's horse shot under him, and the third person shot dead, that Col. Floyds with his Brothers Assistance got to the Salt works. *Sunday* had Acct from different parts of the Country that the Enemy were taking off horses from Duhs [1] River, Salt River etc.; a person fired on near the Crab orchard — they seem to be spread over the country — We are just alarmed with the News that Inglish [2] was Attacked and that the Indians had broken to the Station and were tomahawking the Women, the men being drawn out in quest of Indians. [manuscript illegible] was out with a party and discovered fires on Saturday night in the Nobs of Duhs River and had sent for a reinforcement, expresses were dispatched several ways Col. Logan set off for Whilleys [3] where the men were to rendivous, in the evening they returned and reported that 6 Indians ran up to the house of Michl Woods and one going in the door was shut. Old Mr. Woods, a young woman [4] and negro being in the house,

---

[1] Dicks.   [2] English.   [3] Colonel William Whitley.
[4] The name Mary is here inserted in the manuscript.

that the negro knocked the Indian down whilst the young woman got an ax they got them dispatched the Old woman kept the door shut that before the Indians without could break the door open a man ran up and began firing on them wounded one on which they ran off.

At Col. Logans I observed several petrifactions of the Shells formerly mentioned of Roots and of a hornets nest so that if they were looked for they might I believe be found all over the Country. The Frenchmen from the Illinois informed me that they were never troubled at St. Vincent or Opost either with Fleas or Ratts neither of which could live there, the latter may be accounted by the water being impregnated by Arsenic. . . .

April 14. Were informed that Col. Floyd died on Thursday, he was wounded on tuesday, there was five in Company : one man shot dead, Col. Floyd wounded, all the horses shot except Col. Floyds.

April 15. This day had information that Old Mr. Harbisons son-in-law was killed last night and that [manuscript illegible] Mr. Wallace was elected a delegate for Lincoln, at night Mr. Wimton from Kaskaskias came up but was so indisposed he [was] unable to proceed with us and returned next morning Settled with Col. Logan and began my Journey home, parted with Walker Daniel Atty General for the District, spoke to him to [manuscript illegible] buisness in this Country which he promised to do, but gave him no money having run short. I told him I would give him a writing for it [in] a few days. Encamped on a Branch shoot of to give him time for the Company to [manuscript illegible].

Started in the morning, went the old trace, got alarmed, several fresh horse tracts before us, turned out at a Spring 12 miles from Ingliss to let our horses feed, were joined by Jno. and George May Capt. Brackenridge and two three or others, likewise a party from Salt Lick Creek.

April 17. Encamped on Scago[1] Creek above the Fork,

---

[1] Scaggs.

several horse tracts on the Creek, made a halt till the rear came up. Maj. Mosebys lost his provision horse and provisions — at the crossing of Rockcastle was a black mare which followed us, got to the Hazel patch, a fresh shod horse tract before us, went on to the No. Branch of Lawrel River, encamped, we were detained in the morning, Geo. May having lost four horses which had been frightened by Gun discharged he pursued their tracts and got them in five weeks, halted at Lin Camp C and encamped 7 miles from the Flat Lick, were joined by several in the night, got letters [from] Government by John Reed, who was going to Kentucky and informed me he was going to the Chickesaw nation — passed Flat Lick crossed Cumberland and rested after crossing the Foarding. Encamped on Yellow Creek, Crossed Cumberland mountain, halted at Owins and encamped on Trading Creek, Halted at Valley Station and Scotsplain 3 miles from there.

INDEX

Abecas (Abihkas), Upper Creek Indians, 116 n., 177, 189, 270.

Abicouches (Abikudshi), 508 n., 532.

Acolapissas, *see* Colapissas.

Adair, James, 259.

Addams, Deacon, 320.

Akens, William, 642.

Alabama, fort, *see* Fort Toulouse.

Alabama River, 499 n.

Albany, N. Y., in 1765, 416–417.

Albert, Pierre, 239, 240, 246, 247–450.

Aleck, Captain, great medal chief of the Creeks, 496.

Alexandria, Va., 407.

Alibamu (Alibama) Indians, 270 n., 483.

Allaire, Sieur, 90.

Allibamonts, Mingo, speech of, 273–274.

Altamaha River, report that the English were to erect a fort at the mouth of, 203.

Altem, 354, 355.

America, "Back Part" of, proposal for government of, 424–425.

American Revolution, Dr. Berkenhout's reflections regarding, 579–582.

Amherst, Sir Jeffrey, 407 n., 420, 430 n., 443.

Ancenys, Marquis d', 41.

Anderson's ferry, 586 n.

Andrews, Capt., 10.

Andros, Sir Edmund, 8.

Annapolis, Md., in 1765, 408–409.

Antigua, island of, description, 375–376.

Apalachicola, a Lower Creek town, 184.

Arbre Croche, Mich., 361 n.

Arkansas Indians, villages, 55, 56, 57, 86; food and clothing, 57; moon worship, 57; treatment of smallpox patients, 57; number, 57, 150; belief in metempsychosis, 58; women, 58; attack Frenchmen, 85.

Arkansas River, French settlement on 55–56, 480.

Arlois, Jean, 246, 247, 251, 252.

Arnold, Benedict, 608 n.

Artagnac, Marquis d', 25 n.

Artaguiette, Diron d', journal of his tour up the Mississippi, 15–92; inspector-general of Louisiana, 16; a director of the Western Company, 16; founder of Baton Rouge, 16; talk to the Cahokias, 81; commandant of Fort Condé, 268.

Artaguiette, Pierre d', 32 n.

Atasi (Ottesey), Creek town, 505 n., 540.

Aufaugoulas, 51.

Augusta, Ga., an Indian trading post, 518; treaty of, 547 n.; garrison at, 563.

Aust, 586 n., 587, 590–591, 597.

Aveas, 364.

Ayanabi, Choctaw town, 284 n.

Badons, 536.

Baillie, Richard, 512.

Balize, French post at, 90.

Ballow, William, 103.

Baltimore, Frederick Calvert, sixth lord, 408 n.

Bannister bridge, Va., 605.

Barbara, Don Antonio, 234.

Barbery, 5.

Barbour, James, 618.

Barbour, Capt. Phil., 664, 666.

Barbour, Col., 623, 624.

Barby, synod of, 585.

Bard, manager of salt works in Kentucky, 636.

Baton Rouge, La., 16, 43.

Bauchman, Henry, 654.

Bauchman, Jacob, 654.

Baudouin, Michael, missionary to the Choctaws, 264, 265.

INDEX

INDEX

Buffaloes, hunting of, 53, 54, 60, 83, 84, 465; speed of, 219; great herds of, 468, 469; hump of, 627; uses of, 628–629.
Buffalo Lick, Va., 344.
Bull, Mr., 7.
Bullit, Capt. Thomas, 620 n.
Burges, Indian trader, 552.
Burlington, N. J., 414.
Burnaby, Admiral Sir William, 377.
Burns, 233.
Burton, Ralph, 433.
Butler, Father, 389.
Byrd, Col., 669.

Caderaqui, 428.
Cadet, Marie le, 30.
Cadillac, M. de la Motte, governor of French Louisiana, 69 n.
Cahokia, Ill., French settlement, 474.
Cahokia Indians, village of, 76, 80; Renard Indians prepare to attack, 78; Artaguiette's talk to, 81.
Caimullga, Creek town, 532.
Calaway, Col., 634, 635.
Caldwell, 647, 650.
Cameron, 497, 511.
Campbell, Lieut., 426.
Campbell, Indian trader, 535.
Canaan, Conn., 447.
Canada, Indian captives in, 301, 302–305; description, 431–442; iron works, 435–436; considerations regarding government of French population in, 439–442.
Cannaday, John, 207.
Cannes Brulées, 16, 25, 27, 40.
Cap à l'Ail, 67.
Cap à l'Anguille, 60.
Cap à la Cruche, 66.
Cape Canaverall, 390.
Cap St. Anthoine, 67.
Cap St. Cosmose, 67.
Carbono, 665.
Carland, Thomas, 636.
Carlisle, Earl of, 569.
Carlisle, Penn., Irish settlement, 331.
Carols, Madam, 308.
Carr, Capt., 234.
Carroll's Manor, 609.
Carron, 24.

Carteret, Philip, widow of, 5 n.
Castachas, Choctaw town, 285 n.
Castle William, 540.
Catawba Indians, regulation of trade with, 132–133.
Caughnawaga, Indian village, 431.
Ceard, Sieur, concession of, in French Louisiana, 20, 21.
Chagey, fortified Cherokee town, 131, 143, 149.
Chamberlain, Ensign, 233.
Chambers, Indian trader, 142.
Chambly, Sieur, 264.
Chaouacha-Indians, 25, 29, 41.
Chapitoulas, 40.
Charleston, S. C., trade routes to Cherokee country, 95–96; description, 397, 399; surrenders to the British, 595.
Charlestown, N. H., 301.
Chateaugué, Jean Baptiste Lemoyne, Sieur de, 39, 267 n.
Chaudepisse, Rivière de la, 43.
Chavacleyhatchie, 545.
Chavagne, Sieur de, 42.
Chebucto (Halifax), Nova Scotia, 310.
Chehaw, see Geehaws.
Cheneth, manager of salt works in Kentucky, 621.
Chepar, 88.
Cherokee Indians, trade and regulation of English trade with, 95, 98, 132, 133, 154, 157, 159; number and distribution, 95, 250; relations with the French, 96, 118, 127, 142, 239, 250–251; ceremonies, 101, 102, 110, 113; scarcity of provisions among, 106; urged to build a corn house, 109; hostile relations with the Creeks, 115–118, 120–121, 126–128, 146–149, 152–158, 188–189, 198; attachment to the English, 138; Creeks and Choctaws allied against, 144, 145, 146; relations with the Chickasaws, 156–157, 190; Gen. Oglethorpe receives a delegation of, 222, 239; smallpox among, 239; treatment of prisoners, 242–249; food of, 245; access of northern Indians to, 465.
Cherokey-Leech-che, 193.

677

INDEX

Chesnal du Diable, 45, 60.

Chesne, 64.

Chester, John, 144, 151.

Chester, Peter, governor of West Florida, 493.

Chestertown, Md., 410 n.

Chetimachas, Choctaw village, 42.

Chevalie, Louison, 359.

Chicago River, 362, 363.

Chickasaw Indians, relations with the French, 31, 33, 85, 103, 254; with the English, 103, 254; with the Choctaws, 135; with the Cherokees, 156–157, 190; with the Creeks, 168–172, 201, 211, 520, 526 n.; number of warriors, 216.

Chicken, Col. George, journal of his journey to and through the Cherokee country, 95–172; sketch, 96; talks to Cherokees, 105, 106, 109, 115, 126–131, 145, 146, 161–162; letters to President Arthur Middleton, 106–107, 134–139, 142, 151–153; letters to Eleazer Wigan, 145, 148, 163–165; instructions to commander of Fort Moore, 167–168; letter to Tobias Fitch, 168, 211.

Chigilly, Creek Indian, 185, 215.

Chim, 359.

Chimhucky, 553, 558.

Chippewa Indians, 360, 426.

Choctaw Indians, at war with the Chickasaws, 51, 90, 122, 135; relations with the French, 103, 287, 290; prepare for war against the Cherokees, 144–147; relations with the English, 196, 206, 218, 291; seek an alliance with the Creeks against the Chickasaws, 201–202; English and French factions, 206–207, 259, 269, 275, 289, 290–291; number of warriors, 216; territory of, 259; "Six Villages," 273, 277 n., 278; Creek-Choctaw boundary, 386–387; at war with the Creeks, 519, 534.

Christian, Col. William, 651, 653, 669.

Chunkey, a Choctaw town, 293 n.

Clark, 7.

Clark, George Rogers, 617, 622, 642.

Claycatskee, a Creek village, 548, 549.

Clinton, Sir Henry, 569, 574.

Cody, Elizabeth, 313, 314.

Cohoes, falls of the Mohawk River, 447.

Colapissas, Choctaw Indians, 35 n., 38, 39, 41.

Colbert, Indian trader, 521.

Colliet, Mrs., 564.

Collins, William, 141.

Collys, MM. settlement near Natchez established by, 34, 43, 46, 88.

Commantle Indians, 184.

Comyns, 555, 557.

Conchasbekas, Indian village, 251 n., 253.

Connecticut, description, 447–448; population in 1765, 448.

Continental Congress, character of the members of, 579.

Continental currency, 580, 593.

Conustee, an Upper Cherokee town, 111, 122.

Conway Cabal, 574 n.

Cook, Lieut.-Col., 228.

Cooper, Joseph, Cherokee interpreter, 102, 105, 108, 126, 162.

Cooper, William, Indian trader, 132, 151, 160.

Coosa (Kusa) Old Town, 534.

Coosa Indians, see Kusa Indians.

Coosha, Choctaw town, 206.

Cornall (Cornell), Creek interpreter, 495, 496, 497, 498, 499, 501, 520 n., 543.

Corn Island, 621 n.

Cornwallis, Lord, 575.

Couchas, Choctaw Indians, 269 n.

Couroye Indians, 51, 52.

Coussot, Pierre, Cherokee prisoner, 244, 247, 251, 252.

Coustilas, Sieur, 39.

Coweta Indians, see Kawita Indians.

Cox, Col., 662.

Cox, John, 655.

Crafton, Capt. Edward, 510.

Creek Indians, country of, 175; number of warriors, 216; black drink, 220 n., 502; food and clothing, 220–221; dancing, 220–221; snake dance, 517; polecat dance, 532; occupation of the women, 221; huts, 221; customs,

678

INDEX

INDEX

Fort Massac, purpose of, 469-470.
Fort Massachusetts, 305, 317.
Fort Michilimackinac, 361 n.
Fort Moore, erected for the protection of Indian trade, 95, 165 n.; garrison of, 167; instructions to commander of, 167-168; location, 181 n.
Fort Moosa, 228.
Fort Niagara, importance, 424; garrison, 425.
Fort Ninety-Six, 96.
Fort Nelson, 665, 667.
Fort Oneida, 420.
Fort Ontario, description, 421, 422.
Fort Oswego, 421.
Fort Pensacola, description, 381-382; barracks, 486.
Fort Picolata, 226 n.
Fort Pitt, 464, 488.
Fort Prince George, S. C., 101 n.
Fort Prince George (Palachocolas Fort) on the Savannah River, 222 n.
Fort Rosalie, description, 45, 49.
Fort St. Andrews, 233 n.
Fort St. George, 225 n.
Fort St. John, 308.
Fort St. Joseph, 362.
Fort San Francisco de Pupo, 225 n., 226.
Fort Schuyler, 419.
Fort Stanwix, 418-419.
Fort Ticonderoga, 444.
Fort Tombecbé, 270 n.
Fort Toulouse, 200 n., 250, 536.
Fort Turner, 305.
Fort William, 232 n., 233, 235.
Fort William Augustus, 429-430.
Fort William Henry, 445.
Fortner, Joseph, 314, 317.
Foulton, Indian trader, 142.
Fouquet, Sieur, 25.
Fox Indians, 32, 76, 77, 78.
Francklyn, Capt., 236.
Franklin, Benjamin, 576.
Frederick, Md., 588 n., 590.
French Pirates, 6, 7.
French, Robert, 529, 553.
Friedrichsville, Va., see Winchester, Va.
Frolier, Capt., 671, 672.
Fuhrer, Valentin, 353.
Fulton, James, 150.

Funchal, capital of Madeira, description, 371-373.
Funk, Justice, 335.
Fusihatchi, a Creek Indian town, 510 n., 537.

Gage, Thomas, instructions to Harry Gordon and to George Croghan, 457; letter to the Earl of Shelburne, 458-462; letter to Secretary Conway, 477 n.
Galphin, George, 505 n., 524 n., 526 n., 541, 550, 558.
Garret, Col., 647.
Gaspard, Indian trader, 285, 286.
Gates, Horatio, 574 n.
Geehaws (Chehaw), a Creek Indian village, 545 n., 546, 550.
George, Capt., 665, 666, 668.
Georgetown, S. C., 398.
Georgia, a prohibition province, 215; trade with the Creek Indians, 215; *Report* of a Georgia ranger, 215-236; Spanish attempts against, 223-224, 232-236; description, 394-396.
Gerard, Conrad Alexander, 581 n.
Germain, Lord George, 570, 573.
German Flats, 418.
Germaney, James, 521, 527.
Germantown, Va., 593, 608.
Gibson, Capt., 235.
Gillespey, John, 206, 207.
Givens, Samuel, 672.
Glahan, 668.
Glover, Capt. Charlesworth, 167.
Goggle Eyes (Steyamasiechie), a Creek Indian, 178, 179, 192, 205.
Gold, Major Nathan, 6 n.
Goose Creek, S. C., militia of, defeats the Yamasees, 96; settlement of, 97.
Gordon, Lord Adam, birth, 368; journal of travel in the American Colonies, 367-453; colonel of the 66th Regiment, 367; member of Parliament, 368; commander of Scotch forces, 368; reception in Boston, 368, 451-452; confers with British Secretaries of State, 368.
Gordon, Capt. Harry, journal of an expedition down the Ohio and the

681

INDEX

Houmas Indians, 34, 42, 483, 489.
How, Caleb, 305.
Howard, 539.
Howarth, 560.
Howe, Robert, 367.
Howe, Sir William, 422 n., 574, 575, 579–580.
Hows, John, 165–166.
Hubard, Capt., 318.
Hudson River, description, 415–416.
Hunt, John, 125.
Huspah, a Yamasee Indian chief, 204 n., 205.
Hutchins, Thomas, 457, 487.
Hutchinson, Thomas, 450.

Iberville River, 480, 481 n., 482, 489.
Illinois Country, Jesuit missionaries, 34, 44; sickness, 52; Indian trade, 52, 70, 424, 477; salt making, 68; inhabitants, 70; description, 74, 362–364; inadequate military protection, 383; French government of, 435; expense of defending, 476; confusion of affairs in, 665.
Illinois Indians, villages, 69–70, 71; number, 71; characteristics, 71; food, clothing and shelter, 71–72; occupation, 72; treatment of captives, 72; marriage, 72–73; women, 73; speed, 73; dancing, 74; medicines, 74; warriors, 79; Jesuit missionaries among, 69; hostile relations with the Fox Indians, 32, 75, 77, 364.
Illison, 340, 342.
Indians, medicine men, 35–36, 57; school for education of, 403 n.; at ball play, 262, 517, 546; conservatism of, 461; *see also* names of tribes and towns.
Indian trade, in the Illinois Country, 70; with the Cherokees, 95; regulation of, 98, 102, 106–107, 119, 125–126, 128–129, 132, 133, 136–139, 144, 159, 460–462; with the Creeks, 192, 199–200, 221, 512, 525; in Canada, 310; on the Great Lakes, 424; on the Mississippi and Missouri rivers, 458–460, 475; rivalry between the French and the English in, 476, 477; protection of, 476, 477.

Indian traders, character of, 98, 106, 424, 494, 504–505, 508, 512, 525, 544; alienate the Creeks from the English interest, 215; insolence of, 216; carry smallpox to the Cherokees, 239; encourage the Cherokees to continue war against the French, 250.
Ingepretsen, Erich, 326, 327, 330.
Irwin, Capt., 647, 650.
Isle aux Noix, 443 n.
Isle Perrot, 430.
Itogen, Richard, 631.

Jamaica, island of, description, 377–381.
Jeffreys, 7, 9.
Jenkins, Daniel, 124, 125.
Jerseys, East, and West, description, 413–414.
Johnsen, Robert, 348.
Johnson, 609.
Johnson, George, 315.
Johnson, John, son of Sir William Johnson, 367.
Johnson, Lieut., 320.
Johnson, Sir William, residence of, 417–418; takes Fort Niagara, 424; Indians cede tract of land to, 427; defeats Dieskau, 445; Lord Adam Gordon's appreciation of, 447.
Johnstone, George, governor of East Florida, 385–386; a peace commissioner, 569, 576 n.
Jones, 97.
Jones, Capt., 233.
Jones, Thomas, 206, 540.
Jones, Willie, 401 n.
Jore, Upper Creek Indian town, 123.
Joyeuse, Sieur, 241.
Juchereau de St. Denis, *see* St. Denis.

Kailardshi, Creek Indian town, 515–516.
Kalberlahn, Hans Martin, 326, 327, 328, 336, 338, 346.
Kampf, 588, 589.
Kashita, Lower Creek Indian town, 157, 184, 185, 186, 195, 221.
Kaskaskia, Ill., description, 67–68, 472.
Kaskaskia Indians, 76, 364, 472.
Kawita, Lower Creek Indian town, 133, 184 n., 185, 215, 216, 221, 549.

INDEX

Kearl, Daniel, 151, 160.
Kellwick, 612.
Kent Island, 409, 410.
Kentucky, immigration to, 617, 637; adjustment of preëmption claims, 618, 631, 644, 645–646; salt and salt springs, 620, 623; hardships of early settlers, 622, 630, 636; hostility of Indians, 623, 626, 635, 636, 642, 643, 644, 645, 647, 650, 661, 669, 671, 672–673; game, 624; shell fish, 624 n.; maple sugar, 631–632, 635; climate, 637–638; nettles and nettle cloth, 637, 643; drainage, 639–640; soil, 639–460; wilderness road to, 648–650; commission to settle accounts with officers of, 659.
Keowee, principal town of the Lower Cherokees, 96, 101, 153.
Kerlazious, 37.
Kettlewell, John, 634 n.
Killbrun, 318.
Kincheloe's Station, Ky., 662 n.
Kingston, Jamaica, description, 377.
Kingston, Ontario, 428 n.
Kirk, Edward, 132, 143.
Klaziou, 24.
Knowles, Sir Charles, governor of Jamaica, 381.
Knox, Col., 644, 663.
Koenigsderfer, Gottlob, 326.
Kohl, Robert, 347.
Kornike, Robert, 334.
Kra, Fende, 333.
Krause, Johan, 603.
Kucher, Peter, 329.
Kulumi, Creek Indian town, 501 n.
Kusa Indians, 134–135.

La Babiche, Wea Indian village, 75.
La Bature au Chevreuil, 45.
La Borde, 38, 39.
La Boulaye, Sieur, 56.
Lafavour, Jonathan, 312.
Lake Erie, 426.
Lake George, description, 445.
Lake Michigan, shores of, 361.
Lake Ontario, appearance, 421; navigation, 422–423, 428–429; water, 426.
Lake Ponchartrain, 460, 484.

Lake St. Francis, 430.
Lake St. Louis, 430.
Lake St. Pierre, 435.
Lambert, Samuel, 314.
Langvin, Chickasaw captive, 31, 33, 62, 85, 87.
Larouve, Sieur, 264.
La Tour, M. de, lieutenant-general of French Louisiana, 18, 23, 24, 26, 30, 31, 38, 39.
Lave, 539, 540.
Lavin, 7.
Lau, David, 611.
Laurens, St. Luke, 309.
Law, John, financial operations of, 15–16; concession of, 31, 56.
Le Blanc, 46, 49, 88.
Le Chef or Le Clef, Indian trader, 475.
Lee, Dr. Arthur, 570, 577.
Lee, Philip Ludwell, 407 n.
Lee, Richard Henry, 570, 571, 576.
Le Gras, 53, 54, 241.
Le Gras, Col., 671, 672.
Le Houx, 49.
Leisler, Jacob, 3, 5, 6.
Le Moyne, Charles, Baron de Longueil, governor of Canada, 302 n., 308; letter to, 303–305.
Le Rocher, 363.
Lesslie, James, 508.
Le Sueur, commandant of Fort Toulouse, 270 n.
Letushe, Madam, 309.
Lewis, Francis, 504, 514, 525.
Lewis, General, 629.
Lewse, 309.
Liberge, 246.
Ligonier, Lord, field-marshal, 578 n.
Lindlay, Col., 628.
Lindsey, Sir John, 381, 388.
Linganesue, 308.
Lischer, Johannes, 326, 327, 334, 335.
Lisle, M. de, 32, 75.
Lititz, Penn., 585.
Little Oakchoys (Okchayi), a Creek Indian town, 530–531.
Little Tallassie, a Creek Indian town, 506–507.
Livilliers, 87.
Lloyd, Thomas, 4, 10.

INDEX

Lockyer, Capt., 388.

Loesch, G., 328, 329, 330, 331.

Loesch, Herman, 326, 327, 328, 329, 336, 339, 340, 341, 348, 354.

Loesch, Jacob, 326, 327, 329, 333, 334, 336, 338, 340, 344–345, 349, 354.

Logan, Col. Benjamin, 643, 671.

Logan's Fort, 624.

London, Bishop of, letter by king of England to, 7.

London, Md., 409.

Long Island, description, 415.

Longe, Sawney, 129.

Longueil, M. de, 66.

Looney's Ferry, 341 n.

Loring, Joshua, 367, 422, 426.

L'Orme, principal agent of the Western Company, 28 n.

Louboey, M. de, 263, 297.

Loudoun's Ferry, 447.

Louis, duc de Bourgogne, 311 n.

Louisiana, settlement of, 16, 21–23, 41; hurricane in, 24–25, 27, 28, 29; discontent with government of, 89; Spanish possession of, 481 n., 483.

Louisville, Ky., settlement of, 621–622; description, 663, 667.

Lovell, John, 652.

Lovell, Thomas, 644, 653.

Loving, Adam, 352.

Lower Eufaula, Creek Indian town, 555.

Lunge, Jacob, 326, 327, 338, 339.

Lun-ham-ga, Upper Creek Indian town, 189.

Lunn, Col., 655.

Lydius, John Henry, 306 n.

Lyman, 318.

Lynch's Tavern, 597.

Lyne, Col. Edmund, 618, 628, 629.

Lyttleton, William Henry, governor of Jamaica, 378 n., 381.

McAffee, James, 623 n.

McAffee's Station, Ky., 661 n.

McBain, Laufflin, 104.

McCormick, Alexander, 102, 132.

Macdonald, Joseph, 343.

McDowell, Col. John, 661.

McDowell, Samuel, 660, 669.

Macée, 12.

McFall, an Indian trader, 501, 514, 516, 521, 536, 537, 539.

Machbichemalla, Creek Indian, 532, 553–554.

Mackay, 505 n., 529.

McKenzie, Alexander, 376 n.

Maclane, 235.

McLean, 563.

McQueens, James, 514, 561.

Mad Dog, Creek Indian doctor, 538, 539, 542.

Madeira, island of, description, 370–375.

Madison, Capt., 671.

Madison, Mrs., 651.

Mahoney, Florence, 168, 212.

Malouins (merchants of St. Malo), grievances against the Western Company, 19–21.

Manchac River, 43.

Marin, Sieur, 241, 242.

Markham, William, 4, 10.

Marlot, Sieur, 31, 40.

Marr, Indian trader, 104.

Marshall, Col. Thomas, 660, 667, 668.

Marshall, Frederick William von, 599, 603, 610.

Marston, John, 642.

Martin, Moses, 603.

Maryland, Germans in, 326; description, 408–410.

Mascouten Indians, 362–363.

Maskingonge, plains of, 434.

Mason, 663.

Massachusetts, charged with violating the Acts of Trade, 3; population, 4, 49; overthrow of the Andros Government, 8–9; description, 448–451; and the Stamp Act, 449–450, 451–452 n.; Lord Adam Gordon proposes a change in the government of, 450.

Massy, Sieur, 27.

Matchinkoa, an Indian village, 364.

Matlack, Timothy, 575, 577, 578.

Matulicht, Jerome, 386.

Maxwell, William, 570, 574, 576, 579.

May, George, 673, 674.

May, John, 662, 668, 673.

Meally, John, 558.

Mekchiquamias Indians, 82, 83.

Mellicq, Sieur, 32, 68.

INDEX

Menchaeg River, *see* Manchac.
Mercier, François le, 78, 80.
Merk, John, 328 n., 331.
Merkli, Christopher, 326, 327, 334, 342.
Metchel, Solomon, 314.
Meurer, Philipp, 336.
Miami Indians, 75.
Michigamea, village of Illinois Indians, 70.
Michigan, description, 360, 361, 362.
Michilimackinac, 360, 431.
Mico Lucko, 517, 520.
Middleton, 409.
Middleton, Arthur, 96, 106, 144, 159–160, 190–191.
Mifflin, Thomas, 574 n.
Milborne, Jacob, 10.
Miller, John, 550, 553.
Millikin, James, 104, 119, 131, 141, 158.
Mine au Fer, 479 n., 488.
Mingo Town, 464 n., 488.
Misère, 364, 472 n.
Missellimer Mill, 327.
Missesauga Indians, 423, 429.
Mississippi River, description, 43, 471, 478–479, 482; early settlements on, 458, 472, 474, 479, 480, 481; Indian settlements on, 483; Indian trade on, 458, 475; navigation of, 479, 480–481.
Missouri Country, commandant of, 29.
Missouri Indians, 77, 80.
Missouri River, Indian trade on, 475.
Mobile, Ala., commandant at, 39; sickness of inhabitants, 383; description, 386–388, 485; Indian trading post, 460; trade with New Orleans, 484 n.
Mobilians, Choctaw Indians, 261 n., 262.
Mohawk Indians, 418.
Mohawk Valley, 417.
Molton, John, Creek interpreter, 207–208.
Mongoulacha, Choctaw Indian chief, speech of, 266–268.
Moniack, Jacob, 536, 542, 544.
Monjoy, Creek Indian, 556.
Monocacy, Md., 588, 589.
Montcalm, Marquis de, 444.
Montgomery, Col. John, 671.
Montreal, Indian trade of, 310; description, 321–322, 431–433; number of houses in 1765, 442.

Moore, Marvin, 607.
Moravians, early settlements in America, 325; a travel diary of, 325–356; archives, 326, 585; religious beliefs and practices, 344 n., 348, 353, 355.
Morgan, George, 457, 468.
Morin, 75, 76.
Morrisania, 453.
Morris, Lewis, 453.
Morro Castle, 389, 487–488.
Morter, Creek Indian, 511, 520, 522–523, 529, 531, 542, 544–545.
Moseby, Major, 664, 674.
Moses, Capt., 305.
Mosley, Thomas, 536, 541.
Mouns, 671.
Mount Pleasant, N. Y., 425–426.
Mouy, Sieur de, 40.
Mucklasses, Creek Indian village, 509 n., 541.
Müller, Jac., 328, 336.
Müller, Joseph, 328 n., 331.
Murray, James, 336 n., 443.
Muskingum River, 465.
Myot, 262.

Natchez, Miss., settlement of, 16, 20, 26, 46; hurricane at, 28; fort at, 45, 88, 479, 480.
Natchez Indians, number, 48; relations with the French, 33, 34–35, 36, 37, 41, 86, 90, 255, 531 n.; food, 48; religion, 48–49; festivals, 48–49; villages, 49; orders, 34 n., 49; marriage relations, 49; features, 49; among the Cherokees and the Chickasaws, 251; among the Creeks, 531.
Natchies, a village of Natchez Indians, 531 n.
Natchitoches Indians, 89.
Natchitoches, La., settlement of, 16; garrison, 89; fort, 481.
Navy Island, 426.
Neely, John, 100.
Neilsen, 597.
Neisser, 587, 612.
Nelson, Thomas, governor of Virginia, 659.
Neuschwanger, 334.
Neuser, 329.

686

INDEX

Nevill's Tavern, 593.

New Bern, N. C., 401.

Newbury, 7.

Newcastle, Del., 410.

New Holland (Low Dutch Station), Ky., 664, 667 n.

New Orleans, removal of capital of French Louisiana to, 17; founded by Bienville, 18; defence, 26; hurricane in, 24; engineering affairs in, 29; lack of provisions, 30; famine, 89; sickness, 39; purple fever epidemic, 89; Indian trade, 458–459, 460; description, 482, 483.

Newport, Eng., 369.

New York, City of, description, 414, 415.

New York, description, 414–429.

Niagara Falls, 425, 447.

Nicholson, Francis, governor of Virginia, 3, 6.

Nicola, Col. Lewis, 576 n.

Nielsen, Jeppe, 586 n., 597.

Niverville, Boucher de, 301.

Nocoochee, Cherokee Indian town, 108, 131.

Nogouwee, Cherokee Indian town, 145.

Nolan, 18.

Noland, Thomas, 590, 591, 592, 609.

Norfolk, Va., description, 406.

North Carolina, description, 400–403; Moravians in, 525–526; concession to the Moravians, 585.

North, Lord, 570.

Noyant, Sieur de, 88.

Noyouwee, Cherokee Indian town, 104.

Number Four, see Charlestown, N. H.

Nyberg, Laurentius Thorstansen, 333, 339.

Oakchoys (Okchayi), Creek Indian town, 177, 511 n., 537.

Oakfuskee, Creek Indian town, 157, 176 n.

Occacochee, Upper Creek Indian town, 135.

Ockel, William, 589, 590.

Ocmulgee River, 561.

Oconee, Lower Cherokee Indian village, 154 n.

Ogdensburg, N. Y., see Oswegatchee.

Ogle, Benjamin, 610, 611.

Ogle, Thomas, 609.

Oglethorpe, General James, letter to the Georgia Trustees, 215–216; treats with the Creek Indians, 215–216, 221; tour to the Creek Country, 218–221; receives a delegation of Cherokee Indians, 222, 239; commands forces against St. Augustine, 224–229; cruizes against the Spaniards, 229–232; defends Georgia coast against the Spaniards, 232–236.

Ohio River, thought to be tributary to the Wabash, 66 n., 241 n.; description, 465–471; Falls of, 467–468, 489, 621–622, 665–666.

Oldham, Capt., 662.

Onion, 5, 10.

Onondaga River, 420–421.

Oony, Choctaw Indian town, 276 n.

Orleans, Duke of, 15, 16.

O'Reilly, 389.

Oriskany Fields, 418.

Oswegatchee, 421, 428, 429.

Otis, James, address to Lord Adam Gordon, 451–452 n.

Ottawa Indians, 312–313, 360, 361.

Ottawa River, 430, 431.

Pader, 329, 331.

Paillou, Sieur, major general of French Louisiana, 35 n., 36–37, 41.

Pain Court (St. Louis), 474, 475.

Pain's Ordinary, 595, 606.

Pakamans, Creek Indians, 270 n.

Pakan-Tallahassee, Creek Indian town, 534, 535.

Palachocolas Fort, 222 n.

Pallachocola, Creek Indian town, 554, 557.

Palmes, Major Edward, 6 n.

Parisien, 87.

Parker, Isaac, 319.

Parker, Ruth, 320.

Parris, Alexander, 138 n., 139, 162, 167.

Partoson, Andrew, 205.

Pasquier, Sieur, 40.

Passaic River, description, 413.

Paterson, Robert, 628.

687

INDEX

Pauger or Peauger, Sieur, engineer, 17–18, 23, 26, 90.
Pawling, Capt., 642, 647, 651.
Paya Lucko, Creek Indian, 511, 518, 519 n., 529, 530.
Peacock, 8.
Penn, 5.
Penn, John, 412.
Pennsylvania, Moravians in, 325; description, 410–413.
Penrose, Col., 578.
Pensacola, Fla., commandant at, 38; French take possession of, 39; description, 383–384; fort, 486–487; frequented by Creek Indians, 384–385, 493.
Peoria, Indian village, 363, 474.
Perilaud, 75, 76, 77.
Perkins, 538.
Perkins, Col., 604.
Perrier, 89.
Perry, 320.
Perth Amboy, 414.
Petersburg (Peter Little's Town), Penn., 588 n., 611.
Petersen, Hans, 326, 327, 336, 342.
Petit Gouffre, 50, 497 n.
Petite Pointe.Coupée, 53.
Petits Colas, 41.
Pettit, 246.
Pfeil, Friedrich Jacob, 326, 327, 345.
Philadelphia, description, 410–411; Indian trade, 477 n.; character of members of the Executive Council, 576, 579; in the Revolution, 581.
Phips, Spencer, 301, 303 n.
Pigg, John, 509–510, 522 n., 540, 541, 551, 554 n.
Pimitoui Indians, 32 n.
Pitman's Station, Ky., 652.
Pittman, Philip, 473 n., 478.
Plowman, 4.
Point Pleasant, Battle of, 617.
Pointe Coupée, 16, 43, 54, 254, 480 n., 481, 489.
Ponpon, 78, 79, 80.
Pontual, Sieur de, 38.
Pope's Station, Ky., 663.
Portier, Guillaume, 244, 247, 251.
Port Royal, Jamaica, 377.

Porto Santo, 374–375.
Portsmouth, Eng., 369.
Pottawatomie Indians, 361 n., 362, 363.
Potter, Col. Cuthbert, commissioner from Virginia to New England, 3; journal of his journey, 4–11; his papers searched in Boston, 8–9.
Poussin, 25.
Powell, Samuel, 342.
Power, 578.
Pradel, 29, 84.
Prairie de Roche, Ill., French village, 472.
Prairie des Roches Indians, 32.
Preston, Col., 627.
Pretor, 544, 545.
Priber, Christian, 239–240, 246, 247–250.
Princeton, N. J., 413, 575.
Princeton College, 574.
Pringle, Walter, 377.
Proprietary Provinces, objection to, 409, 412–413.
Providence, R. I., 452.
Pulaski, Count, cavalry of, 580.
Pumpkin King, Creek Indian chief, 469.
Purrysburg, S. C., 222 n.
Putnam, Ebr., 319.
Putnam, Lawrence, 319.
Putnam, Thomas, 319.

Quapaw Indians, 519–520 n.
Quebec, mutiny of soldiers at, 308; mode of passing signals to Montreal, 434–435; description, 437–439; number of houses in 1765, 442.
Quin, 578.
Quirk, Capt., 626.

Rae, James, 546, 548.
Rae, Robert, 546, 548.
Rall, Johann Gottlieb, 575.
Rauch, Christ., 328, 344.
Rawlings, Pemberton, 634.
Rea, Indian trader, 524, 525.
Red House, Va., 593, 604.
Red Shoe, head of the English faction of the Choctaw Indians, 259; see Soulier Rouge, Ymatahatchitou.
Reh, Benjamin, 346–347.

INDEX

INDEX

Seidel, Nathaniel, 326, 328, 335, 337, 338, 339, 340, 342, 343, 344, 346, 352, 354, 355.

Sempoyeffa, Creek Indian, 549.

Seneca Indians, fall upon the Waccamaws, 138; influence with the Creeks, 188–189; characteristics, 417–418, 422; cut off an armed force under Lieut. Campbell, 426.

Sepe Coffee, leader of the Creek Indians against the Yamasees, 183, 184, 185, 194, 209, 210, 211, 212.

Sergeant, John, 212.

Shannon, 661.

Sharp, John, Indian trader, charged with unfair dealings with the Cherokees, 98, 129–130; instructions to, 132–133; takes his slaves into the Indian Country, 138, 159; satisfaction given, 145–146, 197; letter by Col. George Chicken to, 157; Tobias Fitch demands satisfaction of the Creeks for robbery of, 178, 191, 192–193.

Sharpe, Horatio, governor of Maryland, 408–409.

Shawnee Indians, 271 n., 457, 466.

Shelby, Col. Isaac, 650 n.

Shelton, 593, 596.

Shirley, William, governor of Massachusetts, 301, 303.

Shrimpton, Col., 8.

Silver Bluff, S. C., 505 n.

Simory, William, 512, 527, 562.

Simpson, Hugh, 539, 544.

Simsbury, Conn., 448.

Sioux Indians, 66.

Six Nations, 311, 457.

Slaughter (Sloughter), Henry, governor of New York, 6.

Slaughter, Major, 636.

Small, William, 234.

Smith, planter, 564.

Smith, Quaker, 578.

Smith, Col. Daniel, 671.

Smith, Capt. Henry, 622.

Smith, James, 661.

Smith, John, 10.

Smith, Dr. William, 411 n.

Socuspoga, see Secuspoga.

Sotéhouy, village of Arkansas Indians, 55; garrison at, 86.

Soulier Rouge, Choctaw Indian, 284; speech of, 286; nephew of, 291; promises to kill Ymatahatchitou, 291–292; see also Red Shoe.

South Carolina, Indian trade, 95, 137, 215; Stono Slave Insurrection in, 222–223; description, 397–401.

Spangenberg, Bishop Augustus Gottlieb, 325, 328 n.

Spanish Town, Jamaica, description, 377–378.

Speed, James, 662, 670.

Spinola, Don Diego, 224 n.

Spotswood, Alexander, 203 n.

Squire Mickeos, 210–211.

Stamp Act, 368, 449–450.

Stanard, Thomas, 314.

Stark, John, 301, 314 n.

Stauffer, 588.

Staunton, Va., 335 n.

Stedham, Benjamin, 554.

Stephens, Capt., 651.

Sterling, Lieut., 233.

Stevens, Enos, 321.

Stevens, Isaac, 301.

Stevens, Phineas, Indian captive, 301; frontiersman, 301; his mission to Canada for the recovery of prisoners, 301–317; instructions to, 302–303; building his house, 319–321.

Stevens, Samuel, 305.

Stinging-Lingo Indians, 199.

Stocklitea, Creek Indian, 520.

Stoehr, Hr., 594, 599.

Stone Arabia, N. Y., 418.

Stono Slave Insurrection, 222–223.

Stotz, Jac., 597.

Strubb, Samuel, 597.

Stuart, Charles, 540.

Stuart, Capt. John, superintendent of Indian affairs for the Southern District, 386; difficulties with the Creeks, 493; letters to Hillsborough, 493, 494; instructions to David Taitt, 495–496; letters to the Creeks, 518–521, 546.

Stull, Capt., 642.

Sturgis Station, Ky., 671.

Sullivan, Capt., 664.

INDEX

Sutherland, Lieut., 235.
Swaglehatchies, 556.

Taensa Indians, 25, 41.
Taitt, David, journal of a journey to and through the Creek Country, 493–565; ill treatment by Indian traders, 494; in charge of Creek Indian affairs, 494; a loyalist, 494; instructions to, 495–496; letters to John Stuart, 521–526, 552–554.
Taleachey, Creek Indian, 551.
Tallapoosa Indians, 190, 191, 270.
Tallapoosa River, 501; falls of, 511, 526 n.
Tallassee, Upper Creek Indian town, 202 n.
Tallassiehatchie, Upper Creek Indian town, 532, 534.
Tamatley, Indian town, 551 n., 554.
Tampa Bay, 392.
Tamusey, Cherokee Indian village, 132.
Taneytown, Md., 588 n.
Tanneberger, David, 612.
Tanneberger, Johann, 329.
Tapley, John Adam, 509.
Tapoucha Indians, 87.
Tasbe, John, 309.
Taskanamgouchy, Choctaw Indian, speech of, 272, 275.
Tatoulimatâha, Choctaw Indian, 293.
Taylor, Hub., 662.
Taylor, Col. William, 487 n.
Tehr, Carl, 611.
Tellico, Upper Cherokee Indian town, 111–112, 134–135, 245, 246.
Temple, John, 569, 570, 571.
Tennant's Tavern, 333.
Tennessee, Upper Cherokee Indian town, 112; speech by the head warrior of, 112–113, 118; hostile neighbors of, 114.
Tennessee River, 243 n., 245, 470 n.
Terre Blanche, 46, 49.
Terrisse, 90.
Terry, 643, 644, 669.
Test, 10.
Thaumeur, missionary priest, 81.
Thomas, Elias, 169.
Thomas, George, governor of Antigua, 376.

Thompson, 5.
Thompson, John, 624.
Thonniqua Indians, 44, 88, 90.
Thousand Islands, 429 n.
Three Rivers, 435 n.
Three Rivers (river), 436–437.
Tickhomebey, or Tickhoneby, 181, 182, 201.
Tisne, Sieur du, 32, 34.
Todd, Col. John, 662 n.
Todd, Capt. Levi, 629.
Todd's Station, Ky., 629 n., 641.
Tohomes, Choctaw Indians, 267 n.
Tomachichi, see Tomo-chi-chi.
Tomautley, Cherokee Indian town, 107–108, 547.
Tomeche, Creek Indian, 556.
Tommantle Indians, 185, 188, 202–203.
Tomo-chi-chi, chief of the Yamacraw Indians, 223, 555.
Tonica Indians, 25, 29, 488.
Tonty, Sieur de, 36, 75.
Tool, Robert, 561.
Toopoya, Creek Indian, 537.
Topahatkee, Creek Indian, 552, 553, 558.
Tortuga Islands, 389.
Toupaoü, Choctaw Indian, speech of, 274.
Townley, Col. Richard, 5, 10.
Townshend, Col. Roger, 445.
Toxsaah, Cherokee Indian town, 131, 145.
Traverse, 17–18.
Trenton, N. J., 5, 413.
Trigg, Col. Stephen, 618, 637, 646, 661 n.
Trois Chenaux, 44, 45.
Tryon, Col. William, governor of North Carolina, 367, 401, 402.
Tuccareecho, Cherokee Indian town, 108 n.
Tuccaseegee, Cherokee Indian town, 143 n.
Tuckabatchee, Upper Creek Indian town, 501 n., 509, 513, 514, 515, 526.
Tugaloo, Cherokee Indian town, 142, 145, 151.

INDEX

Tunica Indians, 483.
Turpin, Sieur, 246.
Tuskegee, Creek Indian town, 541.
Tyous Indians, 46.

Uchee, *see* Eutchie.
Ulloa, Don Antonio de, 481 n.
Upper Eufaula, Creek Indian town, 527.
Upper Marlboro, Md., 409 n.
Usher, 7.

Van der Dussen, Alexander, 228 n.
Vaudreuil, Marquis de, governor of French Louisiana, 261, 287.
Velden, Vanden, 505–506, 507, 522 n.
Vera Cruz, 392, 460.
Verbois, Chevalier de, 259.
Verbois, Péchou de, 261.
Vermont, burning of the capitol, 301.
Villiers, Sieur de, 241.
Vincennes (St. Vincent), 673.
Virginia, effect of English Revolution of 1688 in, 3; Indian trade, 137; Germans, 326; log cabins, 590; description, 403–407.

Wabash River, 241 n., 469.
Waccamaw Indians, 138.
Wachovia, N. C., 326, 356 n.
Waggoner, Samuel, 603.
Wagner, 598.
Wagner, Hans, 355 n.
Wakokayi, Creek Indian town, 534, 535.
Wallace, Caleb, 660, 661, 673.
Warren, Capt., 228.
Washa (Ouacha) Indians, 35 n., 38, 39.
Washington, George, 574, 575, 578–579, 580, 581.
Watauga, 642 n.
Watteville, Bishop Johannes von, 334 n.
Wea (Wiatanon) Indians, 75.
Webb, Seth, 313, 314.
Weeo-tee-nee Indians, 135.
Welch, Nich., 622.
Weldren, 540.
Weller, 588.

Weoka, Creek Indian village, 535.
Western Company, proprietors of French Louisiana, 15–16; grievances against, 19; administration of, 38, 39.
Wetter, Joh. Jac., 610.
Wetunkey, a Creek Indian village, 536.
Wharton, 457.
Wheeler, 5.
Wheeler, Moses, 321.
Wheelwright, Nathaniel, 302, 303, 305, 306, 308, 309, 312, 315, 316.
Whey, Aaron, 509–510.
White, Andrew, 131, 143, 163.
Whitfield, George, 395.
Whitley, Col. William, 647 n., 672.
Wigan, Eleazer, Indian interpreter and trader, 97, 99, 105, 107–108, 113, 126; letters of Col. George Chicken to, 145, 148, 163–165; letter to Col. Chicken, 155–156.
Wiggin, Capt., 219, 221.
Wiggin, Thomas, 206.
Willard, Joseph, 319.
Willard, Major, 318.
William and Mary College, 403.
Williams, 4.
Williams, 672.
Williamsburgh, Va., 403, 404.
Williamson, Capt., 305.
Wilmington, N. C., description, 401.
Wilson, Henry, 624, 661.
Wilson's Station, Ky., 644.
Wimer, 650.
Wimton, 673.
Winchester, Va., 334 n.
Winston, Richard, 359.
Winthrop, Major Fitz-John, 6 n., 7.
Wolf, Creek king, 385, 509, 510, 527 n., 541.
Wolfe, James, 438 n.
Wood, William, 195.
Wood Creek, 420.
Woods, Joseph, 318, 319.
Woods, Mary, 672.
Woods, Michael, 672.
Woods, Thomas, 662.
Worcester, Mass., 448–449.
Wormeley, Ralph, 3, 4, 10.
Wright, James, governor of Georgia, 395, 396, 520.

INDEX

Wright's Ferry, 586 n.
Wrights Ordinary, 605.

Xander, 329.

Yamasee Indians, 96, 133, 179, 182, 188, 194, 202–203, 204–205, 209.
Yazoo, Choctaw Indian village, 51, 276 n.
Ymatahatchitou, head of the English faction of the Choctaw Indians, 261 n.,
262, 263, 265, 270, 273, 275, 277, 283–284, 287, 290, 292–293, 294.
Ymonguolacha, Choctaw Indian, 267.
You-ho-lo-mecco, head man of the Upper Creek Indians, 135.
Yowani, Choctaw Indian town, 263 n.

Ziegler, 328.
Zinzendorf, Count, 325.